FANNIE MAE AND FREDDIE MAC: SCANDAL IN U.S. HOUSING

FANNIE MAE AND FREDDIE MAC: SCANDAL IN U.S. HOUSING

JAMES R. CRISTIE
EDITOR

Novinka Books
New York

For permission to use material from this book please contact us:
Telephone 631-231-7269; Fax 631-231-8175
Web Site: http://www.novapublishers.com

LIBRARY OF CONGRESS CATALOGING-IN-PUBLICATION DATA
Available upon request

ISBN 1-60021-356-1

Published by Nova Science Publishers, Inc. ✢ New York

CONTENTS

PREFACE

In the late 1980s and 1990s, Fannie Mae grew rapidly into the largest firm in the U.S. housing finance system and a major global financial institution. The Enterprise achieved double-digit growth in earnings per common share (EPS) for 15 straight years and leveraged its extraordinary financial success into enormous political influence. That financial and political success gave rise to a corporate culture at Fannie Mae in which senior management promoted the Enterprise as one of the lowest-risk financial institutions in the world and as "best in class" in terms of risk management, financial reporting, internal control, and corporate governance. This book describes the development and extent of the problems with Fannie Mae's accounting policies, internal controls, financial reporting, and corporate governance that led to the restatement of the Enterprise's financial reports and the actions to remedy that situation that the Office of Federal Housing Enterprise Oversight (OFHEO) has directed the Enterprise to take to date. The book also recommends that actions be taken to enhance the goal of maintaining the safety and soundness of Fannie Mae.

In: Fannie Mae and Freddie Mac
Editor: James R. Cristie, pp. 1-324
ISBN: 1-60021-356-1

Chapter 1

REPORT OF THE SPECIAL EXAMINATION OF FANNIE MAE[1]

Office of Federal Housing Enterprise Oversight

SUMMARY OF THE REPORT

Fannie Mae senior management promoted an image of the Enterprise as one of the lowest-risk financial institutions in the world and as "best in class" in terms of risk management, financial reporting, internal control, and corporate governance. The findings in this report show that risks at Fannie Mae were greatly understated and that the image was false.

During the period covered by this report—1998 to mid-2004—Fannie Mae reported extremely smooth profit growth and hit announced targets for earnings per share precisely each quarter. Those achievements were illusions deliberately and systematically created by the Enterprise's senior management with the aid of inappropriate accounting and improper earnings management.

A large number of Fannie Mae's accounting policies and practices did not comply with Generally Accepted Accounting Principles (GAAP). The Enterprise also had serious problems of internal control, financial reporting, and corporate governance. Those errors resulted in Fannie Mae overstating reported income and capital by a currently estimated $10.6 billion.

By deliberately and intentionally manipulating accounting to hit earnings targets, senior management maximized the bonuses and other executive compensation they received, at the expense of shareholders. Earnings management made a significant contribution to the compensation of Fannie Mae Chairman and CEO Franklin Raines, which totaled over $90 million from 1998 through 2003. Of that total, over $52 million was directly tied to achieving earnings per share targets.

---

[1] Extracted from http://www.ofheo.gov/media/pdf/FNMSPECIALEXAM.PDF

Fannie Mae consistently took a significant amount of interest rate risk and, when interest rates fell in 2002, incurred billions of dollars in economic losses. The Enterprise also had large operational and reputational risk exposures.

Fannie Mae's Board of Directors contributed to those problems by failing to be sufficiently informed and to act independently of its chairman, Franklin Raines, and other senior executives; by failing to exercise the requisite oversight over the Enterprise's operations; and by failing to discover or ensure the correction of a wide variety of unsafe and unsound practices.

The Board's failures continued in the wake of revelations of accounting problems and improper earnings management at Freddie Mac and other high profile firms, the initiation of OFHEO's special examination, and credible allegations of improper earnings management made by an employee of the Enterprise's Office of the Controller.

Senior management did not make investments in accounting systems, computer systems, other infrastructure, and staffing needed to support a sound internal control system, proper accounting, and GAAP-consistent financial reporting. Those failures came at a time when Fannie Mae faced many operational challenges related to its rapid growth and changing accounting and legal requirements.

Fannie Mae senior management sought to interfere with OFHEO's special examination by directing the Enterprise's lobbyists to use their ties to Congressional staff to 1) generate a Congressional request for the Inspector General of the Department of Housing and Urban Development (HUD) to investigate OFHEO's conduct of that examination and 2) insert into an appropriations bill language that would reduce the agency's appropriations until the Director of OFHEO was replaced.

OFHEO has directed and will continue to direct Fannie Mae to take remedial actions to enhance the safe and sound operation of the Enterprise going forward. OFHEO staff recommends actions to enhance the goal of maintaining the safety and soundness of Fannie Mae.

I. Executive Summary

In the late 1980s and 1990s, Fannie Mae grew rapidly into the largest firm in the U.S. housing finance system and a major global financial institution. The Enterprise achieved double-digit growth in earnings per common share (EPS) for 15 straight years and leveraged its extraordinary financial success into enormous political influence. That financial and political success gave rise to a corporate culture at Fannie Mae in which senior management promoted the Enterprise as one of the lowest-risk financial institutions in the world and as "best in class" in terms of risk management, financial reporting, internal control, and corporate governance.

Fannie Mae management expected to write the rules that applied to the Enterprise and to impede efforts at effective safety and soundness regulation. Those rules included managerial latitude in deciding when to comply with Generally Accepted Accounting Principles (GAAP) and engaging in and concealing improper earnings management for the purpose of achieving announced earnings targets.

When Franklin Raines became Chairman and Chief Executive Officer (CEO) of Fannie Mae in 1999, he sought to lead the Enterprise into a new era of growth in business volumes and profits by challenging senior management and employees to double EPS in five years. Mr. Raines also made changes in Fannie Mae's compensation programs that enhanced incentives to achieve that goal.

A combination of factors led Fannie Mae senior management, through their actions and inactions, to commit or tolerate a wide variety of unsafe and unsound practices and conditions. Those factors included the Enterprise's enormous financial resources and political influence, the expectation that senior management could write the rules that applied to Fannie Mae, financial rewards tied to a measure of profits that management could easily manipulate, and the relative disinterest of senior executives in adhering to standards of prudent business operations.

Fannie Mae's Board of Directors contributed to those problems by failing to be sufficiently informed and to act independently of its chairman, Franklin Raines, and senior management, and by failing to exercise the requisite oversight over the Enterprise's operations.

That misconduct ultimately led to the Securities and Exchange Commission (SEC) directing Fannie Mae to restate its financial results for 2002 through mid-2004, the departure of Mr. Raines and the Enterprise's Chief Financial Officer (CFO), Timothy Howard, losses of tens of billions of dollars in market capitalization for Fannie Mae shareholders, and expenses for the restatement process, regulatory examinations, investigations, and litigation that the Enterprise has recently estimated will exceed $1.3 billion in 2005 and 2006 alone.

Improper earnings management at Fannie Mae increased the annual bonuses and other compensation linked to EPS that senior management received. Compensation for senior executives that was driven by or linked to EPS dwarfed basic salary and benefits. For CEO Franklin Raines, for example, two compensation components directly tied to meeting EPS goals accounted for more than $20 million for the six years from 1998 through 2003. Three-year EPS goals also played a crucial role in determining the size of the approximately $32 million awarded to Mr. Raines during that six-year period under a long-term executive compensation program. In total, over $52 million of Mr. Raines' compensation of $90 million during the period was directly tied to achieving EPS targets.

This report describes the development and extent of the problems with Fannie Mae's accounting policies, internal controls, financial reporting, and corporate governance that led to the restatement of the Enterprise's financial reports and the actions to remedy that situation that the Office of Federal Housing Enterprise Oversight (OFHEO) has directed the Enterprise to take to date. The report also recommends that actions be taken to enhance the goal of maintaining the safety and soundness of Fannie Mae.

Corporate Culture and Tone at the Top

During the period covered by this report, the corporate culture of Fannie Mae encouraged a perception of the Enterprise as a low-risk financial institution that was so well managed that it could hit announced profit targets on the nose every year, regardless of the state of the economy, and that compensated its senior executives appropriately for its extraordinary performance. The highest levels of senior management wanted Fannie Mae to be viewed as "one of the lowest risk financial institutions in the world" and as "best in class" in terms of risk management, financial reporting, corporate governance, and internal control. Chairman and CEO Franklin Raines, CFO Timothy Howard, and other members of the inner circle of senior Enterprise executives sought to convey that image to the public, employees, the Board of Directors, and investors.

The image of Fannie Mae communicated by Mr. Raines and his inner circle and promoted by the Enterprise's corporate culture was false. In the words of one current member of Fannie Mae's Board of Directors, the picture of the Enterprise as a "best-in-class" financial institution was a "façade." To maintain that façade, senior executives worked strenuously to hide Fannie Mae's operational deficiencies and significant risk exposures from outside observers—the Board of Directors, its external auditor, OFHEO, the Congress, and the public. The illusory nature of the Enterprise's public image and senior management's efforts at concealment were the two essential features of the Enterprise's corporate culture. Those features, which were both supported by repeated improper manipulation of earnings, are a major theme of the report.

Fannie Mae's corporate culture emerged in the late 1980s and early 1990s, when the Enterprise enjoyed extraordinary financial and political success that lasted until 2004. Over the years Fannie Mae compiled a remarkable track record of achieving its political objectives. As then Chief Operating Officer Daniel Mudd remarked in a memorandum to CEO Franklin Raines in November 2004, "[t]he old political reality was that we always won, we took no prisoners, and we faced little organized political opposition."

Senior management expected to be able to write the rules that applied to Fannie Mae and to thwart efforts to regulate the Enterprise. As Mr. Mudd remarked in the memorandum to Mr. Raines mentioned above, "We used to, by virtue of our peculiarity, be able to write, or have written, rules that worked for us." Writing their own rules included deciding when to comply with GAAP, engaging in and concealing earnings management, and failing to cooperate with and trying to interfere with OFHEO's special examination.

Fannie Mae senior management also skillfully promoted an image of the Enterprise as a private firm whose corporate objectives were essentially identical to the federal government's public policy objectives. The message was: what is good for Fannie Mae is good for housing and the nation. Senior executives used that image and their political influence to try to ensure that Fannie Mae operated under rules that differed from those that applied to other corporations.

The existence of a federal agency with the ability to regulate the Enterprise represented a direct challenge to senior management. To deal with that challenge, Fannie Mae took the extreme position that OFHEO simply had little authority over the Enterprise, while Fannie Mae's lobbyists worked to insure that the agency was poorly funded and its budget remained subject to approval in the annual appropriations process. The goal of senior management was straightforward: to force OFHEO to rely on the Enterprise for information and expertise to such a degree that Fannie Mae would essentially be regulated only by itself.

Fannie Mae's resistance to OFHEO's regulatory efforts intensified after the agency initiated its special examination of the Enterprise in 2003. Senior management made efforts to interfere with the examination by directing Fannie Mae's lobbyists to use their ties to Congressional staff to 1) generate a Congressional request for the Inspector General of the Department of Housing and Urban Development (HUD) to investigate OFHEO's conduct of that examination and 2) insert into an appropriations bill language that would reduce the agency's appropriations until Director Armando Falcon, who had initiated that examination, was replaced.

Fannie Mae's corporate culture was intensively focused on attaining EPS goals. Decisions by Mr. Raines shortly after he became CEO in 1999 set an inappropriate tone at the top that permeated the Enterprise throughout his chairmanship. For the prior year, and forecast for 1998's as yet unreported financials as well, Fannie Mae had not hit the upper end of its EPS target range, a failure that had a direct effect on the compensation of its most senior officials. Those circumstances caused Lawrence Small, an Executive Vice President, to write Mr. Raines during the summer to inform him of Mr. Small's concern that Fannie Mae's "piggy bank" and various "magic bullets" could not make up the shortfall and that there would be much discontent among senior management if they were shortchanged again.

The message from Mr. Raines was clear: EPS results mattered, not how they were achieved. In the following years, time and time again, Fannie Mae employed last-minute adjustments that enabled it to meet its EPS target, whether on a quarterly basis to meet analysts' expectations, or on an annual basis to meet compensation targets.

In 1999, Mr. Raines set a goal to double Fannie Mae's EPS within five years, from $3.23 in 1998 to $6.46 in 2003. Mr. Raines' goal and the related EPS Challenge Option Grants intensified the focus at Fannie Mae on the achievement of EPS targets and reduced attention to other objectives. Most inappropriately, Mr. Rajappa, Senior Vice President for Operations Risk and head of Fannie Mae's Office of Auditing, the corporate financial watch-dog, gave a speech to his internal auditors which encapsulated the tone at the top and corporate culture of Fannie Mae under Mr. Raines' stewardship:

By now every one of you must have 6.46 branded in your brains. You must be able to say it in your sleep, you must be able to recite it forwards and backwards, you must have a raging fire in your belly that burns away all doubts, you must live, breath and dream 6.46, you must be obsessed on 6.46. . . After all, thanks to Frank, we all have a lot of money riding on it. . . .We must do this with a fiery determination, not on some days, not on most days but day in and day out, give it your best, not 50%, not 75%, not 100%, but 150%. Remember, Frank has given us an opportunity to earn not just our salaries, benefits, raises, ESPP, but substantially over and above if we make 6.46. So it is our moral obligation to give well above our 100% and if we do this, we would have made tangible contributions to Frank's goals." [Bold emphasis added, underscore in the original]

Another reason to focus so intently on EPS targets was to preserve the illusion of low risk. Yet Fannie Mae consistently took a significant amount of interest rate risk and, when interest rates fell in recent years, incurred billions of dollars in economic losses. The Enterprise was also exposed to large operational and reputational risks.

The actions and inactions of the Board of Directors inappropriately reinforced rather than checked the tone and culture set by Mr. Raines and other senior managers. The Board failed to be sufficiently informed and independent of its chairman, Mr. Raines, and senior management, and failed to exercise the requisite oversight to ensure that the Enterprise was fully compliant with applicable law and safety and soundness standards. Those failures signaled to management and other employees that the Board did not in fact place a high value on strict compliance with laws, rules, and regulations. That message contributed to the Enterprise's many failures to comply with safety and soundness standards and the many unsafe and unsound practices documented in this report.

The conduct of Mr. Raines, CFO Timothy Howard, and other members of the inner circle of senior executives at Fannie Mae was inconsistent with the values of responsibility, accountability, and integrity. Those individuals engaged in improper earnings management in order to generate unjustified levels of compensation for themselves and other executives. They promoted a false image of the Enterprise as a "best in class" financial institution while neglecting to manage Fannie Mae properly and participating in or permitting a wide variety of unsafe and unsound practices. Those actions set a highly inappropriate tone at the top that was itself an unsafe and unsound practice.

The Executive Compensation Program

The executive compensation program of Fannie Mae provided strong incentives for senior management to engage in improper earnings management and other unsafe and unsound practices. As a direct result, senior management knowingly and purposefully used accounting maneuvers to achieve earnings goals to increase their own compensation. Meeting specific earnings goals took precedence over proper accounting, risk management, internal controls and complete and accurate financial reporting.

Under the executive compensation program, senior management reaped financial rewards when Fannie Mae met EPS growth targets established, measured, and set by senior management itself. Beyond the basic package of salary and benefits, three components of compensation depended directly on reaching EPS targets: 1) the Annual Incentive Plan, under which by 2003 more than 700 employees were eligible for bonuses; 2) the Performance Share Plan, which granted stock to the 40-50 senior executives based on 3-year performance cycles; and 3) the EPS Challenge Grant, a company-wide program championed by Franklin Raines that tied the award of a substantial amount of stock options to the doubling of core business EPS from 1998 to 2003. The AIP bonus pool grew from $8.5 million in 1993 to $65.1 million in 2003. Bonus awards for senior executives often totaled more than annual salary. For senior executives, EPS-driven compensation dwarfed basic salary and benefits.

While companies typically link the compensation of their executives to firm performance, relying heavily on one accounting-based measure such as earnings per share is problematic. Academic literature and practical experience suggests that when such a linkage exists executives can and do act aggressively to maximize their compensation by making accounting adjustments.

For the top senior executives at Fannie Mae, the entire Annual Incentive Plan bonus payout depended on annual EPS performance, increasing the incentive for senior executives to manipulate both EPS and EPS targets. Furthermore, the Annual Incentive Plan provided no incentive for management to add to earnings once the EPS number for a maximum bonus payout was achieved. That encouraged the shifting of income forward in years of plentiful core business earnings to meet EPS targets in future years as well.

Fannie Mae's executive compensation program gave senior executives the message to focus on increasing earnings rather than controlling risk. Senior executives, including the CFO, the Controller, and the head of the Office of Internal Auditing consistently reminded managers and other employees of their personal stake in meeting EPS targets. The effectiveness of senior management in both setting and hitting EPS targets to attain maximum bonus payouts is demonstrated by its track record. From 1996 through 2003, the final EPS number was always at or near the number required for a maximum Annual Incentive Plan bonus payout.

Fannie Mae senior management achieved those earnings targets by regularly manipulating earnings. They did so by, among other things, manipulating accounts and accounting rules, calibrating repurchases of shares and debt to achieve EPS targets, entering into questionable transactions, and misallocating resources. Management routinely shifted earnings to future years when the EPS target for the maximum bonus payout for the current year appeared likely. In addition, Enterprise executives purposely obscured their official disclosures of executive compensation and failed to provide complete information on the post-employment compensation awarded to former CEOs. Those actions were made possible by the failure of members of the Board of Directors to exercise oversight, the failure by senior management to ensure adequate internal controls, and failures of senior management and the members of the Board of Directors to require adequate external and internal audits.

Misapplications of GAAP, Weak Internal Controls, and Inappropriate Earnings Management

The extreme predictability of the financial results reported by Fannie Mae from 1998 through 2003, and the ability to hit EPS targets precisely each quarter, were illusions deliberately and systematically created by senior management. Senior executives exploited the weaknesses of the Enterprise's accounting and internal control system and misapplied GAAP to accomplish improper earnings management. In addition to measures and policies that primarily dampened overall earnings volatility, they used a variety of transactions and accounting manipulations to fine-tune the Enterprise's annual earnings results. The actions and inactions of senior Fannie Mae management constituted unsafe and unsound practices and failed to comply with a number of statutory and other requirements.

Senior management of Fannie Mae took pains to preserve the public perception of the Enterprise as a company that could be relied upon to produce steadily increasing earnings with a minimum of risk. The use of the "core business EPS" measure served as a foundation for implementing inappropriate earnings management techniques that conveyed to investors a false impression of Fannie Mae's financial performance and the inherent risks of its operations. Moreover, because core business earnings formed the basis for determining the amounts paid under Fannie Mae's Annual Incentive Plan, Performance Share Plan, and the EPS Challenge Grant, manipulation of reported earnings also enriched senior managers.

Senior management of Fannie Mae contravened accounting standards and regulatory requirements in a number of ways to manipulate its financial results to achieve earning objectives between the fall of 1998 and 2004. By using a variety of improper accounting techniques and financial transactions, senior executives eliminated or deferred, as needed, current period expenses and income. As a result, they simultaneously created the appearance of stable double-digit earnings growth and generally met, but only once substantially exceeded, the EPS goals that would yield the highest bonus payments.

When faced with new accounting standards that might increase earnings volatility as reported under GAAP, senior management neither initiated the development of a formal, written GAAP-compliant accounting policy nor invested in the new accounting systems needed to implement them properly. Instead, they patched existing systems and ways of doing business to accommodate their preferred interpretations of the new standards. The most significant examples discussed in the report are Fannie Mae's implementation of FAS 115,

Accounting for Certain Investments in Debt and Equity Securities, in a manner that allowed for controlling earnings volatility and minimized investment in accounting infrastructure over GAAP compliance, and the improper implementation of derivative accounting under FAS 133, *Accounting for Derivative Instruments and Hedging Activities*. Management's disregard for GAAP compliance when GAAP numbers were likely to be volatile and their reliance on obsolete systems were not limited to those two areas. Those priorities characterized the implementation of many accounting policies and practices at the Enterprise, including FIN 46, accounting for dollar roll transactions, and accounting for real estate owned.

In order to reduce volatility in reported earnings, Fannie Mae went to extraordinary lengths to avoid recording GAAP-required write-downs of asset values known as other-than-temporary impairment losses. Frequently, when faced with a situation or new accounting standard that could necessitate recording impairment expense, management chose accounting practices that did not conform with GAAP. The Enterprise's efforts to avoid impairment losses focused on manufactured-housing- and aircraft-lease-backed securities, interest-only securities, and buy-ups. With respect to buy-ups, Fannie Mae's incorrect accounting spared it approximately $500 million in impairment losses in 1998. The 1998 earnings impact with respect to interest-only securities may have been of a magnitude similar to that for buy-ups. The amount of avoided impairments related to manufactured-housing- and aircraft-lease-backed securities amounted to approximately $265 million but authoritative amounts and timing of those impairments will not be determined until Fannie Mae completes its restatement of financial results. As with other issues, senior management's preferences for avoiding the expense and effort of developing new systems and for maintaining smooth and steady earnings growth took precedence over GAAP compliance and strong internal control.

Finally, by utilizing the strategies described above as a foundation, Fannie Mae management was in a position to employ several techniques to manipulate and manage earnings more directly. Those strategies included the use of cookie-jar reserves, certain Real Estate Mortgage Investment Conduit (REMIC) transactions to delay federal taxes or defer earnings recognition, debt repurchases, and certain insurance transactions. Those reserves and transactions were utilized and maintained to provide management with the opportunity to make last minute quarter-end adjustments to hit specific earnings targets. The transactions and strategies constituted additional instances of inappropriate earnings management undertaken to achieve annual EPS targets and maximize bonus payouts to senior management, violating safety and soundness standards.

The Role of the Office of Auditing and the External Auditor

Serious failures existed in both the internal and external audit functions of Fannie Mae, creating an environment conducive to inappropriate earnings management and serious accounting failures during the period covered by this report. Fannie Mae's internal audit unit, the Office of Auditing, failed to meet OFHEO safety and soundness standards with respect to (1) the reliability and integrity of financial and operational information, (2) the effectiveness and efficiency of operations, and (3) meeting its stated audit report objectives. The Office also failed to adhere to standards established by both the Institute of Internal Auditors and the Committee of Sponsoring Organizations, including those pertaining to auditor proficiency and the exercise of due professional care. As a result, the Office also failed to meet the responsibilities assigned to it by Fannie Mae's Board of Directors.

The failures of the Office of Auditing manifested themselves in a variety of ways. The Office's audit program failed to properly confirm compliance with GAAP as specified in its audit objectives or to consistently audit critical accounting policies, practices, and estimates in a timely way. Internal audit reports prepared by the Office consistently understated problems and overstated work accomplished. Rather than undertaking independent work to confirm compliance with policies and procedures, the Office often relied on the managers of units under audit to confirm compliance. In addition, the Office had insufficient staff and insufficient expertise at a time when demands on it were increasing due to the increased size and complexity of Fannie Mae's business, major information technology (IT) projects, and new assignments.

The Office of Auditing failed to perform its primary tasks and issued misleading reports about its work. Internal audits, although they indicated otherwise, failed to assure the compliance with GAAP of numerous accounting policies and practices. Internal auditors also failed to exercise due professional care in audits of critical accounting policies, practices, and estimates. That failure included improper testing of accounting procedures and practices and of internal controls, resulting in improper assurances of compliance with GAAP and improper assurances to the Audit Committee of the Board of Directors regarding internal controls. In addition, the Office of Auditing failed to exercise due professional care in investigating allegations of accounting improprieties raised by Roger Barnes, an employee of the Office of the Controller.

When shortcomings were found, they were not adequately addressed or communicated. Rather, the Office of Auditing misstated the extent of their assessments, especially with respect to GAAP. The Office's communications to the Audit Committee of the Board of Directors were frequently incomplete and inadequate, thereby violating its own Board-approved Charter and best practices. Perhaps the most serious communication failure concerned the Office's scope of its duties with regard to testing for GAAP compliance.

Similarly, external audits performed by KPMG failed to include an adequate review of Fannie Mae's significant accounting policies for GAAP compliance. KPMG also improperly provided unqualified opinions on financial statements even though they contained significant departures from GAAP. Both the failure to review adequately significant accounting policies and procedures for GAAP compliance and the representations regarding GAAP compliance indicate that Fannie Mae's external audits contravened requirements established by OFHEO. The failure of KPMG to detect and disclose the serious weaknesses in policies, procedures, systems, and controls in Fannie Mae's financial accounting and reporting, coupled with the failure of the Board of Directors to oversee KPMG properly, contributed to the unsafe and unsound conditions at the Enterprise.

Both the internal investigation of Mr. Barnes' allegations and KPMG's external review of that investigation contravened safety and soundness standards that require an Enterprise both to maintain and implement internal controls that among other things provide for compliance with laws, regulations and policies, and to establish and maintain an effective risk management framework, to monitor its effectiveness, and to take appropriate action to correct any weaknesses. The internal investigation was tainted by an incomplete review of the accounting issues. The external review was not sufficient to make a determination regarding the propriety of the investigation performed by Fannie Mae or to evaluate the Enterprise's conclusions regarding Mr. Barnes' assertions. The external review team had insufficient independent understanding of the accounting issues involved, failed to review Fannie Mae's internal accounting policy for compliance with GAAP, and relied on the auditors that had already expressed an opinion on the questioned accounting practices.

The Role of Senior Management

Fannie Mae senior executives engaged in a number of unsafe and unsound practices to smooth reported earnings, hit the EPS targets that determined their compensation, achieve rapid growth while keeping administrative and other infrastructure-related expenses as low as possible, and limit internal and external criticism of the Enterprise. Those practices include failing to establish a sound internal control system; failing to maintain the independence and objectivity of Fannie Mae's internal auditor; failing to disclose to external parties accurate information about the Enterprise's financial condition and operations; failing to investigate employee allegations and concerns; failing to allow the Board of Directors unrestricted access to members of management; and making efforts to interfere with OFHEO's special examination.

Those failures allowed Fannie Mae senior management, for a time, to avoid questions or criticism about the Enterprise's improper accounting policies and transactions or the accuracy and integrity of its financial statements. Avoiding those topics benefited those same senior executives by helping to obscure the inappropriate executive compensation they received, which was triggered by the inaccurate EPS reported in Fannie Mae's financial statements.

Fannie Mae's internal control system contravened OFHEO's supervisory standards. Senior management failed to ensure appropriate segregation of duties, invest adequate resources in accounting and financial reporting, avoid key person dependencies, implement sound accounting policy development and oversight, and prevent conflicts of interest. Those and other deficiencies in Fannie Mae's internal control system resulted from decisions, actions, or inactions of Enterprise senior management that failed to meet OFHEO standards and constituted unsafe and unsound practices.

Senior management systematically undercut the independence of Fannie Mae's Office of Internal Auditing in three important ways: they required the Office to report to the CFO and barred unfettered communications with the Audit Committee of the Board of Directors; they tied the compensation of senior management of the Office of Auditing to earnings per share, a metric based on financial statements that the Office audited; and they appointed the Enterprise's Controller to head the internal audit unit, effectively allowing him to audit his own work for a year. In addition, Fannie Mae did not devote sufficient and appropriate resources to the Office of Auditing, resulting in serious weaknesses, including insufficient staff and insufficient expertise. By undercutting the independence and objectivity of the Enterprise's internal controls and internal auditors, senior management made it much less likely that they would be challenged to address Fannie Mae's control deficiencies.

Senior management systematically withheld information about the Enterprise's operations and financial condition from the Board of Directors, its committees, its external auditors, OFHEO, the Congress, and the public—or disclosed information that was incomplete, inaccurate, or misleading. Systematically withholding information prevented others from becoming aware of Fannie Mae's earnings management strategies, the fact that the Enterprise's accounting policies did not comply with GAAP, the pervasive weaknesses of its internal control system, and related safety and soundness issues.

When problems were brought to the attention of senior management, executives failed to conduct appropriate internal investigations and to follow up on the results of those investigations. In 2003, three Fannie Mae employees expressed serious concerns about the Enterprise's accounting. Roger Barnes, then a manager in the Office of the Controller, made allegations about Fannie Mae's accounting for deferred price adjustments under FAS 91 to Sampath Rajappa, Senior Vice President for Operations Risk, who then reported those concerns promptly to Ann Kappler, Senior Vice President and General Counsel. Another employee in Securities Accounting also expressed concerns about amortization accounting to Chief Operating Officer Daniel Mudd, and a third employee echoed those concerns. Ms. Kappler and Mr. Mudd initiated flawed investigations into those allegations and concerns. When those investigations were completed, Ms. Kappler made statements about the issues raised and their disposition—in one case, to the Audit Committee of the Board of Directors—that were false and misleading.

Senior executives in the Office of the Chairman at Fannie Mae prevented members of the Board of Directors from having unrestricted access to members of Enterprise management, including preventing Mr. Rajappa from having unfettered communication with the Audit Committee of the Board, despite the fact that Mr. Rajappa ostensibly reported to the chairman of that committee. Imposing restrictions on the access to Fannie Mae management by members of the Enterprise's Board of Directors violated OFHEO's regulatory requirements and impaired the ability of the Board to discharge its fiduciary duties.

The Role of the Board of Directors

The Board of Directors and its committees failed to meet the safety and soundness obligations set forth in OFHEO corporate governance regulations and other applicable standards for corporate governance. The members of the Board were all knowledgeable and qualified individuals, fully capable of understanding the business and corporate governance duties with which they were charged. The sophisticated and prestigious members of the Board failed to stay appropriately informed of corporate strategy, assure appropriate delegations of authority, ensure that Board committees functioned effectively, provide an appropriate check on Chairman and CEO Raines, hire and retain a qualified senior executive officer to manage the internal audit function, initiate independent investigations of Fannie Mae, and ensure timely and accurate reports to federal regulators.

The responsibilities of the Fannie Mae Board of Directors are clearly articulated in OFHEO's corporate governance regulation, which requires the Board to further the safety and soundness of the Enterprise and sets forth affirmative duties of the Board in carrying out those responsibilities. The corporate governance regulation also points the Boards of Directors of Fannie Mae and Freddie Mac to other applicable laws, such as those of the State in which an Enterprise chooses to incorporate, and to publications and other pronouncements of OFHEO for additional guidance on the conduct and responsibilities of the Board. The Fannie Mae Charter Act also sets forth the duties of the Board. Each of those authoritative sources delineates clear and consistent instructions for the Board to fulfill its oversight responsibilities.

The Board of Directors of Fannie Mae delegated important safety and soundness responsibilities to, and relied on reports from, its Audit and Compensation Committees. Those committees failed to meet regulatory and corporate standards in discharging their responsibilities. The failures of the Audit Committee had the most far-reaching safety and soundness implications, both because of the required independence of its directors and the scope of its responsibilities. The Audit Committee failed to safeguard Fannie Mae safety and soundness by providing inadequate oversight of the internal audit function and the performance of the head of the Office of Auditing, including issues of independence and objectivity. The Audit Committee failed to address the conflict of interest created by an inappropriate compensation system that tied auditors' compensation to the Enterprise-wide drive to double EPS. The Audit Committee failed to oversee the preparation of financial statements, to monitor the development and implementation of critical accounting policies, and to develop in-depth or specialized knowledge necessary to its oversight responsibilities. Finally, the Audit Committee failed to initiate a thorough investigation of whistle-blower claims of accounting irregularities when they arose.

The failure of the Audit Committee was compounded by failures of the Compensation Committee. The primary role of the Compensation Committee is to assure that senior management is properly compensated for its role in directing the affairs of the Enterprise. Nevertheless, the Compensation Committee approved a compensation structure that focused on a single measure—EPS—that was easily manipulated by management. The Compensation Committee failed to monitor that compensation system for abuse by senior management. The Compensation Committee also did not align the compensation of Fannie Mae's internal auditors with appropriate objectives. Finally, the Compensation Committee was too passive in allowing management to script its meetings and influence its choice of an independent compensation consultant.

In addition to the failures of the Audit and Compensation Committees, Fannie Mae's full Board of Directors failed in a number of ways that put the safety and soundness of the Enterprise at risk. The Board failed to stay informed of Fannie Mae corporate strategy, major plans of action, and risk policy. Having approved an executive compensation system that created incentives to manipulate earnings, members of the Board failed to monitor against such manipulations. The Board failed to provide delegations of authority to management that reflected the current size and complexity of the Enterprise. The Board failed to assure the effective operation of its own Audit and Compensation Committees. The Board failed to act as a check on the authority of Chairman and CEO Franklin Raines, and allowed him to concentrate considerable power in the hands of one person, CFO Timothy Howard. The Board failed to initiate an independent inquiry into Fannie Mae's accounting following the announcement of Freddie Mac's restatement and subsequent investigations, or the allegations by Roger Barnes, both of which involved earnings management. The Board failed to assure itself that the Enterprise's regulators were properly informed of Mr. Barnes' allegations. The Board also failed to ensure timely and accurate reports to Federal regulators.

The bedrock principle of OFHEO's regulation of Fannie Mae is that the entity must operate safely and soundly. The Board, in turn, must take reasonable steps to be sure that senior management is operating the Enterprise in accordance with that principle. Judging by the actions and inactions of the Fannie Mae Board, standards of prudent operation clearly were not met. Rather than an active, concerned Board that effectively supervised senior management, the Fannie Mae Board of Directors was a passive and complacent entity, controlled by, rather than controlling, senior management. The Board and its committees missed a host of opportunities to uncover and correct the issues and events described in this report. Instead, Fannie Mae suffered an enormous loss in credibility and reputation, and its shareholders suffered large financial losses. An effective Board, operating in accord with generally accepted standards of prudent operation, would have prevented much of what occurred.

Remedial Actions

During the period of the special examination, OFHEO has directed Fannie Mae to take a number of actions, both as a result of the special examination and as part of OFHEO's continuous supervisory program. To prevent the recurrence of improper conduct, those steps have sought to remedy deficiencies and to enhance the safe and sound operation of the Enterprise going forward.

In an agreement with the Board of Directors reached in September 2004, OFHEO directed Fannie Mae to maintain an additional 30 percent of capital above the minimum capital requirement to compensate for the additional risk and challenges facing the Enterprise. Furthermore, OFHEO directed that Fannie Mae submit for approval the Enterprise's strategy to preserve and maintain capital levels at the required level and contingency plans in case those primary methods prove insufficient. OFHEO also directed Fannie Mae to obtain prior written permission from OFHEO before undertaking certain specified corporate actions and to inform OFHEO of any other significant action likely to impair the ability of the Enterprise to maintain capital sufficient to meet the required capital surplus levels.

As a result of those directives, Fannie Mae has taken significant actions to improve its capital position. Those actions included the issuance of $5 billion in preferred stock, a reduction in the Enterprise's common stock dividend, and a reduction in its on-balance sheet assets. The Enterprise will keep the enhanced capital position until the Director of OFHEO releases or modifies the requirement based upon satisfactory resolution of accounting and internal control issues that are the subject of OFHEO examination.

In addition to the capital requirements, OFHEO directed the Board of Directors of Fannie Mae to make significant changes to its corporate governance structure. Those changes include, but are not limited to, separating the Chairman of the Board and Chief Executive Officer positions, creating a new independent Office of Compliance and Ethics to conduct internal investigations, creating a Compliance Committee of the Board of Directors to monitor and coordinate compliance with the Enterprise's agreements with OFHEO, establishing a program for no less than annual briefings to the Board and senior management on legal and regulatory compliance requirements applicable to Fannie Mae, and creating a procedure for the General Counsel of Fannie Mae to report information on actual or possible misconduct directly to the Board, which will in turn notify OFHEO.

In order to address organizational failures at Fannie Mae, OFHEO required a number of changes to the risk management, internal control, internal and external audit, and accounting functions of the Enterprise. Those changes seek to address significant weaknesses, including lack of appropriate separation of duties and insufficient technical expertise. Additionally, OFHEO directed that the Board cause an independent review of organizational, structural, staffing, and control issues, focusing on but not limited to the Chief Financial Officer,

Controller, accounting, audit, financial reporting, business planning and forecasting, modeling, and financial standards functions. As a result of that review, management has effected significant changes in the organizational structure of the Enterprise.

To address accounting problems, OFHEO directed Fannie Mae to restate inappropriate past financial statements, meeting all applicable legal and regulatory requirements, including having the new financial statements reaudited by the Enterprise's new external auditor, and to cease engaging in inappropriate hedge accounting. OFHEO also directed that the Enterprise implement an appropriate policy for FAS 91 accounting, develop and implement appropriate written policies and procedures for journal entries, and develop and implement a plan to address the deficiencies in the accounting systems for Fannie Mae's portfolio. OFHEO directed the Board to conduct reviews of certain control issues, including accounting policies and practices and procedures for journal entries. OFHEO also directed the Enterprise to conduct a complete review of staff skills, past performance, and roles in the revised corporate structure in accounting. Significant personnel changes have been made.

Recommendations

Based on the special examination of Fannie Mae, OFHEO's staff recommends to the Director that the following actions be taken to enhance the goal of maintaining the safety and soundness of the Enterprise.

1. Fannie Mae should be subject to penalties and fines consistent with the findings of this report.
2. Fannie Mae must meet all of its commitments for remediation and do so with an emphasis on implementation—with dates certain—of plans already presented to OFHEO.
3. Fannie Mae must maintain a capital surplus until the Director determines a change in the surplus amount is warranted.
4. Fannie Mae must continue to use independent consultants acceptable to the Director to validate and assure compliance with requirements. Cyclical targeted exams by independent consultants, at least every two years, are needed to assure systems and practices are being implemented properly.
5. Fannie Mae must develop new structures and operational plans for its Board of Directors related to Board reporting, maintenance of minutes, and other changes that will enhance Board oversight of the Enterprise's management.
6. Fannie Mae must review OFHEO's report to determine additional steps to take to improve its controls, accounting systems, risk management practices and systems, external relations program, data quality, and corporate culture. Once OFHEO has approved the Enterprise's plans, an emphasis must be placed on implementation of those plans.
7. Fannie Mae must undertake a review of individuals currently with the Enterprise that are mentioned in this report and provide OFHEO a report as to conclusions regarding terminations, transfers, or other remedial steps (such as disgorgement, restitution, or alteration of benefits) in cases of misconduct.

8. Fannie Mae must assure that departments are fully and appropriately staffed with skilled professionals who have available regular training opportunities in financial services industry standards.
9. Due to Fannie Mae's current operational and internal control deficiencies and other risks, the Enterprise's growth should be limited.
10. OFHEO should continue to develop its program of regulatory infrastructure to add additional rules and regulations that enhance the transparency of its supervision of the Enterprises. With the end of the special examination, OFHEO staff should be directed to address additional items raised during the preparation of this report as part of the regular examination program.
11. OFHEO should continue to support legislation to provide the powers essential to meeting its mission of assuring safe and sound operations at the Enterprises.
12. Matters identified in this report should be referred to OFHEO's Office of the General Counsel for determination of enforcement actions that the Director may wish to consider.
13. Matters identified for remediation by Fannie Mae should be considered by the Director for application to both Enterprises.

II. The History of the Special Examination

This report by the Office of Federal Housing Enterprise Oversight (OFHEO) presents the findings of a special examination of accounting policies, internal controls, financial reporting, corporate governance, and other safety and soundness matters at Fannie Mae. This chapter reviews the history of that examination. The chapter also summarizes the documentation reviewed and the interviews conducted by OFHEO that provide the basis for the facts and conclusions set forth in the remainder of the report.

Initiation of the Special Examination

On July 17, 2003, OFHEO Director Armando Falcon testified before the United States Senate Committee on Banking, Housing, and Urban Affairs that OFHEO intended to conduct a special accounting review of Fannie Mae in order to evaluate independently accounting policies at the Enterprise and examine whether the implementation of those policies complied with Generally Accepted Accounting Principles (GAAP). On July 18, 2003, OFHEO directed Fannie Mae to assure that the document-retention policies of the Enterprise maintain the integrity of written, electronic, and other information media in the accounting area and related internal control functions. In October 2003, OFHEO issued a Request for Proposals from accounting firms to assist OFHEO in conducting the special examination, which resulted in the engagement of Deloitte & Touche to assist OFHEO.

September 2004 Report of Findings to Date

On September 17, 2004, OFHEO issued a *Report of Findings to Date of the Special Examination of Fannie Mae*. That report was based on an exhaustive investigation by

OFHEO of significant problems with respect to the Enterprise's accounting policies and practices relating to premium and discount amortization (FAS 91[1]) and derivatives and hedging activities (FAS 133[2]). The report also dealt with more general problems relating to accounting policy development, poor segregation of duties, and other internal control deficiencies.

OFHEO concluded that the FAS 91 accounting used by Fannie Mae for amortizing purchase premiums and discounts on securities and loans as well as amortizing other deferred charges was not in accordance with GAAP. Management intentionally developed accounting policies and selected and applied accounting methods to inappropriately reduce earnings volatility and to provide themselves inordinate flexibility in determining the amount of income and expense recognized in any accounting period. In that regard, the amortization policies that management developed and the methods they applied created a "cookie jar" reserve. In addition, OFHEO found (among other things) that management:

- Deliberately developed and adopted accounting policies to spread estimated income or expense that exceeded predetermined thresholds over multiple reporting periods;
- Established a materiality threshold for estimated income and expense, within which management could avoid making adjustments that would otherwise be required under FAS 91;
- Made discretionary adjustments to the financial statement for the sole purpose of minimizing volatility and achieving desired financial results;
- Forecasted and managed future unrecognized income associated with misapplied GAAP;
- Capitalized reconciliation differences as 'phantom' assets or liabilities and amortized them at the same speeds as 30-year fixed-rate mortgages;
- Developed estimation methods that were inconsistently applied to retrospective and prospective amortization required by FAS 91 for current and future periods;
- Developed and implemented processes to generate multiple estimates of amortization and varying assumptions in order to select estimates that provided optimal accounting results;
- Failed to properly investigate the concerns of an employee regarding illogical and anomalous amortization results, along with a further allegation by that employee of an intent to misstate reported income; and
- Tolerated significant weaknesses in internal controls surrounding the amortization process; and inappropriately deferred $200 million of estimated amortization expenses in 1998, which had significant effects on executive compensation.

OFHEO also concluded that Fannie Mae implemented FAS 133 in a manner that placed minimizing earnings volatility and maintaining simplicity of operations above compliance with GAAP. OFHEO found (among other things) that Fannie Mae did not assess and record hedge ineffectiveness as required by FAS 133 and applied hedge accounting to hedging relationships that did not qualify. Fannie Mae treated many hedge relationships as perfectly effective when they were not, improperly ignored ineffectiveness in hedge relationships, and failed to perform assessment tests. Fannie Mae applied the "short-cut" method or the "matched terms" method for a broad range of hedge relationships where those methods were inappropriate. In addition, OFHEO identified a number of problems with hedge documentation by Fannie Mae. The lack of appropriate hedge documentation is not only a GAAP violation but is evidence of a poor control framework and is a significant safety and soundness problem.

Further, OFHEO identified control weaknesses in the accounting policy development process at Fannie Mae. OFHEO found that these weaknesses contributed to the implementation of accounting policies that did not conform with GAAP. OFHEO found that a combination of heavy workloads, weak technical skills, and a weak review environment contributed to the development of key person dependencies and inadequate separation of duties. OFHEO also found that Chief Financial Officer Timothy Howard failed to provide adequate oversight of key control and reporting functions within Fannie Mae.

This report provides a comprehensive review of the findings to date of OFHEO's special examination of Fannie Mae and covers the period from 1998 through 2004. Where OFHEO's September 2004 *Report of Findings to Date* provided a detailed discussion of an issue or event, this report generally treats that issue or event in a more abbreviated form.

September 2004 Agreement

On September 27, 2004, OFHEO and the Board of Directors of Fannie Mae entered into an agreement requiring the Board to cause to be conducted a review of the accounting matters detailed in the September 2004 OFHEO report, and to also address and remedy matters pertaining to capital, organization and staffing, compensation, governance, and internal controls. The Board of Directors, with the approval of OFHEO, hired the law firm Paul Weiss Rifkin Wharton & Garrison, LLP, to conduct the review with a team of lawyers and accountants led by former Senator Warren Rudman. This report refers to that team as the Counsel to the Special Review Committee.

SEC Decision

Subsequent to the September 2004 Agreement, Fannie Mae requested that the Office of the Chief Accountant of the Securities and Exchange Commission (SEC) review the Enterprise's interpretation and application of generally accepted accounting principles relating to FAS 91 and FAS 133.[3] On December 15, 2004, the Chief Accountant of the SEC, Donald Nicolaisen, announced that, after reviewing the September 2004 OFHEO report and letters from Fannie Mae explaining its positions, the SEC had found that the accounting policies of Fannie Mae for both FAS 91 and FAS 133 departed from GAAP in material respects, and advised the Enterprise to restate its financial statements for the years 2001 through 2004.[4]

Continuation of the Special Examination

The OFHEO special examination of Fannie Mae continued after the release of the September 2004 OFHEO report, as the agency investigated additional accounting and other issues. After the December 15, 2004, SEC announcement, Fannie Mae replaced its then external auditor—KPMG, LLP—with Deloitte & Touche. The latter firm ended its engagement with OFHEO soon afterward. On February 11, 2005, OFHEO wrote a letter to the Chairman of the Board of Fannie Mae, Stephen Ashley, detailing findings and requesting information about the following areas:

- classification of mortgage securities as either held-to-maturity or available for sale under FAS 115;[5]
- accounting for dollar rolls under FAS 140;6
- classification of mortgage loans as either held for investment or held for sale under FAS 65;[7]
- avoidance of consolidation on its balance sheet, under FIN 46,[8] of mortgage-backed securities when the Enterprise owned 100 percent of the securities;
- accounting for mortgage purchase commitments under FAS 149;[9]
- specific practices relating to the smoothing of interest income and expense;
- internal controls related to journal entries;
- securities accounting systems; and
- controls surrounding database modifications.

March 2005 Supplemental Agreement

On March 7, 2005, OFHEO and Fannie Mae entered into a Supplemental Agreement that called for internal reviews of (1) journal entry procedures; (2) internal controls associated with manual modifications to databases supporting the general ledger; (3) legal and regulatory structures, responsibilities, and personnel; and (4) bylaws and codes of conduct to assure that they support legal and regulatory compliance. The Supplemental Agreement also required the Enterprise to conduct a re-audit and restatement for prior earnings periods, as necessary, and to review its accounting for the accounting standards that were questioned in the February 11, 2005, letter.

Fannie Mae has conducted internal reviews of the issues raised by OFHEO, in compliance with the September 2004 Agreement and March 2005 Supplemental Agreement between the Enterprise and the agency. The findings of those reviews have fully supported the September 2004 OFHEO report.[10] Chapter X reviews the significant changes put in motion by the September 2004 Agreement, the March 2005 Supplemental Agreement, and other actions by the agency.

Documentation Received and Interviews Conducted to Date

The facts and conclusions set forth in this report are based on OFHEO's review of documents and other information provided to us by Fannie Mae, the Counsel to the Special Review Committee of the Enterprise's Board of Directors, KPMG, and Ernst & Young. OFHEO issued its first information request related to the special examination on November 21, 2003, and has made numerous additional requests. Between November 21, 2003, and the date of this report, OFHEO received approximately 2.8 million pages of hard copy documentation and 4.1 million pages of electronic documentation from the Enterprise and the

Special Review Committee; and more that 700,000 pages of work papers and other documentation from KPMG, LLP, and Ernst & Young, the latter firm having assisted Fannie Mae counsel during the special examination. In addition, the Counsel to the Special Review Committee provided to OFHEO documents that it received from Fannie Mae, as well as copies of memoranda documenting 241 interviews it conducted of current and former employees and third parties. OFHEO also reviewed the transcripts of 47 interviews of current and former Fannie Mae and KPMG employees conducted by the SEC.

OFHEO conducted 26 informal interviews and 55 formal, on-the-record interviews of current and former Fannie Mae employees and members of the Board of Directors. In addition, OFHEO conducted formal interviews of 7 current and former KPMG employees who had been assigned to the Fannie Mae engagement.

References

[1] Statement of Financial Accounting Standards (FAS) No. 91, Accounting for Nonrefundable Fees and Costs Associated with Originating or Acquiring Loans and Initial Direct Costs of Leases.

[2] Statement of Financial Accounting Standards (FAS) No. 133, Accounting for Derivative Instruments and Hedging Activities.

[3] Letter from Jonathan Boyles to Stephen Cutler and Paul Berger, Oct. 19, 2004, FNMSEC 2215-64, and letter from Jonathan Boyles to Stephen Cutler and Paul Berger, November 3, 2004, FNMSEC 151-64.

[4] SEC Press Release 2004-172, December 15, 2004.

[5] Statement of Financial Accounting Standards (FAS) No. 115, Accounting for Certain Investments in Debt and Equity Securities.

[6] Statement of Financial Accounting Standards (FAS) No. 140, Accounting for Transfers and Servicing of Financial Assets and Extinguishments of Liabilities.

[7] Statement of Financial Accounting Standards (FAS) No. 65, Accounting for Certain Mortgage Banking Activities.

[8] FASB Interpretation No. 46, Consolidation of Variable Interest Entities (revised December 2003). (II.9)

[9] Statement of Financial Accounting Standards (FAS) No. 149, Amendment of Statement 133 on Derivative Instruments and Hedging Activities.

[10] Counsel to the Special Review Committee, A Report to the Special Review Committee of The Board of Directors of Fannie Mae, February 23, 2006.

III. OFHEO'S AUTHORITIES AND STANDARDS OF REVIEW

The Office of Federal Housing Enterprise Oversight (OFHEO) has broad authorities to prescribe safety and soundness standards, conduct examinations, and enforce compliance with its standards. The agency evaluates the conduct and safety and soundness of the Enterprises in light of standards articulated in relevant statutes, OFHEO regulations and guidance, and other relevant laws and industry practices. The regulatory pronouncements of the Federal banking agencies and related judicial decisions reinforce OFHEO's standards and provide reliable guidance for determining the types of unsafe and unsound Enterprise conduct subject to OFHEO review and action. This chapter reviews OFHEO's authorities and the standards of review that the special examination has applied to the conduct of Fannie Mae.

Authorities

The Congress created the Office of Federal Housing Enterprise Oversight to operate as a "financial safety and soundness regulator."[1] The Congress determined that OFHEO should have the authority to establish capital standards, require financial disclosure, prescribe adequate standards for books and records and other internal controls, conduct examinations when necessary, and enforce compliance with the standards and rules that the agency establishes.[2]

Consistent with that purpose, OFHEO's Director was charged with the duty of ensuring that the Enterprises are adequately capitalized and operating safely,[3] in accordance with the Federal Housing Enterprises Financial Safety and Soundness Act of 1992 ("the Safety and Soundness Act").[4] The Director is authorized "to make such determinations, take such actions, and perform such functions as [he] determines necessary regarding ... examinations of the [E]nterprises ... [and] administrative and enforcement actions ... with respect to ... matters relating to safety and soundness."[5] The Director is charged with causing an on-site examination of each Enterprise annually, and other examinations as-needed basis, "to determine the condition of the [E]nterprise for the purpose of ensuring its financial safety and soundness."[6] OFHEO must report annually to the appropriate committees of the Senate and the House of Representatives, describing the financial safety and soundness of each Enterprise.[7]

OFHEO possesses supervisory responsibilities and powers "essentially similar to those of the Federal bank regulatory agencies."[8]

> The Director [of OFHEO] has powers that closely resemble those of the independent federal regulatory agencies, including specifically the federal banking regulatory agencies.[9]
>
> The [Senate] Committee has looked to federal banking regulation as a model, because it believes that the Director of the Office of Federal Housing Enterprise Oversight ... will have to deal with financial regulatory issues that are similar to, and as complex as, those within the jurisdiction of the banking agencies.[10]

The Congress charged OFHEO with acting to ensure the safe and sound operation of the Enterprises "at all points on the supervisory spectrum between examination and enforcement."[11] Thus, OFHEO is also charged with ensuring that each Enterprise acts prudently in dealing with perceived problems as they emerge.[12]

Standards of Review

OFHEO has produced regulations, guidances and examination documents that provide Fannie Mae and Freddie Mac with information on the expectations of OFHEO with respect to safe and sound conduct and operating methods. In evaluating the conduct of the Enterprises, OFHEO looks to those explicit standards as well as to the Enterprises' own policies, applicable laws, and standards promulgated by industry.

Minimum Standards for Safety and Soundness

In December 2000, OFHEO issued a written policy guidance setting forth minimum safety and soundness standards in eight broad areas of concern.[13] In August 2002, OFHEO published a Safety and Soundness rule that incorporated that guidance.[14] Modeled in large part on similar standards promulgated by the Office of the Comptroller of the Currency,[15] the guidance did not effect a change in the policies of OFHEO but set forth the basic underlying criteria used historically to evaluate safety and soundness.[16] Contravention of the guidance establishes a red flag that the safety and soundness of an Enterprise may be at risk; OFHEO need merely evaluate the conduct and consider it in the context of any harm incurred or that is reasonably foreseeable. The guidance describes the following standards of prudent business operation for Fannie Mae and Freddie Mac. OFHEO has amplified these standards in subsequent regulation and guidance.

> *Asset Underwriting and Credit Quality* – Each Enterprise should "implement policies and procedures to adequately assess credit risks" through "prudent underwriting standards."
>
> *Balance Sheet Growth* – Each Enterprise should manage its balance sheet so that balance sheet growth is prudent, and should consider changes in risk that may occur as a result of balance sheet growth, and appropriate policies and procedures needed to manage risk that may occur as a result of balance sheet growth.
>
> *Market Risks* – Each Enterprise should protect itself from various risks (*e.g.*, changes in interest rates) by developing plans for responding to each contingency.
>
> *Information Technology* – Each Enterprise should have adequate information technology for its operations, with appropriate security measures.
>
> *Board and Management Responsibilities and Functions* – Each Enterprise's Board of Directors must work with management to establish strategies and goals and must ensure (1) that management is held accountable for meeting the goals and objectives of the Enterprise, (2) that the board is provided with accurate information about the operations and financial condition of the Enterprise, (3) that the organization structure and assignment of responsibilities of the Enterprise provide clear accountability and controls, and (4) that management establishes an effective risk management framework including a periodic review of that framework to monitor its effectiveness and take steps to correct any weakness.
>
> *Internal Controls* – Each Enterprise should maintain and implement internal controls that, at a minimum, provide for an organizational structure and assignment of responsibility that provide for accountability and controls including adherence to policies and procedures; a control framework commensurate with

> the Enterprises' risks; policies and procedures adequate to safeguard assets; and compliance with applicable laws, regulations and policies.
>
> *Audits* – Each Enterprise should establish and implement internal and external audit programs (1) to monitor the internal controls, (2) to maintain the independence of the audit function, (3) to assure that qualified professionals and management conduct and review the audit functions, (4) to adequately test and review audited areas and to adequately document findings and recommendations, and (5) to verify and review measures and actions taken to address identified material weaknesses. OFHEO's statute specifically names a failure to maintain adequate books and records as a failure to meet safety and soundness standards.
>
> *Information Reporting and Documentation* – Each Enterprise should establish and implement policies and procedures for generating and retaining reports and documents that, *inter alia*, (1) enable the board of directors to make informed decisions and to exercise its oversight function by providing all such relevant information in an appropriate level of detail as necessary, and (2) ensure decision makers have appropriate and necessary information about particular transactions and business operations, and (3) ensure timely and complete submissions of reports of financial condition and operations, as well as annual and other periodic reports and special reports to OFHEO.[17]

Compliance with those minimum standards will not necessarily preclude a finding "that the Enterprise is otherwise engaged in a specific unsafe or unsound practice," leaving room for OFHEO to determine whether conduct not fitting squarely within the above categories nevertheless is unsafe or unsound.[18]

The standards of prudent business operation set forth in the guidance have been amplified in subsequent regulation. OFHEO has put in place a corporate governance rule that requires the board of directors and senior officers of an Enterprise to undertake focused efforts to meet their obligations and, in particular, for the board of directors to oversee effectively corporate operations. The corporate governance rule establishes the following minimum standards for safety and soundness affecting corporate governance policy and practices of the Enterprise.[19] Those standards recognize existing and accepted practices in the financial services industry for prudent operation, as well as citing other government agencies or standards-setting groups. Departure from any of these OFHEO-recognized standards raises safety and soundness concerns.

- *Board of Directors* – OFHEO requires that the Enterprise's board of directors exercise oversight necessary to ensure policies are in place to assure that (1) qualified managers are hired; (2) management sets policies and controls to implement the strategies of the Enterprise; (3) management is held accountable for meeting the Enterprise's goals and objectives; and (4) management provides the members of the board of directors with accurate information about the operations and financial condition of the Enterprise in a timely fashion and sufficient to enable them to effect their oversight duties and responsibilities.

- *Compensation* – Compensation shall be reasonable and appropriate, commensurate with the duties and responsibilities of the employee, and consistent with the long term goals of the Enterprise, shall not focus solely on earnings performance, and shall take into account risk management, operational stability, and legal and regulatory compliance.[20]
- *Code of Conduct and Ethics* – Each Enterprise shall establish a written code of conduct and ethics designed to assure the ability of the board members, executive officers, and employees to discharge their duties and responsibilities in an objective and impartial manner that includes standards required by section 406 of the Sarbanes Oxley Act.
- *Conduct and Responsibility of the Board of Directors* – The board of directors shall have policies and procedures in place to assure oversight of (1) corporate strategy, legal and regulatory compliance, prudent plans for growth and allocation of resources to manage risk; (2) hiring qualified executive management; (3) compensation programs; (4) integrity of accounting and financial reporting systems including audit and internal control; and, among other things, (5) process and adequacy of reporting, disclosures and communications with investors.
- *Certification of Disclosures* – The chief executive officer and finance officer of each Enterprise shall require and certify each quarterly report and annual report consistent with section 302 of the Sarbanes Oxley Act.
- *Rotation of External Auditor Partner*– An Enterprise may not accept audit services from an external auditing firm if the lead partner who has primary responsibility for the external audit has performed audit services for the Enterprise in each of the previous five years.
- *Compliance and Risk Management Program* – An Enterprise shall establish a compliance program and a risk management program.

Examination guidance issued by OFHEO in 2005 further amplifies safe and sound corporate governance practices of the Enterprises.[21] The examination guidance suggests, among other things, that the Enterprise separate the risk management function (oversight of risk taking) from the control function (oversight of accounting and financial reporting); and that the internal audit unit should function separately and independently of the chief financial officer and should report directly to the audit committee. It provides that each Enterprise should change its external auditing firm no less frequently than every 10 years, and that senior management and the board of directors of the Enterprise should review all consulting work performed by the external auditor.

In addition to the standards set forth in OFHEO guidance and regulations, the Federal National Mortgage Association Charter Act ("the Charter Act") makes certain requirements of Fannie Mae. Any failure to comply with its enabling statute raises serious safety and soundness concerns. Among other things, the Charter Act requires that the Enterprise have an annual independent audit of its financial statements by an independent public accountant in accordance with Generally Accepted Accounting Principles (GAAP).[22] The Charter Act also requires the Enterprise to submit to OFHEO annual and quarterly reports of financial condition and operation, prepared in accordance with GAAP and signed with a declaration that the report is true and correct.[23] The Safety and Soundness Act gives OFHEO the authority to require Fannie

Mae to submit reports in whatever form the Director may request.[24] The disclosure regulations of OFHEO require each Enterprise to prepare disclosures relating to its financial conditions, results of operation, business developments, and managements' expectations that include supporting financial information and certifications.[25]

A lack of appropriate oversight, whether in the form of inadequate board oversight of management, management's lax oversight of employees (including providing inadequate resources), or failing to seek to determine weaknesses, and the lack of appropriate disclosure, whether through disclosure to the board of directors, disclosure to OFHEO, or disclosure to the public, are key areas where the actions of the officers and directors of an Enterprise may be deemed unsafe or unsound.

Other Standards Considered by OFHEO

OFHEO considers other standards beyond the Safety and Soundness Act, the Charter Act and OFHEO regulations and guidance in evaluating the safety and soundness of Fannie Mae and Freddie Mac. First, OFHEO considers the compliance of an Enterprise and its directors, officers, and employees with that Enterprise's stated corporate policies and goals, usually reflected in a code of conduct, in internal manuals for procedures or controls, or in other documents that set forth expectations of the board or senior management for operations and employee conduct. Second, OFHEO regards compliance with other laws that are applicable to the Enterprises as a measure of safe and sound operations; failure to comply with those laws reflects an inherent weakness in Enterprise policies and practices. Third, OFHEO considers conformance with guidance standards such as pronouncements of the Financial Accounting Standards Board (FASB) or Generally Accepted Accounting Principles as significant indicia of safe and sound operations. Finally, OFHEO regards failures to comply with requirements of the New York Stock Exchange or other self-regulatory organizations of which an Enterprise is a member as indicia of unsafe and unsound operations or conduct.

Support for OFHEO Standards Provided by Federal Banking Law

The Federal bank regulatory agencies[26] have operated under a mandate to examine institutions, to enforce safety and soundness at the institutions whose affairs they supervise, and to identify and eliminate practices that are antithetical to safety and soundness: unsafe or unsound practices in conducting an institution's business (or, in the particular context of the regulation of banks, "unsafe or unsound banking practices").[27] As a result, an elaborate literature, including agency supervisory and enforcement documents and case law, has illuminated the concept of "unsafe or unsound practice," especially since 1966 when the Federal bank regulatory agencies were given the power to issue cease and desist orders upon findings that a regulated entity had engaged in unsafe or unsound practices in conducting its business.[28] That and related concepts and their implications are understood by common usage within the bank regulatory community, the banking industry, and the federal judiciary.

The Congress employed the same terminology in the Federal Housing Enterprises Financial Safety and Soundness Act of 1992, which established OFHEO. Accordingly, the regulatory pronouncements of the Federal banking agencies and related judicial decisions provide reliable guidance for determining the types of unsafe and unsound conduct subject to OFHEO review and action.

Definition of "Unsafe and Unsound Practice"

The federal courts accept as authoritative the definition of "unsafe or unsound practice" offered to the Congress in a 1966 memorandum from the chairman of the Federal Home Loan Bank Board, one of the Federal bank regulatory agencies that would be granted cease and desist authority through the legislation that was then being considered. As one United States court of appeals has stated:

The authoritative definition of an unsafe or unsound practice, adopted in both Houses, was a memorandum submitted by John Horne, then chairman of the [Federal Home Loan] Bank Board. See 112 Cong. Rec. 24984 (1966) (remarks of Rep. Patman) (Horne memorandum authoritative in House); id. at 26474 (remarks of Sen. Robertson) (Horne memorandum included in record in Senate). Chairman Horne defined the provision in the following way:

Generally speaking, an "unsafe or unsound practice" embraces any action, or lack of action, which is contrary to generally accepted standards of prudent operation, the possible consequences of which, if continued, would be abnormal risk or loss or damage to an institution, its shareholders, or the agencies administering the insurance funds. 112 Cong. Rec. 24984 (1966).[29]

Several other federal courts have also concluded that the so-called "Horne Memorandum" provides the appropriate definition of the term "unsafe or unsound practice."[30] The principles of that memorandum are accepted by the Federal bank regulatory agencies.[31]

In meeting the responsibilities of a safety and soundness regulator, a regulatory agency must commit over time to the progressive development of the standards of financial and operational soundness that will constitute prudent business operation. Regulators do not evaluate the institutions they supervise solely as to whether they have avoided any particular static "laundry list" of specified practices. Safety and soundness regulators are charged with addressing evolving and rapidly changing forms of unsound behavior.[32] This "expansive" and evolving view was noted as follows:

> The phrase "unsafe or unsound banking practice" is widely used in the regulatory statutes and in case law, and one of the purposes of the banking acts is clearly *to commit the progressive definition and eradication of such practices to the expertise of the appropriate regulatory agencies*."[33]

The concepts of "safety and soundness" and "unsafe or unsound" permit regulatory authorities the latitude to identify the practices whose elimination will preserve the financial integrity of the members of the industry they are bound to protect,[34] inferring them if necessary from the conditions they discover on inspection of the institution,[35] and through prompt and early intervention to permit the public to retain confidence in their financial soundness.[36] As stated by Senator Wallace Bennett of Utah during hearings on the proposed Financial Institutions Supervisory Act of 1966, whose enactment was a crucial enabler of safety and soundness regulation of the banking industry:

> We are trying to add flexibility to the powers of the supervisory agency and it is much easier to add that in general terms and trust to the judgment of those supervisors than it is to try and write the laws of the Medes and Persians by which you have a very rigid basis for judgment.[37]

Specific Practices Deemed to Be Unsafe and Unsound

Courts have found a variety of practices to constitute unsafe or unsound practices, including the following that reinforce safety and soundness regulation by OFHEO:

- operating without adequate supervision by the board of directors and management;[38]
- operating without an effective loan review system;[39]
- operating under management policies that were detrimental to the institution;[40]
- failing to disclose relevant information to a government investigator;[41]
- hindering a supervisory investigation, or attempting to do so;[42]
- failing to keep accurate records;[43]
- falsifying bank records;[44] and
- obligating one's institution to transactions that might be illegal.[45]

The Federal Deposit Insurance Corporation (FDIC) has emphasized that "unsafe or unsound practices" can result from either action or lack of action by management.[46] The FDIC has listed the following *failures to act* as examples of being "unsafe or unsound":[47]

- failure to provide adequate supervision and direction over the officers of the bank to prevent unsafe or unsound practices, and violation(s) of laws, rules and regulations;
- failure to post the general ledger promptly;
- failure to keep accurate books and records; failure to account properly for transactions;
- failure to enforce programs for the repayment of loans; and
- failure to obtain or maintain on premises evidence of priority of liens on loans secured by real estate.

The FDIC has listed the following *actions* as examples of being "unsafe or unsound":[48]

- operating with an inadequate level of capital for the kind and quality of assets held;
- engaging in hazardous lending and lax collection practices which include, but are not limited to, extending credit which is inadequately secured; extending credit without first obtaining complete and current financial information; extending credit in the form of overdrafts without adequate controls; and extending credit with inadequate diversification of risk;
- operating without adequate liquidity, in the light of the bank's asset and liability mix;
- operating without adequate internal controls including failing to segregate duties of personnel;
- engaging in speculative or hazardous investment policies; and
- paying excessive dividends in relation to the bank's capital position, earnings capacity and asset quality.

The FDIC lists the following *conditions* as examples of being "unsafe or unsound":[49]

- maintenance of unduly low net interest margins;
- excessive overhead expenses;
- excessive volume of loans subject to adverse classification;
- excessive net loan losses;
- excessive volume of overdue loans;
- excessive volume of nonearning assets; and
- excessive large liability dependence.

Conclusion

OFHEO has broad authorities to prescribe safety and soundness standards, conduct examinations, and enforce compliance with its standards. The agency has adopted regulations, guidances, and examination documents that provide Fannie Mae and Freddie Mac with standards of prudent business operation. Contravention of any of those standards establishes a sufficient basis to conclude that the safety and soundness of an Enterprise may be at risk.

OFHEO has both explicit and express duties and obligations under its statute—to examine Fannie Mae and Freddie Mac, to review executive compensation, to set capital standards—as well as the general direction of the Congress to oversee safe and sound operations of the Enterprises. The latter standard requires OFHEO to review, under changing business conditions and changing regulatory concerns and directives, the conduct of the Enterprises subject to its supervision. That is well established law and sets the nature of OFHEO's inquiry and the tool by which it measures conduct—to review conduct for the harm it may or does create in line with express, defined matters as well as generally under the goal of seeing safe and sound operating conditions set forth by the Congress.

References

[1] 12 U.S.C. § 4501 et. seq. Section 4511 is entitled "Financial Safety and Soundness Regulator.
[2] 12 U.S.C. § 4501(6).
[3] Id., at § 4513(a).
[4] Act of Oct. 28, 1992, title XIII of Pub. L. No. 102-550, 106 Stat. 3941.
[5] 12 U.S.C. § 4513(b)(5).
[6] Id. at § 4517(a) & (b).
[7] Id. At § 4521(a)(2).
[8] Office of Federal Housing Enterprise Oversight, Final Rule: Prompt Supervisory Response and Corrective Action, 67 Fed. Reg. 3,587 (January 25, 2002).
[9] S. Rep. No. 102-282 at 16 (1992). "The powers of the Director are modeled [sic] in many respects after those of the Director of the Office of Thrift Supervision and to a lesser extent the Comptroller of the Currency ...." Id.
[10] Id. at 17.
[11] Office of Federal Housing Enterprise Oversight, Final Rule: Prompt Supervisory Response and Corrective Action, 67 Fed. Reg. 3,587, 3,588 (Jan. 25, 2002).
[12] Id.

[13] OFHEO Policy Guidance, Minimum Safety and Soundness Requirements, PG-00-001 (December 19, 2000).

[14] OFHEO, Final Rule: Safety and Soundness Regulation, 67 Fed. Reg. 55,691 (Aug. 30, 2002) (codified at 12 C.F.R. Part 1720).

[15] See 12 C.F.R. Part 30.

[16] OFHEO Policy Guidance, Minimum Safety and Soundness Requirements, PG-00-001 (December 19, 2000) 2-3. See generally OFHEO, Safety and Soundness Regulation, 67 Fed. Reg. 55, 691, 55694 (August 30, 2002).

[17] OFHEO Policy Guidance PG-00-001, Minimum Safety and Soundness Requirements (December 19, 2000). OFHEO Safety and Soundness Regulation.12 C.F.R. Part 1720 App. A (August 30, 2002).

[18] OFHEO Final Rule; Safety and Soundness Regulation. 67 Fed. Reg. 55,691 55,694 (August 30, 2002) (codified at 12 C.F.R. Part 1720.

[19] See generally 12 C.F.R. Part 1710 (2005).

[20] See also 12 U.S.C. § 1723a(d)(2) requiring Fannie Mae to pay compensation that is reasonable and comparable with compensation for employment in other similar businesses.

[21] OFHEO Examination Guidance Examination for Corporate Governance. PG-05-002 (May 20, 2005).

[22] 12 U.S.C. § 1723a(l). Fannie Mae "shall have an annual independent audit made of its financial statements by an independent public accountant in accordance with generally accepted auditing standards," and "the independent public accountant shall determine and report on whether the financial statements ... are presented fairly and in accordance with generally accepted accounting principles." 12 U.S.C. § 1723a(l)(1), (2).

[23] 12 U.S.C. § 1723a(k). The Fannie Mae Charter Act mandates that Fannie Mae's financial reporting shall be in accordance with Generally Accepted Accounting Principles (GAAP). In particular, the Act requires Fannie Mae to "submit [to OFHEO] annual and quarterly reports of condition and operations of the corporation which (sic) shall be in such form, contain such information, and be submitted on such dates as the Director shall require." 12 U.S.C. § 1723a(k)(1). Specifically, each annual report shall include: 12 U.S.C. § 1723a(k)(2)(A) – financial statements prepared in accordance with generally accepted accounting principles..., and 12 U.S.C. § 1723a(k)(2)(C) – an assessment signed by the CEO and CFO (or chief accountant) of (i) the effectiveness of the internal control structure and procedures of the corporation, and (ii) the compliance of the corporation with designated safety and soundness laws. Each report also is to contain a declaration by the President, vice president, treasurer, or any other officer designated by the Board of Directors that the report is true and correct to the best of such officer's knowledge and belief. 12 U.S.C. § 1723a(k)(4).

[24] 12 U.S.C. §§ 4513, 4514.

[25] 12 C.F.R. Part 1730.

[26] The Federal bank regulatory agencies are the Federal Deposit Insurance Corporation, the Board of Governors of the Federal Reserve System, the Comptroller of the Currency, and the Office of Thrift Supervision (and before the creation of the Office of Thrift Supervision, its predecessor agency the Federal Home Loan Bank Board), 12 U.S.C. §1813(q).

[27] See generally 12 U.S.C. § 1818.

[28] Holzman, Thomas L., "Unsafe or Unsound Practices: Is the Current Judicial Interpretation of the Term Unsafe or Unsound?" 19 Ann. Rev. Banking L. 425.
[29] Gulf Federal Savings and Loan Association v. Federal Home Loan Bank Board, 651 F.2d 259, 264 (1981).
[30] E.g., De la Fuente v. FDIC, 332 F.3d 1208, 1222 (9th Cir. 2003); Seidman v. Office of Thrift Supervision, 37 F.3d 911, 927 (3d Cir. 1994); Northwest National Bank v. Department of the Treasury, 917 F.2d 1111, 1115 (8th Cir. 1990); First National Bank of Eden v. Department of the Treasury, 568 F.2d 610, 611 n.2 (8th Cir. 1978).
[31] E.g., Federal Deposit Insurance Corporation,Risk Management Manual of Examination Policies, at 15.1-3 "an unsafe or unsound practice embraces any action, or lack of action, which is contrary to generally accepted standards of prudent operation, the possible consequences of which, if continued, would result in abnormal risk of loss or damage to an institution, its shareholders, or the insurance fund administered by the FDIC".
[32] Seidman, 37 F.3d at 927.
[33] Groos National Bank v. Comptroller of the Currency, 573 F.2d 889, 897 (5th Cir. 1978) (emphasis added).
[34] Id.
[35] Northwest National Bank, 917 F.2d at 1115.
[36] Id.
[37] Financial Institutions Supervisory Act of 1966: Hearings on S. 3158 Before a Subcommittee of the Senate Committee on Banking and Currency, 89th Cong., 2d Sess., at 125 (1966).
[38] Northwest National Bank, 917 F.2d at 1113; Bank of Dixie v. FDIC, 766 F.2d 175, 176 (5th Cir. 1985).
[39] Northwest National Bank, 917 F.2d at 1113.
[40] Bank of Dixie, supra note 766 F.2d at 176.
[41] De la Fuente, 332 F.3d at 1224.
[42] Seidman, 37 F.3d at 937-38.
[43] De la Fuente, 332 F.3d at 1224.
[44] Candelaria v. FDIC, No. 97-9515, 134 F. 3d 382, 1998 WL 43167 (10th Cir.)
[45] Seidman, 37 F.3d at 928.
[46] See Federal Deposit Insurance Corporation, Risk Management Manual of Examination Policies, at 15.1-3.
[47] Id.
[48] Id. at 15.1-4.
[49] Id. at 15.1-4.

IV. CORPORATE CULTURE AND TONE AT THE TOP

During the period covered by this report, the corporate culture[1] of Fannie Mae encouraged a perception of the Enterprise as a low-risk financial institution that was so well managed that it could hit announced profit targets on the nose every year, regardless of the state of the economy, and that compensated its senior executives appropriately for its extraordinary performance. The highest levels of senior management[2] wanted Fannie Mae to be viewed as "one of the lowest risk financial institutions in the world"[3] and as "best in class" in terms of risk management, financial reporting, corporate governance, and internal control. Chairman and Chief Executive Officer (CEO) Franklin Raines, Chief Financial Officer (CFO) Timothy Howard, and other members of the inner circle of senior Enterprise executives sought to convey that image to the public, employees, the Board of Directors, and investors. Fannie Mae's annual reports for 1998 and 1999 each stated:

> Fannie Mae's record of steady earnings growth reflects our disciplined and proven management of our business ....[4]

In the 2000 *Annual Report* Mr. Raines stated:

> Indeed, our 14 years of steady earnings growth demonstrates that Fannie Mae defies the conventional wisdom that financial company earnings are always sensitive to changes in the economy or interest rates. Fannie Mae's management of credit and interest rate risk contributes stability to the global financial system.[5]

The 2001 *Annual Report* told investors that Fannie Mae had "been able to deliver double-digit growth in operating earnings per common share (EPS), year after year, through all types of economic and financial market environments for the last 15 years." That report also stated that the Enterprise had been called the "'new global model' for financial institution safety, soundness, transparency, and market discipline."[6]

This report demonstrates that the image of Fannie Mae communicated by Mr. Raines and his inner circle and promoted by the Enterprise's corporate culture was false. The report also describes how senior executives worked strenuously to hide Fannie Mae's operational deficiencies, significant risk exposures, and improper earnings management to smooth earnings from outside observers—the Board of Directors, its external auditor, OFHEO, the Congress, and the public.

The illusory nature of Fannie Mae's public image and senior management's efforts at concealment were the two essential features of the Enterprise's corporate culture. Those features, which were both supported by repeated improper manipulation of earnings, are a major theme of this report. The remainder of this chapter reviews the emergence of Fannie Mae's corporate culture, improper earnings management under Franklin Raines, the business strategy senior management developed to meet earnings targets, how senior executives defended Fannie Mae's image, and the inappropriate "tone at the top" set by the Board of Directors and the highest level of senior management.

The Development of Fannie Mae's Corporate Culture

The corporate culture of Fannie Mae during the period covered by this report emerged in the late 1980s and early 1990s, when the Enterprise enjoyed extraordinary financial and political success lasting until 2004. Senior management expected to be able to write the rules that applied to Fannie Mae and to thwart efforts to regulate the Enterprise. Writing their own rules included deciding when to comply with Generally Accepted Accounting Principles (GAAP), engaging in and concealing earnings management, and failing to cooperate with and trying to interfere with OFHEO's special examination.

A Financial and Political Powerhouse

From Fannie Mae's conversion into a government-sponsored enterprise in 1968 through the 1970s, the Enterprise financed fixed-rate mortgages with short-term debt. Beginning in October 1979, large increases in interest rates raised Fannie Mae's interest expense, and the Enterprise lost money in four of the six years between 1980 and 1985. Fannie Mae began guaranteeing mortgage-backed securities (MBS) in 1981 and, after interest rates fell, became profitable again in 1986. In 1987 the Enterprise doubled its EPS, starting a 17-year pattern that continued through 2003. Through the early 1990s, Fannie Mae sustained rapid profit growth primarily by expanding the share of conventional single-family mortgage debt outstanding in the U.S. financed with its guaranteed MBS.

Fannie Mae's financial success gave senior management steadily increasing amounts of money to use in efforts to influence the regulatory and legislative processes. Over the years the Enterprise compiled a remarkable track record of achieving its political objectives. As COO Daniel Mudd remarked in a memorandum to CEO Franklin Raines in November 2004, "[t]he old political reality was that we always won, we took no prisoners, and we faced little organized political opposition."[7]

A key political victory for Fannie Mae senior management was the inclusion in the Federal Housing Enterprises Financial Safety and Soundness Act of 1992 ("the 1992 Act") of provisions that weakened OFHEO's authorities and subjected the agency to the appropriations process. Those provisions helped Fannie Mae and Freddie Mac grow their retained mortgage portfolios without impediment beginning in 1993. Fannie Mae needed portfolio growth in order to sustain double-digit EPS growth in the 1990s, since the mortgage market as a whole was growing much more slowly than it had in the 1980s. Slower growth in that market limited the ability of the Enterprises to expand its outstanding MBS—and the associated guarantee fee income—at the previous torrid pace.

Fannie Mae senior management also skillfully promoted an image of the Enterprise as a private firm whose corporate objectives were essentially identical to the federal government's public policy objectives. The message was: what is good for Fannie Mae is good for housing and the nation. Senior executives used that image and their political influence to try to ensure that Fannie Mae operated under rules that differed from those that applied to other corporations.

The Effort to Deter Regulation

Although the 1992 Act, which created OFHEO, represented an important victory for Fannie Mae, that statute did give the agency substantial authorities as a safety and soundness regulator. The existence of a federal agency with the ability to regulate the Enterprise represented a direct challenge to senior management. To deal with that challenge, Fannie Mae took the extreme position that OFHEO simply had little authority over the Enterprise, while Fannie Mae's lobbyists worked to insure that agency was poorly funded and its budget remained subject to approval in the annual appropriations process.[8] The goal of senior management was straightforward: to force OFHEO to rely on the Enterprise for information and expertise to such a degree that Fannie Mae would essentially regulate itself.

Soon after OFHEO opened its doors a pattern developed in which Fannie Mae's Office of General Counsel routinely alleged that the agency had no authority for whatever regulatory action was proposed. The Enterprise maintained that OFHEO employees were acting improperly, perhaps even criminally, in releasing information about Fannie Mae. Over the years the Enterprise made allegations of impropriety against OFHEO employees publishing research[9] and, more specifically, that OFHEO could not do so without Fannie Mae's prior review.[10] Those objections were not limited to research but included many types of disclosures, including those made to and at the request of the Congress. Most recently, the Enterprise objected to OFHEO providing Congress with executive compensation information, suggesting that members of Congress might face criminal sanctions if they made the information public.[11] In another context, an attorney in Fannie Mae's Office of General Counsel recommended suing OFHEO because it was seeking congressional action.[12] Similarly, the Enterprise repeatedly objected to OFHEO hiring outside consultants to assist it in conducting examinations and otherwise meeting its responsibilities, on the theory they would be seeing confidential information.[13]

Over time, the strategy of opposing, circumscribing, and constraining OFHEO became a firmly established corporate policy of Fannie Mae. When OFHEO showed a capacity for independent initiative—by proposing regulations or taking other regulatory actions that the Enterprise opposed—it would attempt to create conflict between OFHEO and other agencies. For example, in 2001 an attorney with Wilmer Cutler Pickering Hale & Dorr (WilmerHale), counsel to Fannie Mae throughout OFHEO's special examination, posed the following question to Fannie Mae Senior Vice President and General Counsel Ann Kappler regarding the agency's proposed risk based capital rule opposed by Fannie Mae:

> Ann: Is there any chance the Sec. of HUD or the HUD GC would be prepared to come to our aid? If so, and if we can convince them that there is a legal flaw in the rule…they can kick the legal issue to Justice for resolution under Exec. Order 12, 146. The EO provides that Justice (OLC) is authorized to resolve interagency legal disputes. Here, the dispute would be between OFHEO and HUD or between OMB and HUD….[14]

In 2004 Fannie Mae government relations staff and WilmerHale attorneys discussed a corporate governance regulation proposed by OFHEO in a similar manner:

> Yesterday, Monica [Medina], Ted [Wartell] and I had a discussion with Russ [Bruemmer, Wilmer Hale] about how to proceed on the OFHEO corporate governance regs that will be issued shortly…Russ will have research done on the following…1. "Joint Jurisdiction" issue- Is there legal authority that would support an argument that the SEC (and stock exchanges) and not OFHEO should be doing the rulemaking in this area? ...We should also have further conversations with the SEC about overlap of jurisdiction. They might be more interested in approaching OFHEO or OMB about this orally rather than in writing.[15]

Efforts to generate interagency conflict involved Fannie Mae's most senior executive officers. An e-mail sent by Ms. Kappler in 2004 described actions by Chairman and CEO Franklin Raines:

> Frank [Raines] wants to put a call into [the SEC] to request a meeting on juris. I'm working on talking points so he can place the call today.[16]

An e-mail sent in 2003 recounted similar actions by Mr. Raines' subsequent replacement, Daniel Mudd:

> I spoke to [a Treasury Department official], he had agreed to talk to [the SEC] on "what to do if OFHEO was not falling in line" already ([another Treasury official] had already bent his ear about OFHEO obstructionism) ... promised me he'd check in to see where things were and would call [the SEC] when needed.[17]

The direct impact on Mr. Raines, who opposed OFHEO's proposal to require Fannie Mae to separate his dual positions of Chairman and CEO, resulted in particular attention to using the technique to oppose the proposed OFHEO corporate governance regulation.[18]

With the initiation of OFHEO's special examination of Fannie Mae, the effort to undermine that examination by generating jurisdictional opposition from the SEC went into high gear. An example is an e-mail from Ann Kappler to Catherine Smith quoting Gregory Baer of WilmerHale referencing talking points for Mr. Raines for a call to the SEC:

> -...We do not believe that OFHEO has authority to opine on GAAP, or to order us to restate our financial statements. We would like to reach an understanding with the Commission on this matter. Obviously, all other regulatory agencies have deferred to the staff on these issues. As you saw with the corporate governance rule, though, this is an agency that sees its jurisdiction and competence as limitless...
>
> Thus, we would like to begin a more adult process with FASB and OCA to vent these issues. We are prepared to live with the consequences. We're confident that we got this right ....[19]

Fannie Mae's resistance to OFHEO's regulatory efforts intensified after the agency initiated its special examination of the Enterprise in 2003. Senior management made efforts to interfere with the examination by encouraging and directing Fannie Mae's lobbyists to use their ties to a key Congressional staff member to 1) generate a Congressional request for the Inspector General of the Department of Housing and Urban Development (HUD) to investigate OFHEO's conduct of the special examination and 2) insert into an appropriations bill language that would reduce the agency's appropriations until Director Armando Falcon, who had initiated that examination, was replaced. Chapter VIII describes those actions, which were unsafe and unsound practices.

The decision by Fannie Mae senior management to register the Enterprise's shares with the SEC in 2002 marked a departure from its effort to deter regulation. Prior to registration the Enterprise represented to the public that its disclosures met or exceeded the SEC's requirements of registrants. Actual registration, which entailed the legal commitment to abide by SEC financial disclosure rules, had the potential to bolster the image of Fannie Mae as a "best-in-class" financial institution. Mr. Mudd described what the change in regulatory status meant in the November 2004 memorandum to Mr. Raines cited above:

> We used to, by virtue of our peculiarity, be able to write, or have written, rules that worked for us. We now operate in a world where we will have to be 'normal'. The SEC is our standard for disclosure and our arbiter for the rules, not our own proofreaders.[20]

One month after Mr. Mudd wrote those words, the SEC agreed with OFHEO that Fannie Mae's implementation of FAS 91[21] and FAS 133[22] did not comply with GAAP and directed the Enterprise to restate its financial results.

Concealing Earnings Management Decisions

In the corporate culture of Fannie Mae, writing rules "that worked for us," to use Mr. Mudd's phrase, included implementing accounting policies that did not comply with GAAP and taking care to conceal such actions from executives and employees who might raise questions about them. Those aspects of the culture predated Franklin Raines' tenure as the Enterprise's CEO.

For example, on November 30, 1998, SVP and Controller Leanne Spencer and Director for Financial Reporting Janet Pennewell sent a memorandum to President and COO Lawrence Small that commented on his planned remarks for an upcoming officers meeting. Those comments implied that a decision had been made to implement an accounting change for Low-Income Housing Tax Credits in 1999, and indicated that care should be taken to prevent KPMG, Fannie Mae's outside auditor, from learning about that decision, since KPMG might conclude that the change was improper.

> ...Nothing you state is incorrect. However, we would like to soften it a little. Technically if you 'know' about a [sic] accounting change you are supposed to book it. We haven't informed KPMG that we intend to implement this [referring to the accounting change for the Low-Income Housing Tax Credits[23]] next year and our preference would be to not to talk to them about it prior to year-end 1998 so they don't say 'book it' at year-end. We've limited discussion of this to the inner circle, so wouldn't want to broadcast it to the officer group.[24]

The inner circle wanted to limit dissemination of information about those decisions to prevent them from being scrutinized or challenged by KPMG or other Fannie Mae executives or employees. Mr. Raines was likely aware of the decisions, as he was Fannie Mae's Chairman and Chief Executive Officer-Designate at the time.

Improper Earnings Management under Franklin Raines

Franklin Raines became Chairman of the Board and Chief Executive Officer-designate of Fannie Mae in May 1998 and Chairman of the Board and Chief Executive Officer (CEO) in January 1999. Mr. Raines, who had been the Enterprise's Vice Chairman from 1991 to 1996, understood fully the Enterprise's economic and political power and its corporate culture. In May 1999 he committed to double Fannie Mae's EPS in five years. Later that year he sponsored a new, company-wide addition to the Enterprise's compensation program. That addition created strong incentives to achieve the EPS growth goal by providing substantial financial rewards to senior executives if the goal was achieved.

The strategy that Fannie Mae senior management developed to achieve that goal took advantage of improper accounting policies and employed earnings management to hit announced EPS targets precisely each quarter. Mr. Raines, Chief Financial Officer (CFO) Timothy Howard, and the other members of the inner circle of senior executives constructed an image of the Enterprise as a very low risk company that was "best in class" in order to carry out that strategy. Senior management engaged in a variety of efforts to maintain that image in order to conceal the improper earnings management and other unsafe and unsound practices in which Fannie Mae engaged.

Manipulation of 1998 Earnings

Shortly after Mr. Raines became CEO in early 1999, before he committed to double EPS by 2003, he made decisions that started to set the inappropriate tone at the top that permeated Fannie Mae throughout his chairmanship. The Enterprise fell just short of the upper end of its EPS target range in 1997, by enough to affect the compensation of its most senior executives. Projections of the financial results for 1998, as yet unreported, showed a larger shortfall. Anticipating such a result in the summer of 1998, Lawrence Small, Chief Operating Officer and President, had written Mr. Raines to inform him of Mr. Small's concern that Fannie Mae's "piggy bank" and various "magic bullets" could not make up the shortfall and that there would be much discontent among the senior management if they did not receive maximum bonuses again.[25]

Mr. Raines was determined not to let that happen, and he closely monitored the situation. He was seemingly thwarted when interest rates fell and prepayments increased in the latter half of 1998, causing unanticipated amortization costs of $440 million. Recording that figure would have caused Fannie Mae's EPS to fall below the minimum of its target range, which would have meant no bonuses for Fannie Mae's senior officials.

After the year had ended but before the books were closed, Fannie Mae's Controller had three alternate studies prepared of how Fannie Mae could nonetheless meet its maximum EPS goals. Those "alternatives" were then presented to Fannie Mae's most senior management in an "earnings alternative" meeting chaired by Mr. Raines. All three alternatives would have resulted in Fannie Mae meeting its maximum EPS target. The alternative chosen included an amortization adjustment of $240 million, only part of the $440 million required by GAAP.

When challenged by Fannie Mae's external auditors, the Enterprise was unable to present any analysis that supported the lower adjustment. Nonetheless, it ignored the external auditors' expressed view that the full amount of the disparity should be booked.

That refusal to charge the full amount of the calculated FAS 91 adjustment did not get Mr. Raines all the way to where he wanted to go, since Fannie Mae was still well below the upper end of its EPS target range of $3.23, which was necessary to trigger maximum executive bonuses. At the same meeting of senior management, however, an adjustment of nearly $109 million, after taxes, related to Low Income Housing Tax Credits (LIHTC) was authorized. Fannie Mae had been planning to make that adjustment in 1999, but senior management accelerated booking the adjustment to 1998. Still short, Fannie Mae made a last-minute adjustment from a cookie-jar account that enabled it to hit the top of the EPS target range.

Thus, from the very beginning of Mr. Raines' tenure as CEO, his goal was clear: EPS results mattered, not how they were achieved. In the following years, time and time again, Fannie Mae employed adjustments that enabled it to meet its EPS targets, whether on a quarterly basis to meet analysts' expectations or on an annual basis to meet compensation targets.

The Commitment to Double Earnings per Share

In 1999, Mr. Raines committed to double Fannie Mae's EPS within five years, from $3.23 in 1998 to $6.46 in 2003. The Enterprise's three previous annual reports had highlighted EPS as a measure of profit growth. The 1996 annual report had compared the growth and volatility of Fannie Mae's EPS to those of ten other companies listed on the New York Stock Exchange "whose stock is held most often by our largest investors." That report had noted that Fannie Mae's "steady and predictable EPS growth stands out in the group."[26] The 1997 annual report had noted that the Enterprise had achieved double-digit growth in operating EPS for 11 straight years.[27] The 1998 annual report had noted the achievement of that milestone for a 12th straight year.[28]

To give executives and other employees a strong incentive to double EPS to $6.46 by year-end 2003, in November 1999 Fannie Mae management recommended that the Board of Directors approve a special stock option grant. The Board of Directors approved that recommendation, which it viewed as an initiative of Mr. Raines. All full-time and part-time employees subsequently received EPS Challenge Option Grants scheduled to vest in January 2004 if Fannie Mae doubled EPS by year-end 2003. Chapter V provides more information on that initiative.

Fannie Mae measured earnings and EPS in two ways during the period covered by this report. In 1998 through 2000, the Enterprise used the GAAP measure of EPS. In 2001 and subsequent years, Fannie Mae used a non-GAAP measure that it called operating net income per share (in 2001) or core business earnings per share (in 2002 through 2004).[29] The Enterprise introduced the new measure in response to its implementation of FAS 133 in 2001. Senior management believed that the period-to-period volatility in reported net income that resulted from that accounting standard did not accurately reflect underlying risk or the actual economics of Fannie Mae's portfolio investment business. Senior management argued that investors could use core business earnings to evaluate the Enterprise's profitability in a way that treated comparable hedging transactions in a similar manner. Not only did Fannie Mae encourage investors to evaluate its performance based on core EPS, it also based its bonus compensation program on the achievement of core EPS targets. SEC Regulation G allows the use of a non-GAAP reporting measure as long as the reporting entity follows prescribed disclosure rules.[30]

Effect of the Commitment on Fannie Mae's Corporate Culture

Mr. Raines' commitment and the related EPS Challenge Option Grants intensified the focus at Fannie Mae on the achievement of EPS targets and reduced attention to other objectives. The December 2001 job descriptions for Mr. Raines, Chief Operating Officer Daniel Mudd, CFO Timothy Howard, and Vice Chairman Jamie Gorelick each listed EPS targets as the first performance indicator for their positions. Achieving those targets preceded performance indicators associated with other corporate goals and objectives, affordable housing, and safety and soundness considerations.[31] As described in detail in Chapter V, executive officers—especially Mr. Raines, Mr. Howard, Controller Leanne Spencer, and Vice President for Financial Reporting Janet Pennewell—devoted an inordinate amount of time and effort to managing reported financial performance, at the expense of other goals and objectives associated with safety and soundness and internal control, so that Fannie Mae's reported EPS would hit announced targets. That tone at the top permeated all levels of Fannie Mae, and $6.46, the EPS goal, became the corporate mantra—everything else was secondary to hitting that target. Even Mr. Rajappa, Senior Vice President for Operations Risk and Internal Audit, the corporate financial watch-dog, fell under its spell. In 2000, after becoming the head of the Office of Auditing, Mr. Rajappa gave a speech to the internal auditors that encapsulated the corporate culture of Fannie Mae under Mr. Raines' stewardship. Mr. Rajappa stated:

> By now every one of you must have 6.46 branded in your brains. You must be able to say it in your sleep, you must be able to recite it forwards and backwards, you must have a raging fire in your belly that burns away all doubts, you must live, breath and dream 6.46, you must be obsessed on 6.46. . . After all, thanks to Frank, we all have a lot of money riding on it. . . .We must do this with a fiery determination, not on some days, not on most days but day in and day out, give it your best, not 50%, not 75%, not 100%, but 150%. Remember, Frank has given us an opportunity to earn not just our salaries, benefits, raises, ESPP, but substantially over and above if we make 6.46. So it is our moral obligation to give well above our 100% and if we do this, we would have made tangible contributions to Frank's goals."[32]

Starting from Desired Earnings Results and Working Backwards to Achieve Them

It is clear the corporate culture at Fannie Mae under Franklin Raines focused intensely on attaining EPS goals. Without an element of impropriety, such goals are appropriate and are typical goals for corporations. Improving shareholder value is one of the primary goals for any board of directors, and increasing EPS is a recognized way to improve shareholder value. A problem arises, however, when a goal becomes so dominant that an organization is driven to achieve it at any cost and through any means necessary. That was what happened at Fannie Mae.

If Fannie Mae's earnings exceeded amounts necessary to hit EPS targets, senior management cast about for transactions of marginal business purpose that had the effect of moving income from the immediate period, where it was not needed, to a future period, when it might be needed to hit EPS targets and maximize bonuses. Indeed, as discussed in Chapter V, excess earnings per share above those targets did not result in additional bonuses.

Additionally, in periods in which EPS targets were hit, adjustments were not made that should have been made. For example, Fannie Mae refused to lower its Allowance for Loan Losses even in the face of historical experience showing the Enterprise actually and consistently recovered more monies than predicted on foreclosures. Faced with a clamor from his staff that accounting standards required an adjustment, Mr. Howard, the Chief Financial Officer, writing in a personnel evaluation, set everyone straight that the lack of earnings volatility trumped GAAP. Mr. Howard complained of one of his subordinate's failure to perceive Fannie Mae's true priorities. Mr. Howard noted that he was concerned about being able to "rely on [Janet Pennewell's] business judgment"[33] because of how she had handled the purchase premium and discount amortization and loss reserve policy issues.

The overriding goals of achieving stable growth in earnings and hitting EPS targets encouraged the use of accounting practices that aimed at achieving EPS goals, rather than practices that complied with GAAP. That was exemplified by an e-mail from CFO Timothy Howard to Controller Leanne Spencer in which Mr. Howard state that he had discussed with Mr. Raines the potential EPS for the third quarter of 2003. Mr. Howard noted that

> [Mr. Raines had a] thought for the third quarter—which I think is a good one ... to come in at an EPS number that would be a double-digit increase from the third quarter of 2002 .... If that's what we want to do, doing $400 million buyback tomorrow would cause us to fall short of our objective .... So—we need a lower cap. I'd be inclined to say $350.[34]

Ms Spencer sent a reply e-mail, noting, "I'm comfortable with $350. Let's let that be the cap."[35] Although the email is discussing a $50 million adjustment, there is no discussion, nor apparent concern, about what level of debt buybacks made economic sense for Fannie Mae. Mr. Raines set an EPS target with the apparent understanding that Mr. Howard and Ms.

Spencer would achieve it through any means necessary. As Ms. Spencer noted in an email exchange with Mr. Howard, "I've just learned over time that [Mr. Raines] always has an opinion."[36]

While debt buybacks offered powerful opportunities for adjusting earnings, stock buybacks were very effective for fine-tuning EPS. In notes prepared for a November 1996 board meeting, Mr. Howard explained how EPS, which by then had a direct impact on the bonus amounts paid, could grow at a substantially greater rate than net income:

> You'll see that for the four year period we're projecting average EPS growth of nearly 12 percent—11.8% to be exact. Net income growth is a bit under 10%. The difference between the 9.8% net income growth and the 11.8% EPS growth is the assumed effect of the continuation of our stock buyback program.[37]

Mr. Howard was not the only executive at Fannie Mae who understood the correlation between the stock buybacks and EPS. In the 1997 Performance Assessment for Mr. Howard, COO Lawrence Small encouraged Mr. Howard to "speed up the pace" of the stock buyback program, but added a very specific parameter for the "pace":

> Obviously, we recognize that our buyback pace has to be calibrated to fit our desired EPS growth rate, so don't take the previous statement as anything more than strong encouragement to stay focused on this important aspect of capital management.[38]

Ms. Spencer also saw the connection between stock buybacks and EPS. In her Quarterly Business Review talking points for the first quarter of 2000, under the heading "Double Income Goal," Ms. Spencer referred to a chart that summarized what each business segment would be assigned to achieve the goal of doubling EPS by 2003. She noted, "[f]ortunately, each business segment doesn't need to quite double in order for us to meet our $6.46 goal, because of the benefit of stock repurchases and other corporate actions. We are calling that amount our 'contingency' reserve."[39] Clearly, Ms. Spencer and other Fannie Mae senior executives viewed stock repurchases as a type of contingency reserve to enable the Enterprise to hit its aggressive EPS target of $6.46 by the end of 2003.

Aggressively Growing Fannie Mae While Promoting a False Image of the Enterprise

Franklin Raines' commitment to double Fannie Mae's EPS in five years presented a significant financial challenge for senior management. To fulfill that commitment, the Enterprise would have to increase EPS at an annual average rate of 14.9 percent over the five-year period. In the preceding five years, 1993 through 1998, Fannie Mae's reported EPS had risen at an average annual rate of 11.5 percent.

Senior management developed a business strategy to fulfill Mr. Raines' commitment. That strategy involved aggressively expanding the Enterprise's credit guarantee and portfolio investment businesses. The strategy also involved promoting an image of Fannie Mae as one of the lowest-risk financial institutions in the world, in order to maximize the financial benefits of the Enterprise's special relationship to the federal government. That image was false, since Fannie Mae took a significant amount of interest rate risk in the portfolio investment business and had serious operational deficiencies. The illusory nature of the image was vividly demonstrated in 2002, when declining interest rates imposed large economic losses on Fannie Mae.

The Business Strategy for Fulfilling the EPS Growth Commitment

Fannie Mae management believed that, to double EPS by 2003, the Enterprise would have to achieve three business objectives. First, in the credit guarantee business Fannie Mae would have to securitize a greater share of the single-family mortgage market, in part by penetrating the subprime market and buying conventional loans that might otherwise be insured by the Federal Housing Administration.[40]

Second, in the portfolio investment business management would have to increase rapidly the size of Fannie Mae's retained mortgage portfolio, while avoiding significant compression of the portfolio's net interest margin—the spread between the average interest rate earned on assets and the average rate paid on liabilities. The portfolio investment business had generated the majority of the Enterprise's net income in 1998 (and continued to do so in subsequent years), so that expanding that business offered the best prospect for growing earnings.[41] For Fannie Mae to grow rapidly without margin compression, the mortgage market would have to expand fast enough to accommodate increased demand from the Enterprise without the market prices of mortgages and MBSs being bid up (and their yields declining) significantly.

Third, senior management believed that it would have to achieve steady, rather than irregular, EPS growth. CFO Timothy Howard presented the following argument for that objective to the Board of Directors.[42] The Enterprise's special relationship to the government gives it unparalleled liquidity and low funding costs. To capitalize on those benefits and maximize shareholder value, Fannie Mae "must be, and be perceived to be, a low-risk company." If the rate of growth of the Enterprise's EPS deviates very little from year to year, investors perceive Fannie Mae to be a low-risk firm and its common stock to be a very low-risk investment. Mr. Howard showed the Board a chart comparing the volatility in the EPS of Fannie Mae and a sample of other firms in the S&P 500 that were rated A+ or higher over a multi-year period. That chart indicated that Fannie Mae had almost the lowest volatility of earnings, stated in terms of standard deviation of EPS from trend, of all the companies in the sample, even lower than Freddie Mac.

Problems with the Business Strategy

There were two problems with Mr. Howard's argument for the importance of EPS growth stability that should have troubled the Board. First, the argument ignored the fact that Fannie Mae's strategy for managing the retained mortgage portfolio involved taking a significant amount of interest rate risk, as members of the Board should have been aware. Movements in interest rates alter the rates at which borrowers prepay their mortgages and the durations of the assets in Fannie Mae's retained portfolio. How much changes in asset durations affect the duration gap of that portfolio—a measure of the sensitivity of the net asset value of the portfolio to further rate changes—depends on whether the Enterprise has purchased options on the liability side of the balance sheet that match the prepayment options embedded in the mortgages.

During the period covered by this report, Fannie Mae's strategy was to match between 50 and 60 percent of the optionality of its mortgage assets with comparable options on the liability side.[43] At least some members of the Board should have been aware of the degree of options mismatching practiced by Fannie Mae, and that the associated interest rate risk is a source of earnings volatility that, if reflected properly in the financial reports, would make it difficult for the Enterprise to maintain very stable EPS growth.

Second, accounting rules provided another source of earnings volatility for Fannie Mae that may or may not be related to the returns on the Enterprise's portfolio investment business. The most significant of those rules, FAS 133, requires that a company mark its derivatives to market, but not its liabilities or the assets the company holds to maturity. To the extent Fannie Mae uses derivatives to hedge the risk of the held-for-investment portion of its retained mortgage portfolio, and to the extent that the Enterprise does not elect hedge accounting or upon election its hedges are ineffective, FAS 133 will produce asymmetrical accounting results that will cause fluctuations in earnings that do not accurately reflect changes in the net asset value of that portfolio. The Board should have recognized that FAS 133 was an additional source of earnings volatility.

For those reasons, and as discussed in Chapter IX, the members of Fannie Mae's Board of Director should have recognized the inconsistency between reporting very stable EPS growth, on the one hand, and taking significant interest rate risk and implementing FAS 133 properly, on the other. If they had done so and inquired further, they might have discovered that Fannie Mae was not implementing FAS 133 correctly and was routinely engaging in improper earnings management in order to minimize volatility and hit its announced EPS target precisely in nearly every quarter. The Board might have also discovered the serious weaknesses in the Enterprise's internal control system that facilitated improper accounting and earnings management, and management's practice of withholding information about those weaknesses from the Board, its committees, and Fannie Mae's outside auditor. Those discoveries would have led them to conclude that the image of Fannie Mae as a "'best practices' company" was a "façade," the term used by Leslie Rahl, who joined the Board in February 2004, in a 2005 interview.[44]

A False Image

As those problems suggest, the image of Fannie Mae that CEO Franklin Raines, CFO Timothy Howard, and other members of the inner circle of senior executives communicated during the period covered by this report was false, for two reasons. First, Fannie Mae was not "one of the lowest-risk financial institutions in the world" but was exposed to significant interest rate risk and quite large operational and reputational risks. Second, the Enterprise was not "best in class" in terms of financial reporting, corporate governance, and internal control, but had serious weaknesses in all those areas. Evidence of Significant Interest Rate Risk: Large Economic Losses Resulting from Rebalancing Actions

The interest rate risk to which Fannie Mae was exposed during the period covered by this report is illustrated by the Enterprise's experience when interest rates declined dramatically in 2002 and 2003. Fannie Mae was not well prepared for the resulting surge in refinancings of fixed-rate mortgages. The Enterprise had matched only a portion of the prepayment options held by borrowers whose mortgages it held in portfolio (either as whole loans or MBS) with options in its liability portfolio of debt and derivatives. When rates declined, Fannie Mae engaged in rebalancing actions in order to keep its duration gap, and its interest rate risk exposure, from increasing. Those rebalancing actions took the form of paying substantial sums to cancel pay-fixed swaps that had imbedded losses.

The economic losses associated with those rebalancing actions were not reflected in Fannie Mae's core business earnings in the periods in which they were realized. Even if the Enterprise had implemented FAS 133 correctly and the derivatives it used for hedging had qualified for hedge treatment and been judged to be fully effective, its GAAP earnings would not have fully reflected those losses. The reason is that GAAP, even after the implementation of FAS 133, is not based solely on fair values and, therefore, does not provide a useful basis for gauging Fannie Mae's economic profit or loss on its portfolio investment business. The change in the Enterprise's after-tax net asset value, a measure of the difference between the fair value of assets and liabilities reported in its annual reports, provides a starting point for measuring that profit or loss. Thus, the decline in Fannie Mae's net asset value in 2002 reported in the Enterprise's annual report for that year provides useful information about the losses associated with the rebalancing actions in which the Enterprise engaged, and the return on the portfolio investment business, during the year.[45]

Additional information about how interest rate movements affected Fannie Mae's net asset value over the period covered by this report is provided by a statement in March 2005 by Executive Vice President Peter Niculescu in a "Portfolio Overview" presentation he gave to the

Enterprise's Board of Directors. That presentation states that Fannie Mae's "[accumulated] accounting income was $12 billion more than accumulated economic return before [the] restatement."[46] The magnitude of those losses, although not large enough to threaten the safety and soundness of Fannie Mae, provides evidence that the Enterprise's interest rate risk exposure during the period was significant and is inconsistent with the image of Fannie Mae as a very low-risk institution promoted by senior management.

Efforts by Senior Management to Defend Fannie Mae's Image

To promote and maintain the image of Fannie Mae as low-risk and "best in class," senior executives hid or denied information about their improper earnings management practices and about the Enterprise's operational weaknesses and risk exposures. This section provides a number of examples of those efforts, which reflected the premium that Fannie Mae's corporate culture placed on maintaining that image.

Ignoring Warnings about Improper Earnings Management

On September 28, 1998, and on November 16, 1998, SEC Chairman Arthur Levitt gave speeches to the financial community in which he strongly criticized earnings management practices. Both speeches received wide press coverage.[47] The very practices that Mr. Levitt criticized were already part of Fannie Mae's strategic direction and would soon be reinforced by Mr. Raines' 1999 challenge to employees to double earnings per share by year-end 2003.

In October, 1998 KPMG Partners Joe Boyle, Ken Russell, and Julie Theobald met with Vincent Mai, Fannie Mae Audit Committee Chairman, to discuss earnings management issues "which the SEC has been focusing on recently." They "explained that the SEC has been very vocal about certain financial reporting matters, primarily, that pubic companies are managing their earnings to meet market expectations."[48] Subsequent to that meeting, on November 17, 1998, KPMG briefed the Audit Committee on the SEC's concerns. Chairman Levitt's comments about companies focusing on short-term analyst earnings estimates rather than long-term shareholder value should have raised red flags for management and the Board, and led to serious soul-searching about exactly how Fannie Mae met its earnings estimates unfailingly, quarter after quarter, year after year, to the penny.

There is little evidence that the Board of Directors showed any concern or took any action in response to either the speeches of the SEC Chairman or the KPMG warnings. Members seemed to think the earnings management issue did not relate to Fannie Mae. They accepted the representations of executives that Fannie Mae was simply the best at doing what it did, and that extraordinary success was to be expected.

Neither Freddie Mac's announcement in January 2003 that it expected to restate upward its financial results for 2002, 2001, and possibly 2000,[49] Freddie Mac's statement in March of that year that the restatements would result in material increases in both the level and volatility of earnings reported in prior periods,[50] nor the July 2003 release of the Baker Botts Report detailing Freddie Mac's numerous accounting violations[51] appear to have had much of an impact on Fannie Mae's Board and senior management. They failed to discover that Fannie Mae had engaged in similar abuses that are discussed in Chapter VI—for example, in its accounting for the amortization of premiums and discounts and in setting its allowance for loan losses in order to minimize reported earnings volatility. As described in Chapter IX, Fannie Mae's Board of Directors accepted management's assertions that the accounting and financial reporting abuses at Freddie Mac did not apply to Fannie Mae, and did not question management about the Enterprise's own accounting policies. The current Chairman of the Board of Directors, Stephen Ashley, and the Chairman of the Audit Committee, Thomas Gerrity, stated that they read only the executive summary of the Baker Botts report.[52] That failure to understand thoroughly the implications of information so clearly pertinent to Fannie Mae exemplified a corporate culture and tone at the top that denigrated all information that ran counter to the image of the Enterprise promoted by senior management.

Ignoring Allegations of Improper Accounting

As discussed in detail in OFHEO's 2004 *Report of Findings to Date of the Special Examination of Fannie Mae* and in subsequent chapters of this report, Fannie Mae senior management failed to investigate serious allegations of improper accounting made by Roger Barnes, who was a manager in the Controller's Department, preferring to view him as merely a disgruntled employee. Mr. Barnes was ostracized by his superiors and eventually entered into a separation agreement. Fannie Mae settled with Barnes over his claims of discrimination but failed to thoroughly investigate his charges of accounting irregularities. The failure to thoroughly investigate such allegations is an example of a culture in which senior executives denied the existence of information that challenged their false image of the Enterprise.

Denying that Debt Repurchases Were Undertaken to Manage Earnings

As discussed in Chapter VI, on occasions when senior management wanted to avoid recording earnings above the amount needed to achieve maximum bonus payouts, Fannie Mae repurchased debt and represented the repurchases primarily as risk management actions or cost-saving initiatives. Although it undertook repurchases to affect core business earnings in 2001, 2002, and 2003, only in the 2003 *Annual Report* did the Enterprise even hint at the earnings implications of its action. The disclosure did not make plain the primary motivation behind the repurchase activity. Instead, the report emphasized the secondary objective of risk management, misleadingly described the cost-savings objective, and most importantly, omitting a straightforward discussion of earnings management. That action demonstrated yet again a culture that paid homage to image over fact.

Despite the lack of full disclosure, investors understood well that Fannie Mae used large debt repurchases to smooth earnings in 2003.[53] Nevertheless, when Reuters published a news article on July 15, 2003, that suggested that the Enterprise was managing earnings, Fannie Mae denied that it used debt repurchases for that purpose. The article includes the following quote from a Fannie Mae spokesperson:

> When market opportunities present themselves, we replace our debt. There was no strategy to cut earnings and move them into the future ...

Misrepresenting Risk and the Costs of Rebalancing

In the summer of 2002, interest rates fell 100 basis points in 60 days to a 40 year low, and mortgage prepayments accelerated dramatically. That acceleration caused Fannie Mae's duration gap, the only published measure of the Enterprise's interest rate risk exposure, to move well outside of Board-approved limits. In Fannie Mae's 2002 *Annual Report*, Mr. Raines described the Enterprise's response:

> Even though we took actions to rebalance our portfolio, the actions were routine ... and had no material impact on our business or core business earnings. In fact, our core business earnings per share increased by 21 percent during 2002.[54]

Mr. Raines' statements failed to mention several important facts. First, the change in the duration gap occurred because Fannie Mae had not fully hedged its exposure to mortgage prepayments—in other words, senior management had taken significant interest rate risk. Second, the decline in rates had had a multi-billion dollar economic impact—the market value of the Enterprise's assets had risen much less than the market value of its liabilities, so that its net asset value had declined. The rebalancing required to address Fannie Mae's duration mismatch in 2002—accomplished through the repurchase of high-coupon long-term debt and the cancellation of pay-fixed swaps—was quite costly. Mr. Raines failed to mention that core business earnings did not reflect that cost. Thus, the steadiness of core business earnings conveyed a false image, promoted by senior management, of the Enterprise as a company that took little risk.

Failing to Acknowledge Deficiencies in Accounting Systems

Another example of that behavior occurred during a press briefing on July 30, 2003. During that briefing Mr. Raines attempted to reassure the participants that Fannie Mae did not have the types of accounting problems then plaguing Freddie Mac. His statements about the quality of Fannie Mae's internal control system were categorical and sweeping:

> So it is possible to run these things properly, but you've got to make the investments. You've got to say that this has got to stand scrutiny internal and external. You can't just go get [sic] by saying, Well, let's do the cheapest or easiest thing to do. So Fannie Mae had always made the investments. We made the investments over Y2K. We've made the investments in our accounting systems. We've centralized our accounting so we don't have to go all over the company to find out what the facts are you can to one place.

> So for some reason if we made a mistake in our accounting, and someone said, Oh, it's not A, it should be B. We could go very quickly in a fairly short period of time and change A to B, and tell you what the results were, but that's management. That has nothing to do with them being a GSE, or it being a complicated company, that's just plain old fashioned management. Do you have systems in place or don't you? They have said they didn't do it. I wish to God they had done it, we wouldn't be having these problems, or certainly they would have been able to resolve them in a much shorter period of time.
>
> But there is a difference in management. Management does matter, and a management that cares a lot about internal control does matter. I think that's really the important difference. It would not take 500 people for us to go back, even if we had made the same mistakes, because we have these systems automated and we can go back and quickly adjust them.[55]

Mr. Raines' remarks failed to acknowledge the serious deficiencies that existed in Fannie Mae's internal control system. As described in OFHEO's September 2004 *Report of Findings to Date of the Special Examination of Fannie Mae* and in Chapter VI of this report, the Enterprise had responded to new accounting standards by attempting to rely on existing accounting systems rather than invest in new systems with proper controls. In many cases, the existing systems were incapable of handling the latest requirements of GAAP. The suggestion by Mr. Raines that Fannie Mae's management, overseen by its Board of Directors, invested in control systems to ensure that they were adequate to address the Enterprise's accounting and financial needs was not accurate. Once again, Fannie Mae's culture prevailed, and fact gave way to message.

An Inappropriate Tone at the Top

The phrase "tone at the top" refers to the example that the words and deeds of the members of the board of directors of a company and its senior officers set for its employees. Since the enactment of the Sarbanes-Oxley Act of 2002, the Securities and Exchange Commission (SEC) and business ethicists have stressed the importance of the tone at the top in shaping a firm's corporate culture and the related roles of the board and senior management in setting an example of personal integrity and respect for the law. The following statements are representative of those pronouncements:

> Directors have overall responsibility for the ethics and compliance programs of the corporation. The tone at the top that they set by example and action is central to the overall ethical environment of their firms.[56]
>
> * * * *
>
> The tone at the top of an organization is perhaps more vital than anything else, and the chief executive will set that tone under the oversight of the board.[57]
>
> * * * *
>
> Setting the right tone means letting employees know that no one at the company is above the law; that no matter how important or how senior, someone who has violated an ethical standard will be punished .... By setting a tone of integrity at the top, you can create a climate for long-term success, a climate in which everyone gets it right.[58]

The Board of Directors of Fannie Mae gave the appearance of setting an appropriate tone at the top. The Board adopted each year a Code of Business Conduct that provided standards to guide the conduct of all employees and certain consultants. In several years of the period covered by this report, that Code of Conduct included a section on "General Principles" that contained the following statements:

> Fannie Mae ... has a strong commitment to uphold the highest standards of ethics. We have a duty to conduct our business affairs within both the letter and the spirit of the law. In doing so with honesty and integrity, we strictly comply with the laws, rules, and regulations that apply to our company and with our corporate policies, procedures, and guidelines.[59]

The conduct of the Board of Directors did not live up to those statements. As discussed in Chapter IX, the Board failed to be sufficiently informed and independent of its chairman, Mr. Raines, and senior management, and failed to exercise the requisite oversight to ensure that the Enterprise was fully compliant with applicable law and safety and soundness standards. Those failures contributed to an inappropriate tone at the top at Fannie Mae. They signaled to management and other employees that the Board did not in fact place a high value on strict compliance with laws, rules, and regulations. That message contributed to the Enterprise's many failures to comply with safety and soundness standards and the many unsafe and unsound practices documented in this report.

The highest level of senior management made statements that echoed the language of Fannie Mae's Code of Business Conduct. For example, the 2004 edition of that code included a message from CEO Franklin Raines that stated:

> Fannie is a company with strong values of responsibility, accountability, and integrity.... Our values are our most valuable asset. Our strong values as colleagues are what make Fannie Mae a company with strong values, and a strong value for our shareholders.[60]

The conduct of Mr. Raines, CFO Timothy Howard, and other members of the inner circle of senior executives at Fannie Mae was inconsistent with the values of responsibility, accountability, and integrity. Those individuals engaged in improper earnings management in order to generate unjustified levels of compensation for themselves and other executives. They promoted a false image of the Enterprise as a "best in class" financial institution while neglecting to manage Fannie Mae properly and participating in or permitting a wide variety of unsafe and unsound practices. Those actions set a highly inappropriate tone at the top that was itself an unsafe and unsound practice.

Conclusion

During the years covered by this report, the corporate culture of Fannie Mae encouraged a false perception that the Enterprise took so little risk and was so well managed that it could hit announced earnings per share precisely almost every quarter. That perception furthered the view that Fannie Mae senior executives deserved to be very well compensated for the Enterprise's extraordinary performance, while serving to divert attention from Fannie Mae's risk and serious problems in accounting, financial reporting, and internal control.

That corporate culture ultimately led to declines in the market value of Fannie Mae of tens of billions of dollars. As of the writing of this report, the Enterprise estimates that its expenses associated with the restatement process, regulatory examinations, investigations, and litigation will exceed $1.3 billion in 2005 and 2006 alone.[61]

Although the actions of many members of senior management shaped Fannie Mae's culture, it was influenced to the greatest extent by Franklin Raines, who called for doubling Fannie Mae's earnings per share in five years, molded the Enterprise's compensation program to heighten incentives to achieve that goal, and gave CFO Timothy Howard extraordinary power and authority; and by Mr. Howard, who was most responsible for Fannie Mae's corporate strategy and its execution.

References

[1] "Organizational culture refers to the basic values, norms, beliefs, and practices that characterize the functioning of a particular institution. At the most basic level, organizational culture defines the assumptions that employees make as they carry out their work; it defines 'the way we do things here.' An organization's culture is a powerful force that persists through reorganizations and the departure of key personnel." Columbia Accident Investigation Board Report, National Aeronautics and Space Administration, v.1, August 26, 2003, p. 101.

[2] Consistent with Fannie Mae's annual reports, this report defines the senior management of the Enterprise as the Chairman and Chief Executive Officer, the Chief Operating Officer, the Chief Financial Officer, executive vice presidents, and senior vice presidents (SVPs). See, for example, Fannie Mae 2002 Annual Report, 128-129. During the period covered by the report, Fannie Mae senior management consisted of approximately 40 to 50 individuals.

[3] Remarks Prepared for Delivery by Timothy Howard, Vice Chairman and CFO, Fannie Mae, Merrill Lynch Banking and Financial Services Conference, New York, NY, November 19, 2003, p. 11: "Being recognized as one of the lowest risk financial institutions in the world ... is a distinction that meeting our publicly disclosed [financial] discipline objectives should allow us to sustain."

[4] Fannie Mae 1998 Annual Report; Fannie Mae 1999 Annual Report.

[5] Fannie Mae 2000 Annual Report, p. 4.

[6] Fannie Mae 2001 Annual Report, pp. 7, 9.

[7] Memorandum from Chief Operating Officer Daniel Mudd to Chairman and Chief Executive Officer Franklin Raines, November 16, 2004, FMSE-E_M 0039511-0039517 at 0039512.

[8] Memorandum from William Maloni to Franklin Raines, January 26, 2000: "There are specific budget, spending and CBO matters that I would ask [for]: keeping us out of his budget resolution...keeping OFHEO in the appropriations process; and, possibly, having pressure applied to others [HUD?] through the appropriations process." GIR 0063590.

[9] Letter of Anastastia Kelly, General Counsel of Fannie Mae, to Anne E. Dewey, OFHEO General Counsel, February 12, 1997. "We are extremely concerned that OFHEO staff publicly discussed research based...on data and information obtained in

the course of OFHEO's supervisory and examination activities...We consider [this] to be a serious breach of OFHEO's obligation to protect the confidential and proprietary information that Fannie Mae provides OFHEO."

[10] Letter of February 12, 1997, James A. Johnson to Aida Alvarez, Director of OFHEO: "I am troubled that OFHEO would permit presentation of these papers without any prior discussion with us."

[11] "Fannie Paid $1M+ To 21 Execs in '02," Dawn Kopecki and Jennifer Corbett Dooren, October 6, 2004, Dow Jones Newswires: "Fannie Mae hired Ken Starr...to lobby lawmakers against releasing the data last fall. It said lawmakers and staff who released the information would be subject to criminal prosecution."; "Fannie Could Lose Fight On Release Of Executive Pay Data," Dawn Kopecki, January 30, 2004, Dow Jones Newswires: "Fannie Mae (FNM) is trying to block the release of a report to be delivered to Congress on Monday detailing the salary and benefits of its top 22 highest-paid employees. The company's lobbyists had been able to successfully suppress the data, which was initially disclosed late last year to the House Financial Services Committee, with threats of 'criminal proceedings' and House disciplinary action."

[12] E-mail Donald Remy to Ann Kappler, April 28, 2004 "I think it may be time to sue OFHEO. As a regulatory executive agency, I don't believe it appropriate for them to undertake legislative Congressional action...I suggest we seriously explore an affirmative declaratory or injunctive action against OFHEO. Alternatively, we could wait until their actual regulatory attempts and then stop it through lit. Also, this is one we could jointly pursue with Freddie. Thoughts?" Kd0128886

[13] Those included a Fannie Mae objection to an OFHEO Request for Proposals that sought an executive compensation consultant. "(We) thought it might be helpful for us to outline our view of the respective roles of OFHEO and Fannie Mae's Board of Director [sic] relating to executive compensation...We believe OFHEO should determine whether Fannie Mae provides "excessive compensation" to its executive officers by reviewing the process that the Board of Directors uses to set executive compensation and ensuring that compensation is established pursuant to the process...." May 15, 1996, letter of Anastasia Kelly, General Counsel of Fannie Mae, to Anne E. Dewey, OFHEO General Counsel.

[14] E-mail of Randolph Moss, WilmerHale, to Ann Kappler, General Counsel of Fannie Mae, July 3, 2001. KD0176994.

[15] E-mail from Judith Dunn to Ann Kappler, et al., March 31, 2004, KD0126546.

[16] E-mail from Ann Kappler to Leanne Spencer, April 20, 2004, KD0 128638.

[17] E-mail from Daniel Mudd to Thomas Donilon, January 13, 2003, FNMA SE 702532.

[18] E-mail from Thomas Donilon to Ann Kappler, February 19, 2004: Ann—(i) do you have any sense of the basis on which the agency believes that it has the authority to mandate practices in this area, hard to believe they have a safety and soundness rationale ... There is a huge issue as to multiple enforcement regimes. We should speed up our work on the interaction between bank regulators and the SEC ... When does Russ [Bruemmer, of WilmerHale] think that we should go into OMB? ...Should we start working with the BRT [the Business Roundtable], Chamber [the U.S. Chamber of Commerce], ABA [the American Bankers Association] etc. now? Tom." KD0180594

[19] E-mail from Gregory Baer to Jodie Kelley et al., April 20, 2004, KD0128646.

[20] Memorandum from Chief Operating Officer Daniel Mudd to Chairman and Chief Executive Officer Franklin Raines, November 16, 2004, FMSE-E_M 0039511-0039517 at 0039514.

[21] Statement of Financial Accounting Standards (FAS) No. 91, Accounting for Nonrefundable Fees and Costs Associated with Originating and Acquiring Loans and Initial Direct Costs of Leases.

[22] Statement of Financial Accounting Standards (FAS) No. 133, Accounting for Derivative Instruments and Hedging Activities.

[23] As discussed in Chapter VI, when faced with the audit adjustment related to purchase premium and discount amortization, Mr. Raines, Mr. Howard, and Ms. Spencer decided to accelerate that accounting change.

[24] November 30, 1998 memorandum from Leanne Spencer and Janet Pennewell, with attachment. FM SRC OFHEO 1398917 – 19.

[25] Memorandum from Lawrence Small to Franklin Raines regarding "Fall Financial Planning," August 10, 1998, FMSE-IR 00331264, FM SRC OFHEO 00310414. For 1998, I'm reasonably confident there's enough in the "non-recurring earnings piggy bank" to get us to $3.21. While that number should satisfy investors, you should be aware that last year the AIP paid out just short of the maximum This year, the maximum is $3.23, so at $3.21, the bonus pool will be noticeably lower than in 1997, a fact which will, of course, be rapidly observed by officers and directors come January.

[26] Fannie Mae 1996 Annual Report, p. 9.

[27] Fannie Mae 1997 Annual Report, p. 8.

[28] Fannie Mae 1998 Annual Report, p. 17.

[29] Fannie Mae described Core EPS in its 2003 10K as "... a non-GAAP measure developed by management in conjunction with the adoption of FAS 133 to evaluate and assess the quality of Fannie Mae's earnings from its principal business activities on a consistent basis. Core business earnings is presented on a net of tax basis and excludes changes in the time value of purchased options recorded under FAS 133 and includes purchase options premiums amortized over the original estimated life of the option and any acceleration of expense related to options extinguished prior to exercise." Fannie Mae 2003 10-K, at p. 25.

[30] Regulation G requires public companies that disclose or release non-GAAP financial measures to include, in that disclosure or release, a presentation of the most directly comparable GAAP financial measure and a reconciliation of the disclosed non-GAAP financial measure to the most directly comparable GAAP financial measure. 17 CFR Parts 228, 229, 244, and 249.

[31] FMSE-EC 004985-4990. Fannie Mae Job Descriptions.

[32] "Address to Audit Group on What We Can Do to Help Achieve $646 EPS," Sampath Rajappa, FM SRC OFHEO 00249929-931. Bold emphasis added, underscore in the original.

[33] E-mail evaluation of Leanne Spencer from Tim Howard, December 9, 2000, FMSE-IR 028780.

[34] Email from Leanne Spencer to Timothy Howard, September 24, 2003, FMSE-KD 029309.

[35] Id., at 029308.

[36] E-mail from Timothy Howard to Leanne Spencer, September 25, 2003, FMSE-KD 029310.
[37] Notes for November Board meeting (11/19/96), FMSE-IR 00361756.
[38] SRC OFHEO 030314.
[39] FMSE SRC OFHEO 00266529.
[40] FM SRC OFHEO 00142121.
[41] Fannie Mae 1998 Annual Report, p. 54.
[42] Timothy Howard Presentation, "Corporate Risk Appetite," to Fannie Mae Board of Directors Strategic Review Committee, July 16, 2002, FMSE 017408-426; "Corporate Risk Management Objectives," Presentation by CFO Timothy Howard to the Fannie Mae Board of Directors, July 14-15, 2003, FMSE 017263.
[43] Remarks Prepared for Delivery by Timothy Howard, Vice Chairman and CFO, Fannie Mae, Merrill Lynch Banking and Financial Services Conference, New York, NY, November 19, 2003, p. 12. During the early years and at some other points of that period, the Enterprise matched even less.
[44] Memorandum from Sarah M. Epstein, September 15, 2005, on Interview with Leslie Rahl, February 15, 2006, 13. FM SRC OFHEO 01563414-46 at 26.
[45] Fannie Mae 2002 Annual Report, p. 119.
[46] "Portfolio Overview", presentation by Peter Niculescu to Fannie Mae Board of Directors, March 29, 2005, page 11 (FMSE 515736)
[47] Remarks by Chairman Arthur Levitt Securities and Exchange Commission, The "Numbers Game," NYU Center for Law and Business, New York, N.Y. September 28, 1998. Remarks by Chairman Arthur Levitt Securities and Exchange Commission "A Financial Partnership", The Financial Executives Institute, New York, N.Y. November 16, 1998.
[48] Memorandum to File re: Discussions with Vincent Mae, October 1998. KPMG-OFHEO 389986.
[49] Freddie Mac Press Release, "Freddie Mac to release unaudited 2002 earnings on January 27th," January 22, 2003, *http://www.freddiemac.com/news/ archives/investors /2003/4q02.html.*
[50] Freddie Mac Press Release, "Freddie Mac Restatement Process on Track," March 25, 2003, http://www.freddiemac.com/news/archives/investors/2003/restatement_ 032503.html
[51] Freddie Mac Press Release, "Freddie Mac Releases Board Counsel's Report," July 23, 2003, http://www.freddiemac.com/news/archives/corporate/2003/report_072303.html.
[52] OFHEO interview, Thomas Gerrity, March 14, 2006. On July 25, 2003, Corporate Secretary Thomas Donilon provided the Board of Directors with the executive summary of the Baker Botts report. In the cover memorandum Donilon indicated that management had reviewed the accounting issues addressed in the report and that the companies response was set forth in the "Answer from the CEO" and in the transcript to Frank's [Franklin Raines'] interview on CNBC's Kudlow & Cramer which was also attached. FM SRC M-OFHEO 00020830-842.
[53] Reuters, Fannie Mae smoothes income say unconcerned analysts, July 15, 2003 FMSE 083034.
[54] Fannie Mae 2002 Annual Report, p. 15.
[55] Franklin Raines, Press Briefing, July 30, 2003, FMSE-E_KD0150617-0150618.

[56] Mark S. Schwartz, Thomas W. Dunfee, and Michael J. Kline, "Tone at the Top: An Ethics Code for Directors?" Journal of Business Ethics (2005) 58: 79–100 at 79.

[57] William H. Donaldson, Chairman, U.S. Securities and Exchange Commission, Remarks at the 2003 Washington Economic Policy Conference of the National Association for Business Economics, Washington, D.C., March 24, 2003.

[58] Stephen M. Cutler, Director, Division of Enforcement, U.S. Securities and Exchange Commission, "Tone at the Top: Getting it Right," speech delivered as part of the Second Annual General Counsel Roundtable, Washington, D.C, December 3, 2004.

[59] Fannie Mae Code of Business Conduct, January 1999, page 1 (FMSE-KD 042484); and Fannie Mae Code of Business Conduct, January 2002, page 1 (FMSE-IR 00397351).

[60] Fannie Mae Code of Business Conduct, January 2004, page 1 (FANN 000826).

[61] See Form 12b-25 filed by Fannie Mae March 13, 2006, p. 19; and Form 12b-25 filed by Fannie Mae May 9, 2006, p. 12.

V. The Executive Compensation Program

The Congress has determined that Enterprise executive compensation may represent a safety and soundness problem.[1 Fannie Mae is required by statute to compensate its executives in a manner that is reasonable and comparable with compensation for employees in similar businesses.[2] Safety and soundness standards and OFHEO regulations require that executive compensation be reasonable and appropriate, be consistent with the long-term goals of the Enterprises, not focused solely on earnings performance, and undertaken in compliance with all applicable laws, rules, and regulations.[3] As in all areas of operations, OFHEO regulations and safety and soundness guidance further provide that an Enterprise should implement and maintain internal controls over executive compensation that provide for accountability and written policies and procedures to safeguard and manage assets.[4]

Under the Fannie Mae executive compensation program, senior management reaped financial rewards when the Enterprise met earnings per share (EPS) growth targets established, measured, and set by senior management itself. The structure of the executive compensation program created the incentive and opportunity for senior executives to benefit at the expense of safety and soundness. In addition, Fannie Mae disclosure of executive compensation obscured public understanding of how much compensation senior executives actually received.

Fannie Mae tied major portions of executive compensation to EPS, a metric easily manipulated by management. Beyond the basic package of salary and benefits, three components of compensation depended directly on reaching EPS targets: (1) an Annual Incentive Plan (AIP) under which executives and other managers earned bonuses; (2) a Performance Share Plan that granted stock to senior executives based on three-year performance cycles; and (3) the EPS Challenge Grant, a program for all employees championed by Chairman and Chief Executive Officer (CEO) Franklin Raines, which tied the award of a substantial amount of stock options to the doubling of EPS from 1998 to 2003. For senior executives, EPS-driven compensation dwarfed basic salary and benefits. For CEO Franklin Raines, two compensation components directly tied to meeting EPS goals—the AIP bonus and EPS Challenge Grant—accounted for more than $20 million of his approximately $90 million in compensation in the six years from 1998 through 2003. Three-year EPS goals also played a crucial role in determining the size of Mr. Raines' approximately $32 million in Performance Share Plan awards during that six-year period.

Over the period covered by this report, the measure of EPS Fannie Mae tied to its executive compensation changed. Until the Enterprise implemented a new accounting rule covering the accounting for derivatives instruments and hedges, Financial Accounting Standard (FAS) 133, Fannie Mae tied executive compensation to Generally Accepted Accounting

Principles (GAAP) measures of EPS. The period-to-period volatility in reported net income that resulted from the requirements of FAS 133 did not, in the view of Enterprise senior management, accurately reflect underlying risk or the actual economics of their hedging strategy. Therefore, in conjunction with its adoption of FAS 133 on January 1, 2001, Fannie Mae developed a non-GAAP measure of earnings that it labeled "core business earnings." The result, the Enterprise said, was that investors could evaluate earnings in a way that accounted for comparable hedging transactions in a similar manner.[5] For purposes of this chapter, references to "earning per share" or "EPS" refer to GAAP earnings per share for the years prior to 2001 and to "core business earnings per share" for the years 2001 forward, unless otherwise noted.

The Board of Directors of Fannie Mae allowed the same set of executives, all subject to the same compensation incentives, to set EPS targets, measure EPS, audit and report results—with no apparent concern for conflicts of interest. As a direct result, senior management reaped ongoing and extensive financial rewards through accounting manipulation. Fannie Mae executives regularly manipulated EPS to achieve higher compensation. They did so by, among other things, manipulating accounting related to purchase premium and discount amortization, manipulating tax-related transactions, and timing stock and debt repurchases. Management routinely shifted earnings to future years when the EPS target for the maximum bonus payout for the current year appeared likely to be exceeded. The effectiveness of senior management in both setting and hitting EPS targets to attain maximum Annual Incentive Plan payouts is demonstrated by their track record. From 1998 through 2002, reported EPS always exceeded the Annual Incentive Plan maximum payout target, and in 2003, reported EPS was only slightly below that target.

Fannie Mae executives obscured their official disclosures of executive compensation. For example, prior to registering with the Securities and Exchange Commission, the Enterprise failed to disclose adequately the value of certain deferred compensation. Similarly, preregistration disclosures related to the EPS challenge grants were incomplete. Those disclosures failed to break down the value of grants among executive officers. Additionally, Fannie Mae also failed to include in its disclosures complete information on the post-employment compensation awarded to its former CEOs. Chapter VIII discusses those failures to disclose the Enterprise's executive compensation.

This chapter documents the structure of the Fannie Mae executive compensation program, the incentives that program created, and how senior management used improper earnings management to increase executive compensation in specific years. The executive compensation program provided strong incentives for senior management to engage in improper earnings management and other unsafe and unsound practices documented in subsequent chapters. As discussed in Chapter VI, improper earnings management involves deliberate manipulation of the accounting in order to create the appearance of controlled, disciplined growth.[6] The incentives imbedded in the executive compensation program drove the misconduct in part because the Enterprise lacked policies, procedures, and internal controls that should have provided checks and constraints. Because the program, as designed and in that context, created strong incentives for unsafe and unsound practices and led to unsafe and unsound conditions, it was itself an unsafe and unsound practice.

An Overview of the Program

Throughout the period covered by this report, Fannie Mae compensation for executive officers involved several key components: 1) basic compensation, which included base salary and other annual compensation; 2) Annual Incentive Plan awards ("bonuses"), whose value was linked to meeting annual earnings per share (EPS) targets; and 3) long-term incentive plan awards (LTIP), which included substantial amounts of "performance share" stock awards under the Performance Share Plan to senior executives if EPS and certain non-financial goals were met over a three-year period, as well as stock options.[7] The last two of those three components of executive compensation included major compensation programs—AIP bonuses and PSP stock awards—that depended directly on the attainment of EPS targets.

As Table V-1 indicates, executive compensation directly related to meeting EPS goals played a central role in the overall remuneration of senior Fannie Mae executives. For 1998 through 2003, including the value of stock options that vested in January 2004 from attaining the doubling of EPS associated with the EPS Challenge Grant, CEO Franklin Raines received approximately $90 million in compensation. Of that compensation, two components directly tied to meeting EPS goals—the AIP bonus and EPS Challenge Grant—accounted for more than $20 million. Three-year EPS goals also played a crucial role in determining the size of Mr. Raines' approximately $32 million in Performance Share Plan awards. Similarly, for that same period, all other top executives listed in the Table V-1 received compensation from the three components linked to meeting EPS goals of $61 million, which accounted for 56 percent of their total compensation of $109 million.

In addition to the components of "regular" compensation, Fannie Mae management in 1999 recommended that the Board of Directors approve a special stock option grant to provide an incentive to double earnings per share (EPS) to $6.46 over the five-year period ending in 2003.[8] That recommendation, closely linked to CEO Franklin Raines, in effect committed Fannie Mae to outperform the market over that period. The Board agreed to this "turbo charge" approach to compensation for executive officers and other employees in 1999.[9]

Corporate financial performance can be an appropriate and even essential factor in the determination of any executive compensation, and EPS is one among several factors often used to measure corporate financial performance. A September 2002 report by the Conference Board Commission on Public Trust and Private Enterprise, which recommended that performance-based compensation incentives support long-term strategic objectives, recommended a variety of performance measures, including the cost of capital, return on equity, economic value added, market share, quality goals, revenue and profit growth, cost containment, and cash management.[10] A 2003 review commissioned by Fannie Mae of performance metrics used by comparable firms showed that most based some share of executive compensation on measures of corporate performance. Significantly, many firms that did so tied compensation to more than one performance measure. American Express used shareholder return, earnings growth, revenue growth, and return on equity as financial performance factors to determine annual bonus awards. Citigroup used return on equity. Sallie Mae used "core cash" EPS growth, fee income growth, preferred channel loan origination growth, and operating expense control. CIGNA used earnings, revenue growth, and cost management. Fleet Boston used return on equity and net income.[11]

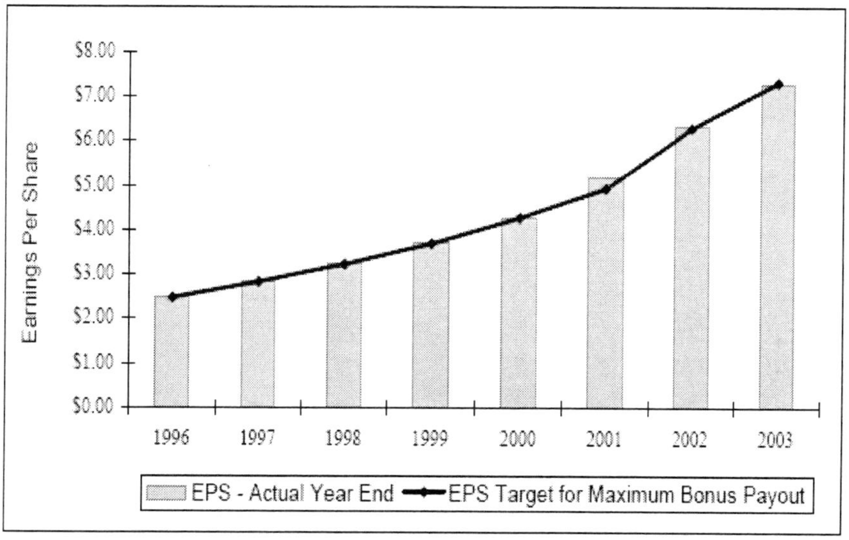

Figure V-1. Maximum Bonus Payout Targets and Reported Earnings per Share (EPS), 1996-2003

Fannie Mae chose EPS as the sole financial performance factor in determining the size of its Annual Incentive Plan bonus pool and made the overall amount of long-term compensation awarded heavily dependent on EPS performance as well. Tying both short-term and long-term compensation to EPS performance had the effect of rewarding senior executives twice for doing the same thing—meeting EPS goals. As shown in Figure V-1, the final reported EPS number closely tracked the maximum bonus payout number, exceeding it substantially in only one year (2001) when market conditions created a "windfall" in EPS.

As described in the September 17, 2004, OFHEO *Report of Findings to Date of the Special Examination of Fannie Mae*, the final 1998 Fannie Mae EPS number that was reported matched the EPS number that resulted in a maximum payout of Annual Incentive Plan bonuses to the penny. That uncanny proximity of the EPS target set for a maximum bonus payout to the EPS number ultimately reported was not an exception to the rule at Fannie Mae; in the years 1996 through 2002, it *was* the rule. That correlation of reported EPS and EPS targets was the result of improper setting of targets and improper adjustment of earnings by senior management to reap financial rewards. Such misconduct can only occur in the absence of appropriate internal controls and proper Board of Directors oversight.

Table V-1. Compensation of Top Fannie Mae Executives, 1998-2003, including Salary, Bonus, Performance Share Plan (PSP) Payouts, Stock Options, and Earnings per Share (EPS) Challenge Grant Awards[a]

	1998	1999	2000	2001	2002	2003	Totals
Franklin Raines							
Salary	$526,154	$945,000	$992,250	$992,250	$992,250	$992,250	$5,440,154
Bonus[b]	1,109,589	1,890,000	2,480,625	3,125,650	3,300,000	4,180,365	$16,086,229
PSP[b]	794,873	1,329,448	4,588,616	6,803,068	7,233,679	11,621,280	$32,370,964
Options	4,052,484	4,358,406	5,829,071	7,945,648	6,680,395	3,006,895	$31,872,899
EPS Grant[b, c]						4,358,515	$4,358,515
Total	$6,483,100	$8,522,854	$13,890,562	$18,866,616	$18,206,324	$24,159,305	$90,128,761
Timothy Howard							
Salary	$395,000	$414,800	$435,540	$463,315	$498,614	$645,865	$2,853,134
Bonus[b]	493,750	518,500	544,425	694,983	781,250	1,176,145	$4,209,053
PSP[b]	909,196	860,464	2,088,542	1,987,119	1,947,368	3,470,578	$11,263,267
Options	938,912	1,154,593	2,035,589	2,166,427	1,749,995	2,491,974	$10,537,490
EPS Grant[b, c]						1,292,085	$1,292,085
Total	$2,736,858	$2,948,357	$5,104,096	$5,311,844	$4,977,227	$9,046,647	$30,155,029
Jamie Gorelick							
Salary	$567,000	$595,400	$625,170	$656,429	$689,124	n/a	$3,133,123
Bonus[b]	779,625	818,675	859,609	1,083,109	911,250	n/a	$4,452,268
PSP[b]	1,055,217	1,292,693	2,458,528	2,591,060	3,049,012	n/a	$10,446,510
Options	1,444,397	1,975,501	2,516,927	2,498,108	n/a	n/a	$8,434,933
EPS Grant[b, c]							
Total	$3,846,239	$4,682,269	$6,460,234	$6,828,706	$4,649,386		$26,466,834
Daniel Mudd							
Salary	n/a	n/a	$537,063	$656,429	$689,124	$714,063	$2,596,679
Bonus[b]	n/a	n/a	735,130	1,083,109	911,250	1,288,189	$4,017,678
PSP[b]	n/a	n/a	414,090	1,188,846	2,339,702	4,674,015	$8,616,653
Options	n/a	n/a	2,516,927	2,498,108	1,776,933	2,355,030	$9,146,998
EPS Grant[b, c]						1,928,049	$1,928,049
Total			$4,203,210	$5,426,492	$5,717,009	$10,959,346	$26,306,057

Table V-1. (Continued)

	1998	1999	2000	2001	2002	2003	Totals
			Robert Levin				
Salary	$395,000	$414,800	$435,540	$457,317	$480,092	$576,706	$2,759,455
Bonus[b]	493,750	518,500	544,425	686,028	575,000	801,237	$3,618,940
PSP[b]	909,196	860,464	2,088,542	1,987,119	1,947,368	2,706,381	$10,499,070
Options	938,912	1,154,593	1,218,212	1,281,658	1,552,496	2,240,652	$8,386,523
EPS Grant[b, c]						1,154,635	$1,154,635
Total	$2,736,858	$2,948,357	$4,286,719	$4,412,122	$4,554,956	$7,479,611	$26,418,623

[a]Executives are among those whose compensation Fannie Mae disclosed in its Annual Proxy Statements for 1998-2003. Valuation of stock options is derived from a modified Black-Scholes pricing model, as disclosed by Fannie Mae in the "Option Grants Table" included in those statements. Those tables do not include the value of the Earnings Per Share Challenge Grants awarded to Mr. Raines, Mr. Howard, Mr. Levin, and Mr. Mudd, but the value of those awards are included in the "EPS Grant" portion of this table. [b]Bonus, PSP, and EPS Challenge Grant components of compensation were tied to attaining EPS goals. [c]Most of the EPS Challenge Grants were granted on January 18, 2000, and all such grants vested on January 23, 2004. Here the value of those grants is included in 2003, the year the Challenge Grant EPS goal was attained. The value of the EPS Challenge Grants is the grant-date Black-Scholes value as estimated by Fannie Mae.

Sources: Summary Compensation Tables and Option Grant Tables in Fannie Mae Annual Proxy Statements, 1998-2003; FMSE-EC 052925.

The desirability of linking executive compensation to corporate performance is rooted in the role of executives as agents of shareholders—tying executives' compensation to corporate performance is intended to align their interests with shareholder interests. Linking corporate performance and executive compensation is a safe and sound practice only if it accomplishes that goal. Fannie Mae failed to meaningfully link corporate performance to executive compensation in such a way that the interests of shareholders and executives were aligned. That failure was rooted in the structure of the Enterprise's executive compensation program, the failure of internal controls, and the absence of effective and proper oversight by the Board of Directors. A result was improperly controlled executive compensation expenses, including the payment of unearned bonuses to senior executives. More importantly, the executive compensation program created perverse incentives that were a root cause of the endemic accounting errors at Fannie Mae.

How Fannie Mae's Executive Compensation Was Determined

As described in the Fannie Mae proxy statements, the performance of each executive officer at the Enterprise involved assessments by the subordinates, peers, and superiors of the officer. In the final step of the performance review process, an overall performance rating reflected a balance of business results and demonstration of leadership. The performance rating determined the individual's bonus and variable long-term incentive award relative to the targets. Each executive was also paid a base salary.

Base Salary

Base salary for executive officers was determined principally by Fannie Mae's judgment as to the market for comparable positions, informed by an annual market comparability review conducted by Fannie Mae's executive compensation consultant.[12] Final salary determinations also reflected individual performance, leadership, and experience level. In general, Fannie Mae targeted annual total cash compensation (salary plus bonus) to the 50th percentile of the comparative market. Mr. Raines' compensation reached as high as the 75th percentile.[13] In addition to base salary, Mr. Raines also received certain perquisites, including the use of the leased corporate jet for personal vacations.[14] Fannie Mae imputed the benefit as income to Mr. Raines for his personal tax purposes.

Annual Incentive Plan

As described below, the Annual Incentive Plan put a portion of each executive officer's annual cash compensation at risk. Fannie Mae established financial goals, measured by earnings per share ("EPS") growth, at the beginning of the year and based funding for the Annual Incentive Plan bonus pool on EPS performance relative to those goals. For the years 1998-2001, the range of funding of the Annual Incentive Plan bonus was 50 percent of a target amount for minimum corporate EPS achievement to 150 percent of a target amount for maximum achievement. Beginning in 2002, the Board tightened the funding range to 75 percent for minimum achievement of EPS goals and 125 percent for maximum achievement.[15] By 2002, Annual Incentive Plan bonus award eligibility included the CEO, two Vice-Chairs, six Executive Vice Presidents, 35 Senior Vice Presidents, 117 Vice Presidents, and 495 Directors.[16]

Long-Term Incentive Awards

Long-term incentive awards to senior Fannie Mae executives came in the form of performance shares, stock options, or restricted stock. All long-term incentive compensation programs were paid in Fannie Mae common stock. Senior executives typically received about half of the value of their annual long-term incentive award in the form of performance shares under the Performance Share Plan (PSP) program and half in the form of stock options.

Performance Shares

Fannie Mae used performance shares to compensate senior management for meeting performance objectives over a three-year horizon. Accordingly, Fannie Mae established designated three-year award cycles. At the beginning of each cycle, the Board of Directors established Performance Share Plan targets for both financial and non-financial goals. The financial goals were tied directly to EPS targets. The non-financial goals were tied to the Fannie Mae strategic plan. The Committee established a scorecard to measure achievement of that plan. Recently, the scorecard reflected the following: leadership in increasing access to affordable housing; leading presence in the secondary mortgage market; optimal interest rate, credit, and policy risk management; development of a corporate culture to enhance strategy execution; and development of an e-commerce infrastructure to increase capabilities and lower costs.

The EPS goals and the strategic goals were equally weighted (*i.e.*, 50 percent each) in determining performance share awards at the conclusion of each cycle. While in theory an actual Performance Share Plan payout could range from 40 percent of the performance shares granted for threshold achievement to 150 percent for goal achievement at maximum levels, in practice, for the period covered by this report, the stock payouts were always at or near the maximum.

Stock Options

To link the interests of executives and shareholders, Fannie Mae awarded stock options to senior executives. Those options provided value to the executive only when the stock price increased over a number of years. Stock options generally vested over a four-year period at the rate of 25 percent per year and expired in ten years. As a group, Fannie Mae executive officers received stock options that, when combined with performance shares, brought their targeted total compensation to the 65th percentile of the comparative market.

How the Annual Incentive Plan Bonus Program Worked

The Annual Incentive Plan bonus program, in theory, put a portion of each officer's annual cash compensation "at risk." Fannie Mae would establish corporate financial goals, measured by annual earnings per share (EPS), at the beginning of the year. Whether these goals were met determined whether payouts would occur under the Annual Incentive Plan and, if so, at what level. The Fannie Mae *1999 Report to Congress* on compensation explained how the Annual Incentive Plan worked.

> The company must attain a specific corporate performance threshold before any awards become payable. If this threshold level of performance is met or surpassed, then one is eligible for payments linked to a mix of personal and corporate performance. The more senior the employee, the greater the weight given to corporate performance.[17]

The Annual Incentive Plan program was structured to provide a disincentive to management to add to earnings once Fannie Mae hit the EPS number for the maximum payout under that plan. Leanne Spencer, Senior Vice President and Controller, described how the process worked in a draft memo forwarded to Mr. Raines dated November 16, 2001, a year in which market forces caused the EPS number to exceed targets substantially.[18] Ms. Spencer noted that within the structure of the Annual Incentive Plan, payouts to participants increased by about ten percent for every penny that EPS exceeded target (until it reached the maximum). She also wrote:

> The company structures itself and runs its business to be a steady, predictable performer. Its compensation system is structured to reward management for steady, predictable performance. In the AIP program, the rewards tie to the earnings goals set by the company to be on the path to doubling earnings per share by the end of 2003 or 14.9% as max. The range around achievements between threshold, target and max are very narrow-five and one half cents of earnings per share, or roughly $82.5 million in pre-tax earnings that would separate each range. This reflects the low volatility of results we typically produce.
> Under our AIP structure, for every one cent we earn above our target EPS, we add about $2.5 million to the AIP pool. Once we get to six cents above our target EPS, however, the AIP pool taps out. 19

In an OFHEO interview, Lorrie Rudin, Director for Executive Compensation and Benefits, also stated that executives did not receive additional bonus compensation when EPS exceeded the maximum target.[20]

needed to assure marketplace competitiveness.

Table V-2. Annual Incentive Plan Cost, 1993 – 2003

Performance Year	Number of Participants	Total Annual Incentive Plan Dollars Paid(dollars in millions)	Percent of After-Tax Profits
1993	394	8.5	0.46
1994	429	12.3	0.58
1995	444	12.6	0.59
1996	482	19.7	0.72
1997	531	22.7	0.74
1998	547	27.1	0.79
1999	585	28.7	0.73
2000	618	35.2	0.79
2001	643	37.9	0.75
2002	707	51.3	0.80*
2003	744	65.1	0.89*

*Percent of core earnings.

Sources: FMSE-KD 029844 (V.9).

As shown in Table V-2, the Annual Incentive Plan program grew markedly over the course of the 1990s. In 1993, for example, bonuses for approximately 394 employees totaled $8.5 million. By 2003, the number of eligible participants in the bonus program had nearly doubled to 744. The total Annual Incentive Plan dollars paid out increased nearly eightfold to $65.1 million. Such bonuses accounted for approximately 0.46 percent of after-tax profit in 1993. A decade later (2003), Annual Incentive Plan payouts accounted for approximately

0.89 percent of after-tax profit.[21] The size of the Annual Incentive Plan bonus pool was set by the Compensation Committee of the Board of Directors, based in part on the recommendations of the executive compensation consultant or consultants on the amount For the top senior executives (Chairman, Chairman-designate, President and Vice Chairman), the entire annual bonus payout depended on annual EPS performance.[22] A Hewitt Associates description of the 1998 employment contract of Mr. Raines noted regarding his bonus: "The size of the actual bonus is wholly a function of the performance of the company. Company performance is gauged by the Earnings Per Share (EPS) produced by the company."[23] Table V-3 shows the size of annual bonuses, which were tied to EPS targets, for top Fannie Mae executives. The size of the annual bonus received by Chairman and CEO Franklin Raines, in particular, increased substantially over the years.

Table V-3. Bonuses Paid to Fannie Mae Senior Executives, by Year, 1998-2003

Executive	1998	1999	2000	2001	2002	2003	Totals
Franklin Raines	$1,109,589	$1,890,000	$2,480,625	$3,125,625	$3,300,000	$4,180,365	$16,086,204
Daniel Mudd	n/a	n/a	$735,130	$1,083,109	$911,250	$1,288,189	$4,017,678
Timothy Howard	$493,750	$518,500	$544,425	$694,983	$781,250	$1,176,145	$4,209,053
Thomas Donilon	n/a	n/a	n/a	$562,751	$600,000	$727,070	$1,889,821
Robert Levin	$493,750	$518,500	$544,425	$686,028	$575,000	$801,237	$3,618,940
Jamie Gorelick	$779,625	$818,675	$859,609	$1,083,109	$911,250	n/a	$4,452,268
James Johnson	$1,932,000	n/a	n/a	n/a	n/a	n/a	$1,932,000
Lawrence Small	$1,108,259	$1,163,672	n/a	n/a	n/a	n/a	$2,271,931

Source: Notice of Annual Meeting of Shareholders. March 29, 1999 at 13; Notice of Annual Meeting of Shareholders. March 27, 2000 at 14; Notice of Annual Meeting of Shareholders. April 2, 2001 at 14; Notice of Annual Meeting of Shareholders. April 2, 2002 at 14; Notice of Annual Meeting of Shareholders. April 14, 2003 at 24; Notice of Annual Meeting of Shareholders. April 14, 2003 at 24. Notice of Annual Meeting of Shareholders. April 23, 2004 at 25.

Under direction from the Compensation Committee of the Board of Directors, Fannie Mae set the size of the Annual Incentive Plan bonus pool so that, if the target EPS was achieved, the total of the basic compensation (e.g. annual salary) and bonus would fall at the median compensation for executives in peer firms. Ultimately, how reported EPS compared to EPS targets determined the size of the annual bonus payout pool. In 1998, for example, a threshold EPS of $3.13 would bring the "minimum" payout to the bonus pool, $3.18 was the "target" and an EPS of $3.23 would bring the maximum payout.[24] This meant that for Fannie Mae to pay out the *maximum* amount in 1998 Annual Incentive Plan bonus awards ($27,094,679), the EPS for that year would have to be at least $3.23. If EPS was below the $3.13 minimum payout threshold, no Annual Incentive Plan bonus payout would occur.[25] If EPS surpassed $3.23, the bonus pool would not be increased any further—it would be "tapped out".

Senior executives consistently reminded those participating in the Annual Incentive Plan of the personal stake in meeting EPS targets. Chief Operating Officer Lawrence Small described how things worked to senior Fannie Mae executives at a critical moment in December 1998. Referring to bonuses that were to be "divvied up by those in this room," Mr. Small emphasized how important a particular EPS number was in determining the size of the bonus pool and, ultimately, the dollar amount of bonuses for individual officers. Using slides to illustrate his points, Mr. Small said: 26

> And earnings per share have to do with the annual incentive plan, the bonus pool for the people in this room and others because the bonus pool is based one hundred percent on earnings per share. And this slide shows you how.
>
> Our budgeted EPS target was three dollars and eighteen cents a share. That's the lighter yellow band sort of in the middle of the slide, three-eighteen right in the middle of the slide. And you can see that at three-eighteen, the AIP pool would be $18.1 million dollars. Now from the moment we put together the 1998 plan a year ago, we were quietly thinking that if things broke our way, we could hit three dollars and twenty-one cents as share. At three twenty-one, go down the slide a bit, you'll see that in the light green, at three twenty-one, the AIP pool, to be divvied up by those in this room would be 23.5 million dollars. That's 5.4 million dollars more than at three dollars and eighteen cents a share. In other words, thirty percent more bonus money if we got this stretch target that we set for ourselves.

Mr. Small went on to describe how competitive conditions in the market in 1998 had threatened to reduce the size of the bonuses for that year:

> Now by the time the early summer rolled around, our ambitious stretch goal of three dollars and twenty-one cents a share was just crumbling because the market had gotten so competitive and, remember when Tim talked to you yesterday, by the time we got to that time, we thought we were going to be in the year at three dollars and sixteen cents a share, appropriately in red, which is two cents below our plan of three eighteen and five cents away from the stretch target of three twenty one. Now you can see that each cent here on the slide is worth about 1.8 million dollars to the bonus pool. So, being two cents down from the three-eighteen to three sixteen would meant, would mean that we have 3.6 million less in the pool.
>
> And obviously, if you were looking at it against the three twenty one stretch target, it would mean that we'd have nine million dollars less in the pool...

In fact, the "stretch goal" for Fannie Mae senior management bonuses in 1998 was not the $3.21, to which Mr. Small referred in his address but $3.23—the EPS number senior management needed to hit to ensure they would receive a *maximum* payout from the Annual Incentive Plan bonus pool.

A November 18, 1998, memorandum to senior vice presidents from Thomas Nides, Senior Vice President (SVP) for Human Resources, had already placed senior executives on notice that the size of their bonus might be reduced because EPS growth was not sufficient. Mr. Nides warned:

> You know that as a management group member, you help drive the performance of the company. That's why your total compensation is tied to how well Fannie Mae does each year. Annually, the Board sets earnings per share goals that determine the size of the pool for the AIP, from which your bonus is awarded.

Current estimates indicate that we are exceeding the aggressive EPS target set by our Board of Directors. However, currently we do not expect to exceed the target to as great an extent as we did last year. As a result, the AIP bonus pool is somewhat smaller than it was last year, which means your bonus may be smaller than last year. (Emphasis in original)[27]

Problems with the Annual Incentive Plan

The structure of compensation under the Annual Incentive Plan, which had been in place at Fannie Mae since 1985,[28] was problematic in several respects. There were incentive conflicts created by setting an EPS minimum for executives to receive any bonuses and by setting an EPS maximum beyond which bonuses no longer increase. Designating EPS as the sole measure tying executive compensation to corporate performance to determine the size of the bonus pool, in the absence of effective internal controls or board oversight, increased the incentive for senior executives to manipulate both EPS and EPS targets.[29]

As OFHEO pointed out in the *Report of the Special Examination of Freddie Mac*, earnings per share figures, unlike certain other measurements of corporate performance such as stock prices, are generated internally and are not the best gauge of corporate performance when it comes to executive compensation.[30] Awarding such compensation based on accounting performance measured by an internally derived target is generally not advisable.[31] Given management's self-interest, executives can be expected to manipulate accounting earnings to achieve a personal agenda, such as bonuses. For example, management could attempt to raise current bonuses by increasing accounting earnings.[32] Income smoothing is prevalent in companies using internally derived performance standards, but not in companies using external standards.[33] When financial incentives for executives are based directly or indirectly on accounting results, the motivation behind earnings management may become strong enough to result in fraud.[34] In some instances, executives may manipulate earnings downward when the "true" earnings are either too low for a bonus to be awarded or so high that the cap on the bonus has been reached.[35] By making use of flexible accounting rules, executives can shift income between years and thereby increase total bonus payoffs.[36] Compensation packages heavily weighted to stock-based compensation may lead to incentives for earnings management [37] and may increase the likelihood of fraud as well.[38] There are metrics other than earnings per share that could be used to measure performance that are less susceptible to management influence.[39]

An Incentive "To Achieve That Goal at Any Cost"

The OFHEO *Report of the Special Examination of Freddie Mac*, issued in December 2003, found that the executive compensation program at Freddie Mac contributed to improper accounting and management practices. As at Fannie Mae, the Freddie Mac executive compensation program tied the size of the annual bonus pool, in large part, to meeting or exceeding annual specified EPS targets.[40] The sharp criticism by OFHEO of the undue reliance by Freddie Mac on EPS as a performance metric for compensation presaged such a review of Fannie Mae by OFHEO.

Johnson Associates, the company's compensation consultant, pointed out to Fannie Mae that tying Annual Incentive Plan funding to a minimum threshold or "cliff" EPS goal provided incentives to "achieve the goal at any cost." A July 2004 Compensation Committee Update noted the following in reference to a failure to meet the Annual Incentive Plan (AIP) minimum EPS threshold:

> Should AIP funding drop to zero for goal achievement below minimum levels? External consultants advise us of the need to fund bonus pools at some threshold level to ensure ability to remain within competitive range of market for retention and recruitment. Corporate governance issue is generated by having a cliff that reduces the bonus pool to zero, which could incent people to achieve that goal at any cost.[41]

In an interview with OFHEO, Ms. Rudin, the internal executive compensation expert at Fannie Mae, said she shared this portion of the report with Johnson Associates, the compensation consultant for Fannie Mae, to make certain the views stated accurately reflected the views of Johnson Associates.[42]

Executive compensation expert David Yermack, a New York University associate professor of finance, told Fannie Mae staff in 2004 that a 20-year history of research showed that accounting targets could be manipulated so that managers could hit the target. He also advised that it was relatively easy for a financial company to smooth earnings in a way most convenient for managers.[43] In an e-mail, Yermack told Fannie Mae:

> EPS is very much in disrepute among academics (as well as compensation professionals) because it is a statistic that managers can manipulate very easily. Research as far back as the 1980s has shown that managers 'smooth earnings' across time quite aggressively, and it has never been done more obviously than in the situation involving Freddie Mac. The managers at Fanne [sic] Mae, and just about everywhere else, should have their incentive compensation linked to the stock price, not to accounting targets.[44]

The use of market-based financial performance metrics for Annual Incentive Plan bonuses in addition to EPS would have made it more difficult for senior executives to enrich themselves inappropriately through the manipulation of accounting earnings. While stock price, for example, was a component in the long-term incentive plan (LTIP) compensation received by senior executives, particularly as it affected the value of stock options, it played no role in the Annual Incentive Plan bonus.

Link between Compensation Earnings Targets and Earnings Management Noted by KPMG

Fannie Mae's external auditor, KPMG, noted the link between compensation and earnings management in 1999. In a strategic analysis memorandum, KPMG observed:

> The earnings objective is tied to the employees' incentive goals and performance based compensation, which could result in the managing of earnings to meet corporate goals and objectives.[45]

The likelihood of such an occurrence, KPMG said in the analysis, was "possible" and the magnitude of impact "high."

KPMG described how earnings-based incentives could contribute to fraudulent revenue recognition and financial reporting, due in part to a desire by executives to preserve personal wealth. Referring to Fannie Mae compensation, KPMG noted in a 2002 risk analysis:

> Management has incentive to meet earnings targets in order to meet analyst expectations and to preserve their personal wealth as incentive compensation is linked to meeting established targets and because of ownership of company stock and stock options.

KPMG also noted that adequate allowance for credit losses and proper recognition of FAS 91 amortization was an area of concern:

> The risk of fraudulent revenue recognition has been identified as a significant opportunity for fraudulent financial reporting in light of Management's incentive program, which is designed to reward higher earnings, among other things. This presents a fraud risk factor with respect to revenue recognition and the significant judgment areas in the financial statements.[46]

Conflicts of Interest in Setting EPS Targets

Allowing executives who stand to benefit from their own decisions to control the establishment of the annual EPS growth target for Annual Incentive Plan bonuses, the actions that directly influence the rate of EPS growth, and the reporting of the final EPS number which determines the size of the overall bonus pool creates a conflict of interest. Senior executives can anticipate EPS growth, can exercise substantial influence over such growth, and stand to gain financially from meeting compensation targets tied to that growth. As a result, they may set growth targets that are consistently achieved, sometimes through transactions that create no value for shareholders.

Chief Financial Officer Timothy Howard, in consultation with the CEO, set the financial targets for the Annual Incentive Plan bonus that included the target for maximum payouts as well as the minimum threshold which determined whether there would be payouts at all from the Annual Incentive Plan bonus pool. Ms. Rudin confirmed the financial targets were set by Mr. Howard in consultation with the CEO at the time in an interview with OFHEO:

> Q: Who sets the targets?
> A: The financial –
>
> Q: The EPS targets.
> A: The financial targets or whatever targets for the Annual Incentive Plan are established for each year. When there were financial targets were established -- let me say I would get -- I got them from Tim Howard –
>
> Q: Okay.
> A: -- and I put them into the book.
>
> Q: So that decision was made at the Office of the Chairman level?
> A: What I know is I got them from Tim Howard.
>
> Q: Okay. Do you think he decided on his own?
> A: I believe he consulted with whoever the CEO was at the time.[47]

According to Shaun Ross, Director for Business Planning, Mr. Howard acted based on preliminary recommendations by Senior Vice President and Controller Leanne Spencer.[48] Mr. Raines reviewed and approved the goals set by Mr. Howard, which were ultimately approved by the Compensation Committee of the Board of Directors. A handwritten note with the notation "per FDR 1/14/03" included the specific Annual Incentive Plan goals for 2003 that were eventually established by the Compensation Committee of the Board of Directors on January 20, 2003.[49] Ms. Rudin indicated that the "per FDR" portion of the note was in her handwriting and that she had been informed that targets had come from Mr. Raines. The source of information was likely Christine Wolf, Vice President for Compensation and Benefits, or Kathy Gallo, Senior Vice President for Human Resources.[50]

As Chief Financial Officer Mr. Howard was responsible for the final earnings per share number, the metric that determined whether the EPS bonus targets were met and, accordingly, the metric that determined the size of the Annual Incentive Plan bonus pool. Ms. Rudin noted in her interview with OFHEO: "That assumption about how big the pool should be funded was based on or was -- not even based on, was given to me by the -- by Tim Howard."[51] In that process, Mr. Howard had direct interaction with Ms. Rudin.[52] Ms. Rudin actually reported to the Senior Vice President for Human Resources, who did not report to Mr. Howard. Regarding former Senior Vice President for Human Resources Kathy Gallo, Ms. Rudin indicated in an OFHEO interview:

> [OFHEO]: Who did Kathy Gallo report to? Did she report–
>
> [Ms. Rudin]: Kathy Gallo reported to Dan Mudd [Chief Operating Officer]
>
> [OFHEO]: So, Human Resources reported to Dan Mudd, yet most of what we've talked about today was going through Tim Howard. I'm just--this is the first time Dan Mudd's name has come up, even though in the line of command, when we look at the chart, he was in charge, is that correct? He was in charge?
>
> [Ms. Rudin]: That's correct. Well, yeah. Dan Mudd was Kathy's boss.[53]

Mr. Howard's guidance on executive compensation targets was usually on the mark. Ms. Rudin also noted in her OFHEO interview:

> Q: Did there ever come a time when you were given a preliminary number and you funded [the AIP bonus pool] at the certain level that Mr. Howard told you to fund it at and then later on at the close of the year, Mr. Howard said oops, unfund it?
> A: That never happened.[54]

The setting of EPS growth targets for Annual Incentive Plan Bonuses and the reporting of the final EPS number were actions that fell within the purview of a small number of very senior Fannie Mae officers. That circumstance resulted in an inherent conflict of interest.

How the Performance Share Plan Worked

The Performance Share Plan (PSP) was another key component of the executive compensation program tied to consistent, double-digit growth in EPS. The members of senior management—a relatively small group of 40 to 50 officers—received Performance Share Plan shares. In the early years of the Performance Share Plan, which was inaugurated with a four-year cycle covering the years 1982-1985,[55] payouts were tied to multiple measures of performance, including cumulative pre-tax earnings, return on assets (for both the retained portfolio and mortgage-backed securities held by others), and administrative expense growth. Beginning in 1992, EPS growth goals and "strategic" goals determined payouts at the conclusion of each three-year cycle, as described above. By 1994, the EPS and strategic goals were given equal weighting (*i.e.* 50 percent each) in determining actual achievement at the conclusion of each cycle.[56] The amount of the total award represented the sum of the results of the EPS growth-related portion (50 percent) and the evaluation by the Compensation Committee of the Board of Directors of the Corporate Performance

Assessment (50 percent).[57] As a result, EPS growth became a critical factor in long-term compensation.

As with the Annual Incentive Plan, Fannie Mae set the size of Performance Share Plan payouts under direction from the Compensation Committee of the Board of Directors.[58] Again, how reported EPS compared to EPS targets (along with achievement relative to "strategic goals") determined the size of the Performance Share Plan payout for any three-year cycle. As the chart below shows, achievement of the Performance Share Plan maximum goals payout (150 percent) was nearly automatic after the 1995-1997 cycle, and executives were compensated accordingly. The 150 percent maximum payout under the Performance Share Plan program assumed a maximum achievement of EPS goals (75 percent) plus a maximum achievement of Corporate Performance Assessment (75 percent).

As figure V-2 indicates, for Performance Share Plan cycles in years that began in 1996 onwards, Fannie Mae met the Performance Share Plan 150 percent maximum payout target every cycle except for that of 2000-2002. That cycle achieved a 145 percent payout. The Performance Share Plan total award value at the completion of the 2001-2003 cycle reached $51.9 million.

Problems with the Performance Share Plan

The Performance Share Plan suffered from many of the same structural problems as the Annual Incentive Plan. The Performance Share Plan payouts required minimum achievements and were capped beyond a set level of EPS attainment. The reliance on EPS as the principal measure of financial performance multiplied executives' rewards since EPS also determined the size of the Annual Incentive Plan annual bonus pool. It also aggravated problems already associated with the Annual Incentive Plan reliance on that measure, primarily the ease with which managers could manipulate EPS both as a target and as a measure of performance achieved, especially in an environment of lax controls and oversight.

Completed PSP Cycles-Payments to Date

			Completed Payments		
PSP Cycle	Achievements Against Goals	Completion of Cycle	Shares	Cash	Shares to be Paid
1988-1990	129,250%	$15.6MM	$30,024	$7.2MM	0
1989-1991	141,400&	16.1	1,018,760	0.2	0
1990-1992	120,240%	9.1	425,528	0	0
1991-1993	142,780&	19.2	356,012	0	0
1992-1994	146,000%	7.2	392,699	0	0
1993-1995	33,621%	12.6	311,552	0	0
1994-1996	127,187%	16.7	439,799	0	0
1995-1997	145,104%	41.1	658,237	0	0
1996-1998	150,000%	34.5	538,436	0	0
1997-1999	150,000%	24.8	383,146	0	0
1998-2000	150,00%	39.6	479,537	0	0
1999-2001	150,000%	26.1	351,513	0	0
2000-2002	145,000%	37.8	545,078	0	0
2001-2003	150,000%	51.9	362,961	0	286.557 (a)
2002-2004 (b)	N/A	N/A	N/A	N/A	N/A

(a) Originally scheduled to have been paid in January 2003.

(b) Cycle concluded in December 2004 and the first payment was originnaly scheduled to have been maid in January 2005.

Source: FMSE 535230.

Figure V-2. Performance Share Plan Payouts for Cycles Ending from 1990 to 2003

As with the one-year Annual Incentive Plan targets, Chief Financial Officer Timothy Howard monitored the Performance Share Plan payouts closely.[59] In an e-mail chain from Mr. Howard to Ms. Rudin dated September 29, 2003, Mr. Howard made the point that even a 2004 year in which EPS was in the 7 percent range would result in a "max out" in the EPS portion of the Performance Share Plan (PSP) payout (75 percent) in an upcoming cycle:

> For the 2001-2003 cycle (PSP 17) we will definitely max out on the EPS component. We are also very likely to max out on the 2002-2004 cycle (for us not to, we would need core business EPS growth in 2004 to be less than 7% above our estimate for 2003). So I'd use 75% attainment for the EPS portion in both cycles. For 2003-2005, it's too early to change from a 50% estimate.
> What has been this history of our award on the corporate report card? Other than last year, when we were at 70%, I can't recall any recent year when we weren't at the max of 75%.[60]

The recollection of Mr. Howard was accurate. The Performance Share Plan indicators were expected to hit the maximum during the period examined, as they nearly always did.

Executive compensation consultant David Yermack told Fannie Mae staff that the Performance Share Plan targets were much too achievable. A summary of a discussion with Mr. Yermack recounted his view that management had an idea where earnings would be and set goals accordingly:

> Many cycles paid out at 150% or close. This suggests to him [Mr. Yermack] that targets are too low and management had an idea of where earnings would be and suggested targets accordingly.[61]

Regarding the ill-defined Corporate Performance Assessment metric, executive compensation consultant Semler Brossy noted in a February 2005 internal report:

> The six factors represent broad areas of performance (mission, risks, etc) without explicit objectives.
> The discretion in question covers a three-year period, which we think is an unrealistic period to track without specific objectives, especially given the normal rotation of Directors on and off Board Committees.[62]

For Mr. Raines, the combination of salary, bonus, and Performance Share Plan awards provided substantial compensation, as indicated in Table V-1. As previously described, meeting annual EPS goals played a key role in the size of the bonus pool available under the Annual Incentive Plan program and also on the size of the bonuses actually received by Fannie Mae executives. Meeting three-year EPS goals under the Performance Share Plan program had an even larger financial impact on senior executives, as Table V-4 indicates. Such was the concern about meeting the three-year Performance Share Plan goals that a January 2003 analysis prepared by the Office of the Controller noted the adverse effect an anticipated slowdown in EPS growth would have on Performance Share Plan payouts. In the document, reproduced below as Figure V-3, Plan Operating EPS for those years is projected to have an average growth rate of 10.4 percent for the cycle—slightly above the Performance Share Plan (PSP) minimum threshold. A margin note on the document indicates that "we need to stretch to get to a 100% PSP payout."[63] The "stretch" to meet the 12% target

Performance Share Plan payout required an additional $571.9 million in earnings for the cycle; a maximum payout would require an additional $1.311 billion in the period. Figure V-3: Office of the Controller Plan Operating Earnings Per Share (EPS), Annual Incentive Plan (AIP) and Performance Share Plan (PSP) Analysis: January 2003

Fannie Mae proxy statements show that the cumulative total of EPS-influenced Performance Share Plan awards for Mr. Raines and Mr. Howard from 1998 to 2003 was sizable, as indicated in Table V-4.

Table V-4: Mr. Raines and Mr. Howard Performance Share Plan Awards

	1998	1999	2000	2001	2002	2003	Total
Mr. Raines	$794,873	$1,329,448	$4,588,616	$6,803,068	$7,233,679	$11,621,280	$32,370,964
Mr. Howard	$909,196	$860,464	$2,088,542	$1,987,119	$1,947,368	$3,470,578	$11,263,267

Source: Fannie Mae proxy statements.

The Raines Initiative: Earning Per Share (EPS) Challenge Option Grants to "Turbo-Charge" Compensation

In May 1999, incoming CEO Franklin Raines told investors that "the future is so bright that I am willing to set as a goal that our EPS will double over the next five years."[64] In conjunction with that initiative and in anticipation of the planned fall 1999 meeting of the Compensation Committee, Mr. Nides, Senior Vice President for Human Resources, reported to Mr. Raines on planned revisions to the Fannie Mae executive compensation system. Those revisions eventually resulted in the establishment of the Earnings Per Share Challenge Grant. In an August 20, 1999, memo to Mr. Raines, Mr. Nides affirmed that changes in the compensation program were directly related to the doubling EPS challenge: "First and foremost, our executive compensation program should be strongly linked to your goal to double EPS by the year 2003."[65]

In 1999, Fannie Mae management recommended that the Board of Directors approve a special stock option grant to provide an incentive for employees to double EPS to $6.46 by yearend 2003. The Board of Directors implemented the recommendation, which it viewed as a Raines initiative. All full-time and part-time employees subsequently received EPS Challenge Option Grants scheduled to vest in January 2004 if Fannie Mae doubled EPS by year-end 2003.

On January 23, 2004, the Board of Directors determined that Fannie Mae had indeed doubled EPS, vesting employees with 4,896,542 stock options ("EPS Challenge Grants") with an estimated present value on the date of the grant of $103,248,130.[66] For most senior officers, the "strike price" for the bulk of the options awarded was $62.50 with an expiration date of January 18, 2010. Senior executives received substantial value from these EPS Challenge Option Grants, as Table V-5 indicates. According to Fannie Mae, the grant date present value of the 213,548 options awarded to Mr. Raines, for example, was $4,358,515. For Mr. Howard, the value of the 63,791 options awarded was $1,292,085. Those values reflect the ability of the executives to exercise those options until January 2010.

($ in millions, except EPS)

Plan Summary

	2002	2003	2004	2005	03-05 CAGR
Plan Operating EPS	$6.3125	$ 7.1016	$ 7.5796	$ 8.4944	
Growth	21.3%	12.5%	6.7%	12.1%	10.4%
Average Shares Outstanding	997.1	993.0	993.9	993.3	

2003 AIP

03 AIP

	EPS %	EPS $	Variance To Plan	Payout 1/
Max	16.0%	$7.3225	$ (337.5)	125%
Target	13.0%	$7.1332	$ (48.2)	100%
	12.0%	$7.0700	$ 48.2	
Min	10.0%	$6.9438	$ 241.1	75%

Below 10% constitutes zero payout

1/ Payout scaled linearly

We need to stretch to get a 100% PSP payout

PSP

'03-'05

	EPS %	2005 EPS $	Variance To Plan
Max	14.0%	$9.3523	$ (1,311.0)
Target	12.0%	$8.8687	$ (571.9)
Min	10.0%	$8.4020	$ 141.2

EPS performance represents weight of 50%

Source: Controllers

compplans03final.xls FinalComp
1/16/2003 11:10 AM

Source: FMSE SRC OFHEO 00254575.

Figure V-3. Office of the Controller Plan Operating Earnings Per Share (EPS), Annual Incentive Plan (AIP) and Performance Share Plan (PSP) Analysis: January 2003

Problems with the EPS Challenge Grants: To Live, Breathe and Dream $6.46

The EPS Challenge Grants worsened the problems with the other components of executive compensation. By further concentrating management on EPS as the sole relevant measure of financial performance, those grants intensified incentives to manipulate EPS reporting improperly. In addition, the provision of challenge grants to all employees aligned incentives throughout Fannie Mae, most inappropriately among those charged with establishing and maintaining internal controls. If the annual or cyclical minimum performance targets created a go-for-broke incentive to achieve minimum payout levels, the EPS Challenge Grant magnified that incentive further.

Table V-5. Fannie Mae EPS Challenge Options Grants Vested January 2004

Officer	Title	EPS Challenge Grant Options Award	Grant Date Black-Scholes Value
Franklin Raines	Chairman & CEO	213,548	$4,358,415
Timothy Howard	Vice Chair & CFO	63,791	$1,292,085
Daniel Mudd	Vice Chair & COO	116,710	$1,928,049
Robert Levin	EVP, Housing and Comm. Development	56,572	$1,154,635
Adolfo Marzol	EVP, Finance and Credit	48,086	$981,435
Thomas Donilon	EVP, Law and Policy, & Corporate Secretary	37,257	$900,211

Source: Letter from Pamela F. Banks, Vice President for Regulatory Compliance, Fannie Mae to Brian Doherty, Senior Policy Analyst, OFHEO, dated February 20, 2004.

The challenge to double EPS by the end of 2003 galvanized all parts of the Enterprise. Sampath Rajappa, Senior Vice President for Operations Risk and head of Internal Audit, in remarks prepared for an address to the internal audit group in 2000, made clear the importance attached to hitting the $6.46 goal. In a prepared text he shared with Mr. Raines, Mr. Rajappa, the head of internal audit, said:

> By now every one of you must have $6.46 branded in your brains. You must be able to say it in your sleep, [sic] you must be able to recite it forwards and backwards. You must have a raging fire in the belly that burns away all doubts, you must live, breathe and dream $6.46. You must be obsessed on $6.46. After all, thanks to Frank, we all have a lot of money riding on it.

Mr. Rajappa emphasized the role internal auditors would play, in achieving hat earnings target, and the monetary reward they would receive, if Fannie Mae met "Frank's goals":

> We must do this with fiery determination, not on some days, not on most days, but day in and day out, give it your best, not 50%, not 75%, not 100%, but 150%. Remember, Frank has given us an opportunity to earn not just our salaries, benefits, raises, ESPP [Employee Stock Purchase Program] but substantially over that if we make $6.46. So it is our moral obligation to give well above and above our 100% and if we do this, we would have made tangible contributions to Frank's goals.[67]

In view of the responsibility of his office to monitor compliance with accounting and other standards, those remarks prepared by Mr. Rajappa for delivery to his Operations Risk and Internal Audit employees were inappropriate.

The EPS Challenge focused senior executive officers on the precise income numbers needed to hit the target in the out-years. Chief Operating Officer (COO) Daniel Mudd had the number in mind in an October 12, 2000, memorandum to senior executives:

> We also need to continue to focus on our 2003 challenge. Our outlook for that year has improved from the last forecast, but we still have a gap of nearly $375 million in pre-tax income.[68]

In the memorandum, Mr. Mudd also noted: "I know that the numbers in our Q3 forecast around our 'big bets' are still being refined as we iron out the issues—and that those revenue numbers may well change. It is clear that these new products may not be sufficient to get us to our $6.46 goal—and we as a company must be looking hard at what it will take to make it."

Fannie Mae nearly met the $6.46 EPS doubling goal at the end of 2002. By early 2003, the company was operating on the assumption that the $6.46 goal would be met or exceeded.[69] The final EPS number for 2003 was $7.29. While EPS generally made an unrelenting, sharply upward climb during the EPS Challenge Grant years (1999-2003), EPS declined once the Challenge Grant target was met in January 2004, due in part to a less favorable mortgage market environment.

Manipulation of EPS Targets and Reported EPS to Increase Executive Compensation

So far this chapter has documented the structure of executive compensation at Fannie Mae and the potential of that structure to induce behavior inconsistent with safety and soundness. This section documents that Fannie Mae executives knowingly and purposefully used accounting maneuvers to achieve earnings goals to increase their own compensation over an extended period. With compensation goals as an incentive, senior executives consistently managed to hit the EPS goal that ensured a maximum bonus payout, generally without significantly exceeding that goal. The effectiveness of senior management in both setting and hitting EPS targets to attain maximum Annual Incentive Plan payouts is demonstrated by their track record. From 1996 through 2002, a very good predictor of the EPS reported at the end of any given year was the EPS maximum payout bonus target established at or near the beginning of the year. The accounting maneuvers documented here and in more detail in chapter VI were inconsistent with the interests of safety and soundness.

A Long History of EPS Manipulation: The Fannie Mae Bonus Program

The fact pattern that connects Fannie Mae's focus on earnings goals, the relationship of those goals to executive compensation, and the corresponding accounting maneuvers that resulted, can be documented back to the early 1990s. This sub-section describes the development of the Fannie Mae Annual Incentive Plan (bonus) plan, which used net income, rather than EPS, as a performance metric in the early 1990s. It also describes how, after Fannie Mae began to use EPS as the Annual Incentive Plan performance metric in 1995, it used stock and debt buybacks to influence the EPS growth rate, which by then determined awards under the two major portions of executive compensation (the Annual Incentive Plan and the Performance Share Plan).

Chief Financial Officer Timothy Howard advocated transferring net-income from one year to another in his October 2, 1992, self-evaluation memorandum to then Vice Chairman Franklin Raines and Chief Operating Officer Lawrence Small. Mr. Howard stated, in part:

> We currently are projecting 1992 net income of $1.620 billion, nearly $100 million over plan. (This, I would add, is almost too much over plan, as far as the credibility of the plan is concerned.) The work done on the foreclosed assets accounting standard will give us a boost

> in 1993 and 1994 net income that investors will not discount as a "windfall" event. We have been able, through repurchase of high-cost debt, to transfer over $12 million in after tax net income from this year into 1993 and 1994.[70]

Mr. Howard discussed the relationship between accounting and earnings management in a section of that self-evaluation entitled "Earnings Management." His early October 1992 projection of $1.620 billion in net income for 1992 was quite accurate. Table V-6 shows after-tax net income for that year was $1.623 billion.

Table V-6. Maximum Annual Incentive Plan (AIP) Bonus Targets and Actual After-Tax Net Income (in billions), 1991 – 1995

Year	After-Tax Net Income Target for Maximum AIP Bonus Payout	Actual Year-End After-Tax Net Income
1991	$1.345	$1.363
1992	$1.575	$1.623
1993	$1.883	$1.873
1994	$2.173	$2.132

Source: FMSE-EC 068115

EPS and Stock Repurchases

Fannie Mae adopted EPS goals for Annual Incentive Plan bonuses in 1995 partly to bring that measure into conformity with its long-term compensation program, which was by then EPS-based.[71] That management-recommended and Board of Directors-approved[72] shift from a net income performance metric to EPS gave management another tool with which to target a specific EPS number: stock buybacks.[73] In a bonus compensation system based on net income targets, stock buybacks, which can reduce net income, can thereby have an adverse effect on meeting the bonus goal. In notes prepared for a presentation to a November 1996 Board of Directors meeting, Mr. Howard described how earnings per share, which by then directly impacted the Annual Incentive Plan bonus program metric, could grow at a substantially greater rate than net income:

> You'll see that for the four year period we're projecting average EPS growth of nearly 12 percent—11.8% to be exact. Net income growth is a bit under 10%. The difference between the 9.8% net income growth and the 11.8% EPS growth is the assumed effect of the continuation of our stock buyback program. In the forecast we assume that we repurchase the six percent of outstanding shares authorized in our December 1996 capital restructuring program evenly over 1997, 98 and 99. This has two effects. First, the additional debt costs we incur to repurchase the shares reduce our net interest income, and also our net income, by about one percent. (That is, were it not for the buyback, our net income would grow by about 11%, rather than 10%.) But the effect of having significantly fewer shares pushes our EPS growth above the 11 percent growth we would have had without the buyback, to the 11.8% shown here.[74]

The Board of Directors was aware of the use of stock buybacks to influence EPS goals and approved such buybacks. There is no indication that the Board considered the impact of those buybacks when setting EPS targets for bonus compensation at the beginning of each year.[75]

Fannie Mae calibrated share repurchases to hit a desired EPS growth rate. The 1997 Performance Assessment for Mr. Howard, which includes the signature of COO Lawrence Small, encourages Mr. Howard to "speed up the pace" of the share buyback program, but added a very specific parameter:

> Obviously, we recognize that our buyback pace has to be calibrated to fit our desired EPS growth rate, so don't take the previous statement as anything more than strong encouragement to stay focused on this important aspect of capital management.[76]

In an interview with OFHEO, Mr. Small discussed the calibration of share buybacks to reach a desired EPS growth rate:

> Q: By growth rate, do you mean growth rate of the EPS shares outstanding or growth rate of earnings per share generally.
> A: I think what this is—my reading of this is that this is the—focused on the issue of calibration and that what it's saying is that there's—desired growth rate means whatever we had in the plan...
>
> Q: Right.
> A: ...and that to make sure that whatever you're doing in this aspect of achieving the plan is in synchrony with the rest of the plan.[77]

Mr. Small went on to say, in the context of the shift from a net income AIP metric to an EPS metric: "So, I think we said for the health of the company and to get the plan so it does what you want it to do, you change it to the growth figure because the growth obviously would not be impaired by doing that. That was the idea." Mr. Small was then asked:

> Q: Now, not only would it not be impaired, I think, but by calibrating it, as you suggested or somebody, in the review of Tim Howard that you helped write, by calibrating the purchase of stock buy backs, you could get the particular earnings per share numbers?
> A: Right. It could help you do that, always within the context of having been authorized to do so by the Board.[78]

The Board of Directors authorized share buybacks for multi-year periods. Senior management then made month-to-month decisions related to such buybacks.[79]

Management also viewed stock repurchases as a type of contingency reserve for meeting the EPS Challenge Grant earnings goal of $6.46 by the end of 2003. In Quarterly Business Review talking points for the first quarter of 2000, under the heading "Double Income Goal," Leanne Spencer, Senior Vice President and Controller, referred to a chart which indicated that each business segment would be assigned a goal for doubling net income by 2003. Ms. Spencer noted:

> Fortunately, each business segment doesn't need to quite double in order for us to meet our $6.46 goal - because of the benefit of stock repurchase and other corporate actions. We are calling that amount our "contingency" reserve.[80]

Because the Board of Directors approved the dollar amount of stock repurchases, a lower stock price increased the effectiveness of repurchases in boosting earnings per share and thereby meeting earnings and bonus targets. In describing stock repurchases, Ms. Spencer further predicted that the cumulative impact of actual and projected repurchase activity would contribute $0.19 to EPS in 2003. That scenario required the Fannie Mae stock price to remain low. "We estimate that because of the lower stock price assumption in the Q1 forecast, we pick up almost $.05 in 2003."[81]

Debt Repurchases Tied to EPS Goals

Debt repurchases were another tool management used to attain EPS goals. As described in Chapter VI, contrary to assertions in the public disclosures of Fannie Mae, e-mail exchanges indicate that a primary reason for conducting debt repurchases was to achieve specific EPS goals. Documents show that, prior to a repurchase announcement, senior management engaged in discussions to determine the specific amount of repurchases to execute in order to achieve the annual EPS goal.

While the debt repurchases were transparent, the EPS targets for payout of Annual Incentive Plan bonuses, for example, were not publicly disclosed. The repurchase activity was orchestrated by a few members of senior management who were the sole decision-makers in establishing the budget, the amount, and the timing of the repurchases.[82] In response to analysts, Fannie Mae denied employing a strategy to use debt repurchases to hit earnings targets.[83]

An Uncanny Coincidence: Maximum Bonus Payout Targets and Reported EPS

The annual year-end EPS number that triggered maximum Annual Incentive Plan payouts was the number to watch at Fannie Mae. From 1996 through 2002, an exceptionally good predictor of the EPS number at the end of a given year was the EPS maximum bonus payout target set by management and approved by the Compensation Committee of the Board of Directors at or near the beginning of each year. In some years, the difference between the maximum bonus payout number and the actual EPS number was fractions of a cent. The only significant exception was in 2001, when a short-term interest rate decline of more than 400 basis points created a "windfall" effect on EPS for Fannie Mae. That resulted in a year-end EPS number much higher than necessary to achieve a maximum bonus payout.

Table V-7. Maximum Annual Incentive Plan (AIP) Bonus Payout Targets and Actual Annual Earnings per Share (EPS), 1995 – 2003

Year	EPS Target for Maximum AIP Bonus Payout	Actual Year-End EPS Performance	
1995	$2.195		$2.1515
1996	$2.480		$2.4764
1997	$2.840		$2.8325
1998	$3.230		$3.2309
1999	$3.690		$3.7199
2000	$4.274		$4.2874
2001	$4.926	(14.9%)*	$5.1963
2002	$6.288	(21.0%)*	$6.3137
2003	$7.3240	(16%)*	$7.2947

* Fannie Mae established EPS goals as a percentage, rather than a dollar number, beginning in 2001.
Source: FMSE 535220 and FMSE1 1001866-67.

As Table V-7 indicates, the actual year-end EPS numbers hover at or near the maximum bonus payout target. Except for 2001, the final reported EPS number was never substantially *more* than that target, in part due to the perverse incentive caused by the ceiling on the Annual Incentive Plan payout structure.

In most years, Fannie Mae avoided the "tapping out" problem described by Controller Leanne Spencer by posting an EPS at or near the maximum bonus payout target, thereby ensuring maximum or near-maximum payout of the bonuses. When earnings were plentiful, the compensation system encouraged pushing income to future years to ensure that EPS and compensation goals for those years would be met.[84] That was not possible in the "windfall" year of 2001, and the Board of Directors, following what was described as a "hard sell" by Fannie Mae staff, approved a "special award" for employees. The Board approved a "Special Award" for executive officers in November 2001 equal to 20 percent of the 2001 Annual Incentive Plan bonus to be paid in stock.[85]

The effort to secure special awards in 2001 was described in an e-mail from the internal compensation expert, Lorrie Rudin, Director for Executive Compensation and Benefits, to Kathy Gallo, Senior Vice President for Human Resources, with a copy to Christine Wolf, Vice President for Compensation and Benefits, dated October 31, 2003. The e-mail, entitled "Follow-up to your meeting with Dan [Mudd, then Chief Operating Officer]," provided a historical perspective on the possibility of another round of special bonuses. The e-mail from Ms. Rudin read, in part:

> Special Bonus for Hard Work and Morale – Chris asked if we had ever done this before. Answer – yes, but only once in my 16-year tenure and even then it was hard to sell to the Board. This was at the end of 2001, after a year when we made a ton of money and we proposed a special award for all employees. Rather than approve it immediately, the Board asked what it was that we did that was so special as opposed to being income simply generated by market conditions. Leanne and her team spent all weekend preparing data to prove the case. They did eventually approve it and payments were made in January 2002. This was a pretty big deal. A very small group of us worked on this for six months and we were able to keep it a secret even from the EVPs.[86]

Fannie Mae did not actually award the stock related to the "Special Award" to officers until 2002. Nonetheless, the Enterprise accrued compensation expenses related to the stock grants at December 31, 2001, conveniently taking the expense in the EPS-laden "windfall" year.[87]

While the 2001 EPS was substantially greater than the maximum bonus payout target that year, Fannie Mae appeared to make a "mid-course correction" on its projected earnings number in mid-2001. That mid-year estimate of 2001 EPS may have had the effect of setting the limit on the final EPS number for that year. In a "10-Year Financial Outlook" presentation by Ms. Spencer on June 24, 2001, to executives at a retreat, she projected the revised year-end 2001 EPS number to be $5.20, reflecting EPS growth over the prior year of 21.3 percent.[88] That revised, mid-year prediction turned out to be on target—to the penny.

Continuing Manipulation of EPS Compensation Targets and Reported Earnings

Fannie Mae senior executives managed earnings over an extended period. That practice originated before Mr. Raines became CEO and was perfected during his tenure. While the techniques varied, the result was predictable: from 1996 through 2002 (except for 2001, when market forces caused an unexpected earnings surge) the final EPS number was always at or near the number required for a maximum Annual Incentive Plan bonus payout. In 2003, EPS was only slightly below the maximum payout target. In 2004, Fannie Mae was unable to report an EPS number.

In that period, Fannie Mae executives used accounting maneuvers to achieve earnings goals to increase their own compensation. With compensation goals as an incentive, senior executives consistently managed to hit, but rarely exceed by much, the annual EPS goals that ensured a maximum bonus payout. This sub-section documents that from 1996 through 2002, the EPS number at the end of a given year was typically very close to the EPS maximum bonus payout target set at or near the beginningof each year, sometimes within fractions of a cent.

1996— Maximum Bonus Payout Number: $2.48
Actual EPS Number: $2.4764

As early as 1996, Fannie Mae engaged in managing earnings per share to a number that matched the maximum bonus payout number. Mr. Howard's talking points for an October 1996 Board of Directors meeting noted that Fannie Mae was on track to produce a $2.48 EPS.[89] That number—$2.48—was the EPS target for a maximum Annual Incentive Plan payout set earlier that year by the Compensation Committee of the Board of Directors. The October 1996 presentation included handwritten margin notes in a forecast chart ("Long Term Forecast: 1996-2000") that projected the year-end 1996 EPS to be $2.4761. The difference between that projection and the final actual EPS number ($2.4764) was a scant 3 basis points (three one-hundredths of a cent).[90]

A mid-November 1996 memorandum from Ms. Spencer to Mr. Howard updated the 1996 3Q forecast after the reversal of a tax entry. Ms. Spencer noted:

> So, what this results in is a forecast that now rounds down to 2.47—2.4744. And, I have now held nothing back such as the previous earnings management items that I've been plugging to the tax line over the last several forecasts, with the reversing of the tax entry.[91]

Ms. Spencer's mid-November EPS forecast of $2.4744 differed from the final actual EPS number by only 20 basis points.

In that memorandum, Ms. Spencer also described the following options that could provide an earnings "cushion" in the event of a shortfall, including revising the accrual rate of foreclosed property closing costs:

What do I Have up my Sleeve to Solve an Earnings Shortfall?

1. 996K of misc income related to lender loss recoveries. An item identified by WRO and we told them not to book it until we told them to.
2. $1.8 million on the tax line relating to an environmental tax that we previously accrued and now apparently will not have to pay, so Marian has told us we could reverse.
3. Foreclosed property expense line. Mike offered up last night the ability to change again the accrual rate on closing costs in the Falcon [single family charge-off and foreclosed property expense] system. You'll recall we did that in June to help the

> second quarter. When we did it, we brought the accrual rate down to 8.25%. His actual experience rate is 7.9% and we wanted to leave a little cushion. He told me last night if I wanted him to he could bring it down to 7.9%, adjust the inventory and he would pick up about $2.2 million dollars."

These three items give me roughly $6 million pre-tax of cushion to earnings. So this is how I would solve a small problem.

We still have other cushion in the bucket account, but it's mostly nii [net interest income] related and we're very protective of this account to resolve margin fluctuation when it occurs.[92]

1997—	*Maximum Bonus Payout Number:*	*$2.840*
	Actual EPS Number:	*$2.8325*

A second quarter 1997 earnings forecast, noting that "we have lost earnings momentum since our first quarter earnings projection," described the response:

> During this forecast we attempted to overcome some of our earnings challenge by introducing an even more accelerated stock repurchase pace and incorporating reduced credit losses and provision cuts.[93]

A subsequent "EPS Update," part of a series of slides which appear to have been presented in December 1997, notes that EPS for the first three quarters of 1997 was $2.08 and that $0.75 in the fourth quarter was "required to hit $2.83."[94] A slide entitled "December Earnings Actions" noted several ways in which the forward-shifting of income or the deferral of expenses had already been accomplished. In addition, it listed several proposed actions "[t]o [a]chieve $2.8325."[95] Earnings actions "[a]ccomplished-[t]o-[d]ate" involved early retirement of debt and deferral of expenses related to such areas as Corporate-Owned Life Insurance. Fannie Mae achieved the projected EPS number of $2.83 in December.[96] In January 1998, Fannie Mae CEO James Johnson reminded Annual Incentive Plan recipients that the size of the Annual Incentive Plan bonus pool, and their Annual Incentive Plan awards, was directly related to EPS targets. In a memorandum, he wrote:

> As you know, the size of the AIP bonus pool is based on corporate financial performance. Thanks to your collective commitment and hard work, we were able to achieve greater than anticipated earnings per share, which resulted in higher AIP awards.[97]

As previously noted, Mr. Raines later sent a nearly identical memorandum to Annual Incentive Plan bonus recipients in January 1999.[98] Ironically, none of the hard work related to the shifting of the recognition of income or expenses between accounting years and provided economic or safety and soundness benefits.

1998—	*Maximum Bonus Payout Number*	*$3.230*
	Actual EPS Number	*$3.2309*

The Fannie Mae 1999 proxy statement said that 1998 "was the most successful year in Fannie Mae history."[99] As described in the September 2004 OFHEO report and Chapter

VI, the deferral of a 1998 expense related to FAS 91 allowed Fannie Mae to meet an EPS target ($3.230) that ensured a maximum payout to the bonus pool.

A July 28, 1998 memorandum from Ms. Spencer and Janet Pennewell, Director for Business Planning, to Mr. Raines and other senior executives noted:

> We will be working closely with Tim [Howard], Ann [Kappler], Rob [Levin] to develop strategies for reaching our minimum EPS targets for 1998, 1999 and beyond. We still need to add almost $30 million in pre-tax income to reach analyst consensus of $3.21 for 1998. We also need to add additional income to achieve double-digit growth for 1999.[100]

Fannie Mae executives managed earnings to an exact EPS target in 1998. A September 22, 1998 "Risk Review with the CFO" meeting included material that listed several goals, including:

1. Establish as priority one the goal of making $3.21 per share in 1998.
2. Manage earnings to that target and manage to the net interest margin implied in the Q2 forecast against which we have set expectations. To the extent that we have "surplus" NII or extraordinary NII/g-fee adjustments that manifest during the remainder: apply these amounts to increase the topside adjustments.[101]

By September 29, 1998, Mr. Howard was expressing concern about the possibility of not "maxing out" in 1998. In a self-evaluation addressed to COO Lawrence Small, Mr. Howard said:

> It's disappointing not to be "maxing out" given that we're in the midst of the strongest origination year in our history. Moreover, with this year's increased liquidations and the impacts successive declines in interest rates are having on the value of our unamortized purchase premiums, buyups and certain REMIC and strip tranches, we are going into 1999 in somewhat weaker shape than I would have liked.[102]

Mr. Howard went on to explain that several factors, including lower-than-forecast spreads on new business, would mean a $70 million shortfall in portfolio net income but indicated he was confident Fannie Mae could "fill the gap":

> Moreover, the effect of this year's net interest margin shortfall has a full year impact in 1999, putting us in a worse position to hit the analysts' consensus than we were at the beginning of the year. I am confident we will come up with a means to fill the gap, but the source is unlikely to be the portfolio business.[103]

One method of "filling the gap" was a non-recurring earnings event of the "cookie jar" type, described in detail in Chapter VI. Mr. Small, in an August 10, 1998 memorandum to Mr. Raines, approximately a month-and-a-half before the Chief Financial Officer "risk review" meeting described above, provides "tone at the top" guidance on how earnings targets are to be met. In a remarkably candid description, Mr. Small advised that earnings targets could be met via "a non-recurring earnings piggy bank." He also described the perils of missing the 1998 maximum bonus payout number of $3.23 to Mr. Raines:

> For 1998, I'm reasonably confident there's enough in the "non-recurring earnings piggy bank" to get us to $3.21. While that number should satisfy investors, you should be aware that last year the AIP paid out just short of the maximum This year, the maximum is $3.23, so at $3.21, the bonus pool will be noticeably lower than in 1997, a fact which will, of course, be rapidly observed by officers and directors come January.[104]

As previously discussed, senior Fannie Mae executives were warned, via staff memoranda in September 1998 and November 1998, that Annual Incentive Plan bonuses would likely be reduced if EPS performance did not measure up.[105]

The "tone at the top" was further reflected in another "piggy bank" approach floated by Mr. Small that involved the establishment of a reserve account linked to the amortization of purchase premiums and discounts. In a July 13, 1998, memorandum to Mr. Small, Ms. Spencer advised against that approach, noting that there was no accounting concept that supported an allowance in that context.[106] Ms. Spencer further advised:

> My final concern is the SEC has stated in the past that they are against companies setting up general "corporate allowances" because they are viewed as piggy banks for the company and do not have any basis in accounting theory.

By November 24, 1998, Fannie Mae was assuming a year-end EPS number of $3.2240 for the purpose of estimating the bonus amounts payable to Mr. Raines and others.[107] The $3.23 maximum payout bonus number was eventually met to the penny (at $3.2309), partly by tapping the "non-recurring earnings piggy bank." In addition to the deferral of the FAS 91 expense described in the September 2004 OFHEO report and Chapter VI, in 1998 Fannie Mae used a "piggy bank" non-recurring accounting action related to the Low Income Housing Tax Credit (LIHTC) that had a powerful effect on EPS. Mr. Small was informed of the potentially powerful EPS effect of that accounting change in a November 25, 1998 memorandum from Ms. Pennewell. Writing in response to a query from Mr. Small, Ms. Pennewell described the anticipated accounting-related contributors to *1999* EPS growth (rather than 1998), listing several "major contributors," including the LIHTC. Ms. Pennewell wrote:

> The biggest contributor is the accounting change for the low income tax credit investments (LIHTC) which adds 3.4 percent to EPS growth. This includes changing from a cash to accrual basis of accounting and changing our depreciation method.[108]

Fannie Mae did not utilize that earnings "contributor" in 1999, as projected in the November 25, 1998 memorandum. That contribution was used only in 1998, which proved a difficult year for meeting earnings targets.

As described in Chapter VI, on January 9, 1999, a journal entry in the amount of $3.9 million recorded a debit to what was known as the 162200 account and a credit to miscellaneous income. Additionally, the journal entry was effective for year-end 1998. The Fannie Mae 1998 Earnings Plan called for net income of $3,349.4 billion for an EPS of $3.22 compared to actual earnings of $3,351.5 billion for an EPS of $3.23. It is apparent that had this journal entry from the 162200 account had not been recorded, the Enterprise would not have met the planned maximum bonus target.[109]

1999 — Maximum Bonus Payout Number $3.690
Actual EPS Number $3.7199

Setting the multi-year goal of doubling EPS had the effect of linking earnings growth targets across years, which required senior management periodically to review and revise its projections. Once management determined that it likely would achieve the maximum bonus payout EPS number in a given year, discussion turned to pushing additional projected income into future years, thereby making it more likely the EPS targets for those years also would be achieved. Management regularly engaged in making such EPS projections and target setting. For example, in 1999, the maximum bonus payout EPS target was $3.69. By July 14, 1999, a document entitled "1999 and 2000 EPS Targets" (which includes the identifier "frankeps.xls sheet (2)"), includes explicit strategies for moving income to contribute to meeting, but not overshooting the EPS targets associated with maximum AIP bonuses in both years.[110]

2000— Maximum Bonus Payout Number $4.274
Actual EPS Number $4.2874

By mid-year 2000, a $4.28 EPS was viewed at Fannie Mae as "delivering on 2000." An August 3, 2000 Quarterly Business Review Document entitled "Delivering on 2000 Then Shifting the Focus to 2001" projects the final EPS number for 2000 as $4.28.[111] A slide in that presentation entitled "The Second Half is Important" illustrates that to achieve the necessary additional $2.20 in EPS in the July-December 2000 period (EPS was $2.08 in the first half of 2000), portfolio growth in the second half of the year would have to be at a 22.6 percent rate (compared to 10.4 percent growth in the first half) and growth of all single-family mortgages would have to be 12.2 percent, (compared to 6.6 percent growth in the first half).[112] A slide entitled "Dimensioning 2001 EPS" predicted a net income shortfall of $100 million in the following year, based on an anticipated 14.9 percent EPS growth goal for that year.[113]

Christine Cahn, Vice President for Budget and Expense Management, indicated to Mr. Howard in an e-mail chain of November 27, 2000, that the maximum EPS target number was $4.27. Mr. Howard, however, was interested in a more precise maximum payout target number—out to the fourth decimal—with an eye not only toward that year's EPS number but the next year's as well. Mr. Howard wrote:

> Do you know if we were intending to base the AIP payouts on the percentages or the EPS numbers (calculated to the fourth decimal)? It won't make a difference this year if we hit $4.28, but it will next year.[114]

In a December 22, 2000, e-mail to Ms. Spencer, Mr. Howard discussed hitting a $4.28 EPS number. The e-mail, with a subject line of "Year-end Planning," advised that debt calls, which looked to be showing a modest gain, should actually show a small extraordinary loss. In his e-mail, Mr. Howard wrote, in part:

> I am still a little confused as to where we are on year-end income planning.
>
> Janet showed me some numbers that had us coming in right at $4.2850, which I thought was pretty close to the figure we needed to hit. If that's the case, it's not obvious that we need to

> do much in the way of 'pre-positioning' for year-end. I recognize that there is unpredictability in our actuals, but I don't know that the unpredictability necassarily [sic] runs in a particular direction.
>
> Janet had been asking Linda about potential year-end losses. Linda came up with a repurchase of some very long debt (2038!) that I nixed because of the extremely long payback period. (I'd do more of the Xerox bonds at a straight loss before I do the long debt.) But I was puzzled as to why she was looking for losses.
>
> Could you make sure to stay on top of this (in absentia)?
>
> Also, Rick Swick mentioned at PIC [Portfolio Investment Committee] that with the debt calls we've done we'll now show a modest extraordinary gain. I assume that we don't want that, and that someone will tell the appropriate portfolio business person that a small extraordinary loss is preferable. 115

There was, in fact, little unpredictability in the actuals that late in the year. The final EPS number "hit" by Fannie Mae at year-end 2000 was $4.2874, a slight twenty four basis points difference from the number referred to in the "year-end planning" e-mail.

2001—	*Maximum Bonus Payout Number*	*$4.926 (14.9 percent growth)*
	Actual EPS	*$5.1963*

With an unanticipated surge in earnings in 2001, due mainly to a sharp drop in interest rates, it was clear to senior executives by the middle of that year that Fannie Mae would easily exceed its maximum EPS bonus payout number. As a result, senior management focused on shifting earnings to future years.

In a "10-Year Financial Outlook" presentation to executives on June 24, 2001, Controller Leanne Spencer projected the year-end 2001 EPS number to be $5.20, reflecting an EPS growth over the prior year of 21.3 percent.[116] The $5.20 number projected by Ms. Spencer in June was still the target in November.

In a November 4, 2001 memorandum from Ms. Spencer to Mr. Raines entitled "Update on Earnings," Ms. Spencer described her recent Quarterly Business Review "Financial Outlook" presentation and discussed earnings management and "smoothing ideas."[117] To meet the $5.20 target, Ms. Spencer told Mr. Raines, required debt repurchases combined with a special contribution to the Fannie Mae Foundation, actions which would have the effect of reducing reported earnings for that year. In further describing a portion of the presentation related to a downturn scenario, Ms. Spencer advised Mr. Raines: "Under Q3 the Modest Downturn Scenario, IF (sic) we were unable to come up with any smoothing ideas to move income you see that we'd be flush in 2002 and then 03 and 04 are negative to low and unacceptable growth."[118] Ms. Spencer also described to Mr. Raines plans to "pull the earnings down" to $6.30 EPS in the following year (2002), with an indication that CFO Timothy Howard had asked Senior Vice President for Portfolio Strategy Peter Niculescu for ideas on how to accomplish that. As Ms. Spencer described it to Mr. Raines:[119]

> For 2002, I plugged in (sic) an amount into the gain/loss line item just to pull the earnings down to $6.30. It is purely a plug with no actions identified as yet. Tim has Peter working on ideas.

Any plan to "pull the earnings down to $6.30" in 2002 should be viewed in an executive compensation context. As noted in the section below, the EPS number reported at year-end 2002 was $6.3137, and the maximum EPS AIP bonus payout number was $6.288.

2002—	*Maximum Bonus Payout Number*	*$6.288 (21.0 percent growth)*
	Actual EPS	*$6.3137*

According to Roger Barnes, Manager for Premium Discount Amortization, whose allegations of earnings management are discussed in Chapters VII and VIII, by 2002 it was clearly Fannie Mae policy to use such instruments as REMICs to reduce short-term income and to push out income to future years. In a May 2002 e-mail, Mr. Barnes noted:

> Top management is creating the structured transactions to take losses now. Per Janet, Frank and Tim feel there is enough income locked in for 2002 that we do not need to worry about meeting this year's goals. Further, she indicated the amortization of deferred items provides a vehicle to manage to "Plan."[120]

Mr. Barnes also expressed concern with the lack of detailed disclosures regarding REMICs. Mr. Barnes wrote:

> Investors and analysts are clamoring for the data but the company is refusing to provide it because of the uproar it would cause if Wall Street know [sic] we were so heavily "managing income" as to take losses needlessly. There is more concern about maintaining a desired level of income than maximizing income. It is unbelievable. People are buying the stock thinking every effort is being made to maximize earnings but that is not the case.[121]

Mr. Howard, according to notes taken from a May 9, 2002 Quarterly Business Review discussion, confirmed the strategy to push income from 2002 into future years. In notes describing a discussion about pulling in certain low income housing tax credits into 2002 by buying up portfolios of mature loans, or by pushing up the construction schedule, the following is attributed to Mr. Howard:

> Why are we working to increase income in 2002 when the corporation is trying to push income out of 2002 to 2003 and 2004? We need to talk about this as a follow up.[122]

A summary of that Quarterly Business Review, under the heading "Follow ups" reflected the company position expressed by Mr. Howard in the discussion:

> It was mentioned that the LIHTC group is working on ways to pull income into this year by buying portfolios of mature loans or moving up construction timelines. This is inconsistent with the overall corporate effort to move income out of 2002 and into later years. (Pennewell, Neill [likely, Edwin Neill, Vice President for Tax Credit Investments])[123]

A July 26, 2002, "Q2 Earnings Forecast" from Janet Pennewell, Vice President for Financial Reporting and Planning, and Shaun Ross, Director for Business Planning, noted that Fannie Mae was on track that year to achieve planned EPS of $6.30 or EPS growth of 21.2 percent.[124]

Kathy Gallo, Senior Vice President for Human Resources, was informed via an e-mail chain from Christine Wolf, Vice President for Compensation and Benefits, on November 14, 2002, that a $15 million change in pre-tax earnings would change EPS by a penny, as would a $10 million after-tax change in earnings.[125] The mid-year projection from Ms. Pennewell and Mr. Ross was on target: the reported $6.3137 EPS figure, later restated as $6.3017, slightly exceeded the $6.288 maximum EPS payout bonus target number. The result was a maximum payout to the Annual Incentive Plan bonus pool.

2003—Maximum Bonus Payout Number	*$7.3240 (16.0 percent growth)*
Actual EPS	*$7.2947*

In a January 14, 2003 meeting that included Mr. Raines, Mr. Howard and Mr. Mudd, Annual Incentive Plan bonus targets were set for 2003, with an eye towards 2004. Ms. Spencer, in an e-mail to Ms. Cahn, Ms. Pennewell, Mr. Ross and Peter Niculescu, Executive Vice President for Mortgage Portfolio Business, described that meeting with senior executives in which the EPS minimum payout target was set at 10 percent, and the maximum at 16 percent, noting that "Frank was emphatic" that there be no bonus payout if EPS growth were "below 10%." Mr. Raines predicted actions, including debt repurchases, to shift earnings to future years, according to Ms. Spencer. In this e-mail, Ms. Spencer wrote:

> Frank said he will be telling people to start on plans for 2004 now. (I'm sure he will communicate this at the SLT [Senior Leadership Team]). And, he plans to communicate that people should expect no more than target bonuses for the next two or more years if the outlook remains as it does because if we have excess earnings we will be deploying them in debt repurchases or other management actions to make "tomorrow" better.[126]

A February 11, 2003 Quarterly Business Review (QBR) presentation by Ms. Spencer projected 2003 EPS growth at 12.5 percent. EPS growth for the next year—2004—was projected at 6.7 percent, with the pre-tax revenue shortfall to meet double digit (10 percent) EPS growth for that year listed as $355.1 million.[127] Notes for the "QBR Presentation February 11, 2003" link EPS projections directly to Annual Incentive Plan maximum bonus payout goals:

> January is off to a good start, but sustained low mortgage rates could really hurt us this year if liquidations continue to run higher than plan. Our 2003 AIP calls for target EPS of 12-13%. If we want to hit max of 16% we have some work to do. We need to generate about $340 million more in revenue.[128]

Debt repurchases were levers for attaining EPS targets. In a June 6, 2003 forecast-related memorandum to Mr. Howard, Mr. Ross noted: "We have also included smaller debt repurchases in the third and fourth [quarter] of this year to keep earnings growth to 12.5% for the year."[129]

In notes prepared for the second quarter 2003 earnings press release and conference call, Mr. Howard was explicit about managing EPS to an Annual Incentive Plan bonus target so that earnings could flow forward to 2004 while hitting 100 percent of the Annual Incentive Plan target in 2003:

> Manage EPS growth in the 12 to 13 percent range this year, consistent with our original plan. This will reduce, but not eliminate, the possibility of our having a down year in 2004. It will also allow us to pay out 100 percent of target (but not more than that) in incentive compensation to our officers.[130]

Ms. Spencer indicated that Mr. Howard shared the draft presentation with Mr. Raines.[131]

Mr. Ross, in an August 28, 2003 e-mail to Ms. Spencer, advised on 2003 and 2004 portfolio net interest income (NII) and net interest margin (NIM) scenarios and projected EPS growth in both 2003 and 2004:

> If we ended this year with EPS growth of 13.0 percent and wanted 2004 EPS growth to be 11.0 percent, portfolio NII could be $8,532m, which is $1,216m lower than the long-term forecast shared yesterday. This would make the 2004 NIM 98.3 bps, down 18.7 bps from 2003.[132]

By the third quarter, the earnings outlook appeared to improve, but earnings management actions related to debt buybacks, described in Chapter VI, were still being contemplated. Mr. Raines was fully engaged in that process. For example, in an e-mail dated September 24, 2003, Mr. Howard described for senior management certain earnings targets proposed to him by Mr. Raines and elicited Ms. Spencer's feedback on the "right cushion." Mr. Howard wrote:

> I was able to get to Frank [Raines] this evening on the buyback loss for the third quarter. (I also showed him the sheet that had $8.87 EPS in 2004, but told him that it was the result of front-ended income that we did not intend to let flow through.)
>
> His thought for the third quarter, which I think is a good one—was to come in at an EPS number that would be a double digit increase from the third quarter of 2002. A third quarter EPS of $1.79 would do that—it would be 10.5% above the $1.62 we reported in the third quarter of 2003.
>
> If that's what we want to do, doing [a] $400 million buyback tomorrow would cause us to fall short of our objective. Using Leanne's numbers, a $400 million buyback would put us at $1.78. And of course, that's without any cushion.
> So—we need a lower cap. Without doing any analysis, I'd be inclined to say $350. A $375 million cap would give us a penny of cushion ($1.80 versus our $1.79 target). Leanne, how much of a cushion would you like, if we're shooting for double digit growth from Q3 2003? Your view of the right cushion should determine the maximum loss number we give to Dave.[133]

Ms. Spencer's response suggests that senior management was obliged to solicit Mr. Raines' views on the use of debt buybacks to hit EPS targets. Having been advised as to the suggestion by Mr. Raines about the proper size of the third quarter EPS number, and the notification to Mr. Raines that Fannie Mae would not let front-ended income flow through to 2004, Ms. Spencer commented: "Thank you. I feel better. I've just learned over time that he always has an opinion."[134]

By the fourth quarter, due in part to a FAS 149 transition adjustment that brought in approximately $285 million in additional pre-tax income, Fannie Mae was "overshooting"

EPS relative to plan. In an October 16, 2003 e-mail to Jayne Shontell, Senior Vice President for Investor Relations, entitled "Rationale for 'overshooting' on EPS," Mr. Howard noted:

> In the fourth quarter, we anticipate future opportunities for debt buybacks. That's why we've updated our guidance to core EPS growth for the full year of "only" around 15 percent. If we can't find enough debt on attractive terms to buy back we could come in higher than that. But 15 percent growth is our current best estimate.[135]

The final EPS growth number for 2003 was, as predicted by Mr. Howard, "around" 15 percent.

2004—	*Minimum Bonus Payout Number*	*$7.8782 (8 percent growth)*
	Actual EPS	*Not reported*

Double-digit earnings growth came to a halt in 2004 as Fannie Mae found itself in a new position in an evolving mortgage market. As a result, senior management began to focus on the *minimum* EPS payout number, rather than the maximum. The focus on hitting that number, particularly by Mr. Howard, was laser-sharp.

The reality of slower growth resulted in a sharp downward revision in 2004 Annual Incentive Plan bonus EPS goals: the minimum Annual Incentive Plan payout threshold was set at EPS growth of 8 percent, the target was set at 10 percent growth, and the maximum Annual Incentive Plan payout cap was set at 12 percent growth.[136] In a January 11, 2004 e-mail exchange with Mr. Howard, Ms. Spencer noted that,

> For AIP, I looked back as far as 1996 and min [minimum] has not been lower than 10.5%. It hasn't been that low since the 96-98 timeframe. Lowest "target" is 12%. Lowest max [maximum] was 14% in 98.

Ms. Spencer noted that recent Performance Share Plan (PSP) targets had set thresholds of minimum compound core EPS growth of 10 percent per year over three years, target growth at 12 percent, and maximum growth at 14 percent.[137] Mr. Howard said in an e-mail to Jonathan Roman, Vice President for Corporate Finance, that a 7 to 8 percent long-term earnings growth rate "will become increasingly more reasonable for us the bigger we get."[138] Citing the prospect of near-term EPS growth in the single-digit range, Mr. Howard suggested to Ms. Spencer that the new Performance Share Plan goals be revised downwards, noting the substantial income hurdles to achieve payouts:

> The four year plan you reviewed with me on Friday has compound annual core EPS growth of 5.9% through 2006. To get to 11% we'll need an extra $1.37 billion. To get to 8% we'll need $600 billion. I think I'd be inclined to notch the range down a bit, since we're coming off three exceptionally high years. I'd probably suggest 7.5% - 10.5% -13.5%.[139]

The post-EPS Challenge Grant Fannie Mae, at least for the near term, was one of single-digit annual EPS growth. Over the next several months, it became clear that Fannie Mae was not likely to fund the Annual Incentive Plan bonus pool at or near the maximum payout levels.[140]

Shortly after OFHEO provided the September 2004 *Report of Findings to Date of the Special Examination of Fannie Mae* to the Board of Directors, questions arose at a September

27, 2004, meeting of the Fannie Mae Senior Leadership Team[141] about the amount of the 2004 Annual Incentive Plan bonus payout. On September 29, 2004, Mr. Howard informed the senior executives that if Fannie Mae achieved target growth, the Annual Incentive Plan bonus payout would be $76,059 million; if Fannie Mae achieved minimum growth, the payout would be $57,805 million.[142]

Significantly, however, as a result of an action taken by the Compensation Committee of the Board of Directors at the July 2004 meeting, the bonus pool for that year was funded at a substantially *higher* level than in prior years. The Compensation Committee acted to increase compensation incentives by 18 percent, allocating 75 percent of the increase to the Annual Incentive Plan program, and 25 percent to long-term incentives. [143] The stated reason for that increase was to ensure Fannie Mae executives were compensated in keeping with the market. For senior management the increase had the felicitous result of mitigating the effect of the sharp decline in EPS growth, thereby ensuring a relatively "soft landing" if the Annual Incentive Plan payout was near the minimum. At the minimum Annual Incentive Plan payout (resulting in the funding of the Annual Incentive Plan bonus pool at 75 percent of target), Mr. Raines could expect a bonus of $3.237 million and Vice Chairs, including Mr. Howard, an average of $1.103 million.[144] Not meeting the minimum threshold meant no bonuses would be paid, except at the discretion of the Board of Directors.[145]

Less than two weeks after the October 6, 2004, testimony before the Congress in which Mr. Raines and Mr. Howard disputed findings included in the September 2004 OFHEO report regarding hitting 1998 Annual Incentive Plan earnings targets, Mr. Howard engaged in a detailed series of e-mails about how to hit those very targets in 2004. On Tuesday, October 19, 2004, Mr. Howard, again citing Annual Incentive Plan bonus numbers out to the fourth decimal point, wrote in an e-mail to Mr. Ross:

> I'm fine (I think!) for the Board meeting, but I'd like to make sure I have a good sense of where we stand, in our latest projection, relative to the 8% adjusted EPS growth rate (i.e., adjusted for the OFHEO-mandated impairments) for 2004 that will trigger AIP payments. It seems from your note, that we're $55 million pretax above it, but that doesn't, I think, subtract the OFHEO-related impairments we are bringing back into income this year. If we subtract those, how big is our cushion over the 8% adjusted rate? And are there any other adjustments we should be making?[146]

Following an e-mail from Janet Pennewell, Senior Vice President for Financial Reporting and Planning, in which she provided numbers and indicated that she "[t]hought it might be helpful to lay out our math quickly on this, [so] we'll still get on your calendar though,"[147] Mr. Howard replied with an analysis of how to meet the Annual Incentive Plan bonus payout target. The length, breadth, detail, and timing of that e-mail from Mr. Howard, who at that point was Vice-Chair of Fannie Mae, a member of the Board of Directors, and Chief Financial Officer, reflects intense interest in the ability of Fannie Mae to "trigger the AIP payout." Mr. Howard, once again working in detail with Annual Incentive Plan bonus figures out to the fourth decimal point, wrote:

> We need to do the math on this carefully, not quickly.
> First, we have to determine the precise target we're shooting for. My understanding is that last year the core EPS growth rate (15.54%) we used to determine the AIP payout percentage, 121.17 percent of target, was calculated using unrounded core EPS numbers (to four decimal places) for 2002 ($6.3139) and 2003 ($7.2950). (We used the originally reported 2002 core

EPS number, not the revised number that included the higher preferred stock dividends mandated by the change in the way issuance costs on called preferred issues were treated.)

If that's correct—and someone will need to verify it—then 8.0% growth from the unrounded 2003 core EPS number is $7.8786 (which rounds to $7.88). Using our current forecast for weighted average diluted shares outstanding of 972.2, which we recognize can change, that means we would need to earn at least $7659.6 million this year to trigger an AIP payment. That's $9.2 million higher than the number you show below.

Second, we'll need to decide how to adjust for OFHEO-mandated impairments. There are two ways to do this, by adjusting the plan or adjusting the actuals. If you adjust the plan, you'd take our plan core EPS of $7953.0 million, subtract the OFHEO impairments to date ($302.6),compute a new plan core business earnings number ($7650.4), core EPS number ($7.9164) and growth rate (8.5 percent). You'd then do the same thing for the old 8.0 % scenario -- $7659.6 less $302.6, or $7357.0, divided by the shares outstanding of 966.4, to equal $7.6128. To hit $7.6128 now, though, given that we think we'll have 972.2 million shares outstanding, we'll need to earn $7401.1 million. That's $44.1 million more than we'd need to earn if we adjust the actual, by adding $302.6 million to the core EPS we earn. Doing the latter, we'd only need to earn $7357.0. We have to decide which approach we're going to use before we determine what our overage or shortfall is.

Finally, we need to see what "cushions" or risks we have in our current projection. We've got the $30 million assumed impairments in the fourth quarter, which if they do happen would reduce both actual earnings and the "OFHEO-adjusted" earnings. There also is some dollar amount by which our current projection is different from the number we need to trigger the AIP payout, but that number depends on how you define the target. I'm not aware of any other cushions in the forecast. And, of course we know we're high on portfolio growth, and probably purchase spread as well.

As I've noted, I want to be very precise on the way we gauge and track this. And I want to monitor it very closely.

I'd like to meet on this when everyone is ready, but I don't want to rush a meeting if we're not. 148

In his interview with OFHEO, Shaun Ross, Director for Business Planning, indicated that the "precise target we're shooting for" referred to by Mr. Howard was the EPS growth target:

Q: Okay. So, this first paragraph, "The precise target we're shooting for," what are we talking about here? The EPS target, the growth rate, AIP pay-out, percentage of the pay-out?
A: In general, when I hear the word target, it referred to the earnings per share that the company was targeting.

Q: You also determined the AIP pay-out based on a percent of target, right?
A: Again, I mean, as I talked about this morning, I think that was my understanding of '03 and '04. That was at least part of the calculation, to my knowledge.[149]

Notes prepared for an October 19, 2004, presentation by Mr. Howard to the Board of Directors, including Board of Directors Chairman and Chief Executive Officer Franklin Raines, included the following: "Without the additional impairments, our projected 2004 core EPS growth would be $7.90. That's three cents above the $7.87 we need to achieve in order to trigger the minimum payout on our annual incentive plan based on our EPS performance."[150] On October 26, 2005, Mr. Ross informed Mr. Howard by memorandum: "The current Q3 forecast would put us at an 86% payout...."[151]

The detailed analysis and positioning were for naught. Following the issuance of the September 2004 OFHEO report and subsequent guidance from the SEC, Fannie Mae management was unable to report a GAAP or core business EPS number in 2004. The Board of Directors made no Annual Incentive Plan bonus awards to senior executives for 2004.

Conclusion

Fannie Mae tied major portions of executive compensation to earnings per share without establishing appropriate internal controls or Board of Directors oversight. Senior executives had a powerful incentive and opportunity to increase personal wealth through accounting manipulations that directly affected EPS and, as a result, their own compensation. The structure of the Annual Incentive Plan, which provided no incentive for management to add to earnings once the EPS number for a maximum bonus payout was achieved, encouraged in times of plentiful earnings the shifting of income forward to meet EPS targets in future years. The chapters which follow discuss in detail the improper earnings management and lack of internal controls that facilitated maximum or near-maximum executive compensation payouts.

References

[1] 12 U.S.C. § 4518, Prohibition of Excessive Compensation, and Preamble, Corporate Governance regulation, 70 Fed. Reg. 17303, 17306 (April 6, 2005) (12 C.F.R. Part 1710).

[2] 12 U.S.C. § 1723a.(d)(2).

[3] 12 C.F.R. § 1710.13, Corporate Governance regulation, and OFHEO Examination Guidance, Examination for Corporate Governance, PG-05-002 (May 20, 2005).

[4] 12 C.F.R. § 1710.15, Corporate Governance regulation, OFHEO Policy Guidance, Minimum Safety and Soundness Requirements, PG-00-001 (December 19, 2000), and 12 C.F.R. Part 1720 App. A, Safety and Soundness regulation.

[5] Fannie Mae previously referred to core business earnings as "operating net income." Fannie Mae 2002 Annual Report at 23.

[6] Michael R. Young, Accounting Irregularities and Financial Fraud: A Corporate Governance Guide (2000 Edition), at 13 n.1, cited in Report and Recommendations from Public Oversight Board's Panel on Audit Effectiveness, at 77 (August 31, 2005).

[7] Fannie Mae Vice-Chair Jamie Gorelick alluded to the role EPS goals played in producing large payouts of Fannie Mae shares to senior executives in draft, light-hearted opening remarks to a 1998 Operating Committee Retreat. The draft remarks included a "Top Ten List" of reasons Fannie Mae had not been able to launch a new product or service and included as "Reason #3." "There's no available budget…[Fannie Mae Chief Operating Officer] Larry Small is concerned that we might not meet his retirement, no I mean, the company's PSP [Performance Share] plan earnings goal." Draft—"Clearing a Path to Growth Through the Legal and Regulatory Thicket,"

Remarks for Jamie Gorelick, 1998 Operating Committee Retreat, Sun Valley, Undated, FMSE KD 042626-650 at 631.

[8] The resolution of the Board of Directors refers only to EPS, but Fannie Mae has indicated that Challenge Grants are tied to achieving a "core business diluted earnings per share goal." Fannie Mae 2002 Annual Report at 108.

[9] A November 16, 1999 resolution of the Board of Directors approved the EPS Challenge Option Grant. A January 18, 2000 Board of Directors resolution approved a modification of the EPS Challenge Grant. Letter from Pamela Banks, Vice President for Regulatory Compliance, Fannie Mae to Brian Doherty, Senior Policy Analyst, OFHEO, February 20, 2004. FMSE-EC 024460–62 at 60.

[10] "Findings and Recommendations—Part 1: Executive Compensation. The Conference Board Commission on Public Trust and Private Enterprise," September 17, 2002 at 9.

[11] The study was conducted by Johnson Associates, which determined that it was appropriate for Fannie Mae to continue to use EPS as a performance metric because other metrics did not correlate well to the Fannie Mae business model. Discussion Draft, "Fannie Mae Performance Metrics Study," October 9, 2003, FMSE KD008125–150.

[12] Notes of the Compensation Committee of the Board of Directors meetings suggest that the Committee appeared to view management's compensation consultant—Johnson Associates—as the "company consultant" rather than as a consultant to the Committee itself. In 2003, that Committee retained compensation consultant Semler Brossy with the intent of having that firm work directly for the Committee to provide an independent view. In notes of a Compensation Committee conference call of September 23, 2003, that included a discussion of the hiring of Semler Brossy, Committee member Taylor Segue asked specifically about the relationship between the committee consultant and the company consultant. Compensation Committee Chair Anne Mulcahy indicated in response that the relationship was arms-length. FMSE 105358.

[13] OFHEO Interview, Lorrie Rudin, Director for Executive Compensation and Benefits, January 31, 2006 at 197-200.

[14] OFHEO Interview, Jill Blickstein, Vice President and Assistant to the Chairman, January 26, 2006 at 222-223.

[15] FMSE KD 029842.

[16] "2002 Executive Compensation Program Overview." FMSE-EC 047734.

[17] Fannie Mae 1999 Report on Compensation to the Committee on Banking and Financial Services of the U.S. House of Representatives and the Committee on Banking, Housing, and Urban Affairs of the U.S. Senate, Pursuant to P.L. 102-550 Section 1381(j)(2) at 7.

[18] "We've had a lot of good years, but this year all the planets lined up, and like the Leonid meteor shower a few weeks ago, these results are rare phenomena." Draft Weekly Message by Franklin Raines, December 7, 2001. FM SRC OFHEO 00257305.

[19] E-mail from Leanne Spencer to Denise Grant, Daniel Mudd, Timothy Howard, Franklin Raines, et al., "Comp Committee/Vincent," November 11, 2001, FMSE-E_EC0033521–23 at p. 3. The draft was incorporated into a presentation on special awards to the November 19, 2001 Board of Directors Compensation Committee meeting. FMSE EC 028058-74 at 70–71.

[20] OFHEO Interview, Lorrie Rudin, January 31, 2006 at 122.

[21] FMSE-KD 029844.

[22] "Notice of Annual Meeting of the Stockholders," March 29, 1999 at 10. For the two executive vice-presidents listed in the proxy statement, approximately 75 percent of the annual bonus was based on one-year EPS performance, and 25 percent based on individual contributions.

[23] Fannie Mae replaced Hewitt Associates with Johnson Associates in 2002. "Fannie Mae Executive Compensation Programs," prepared for Mary Ellen Taylor, Senior Policy Advisor, OFHEO, June 25, 2004. FMSRCZTZ 00618384-422 at 398.

[24] An annual EPS of $3.18 was the "target" payout to the bonus pool. FMSE 017771–73.

[25] The Board of Directors had the discretion to provide for payment of some or all awards for individual performance, regardless of whether the minimum corporate goals have been met, and to adjust corporate goals because of extraordinary or nonrecurring events. FM SRC M-OHFEO 00007481. The issue of whether to award bonuses when minimum EPS thresholds are not met was considered in 2004 by the Board of Directors. Compensation Committee Update, "Review of Current Practices," July 2004 at FMSE 224829 and FMSE 224831.

[26] Address by Fannie Mae Chief Operating Officer Lawrence Small to the 1998 Officers Meeting, "Luck, Smarts and the Capacity to Act," December 10, 1998, Biltmore Hotel and Resort, Phoenix, FMSE 700969–1016 at 977–979.

[27] Memorandum from Thomas Nides, Senior Vice President for Human Resources, to Senior Vice Presidents, "1998 Compensation Actions," November 18, 1998, FMSE-EC 020741–43 at 41. A September 21, 1998 memorandum from Mr. Nides to "All Officers" also advised that EPS performance meant that the Annual Incentive Plan bonus pool would be smaller and, as a result, so would Annual Incentive Plan Awards. Memorandum from Thomas Nides to All Officers, "1998 Compensation Performance and Review Process," September 11, 1998, FMSE-EC 091147–49 at 49.

[28] "Annual Incentive Plan." FMSE-EC 001898–1901 at 1898.

[29] In describing emerging themes from interviews with all members of the Office of the Chairman, all Executive Vice Presidents, 10 Senior Vice Presidents, members of the Compensation Committee of the Board of Directors and others, a 2002 internal compensation study included a key comment: "Incentive plans have 'always' hit max." This reflected the view of some senior executives that Annual Incentive Plan goals were designed and set to ensure that competitive compensation would be paid. Update on Executive Compensation Study. July 1, 2002 FMSE EC 014739–742 at 741.

[30] Office of Federal Housing Enterprise Oversight, Report of the Special Examination of Freddie Mac, December 2003 at 69.

[31] "Accounting performance is often measured relative to a 'target' set by the board and the top management team at the beginning of the year. Although targets are a sensible outgrowth of the corporate strategy-setting process, it is generally not advisable to base compensation on performance measured against an internally derived target. Targets (and overall strategy decisions) cannot be made without substantial input from the top management team, and basing pay on targets may pressure executives to support attainable targets and strategies rather than those that increase shareholder wealth. Externally based industry, financial, and market targets (not set or influenced by top managers) offer viable alternatives." "Report of the National Association of Corporate Directors Blue Ribbon Commission on Executive Compensation: Guidelines for

Corporate Directors," National Association of Corporate Directors, Washington, D.C. 2000 at 26. See also: "A compensation structure in which the payout is contingent on reported earnings cannot simultaneously incentive the managers to maximize profits and to report those profits honestly." Crocker, K.J. and Slemrod, J. "The Economics of Managerial Compensation and Earnings Manipulation: A Problem of Contract Design in the Presence of Hidden Information and Hidden Actions," at 17. April 6, 2004.

[32] Giroux, G. Detecting Earnings Management. (John Wiley and Sons, 2004) pp. 4-5. See also Imhoff, G., "CEO Pay and Accounting Performance Measures: The Role of Earnings Management," University of Michigan Business School, November 2003.

[33] Murphy, K. J. "Performance Standards in Incentive Contracts," Marshall School of Business, University of Southern California, December 4, 2000 at 2.

[34] Public Oversight Board, Report and Recommendations from Public Oversight Board's Panel on Audit Effectiveness, August 31, 2000, at 80.

[35] Gao, P. and Shrieves, E. "Earnings Management and Executive Compensation: A Case of Overdose of Option or Underdose of Salary," at 5, presented to EFA 2002 Berlin Meetings, Humboldt University, Berlin, July 29, 2002. The authors note at 4 that actions to decrease reported earnings in a given period which result in an increase in earnings in a future period may imply that there is a dynamic aspect to earnings management, manifested by such actions as the establishment of "cookie jar" reserves. See also Holthausen, R.W., Larcker, D.F., and Sloan, R.G.,"Annual Bonus Schemes and the Manipulation of Earnings," Journal of Accounting and Economics, 19 (1995) 29-74, and Healy, P.M. and Wahlen, J.M., "A Review of Earnings Management Literature and its Implications for Standard Setting," Preliminary Draft, November, 1998; and Bollinger, G. and Kast, M. "Executive Compensation and Analyst Guidance: The Link Between CEO Compensation and Expectations Management," November 2003, EFA 2003 Annual Conference Paper No. 861. Regarding the manipulation of "true" earnings based on bonus incentives, see Lin, Z.X. and Shih, M. "Variation of Earnings Management Behavior across Economic Settings, and New Insights into Why Firms Engage in Earnings Management," Undated unpublished manuscript, National University of Singapore at 21. Regarding Fannie Mae incentives to increase earnings for compensation purposes, see also Bebchuk, L. and Fried, J. "Executive Compensation at Fannie Mae: A Case Study of Perverse Incentives, Nonperformance Pay, and Camouflage." January 2004. FMSE-KD 025896 – KD 026009.

[36] "To perform smoothing of earnings, managers sometimes pay more attention to the accounting consequences of major decisions than to the economics. It is believed that managers devote such attention to earnings because they believe that it is what matters most to shareholders. Reports that please shareholders serve a manager's self interest. Managers appreciate a lot of their bonuses and the other [prerequisites] that are tied to reported earnings." Naciri, A., "Earnings Management and Bank Provision for Loan Losses," Working Paper 04-2002, Centre de Recherche a Gestion, January 2002 at 5. See also "Report of Investigation of Enron Corporation and Related Entities Regarding Federal Tax and Compensation Issues, and Policy Recommendations Volume I: Report," Prepared by the Staff of the Joint Committee on Taxation, United States Congress, February 2003. The report notes at 664: "While some argue that linking shareholder and executive success is beneficial for the shareholders, conflicts may arise. Linking compensation of executives to the performance of the company can result in

executives taking measures to increase short-term earnings instead of focusing on longer-term interests."

[37] Cheng, Q. and Warfield, T., "Equity Incentives and Earnings Management," November 2004 at 28. Tying management incentives to stock price, which was viewed as a method of aligning the interests of stockholders and executives, may have had the perverse incentive of encouraging managers to exploit their discretion in reporting earnings, with an eye to manipulating company stock price. See also Bergstresser, D. and Phillipon, T., "CEO Incentives and Earnings Management," December 2004. The paper finds evidence that 'incentivized' CEOs lead companies with higher levels of earnings management and that CEOs exercise large amounts of options and sell large quantities of their firm's shares during years where accruals comprise a larger part of reported earnings.

[38] Erickson, M., Hanlon, M. and Maydew, E., "Is There a Link between Executive Equity Incentives and Accounting Fraud?," Journal of Accounting Research, 44 (2006) at p. 113.

[39] A September 2002 report by Conference Board Commission on Public Trust and Private Enterprise recommended that performance based incentives support long-term strategic objectives established by the Board of Directors. The Board recommendations included such measurements cost-of-capital, return on equity, economic value added, market share, quality goals, compliance goals, environment goals, revenue and profit growth, cost containment, and cash management. "Findings and Recommendations—Part 1: Executive Compensation. The Conference Board Commission on Public Trust and Private Enterprise," September 17, 2002 at 9. Notably, the Board Commission recommended, also at 9, that compensation committees "should adopt specific policies and programs to recapture incentive compensation from executives in the event that malfeasance on the part of such executives results in substantial financial harm to the corporation." See also: "CEOs in weakly governed firms increase the weight of controllable performance measures at the expense of more complete but also noisier measures." Davila, A. and Penalva, F., "Governance Structure and the Weighting of Performance Measures in CEO Compensation," Working Paper No. 601, July 2005 at 15. IESE Business School, University of Navarra, Barcelona. Available online at http://www.iese.edu/research/pdfs/DI-0601-E.pdf. Compensation metrics used by Fannie Mae "comparator" financial firms include, return on equity, return on equity with hurdles, return on assets, revenue, book value, cash flow, fee income growth, profit margins, operating income, operational expense control, stock price, stock targets/hurdles, shareholder value added, total shareholder return, EPS and operating EPS. "Fannie Mae: Performance Metrics Study—October 9, 2003. Johnson Associates, Inc" at 5. FMSE 221678.

[40] OFHEO, Report of the Special Examination of Freddie Mac, December 2003, at iv.

[41] Compensation Committee Update, "Review of Current Practices," July 2004 at FMSE 224829.

[42] OFHEO Interview, Lorrie Rudin, January 31, 2006 at 137.

[43] E-mail from Judith Dunn, Vice President and Deputy General Counsel, to Thomas Donilon, Ann Kappler, Anthony Marra et al., "Executive Comp," March 5, 2004, FMSE-EC 069878.

[44] E-mail from David Yermack to Judith Dunn, "Re: Fannie Mae – Exec. Comp," February 3, 2004, FMSE SRC OHFEO 00280233–34 at 34.

[45] KPMG Fannie Mae Strategic Analysis Memorandum December 31, 1999 KPMG-OFHEO-058985–9026 at 9006.

[46] "Risk Analysis Document.-US (10/02 Rev)." Prepared by Marissa Wheeler. Date 7/03. KPMG-OFHEO- 001045–66 at 52.

[47] OFHEO Interview, Lorrie Rudin, January 31, 2006 at 45-46. In a memorandum to Vice-Chair Jamie Gorelick dated January 8, 1999—the same day a senior management "Earnings Alternative" meeting discussed critical 1998 earnings decisions—Ms. Rudin made clear the role Mr. Howard played in the Annual Incentive Plan (AIP) and Performance Share Plan goal-setting process. "Tim Howard still is working on the earnings goals for the 1999 AIP and the 1999-2001 cycle of the Performance Share Plan." Memorandum from Lorrie Rudin to Vice-Chair Jamie Gorelick, "Compensation Committee Meeting," January 8, 1999, FMSE-EC 001889. Mr. Howard informed Ms. Rudin in an e-mail four days later that the Annual Incentive Plan target for 1999 would be $3.64, with a high of $3.69 and a low of $3.59. E-mail from Timothy Howard to Lorrie Rudin, "Re: 1999 AIP and 1999-2001 PSP Goals," January 12, 1999, FMSE-EC 042891.

[48] OFHEO Interview, Shaun Ross, May 25, 2005 at 84-85.

[49] FMSE-EC 015593 and FMSE EC 015996. "Agenda. Compensation Committee of the Board of Directors. Fannie Mae. January 20, 2003." FMSE-EC 003627-628. "Annual Incentive Plan." FMSE-EC 003646-650 at FMSE-EC 0036649.

[50] OFHEO Interview, Lorrie Rudin, January 31, 2006 at 103. "Q. So I can only assume that because of the way the paper is set up, you had received those numbers and then you put "per FDR 1/14." A. Yes, and I'll expand on that. I can only assume that I wrote "per FDR" because someone told me this was from Frank [Raines]."

[51] OFHEO Interview, Lorrie Rudin, January 31, 2006 at 51.

[52] Id., at 108.

[53] Id., at 119-120.

[54] Id., at 55.

[55] "Performance Share Plan," FMSE-EC 001917-927 at 001917.

[56] FMSE KD 029848–49. Notice of Annual Meeting of Shareholders. April 14, 2003 at 17-18. FMSE-E_EC0111857–861.

[57] FMSE-E EC00111857–861 at 859.

[58] Fannie Mae used the awards of Performance Share Plan stock and stock options to help ensure a total compensation package at the 65th percentile for executives in peer firms if targets were met.

[59] "Q: Okay. So, who sets the three-year target and how is it set? A: The target is given to me again by Mr. Howard, and it would be performance over the three-year period, either an average rate or a compound rate." OFHEO Interview, Lorrie Rudin, January 31, 2006 at 59.

[60] E-mail chain from Timothy Howard to Lorrie Rudin, "Re: PSP estimated achievement percentages," September 23, 2003, FMSE E EC 0091143.

[61] E-mail from Judith Dunn, Vice President and Deputy General Counsel, to Thomas Donilon, Ann Kappler, Anthony Marra, et al., "Executive Comp," March 5, 2004. FMSE KD010482.

[62] Report to the Board Compensation Committee on Appropriate Compensation Structure and Incentives for Fannie Mae Management, Semler Brossy Consulting Group, February 23, 2005, at FMSE EC 008834.

[63] "compplans03final.xls FinalComp," January 16, 2003, FM SRC OFHEO 00254575.

[64] Remarks of Franklin Raines, Biennial Investor/Analyst Conference, Washington DC, May 6, 1999. FM SRC OFHEO 00250595-604 at 604.

[65] Memorandum from Thomas Nides to Franklin Raines, "Fannie Mae's Executive Compensation Program," August 20, 1999, FMSE EC 017515–543 at 515.

[66] Minutes of a meeting of the Board of Directors of Fannie Mae, January 23, 2004, FMSE 222118-222146; Had the EPS goal not been met, the EPS challenge option would have been delayed for one year. Beginning in January 2005, vesting would begin at the rate of 25 percent a year. The Board had the discretion to reduce or eliminate future compensation awards to offset such a vesting. FMSE EC052924.

[67] "Address to Audit Group on What We Can Do to Help Achieve $6.46 EPS" FM SRC OFHEO 00249929- 931. Emphasis in original.

[68] Memorandum from Daniel Mudd to Thomas Donilon, et al., "QBR-November 1-2," October 12, 2000. FMSE 332824 – 332825.

[69] "According to the company's estimate, the target $6.46 earnings per share goal will be met or exceeded by the end of 2003." Memorandum from Thomas Donilon to the Compensation Committee of the Board of Directors regarding the termination of Vice-Chair Jamie Gorelick, April 3, 2003, FMSE 020173. As early as May 2002, Jonathan Boyles, Vice President for Financial Accounting, in response to at least two queries from Anthony Marra, Senior Vice President and Deputy General Counsel, as to whether Fannie Mae could accelerate the vesting of the EPS Challenge Grant if the earnings target was met early, indicated KPMG would object to such an action because other stock option plans might be deemed to be variable, thereby causing significant earnings issues. E-mail from Jonathan Boyles to Anthony Marra and Leanne Spencer, "Acceleration of Vesting on $6.46 grant," May 31, 2002. FMSE-SP 072510.

[70] SRC OFHEO 020436 – 020442 at 020439–440.

[71] "Annual Incentive Plan." FMSE 020632.

[72] OFHEO Interview, Lorrie Rudin, January 31, 2006 at 83.

[73] "Starting in 1995, we moved to an EPS measure both to bring this measure into conformity with our PSP target (which also is EPS-based) and to provide us with the flexibility to repurchase shares without penalizing AIP participants." FMSE-EC 058609. Share buybacks provided flexibility in another area as well: "If you have a share buy-back program, it's more likely to appeal to institutional investors because the institutional investor is able to get their returns out of the stock price basically and they understand that if the earnings increase, the stock price is likely to increase at some point in time. They're less oriented to dividends. So, it depends on what kind of an investor base you have. So, the principal advantage of a stock buy-back program is that it's more flexible than a dividend increase." OFHEO Interview, Lawrence Small, February 10, 2006 at 39.

[74] "Notes for November Board meeting (11/19/96)" FM SRC OFHEO 00311185-87 at p. 1. A rise in the Fannie Mae stock price meant fewer shares could be repurchased for the same dollar of capital spent. FM SRC OFHE0 023402.

[75] Stock buybacks are a common way to provide value to shareholders. In the tax regime before 2003, it was more tax efficient for many shareholders to receive value from stock buybacks rather than from dividends. Dividends were taxed annually at the ordinary tax rate, but the value returned through buybacks was taxed only on the sale of stock and then usually at the reduced tax rate applied to capital gains. That discrepancy was one of the arguments supporting the 2003 reduction in the tax rate applied to dividends.

[76] "Tim Howard 1997 Performance Evaluation." SRC OFHEO 020377.

[77] OFHEO Interview, Lawrence Small, February 10, 2006 at 51.

[78] Id., at 132.

[79] Id., at 41.

[80] "Q1 QBR Presentation Talking Points-Leanne Spencer." FM SRC OFHEO 00266529.

[81] Id.

[82] Based on available documentation, Mr. Raines, Mr. Howard and Ms. Spencer had primary roles in determining the amount and timing of the debt repurchases to achieve specific earnings targets. See e-mail series, "Re: EPS AND BUYBACK LOSSES FOR THIRD QUARTER," September 24, 2003, OFH-FNM00124614.

[83] Reuters, Fannie Mae smoothes income say unconcerned analysts, July 15, 2003, FMSE 083034.

[84] As noted below, Mr. Howard advised senior executives in 2002 that income should be pushed forward to 2003 and 2004. "Notes from QBR. 5/9/02." FM SRC OFHEO 0031279–283 at 280.

[85] "Board Resolution. November 30, 2001." FMSE 191703-FMSE 191704.

[86] E-mail from Lorrie Rudin to Kathy Gallo with cc: to Christine Wolf, "Follow-up to your meeting with Dan," October 31, 2003, FMSE EC 015847.

[87] Memorandum from Harry Argires (Engagement Partner, KPMG) to Fannie Mae File, "Summary of DPP Consultations Related to 2001 Audit," KPMG-SEC-031594.

[88] Presentation by Leanne Spencer to the Nemacolin SVP Retreat, "10-Year Financial Outlook," June 24, 2001, FMSE-KD 005137–157 at 142.

[89] FMSE SRC OFHEO 00311217–221 at 218.

[90] FM SRC OFHEO 00311226–27.

[91] FMSE SRC OFHEO 00311203–05 at 03.

[92] Id. at 04.

[93] Memorandum from Leanne Spencer and Janet Pennewell (Director, Office of the Controller) to Timothy Howard and Robert Levin (then Executive Vice President for Marketing), "Q2 Earnings Forecast-Base Case," July 8, 1997, SRC OFHEO 023337–342 at 337. The forecast lowered the provision for single-family credit losses beginning with the third quarter of 1997. SRC OFHEO 02337- 42 at 37.

[94] FM SRC OFHEO 00197273.

[95] FM SRC OFHEO 00197274.

[96] "And because of our stock repurchase program—where we reduced outstanding shares by over two percent—our earnings per share rose by 14.1 percent compared with a year ago, to $2.83." Notes for January 1998 Board of Directors Meeting. FMSE-E_EC0026239–245 at 239.

[97] Memorandum from then-CEO James Johnson to Annual Incentive Plan Award Recipients, "Annual Incentive Plan Check," FMSE-EC 021984.

[98] Memorandum from Franklin Raines to Annual Incentive Plan Award Recipients, "Annual Incentive Plan Check," January 20, 1999. FMSE-EC 042719.

[99] Notice of Annual Meeting of Stockholders. May 20, 1999 at 11.

[100] Memorandum from Leanne Spencer and Janet Pennewell to Franklin Raines et al, "Q2 Earnings Forecast Analysis," July 28, 1998, SRC OFHEO 023932-023963 at 933.

[101] "Risk Review with CFO," Tuesday, September 22, 1998, FM SRC OFHEO 00269113–127 at 116. Attendees listed included Timothy Howard, Tom Lawler, Sampath Rajappa, Joseph Amato, Vice President, Portfolio Strategy, Leanne Spencer and Jonathan Boyles.

[102] Memorandum from Timothy Howard to Lawrence Small, "1998 Performance self-evaluation," September 29, 1998, FMSE 699020-24 at 20.

[103] Id., at 21.

[104] Memorandum from Lawrence Small to Franklin Raines, "Fall Financial Planning," August 10, 1998. FMSE-IR 00331263–65. FM SRC OFHEO 00294503-505 at 504.

[105] Memorandum from Thomas Nides, Senior Vice President for Human Resources, to Senior Vice Presidents, "1998 Compensation Actions," November 18, 1998, FMSE-EC 020741–44 at 41. See also Memorandum from Thomas Nides to All Officers, "1998 Compensation Performance and Review Process," September 11, 1998, FMSE-EC 091147–49 at 49.

[106] Memorandum from Leanne Spencer to Lawrence Small, with copies to Timothy Howard and Sampath Rajappa, "Setting up and Allowance for Discount and Premium Amortization," July 13, 1998, FM SRC OFHEO 00141647.

[107] "1998 Compensation Actions." 11/24/1998. FMSE-EC 000947-970 at 948.

[108] Memorandum from Janet Pennewell to Lawrence Small, with copies to Timothy Howard and Leanne Spencer, "Your Question on 1999 EPS Growth," November 25, 1998, FM SRC OFHEO 00183511.

[109] "1999 Plan – Earnings Scenarios." FMSE 556060.

[110] FMSE SRC OFHEO 00237128.

[111] "Delivering on 2000 then Shifting the Focus to 2001," August 3, 2000, Quarterly Business Review, FMSE 332726–751 at 727.

[112] Id. at FMSE 332728.

[113] FSME 332731. The 14.9 percent "goal" figure is based on the annual amount of EPS growth necessary to double earnings by 2003. Fannie Mae EPS growth in 2001 turned out to be substantially greater than 14.9 percent.

[114] E-mail chain from Timothy Howard to Christine Cahn, "Re: your question," November 27, 2000, FMSE-E_2275138.

[115] E-mail from Timothy Howard to Leanne Spencer, "Year-end planning," December 22, 2000, FMSE-KD 029307. Emphases in original. The references by Mr. Howard to numbers provided by "Janet' appears to be to Janet Pennewell, and the reference to "Linda" appears to be to Linda Knight, Senior Vice President and Treasurer.

[116] Presentation by Leanne Spencer to the Nemacolin SVP Retreat, "10-Year Financial Outlook," June 24, 2001. FMSE-KD 005137-157 at 142.

[117] Memorandum from Leanne Spencer to Franklin Raines, "Update on Earnings," November 4, 2001, FMSRC-Z 00000133 -00000134.

[118] Id.

[119] Id.

[120] E-mail from Roger Barnes, Manager for Premium Discount Amortization, to Stephen Spivey, Senior Developer, "Items Today," May 7, 2002, FMSE 341795.

[121] Id.

[122] "Notes from QBR," May 9, 2002, FM SRC OFHEO 00311279–283 at 280.

[123] "QBR Summaries. Notes 5/02." FM SRC OFHEO 00311277-278 at 277.

[124] Memorandum from Janet Pennewell and Shaun Ross to Distribution, "Q2 Earnings Forecast," July 26, 2002, FM SRC OFHEO 00198925–932 at 925. The EPS growth rate for 2004 was forecast to be a meager 4.5%.

[125] E-mail from Christine Wolf to Kathy Gallo, "[Fwd: question]," November 14, 2002, FMSE EC 007682.

[126] E-mail from Leanne Spencer to Christine Cahn, Janet Pennewell, Shaun Ross and Peter Niculescu, "Plan/AIP/PSP Targets," January 14, 2003, FM SRC OFHEO 00243136.

[127] Presentation by Leanne Spencer, "2003 Plan. Key Challenges and Opportunities," February 11, 2003. FMSE 335124–140 at 136.

[128] "QBR Presentation—February 11, 2003." FM SRC OFHEO 00270093–98 at 98.

[129] Memorandum from Shaun Ross to Timothy Howard, "Capital Reports—Q2 Forecast Down 50 bps," June 6, 2003, FM SRC OFHEO 00244157.

[130] Managing EPS to the Annual Incentive Plan target (but not more) in 2003 and moving income to 2004 would make it easier to meet Annual Incentive Plan goals in 2004—a year which management anticipated could be a "down year." FM SRC OFHEO 00227948–953 at 951.

[131] E-mail from Leanne Spencer to Janet Pennewell, "[Fwd: Re: Investor Message]," June 15, 2003, FM SRC OFHEO 00227948.

[132] E-mail from Shaun Ross to Leanne Spencer, "2004 NII," August 28, 2003, FMSE E-EC0044837.

[133] E-mail chain from Leanne Spencer to Timothy Howard, "Re: EPS and buyback losses for the third quarter," September 24, 2003, FM SRC OFHEO 0034929.

[134] Id.

[135] E-mail from Timothy Howard to Jayne Shontell, Senior Vice President for Investor Relations, et al., "Rationale for 'overshooting' on EPS," October 16, 2003, FMSE-KD 030911–12.

[136] FMSE-E_EC012563.

[137] E-mail from Leanne Spencer to Timothy Howard, "Re: aip/psp," January 11, 2004, FMSE-E_EC0100120.

[138] E-mail from Timothy Howard to Jonathan Roman, "Re: Compensation Comparisons," January 6, 2004, FMSE-E_EC0023913–15 at 13.

[139] E-mail from Leanne Spencer to Timothy Howard, "aip/psp," January 11, 2004, FMSE-E_EC0100120.

[140] In May 2004, Christine Cahn indicated to Leanne Spencer in an e-mail that a "sensitivity run" had been done on the prospects of Annual Incentive Plan payouts of 75 percent and 87 percent. E-mail from Christine Cahn to Leanne Spencer, "misc.," May 16, 2004, FMSE-E_EC0044617. In July 2004, management recommended that the Compensation Committee of the Board of Directors, chaired by Anne Mulcahy, consider an unusual option: revise the 2004 Annual Incentive Plan performance criteria in the middle of a program year so that EPS targets, once dominant in determining the size of the Annual Incentive Plan bonus pool, played a lesser role in determining the

size of the pool in 2004. In an interview with OFHEO, Ms. Rudin indicated that changing incentive compensation goals in the middle of a program year was not common practice and that management knew that to be the case. The Compensation Committee of the Board of Directors did not agree to that option, deciding instead to institute an alternative that would make such changes beginning in the 2005 program year. OFHEO Interview, Lorrie Rudin, January 31, 2006 at 140-141. See also E-mail chain from Daniel Mudd to Rebecca Senhauser, Senior Vice President for Human Resources, "Re: Updates," July 16, 2004, FMSE – E_EC0117032-33 and "Proposed Goals for 2004 AIP July 14, 2004 Draft." FMSE-EC 036830–31.

[141] The Fannie Mae Senior Leadership Team included Franklin Raines, Chairman and CEO, Daniel Mudd, Vice Chair and COO, Timothy Howard, Vice Chair and CFO, Thomas Donilon, Executive Vice President for Law and Policy and Corporate Secretary, Michael Williams, President for Fannie Mae eBusiness, and Executive Vice Presidents Louis Hoyes, Robert Levin, Peter Niculescu, and Julie St. John.

[142] E-mail from Timothy Howard to Franklin Raines, Daniel Mudd, Thomas Donilon, Louis Hoyes, Executive Vice President (EVP) for Single Family Mortgage Business, Robert Levin, EVP for Housing and Community Development, Michael Williams, President for Fannie Mae eBusiness, Julie St. John, EVP for Enterprise Systems and Operations and Chief Information Officer, and Peter Niculescu, EVP for Mortgage Portfolio Business, "FW: forecast," September 29, 2004, FSME-E_EC0025606.

[143] "Minutes of the Compensation Committee of the Board of Directors of Fannie Mae." July 19, 2004. 6 p.m. FMSE - EC 035660–64 at 63.

[144] AIP Fall 2004 Average AIP Awards—Alternative Funding Assumptions ($000). FMSE-E_EC0127392–97 at 96.

[145] OFHEO Interview, Lorrie Rudin, January 31, 2006 at 154-155.

[146] E-mail from Timothy Howard to Shaun Ross, with copies to Leanne Spencer and Janet Pennewell, "RE: Talking Points," October 19, 2004, 8:17 a.m., FMSE-E_EC0127942. Mr. Ross described his reaction to the Mr. Howard e-mail in an OFHEO interview: "I think that my recollection is that the -- he wanted to know where the latest earnings forecast was in relation to an eight percent EPS growth target, -- Q Okay. A -- and my recollection is that he was thinking about -- I don't know that this ever was recommended or not. He was thinking about excluding the amount of impairments that were taken in 2004 from that calculation. The focus was on the Annual Incentive Plan EPS growth minimum payout number. Mr. Ross indicated that "the minimum amount for AIP pay-out was eight percent." Mr. Ross indicated in OFHEO interview that the reference to a "cushion" related directly to the Annual Incentive Plan EPS minimum target. OFHEO Interview, Shaun Ross, February 7, 2006, at 139-143.

[147] E-mail from Janet Pennewell to Timothy Howard and Shaun Ross, copy to Leanne Spencer, October 19, 2004, 3:07 p.m. FM SRC OFHEO 00226623-27 at 24.

[148] E-mail from Timothy Howard to Janet Pennewell and Shaun Ross, with a copy Leanne Spencer, "RE: Talking Points," October 19, 2004, 5:49 p.m., FM SRC OFHEO 00226623–27 at 23. In an e-mail from Timothy Howard to Janet Pennewell and Shaun Ross, with a copy to Leanne Spencer, October 20, 2004, 12:35 p.m., Mr. Howard indicated that some of the numbers in his prior e-mail were incorrect. He noted that: "Before we meet, however, someone should do an illustration of the difference between adjusting the plan for the OFHEO impairments and adjusting the actuals for the

impairments. We'll need to make a call on that, and also have a rationale for why that call is the correct one." FM SRC OFHEO 00226623

[149] OFHEO Interview, Shaun Ross, February 7, 2006 at 151-152.

[150] "Notes for October 19, 2004 Board Presentation." FM SRC 00192838–842 at 842.

[151] Memorandum from Shaun Ross to Timothy Howard, "Follow Up Items," October 26, 2004, FM SRC OFHEO 00225740.

VI. Misapplications of GAAP, Weak Internal Controls, and Improper Earnings Management

As noted in previous chapters of this report, the extreme predictability of the financial results reported by Fannie Mae from 1998 through 2003 was an illusion deliberately and systematically created by senior management. This chapter provides specific examples how senior executives exploited the weaknesses of the Enterprise's accounting to accomplish improper earnings management and misapply Generally Accepted Accounting Principles (GAAP), and how they used a variety of transactions and accounting manipulations to fine-tune the Enterprise's annual earnings results. Those actions aimed to perpetuate management's reputation for achieving smooth and predictable double-digit growth in earnings per share and for keeping Fannie Mae's risk low, while assuring maximum funding of the pool from which senior management would receive bonus payments under the Enterprise's Annual Incentive Plan as well as maximum payments under other, longer-term executive compensation plans.

To provide context for the technical material that follows, the chapter first expands on several issues raised in the previous chapters by elaborating on the concept of improper earnings management and describing the circumstances that demonstrate that Fannie Mae senior management must have been aware of the evolving official concerns about such practices. Following those discussions, the chapter reviews the improper accounting policies and control weaknesses that created opportunities for inappropriate manipulation of earnings at the Enterprise. The chapter then describes inappropriate accounting undertaken to avoid recording other-than-temporary impairment losses to avoid earnings volatility. The chapter concludes with discussions of several additional techniques used by senior management to fine-tune reported earnings results.

The actions and inactions of Fannie Mae senior management described in this chapter constituted unsafe and unsound practices that involved failures to comply with a number of statutory and other requirements. Several independent authorities, for example, require the Enterprise to verify and submit financial information. The Fannie Mae Charter Act—the statute that created the Enterprise—specifically requires that quarterly and annual reports of financial conditions and operations be prepared in accordance with GAAP.[1] The Federal Housing Enterprises Financial Safety and Soundness Act of 1992, OFHEO's organic statute, requires Fannie Mae to provide OFHEO with reports on its financial condition and operations.[2] Similarly, regulations promulgated by OFHEO under that statute require the Enterprise to prepare and submit financial and other disclosures that include supporting financial information and certifications, on matters such as its financial condition, the results of its operations, business developments, and management's expectations.[3]

Moreover, in accordance with applicable safety and soundness authorities, Fannie Mae should have had an effective system of internal controls in place under which:

- policies and procedures would be sufficient to assure that the organizational structure of the Enterprise and the assignment of responsibilities within that structure would provide clear accountability;
- policies and procedures would be adequate to manage and safeguard assets, and assure compliance with applicable law and regulation;[4]
- policies and procedures would assure reports and documents would be generated that are timely, complete, and sufficient for directors and management to make informed decisions by providing relevant information with an appropriate level of detail;[5] and
- policies and procedures for managing changes in risk would be sufficient to permit the prudent management of balance sheet growth.[6]

By failing to fulfill those obligations, the senior management of Fannie Mae did not meet the minimum standards for safety and soundness with respect to internal control, audits, information and document reporting, and balance sheet growth[7] in derogation of the standards for safe and sound conduct and operating methods as set forth by statute, OFHEO regulations and guidance, and industry standards.[8]

Earnings Management

There is no single, generally accepted definition of "earnings management." The term is used to describe a spectrum of actions from legitimate managerial activities at one end to fraudulent reporting at the other.[9] One authority describes two types of managed earnings: "One type is simply conducting the business of the enterprise in order to attain controlled, disciplined growth.

The other type involves deliberate manipulation of the accounting in order to create the appearance of controlled, disciplined growth...."[10]

As described in Chapter IV, certain members of the senior management at Fannie Mae took pains to preserve the public perception of the Enterprise as a company that could be relied upon to produce predictable and steadily increasing earnings with a minimum of risk. One technique they employed to foster that image was to use otherwise unexceptionable disclosure measures in inappropriate ways or to provide inadequate disclosure. For example, as a way to direct investors' attention away from the earnings volatility introduced by FAS 133, the Enterprise began using "core business earnings," a non-GAAP reporting measure.[11]

There was nothing inherently improper in that action. The SEC allows the use of non-GAAP reporting measures, provided that the company doing so provides public notice of that action and satisfies the other requirements of Regulation G.[12] In the only 10K filings Fannie Mae has made—for the years 2002 and 2003—it reported both GAAP and core business earnings and provided a reconciliation of the two numbers in accordance with Regulation G.[13]

In contrast to the ostensibly compliant posture assumed in the SEC filings, however, senior management at Fannie Mae also used the core business earnings measure as a foundation for implementing the inappropriate earnings management techniques that would convey to investors a false impression of its financial performance and the inherent risks of its operations. Moreover, because core business earnings formed the basis for determining the amounts paid under Fannie Mae's Annual Incentive Plan, manipulation of reported earnings also affected bonus payments. [14] The specific transactions and strategies employed for those purposes are described later in this chapter.

In some circumstances, it is also possible for publicly disclosed transactions to be inappropriate, for example through inadequate disclosure of debt repurchases. Debt repurchases have become an accepted part of the risk management strategy of Fannie Mae and other companies,[15] but such transactions should not be undertaken primarily to achieve earnings targets and never without proper disclosure of their principal objective.[16] As discussed below, when the senior management of Fannie Mae wanted to avoid recording earnings above the amount needed to meet earnings targets and assure maximum funding for bonus payouts, they repurchased debt and represented the repurchases primarily as risk-management actions or cost-saving initiatives. Although they undertook repurchases to affect core business earnings in 2001, 2002, and 2003, only in 2003 did the senior management reveal their motivation for those activities.[17]

Other types of transactions are simply improper, such as those entered into solely to affect the timing of recognition of certain revenues and expenses, whether or not they have been publicly disclosed. As described later in this chapter, senior management at Fannie Mae entered into certain structured securities and insurance transactions solely for the improper purpose of shifting income between years.[18]

Senior management was well aware of the risks posed by improper earnings management. In August 1998, Kenneth Russell, the KPMG partner who led Fannie Mae's external audits, met with Timothy Howard, the Chief Financial Officer (CFO) of Fannie Mae, to alert him to growing concerns at the SEC about earnings management practices. Although Fannie Mae was not then registered with the SEC, management had represented to the Audit Committee of the Board of Directors that the Enterprises adhered to the SEC standards governing registrants.[19] In a memo recording his meeting with Mr. Howard, Mr. Russell wrote:

> I advised Tim [Howard] that there is a new chief accountant at the SEC and his current hot button is "earnings management." We discussed the numerous restructurings being disclosed my [sic] significant public companies, which Tim believes puts Fannie Mae at a competitive disadvantage in regards to investors. I pointed out to him how conservative accounting methods are being criticized as much as liberal accounting, especially with the use of allowances and reserves.[20]

In a speech at New York University six weeks after the meeting between Mr. Russell and Mr. Howard, Arthur Levitt, the former Chairman of the SEC, referred to earnings management as "[a] gray area where the accounting is being perverted; where managers are cutting corners; and, where earnings reports reflect the desires of management rather than the underlying financial performance of the company." Mr. Levitt included "cookie jar" reserves, the premature recognition of revenue, and the abuse of the concept of materiality among the five most common and popular forms of inappropriate earnings management. In discussing abuses of the materiality concept, Mr. Levitt said he had "a hard time accepting that some of those so-called non-events do not matter"..."in markets where missing an earnings projection by as little as a penny can result in a loss of millions of dollars in market capitalization." He characterized such practices as eroding the quality of earnings and the significance of financial reporting, and deceiving users of financial statements.[21]

On November 6, 1998, three months after the meeting between Mr. Russell and Mr. Howard, Lynn Turner, then Chief Accountant at the SEC, delivered a speech at an American Institute of Certified Public Accountants banking conference, in which he raised concerns about earnings management, misuse of the materiality concept, and cookie jar reserves:

> You will find very few instances in generally accepted accounting principles (GAAP) where materiality is defined as a specified amount. Instead, both the legal statutes and accounting literature spell out clearly both qualitative and quantitative factors that must be considered when assessing materiality. This is an area in GAAP where professional judgment is required. But it is also an area where the Commission staff has seen numerous instances of non-GAAP entries, in some cases intentionally made, that changed earnings trends or perhaps allowed the company to make the earnings forecast for the quarter. The argument we have heard to justify these entries, both from companies and their auditors, is that the amounts are less than a rule of thumb 5% or 6% of net income, or whatever test they use for materiality.[22]

Abuses of materiality were among a series of actions by senior management that enabled Fannie Mae to meet its earnings target for 1998 thereby fulfilling the expectations created among analysts and investors and meeting the target for potential maximum payout of 1998 bonus compensation. One of those abuses of materiality was the failure to record as current expense approximately $200 million of net premium amortization expenses at year end.[23] KPMG characterized the deferral of this expense as an "Audit Difference." KPMG advised Thomas Gerrity, Chair of the Audit Committee, of that Audit Difference. Fannie Mae's management justified their refusal to record the additional $200 million of expense on the grounds that the calculation and projection of premium/discount amortization is complicated and imprecise. KPMG ultimately waived its characterization on the basis that the amount was immaterial.[24]

A second example of senior management's improper use of the materiality concept was its accounting adjustment of nearly $109 million, after taxes, for Low Income Housing Tax Credits (LIHTC), discussed in more detail later in this chapter. That adjustment was used to partially offset the $240 million of net premium amortization expenses that was recorded, which represented about $156 million on an after-tax basis, an amount that was material. Even though KPMG did not cite the LIHTC adjustment as an audit difference, the fact that the adjustment made the difference between Fannie Mae's meeting and not meeting the predicted earnings target for 1998 rendered it material.

In light of Mr. Russell's warning to Mr. Howard and the highly publicized speeches by top-ranking SEC officials raising concerns about earnings management, by the middle of November 1998, members of senior management at Fannie Mae could not plausibly claim to be unaware of that subject. Nevertheless, in addition to the manipulative accounting practices described above in relation to the 1998 fiscal year, they also made a last minute adjustment—a $3.9 million miscellaneous-income journal entry—to assure earnings reached the top of the potential bonus payout range so that maximum bonus payments could be made under the Annual Incentive Plan. The adjustment also caused Fannie Mae to meet analysts' earnings expectations to the penny. The journal entry issue is described in more detail in the discussion of Other Accounts Receivable, below.

The remainder of this chapter describes a number of the ways the senior management of Fannie Mae took advantage of the weak accounting policies, processes, and systems at the Enterprise and, in contravention of accounting and regulatory standards, manipulated its financial results in order to achieve predetermined earning objectives between the fall of 1998 and 2004.[25] By using a variety of improper accounting techniques, senior management eliminated or deferred, as needed, current period expenses and income. As a result, they simultaneously created the appearance of predictable double-digit earnings growth and met, but did not exceed, the earnings per share (EPS) goals that would yield the highest bonus payments. The improper accounting activities and transactions described below fall into one of the following three categories:

1) Accounting misapplications that directly minimized earnings volatility and, together with weak internal controls, provided earnings management opportunities;
2) Accounting misapplications that masked impairment losses; and
3) Transactions and accounting misapplications that allowed management to improperly shift annual reported earnings.

Improper Accounting Policies and Weak Internal Controls

This section describes the environment that made it possible for senior management at Fannie Mae to adopt non-GAAP-compliant accounting policies and the weak internal control system that enabled them to ignore or transact around the few GAAP-compliant policies that did exist. In its March 13, 2006, 12b-25 filing with the SEC, Fannie Mae reported accounting errors in over twenty separate categories.[26] The sheer number and diversity of those errors reveals an accounting environment pervaded by weak internal control and poor financial management. It highlights a corporate culture that chose to oppose changes to the status quo of smooth earnings recognized through accrual accounting and reliance on obsolete accounting systems rather than correctly implementing GAAP.

When faced with new accounting standards that might show heightened earnings volatility, senior management neither required the analysis to be performed nor invested in developing the new systems needed to perform the accounting required to implement them properly. Instead, they repeatedly attempted, without success, to superimpose those new standards onto existing systems and ways of doing business.

Derivative and Hedge Accounting

OFHEO's September 2004 *Report of Findings to Date* focused on Fannie Mae's application of the Financial Accounting Standards Board Statement of Financial Accounting Standard No.133,

Accounting for Derivative Instruments and Hedging Activities (FAS 133). FAS 133 was issued in 1998 and became effective on January 1, 2001. It required companies to mark to market their derivatives and had the potential to cause significant volatility in reported earnings. Hedge accounting, an approach that gave credit for certain highly effective hedges, was available under FAS 133 and could mitigate that volatility but posed operational challenges for companies like Fannie Mae. Nevertheless, senior management at Fannie Mae elected to adopt hedge accounting.[27]

To apply hedge accounting under FAS 133, companies must initially perform an assessment test, monitor the hedging relationships, and measure and record the ineffectiveness of those relationships over time. Companies using simple, passive hedging approaches—those in which hedges are established and then allowed to run their course—could easily adopt hedge accounting. For an entity with a large and dynamic hedging program like Fannie Mae, however, hedge accounting posed much greater challenges, involving new administrative procedures, documentation, and systems.[28] By inappropriately assuming that the vast majority of its derivatives were "perfectly effective" hedges, the hedging system adopted by Fannie Mae management achieved the volatility-dampening benefits of hedge accounting without the need to address the associated operational challenges. As a result of their preoccupation with reducing earnings volatility and minimizing infrastructure investment, senior management caused the Enterprise to adopt a FAS 133 policy that did not comply with GAAP.

Fannie Mae uses derivatives to create synthetic debt. For example, the Enterprise may combine a discount note with a 10-year pay-fixed swap to create a synthetic ten-year note. Or Fannie Mae may combine straight debt with receive-fixed swaptions to create synthetic callable debt. Prior to the implementation of FAS 133, the Enterprise accounted for synthetic debt on an accrual basis, consistent with GAAP. The senior management at Fannie Mae had a strong incentive to retain the accrual accounting of synthetic debt instruments employed before FAS 133 became effective because that provided smoother accounting of earnings and made reported financial results more predicatable. As Chief Financial Officer Timothy Howard put it: "We account for those [options] the way that we were permitted to prior to this accounting standard [FAS 133] and that's by amortizing the amount we pay evenly over the life of the option, until it is either exercised or expires."[29] The Fannie Mae derivatives accounting policy made several references to transaction accounting that was intended to mimic accrual accounting of synthetic debt instruments even after the FAS 133 became effective.

A memorandum from then-Vice President for Financial Standards and Taxes Jonathan Boyles in March 2003 articulated the reasoning behind Fannie Mae's approach to FAS 133. He stated that management's implementation of FAS 133 was driven by the desire to: minimize earnings volatility, continue to use existing systems, and make the non-GAAP measure of "operating earnings" simple and easy to understand.[30] Mr. Boyles specifically said that those goals "were intertwined in many of the decisions we made during the implementation process," and that they "were often the joint decision of management including the CFO." He also observed that "in hindsight these decisions may not have been the best decisions given what we know now."[31]

Fannie Mae's documentation of its implementation of FAS 133 identified minimizing earnings volatility and maintaining the simplicity of operations as primary objectives. That documentation also recognized that earnings volatility would arise naturally from those derivatives that did not qualify for hedge accounting as well as from any hedge ineffectiveness arising from those hedging relationships that did qualify for hedge accounting. The overarching concern of Fannie Mae management with minimizing earnings volatility, keeping operations simple, and avoiding the expense connected with developing systems that were compliant with the standard led to failures to assess hedge effectiveness or measure hedge ineffectiveness when required as well as failures to apply hedge accounting to hedging relationships that did not qualify for such treatment. A detailed discussion of the misapplication of FAS 133 is provided in the *Report of Findings to Date*.[32]

Fannie Mae's improper implementation of FAS 133 masked billions of dollars of earnings volatility. In its most recent 12b-25 filing with the SEC, Fannie Mae estimated a cumulative reduction in reported earnings through the end of 2004 of $10.6 billion for the two accounting areas with the most significant impact—hedge accounting and accounting for mortgage commitments.[33]

Investment Accounting

Under FAS 115, an enterprise must classify securities in one of three categories at the time of acquisition: Held-to-Maturity, Available-for-Sale, or Trading.[34] Senior management at Fannie Mae ignored that requirement and implemented a policy under which the securities were classified at the end of the month of acquisition. No one from Fannie Mae has provided a credible rationale for interpreting the accounting literature in that manner.[35] While the Enterprise does not appear to have used those classification delays to manage earnings, it implemented FAS 115 policy in an improper manner that enabled it to continue to use preexisting accounting systems, avoid making costly investments in new ones, and which resulted in a misapplication of GAAP.

In April 1993, one month before FAS 115 was issued, James Parks, Vice President for Financial Standards, sent a memorandum to CFO, Timothy Howard, and Michael Quinn, Senior Vice President and Controller, that explained the possible effects of FAS 115 on Fannie Mae's operations. He discussed the requirements for the separate classifications of securities types and the transfer restrictions placed on the Held-to-Maturity category. The Held-to-Maturity category allowed investors to account for the securities at amortized cost as opposed to the Available-for-Sale and Trading categories, which required fair value accounting. Mr. Parks also noted that FAS 115 would largely curtail Fannie Mae's ability to manage earnings through portfolio sales, but that earnings management would still be possible, to some extent, by establishing a separate portfolio of Available-for-Sale securities.[36] Earnings might be managed by opportunistically selling securities with unrealized gains or unrealized losses in order to produce the desired effects on income statement. If securities were placed in the Held-to-Maturity category, that practice would not be possible.

Leanne Spencer, Senior Vice President and Controller, and Jonathan Boyles, Senior Vice President for Financial Standards, suggested to OFHEO that the approach by Fannie Mae to investment accounting was a holdover from its practice before FAS 115 became effective. Following its past practice of Intra-Month Redesignation rather than developing and implementing GAAP-compliant practices enabled Fannie Mae to continue using existing systems.[37] The practice provided the Enterprise with additional time to analyze which securities to retain and which to sell, and it was precisely that type of flexibility that the Financial Accounting Standards Board was attempting to eliminate with the "at acquisition" requirement and the strict requirements related to the transfer of securities out of the Held-to-Maturity category established by FAS 115.[38] In addition, by postponing the classification of a security until month end, Fannie Mae could factor post-purchase changes in the value of a security into the classification decision.

Fannie Mae's approach to FAS 115 implementation further reflects a corporate culture where controlling earnings volatility and minimizing infrastructure investment took precedence over GAAP compliance. Fannie Mae's implementation of FAS 115 did not satisfy the requirements of that standard, did not comport with its general obligations under GAAP, and violated its duty to operate in a safe and sound manner by creating opportunities for unsafe and unsound practices.

Securitization Accounting

In order to avoid additional operational complexity, investment in new IT systems, and earnings volatility, senior management at Fannie Mae failed to properly implement Financial Accounting Standards Board Interpretation (FIN) 46, an accounting rule governing when an issuer of mortgage-backed securities (MBS) must consolidate them on its balance sheet.[39] Under FIN 46 an investor (the beneficial interest holder) who owns 100 percent of an entity's certificates is presumed to have the unilateral right to dissolve the trust.[40] As a result, in cases when Fannie Mae owned 100 percent of a given MBS pool, the trust would no longer meet the definition of a qualified special purpose entity, the method Fannie Mae used to account for MBS trusts, and the trust collateral—the loans underlying the MBS—would have to be consolidated on Fannie Mae's balance sheet. Fannie Mae's FIN 46 policy provided two ways to avoid consolidation: the transfer of wholly-owned pools of securities from Available-for-Sale to Held-to-Maturity (because the accounting results would not be materially different from consolidation), and the sale of 1 percent of the wholly-owned pool to a third party.[41] In order to sell 1 percent interests more efficiently, the Enterprise formed "mega pools," with collateral comprising multiple wholly-owned pools, and sold 1 percent interests of the "mega pools."[42]

Shortly after OFHEO released the *Report of Findings to Date*, Fannie Mae's Financial Standards group issued a new policy memo reversing the earlier policy[43]. That memo stated the conclusions that mega pools are subject to consolidation unless at least 10 percent of the fair value of a trust is held by a third party, and that redesignation of securities from Available-for-Sale to Held-to-Maturity would not allow Fannie Mae to avoid consolidation. The 2004 memo demonstrated management's recognition that the earlier policy was not GAAP-compliant.

In November 2004, the Financial Standards group conducted an analysis and concluded that Fannie Mae's improper implementation of FIN 46 resulted in a cumulative impact on the Enterprise's earnings of $17.4 million.[44] OFHEO has questioned the reliability of that analysis. Current Fannie Mae management has agreed to restate the Enterprise's financial statements related to the issue and has acknowledged to OFHEO that FIN 46 compliance is one of the most complicated, time-consuming, and system-intensive areas of the restatement.[45]

In implementing FIN 46, as it did with FAS 133 and FAS 115, Fannie Mae responded to new standards by developing policies that would help to preserve the operational status quo. In the case of FIN 46, the goal was to avoid the complexity and expense of consolidation accounting. Instead of determining and implementing the accounting methods and the systems needed to comply with those requirements, Fannie Mae misapplied its resources in an attempt to circumvent the burdens FIN 46 created.[46] Avoiding GAAP compliance, because it is burdensome or for any other reason, violated Fannie Mae's Charter Act and is an unsafe and unsound practice.

Dollar Roll Accounting

Fannie Mae did not follow GAAP when accounting for dollar roll transactions during much of the period covered by OFHEO's Special Examination. Dollar rolls provide low-cost, short-term funding. In a typical dollar roll transaction, an entity sells mortgage-backed securities and simultaneously agrees to repurchase substantially the same securities from the same counterparty at a later date. Properly executed, even though the counterparty to such an agreement acquires legal ownership of the transferred securities, the accounting rules allow the transaction to be accounted for as a secured financing. Although it did not use dollar rolls to manage earnings, Fannie Mae did not develop the policies, processes, and systems needed to account for the dollar roll transactions properly. The inadequate manner in which it accounted for dollar roll transactions provides another example of the weak control system that existed at Fannie Mae.

If a dollar roll transaction does not meet GAAP requirements for a secured financing, it must be accounted for as a sale, creating earnings volatility to the extent that the value of the rolled security changes before repurchase. Because it did not have appropriate procedures for monitoring the collateral pledged to support its dollar roll transactions, Fannie Mae did not ensure that the securities returned to it were substantially the same as those it had conveyed, as required both by GAAP and its own policies.[47] Fannie Mae did not appear to correctly apply the accounting principles used to calculate the weighted average maturities—one of the criteria used to assure that the securities delivered by the counterparty were substantially the same. In addition, Fannie Mae failed to obtain the proper understanding of the accounting principles, that is, if its dollar rolls were sales rather than financings, the use in dollar rolls of MBS from its held-to-maturity portfolio would "taint" that portfolio, requiring the reclassification of the entire Held-to-Maturity portfolio as Available-for-Sale, or Trading. Because Available-for-Sale and Trading are marked-to-market, this taint would have had an even more dramatic impact on Fannie Mae's financial statements.[48]

In addition, the inability of Fannie Mae's securities accounting systems to handle dollar roll transactions caused errors in calculating the premium and discount amortization of the securities involved in dollar rolls. In early 2004 Fannie Mae discovered an error during a review of the accounting system it used for dollar roll transactions.[49] The system had calculated the original premium/discount by using the date on which the counterparty returned securities under the dollar roll agreements instead of using the securities acquisition date, as it should have. The error had gone undetected since September 2002 when the Enterprise last updated the securities accounting system. Fannie Mae performed an analysis of the error and determined that it was immaterial.[50] In an undated presentation, Senior Securities Analyst Anthony Lloyd stated that the securities accounting system was not designed for dollar rolls, and that it was incapable of handling even "plain vanilla" dollar roll transactions.[51]

Fannie Mae's dollar roll transactions provide an example of the Enterprise's entering a new line of business without the proper internal controls and systems in place to account properly for them. Such action constitutes an unsafe and unsound practice. Although senior management engaged in dollar rolls as a low-cost source of funding to supplement its discount notes rather than for earnings management purposes, the tainting of its Held-to-Maturity portfolio raises questions about Fannie Mae's reported earnings.

Foreclosed PropertyAccounting (Real Estate Owned)

Fannie Mae's real estate owned (REO) accounting did not comport with GAAP. Due to a weak operating environment, numerous errors existed throughout the REO accounting process. In addition, Fannie Mae inappropriately set annual Enterprise-wide REO charge-off and expense targets for appraiser analysts working in its National Property Disposition Center, when it should have emphasized accurate and efficient appraisal work.

Accounting for REO includes three stages: 1) foreclosure, which entails accounting for reclassification of the loan receivable to REO and establishing an initial valuation; 2) possession, which is the period from foreclosure to property disposition that involves monitoring both REO classification and the carrying amount for impairment, as well as recording costs for maintenance and disposition; and 3) disposition, which entails recording the sale of REO and related accounting entries.

Errors Related to Foreclosures

Fannie Mae made a number of errors at the time of foreclosure.[52] Two were related to timing. The Enterprise should have recorded a foreclosure, i.e., reclassified the loan receivable to REO, when it took physical possession of a mortgaged property or when it took title to the property, whichever came first. Instead, Fannie Mae waited until it received notification of title transfer, which, in most cases occurred after it took possession.[53] For loans where Fannie Mae shared risk with counterparties (e.g., back-end credit enhancements, recourse, etc.), it neglected to reclassify them as REO until after the properties were sold and Fannie Mae was made whole by the credit enhancement.

Additional errors relating to the foreclosure stage shifted losses from charge-offs, which reduced the Allowance for Loan Losses, to Foreclosed Property Expenses, (FPE) and vice versa (the former included all losses determinable at the time of foreclosure; the latter included expenses incurred after foreclosure and any adjustments to amounts estimated at foreclosure). Before it foreclosed on delinquent loans that backed its mortgage-backed securities, Fannie Mae repurchased them out of those securities, so it owned them at the time of foreclosure. During the period for which Fannie Mae intends to restate its financials—2002-2004—the Enterprise improperly failed to include adjustments to the face values of such loans—*i.e.*, premiums or discounts—when determining charge-offs.

Fannie Mae should have written off accrued interest on foreclosed loans only to the extent it was sure it could not recover that accrued interest. The Enterprise prematurely reversed a portion of the accrued interest when determining the related REO investment and associated charge-off.

In calculating the fair market value of REO assets at foreclosure, Fannie Mae did not subtract selling costs. Fannie Mae charged the incremental losses to the Foreclosed Property Expenses when the REO was finally sold, but those incremental losses should have been charged to the Allowance for Loan Losses at the time of foreclosure.

An entity may write down the value of loans and record charge-offs prior to foreclosure, when it believes it has already incurred those losses. If, upon foreclosure, the entity calculates net gains, it should credit such gains against the Allowance for Loan Losses only to the extent of prior charge-offs.[54] During the restatement period Fannie Mae recorded all charge-off gains as credits to the Allowance for Loan Losses without regard to the amount or existence of a prior loan charge-off. That error caused excessive amounts to be credited to the Allowance for Loan Losses instead of reducing Foreclosed Property Expenses.

While performing Sarbanes-Oxley testing, KPMG found a second accounting error with respect to charge-off gains. Fannie Mae had accrued a mortgage insurance receivable above the contractual amount owed. Mortgage insurance companies are only obligated to pay an amount that, at most, makes the insured whole. Because the accrued mortgage insurance proceeds were not capped at the estimated charge-off loss amount (the make-whole amount), the financial statements reflected charge-off gains that were not likely to materialize. That error also inflated the Allowance for Loan Losses.

The senior management of Fannie Mae was well aware that its accounting for charge-off gains at foreclosure was incorrect for years prior to taking action to correct it.[55]

Errors Related to Possession

Fannie Mae made a number of errors related to the possession stage that affected either the allocation of losses between charge-offs and FPE or the timing of the recognition of those expenses. Accounting guidance permitted Fannie Mae to use a temporary property valuation in determining charge-offs and adjust that amount only if it obtained a fair market value within a reasonable period. Because appraisals were frequently not available at the time of foreclosure, Fannie Mae often recorded such temporary valuations. Then, regardless of how much later it received an appraisal, the Enterprise increased or decreased the REO investment and adjusted the related charge-offs. In the case of unreasonably late appraisals, Fannie Mae should not have recorded resulting gains until they were recognized through the sale of the REO. The Enterprise should have credited these gains against FPE, not charge-offs.

Under FAS 144, an entity must institute the Lower of Cost or Market principle for REO.[56] Impairment losses that occur when the fair value of a property falls below its carrying amount are charged to Foreclosed Property Expense. Fannie Mae's written policy conformed to industry practice and called for at least quarterly review of its REO valuations to determine the extent of such impairment losses. OFHEO was unable to confirm that policy was followed. Failure to perform the impairment assessments or to document their performance reflects a breakdown in internal control. Lack of impairment assessments creates the potential for unrecorded impairments that would understate Foreclosed Property Expense and overstate asset value during the possession period.

A company should capitalize costs incurred for improvements, rehabilitations, replacements, and repairs only when they appreciably extend the life, increase the capacity, or improve the safety of the property. (Otherwise, costs associated with REO should be immediately charged to Foreclosed Property Expense.) Fannie Mae charged all costs related to maintaining and repairing the REO properties to Foreclosed Property Expense, thus overstating it. (Upon sale of the REO, that error would have been offset.)

Errors Related to Disposition

In certain instances Fannie Mae inappropriately recognized all profit when it sold REO, overstating revenue. Financial Accounting Standard No. 66, *Accounting for Sales of Real Estate* (FAS 66) calls the "[r]ecognition of all of the profit at the time of sale" "the full accrual method." To qualify for that method, "the collectibility of the sales price [must be] reasonably assured," and the seller must not be "obliged to perform significant activities after the sale to earn the profit. Unless both conditions exist, recognition of all or part of the profit shall be postponed."[57] In some instances when Fannie Mae extended financing to parties purchasing their REO, those conditions did not exist.

Inappropriate Incentives for Appraisers

Apart from specific accounting errors, Fannie Mae created inappropriate incentives for its appraisal staff that were inconsistent with safety and soundness. Those incentives suggest that the obsession of management with low volatility extended to the loss line. During the course of its special examination, OFHEO obtained seven National Property Distribution Center (NPDC) performance plans for appraiser analysts that required them to "[m]anage the quality of values [of REOs] such that ... NPDC goals [for all appraisal analysts] are supported to maintain charge-off and REO expense at $127.3 million, while monitoring exceptions to avoid ...audit findings."[58] The phrasing of that performance standard shows that management created incentives for employees to obtain specific numbers rather than accurate values.

The majority of Fannie Mae's accounting policies for REO was not in compliance with GAAP and, therefore, violated the Charter Act. The number and dispersion of the errors throughout all three stages of the REO cycle demonstrates a complete breakdown in internal controls and management oversight as well as weak accounting expertise. Failed internal controls and ineffective oversight, in turn, created conditions that management could exploit to manage earnings. The extent of the breakdowns in overseeing the National Property Distribution Center and accounting for its activities, together with the inappropriate incentives created by setting specific charge-off goals, reflect unsafe and unsound practices.

Lack of Journal Entry Controls

In a sound internal control environment, journal entries for financial records are prepared by personnel with knowledge of the transactions being recorded. Entries are independently reviewed, validated, authorized, and properly recorded. Procedures for preparing journal entries should provide a roadmap for multiple individuals performing independent tasks for the analysis, preparation, and approval of the entries.

Supporting documentation is another critical control in the journal entry process. Such documentation memorializes the rationale for each journal entry and ensures that the personnel who approve and execute each entry have the authority to do so. The adequacy of the documentation and levels of approval required for each entry are determined by the purpose and timing of the entry. Supporting documentation consists of all analyses performed to determine that the entry is necessary, as well as signatures of the preparer, reviewer, and the authorizer of the entry.

Statement on Auditing Standard No. 99, *Consideration of Fraud in a Financial Statement Audit* (SAS 99), which the American Institute of Certified Public Accountants issued in October 2002, relates to the consideration of fraud in a financial statement audit. SAS 99 specifies the requirements for auditors reviewing journal entries. The standard identifies the importance of exercising professional skepticism in reviewing journal entries, the risks of material misstatement due to fraud, and the importance of considering the risk of management's override of controls. SAS 99 states that:

> [Material] misstatements of financial statements due to fraud often involve the manipulation of the financial reporting process by (*a*) recording inappropriate or unauthorized journal entries throughout the year or at period end, or (*b*) making adjustments to amounts reported in the financial statements that are not reflected in formal journal entries, such as through consolidating adjustments, report combinations, and reclassifications.[59]

Fannie Mae used manually prepared journal entries to record adjustments, called "catchup adjustments," to alter premium and discount amortization balances. Those catch-up adjustment entries were almost always recorded post-closing in what the Enterprise referred to as "on-top" adjustments.

OFHEO's review of journal entries relating to amortization adjustments revealed several significant problems, including: falsified signatures on journal entries; the failure to require that journal entry preparers understood the purpose for which the journal entry was being made and that the individual responsible for reviewing and approving journal entries determined that each entry was valid and appropriate; the failure to require supporting documentation for journal entries; the lack of an independent review of journal entries; and the absence of written policy guidance concerning journal entry procedures.

Patricia Wells of the Controller's Office told OFHEO that for the period 1999 through 2002 she did not actually prepare some of the journal entries related to amortization that bore her name.[60] Those entries were created after the closing process, a time when journal entries require a higher level of scrutiny than usual. Ms. Wells stated that one particular entry bearing her name that she did not prepare was for an adjustment of $80 million in January 1999. Ms. Wells said it was her belief that the entry was related to recording "catch-up" amortization for 1998.[61] Many other journal entries relating to amortization adjustments were signed by Gary Robinson, another employee working in Fannie Mae's Controller's Office. Mr. Robinson's duties, however, related to business planning and budgeting, not amortization, and Ms. Wells indicated her belief that Mr. Robinson had knowledge and awareness of the falsified signatures.[62]

When questioned about specific journal entries relating to amortization that she had prepared, Ms. Wells could not provide explanations for them. She stated that she did not know that the preparer of a journal entry had a responsibility to assure that it was appropriate.[63] Although the Controller, Leanne Spencer, told OFHEO that the preparer of journal entries was, in fact, responsible for determining that a journal entry was appropriate,[64] Ms. Wells said her "feelings personally were that if management asked me to do an entry, that they had a reason for it and that it was a reasonable request."[65] When asked if she had a role in validating the journal entries she prepared, specifically defining "validation" as determining that the amount stated on an entry was the correct amount, Ms. Wells replied that she did not.[66] Further, when asked whether her role in preparing journal entries involved discretionary decision-making or was clerical, Ms. Wells replied, "[i]t's clerical."[67]

Given the significance of her role as the preparer of many entries relating to amortization, Ms. Wells' assertions that she was not responsible for assuring the appropriateness of those entries illustrates the poor control environment that existed in the Office of the Controller.

Richard Stawarz, Director for Accounting and Audit, told OFHEO that in 2003, before controls were enhanced in compliance with the Sarbanes-Oxley Act, he was unaware of any requirement for either the reviewer or approver to understand the purpose of a journal entry or to verify that such an entry was valid.[68] Regarding adjustments to premium and discount amortization, Mr. Stawarz also said that amortization entries showing Ms. Wells' signature as preparer and his signature as approver were made at the direction of Janet Pennewell, Vice President for Financial Reporting and Planning, based upon analysis performed by Jeffrey Juliane, a Director in the Office of the Controller. Mr. Stawarz was unable to provide a satisfactory explanation why Mr. Juliane and Ms. Pennewell did not serve as preparer and reviewer respectively, even though he stated that neither he nor Ms. Wells would have reviewed the analysis upon which the entries were based.[69]

Ms. Wells also told OFHEO that there were instances of journal entries for which she believed documentation was inadequate. In particular, she indicated that she did not receive hard copy support for some catch-up adjustments related to amortization and was only given oral instructions to prepare the entries.[70] For example, in the second quarter of 2004, Mr. Julianne instructed Ms. Wells to zero-out the sub-ledger accounts associated with catch-up. Ms. Wells testified that the only explanation she received was that it needed to be done.[71] Mr. Stawarz also stated that it was not the practice of the company to maintain supporting documentation with journal entries.[72]

OFHEO found that management often only provided oral instructions for journal entries relating to catch-up adjustments. In a properly controlled accounting system, such adjustments would normally be the result of an analysis. The lack of documentation at Fannie Mae further demonstrates the poor control environment that existed in the Office of the Controller. In addition, although Ms. Spencer, Ms. Wells, and Mr. Stawarz all referred to the Fannie Mae policy for journal entries, none knew whether that policy was actually documented.[73]

The absence of policy guidance and a well controlled process for recording journal entries and the falsifying of signatures in journal entries raise significant risks to any financial institution and were clearly unsafe and unsound practices.

Misapplications of GAAP to Avoid Impairment Losses

Because other-than-temporary impairment losses would have resulted in volatility in reported earnings, senior management at Fannie Mae went to extraordinary lengths to avoid recording those losses.[74] This section reviews their efforts to avoid such losses with respect to certain classes of investment securities and two types of interest-only (IO) instruments—IO securities and buy-ups. With respect to the latter, Fannie Mae's incorrect accounting spared it approximately $500 million in impairment losses in 1998, an amount that exceeded the known effects of other manipulations by the Enterprise that year. Quantification of the impact of impairments avoided with respect to investment and IO securities must await Fannie Mae's restatement of financial results, but OFHEO believes the 1998 earnings impact with respect to IO securities may have been of a magnitude similar to that for buy-ups. The misapplications of GAAP discussed in this section which served to hide losses, plainly violated the Charter Act and constituted unsafe and unsound practices.

Investment Securities

In May 2004, OFHEO determined that Fannie Mae's impairment policies and practices related to two classes of investment securities—manufactured housing loan-backed securities and aircraft lease-backed asset-backed securities— were inconsistent with GAAP.[75] In response, Fannie Mae altered its impairment methodology on a going-forward basis, and recognized an additional $265 million of impairments in the second quarter of 2004.[76] Fannie Mae will apply the proper impairment methodology for the entire restatement period. Current Fannie Mae management anticipates the restatement impairment methodology will primarily affect the timing rather than the overall magnitude of impairment losses.

Although senior management had adopted high-level policies related to impairment accounting, the policies provided no guidance for conducting the periodic and systematic review of assets for potential impairment losses that GAAP requires. In 2003, management appeared to adopt a more structured approach to impairment accounting when it formed an impairment committee, but the committee was not effective. Members rarely participated in decision-making; instead, they delegated authority for making decisions about impairment losses to lower-level employees. The Impairment Committee's charter specifically excluded from its purview manufactured housing securities, over which the Credit Policy team retained responsibility.[77] Additionally, during 2002 and 2003, when manufactured housing securities became seriously impaired, CFO Timothy Howard played a major role in valuation decisions determining the recorded impairments.

After Fannie Mae purchased manufactured housing securities and the aircraft asset-backed securities, both market sectors experienced significant credit events. In the manufactured housing securities market the crucial events were a downturn in the manufactured housing industry and the resulting bankruptcy of Conseco, the largest issuer of manufactured housing securities, and a provider of limited credit enhancements for them.[78] In the aircraft asset-backed securities market, the key events were the al-Qaeda attacks of September 11, 2001, and the resulting fear of further acts of terrorism, which produced an airline industry downturn.[79] The values of securities in both markets fell, and the markets became less liquid, thereby increasing the possibility of impairment recognition under GAAP.

In measuring the fair value of assets, accounting rules require that companies follow a hierarchy of valuation methods. At the top of the hierarchy are prices for identical securities trading in the market. When market prices are not available, values extrapolated from market prices of similar securities that are actively traded may be substituted. Still lower in the hierarchy are prices based on the discounted present values of modeled cash flows.[80] Prices for identical securities trading in the market were low, but they were available; management chose not to use them.[81] Instead, they used discounted cash flow models, but did not document procedures and controls governing their use, which allowed senior management directly to influence the results. Mr. Howard, for example, frequently made the final decisions with respect to model assumptions.[82] Neither his decisions nor the rationales supporting them were formally documented. In addition, Controller Leanne Spencer revised accounting policies affecting the use of loss projections for determining impairments in order to, among other things, "prevent unnecessary volatility."[83]

Over the course of the ongoing restatement process, current management at Fannie Mae has confirmed a number of significant shortcomings in the Enterprise's prior practices relating to accounting for impairments of investment securities, including:[84]

- Lack of robust impairment policies from 2001 through mid-2004;
- Failure to follow policies that did exist, *e.g.*, failure to review all available-for-sale and held-to-maturity securities for potential impairment;
- Failure to determine fair values at the security level for held-to-maturity securities, thereby preventing Fannie Mae from asserting that it had evaluated the complete population of securities, as GAAP requires;
- Failure to maintain complete documentation of impairment evaluations, and failure of the documentation that was prepared to meet GAAP standards;[85]

- Failure, when the Enterprise did record impairments, to properly account for interest earned on the impaired securities going forward.[86]

Interest-Only Securities

In 2004 OFHEO concluded, and the SEC concurred, that Fannie Mae's accounting for Interest Only (IO) securities was not in compliance with GAAP.[87] IO securities are financial assets that are particularly sensitive to changes in interest rates. In a decreasing interest rate environment IO securities rapidly fall in value because the underlying loans are paid off and refinanced and, under GAAP, they should be subject to impairment analysis.

Given the potential for other-than-temporary impairments of IO securities and the desire by senior management to avoid recording such impairments, in late 1995 the Controller's Office presented to KPMG an approach that grouped IO securities with other mortgage-backed securities (MBS), including single-class MBS, REMIC tranches, and principal only securities (POs), and accounted for them as "synthetic MBS KPMG accepted that ."[88] By accounting for those IO bundles as MBS—which would have been acceptable if they were legally bundled in REMIC securities, or if the IOs were linked only to PO securities purchased on the same day from the same trust (*i.e.*, with the same underlying collateral) – Fannie Mae not only avoided impairments, but also avoided the substantial investments in systems necessary to accurately value the individual IO securities to determine impairments.[89] The approach by Fannie Mae did not conform with GAAP and represents another example of efforts by the Enterprise to avoid the effects of compliance with GAAP impairment losses would have increased earnings volatility and required investment in new systems.

Although KPMG approved its synthetic MBS accounting in 1995, some members of Fannie Mae staff questioned it. On the same day that Richard DePetris, Director for Financial Standards, documented a meeting with KPMG, he wrote in an e-mail to James Parks, Vice President for Financial Standards that:

> My concern is that the more we stretch the package concept, the greater the possibility exists that Peat [KPMG] might question the substance over form position we presented to them.[90]

By the end of 1998, falling interest rates and the resulting dramatic increase in mortgage prepayments would have generated very large IO impairments—likely hundreds of millions of dollars—under GAAP-compliant accounting.[91] By that time as well, many members of the KPMG staff who had been involved in the approval of Fannie Mae's bundling approach had left the assignment. In light of the potential for IO impairments in 1998, Jonathan Boyles, Director for Financial Standards, communicated his ongoing concern about the questionable IO security accounting in a briefing given to Mr. Howard in March 1998. In materials prepared for that briefing, Mr. Boyles suggested that current KPMG staff were unaware of the accounting treatment for the securities bundles that the Enterprise was using, and he noted his concern that the external auditors would disallow that accounting treatment if they did become aware of it:

> KPMG has apparently forgotten about these transactions, and we have not brought these issues to their attention. They [KPMG] have experienced significant turnover since we originally adopted the "package" accounting and, as a result, there is currently only one member of the audit team that remaining from the fall of 1995. The accounting team they

> currently have on the audit is more technically proficient, and if they stumble across these packages, may not be as easily convinced of the current accounting treatment. We have made every effort to keep our analysis confidential.[92]

In 2005 Mr. Boyles claimed to have no recollection of writing that paragraph and denied trying to withhold the analysis from KPMG. He said that during the 1998 through 2004 timeframe he had spoken with several KPMG partners about the issue, including Kenneth Russell, Harry Argires, David Britt, and Mark Serock.[93] OFHEO could not verify those assertions and found only one reference to IO accounting among all of KPMG's workpapers for the 1998 Fannie Mae audit: "Fannie Mae bundles (*i.e.* combines) IOs, POs, (Interest Only/Principal Only) and various REMIC structures to synthetically create an MBS with yields Fannie Mae would normally purchase for their portfolio."[94] KPMG did not document any concerns about the potential for major IO impairments in 1998, casting serious doubt upon Mr. Boyle's credibility or recollection.

After OFHEO raised questions about Fannie Mae's IO securities accounting in April 2004, Mr. Boyles wrote a letter to the SEC requesting support for Fannie Mae's synthetic MBS accounting method.[95] The letter reflected seriously misleading omissions. It posed for the SEC's consideration a special case in which Fannie Mae IOs and POs had the same notional amount, were issued from the same trust, and were purchased in contemplation of each other. That was arguably the case that the SEC would not likely object to. Mr. Boyles did not mention the fact that prior to 1996 Fannie Mae bundled almost all the IOs it purchased with unrelated securities. Nevertheless, in the fall of 2004, the SEC notified Fannie Mae that IO and PO securities should be accounted for separately on a prospective basis starting in the third quarter of 2004, and that the IOs should be accounted for pursuant to EITF 99-20.[96]

By virtue of Fannie Mae's misapplication of FAS 91[97] accounting, IOs contributed $180 million of the $439 million under-amortized premium expense at year-end 1998.[98] Because Fannie Mae tracked its IO securities in combination with other securities and did not monitor their market values, OFHEO cannot determine the amount of IO impairment losses the Enterprise should have recognized. It is likely, however, that the losses would have substantially exceeded the $180 million under-amortization under FAS 91.

Misapplications Relating to Buy-ups

Buy-ups and buy-downs are price adjustments Fannie Mae pays or charges to increase or decrease, respectively, the guaranty fee rate lenders pay for Fannie Mae's guarantee of MBS backed by the lender's mortgages.[99] Buy-ups (often referred to in internal Fannie Mae communications as "buyups" or "BUs"; buy-downs are similarly referred to as "buydowns" or "BDs") are IO-like instruments and are subject to the same impairment accounting as IO securities. To avoid recording hundreds of millions of dollars of impairments on its buy-up portfolio, senior management at Fannie Mae misapplied GAAP, diverted KPMG's attention from that misapplication, and provided incomplete information about its IO accounting to the Financial Accounting Standards Board and the Securities and Exchange Commission. Through its misapplication of GAAP, Fannie Mae avoided recording approximately $500 million of buy-up impairment losses in 1998, an amount that exceeded the combined effects of the other GAAP misapplications that the Enterprise employed to meet its maximum bonus pay-out targets that year. Fannie Mae's approach to buy-up accounting was the same as its approach to the implementation of accounting standards generally, that is, to minimize earnings volatility and expenditures on the development of systems to support proper accounting.

Until the spring of 2004, Fannie Mae applied FAS 91 to both buy-ups and buy-downs. FAS 91 is consistent with accrual accounting in that the reporting entity carries premiums and discounts (in this case, buy-ups and buy-downs, respectively) on its books at amortized cost, and it amortizes them into expense or income using the effective-yield method.[100] Amounts amortized into income or expense either offset (in the case of buy-ups) or augmented (in the case-of buy-downs) the guaranty fees received over the lives of securitized mortgages. As discussed below with respect to buy-ups, that accounting treatment violated GAAP. Accounting rules required that Fannie Mae account for buy-ups as financial instruments similar to IO securities by marking the instruments to market through equity and recognizing impairments through earnings when market values declined substantially below their book values.

In connection with Fannie Mae's ongoing restatement, current management revisited past policy and confirmed that since January 1, 1997, the effective date of FAS 125, Fannie Mae should not have accounted for buy-ups under FAS 91.[101] Rather, as discussed further below, buy-ups should have been marked-to-market through equity and evaluated for impairments (i.e., accounted for as financial assets subject to paragraph 14 of FAS 125 and FAS 140 and the income recognition and impairment provisions of EITF 99-20).[102]

Determining Accounting Treatment—FAS 125 and 115 and EITF 93-18

FAS No. 125, Accounting for Transfers and Servicing of Financial Assets and Extinguishments of Liabilities (FAS 125) ,became effective in January 1997. Paragraph 14 of FAS 125 provides:

> Interest-only strips, retained interest in securitization, loans, other receivables, or other financial assets that can contractually be prepaid or otherwise settled in such a way that the holder would not recover substantially all of its recorded investment ..., [s]hall be measured like investments in debt securities classified as available-for-sale or trading under Statement 115, as amended.[103]

Debt investments classified as available-for-sale are marked to market through equity; that is, changes in their market value do not flow through earnings, but are recorded in Accumulated Other Comprehensive Income (AOCI), a component of shareholders' equity. Trading securities are marked to market through earnings. FAS 91 provides for the amortization into earnings of premiums and discounts of held-to-maturity investments, which are subject to accrual rather than fair value accounting. FAS 91 does not apply to available-for-sale and trading investments because they are marked to market.

The Emerging Issues Task Force consensus on Issue No. 93-18, Recognition of Impairment for an Investment in a Collateralized Mortgage Obligation Instrument or in a Mortgage Backed Interest-Only Certificate (EITF 93-18), established what constituted "other-than-temporary" impairments for interest-only instruments. Under EITF 93-18, an IO was other- than-temporarily impaired when the projected future cash flows, discounted at the risk-free rate, fell below its amortized cost. Because market values are determined by discounting cash flows at a market yield, which is higher than the risk-free rate, market values are lower than values determined using the risk-free rate. Thus, when an asset met the EITF 93-18 definition of other-than temporarily impaired, its market value typically had fallen significantly below its book value.

Questions About Buy-up Accounting That Arose in 1997

With the issuance of FAS 125 Fannie Mae should have stopped accounting for buy-ups under FAS 91. Freddie Mac intended to do just that. On March 20, 1997, Sampath Rajappa, then Fannie Mae's Controller, sent Timothy Howard a memorandum informing him that Arthur Andersen, then Freddie Mac's auditor, had taken the position that FAS 125 applied to buy-ups, which meant that Freddie Mac should mark them to market though equity.[104]

The switch from FAS 91 to FAS 125 and EITF 93-18 in accounting for buy-ups had significant implications for the volatility of Fannie Mae's equity and earnings.[105] Under FAS 91, a company reflects the effects of prepayment variations on net buy-up/buy-down positions via relatively small upward and downward adjustments to earnings. Application of FAS 125, however, would reflect the effects of those variations on gross buy-up positions through larger adjustments to equity. If market values of buy-ups were to fall far enough, impairment analysis under EITF 93-18 would result in large downward adjustments to earnings.

Mr. Rajappa told Mr. Howard that Fannie Mae's own auditor, KPMG, had not yet raised with Mr. Rajappa the issue of Freddie Mac's accounting change. Because Mr. Rajappa thought Freddie Mac would make the accounting change in its first quarter financial statement, he recommended that Fannie Mae raise the issue with KPMG.[106] Although his memo did not specifically address the applicability of FAS 125 to Fannie Mae, Mr. Rajappa recommended that the Enterprise "not record any mark-to-market through equity at this stage." He noted that at January 31, 1997, the market value of Fannie Mae's buy-up portfolio exceeded the book value by approximately $250 million (reflecting a recent rise in interest rates, increasing projected guaranty fee cash flows), that he believed "the amount of the mark-to-market would be relatively immaterial in relation to the size of our balance sheet and amount of our equity," and that Fannie Mae should monitor the market value of its buy-up portfolio relative to its book value and "reevaluate recording any adjustment through equity based on materiality."[107] Mr. Rajappa's recommendations are another example of Fannie Mae understanding the rules but choosing not to apply them.

To avoid a possible future restatement, Mr. Rajappa argued for approaching KPMG in the near future, pointing out that "any differences in the accounting for buy-ups between Freddie Mac and Fannie Mae will likely result in analysts and/or OFHEO raising questions (and) in these situations it's best to have KPMG's concurrence with our position."[108] Two days later, Mr. Howard responded to Mr. Rajappa, saying he was not sure of "the logic of approaching Peat on this right away." Mr. Howard thought it "highly unlikely that Peat would ask us to restate for something like this -- particularly since that restatement would result in a gain .... If we go to Peat before the fact, it seems it can't do anything but reduce the chance of our coming out where we'd like to."[109]

In spite of the reluctance of Mr. Howard, Fannie Mae did approach KPMG on the issue shortly before Freddie Mac's earnings release. In an April 4, 1997, e-mail message Jonathan Boyles, Director for Financial Standards, circulated "a few talking points for meeting with KPMG on the buyup issue." Mr. Boyles proposed, first, that Fannie Mae ask KPMG to confirm that Fannie Mae's buy-up program would not be affected by FAS 125; second, that Fannie Mae tell KPMG that the mark-to-market calculation required under FAS 125 would be difficult, and the balance sheet impact "immaterial;" and third, to tell KPMG that "we examined the issue and do not intend to mark-to-market the portfolio and ask for confirmation from them that it's the right thing to do."[110] Responding back to Mr. Boyles, James Parks, Vice President for Financial Standards, said, "I wouldn't focus on 'right thing to do' which might suggest recording any entry in their mind; just tell them our conclusions and why."[111]

Someone wrote "agree" next to Mr. Parks' comment.[112] In an April 15, 1997, e-mail message to Mr. Rajappa, Ms. Spencer, Matthew Douthit, Thomas Lawler, Mr. Howard, and others, Mr. Boyles said: "As most of you know, we brought the issue to Peat Marwick's attention last week and told them why we didn't think it was an issue for us. We have never heard back from them."[113] An undated, unsigned document entitled "Buyup Accounting History" states that "after review and conversations with the CFO, the decision was made not to mark the buy-ups to market through equity"[114] (i.e., not to follow FAS 125).

Mr. Boyles also informed Mr. Rajappa, Ms. Spencer, Mr. Douthit, Mr. Lawler, and Mr. Howard that Freddie Mac's first quarter 1997 financial disclosure reported a $26 million gain (net of taxes) due to the adoption of FAS 125. He pointed out that the disclosure "does not specifically say 'buyup'" but read "'Under FAS 125, I/O and I/O-like assets are reported at market value with unrealized gains/losses reported through equity." Mr. Boyles reassured them that, "[t]he disclosure by Freddie Mac is vague enough that I don't think it will raise any questions from Peat Marwick."[115]

Economic and Accounting Concerns Mount

Although Fannie Mae chose to ignore FAS 125, it tracked the market versus book values of its buy-up portfolio. As interest rates started to decline and buy-ups fell in value the Enterprise demonstrated a growing concern about the implications of applying FAS 125. According to a document entitled "Buyup Accounting History," "market value calculations were performed in June 1997, November 1997, January 1998, and August 1998." Those calculations showed that "the sustained decline in interest rates during 1998 caused prepayments to accelerate to such a level that resulted in certain buckets to fall into impairment."[116] As of March 25, 1998, (based on January 31, 1998, book balances, and thus, presumably the "January 1998" market value calculations referred to in the preceding quotation from the "Buyup Accounting History), the aggregate book value of Fannie Mae's buy-ups on 30- and 15- year fixed-rate mortgages (FRMs) exceeded their market value by $278 million ($1.497 vs. $1.219 billion).[117]

On March 25, 1998, Fannie Mae performed an analysis to determine the extent of other-than-temporary buy-up impairments under EITF 93-18. That analysis showed that had Fannie Mae followed FAS 125 and EITF 93-18, it would have recorded an impairment write-down totaling $5.1 million.[118]

An unsigned document dated February 4, 1998, entitled "Buyup and Buydown Discussion" indicated growing concern at the Enterprise about the economic and FAS 91 accounting implications of falling buy-up valuations in addition to concerns about the impact of applying FAS 125. The document stated:

> As of December 31, (1997) Fannie Mae's net long IO position exceeded $500 million. The financial risks are that a) IO revenue continues to fall short of levels anticipated at pricing .... This could lead to b) an accounting write-down; with revenues falling below expectations, the

market value of our book is in danger of falling below prices paid (amortized book price). When this occurs, the loss must be reported to shareholders.[119]

Unsafe and Unsound Buy-Up Pricing

The concern of Fannie Mae management about the growing excess of buy-ups over buy-downs in 1998 arose from its competition with Freddie Mac for market share in a period when falling interest rates caused a surge of refinancing. Fannie Mae's strategy was to increase its share of the securitization market by overpaying for buy-ups. In April 1998, Ms. Spencer wrote to the Executive Vice President for Housing and Community Development, Robert Levin:

> [I]n order to purchase $4.2 billion of business in the first two months of the year we overpaid for guaranty fee buyups by approximately $8.4 million .... Until last week, I was not aware that the 'enhanced' buyup meant that we were paying materially above market for an 'IO-Like' instrument. I do not believe that we can continue to amortize this above-market pricing differential.[120]

Around the same time that Ms. Spencer wrote her note to Mr. Levin, Mr. Boyles made a presentation on buy-ups to the Assets and Liabilities Committee of the Board of Directors. His presentation addressed two main issues: "the risk of impairment if interest rates fall and the volume of the BU book continue[s] to grow," and the "use of BUs as a tool for competing on price."[121] Mr. Boyles' presentation slides illustrated the following:

> BUs have grown disproportionately to BDs during the last three years but the trend has accelerated in 1998 .... The dollar value of 'enhanced' buyup activity (where we pay more than our posted ratios) has increased since 1996 .... Capping (the buyups of lenders from which Fannie Mae had agreed to purchase in excess of 20 basis points) would have saved $2 million .... The consequence, however, would likely have been lost share.[122]

During his presentation, Mr. Boyles also speculated about the feasibility of a hedging strategy involving "linking MBS in portfolio with buyup IO ... in order to reduce the severity of impairment ...."[123] Thus, Mr. Boyles suggested the possibility of masking buy-up impairments the same way senior management was improperly masking IO security impairments, by bundling them with other mortgage-backed securities, to offset the premiums represented by buy-ups, as well as to justify accounting for IO securities under FAS 91 instead of FAS 125.[124]

Through the spring of 1998 Fannie Mae continued to overpay for buy-ups in its competition with Freddie Mac for a greater share of the mortgage securitization business. On May 19, 1998, Matthew Douthit, Director for Portfolio Management, e-mailed Adolfo Marzol, Executive Vice President and Chief Credit Officer, and Ms. Spencer (who, in turn, forwarded the e-mail to CFO Howard, among others), expressing his concern. He said:

> I now see April being the biggest month of the year in terms of using the enhanced pricing grids. We've added to our buyup position in the first four months of the year $230 million in buyups with an estimate that we have paid over and above the market price for the IO by $22 million ytd. to get business on the books. This is for 30 year product only I am staring at a report that is telling me that we are under amortized in the amount of $63 million of expense against the gfee line on our p & l because of the faster pace of prepayments we are seeing.

> I remain concerned that the hole gets bigger faster than I can come up with a strategy to dig out of it from an earnings perspective.[125]

Mr. Douthit focused not on accounting, but on a more fundamental safety and soundness issue—the economic risk posed by Fannie Mae's buy-up pricing practices. The $63 million of expense Mr. Douthit cited, which resulted from an unexpected increase in mortgage prepayments as a consequence of declining interest rates, represented accounting losses Fannie Mae would have to recognize under its inappropriate application of FAS 91, which treated buy-ups as purchase premiums rather than IOs. (As discussed earlier, IO accounting, involving impairment analysis and the recording of other-than-temporary impairments, would have resulted in much higher losses.)

Mr. Douthit observed, in effect, that the buy-up pricing of Fannie Mae represented a risky bet on interest rates that had gone bad. Until that point, Fannie Mae does not appear to have focused properly on the risk of that strategy. For example, in a May 19, 1998, e-mail to Robert Weiss, Vice President for Marketing and Sales, Mr. Howard wrote:

> [A]lthough we do use buyups as a means for competing on price, we also have to think of and manage them as a business. We need to price them to produce an appropriate return (except where we're deliberately mispricing them to get share, in which case we should be clear on and keep track of the degree of mispricing), track and measure our exposure, and develop and execute an explicit strategy for hedging our buyup exposure. I was expecting this to have been a part of our buyup discussion [a presentation to the Assets and Liabilities Committee]. Is that something that's being done separately?[126]

The response by Mr. Marzol to Mr. Douthit's e-mail confirmed Fannie Mae's lack of a capability to respond in a systematic way to competition for market share. He wrote:

> Lack of capabilities: If our competitor continues to entice business with buyups at values we believe are greater than market, we must counter to maintain our commitment to share. Without using buyups the only alternative is to cut gfee [guarantee fee]. We are very constrained in our ability to cut gfee at a precise level (meaning by lender by coupon or note rate), and absent a precise capability, we have to give the gfee up across the board, which is costly and results in perhaps more buyup coming back to us (although at least valued at market).[127]

A follow-up by Thomas Lawler further reveals the lack of a policy and systems infrastructure to properly manage a competition for market share based on buy-up pricing:

> buyups are by their nature extremely difficult to hedge, are [sic] many traders over the past decade who have hedged ios are out of that business now ... net/net, I agree with Adolfo in that any real strategy should incorporate a plan to dramatically reduce the amount of buyups we do.[128]

Tracking Buy-up Impairments under FAS 125

Reflecting a global recession, interest rates fell steadily during the first eight months of 1998; the constant-maturity ten-year treasury rate fell over 70 basis points. Falling rates steadily eroded the value of buy-ups and other interest-only-type investments. Although Fannie Mae continued to account for buy-ups under FAS 91, on August 21, 1998, in the midst of the Russian Currency crisis,[129] the Enterprise estimated impairment write-downs of buy-ups under FAS 125 of $599.4 million.[130] In calculating that amount Fannie Mae chose the highest of three market value calculations.[131]

On Friday September 18, 1998, with the Long Term Capital Management (LTCM) hedge fund on the verge of collapse (fourteen banks would bail it out ten days later),[132] Fannie Mae recalculated impairments using two different approaches. In one approach, assuming current market conditions, and thus capturing current market values, Fannie Mae projected impairment losses of $592.7 million.[133] A second approach, which applied Fannie Mae's long-term planning assumptions and effectively assuming away the LTCM crisis,[134] estimated much lower losses, $189.9 million. In future exercises to estimate the amount of buy-up impairments under FAS 125, Fannie Mae applied the second approach.

Applying the latter approach on October 30, 1998, with the LTCM crisis easing, Fannie Mae estimated other–than-temporary impairments of $346.7 million.[135] Using the same approach at December 8, 1998, impairment write-downs under FAS 115 would have been $309 million, [136] close to the October 30 figure. Demonstrating his awareness of the disastrous effect the application of IO accounting would have on earnings, Mr. Boyles transmitted the December 8 analysis to Ms. Spencer with penciled-in figures -- $75 million – reflecting "what we would have to write down the book balances by to fall just under the impairment cliff."[137] Mr. Boyles' expression "impairment cliff" referred to the phenomenon described earlier—EITF 93-18 establishes an "other-than-temporary" threshold under which impairment write-offs are taken only after an asset is seriously impaired. Mr. Boyles calculated that if Fannie Mae's 30- and 15- year fixed-rate mortgage buy-up balances were $75 million lower, the remaining impairments would not reach the threshold for "other-than-temporary."[138] In other words, if Fannie Mae could find a way to write down its buy-up book balances by $75 million, the Enterprise could avoid four times higher write-downs associated with what would otherwise, under FAS 125, be considered other-than-temporary impairments. Mr. Boyles noted, however, the favorable assumptions used in the October 30 and December 8 analyses, and that they understated the impairments. He pointed out the analyses used "a 400 bp [basis point] spread to treasuries [*i.e.*, Option Adjusted Spread] in valuing the buyups [sic]. This is based on a long view of spreads. In reality, spreads on these could be over 1000 bps and therefore the market value much less."[139]

It is not clear how Fannie Mae could have accomplished the $75 million write-down that Mr. Boyles said Fannie Mae would need to avoid recording impairments under FAS 125. Poor controls over Fannie Mae's Purchase Discount Amortization System (PDAMS—the system used to amortize purchase premium and discount under FAS 91) might have provided the opportunity to effect such a write-down. In September 1998, in a "Risk Review with CFO," Ms. Spencer suggested that Fannie Mae "consider charging directly to expense each month any 'excess' buyup." She made the suggestion in connection with using PDAMS to "book additional amortization expense as we generate additional portfolio income growth during the remainder of the year while managing to EPS expectations of $3.21."[140] As discussed below in the section on Purchase Premium and Discount Amortization, Fannie Mae misused the PDAMS system to manipulate earnings.

At January 4, 1999, potential impairment write-downs under FAS 125 for 30- and 15-year FRMs had grown to $495.9 million. That analysis shows the sensitivity of buy-ups to further declines in interest rates. The analysis indicated that further downward parallel interest rate shifts of 50 and 100 bps increased the potential impairment write-down to $882.1 and $1,038.8 million, respectively.[141]

Obscuring the Issues

Although Fannie Mae continued to amortize its net buy-ups inappropriately under FAS 91, Mr. Boyles and Mr. Douthit, Vice President of Portfolio Management, continued to assess the potential impairments on its buy-up portfolio under FAS 125. Mr. Boyles claimed he was aware only of the September 1998 buy-up analysis and unaware of the other analyses.[142] The "History" document, however, which includes schedules showing impairment analysis as of August 21, 1998, came from the hard drive of his computer.[143] Clearly Mr. Boyles was aware of analysis after September 1998 because he wrote a cover-note for Mr. Douthit's December 10, 1998, memo transmitting the results of a December 8th impairment analysis that referenced similar analysis from "last March."[144] Another memo from Mr. Douthit, subject: "IO Book (buyups [sic])," which transmitted potential impairment analysis at January 4, 1999, has Mr. Boyles' name handwritten on the top, presumably identifying his copy (the document was found in his files), and Mr. Boyles was formally copied on that memo.[145] He was also copied on a similar memo dated April 5, 1999.[146]

An undated, unsigned presentation document entitled "Managing the Buyup/Buydown Book,"[147] that appears to date from late 1998, further demonstrates management awareness of Fannie Mae's "potential accounting exposure [*i.e.,* exposure under FAS 125] from its buyup /buydown book." It states that "there is some risk that could affect our accounting on our gross, and not net, buyup position that in turn could require an even bigger write-down if interest rates were to fall."

In 1999, Mr. Boyles and Ms. Spencer demonstrated their continued awareness of the potential earnings volatility created by buy-ups under FAS 125. Karen Pallotta, Director for the Single Family business, and Bud Riley asked Mr. Boyles for his opinion about a proposed purchase by Fannie Mae from one of its seller/servicers of an IO strip from a mortgage pool.[148] He responded:

> IO's are classified as available-for-sale (AFS) and are marked to market through equity (This isn't the bad part). IO's also are subject to special accounting rules. We currently don't have a system in place to properly accounting for IO's, and as a result, have a much greater exposure to IO impairment risk. The impairment risk is like jumping off a cliff, if you are impaired (and you're never a little impaired) the hit to earnings could be quite large.[149]

Ms. Pallotta responded by asking whether "the risk we would take ... would be commensurate with the risk we take in purchasing excess servicing via our buyup program."[150] Mr. Boyles prepared a draft response for Ms. Spencer's review, stating:

> Economically this deal is the same as a buyup, however, there are other concerns that make it different. KPMG has not questioned our accounting treatment for buyups even though we have not necessarily been faithful to IO accounting. One of the reasons they have not questioned our treatment is that the cash flows are part of a guarantee fee payment and don't 'sound' like an IO.

Mr. Boyles told Ms. Spencer that he planned to send the e-mail only to Ms. Pallotta and Mr. Lawler. Ms. Spencer told him not to send the e-mail, but to brief Ms. Pallotta in person.[151] That exchange, reflecting the concern of Mr. Boyles and Ms. Spencer about public discussion of Fannie Mae's buy-up accounting, demonstrates their knowledge that

Fannie Mae was intentionally misapplying GAAP related to buy-ups and their focus on concealing the information rather than correctly applying GAAP.

New FASB Pronouncements Affecting Buy-up Accounting

Two FASB pronouncements relating to buy-ups became effective in 2001, EITF 99-20[152] and FAS 140.[153] EITF 99-20, effective in April, slightly modified EITF 93-18 criteria for determining whether an impairment is other than temporary.[154] Under EITF 99-20, in an unfavorable interest rate environment buy-ups are more likely to be other-than-temporarily impaired than under EITF 93-18. FAS 140, also effective in April, superseded FAS 125 but included a paragraph 14 identical to that in FAS 125. That paragraph provided that IOs and IO-like instruments should be accounted for under FAS 115,[155] making them subject to mark-to-market adjustments through equity and impairment write-downs under EITF 99-20. Fannie Mae continued to account for its buy-ups as if neither FAS 125 nor its successor FAS 140 applied, and thus, consequently, as if EITF 99-20 did not apply.

KPMG Left in the Dark

An e-mail dated January 28, 2002, from Ms. Spencer to Mr. Howard and copied to Mr. Boyles, further shows that Fannie Mae was taking advantage of KPMG's lack of attention to the Enterprise's questionable buy-up accounting practices. In the wake of the Enron scandal, Freddie Mac had recently fired Arthur Andersen and apparently was considering retaining KPMG, Fannie Mae's auditor, as a replacement. In the e-mail, Ms. Spencer conveyed the "combined thoughts of Jonathan and myself regarding KPMG doing audit and other services for Freddie Mac." She wrote:

> We believe it is a good thing for the 'industry of two' to have different auditors. It gives us a vehicle to get a second opinion at times .... There is at least one thing that we know of where we have a favorable accounting treatment and that is on the IO's we have on our books. Freddie is doing IO accounting and we are not. KPMG hasn't figured that out—but Jonathan reminded me of this.[156]

Discussions with the FASB and the SEC

At the beginning of 2003, another FASB pronouncement, FIN 45, became effective.[157] In earlier discussions with the FASB about the implementation of FIN 45, Mr. Boyles, along with representatives of Freddie Mac, raised the issue of the applicability of EITF 99-20 to buy-ups. According to Mr. Boyles, conversations with FASB confirmed that EITF 99-20 did not apply.[158] Mr. Boyles did not, however, raise the underlying issue that would determine the applicability of EITF 99-20—whether or not paragraph 14 of FAS 140 (the paragraph identifying buy-ups as interest-only instruments) applied.[159] Thus, Mr. Boyles only inferred from FASB's position on the inapplicability of EITF 99-20 that FASB supported Fannie Mae's position that paragraph 14 of FAS 140 did not apply.

When Boyles consulted with the SEC in 2002 regarding the implementation of FIN 45 by Fannie Mae, he again did not bring up the issue of paragraph 14 of FAS 140. He memorialized his understanding with the SEC in a letter to the SEC staff, saying "the SEC staff does not object to our accounting treatment of our guaranty fee income in accordance with EITF Issue No. 85-20, *Recognition of Fees for Guaranteeing a Loan.*"[160] As discussed below, Mr. Boyles would later try to infer from that SEC consultation, in which the

SEC affirmed that EITF 85-20 applied to guarantee fees, that the SEC supported his position that paragraph 14 of FAS 140 and EITF 99-20 did not apply to Fannie Mae's buy-ups.

Impact of Freddie Mac Restatement

On November 21, 2003, Freddie Mac announced the results of its restatement for 2000, 2001, and 2002. With the restatement, Freddie Mac publicly acknowledged its 2001 adoption of Fannie Mae's approach to buy-up accounting was in error and informed the public that:

> the accounting during the restatement period was incorrect because it (i) netted buy-ups and buy-downs (buy-down fees represent cash received from counterparties to reduce the guarantee fee rate); (ii) stopped reporting the change in fair value of buy-up fees as a component of Accumulated Other Comprehensive Income as required under FAS 125 for financial assets with significant prepayment risk on April 1, 2001, the effective date of EITF 99-20, "Recognition of Interest Income and Impairment on Purchased and Retained Beneficial Interest in Securitized Financial Assets," ("EITF 99-20"), thereby avoiding recording impairments of these assets; (iii) used an incorrect amortization method, including allocating buy-up and buy-down fee amortization between net interest income and management and guarantee fee income; and (iv) failed to follow an acceptable impairment valuation method.[161]

Understandably, Freddie Mac's announcement raised concern at Fannie Mae. As Mr. Boyles later told senior management, he believed that of all the issues raised in the Freddie Mac restatement, buy-up accounting was the most significant.[162] For years Fannie Mae had avoided questions about its buy-up accounting, and the Freddie Mac restatement invited questions, particularly from the SEC. Fannie Mae staff reacted immediately, drafting talking points for a phone call with the SEC.

The unidentified author of the talking points proposed raising "four issues where we identified that Freddie Mac's new accounting policies different [sic] from our own for similar transactions," adding that:

> With respect to one area of different accounting, we reviewed our accounting treatment and consulted KPMG, and remain comfortable with our accounting treatment. We also believe that there are structural differences between our mortgage-backed securities and Freddie Mac PCs that may be the source of the difference. However, given the scrutiny public companies are under, and especially GSE's, I wanted to take this opportunity to request your advice on how we should handle this issue.

The Talking Points Continue:

> I don't know that he will ask what the issue is but if he does say: The issue is how to account for deferred price adjustments related to guaranty fees ... Freddie Mac has decided to account for their buy-ups at fair value while we have always applied a level yield amortization approach to these as well as the flip side to the transaction 'buy-downs.' [163]

Resolving the Issue with the SEC

On February 20, 2004, Mr. Boyles had a conversation in which SEC staff asked why Fannie Mae didn't view buy-ups like interest-only securities. The SEC advised him that Fannie Mae should provide that information via its standard pre-clearance process—providing a description of a transaction and presenting the possible differing views regarding the accounting.[164]

In a February 24, 2004, letter, Mr. Boyles laid out for the SEC the arguments he developed in support of the current accounting practice of Fannie Mae—that buy-ups are a component of guaranty fees that are not financial assets or retained interests in securitizations, and therefore are not subject to paragraph 14 of FAS 140 or EITF 99-20. Mr. Boyles supported his argument by referring to FASB's supposed "confirmation" that buy-ups were not subject to EITF 99-20. The SEC staff asked, "when Jonathan Boyles discussed buy-ups and EITF 99-20 with the FASB, did paragraph 14 of FAS 140 come up as relevant literature?"[165]

Mr. Boyles later told his Fannie Mae colleagues that he had not discussed the applicability of FAS 140 with the FASB. Responding to the SEC question, he wrote to a subordinate:

> The discussion we had with the FASB was specifically around the implementation of EITF 99-20 because it was about to become effective and we needed clarification as to its applicability to buy-ups. We did not specifically address paragraph 14 because at Fannie Mae we'd already determined it did not apply so I didn't ask."[166]

With language crafted in consultation with Ms. Spencer, Scott Lesmes, Vice President and Deputy General Counsel, and Harry Argires of KPMG, Fannie Mae sent the following response to the SEC:

> No [paragraph 14 of FAS 140 did not come up as relevant literature]. The discussion we had with the FASB was specifically around the implementation of EITF 99-20 because it was about to become effective and we needed clarification as to its applicability to buy-ups. We concluded from this discussion that the bought-up portion of the future guarantee fee receivable could not be considered either a purchased or retained beneficial interest. This confirmed our previous conclusion that paragraph 14 of FAS 140 could not apply.[167]

In a March 10, 2004 phone call, the SEC disagreed with Fannie Mae's buy-up approach and concluded that buy-ups were not guarantee fees but rather financial assets subject to paragraph 14 of FAS 140.[168] As a result, Mr. Boyles told his colleagues in a March 13, 2004, memo, Fannie Mae would have to create the systems necessary to mark buy-ups to market through equity.[169] That memo suggests that Mr. Boyles overstated to the SEC Fannie Mae's operational ability to apply FAS 140. He included "a list of items I think we need to get done to comply with what we told the SEC." For example, under its existing FAS 91-based accounting, Fannie Mae netted buy-ups and buy-downs within FAS 91 types. Applying FAS 140 would require netting within individual MBS trusts, a far more complicated, systems-intensive approach. Mr. Boyles said he had told the SEC "we would address this and net in future filings," implying that this could be done easily. As Mr. Boyles himself observed in his memo, however, "[o]n the surface this sounds simple but I believe the devil is in the details." Responding to the implication of Boyles' memo that he oversold Fannie Mae's systems capabilities, Attorney Denise Grant wrote Ann Kappler, "I'm sure you'll have the same reaction that I did to certain passages. Someone should talk to the accounting folks about how they phrase things in written documents on such sensitive topics."[170]

On March 15, 2004, Mr. Boyles provided a confirming letter to the SEC. That letter implies that the SEC accepted his idea that the implementation of FIN 45 (which created the concept of a Guarantee Asset consisting of the fair value of future guarantee fees offset by unamortized buy-ups fees) triggered the application of FAS 140 for Fannie Mae. Mr. Boyles wrote:

> We acknowledge your view that, contemporaneous with the adoption of FIN 45, the method of accounting for buy-ups created after January 1, 2003 is paragraph 14 of FAS 140. The adoption of FIN 45 ... changed the historical accounting for guarantees that formed our historical view, resulting in the recognition of buy-up fees as a financial asset subject to paragraph 14 of FAS 140.[171]

Fannie Mae misapplied GAAP when it neglected to apply paragraph 14 of FAS 125 and later FAS 140 to buy-ups. The Enterprise raised the issue internally as early as March 1997 but chose to continue with past practice, which was operationally easier and minimized the possibility of having to recognize impairment losses. As discussed above, at that time the market value of Fannie Mae's buy-ups exceeded their book value by about $250 million. Mr. Rajappa had suggested that Fannie Mae monitor the market value of its buy-up portfolio and consider the application of FAS 125 "based on materiality,"[172] but that simply did not happen. When interest rates fell during 1998, rapidly eroding the value of buy-ups, the consequences of applying FAS 125 became very material. Significantly, if properly recorded, such consequences would have made it impossible for Fannie Mae to meet its 1998 AIP bonus goals and analysts' expectations. Fannie Mae's reaction was to avoid calling KPMG's attention to the matter.

Mr. Boyles' letter to the SEC of March 15, 2004, emphasizes the insignificant effect of FAS 140 at December 31, 2003: "[w]e evaluated the effect of marking to market the unamortized buy-up amount as of December 31, 2003, and have determined that this amount was immaterial relative to our total assets and equity" -- just $21 million.[173] As mentioned previously, current management has revisited that area as part of the restatement efforts, determined past practice was in error, and agreed to restate.

Staff in the Office of the Controller went to great lengths to avoid recording impairment expense. Frequently, when faced with a situation or new accounting standard that could lead to the need to record impairment expense, management rationalized inappropriate applications of internal policies and/or GAAP. As seen with other issues (*e.g.*, FAS 133, FAS 115, Dollar Rolls, and REO) the preference for avoiding the expense and effort of developing new systems and for maintaining smooth and steady earnings growth took precedence over GAAP compliance and strong internal controls. By their various actions to avoid recording impairment expenses, personnel in Fannie Mae's Office of the Controller were knowingly misapplying GAAP, and the manner in which management handled the buy-ups issue again demonstrates its belief that it did not have to provide complete information to regulatory authorities. This failure to apply GAAP violated the Charter Act, served to mask losses, volatility, and risk, and constituted an unsafe and unsound practice.

Improper Transactions and Accounting to Fine-Tune Results

The accounting misapplications described in earlier sections of this chapter dampened Fannie Mae's earnings volatility sufficiently to permit other accounting misapplications and improper (or improperly disclosed) securities transactions to fine-tune earnings results. Those strategies included the use of cookie-jar reserves, certain Real Estate Mortgage Investment Conduit (REMIC) transactions used to delay federal taxes, debt repurchases, and certain REMIC and insurance transactions.

Short-Term Investment Securities

The two Short-Term Investment Securities (STIS) transactions that Fannie Mae entered into are another example of the management at the Enterprise investing a great deal of time and effort, plus $2 million in issuance costs, on a mechanism having as its sole purpose the inappropriate management of an accounting outcome. The STIS transactions had no meaningful business purpose; their function was to partially defer Fannie Mae's 1998 and 2000 tax liabilities to later years and thereby increase reported earnings in 1998 and 2000. The 1998 transaction reduced Fannie Mae's 1998 tax liability by $341 million.[174] Assuming a 35 percent tax rate, the 2000 transaction reduced that year's tax liability by $163 million.[175] Entering into improper tax deferral transactions with no business purpose other than tax liability reduction is an unsafe and unsound practice.

Until less than two weeks before the first STIS transaction was executed on April 1, 1998,[176] neither internal nor external Fannie Mae communications mentioned business objectives related to the transaction other than tax deferral. On March 19, 1998, a memo seeking formal senior management approval of the transaction mentioned "benefits" other than tax deferral for the first time.[177]

In addition to its inappropriate use of STIS to avoid taxes, the transactions created the appearance of a conflict for KPMG in its role as Fannie Mae's auditor. Fannie Mae paid KPMG fees of $1.8 million and $250,000 in connection with the 1998 and 2000 STIS transactions, respectively, for tax consulting and other services.[178]

A STIS transaction involves the issuance of REMIC securities backed by the first several months of interest payments from a pool of residential mortgages. It exploits a provision of IRS Original Issue Discount rules that exempt discounts of less than 0.25 percent from those rules.[179] Applying that provision, Fannie Mae planned to recognize early months' interest income from a pool of mortgages (proceeds from the STIS sale corresponded to the present value of seven months of interest payments) over the life of the pool. The IRS ruled in 2005 that the 1998 STIS transaction was abusive, and reached a settlement with Fannie Mae disallowing 75 percent of the related 1998 tax deduction.[180] The dispute with IRS over the 2000 STIS transaction, in which the relevant facts and issues are functionally identical to the 1998 transaction, was still ongoing as of April 2006.[181]

Management of the Enterprise viewed the initial STIS transaction as an effort to meet earnings goals. In a July 14, 1997, e-mail requesting staff assistance to pursue an initial STIS transaction, Deborah Cohen, Vice President for Portfolio Management, wrote, "Tim Howard is VERY interested in this as a way to improve income in these difficult times."[182]

The Lehman Proposal

On May 13, 1997, Lehman Brothers, with Ernst and Young as its tax advisor, proposed a STIS-type transaction to Fannie Mae, and a Fannie Mae team began work with that firm on the project.[183] William Einstein, Vice President for Corporate Taxes (who reported to Mr. Howard), appears to have been the lead and worked closely with Ms. Cohen of Portfolio Management.[184] After substantial work by the Fannie Mae/Lehman team, on September

17th Lehman Brothers sent Fannie Mae a draft agreement for Mr. Einstein's signature committing Fannie Mae to work exclusively with Lehman on the deal.[185]

Between September 17th and September 26th Fannie Mae's Controller, Sampath Rajappa, who previously had not been involved in the undertaking, appears to have taken over leadership of the project. In an interview with OFHEO, Mr. Rajappa said that he had no knowledge of the previous work done by Mr. Einstein and Ms. Cohen with Lehman Brothers.[186] Mr. Rajappa explained that Mr. Howard asked him to get involved because the project "was not getting traction or it was languishing under Bill Einstein."[187] Mr. Rajappa said, however, that before he got involved, he thought Mr. Einstein had been working on the project.[188]

Mr. Rajappa was the primary liaison with Fannie Mae's auditor, KPMG. Shortly after Mr. Rajappa took over leadership of the STIS transaction, Fannie Mae stopped working with the Lehman/Ernst & Young team. KPMG ultimately earned a substantial fee for its services on the deal. Those facts suggest a potential conflict of interest with respect to the roles of Mr. Rajappa and KPMG.

Work on the Project with KPMG

There is no record of any further work with Lehman Brothers on STIS after September 17th. Undated, unsigned handwritten notes state: "After working w/ Lehman, we concluded 1) tax issues existed w/ their structure 2) The idea was not proprietary 3) We could not agree on reasonable fees 4) KPMG presented a better structure at reasonable fees."[189] Documentation of KPMG's role takes the form of an unsigned draft letter dated September 25, 1997, from Stephen M. Rosenthal, a principal in KPMG's tax practice, to Mr. Rajappa. The letter begins "[t]he purpose of this letter is to update a tax planning idea that we originally presented to Fannie Mae in 1993. This tax planning strategy could result in significant tax deferral."[190] From that date forward, work on the STIS project proceeded with KPMG, under Mr. Rajappa's oversight and with Mr. Einstein's day-to-day management.

Tax Benefits. Mr. Rajappa told OFHEO he viewed "the principal benefits of this transaction [to be] postponement of payment of taxes."[191] The deep involvement of Mr. Einstein, Fannie Mae's tax expert, further reflects that the STIS was viewed primarily as a tax transaction. The first reference to non-tax objectives appears in notes (they appear to be in Mr. Einstein's handwriting[192]) on an October 29, 1997, fax transmittal sheet from Mr. Rosenthal at KPMG: "Subject: Comparison of Structures." The notes ask: "How critical is it that we have a business purpose?—w/no prepayment risk, we don't reach any new investors."[193]

The March 19, 1998, memo from Mr. Einstein and Mr. Rajappa to Mr. Howard formally requesting approval for the transaction listed as benefits (in addition to tax deferral) broadening the market for Fannie Mae's short-term debt, providing "prepayment risk management," and accelerating cash receipts (mortgage interest payments that Fannie Mae would otherwise receive over six to seven months). It also mentioned in passing that the structure of the transaction "generally will result in a deferral of taxable income, which enhances the economics of the STIS product for the company."[194] Mr. Rajappa transmitted the memo to Mr. Howard with a handwritten note stating: "This is the 'business justification' memo on STIS and as such influenced quite heavily by the lawyers (Internal Counsel and External Counsel)."[195]

The memo captured the benefits of tax deferral in a section entitled "Positive financial statement impact" that did not explicitly mention tax deferral. The other benefits mentioned in the memo are discussed below.

Analysis of Supposed Non-Tax Benefits. An analysis that accompanies the memo showed a "Pre-Tax Economic Profit" of $900,000. That analysis excluded from consideration, however, $1.735 million of $2.5 million in initial transactions costs ($1.8 million fee to KPMG, the $0.2 million fee to the law firm of Arnold & Porter, and additional unspecified costs associated with developing the STIS structure).[196] It also excludes substantial investment in systems infrastructure to process the very complex transaction, including $100,000 that Lawrence Small approved on February 20, 1998, at Mr. Rajappa's request. The excluded costs exceeded the stated profit.

In that analysis, the "profit" resulted from what Fannie Mae earned by reinvesting the proceeds of the STIS transaction, that is, what the STIS investor paid for the seven monthly mortgage interest payments that Fannie Mae would otherwise have received. Because the transaction was a short-term borrowing, a more appropriate analysis would have compared the STIS transaction to a discount note borrowing. The memo itself stated that the rate of the STIS borrowing would be "30-35 b.p. [basis point] higher than that comparable discount note borrowings."[197] The memo also failed to include the high transactions costs in the calculation.

The March 19th memo claimed that STIS would "increase [Fannie Mae's] debt market penetration."[198] In fact both STIS issues were sold to investment banks (the first to Bear Stearns, the second to CSFB) in private transactions and do not appear to have been subsequently placed with investors. Transaction documents prohibited the transfer of the STIS securities to another investor unless that investor accepted, in writing, Fannie Mae's option to repurchase the securities at a specified price.[199] Among records produced by Fannie Mae, OFHEO has not located any documents from any subsequent investors accepting such an option. Accordingly, OFHEO believes no such transfers occurred, the STIS were held to maturity by the investment banks, and the securities did not in any way increase Fannie Mae's debt market penetration.

One statement among the handwritten notes on the October 29, 1997, fax transmittal sheet cited above—"How critical is it that we have a business purpose? w/no prepayment risk, we don't reach any new investors"—contradicted the ostensible justification for the transaction (STIS could induce new investors to purchase Fannie Mae's short-term debt) and undermined the argument that STIS provided "prepayment risk management." That reference alluded to the fact that in those transactions Fannie Mae held "support tranches" that absorbed almost all of the prepayment risk, to protect STIS investors. Thus STIS would only provide protection from improbably high rates of prepayment.

Finally, because Fannie Mae's access to the short-term debt markets allowed it to borrow, virtually without limit, at rates substantially lower (the 30-35 b.p. mentioned earlier) than those of the STIS securities, Fannie Mae did not obtain any meaningful benefit from monetizing the early interest payments from its retained mortgages.

Income-Shifting REMICs

In December 2001 and March 2002, Fannie Mae created $20 billion and $10 billion Real Estate Mortgage Investment Conduit (REMIC)[200] transactions—Fannie Mae REMIC Trusts 2001-81 and 2002-21, respectively—to shift $107 million of earnings into future years.[201] Neither transaction had another economic purpose. Entering into transactions that have no economic purpose other than shifting income, even when otherwise GAAP-compliant, are violations of GAAP. Fannie Mae did not make the appropriate disclosures about the transactions in the associated prospectus supplements or financial statements. In addition, the transactions highlight a number of internal control deficiencies, including Fannie Mae's lack of systems to account for them properly.

Income-Shifting Effects

The income-shifting REMICs transformed a 90 percent pro rata share of cash flows from a pool of mortgages into sequential pay-bond tranches, which Fannie Mae retained. Goldman Sachs underwrote the sale to investors of the remaining 10 percent of the collateral cash flows configured as REMIC tranches with varying characteristics. The income-shifting REMICs were highly unusual both because of their large size, and because Fannie Mae provided the collateral and retained most of the resulting securities. The initial $20 billion transaction was twice as large as any REMIC Fannie Mae had previously issued.[202]

The sequential-pay securities Fannie retained were priced to yield increasing rates of interest, consistent with their average lives. The securities bore the coupons of the underlying MBS collateral, 6.0 and 6.5 percent. Varying yields were effected through premium and discount pricing; shorter tranches were priced at premiums and larger tranches at discounts (under FAS 140, the aggregate carrying amount of the retained tranches was not affected). As a result, instead of recognizing income at a constant yield on the MBS, after the transactions Fannie Mae recognized lower income in the early years, and increasingly higher income as the shorter, lower yielding tranches paid down.

Table VI-1 shows the anticipated impact on earnings of the December 2001 and March 2002 transactions based on contemporaneous assumptions concerning collateral prepayment speeds.[203] The negative numbers reflect reductions, the positive numbers increases in earnings for the referenced years relative to what the Enterprise would have recorded without the transactions.

Table VI-1. Anticipated Effect on Earnings of Income-Shifting REMICs ($ in millions)

Year	REMIC Trust Number	
	2001-81	**2002-21**
2002	-61	-13
2003	-26	-4
2004	-3	3
2005	10	3
2006	15	3
2007	18	3
2008	18	2
2009	17	2
2010	15	1
2011	12	1
2012+	52	5

Relevant Accounting Rules

FAS 140 governs whether assets transferred to an independent trust by an entity such as Fannie Mae must be consolidated on the balance sheet of that entity. FAS 140 calls such trusts Qualifying Special Purpose Entities, or QSPEs. Under FAS 140, when an entity transfers assets to a QSPE, it can sell as little as a 10 percent interest in the QSPE and receive sales treatment, recognizing a gain or loss, on the sold portion.[204] Ownership interests retained by the transferring entity are re-characterized as interests in the QSPE (in this case, the REMIC tranches Fannie Mae retained). The carrying value on the entity's books of the retained portion is reallocated to the retained interests based on their relative fair values.[205]

In order to maintain QSPE status and avoid consolidation, FAS 140 requires independent parties to hold at least 10 percent of the fair value of the interests in the QSPE.[206] A transferor that retains interests in a QSPE must disclose its methodology for valuing retained interests both at inception and at every subsequent reporting date.[207] In the case of the income-shifting REMICs, meeting its earnings management objective required that Fannie Mae never own more than 90 percent of the REMIC securities. FAS 140 does not address measurement of retained assets relative to the overall QSPE going forward.

Genesis of the Income-Shifting REMIC Transactions: Project Libra

According to Thomas Lawler, Senior Vice President for Portfolio Management, when Fannie Mae entered the income-shifting REMIC transactions, the Enterprise was concerned that the steep decline in interest rates in 2001 would cause higher near-term and lower long-term recognition of income under GAAP. Mr. Lawler explained that in the context of developing strategies to address that concern, Peter Niculescu, Senior Vice President for Portfolio Strategy, may have suggested the income-shifting REMIC idea. He was not aware of anyone senior to Mr. Niculescu playing a role in initiating the transactions.[208]

Andrew McCormick, Senior Vice President for Portfolio Management (then reporting to Mr. Lawler), indicated he believed Goldman Sachs (Mr. Niculescu's former employer and the underwriter of the transactions) was the source of the idea.[209] In fact Goldman Sachs described the proposed transaction in a November 19, 2001, presentation to Fannie Mae. David Rosenblum, a Goldman Sachs managing director, attached PowerPoint slides for the presentation to a December 3, 2001, e-mail to Mr. Niculescu. Mr. Rosenblum referred to the project as "Project Libra."[210]

Rationale for the Transactions. The Goldman Sachs Presentation Stated:

> Replacing a MBS pass-through portfolio with a sequentially tranched basket of CMO [i.e., REMIC] classes representing the same cash flows allows FNMA to better manage the recognition of income for GAAP purposes. By replacing a single asset yield with multiple asset yields, FNMA can substantially reduce the GAAP accounting mismatch between asset yields and the term structure of its financing costs. The current steep yield curve environment exaggerates the mismatch between the recognition of interest income and interest expense and makes the transaction more compelling than in a flat yield curve environment.[211]

The Goldman Sachs presentation did not present any other reasons for the transaction.

Mr. Lawler acknowledged that a motive for creating the REMICs was to effect "a change in the expected [pattern of] recognition [of income]."[212] He also emphasized that without the income-shifting REMICs he did not believe the GAAP earnings that the company would have realized would have accurately reflected the underlying economics.[213] Although he referred to economics, Mr. Lawler was actually talking about the GAAP accounting mismatch Goldman Sachs cited. In an e-mail to a colleague, Jeff Juliane, who, as a member of the Office of the Controller had operational responsibilities for accounting for premiums and discounts on the tranches Fannie Mae retained, "these (REMICs) were structured to transfer income from 2002 to out-years."[214]

Mr. Lawler cited as an additional, non-economic objective of the December 2001 transaction the desire to "dramatically increase our REMIC volume relative to Freddie Mac's" at the end of the year.[215] "The size of the transaction ... would give Fannie Mae's REMIC program a 'boost' through increased volume."[216] Ramon DeCastro, Vice President for Portfolio Management, characterized that transaction as economically neutral, as opposed to economically enhancing, pointing out that the risks and cash flows were the same before and after the transactions.[217] Andrew McCormick, Senior Vice President for Portfolio Management, recalled that "Goldman's pitch centered on the 'income effects' of the transaction."[218] He said that the transaction appealed to him because "the exposure associated with such a large REMIC transaction would gain the attention of dealers and the market, and potentially result in future pitches to Fannie Mae for similar REMIC transactions," and that it "would help familiarize the accounting employees and back offices with the handling of such transactions."[219]

Staff Involved in the Transaction. In a meeting with Ms. Spencer, Mr. Niculescu, and several Portfolio Management executives, Mr. Howard made the selection of the structure for the December 2001 transaction which had the greatest income-shifting effect.[220] The structure was one of two proposed in an undated "Summary of Potential December REMIC transactions."[221]

Thomas Lawler, Senior Vice President for Portfolio Management, believed that Portfolio Strategy, Mr. Niculescu's group, took the lead in developing the income-shifting REMIC transactions.[222] Mr. Lawler also stated that Mr. Howard "likely would have been involved or briefed because of the potential impact on the income forecast." He said he did "not recall specific meetings or discussions about the transaction but is sure that they occurred."[223] When OFHEO asked Mr. Lawler whether someone from the Office of the Controller would "have reviewed this change in income recognition and proved [sic] the impact on the company's financial reporting?" he responded by saying only that, "[A]s part of the normal process, this transaction would have been reviewed ... in terms of ... correct accounting."[224]

Jonathan Boyles, and his subordinate, Paul Salfi, provided accounting advice for the first income-shifting REMIC. In an e-mail exchange with Laurie Zeller, Mr. Boyles noted the importance of ensuring that Fannie Mae sell over 10 percent of the QSPE interests to investors to satisfy the requirement of FAS 140.[225]

Sharon Stieber, Vice President for Structured Transactions, and head of the division responsible for processing all REMICs, was involved in operational aspects of the transactions in the same way she was for all of Fannie Mae REMICs. She said she did not believe they were unique.[226] According to Ms. Stieber, Fannie Mae's auditor, KPMG, was involved in all the routine functions such as providing comfort letters, bond validation, and tax reporting. Neither Mr. Lawler nor Mr. McCormick recalled consultations with KPMG, although Mr. Lawler "stated he would be surprised [if outside advisors were not consulted] given the size of the transaction."[227] Ms. Stieber could not remember consulting with KPMG on the special earnings management aspects of the income-shifting transactions and their disclosure.[228]

Public Comment. Fannie Mae's December 2001 income-shifting transaction, which was twice as large as any REMIC transaction the Enterprise had previously issued, generated much discussion in the marketplace.[229] Fannie Mae never disclosed its true role in the transaction, that transaction's economic purpose, or that the $20 billion issuance masked the fact that only $2 billion of the transaction was actually sold to investors. Shortly after the December REMIC was priced, rumors circulated on Wall Street that Fannie Mae had done "a $20 billion 'tax driven' REMIC." Although Fannie Mae wanted to hide the true nature of the transaction, it also wanted to dispel inaccurate, unfavorable rumors. Ramon DeCastro drafted talking points to respond to public inquiries. As Mr. DeCastro put it, "The talking points are light because they are very close to saying 'no comment.'" The talking points evaded questions asking whether collateral from the transaction came from Fannie Mae's portfolio and the motivation for the transaction. Mr. Howard showed a specific interest in that aspect of the transaction, asking "Who's working on the public response? I'd like to see it before it goes final."[230]

An e-mail from "Fannie Mae User" (OFHEO has not been able to determine whether the e-mail was sent or to whom it was sent) provided slightly more information. Attached to the e-mail is a brief statement acknowledging that a significant part of the December REMIC was "bought by Fannie Mae's portfolio .... We are confident [this] new REMIC ... will contribute to producing a stable and balanced growth path for our portfolio earnings."[231] When shown the e-mail, Mr. DeCastro, who had not seen it before, expressed his opinion that the transaction did not create any balance-sheet growth.[232]

Formal Disclosure. Fannie Mae should have made disclosures about the income-shifting REMICs both in the prospectus supplements and in its annual information statements. The prospectus supplements for the income-shifting REMICs did not mention Fannie Mae's role as transferor of the collateral or that it had retained just under 90 percent of the securities issued. That contrasts with what Ms. Stieber told OFHEO during a general discussion of her REMIC responsibilities: that in the few cases in which Portfolio Management provided the underlying collateral for a deal and took back a security, there was a line item in the prospectus supplement stating that the security had been retained by Fannie Mae.[233] For example, offering materials for a similar, but differently motivated transaction -- Fannie Mae Grantor Trust 2002-T8 -- stated in the Plan of Distribution that "initially, we (Fannie Mae) will retain a substantial majority of the Certificates."[234]

Attorneys at Sidley Austin Brown & Wood, which served as issuer's counsel for Fannie Mae in most of the REMICs, said that the Enterprise never informed them of the unique nature of the two income-shifting REMICs—that is, Fannie Mae provided the collateral and retained most of the resulting securities. The attorneys averred that had they been so informed, they would have recommended that Fannie include the information in the prospectuses. They also indicated that in subsequent deals where Fannie Mae retained securities, Fannie Mae conveyed that information to Sidley and included it in the prospectuses.[235]

In its Annual Reports Fannie Mae mentioned neither the Goldman transactions themselves, nor their expected effects on the timing of earnings. The 2002 Report stated only: "In some cases, we create REMICs using assets from our mortgage portfolio and retain an interest in the REMICs."[236] The 2001 Report did not even include that vague language. That lack of disclosure appears inconsistent with guidance that Annette L. Nazareth, Director of SEC's Division of Market Regulation provided in testimony before the Senate Permanent Subcommittee on Investigations, Committee on Governmental Affairs. She observed that "structured finance transactions ... have at times been used inappropriately to achieve a specific accounting or tax result or provide "window dressing" for financial statements." She said that "[i]f a company relies on a structured transaction for a one-time boost in earnings or liquidity, or a series of structured transactions to continue a trend, the investing public absolutely must understand that when evaluating the company. Transparent financial reporting facilitates this evaluation process."[237]

In addition to lack of transparency regarding the income-shifting REMICs, Fannie Mae does not appear to have met the corporate disclosure requirements of FAS 140 for the 2001 reporting year. Under FAS 140, if an entity has securitized financial assets, it must disclose its policies for valuing any retained interests both at inception and at every subsequent reporting date. Although Fannie Mae disclosed such information in its 2002 annual report,[238] it did not in its 2001 annual report.[239]

Compliance with FAS 140 Requirements for QSPEs. As discussed above, although FAS 140 does not include specific guidance regarding the determination of compliance with the requirement that at least 10 percent of a QSPE be sold to investors, it clearly contemplates ongoing compliance in order to avoid consolidation over the life of the QSPE. FAS 140 does not address the measurement of retained assets relative to the overall QSPE over its life.

In a December 27, 2001, e-mail exchange with Mr. Boyles, Laurie Zeller, stated "we have been under the assumption that we needed to sell 10 percent of the collateral/tranches in principal." Mr. Boyles responded "you'd want to make sure that the 10 percent would stay true throughout the pay-down of the REMIC." Ms. Zeller's reference to "principal" suggests she did not understand that the 10 percent related to the fair value of all the REMIC interests. In the e-mail exchange, Boyles did not correct that misunderstanding.[240]

The *Fannie Mae 2002 Annual Report* states "we measure our retained interests by allocating the carrying amount of the assets we retained based on their fair value at the transfer date relative to the assets we sold," implying the Enterprise only evaluated its percentage ownership in the income-shifting REMICs at inception.[241] OFHEO has learned nothing that suggests Fannie Mae systematically evaluated the potential for its retained percentage to exceed 90 percent over time, which would be necessary to meet the requirements of FAS 140 for avoiding consolidation of the income-shifting REMICs.[242]

Cost to Fannie Mae. Although Fannie Mae paid no fees to Goldman Sachs related to the income-shifting REMIC securities the Enterprise retained, the transactions were not without cost to the Enterprise. For the 2001 transaction, the principal cost was $100,000 of "additional REMIC production costs" -- legal and accounting fees associated with all REMIC issues. Fannie Mae paid Goldman Sachs a standard underwriting fee for the $2 billion of REMIC securities that it sold to investors (the fee was 1/32 of one percent, or $625,000). Given that the transaction was largely for Fannie Mae's benefit, the Enterprise also waived the standard REMIC formation fee it charges Wall Street firms, on transactions they initiate, for providing the collateral and marketing the resulting REMIC securities to investors. That fee would have amounted to $1.5 million. REMIC formation fees provide the revenues for most of Fannie Mae's REMIC production, which is a profit-making activity of the Enterprise.[243]

Internal Controls and Approvals Relating to Income-Shifting REMICs

Although Fannie Mae maintained extensive controls and procedures relating to its REMIC production, they focused on routine transactions in which dealers supplied collateral and Fannie Mae provided the guarantee of the resulting REMIC securities. Fannie Mae applied all those controls and procedures to the production of the income-shifting REMICs, but they were inadequate to respond correctly to the issues raised by the unique nature of the REMICs. Fannie Mae supplied the collateral and retained by far the largest portion of the REMIC securities created.

First, Fannie Mae had no formal procedures for the approval of income-shifting REMICs. As discussed above, Mr. Howard ultimately approved the transaction, but did not follow any established formal process in so doing. Second, there was inadequate communication among Portfolio Management, which initiated the transactions; Fannie Mae's Legal Department (outside counsel was unaware of any involvement by the Legal Department); Structured Transactions, which executed the deals; and the Corporate Controller's office, which had responsibility for ongoing accounting for the transactions. Third, Fannie Mae had no formal written procedures for approving or processing that kind of transaction,[244] or for obtaining necessary outside tax and accounting advice. Fourth, Fannie Mae had no system in place to ensure that issuer's counsel (in this case, Sidley Austin) was informed of any special characteristics of a given REMIC that might require disclosure. Finally, at the time the transactions were executed, Fannie Mae's Purchase and Discount Integration (PDI) system could not accurately account for the resulting security premiums and discounts under FAS 91. Ironically, the income-shifting objectives of the transactions were a function of premium and discount amortization accounting. (The different yields on the shorter and longer lived tranches were effected through premium and discount pricing, as all tranches had the same interest coupons).

At the time Fannie Mae executed the December 2001 REMIC, Ramon DeCastro reminded his colleagues that "there are a whole lot of steps still left in this transaction before these are realized income effects."[245] Accomplishing income-shifting required the amortization of individual tranche discounts and premiums on a level-yield basis.[246] Fannie Mae's implementation of FAS 91, the accounting rule governing the amortization of premiums and discounts, involved aggregation of many securities into a number of amortization buckets. Aggregating the cash flows from the different REMIC tranches obscured the differential yields on the various securities, so the income-shifting effect could not be captured. Jeff Juliane, responsible for discount and premium amortization, indirectly described this problem when he stated that "the current infrastructure of the REMIC model could not support the underlying structure of the deals."[247] According to Mr. Juliane, work-arounds to address that problem resulted in errors, discovered in mid-2002, that caused the understatement of income by $9 million, and the subsequent revision of FAS 91 amortization factors for the affected buckets. On June 27, 2002, Rene LeRouzes, who worked for Mr. Juliane, sent an e-mail to Roger Barnes requesting the factor revisions.[248] The inadequate justification for those factor revisions was one of a number of concerns Mr. Barnes raised concerning Fannie Mae's misuse of its systems implementing FAS 91.[249]

Debt Repurchases

Fannie Mae misled investors about a principal purpose of its 2001 and 2002 debt repurchases: its desire to postpone the excess earnings to future years when it expected to overshoot its earnings targets. In 2003, when losses from debt repurchases—also known as early debt extinguishments and debt buy-backs—reached record levels, the Enterprise made a somewhat more accurate, but still incomplete disclosure of its motivation. In those three years, Fannie Mae recorded losses on debt repurchases of $524 million, $710 million, and $2.261 billion,[250] which resulted in reductions in core earnings per share of $0.52, $0.71, and $2.30, respectively.[251] In contrast, in 1998, 1999, and 2000, Fannie Mae recorded losses of only $40 million and $14 million, and a gain of $49 million, respectively.[252]

Although GAAP allows for the repurchase of debt and the recording of a gain or loss on the repurchase, companies must provide accurate and adequate disclosures in their financial statements, so that the transactions and their impact can be understood.[253] The information provided by Fannie Mae management was inadequate and misleading, and in response to inquiries by analysts, the Enterprise denied employing debt repurchases to achieve earnings targets.

Reasons for Debt Repurchases

In addition to shifting income, Fannie Mae might choose to repurchase debt for three other reasons: (1) to manage interest rate risk (by altering its liability structure),[254] (2) to take advantage of arbitrage opportunities (by repurchasing debt that is trading at a higher yield than debt it could currently issue, thus resulting in a small, but real net economic benefit). and (3) to support the liquidity of its benchmark debt program (by repurchasing odd lots of off-the-run securities[255] that are trading at a slightly higher yield (and lower price) than on-the-run securities, reflecting the relative illiquidity of the former).[256] The second and third of those reasons are very similar, in that they both involve repurchasing securities priced to provide slightly higher yields than those they could be replaced with.

Fannie Mae did engage in limited analysis to determine securities it might purchase to advance liquidity and arbitrage objectives.[257] Staff in the Treasurer's department would make recommendations about which securities might be potential candidates for repurchase.[258] Peter Niculescu described a buy-back budget, under which buy-back transactions resulting in a net quarterly gain or loss of over $30 million required approval from a higher-ranking official.[259] It was well known within the Enterprise, however, that Fannie Mae conducted debt repurchases when its earnings position for the period was clear, which corroborates the earnings management motive.[260] In any case, the standard analysis to support liquidity and arbitrage-related buy-backs was not an element of the justification for the massive buy-backs Fannie Mae used to avoid overshooting earnings targets.

Planning for Earnings Management

The large-scale repurchase activity of 2001-2003 was orchestrated by members of senior management, who determined the amount and timing of the repurchases.[261] E-mail exchanges among Mr. Raines, Mr. Howard, and Ms. Spencer show their understanding that the primary reason for conducting debt repurchases was to achieve specific EPS goals. Prior to a repurchase announcement, documents show that they engaged in discussions to determine the specific amount of repurchases to execute in order to achieve those goals, which were the same ones Messrs. Raines and Howard often shared with analysts, such as achieving double digit earnings growth year after year and maintaining stability of earnings.

In late September 2003, just prior to the end of the third quarter, Mr. Howard discussed an upcoming debt repurchase with Mr. Raines. Mr. Raines stated that the Enterprise should come in at a double-digit increase in EPS over the previous year. Mr. Howard agreed with the rationale and relayed that guidance to several of his direct reports, including Ms. Spencer, Mr. Niculescu, Mr. Lawler, and William Quinn, Vice President for Risk Management Strategies:

> I was able to get to Frank this evening on the buyback loss for the third quarter. (I also showed him the sheet that had $8.87 EPS in 2004, but told him that it was the result of front-ended income that we did not intend to let flow through.)
>
> His thought for the third quarter—which I think is a good one—was to come in at an EPS number that would be a double-digit increase from the third quarter of 2002. A third quarter EPS of $1.79 would do that—it would be 10.5% above the $1.62 we reported in the third quarter of 2003 [sic].
>
> If that's what we want to do, doing $400 million buyback tomorrow would cause us to fall short of our objective. Using Leanne's numbers, a $400 million buyback would put us at $1.78. And of course, that's without any cushion.
>
> So—we need a lower cap. Without doing any analysis, I'd be inclined to say $350. A $375 million cap would give us a penny of cushion ($1.80 versus our $1.79 target). Leanne, how much of a cushion would you like, if we're shooting for double-digit growth from Q3 2003 [sic]? Your view of the right cushion should determine the maximum loss number we give to Dave [Benson].[262]

There is no evidence that management documented its reasons to proceed with the large-scale debt repurchases. Mr. Howard stated that his preferred repurchase amount was developed with no analysis.[263] As noted above, Fannie Mae staff did perform analysis to support buy-backs to promote liquidity and take advantage of arbitrage opportunities, but at times the analysis was performed in reverse. Staff in the Treasurer's Office noted that they "need to begin to look at the possibility that the buyback may need to produce $200-$300mm in losses."[264]

Disclosure. Fannie Mae has always disclosed its debt repurchase activity and resulting gains and losses in its annual reports (its 10Ks in 2002 and 2003, after it registered with the SEC), but began to provide an explanation of those activities only with its 1999 Annual Report. That report mentioned only one of the four reasons for repurchasing debt: "[t]he repurchase and call of debt and related interest rate swaps are part of Fannie Mae's interest rate risk management strategy and are designed to benefit Fannie Mae's future cost of funds."[265] Fannie Mae's 2000 Annual Report included similar language.[266]

That language conflated the redemption of callable debt with the repurchase of non-callable debt at its market price, implying incorrectly that the debt buy-backs had the same benefits as the redemption of callable debt. When Fannie Mae exercises call or cancellation options on debt and swaps with yields above current market levels and replaces them with new debt or interest rate swaps, it incurs no current expenses but lowers future funding costs. When it repurchases debt or swaps at their market prices, it recognizes losses equal to the present value of the savings it would recognize had the debt or swaps been callable. The repurchase of non-callable debt and the close-out of non-cancelable swaps does not result in lower costs on an economic basis but converts future costs into current losses (the equivalent of shifting current income into the future).

Fannie Mae's Annual Reports did not disclose the clear earnings management motivation of its 2001 and 2002 debt buy-backs—the smoothing away of what otherwise would have been earnings higher than necessary to meet bonus targets and analyst expectations. The Enterprise did add an additional, somewhat misleading, explanation along with its earlier risk-management explanation, saying that the repurchases took advantage of favorable market conditions. The 2000 Annual Report said, "[f]luctuations in interest rate volatility and market pricing during 2001 gave Fannie Mae a valuable opportunity to repurchase $9 billion of debt that was trading at historically wide spreads to other fixed-income securities." The 2002 report said, "[w]e took advantage of opportunities to repurchase $8 billion of debt in 2002 and $9 billion of debt in 2001 that was trading at historically wide spreads to other fixed-income securities." That the repurchased debt was trading at wide spreads to other fixed-income securities was not a justification for the repurchases because it did not result in any economic benefit for Fannie Mae. Economic benefit would only result from arbitrage activities, which Fannie Mae has never mentioned in public disclosures.

Fannie Mae's 2003 10-K included the 2002 language and additional language that explained the unusually large debt repurchases that occurred that year. The Enterprise first described the low interest rate environment in the first half of the year that induced it to redeem high cost debt callable at par. The report continued:

> In anticipation of increasing liquidations in our mortgage portfolio as a result of heavy refinancing activity, we replaced the higher cost debt with shorter-term, lower-cost debt. This dynamic resulted in a temporarily elevated spread between the yield on our mortgage assets and our funding cost. We chose to reinvest a portion of the income generated from these temporary circumstances in debt repurchases to reduce our future debt costs.[267]

In other words, instead of booking greater-than-planned income generated by "the temporarily elevated spread between the yield on our mortgage assets and our funding cost," Fannie Mae accelerated losses into 2003 that would have otherwise lowered income in future years.

Despite the lack of full disclosure, the investor analyst community understood well that Fannie Mae had used large debt repurchases to smooth earnings in 2003.[268] Nevertheless, in response to inquiries, Fannie Mae publicly denied employing debt repurchases to achieve earnings targets.[269]

It does not appear that Fannie Mae violated GAAP in the recording of the debt repurchase activities, which were transparent to the extent that Fannie Mae reported the earnings affects in its Annual Reports and 10-Ks. On the other hand, the Enterprise failed to honestly disclose the primary motivation behind its repurchase activity. It emphasized a secondary objective—risk management—misleadingly described the cost-savings objective, and, most importantly, omitted a straightforward discussion of earnings management.

Fannie Mae's debt buy-back practices also reveal a lack of adequate delegations of authority, controls, and procedures. As such they raise operations and litigation risk and constitute an unsafe and unsound practice. At a minimum, an appropriate, written policy on debt repurchases was required. Such a policy should have specified the appropriate economic or risk management rationales for debt repurchases, the approval process for undertaking such repurchases, and clear documentation of the process, so that the process could be readily understood.

Insurance Transactions

Finite insurance is insurance that carries a limited amount of risk for the company that writes the policy. Under insurance accounting, premiums are expensed when incurred. When an insurance policy transfers insufficient risk to be treated as an insurance policy, the premium is accounted for as a loan and, therefore, does not affect expenses.[270]

Fannie Mae explored the use of finite insurance policies as a means to manage earnings and entered into one small policy for which it inappropriately applied insurance accounting in order to postpone earnings in a year when Fannie Mae expected to exceed earnings targets. That policy was a pool insurance policy covering a higher-risk loan purchase program—Expanded Approval/Timely Payment Rewards—purchased from Radian Insurance. Current Fannie Mae management has determined that policy was not eligible for insurance accounting, the accounting used to achieve the income-shifting effect, and that Fannie Mae should have accounted for it as a loan. The improper accounting and its income-shifting effect will be reversed in the restatement.

In addition to the Radian policy, Fannie Mae actively explored but did not enter into major finite policies with insurance companies caught up in New York Attorney General Spitzer's investigation of bid rigging, finite insurance, and accounting irregularities in the insurance industry. Those companies were insurance broker Marsh & McLennan and the U.S. subsidiary of the Bermuda-based ACE Companies, both of which admitted involvement in improper finite insurance transactions.[271]

Exploration of Finite Insurance to Substitute for an ExcessiveLoss Allowance

As early as 1997, Office of the Controller staff at Fannie Mae expressed concern that the Enterprise's loss allowance was too high, with the implication it could be seen as a cookie jar reserve used to smooth earnings. Using cookie jar accounts to smooth earnings is a practice not in compliance with GAAP. Pressure grew to revise Fannie Mae's loss allowance methodology as the likelihood increased that the Enterprise would register with the SEC. In early spring 2001, Fannie Mae began discussions with Marsh McLennan Companies (MMC) about a possible finite risk policy that might serve as an alternative to an inflated loss allowance. Notes attached to an e-mail from Marsh McLennan Companies to Robert Schaefer, Director for Finance, describe "Fannie Mae's interest in a structured insurance policy (i.e., finite risk) to replace some portion of the $800mm+ loss reserve accrued on Fannie Mae's Balance Sheet …." and Fannie Mae's principal objective to "spread the volatility of the loss reserve over time, whether that volatility resulted from accounting pressure to reduce or increase the reserve or from actual experience."[272]

A May 25, 2001, e-mail from Mr. Schaefer to Brian Graham, Senior Vice President for Credit Portfolio Strategies, "Subject: MMC Update," referred to the policy being considered under the heading, "Income Smoothing." Demonstrating the sensitivity of Credit Policy to Fannie Mae earnings goals, Mr. Schaefer mentioned that Morgan Whitacre, Director for Accounting and Audit, "mentioned that less concern surrounding $6.46, there was less inertia behind an immediate reduction to the loss reserves. If anything, there is more concern about an earnings drop-off after 2003 …. A new focus on 2003 and beyond might fit well with Marsh McLennan Companies' proposal which would preclude us from reclaiming premiums … until after a 3 yr window."[273]

On June 12, 2001 Mr. Schaefer wrote Mr. Graham: "Yesterday we held a meeting with the 'Loss Smoothing' team ….We agreed that the current MMC proposal really does not counter any arguments for reducing the loss reserve. The MMC policy might make the case for a larger reduction in the allowance …the MMC policy provides more deferral, than smoothing, benefit; but the former would be more attractive given the current environment."[274] Two weeks later Mr. Graham suggested: "If we really wanted to get fancy, we could structure this conversion option such that Tim [Howard] could argue that, upon conversion, we should reduce our loss reserve by the amount of coverage we now have (which would generate positive income) and then separately receive the claims payments over time."[275]

Finite Insurance to Shift Income

On June 29, 2001, Mr. Graham sent Mr. Schaefer a spreadsheet showing how a pool insurance policy along the lines of what Fannie Mae was discussing with Marsh McLennan Companies could shift $100 million of income from 2001 to 2004.[276] Michael Goldberg, Vice President for Lending, emphasized the income-shifting objective a few days later, writing:

> Now that we seem to be hitting our earnings targets through 2003, there is some discussion as to whether there is a strategy for redistributing some of our near-term earnings until after 2003. The strategy that has been discussed most frequently is that of smoothing out our losses. To that end we have a proposal that offers to provide insurance for our loss reserves.[277]

By July 18, 2001, the need to pass a risk-transfer test proving the policy transferred sufficient risk to be considered insurance was clearly a significant concern. The term "risk-transfer test" refers to rule of thumb audit firms have implemented to evaluate whether a reinsurer qualifies as having a reasonable possibility of realizing a significant loss. One such rule is the "10/10 rule" whereby, if the reinsurer has a 10 percent or greater chance of incurring a 10 percent or greater present value loss under the contract, then the contract is deemed to have transferred risk. Although not documented, the "10/10 Rule" is generally accepted and applied in practice.[278]

In the e-mail chain including Michael Goldberg's comments quoted above, Director David Kightlinger appears to discuss risk transfer analysis of the proposal: "Rob Haar and his group should have the data to calculate the 90th percentile for 1, 2, 3, 4, 5 years for accounting losses."[279] Later Mr. Goldberg e-mailed Mr. Whitacre, asking "how do we calculate losses for the 10-10 rule of a 10% chance of a 10% loss?"[280]

At the same time this was going on, Mr. Boyles raised the issue of cookie-jar loan loss accounting (which the Marsh McLennan Companies deal was designed to help address), writing to Ms. Spencer, with copies to Mr. Marzol, Mr. Graham and others. In informing his colleagues of the SEC's Staff Accounting Bulletin No. 102, "Selected Loan Loss Allowance Methodology and Documentation Issues," Mr. Boyles pointed out a finding in a 1994 GAO report that most depository loan loss allowances included "unjustified supplemental reserves [that could] conceal crucial changes in the quality of an institution's loan portfolio and undermine the credibility of financial reports."[281]

It appears that in the late summer or early fall of 2001 Fannie Mae terminated negotiations with Marsh McLennan Companies but continued to pursue a similar transaction with its traditional mortgage insurance partners. Although Mr. Graham was a recipient of Mr. Boyles' e-mail to Ms. Spencer, he continued pursuing various cookie jar options. In October 2001 Mr. Graham wrote to his subordinates Mr. Perez and Mr. Schaefer,

> [s]hould we consider … 2.) Any progress on the earnings mgt strategy now that we have lifted the 'have to get our money back' constraint? What about the idea of buying a slug of first loss pool cover on the risky stuff we have on our books? 3.) Have you guys done any work on the ability to offset the cost of credit enhancement with draw-downs from the loss reserve. For

> instance, we buy $100 million a year in premiums. We then argue that we 'expect $30 million in credit losses out of this pool so let's lower our loss reserve by that amount.[282]

Presumably, Mr. Graham's reference to the lifting of the "have to get our money back" constraint reflected Mr. Raines' personal guidance. On October 17, 2001 Mr. Marzol wrote to Mr. Graham, Mr. Mudd, Mr. Howard, and Ms. Spencer, that "FDR [Mr. Raines] ... personally reiterated guidance he had given through Dan last week—that he views keeping the credit loss line under control as a top priority. He is more than prepared to trade revenues for losses as he feels the market will be punishing to a swing in the loss line more so than a swing in the gfee line."[283]

Radian Expanded Approval/Timely Payment Reward Policy

In 2001 Fannie Mae substantially broadened the Expanded Approval/Timely Payment Reward (EATPR) program begun in 1999. EATPR provided loans to higher-risk borrowers, so Fannie Mae anticipated losses to be greater than usual. Given the typical pattern of such losses, they were anticipated to occur three to four years after loan origination. A finite insurance policy would provide an opportunity to shift those losses forward.

The EA/TPR program, for which Fannie Mae had obtained a basic pool insurance policy with a 1 percent deductible, presented an opportunity for "buying a slug of first loss pool cover on the risky stuff" to which Mr. Graham referred in the October 2001 e-mail quoted above. Mr. Graham summarized thoughts from a brainstorming meeting, "[b]uy coverage that caps the amount of our EATPR deductible that we can 'use' in any one year to ensure we don't have big bumps in the road." He continued: "[i]dentify product with higher risk characteristics and put into a pool on which we buy coverage (could include buying first loss cover on EATPR)."[284] According to Mr. Schaefer, Fannie Mae ultimately purchased coverage of the EATPR deductible.[285]

At the end of October and in early November, Mr. Graham's team began to focus on how to structure a deal to obtain insurance accounting. They appear to have applied the model used to model the pmiSELECT policy described in the following section. Mr. Goldberg wrote: "if we have an experienced-based policy with a stop loss, we are essentially guaranteeing that the MI gets their money back. This seems to add another layer of difficulty in getting this structure to be defined as insurance."[286]

Apparently, Fannie Mae sought bids on the policy from some or all of its traditional mortgage insurance partners, including MGIC, GE, and Radian.[287] The only attractive bid came from Radian.[288] At the end of November, Fannie Mae began negotiating in earnest with Radian on the EATPR policy. It appears the question of whether the policy met the requirements of risk transfer was dealt with internally and may not have been raised with KPMG. In a March 2002 memo to the file concerning the consultations with KPMG's Department of Professional Practice in connection with KPMG's 2001 Fannie Mae audit, audit partner Harry Argires wrote that Wall Street firms pitched a number of insurance transactions that the KPMG Department of Professional Practice concluded "would not qualify as 'insurance policies' and accordingly Fannie Mae abandoned the transactions." Notably, Mr. Argires' memorandum did not mention the Radian deal, which was struck at the end of 2001, and which may well not have qualified as an insurance policy.[289]

On November 26, 2001, Mr. Graham wrote to Mr. Schaefer: "With respect to meeting the 'insurance' test, we should check with Mr. Boyles but I'm thinking we could probably be aggressive given how similar it is to stuff we do every day."[290] It is clear that Fannie Mae anticipated that it would collect as much in claims from the Radian pool policy covering EATPR as it would pay in premiums. On December 11th Mr. Goldberg wrote to Mr. Schaefer: "If Radian's single premium bid … could be written off immediately, this cost would be … effectively a net wash on the transaction."[291] Fannie Mae analysis of the Radian policy showed they were skating close to the line in terms of the risk transfer test. On December 13th, Mr. Goldberg wrote Mr. Schaefer: "[f]or a 30% defined benefit, it looks like Radian 'makes' money less than 25% of the time … and only when they have the right to cancel the policy at the end of three years."[292] The following day Mr. Goldberg wrote "[h]ow much risk is there for Fannie Mae in the proposed transaction? Not much. We're getting the premiums back over 90% of the time."[293]

In fact, the Radian policy accomplished the same income-shifting objectives as the scuttled Marsh McLennan Companies policy. The Radian policy shifted income from 2002 to 2003 and 2004, as demonstrated in a spreadsheet Mr. Schaefer sent to Mr. Perez on December 14.[294]

Mr. Howard was fully briefed on the purchase of the Radian policy, which he approved. On December 21st, he wrote Mr. Graham and Mr. Schaefer, with a copy to Ms. Spencer, "Brian and Rob: I'm fine on going ahead with this. It's not a 'table pounder' for me, but on balance probably worth doing." Ms. Spencer realized the value lay more in helping with earnings management rather than economic value, writing to Mr. Howard, "it helps some with our challenge … on the negative side, we don't think the economics are very compelling."[295]

Lou Hoyes, Executive Vice President for the Single-Family Mortgage Business, learned of the Radian deal on January 9, 2002, the day before it was consummated. He was very unhappy about the policy when Mr. Marzol laid it out in detail, saying that "[t]he transaction pays a one time premium to Radian of … (roughly $40MM) …. The net income after tax impact is a reduction … for 2002 and 2003, then turning into positive P/L … The higher the foreclosures, the faster we get claims and the better the policy value." Mr. Hoyes responded, "I would like to express an EXTREMELY STRONG NO VOTE … I am terrified of the negative public relations aspects of a disclosure of a transaction like this. Should we be exposing Fannie Mae to this type of political risk to 'move' $40 million of income? I believe not."[296]

Exploration of a Finite Insurance product for the Dedicated Channel. Fannie Mae introduced the Dedicated Channel in 2001 to assist internet-based originations and increase the efficiency of the loan origination process. Dedicated Channel acquisitions are originated using Fannie Mae's origination technology (e.g., Desktop Underwriter). Charter-compliant credit enhancement is provided by primary mortgage insurance coverage purchased in bulk by Fannie Mae, or, as an alternative, lender recourse (as opposed to borrower-paid mortgage insurance).

In June 2000, Fannie Mae entered into a "pmiSELECT" policy to provide required Charter-required credit enhancement for mortgages without lender recourse (most loans originated via the Dedicated Channel). PmiSELECT is an experience-based insurance policy under which premiums are adjusted based on past lost experience. Fannie Mae pays PMI Mortgage Insurance a constant base premium for the first four years of the policy. At the end of the fourth coverage year and annually thereafter, Fannie Mae pays a premium based on the ratio of cumulative claims paid to premium paid since the beginning of the policy.[297]

In negotiating the pmiSELECT policy, Fannie Mae consulted outside counsel to determine whether the policy would be considered insurance for tax purposes, so that the Enterprise might deduct premiums paid. Attorneys at Sutherland Asbill & Brennan, Fannie Mae's outside insurance counsel, opined that it would because "the Policy's terms do not prevent the shifting of insurance risk from Fannie Mae to PMI. The Policy provides for limitations on the premiums ultimately due under the Policy, creating the possibility that PMI may sustain losses on the Policy." Those attorneys suggested, however, that the "experience rating feature" be worded to emphasize provisions "making the experience rating feature clearly prospective."[298]

In 2001, in the context of exploring other insurance options, internal Fannie Mae documents refer to Fannie Mae's interest in a "PMI Select-type structure."[299] In connection with exploring options for coverage of Fannie Mae's Expanded Approval/Timely Payment Rewards (EATPR) program, Fannie Mae's analysts used a spreadsheet "built to model the proposed experienced-based policy,"[300] to determine whether the policy generate sufficient probability of loss to the mortgage insurer to be considered insurance. At that point, Fannie Mae appeared less concerned about the possibility that a policy would not properly be considered insurance for accounting purposes than that insurance premiums might be taxable.[301]

In mid-2003 Fannie Mae began exploring the possibility that a potential new entrant into the mortgage insurance (MI) business, ACE, could provide a less-expensive alternative to the pmiSELECT policy. An internal Fannie Mae presentation stated that ACE policy's "objective is to provide Primary MI in an operational and cost effective manner … [and b]roaden the spectrum of credit enhancement providers for Fannie Mae."[302]

In its negotiations with ACE, proper GAAP accounting for the insurance premiums appears to have become an important issue for Fannie Mae. On September 8, 2003, Angela Hairston of Financial Standards wrote to Harry Argires of KPMG that "we want to understand better the difference between deposit accounting for insurance contracts that don't transfer risk as defined under FAS 113 … Do you have a KPMG insurance expert that we could talk to?"[303] The following month Ms. Hairston wrote to Paul Salfi, Director for Financial Standards, "I found some information from E&Y on insurance accounting. I think the ACE contract fails the 9(a) risk transfer test of FAS 113 because the insured's financial results is [sic] not subject to a variability with respect to the amount and timing of the underwriting results until losses exceed 80 bp."[304]

In a November memorandum from Dan Smith to Thomas Donilon, Executive Vice President for Law and Policy, pitching the ACE policy, Mr. Smith characterized the ACE policy as "similar to pmiSELECT (providing) 'experience rated' insurance …. This is insurance for accounting purposes. (Until the right to cancel annually was added to the structure, our accountants were unwilling to treat all premiums as premiums paid for insurance.)"[305]

For reasons that are not entirely clear but that likely relate to the political problems that would ensue were Fannie Mae to enter into an insurance contract with a company other than one of its traditional mortgage insurance partners, the Enterprise never entered into a contract with 300 ACE. Its outside auditors, however, were by then apparently sensitized to the risk transfer issue. PmiSELECT remained the bulk-purchased primary mortgage insurance policy for non-recourse loans originated through the Dedicated Channel.

In March 2004 Fannie Mae submitted a risk transfer analysis of the pmiSELECT policy to KPMG. Roger Wade of KPMG responded that, "[f]or a regional book of business, there is sufficient risk to pass the risk transfer requirements. Under a broadly dispersed countrywide book of mortgages, it is less likely that risk transfer is present .... A critical assumption in reaching this conclusion is that Fannie Mae has the ability to cancel the contracts, and a potential business reason to do so ...." [306] The following day Mr. Argires of KPMG added, "we have not audited the detailed data within the model and if during our audit process this ends up being an area of audit focus and we find discrepancies in the data it could alter our conclusions ...."[307]

Apparently KPMG's belated "approval" of the pmiSELECT structure was delivered orally.[308] In any case, the reaction of Fannie Mae's credit policy staff to having to prepare the risk transfer analysis suggests that was one of very few times KPMG ever requested it. According to the April 16, 2004, *Credit Portfolio Strategies Weekly Status Report*, prepared weekly by Mr. Graham's group, "Met with KPMG (Roger Wade, Harry Argires) to discuss their rationale for confirming the pmiSELECT structure should be treated as insurance. We discussed when it was necessary to even conduct this risk transfer analysis, and how cumbersome this would be if it were required for all 120 deals that we do every year. We agreed that what drove the analysis for this deal was the performance-based adjustment to the premium."[309]

Corporate-Owned Life Insurance. By late 2001, Fannie Mae executive officers realized the Enterprise was likely to earn significantly more than necessary to meet maximum Annual Incentive Plan payout targets in both 2001 and 2002. There was strong pressure throughout the company to accelerate expenses and push income into future years, when expected rising interest rates likely would reduce earnings.

To help his Credit Policy unit contribute to this effort, Mr. Graham developed a strategy to accelerate expenses associated with the Enterprise's Corporate-Owned Life Insurance policies. That would be accomplished by accelerating the amortization of deferred acquisition costs (DAC), state premium tax, and broker commissions into 2002. The effect would be to increase current expenses in 2002 and reduce expenses amortized in future years, thus shifting income into the future.[310]

Fannie Mae reached an understanding with MetLife, one of its Corporate-Owned Life Insurance (COLI) providers, that would allow Fannie Mae to accelerate $12 million of expenses into 2002 in exchange for a 45 bp increase in the yield on the COLI policy (the yield increase was the form the reduction in future expenses would take). The change resulted in a barely positive economic impact on the Enterprise, and, thus, was effectively neutral.[311] That change could have no meaningful business purpose other than to accelerate expenses and postpone income. On May 2, 2002, Fannie Mae booked $11.6 million of "DAC expenses for COLI Met Life Insurance," reflecting the execution of the loss acceleration.[312]

Inappropriate Use of Cookie Jar Reserves

Many companies quite appropriately maintain reserves to use in responding to uncertainties in their business. The senior management at Fannie Mae, however, maintained inappropriate cookie-jar reserves to generate the appearance of steady earnings growth and achieve specific earnings targets. Those reserves allowed management to make last minute, quarter-end adjustments to earnings so that the predicted earnings per share result could be achieved within a fraction of a cent.

Other Accounts Receivable 1622-00

Fannie Mae's Other Accounts Receivable Account 1622-00 was one such cookie jar reserve. Fannie Mae maintained numerous questionable items in the account until late 2003. However, the most egregious use of the account was a $3.9 million draw-down in 1998 that allowed Fannie Mae to meet its 1998 earnings target to the penny, thereby maximizing Annual Incentive Plan bonus payouts.

Inappropriate Characterization of the Account. Fannie Mae inappropriately characterized Account 1622-00 in the category of "other accounts receivable."[313] In practice, the Enterprise treated it as a suspense account established for the month-end posting of certain normal, recurring entries that would subsequently clear in the following month. On September 30, 2003, the account had a balance of $307.0 million.[314] Of that amount, approximately $25.6 million comprised numerous entries dating from October 1990 through November 1999 that related to interest and amortization accruals. More recent items related to loan foreclosures, credit enhancements, mortgage payoff estimates, and short-term interest strips transactions.

An "other accounts receivable" account should hold true accounts receivable—for example, accruals for miscellaneous fees, other prepaid expenses, and payroll deductions receivables. The contents of 1622-00 belonged in a suspense account, which generally holds amounts related to items recorded and held pending classification and transfer to the proper account. (Suspense accounts are generally recorded within "other liabilities" in the balance sheet but may have debit balances.)[315]

Members of the financial reporting staff raised questions about the characterization of the account as "other accounts receivable." Gary Robinson expressed concern about the age of the reconciling items in the account, noting that the account had been used to account for true short-term receivables and accrued amounts as well as to hold reconciling items while an accounting system was being updated.[316] Similarly, Richard Stawarz, Director for Accounting and Audit in the Controller's Office, described the account as a financial reporting clearing account that represented timing items that were not to hit the individual business units.[317]

Evidence of a Cookie Jar Reserve. Internal communications of Roger Barnes and Leanne Spencer suggest staff knowledge that 1622-00 served as a cookie jar reserve. In an e-mail Mr. Barnes observed that Fannie Mae was posting needlessly high reserves to be used later to manage income. He said he believed that account 1622-00 was being used for income adjustments, plugs, contingencies, and excess income.[318] In a memo to Mr. Howard discussing the forecasted EPS for 1996, Ms. Spencer identified a list of items that were "up [her] sleeve to solve an earnings shortfall," including what appears to be the 1622-00 account, which she describes as containing a "cushion" available for that purpose.[319]

Given the length of time items remained in the account, management appears to have made no effort to determine the proper classification of the aged items in the 1622-00 general ledger account. Regardless of the characterization of the account, Fannie Mae should have written off those older items.[320] In 1998 KPMG proposed that Fannie Mae clear $22.5 million in items from the account and take them into income. When Fannie Mae did not agree, the following year KPMG recorded an audit difference in that amount.[321] Instead, Fannie Mae transferred $3.9 million from 1622-00 to income, exactly what management needed to meet its maximum AIP bonus payout target for 1998.[322] Fannie Mae finally addressed the 1999 audit difference in October 2003 when it cleared $25.6 million of stale-dated STAR and STATS reconciling items from the account through income, explaining the move as associated with a system conversion.[323]

Poor controls around the account, notably the lack of documentation, policies, and processes, allowed Account 1622-00 to be used as a cookie jar. Huong Pham, who actually prepared the $3.9 million journal entry, indicated that obtaining supporting documentation was handled loosely; noting that support for journal entries was sometimes lost. She reported that typically she would not be given the supporting documentation at the time an entry was made and the expectation was that she would find such documentation on her own.[324]

The nature of the account, and the absence of documentation and controls surrounding it, allowed Fannie Mae management to use Account 1622-00 as a cookie jar reserve for earnings management purposes. That account was not only the product of and the vehicle for an unsafe and unsound practice, but also constituted an unsafe and unsound condition.

Purchase Premium and Discount Amortization

OFHEO's September 2004 Report of Findings to Date detailed significant misapplications by Fannie Mae of FAS 91, Accounting for Nonrefundable Fees and Costs Associated with Originating or Acquiring Loans and Initial Direct Costs of Leases. OFHEO concluded that the accounting used by Fannie Mae for amortizing purchase premiums and discounts on securities and loans, as well as for amortizing other deferred charges, was not in accordance with GAAP, and that the control environment surrounding the FAS 91 amortization process was weak or nonexistent. Capitalizing on that lack of controls, management knowingly developed improper accounting policies and selected and applied accounting methods that would inappropriately reduce earnings volatility and would provide inordinate flexibility to determine the amount of income and expense recognized in any accounting period. That amortization policy provided management with a reserve that could be utilized as needed at the end of each quarter.[325]

Fannie Mae senior executives developed and adopted accounting policies to spread estimated premium and discount income or expense that exceeded predetermined thresholds over multiple reporting periods. They established a materiality threshold for estimated income and expense, within which management could avoid making adjustments that would otherwise be required under FAS 91.[326] Likewise Fannie Mae management made discretionary adjustments to the financial statements, for the sole purpose of minimizing volatility and achieving desired financial results.

Adoption of FAS 91 The senior management at Fannie Mae was both unable and unwilling to implement FAS 91 fully. For example, a document dated December 31, 1993, indicates that the Enterprise was unable to calculate FAS 91 amortization factors on a monthly basis.[327] That document shows that at that time, Fannie Mae only calculated amortization factors annually and thus needed to create "smoothing adjustments" that ran through general ledger account 1200-00. (Although that account, listed on the December 1997 Trial Balance as "Purch Disc Fract Rate Adj.," was discontinued in subsequent periods, there is little doubt as to its function: the December 31, 1993, document identified above refers to Account 1200-00 as the "smoothing account.") The document also describes reconciliations between the general ledger, the Purchase Discount System (PDS), and LASER and indicates that reconciliation differences were deferred and amortized, instead of being immediately recognized. That indicates that the practice of deferring and amortizing accounting errors was a long-standing one at Fannie Mae.

An unsigned document dated November 7, 1995, contains an outline comparing the FAS-91 level-yield method to "Fannie Mae Practice."[328] That outline states that because "true FAS-91 would introduce excessive variance in income recognition from quarter to quarter," Fannie Mae adopted what the author described as a "prospective method" that was not GAAP-compliant. "The prospective method did not make the retrospective amortization adjustments required by FAS 91, but instead made all adjustments based on "level yield from the current period forward, using updated prepayment expectations." Though it would introduce less earnings volatility than proper implementation of FAS 91, the document noted increased earnings sensitivity under rising and falling rate scenarios would result from the resulting "changes in the long-term CPR [constant prepayment rate], changes we may be reluctant to make." The author listed a series of options involving varying levels of earnings volatility and inappropriate management discretion, including the option to simply "monitor catch-up and wait for catch-up to grow before making any prospective yield adjustments." The author then recommended limited and somewhat discretionary implementation of that prospective method.

In late 1996 Leanne Spencer wrote to Timothy Howard describing an earnings forecast that was slightly short of management's EPS target of $2.48 for that year.[329] Ms. Spencer asked rhetorically: "What do I have up my sleeve to solve an earnings shortfall?" and went on to describe possible adjustments to miscellaneous income, tax accruals, and foreclosed property expense. "We still have other [*sic*] cushion in the bucket account," she wrote, "but its [*sic*] mostly nii [net interest income] related and we're very protective of this account to resolve margin fluctuation when it occurs." As described in the September 2004 *Report of Findings-to-Date*, Fannie Mae management used this account to defer and amortize various premium and discount amounts, including those relating to system realignments. Ms. Spencer's note to Mr. Howard indicates that the amounts in the "bucket" may have been deliberately manipulated to dampen net interest income volatility.

A November 2004 memorandum from an employee in the Controller's Office provides an historic analysis of amounts recorded in the FAS 91 type "BUCKET."[330] The memo states that amounts amortized using the "BUCKET" were recorded in the general ledger account 1201-01. The analysis details amounts that management recorded in that account going back to October 1991 and describes various adjustments that management made to smooth the recognition of amortization income and expense. The analysis includes many large entries to the account for which there is "no information available" to identify the reason those entries were made to the account.

Manipulation of Premium and Discount Amortization Factors. Management also manipulated the Amortization Integration Modeling System (AIMS), which calculated yields and amortization factors for premium and discount amortization, to achieve desired accounting results. AIMS included functionality that allowed management to manually adjust amortization factors. Such an adjustment had essentially the same effect as posting an on-top general ledger entry, except that manual factor adjustments made increases to income or expense more difficult to detect.[331] Rene LeRouzes, an employee in the Controller's Office who reported to Jeff Juliane, indicated that if he wanted to make a $10 million adjustment, he would simply enter that amount into a screen in AIMS. He further indicated that he simply allocated those improper adjustments to the FAS 91 types with the largest catch-up associated with them.[332] That process for allocating adjustments provides further evidence of the lack of reliability of the unamortized premium and discount accounting balances for the various groups of mortgages and securities.

The ability of a user to input on-top adjustments directly into AIMS is indicative of the lack of controls around the amortization process. Indeed, it appears that AIMS may have been intentionally designed to make auditing that process difficult, if not impossible. A March 12, 1999, memorandum detailing the original objectives for AIMS had as one objective, "[i]s easily auditable." However, a hand-written note alongside that proposed objective asks, "are we sure this is a prime objective?"[333]

Abuse of FAS 91 in 1998. In 1998 the Enterprise used non-GAAP FAS 91 accounting and its materiality threshold policy to justify deferring $199 million of $439 million of premium and discount amortization (PDA) expense.[334] That deferral, along with the LIHTC adjustment described in the following section, allowed management to meet its 1998 earnings targets and achieve maximum AIP bonus payouts. On January 8, 1999, the Office of the Chairman and KPMG were both made aware that the $240 million PDA expense adjustment for 1998 was significantly understated. Ms. Spencer indicated that Mr. Raines was aware that the full amount was not recorded.

> Ms. Spencer believed that the full amount of the catch-up had been disclosed to the Chairman. She recalled a discussion at the 1999 Plan meeting in which the attendees were informed about the work that had been done with respect to the catch-up, that $240 million would be recorded, and that $200 million would be left on the table to be "remeasured." According to Ms. Spencer, the rationale for the decision to leave $200 million unrecorded was fully disclosed and Raines was comfortable with it. [335]

KPMG workpapers show that the outside auditors knew that the full amount of the PDA adjustment was not recorded in 1998 and that Fannie Mae senior management intended to defer the unrecorded portion to future years. They also disclose the KPMG auditor's position that the additional $199 million should be recorded:

> ...the SFAS 91 adjustment for the entire portfolio was estimated at approximately $439 million.
>
> The company has proposed recording an adjustment of $240 million in 1998 and $135 million in 1999. The Company has made this proposal based on the facts that the calculation and projection of premium/discount amortization is complicated and imprecise.
>
> While the company can support its argument that premium/discount amortization is based on numerous assumptions and is a subjective calculation, their budgeting and planning processes use the same projected interest rate environment as the premium/discount calculation, and therefore, it is KPMG's position that the company should book the full amount of the indicated SFAS 91 adjustment and therefore proposes the following audit difference. [336]

Although the KPMG auditors initially took the position that the additional $199 million should be recorded and therefore posted an audit difference for that amount,[337] KPMG subsequently agreed to waive its audit difference on the grounds that it was immaterial.[338]

Partners Ken Russell and Julie Theobald, and senior manager Eric Smith, signed the following statement in waiving the $199 million PDA and other audit differences as of December 31, 1998:

> I have evaluated the above audit differences individually and in the aggregate, and determined that the waived audit differences would not have material effect on the financial statements as a whole.

The unrecorded additional $199 million ($439 million less $240 million) of PDA expense was, however, material to 1998 earnings. Not booking that expense increased EPS by about 12.5 cents – from $3.11 to the $3.23 that was actually reported to the public on January 14, 1999, and in the 1998 Annual Report, including the audited financial statements.[339]

> In waiving the audit difference, KPMG auditors failed to implement the materiality guidance issued by their own Department of Professional Practice. During the three months prior to the waiver, that department had issued several letters describing the focus on earnings management by the SEC and the press. In a discussion of former SEC Chairman Levitt's September 28, 1998, speech, one of those letters noted an earnings management gimmick related to materiality that was particularly relevant to Fannie Mae's FAS 91 accounting:
>
> "Materiality" or "abuse of materiality," by intentionally recording errors within a defined percentage ceiling that is deemed "immaterial" to achieve a desired reporting result. [340]
>
> The SEC staff has indicated that they view materiality with respect to "on purpose" errors as close to zero.

Another KPMG letter also referred to Chairman Levitt's speech on September 28, 1998:

> One of the "gimmicks" identified was "the misuse" of the concept of materiality in preparing financial statements by intentionally not adjusting for errors that are less than a defined materiality level (i.e., immaterial misapplications of generally accepted accounting principles). The SEC rejects the notion that the concept of materiality can be used to excuse deliberate misstatements and has further indicated that materiality is not a bright-line cutoff of three or five percent.

Rather, it requires consideration of all relevant factors (qualitative as well as quantitative) that could impact an investor's decision.[341] The KPMG lead and engagement partners and senior manager appear not to have adequately considered the firm's own practice letters at the time of their January 13, 1999, audit sign-off, which was the day before Fannie Mae issued its earnings release.[342] Neither senior management nor KPMG disclosed the $199 million audit difference to the Audit Committee of Fannie Mae's Board of Directors at the Committee's February 16, 1999, meeting, although KPMG had previously disclosed it to Audit Committee Chair Thomas Gerrity.[343] The minutes of that meeting report the following pronouncement delivered by Mr. Russell:

> Mr. Russell advised the Audit Committee that during their 1998 audit, KPMG had no disagreements with management, did not become aware of any consultations management may have had with other auditors, discussed no major accounting or auditing issues with management in connection with their reappointment as auditors, and encountered no difficulties in completing the audit.[344]

At the same meeting, the minutes report Mr. Howard's praise of Mr. Russell's keen technical knowledge in introducing a proposed resolution to appoint KPMG to be the company's external auditors for the 1999 fiscal year:

> Mr. Howard introduced a proposed resolution to appoint KPMG to be the corporation's auditors for 1999. He stated that KPMG has maintained a high rate of staff continuity which has ensured excellent service and minimum disruption of daily activities. He noted Mr. Russell's keen technical knowledge has added much value to the company over the past couple of years.

Low Income Housing Tax Credits (LIHTC)

Before 1998, Fannie Mae accounted for its low income housing tax credit (LIHTC) equity investments on a cash basis. Cash-basis accounting did not comply with GAAP and created a cookie jar reserve of deferred earnings that Fannie Mae used to manipulate income to achieve earnings targets in 1998.[345]

Although management had planned to release the deferred earnings from its LIHTC investments into 1999 income, it made a year-end adjustment to book the earnings for 1998 in order to offset the year-end expense adjustment associated with premium and discount amortization discussed in the previous section. Had senior management not dipped into the LIHTC cookie jar to offset the PDA adjustment, Fannie Mae would not have met the predicted earnings per share targets. While Fannie Mae's 1998 Annual Report disclosed that additional LIHTC tax benefits and PDA amortization were recorded in the fourth quarter of 1998, the report and the attendant audited financial statements did not adequately disclose the true nature and appropriate accounting for those year-end adjustments.

The Tax Reform Act of 1986 created the LIHTC Program, and the Omnibus Budget Reconciliation Act of 1993 made it permanent.[346] The tax credits are allowable each year over a 10-year period and are subject to recapture of losses over a 15-year period, starting with the first year tax credits are earned.[347] Fannie Mae, a large investor in LIHTC limited partnerships, first purchased such interests in 1987.[348] From 1987 to 1998, Fannie Mae accounted for its limited partnership interests on a cash or tax basis instead of on an accrual basis, as required by GAAP.[349]

Fannie Mae's management was aware that accounting for its LIHTC equity investments on a cash basis created an off-balance sheet cookie jar reserve of deferred earnings at least as early as May 1996 when a document prepared by Ms. Spencer indicated that management was able to choose a fiscal period in which to change from cash to accrual accounting and thereby recognize two years worth of LIHTC tax credits: [350]

> In the period we should chose [*sic*] to change to an accrual method, you simply pull forward the projections and in the year of change, you recognize two year's worth of activity.

In 1998, Fannie Mae's forecasts had indicated that the extra earnings boost from a LIHTC accounting change would be needed in the following year. A number of documents from 1998 plainly reveal the intent of Fannie Mae management to boost 1999 earnings per share by switching LIHTC from cash to accrual accounting.[351] An example is a note from Ms. Spencer and Janet Pennewell, Vice President for Financial Reporting and Planning, to Larry Small, President and Chief Operating Officer, in November 1998 while he was preparing remarks for an officers' meeting. The note suggested not disclosing to officers outside "the inner circle" or to the KPMG auditors Fannie Mae's intent to release the deferred earnings into 1999 income:

> Were you talking about the accounting change [?] Nothing that you state is incorrect. However, we would like to soften it a little. Technically, if you "know" about a [*sic*] accounting change you are supposed to book it. We haven't informed KPMG that we intend to implement this next year and our preference would be to not talk to them about it prior to year-end 1998 so they don't say "book it" at year-end. We've limited discussion of this to the inner circle, so wouldn't want to broadcast it to the officer group at this point.

Suggested Re-wording

> ...on it in the 90's. In 1999 the biggest incremental gain on our tax line will come from our low income housing tax credit portfolio. We will get to recognize some serious book accounting benefit from this portfolio in 1999 which will improve the tax line by $138 million in 1999 alone. 352

That note shows the initial determination of Fannie Mae senior management to wait and book the LIHTC accounting adjustment for the 1999 fiscal year.[353] Near year-end 1998, however, management realized that a substantial adjustment increasing premium and discount amortization expense would be required under FAS 91 because mortgage prepayments were higher than expected.[354] Accordingly, they decided to book $240 million of additional PDA expense. Because that increase in PDA expense would have an adverse impact on 1998 earnings, they decided in January 1999 to help offset that expense by taking the LIHTC cookie jar of deferred earnings into 1998 income. Using a January 8, 1999, catch-up journal entry, Fannie Mae recorded the LIHTC accounting change as of December 1998, which net of tax effect produced a gain of $109 million.[355] The $240 million PDA adjustment on an after-tax basis was $156 million.[356] The PDA adjustment and the partially offsetting LIHTC adjustment were presented separately on January 8, 1999, to the Office of the Chairman and to the KPMG auditors, just six days before they were reflected in the 1998 earnings numbers that Fannie Mae released on January 14, 1999.[357]

The timing of the LIHTC adjustment increased EPS by nearly 10.5 cents.[358] Aggregate EPS without the LIHTC adjustment and $199 million FAS 91 expense deferral would have been about $3.00 per share or about 22 cents less than the $3.22 analyst consensus at the end of the year. [359] The growth in EPS for 1998 over 1997 would have been about 6 percent, substantially less than the 14 percent that Fannie Mae management was able to report thanks to the manipulative timing of the LIHTC adjustment and the $199 million underreporting of PDA.[360] Had Fannie Mae not dipped into the $109 million LIHTC cookie jar and also not deferred, but instead recorded, the $199 million of PDA expense, the Enterprise would have been unable to (1) meet or exceed Wall Street analysts' EPS expectations, (2) produce impressive double-digit growth in EPS, and (3) ensure the payout of 1998 bonuses to Fannie Mae executives.[361]

The 1998 KPMG "tax" workpapers indicate that the external auditors verified the amount of the $109 million LIHTC adjustment. Those workpapers record the following statement regarding Fannie Mae's tabulation of the components of that adjustment:

> Fannie Mae was recording current year low income housing tax credits for GAAP based on prior year numbers. In 1998 a system was implemented which will allow Fannie Mae to record actual credit amounts for GAAP. Also, for GAAP, depreciation was calculated on a tax

basis. This was adjusted to a GAAP basis in 1998. KPMG assurance tested Fannie Mae's calculations.[362]

While the KPMG personnel may have tested Fannie Mae's calculations of the $109 million amount, they failed to recognize that taking the entire $109 million cookie jar into 1998 income did not conform to GAAP. The LIHTC adjustment was significant and should have been have treated as a correction of an error with adjustments to prior periods.[363] The theoretical basis for correcting an error in accounting for LIHTC was stated by Fannie Mae's Kim Rawls in an April 14, 1998 memorandum, which was shared with KPMG, on a change in the method of depreciating LIHTC housing units.

> Because we are accounting for these investments using the equity method, we should have been recording our share of "book" losses, not "tax" losses. As a result, the proposed change is closer to a correction of an error, however, the amount of the adjustment is immaterial and does not warrant recording a prior period adjustment through retained earnings. Because the amount of the adjustment is immaterial, I concluded that it should be accounted for in current earnings and included in miscellaneous income. 364

Because the adjustment allowed Fannie Mae to meet earnings targets and maximize Annual Incentive Plan payouts, the adjustment should have been considered material. KPMG was aware of senior management's focus on maintaining double-digit earnings growth and also the EPS link to executive compensation, both qualitative factors to be considered in evaluating the materiality of year-end adjustments. A KPMG workpaper observed:

> KPMG has initially assessed the overall inherent risk as low. Inherent to all aspects of Fannie Mae's operations is Senior Management's pressure to maintain double digit earnings growth each reporting period. In conjunction with this risk, Fannie Mae's management compensation is linked to earnings per share and stock performance.[365]

KPMG lead partner Kenneth Russell acknowledged last year that the LIHTC adjustment was significant. Other than KPMG's receipt of the Rawls memo, however, OFHEO is not aware of any documentation indicating KPMG's contemporaneous awareness or consideration of the view that the year-end 1998 LIHTC adjustment to adopt GAAP accrual accounting needed to be recorded as a correction of an error or that the amount was not material.[366]

In addition to the January 8, 1999, LIHTC journal entry not being recorded as a correction of an error, the journal entry also did not record deferred equity contributions, as required under GAAP.[367] In the course of its restatement Fannie Mae has identified other historical deficiencies in LIHTC accounting that OFHEO has confirmed.[368]

In Fannie Mae's *1998 Annual Report*, the disclosures for the year-end 1998 adjustments for LIHTC and PDA expense were deficient. The adjustments were not described as the last minute year-end adjustments that they really were, but rather as additional amounts recorded in the fourth quarter. In the case of the LIHTC adjustment, the annual report did not reveal the true nature and purpose of the underlying transaction or its dollar amount. The LIHTC disclosures on page 22 of the Annual Report made a vague reference to the recording of additional and nonrecurring LIHTC in the fourth quarter of 1998 and indicated that the additional credits resulted from improvements in systems and information to refine the timing of benefits:

> The reduction in federal income tax expense and the effective federal income tax rate for 1998 reflect the recording of additional low-income housing tax credits in the fourth quarter of 1998. The additional tax credits were a result of the corporation using improved systems and information to refine the timing of the recognition of the tax benefits associated with investments qualifying for low-income housing tax credits.

A footnote to the financial statements audited by KPMG on page 54 of the 1998 annual report contains the following statement about the additional LIHTC and PDA in a very small font size:

> Results include the recognition of additional non-recurring tax benefits associated with investments qualifying for low-income housing tax credits, and additional amortization of premiums or discounts and deferred or prepaid guaranty fees that were recorded in the fourth quarter of 1998.[369]

As to the additional PDA expense, the Management's Discussion and Analysis of Financial Condition and Results of Operations in the 1998 Annual Report discloses that additional amortization of premiums on mortgages held in portfolio and additional amortization of prepaid or guaranty fees were recorded in the fourth quarter. The dollar amounts of the additional amortization are not given, as also is not disclosed the company's decision to not record $199 million of 1998 amortization expense.[370]

While not disclosed in the *1998 Annual Report* to shareholders, dollar amounts related to the LIHTC and PDA adjustments were provided to the Board of Directors at the Board's meeting five days after the January 14, 1999, earnings release. Mr. Howard's notes from that meeting that concern the Exhibit 2 Income Statement Summary not only show the amounts of the adjustments made in the fourth quarter but also provide the following unfiltered glimpse of his *modus operandi*:

> I should note that we have not disclosed the size of these fourth quarter adjustments publicly, so you are seeing figures here that investors and analysts do not know with precision."[371]

The next page of the Mr. Howard's notes contains the following statement concerning the fourth quarter PDA adjustment:

> Taking these adjustments now will mean that we can report higher levels of net interest income and guaranty fees over the next year or two. That's one reason we made them. Another is that we had the 'room' to make them while still coming above the analysts' consensus for the year, thanks to the tax credit adjustment and the exceptional strength in net interest income due to extremely rapid growth in the second half of the year.[372]

OFHEO concludes that disclosures for the LIHTC and PDA adjustments contained in Fannie Mae's *1998 Annual Report* were inadequate and meant to mislead investors, other stakeholders, and public and private entities with non-pecuniary needs for accurate financial information concerning the Enterprise about the additional tax credits and PDA expense recorded in the fourth quarter of 1998. Given the materiality of the two adjustments and the erroneous and incomplete accounting used, OFHEO believes that the following additional disclosures should have been considered for the Annual Report:

1. That the additional amounts recorded in the fourth quarter 1998 for LIHTC and PDA were in fact year-end adjustments that were made in early January 1999, just days before the audit sign off and earnings release;
2. For the LIHTC adjustment, the dollar amount of the additional LIHTC tax benefits—$109 million on a tax-effect basis;
3. That the LIHTC accounting change resulted in including in 1998 earnings two years worth of tax credits;[373]
4. That the LIHTC adjustment resulted from changing from cash to accrual-basis accounting and therefore should have been recorded as a correction of an error;
5. The financial impact for 1998 and prior periods had the LIHTC adjustment been recorded as a correction of an error;
6. The reasons why it was not possible to implement improved LIHTC systems and information in earlier years;
7. That the LIHTC adjustment was timed to specifically offset a $240 million PDA adjustment that was recorded, which was $156 million on a tax-effect basis; [374]
8. That $199 million of 1998 PDA expense was not recorded, which was $129 million of a tax effect basis; [375] and
9. The aggregate and individual effect on 1998 net income and EPS of not recording the LIHTC adjustment as a correction of an error and failing to record $199 million of PDA expense.

Overall, the accounting and external auditing practices, internal controls, and management oversight relating to the 1998 LIHTC and FAS 91 PDA amortization adjustments were seriously deficient and allowed for unsafe and unsound financial reporting practices by management. Those reporting practices subverted the accuracy of 1998 financial reporting of earnings and earnings trends to investors and regulatory authorities and also allowed for the improper payment of Annual Incentive Plan bonuses.

Allowance for Loan Loss (ALL)

The senior management at Fannie Mae did not maintain its allowance for loan loss (ALL) at a level commensurate with the risk of its credit portfolio, as GAAP requires. Instead, CFO Timothy Howard insisted that the allowance be kept at an excessive level, maintaining that it was a cushion to protect against volatility in the loan loss line. Fannie Mae did not have adequate internal controls, policies, practices, and procedures to determine the adequacy of the allowance account, which provided management with the opportunity to use the ALL to manage earnings.

Authoritative Accounting Literature. GAAP stipulates that the allowance for loan loss should be established at a level adequate but not excessive to cover probable credit losses (1) related to specifically identified loans and (2) inherent in the remainder of the loan portfolio as of the balance sheet date.[376] Under SEC Staff Accounting Bulletin (SAB) 102, financial institutions and SEC registrants must provide a description of the process used to establish the allowance, an explanation of how estimates were derived and applied, and an analysis of changes in the allowance. Relevant accounting literature acknowledges that management's determination of an adequate allowance requires significant judgment, applied in a systematic, consistent, and disciplined manner.

Mr. Howard's Cushion. As described below, for a number of years, several members of Fannie Mae's staff viewed its allowance for loan loss as excessive. The allowance was approximately $800 million in 1998 and remained relatively unchanged through 2003.[377] Fannie Mae's current accounting policy staff has been unable to find documentation to support the ALL during the restatement period (2002-2004) and believes that there was minimal documentation.[378] That lack of documentation, together with Fannie Mae's failure to maintain an appropriate allowance level, resulted in the misstatement of the Enterprise's operations and overall financial condition, and, as such, represents a serious lapse in safety and soundness.

Beginning as early as 1997, Office of the Controller staff—Ms. Spencer, Mr. Boyles, then-Director for Accounting and Audit, and Morgan Whitacre, Manager for Business Planning—were uncomfortable with the size of Fannie Mae's loss allowance. They cited a typical industry coverage ratio of two times total annual credit losses and said that, given projected base case losses and the current allowance level, Fannie Mae would not have to add to the allowance for five years.[379] A principal source of the problem was Fannie Mae's exclusion from loan losses of selling costs, which lowered reported losses. Fannie Mae offset reported losses with proceeds from mortgage insurance and other credit enhancements, which included amounts for selling costs, in many cases resulting in accounting gains. In a rising housing price environment, and with the Enterprise's increased use of mortgage insurance and other credit enhancements, Fannie Mae's net charge-offs became negative, requiring a negative provision to keep the allowance balance at $800 million.[380] Charge-offs were negative from 1998 through 2002.[381]

Fannie Mae staff continually lobbied Mr. Howard to change Fannie Mae's loss allowance methodology over that period. During a "methodology review," in the fall of 1998 Mr. Whitacre sent Mr. Howard an analysis that reflected that the allowance was too high in all except very unfavorable loss scenarios.[382] At year-end 2000, Mr. Whitacre prepared a presentation specifically pointing to SEC, FASB, and AICPA concerns "that loss reserves were being used to manage earnings."[383]

Mr. Howard consistently resisted lowering the loss reserve, which he wished to use, counter to its proper purpose, as a cushion to protect against volatility in the loss line. In his year-end performance evaluation of Ms. Spencer, he objected to Mr. Whitacre's presentation, apparently delivered by Mr. Whitacre's boss, Ms. Pennewell, writing: "My main concern on this issue is that we not get into a situation where, when losses start rising, our proposed new policy results in our needing to add large amounts to our loss allowance in addition to covering our credit losses. Yet the proposal she presented to me a few weeks ago would, in my view have done exactly that."

Fannie Mae appears to have reviewed its loan loss allowance approach near the end of every year, and every year Mr. Whitacre and other members of the Controller's staff raised the issues of loan loss accounting, excessively high loss reserves, and proposed methodology changes. At year-end 2001, Office of the Controller staff again recommended a change in loss allowance methodology, pointing out that Fannie Mae was not operating consistent with SAB 102, issued earlier that year.[384]

Management Considers Inappropriate Uses of the Cookie Jar. Although Fannie Mae does not appear ever to have drawn down the loss allowance for inappropriate purposes, there are instances where the Enterprise considered using it in that way. In a January 1999 planning exercise, an analysis prepared by Mr. Whitacre appears to have considered drawing down

$100 million of loss reserves to meet EPS goals. (That drawdown still would have left loss reserves excessively high.) The drawdown apparently did not occur.

In 2002 Adolfo Marzol, Executive Vice President and Chief Credit Officer, was concerned about the potential volatility in the markets for the manufactured housing bonds, noting that Other-Than-Temporary Impairments could affect earnings. Fannie Mae held discussions with KPMG to gain approval for a credit loss accounting model in which the Enterprise would charge manufactured housing bond impairments against the allowance so those expenses would not flow through fee and other income. KPMG advised Fannie Mae that the impairments must flow through earnings.[385]

Evidence of Managing the Loss Line. For the period during which Fannie Mae maintained the Loss Allowance steady at $800 million, the Enterprise's effective policy was to set provisions equal to charge-offs. The consistency of forecast charge-offs with actual charge-offs two years hence suggests Fannie Mae may have manipulated its reported losses to meet earnings goals. A January 1999 planning document showed four possible alternative loss scenarios for the years 1998 through 2000, and actual losses recorded in 1999 and 2000 exactly equaled the amounts shown in most of those scenarios.[386] When asked by OFHEO how Fannie Mae could so precisely forecast losses two years away, during a period of volatile interest rates and credit losses, Mr. Whitacre, who was responsible for the Allowance, responded, "[w]e were good at forecasting."[387]

Despite all the discussion and emphasis on the proper accounting literature, at the end of the third quarter of 2003, KPMG concluded that the allowance for loan loss, which then totaled $799.6 million, conformed to GAAP and SEC guidance.[388] However, KPMG contradicted that conclusion when it commented that Fannie Mae was continuing to improve its documentation for certain exposures that fell outside of the formalized models and noted that it was continuing discussions with Fannie Mae regarding the documentation for the other projected risks that were part of the unallocated portion of the allowance.[389]

Lack of Supporting Documentation and Controls. OFHEO and Fannie Mae's internal auditors found inadequate support and documentation for the Enterprise's allowance for loan loss throughout the period under review. An October 28, 2004, OFHEO examination memorandum recommended that Fannie Mae implement corrective action necessary to comply with the provisions of the SEC's SAB 102.[390] An internal audit report of December 15, 2003, raised several key concerns, including lack of consistent application of key assumptions, application controls, and data limitations, during the review of the allowance for loan loss.[391] With respect to application controls, the audit noted that there were no built-in system controls or formal manual process in place to ensure integrity. There was also no evidence of reconciliations to ensure data integrity. As a result, unauthorized changes could be made to programs and data due to shortfalls in access security.

Income Tax Reserves

Income tax reserves, like certain aspects of the allowance for loan loss, are governed by FAS 5, *Accounting for Contingencies*.[392] FAS 5 requires that a liability for a tax contingency be recognized when it is probable and the amount can be reasonably estimated. A company may not reserve for general contingencies.[393] Fannie Mae did not have a written accounting policy for determining tax reserves. The Enterprise did not maintain documentation to support the process for determining the quarterly tax reserve figures. Nonexistent or weak controls surrounding the tax reserve process may have allowed the recording of amounts in the tax reserve that were not connected directly to a known tax liability.

Management at Fannie Mae maintained that they reviewed the income tax reserve on a quarterly basis at a meeting attended by personnel from the Corporate Tax and Legal Departments. It has been asserted that participants at those meetings came to a consensus by considering existing precedent and the degree of uncertainty surrounding each issue.[394] Minutes of the meetings were not kept, however, and Fannie Mae has produced no written policies surrounding the meetings. Inadequate documentation to support the tax reserve was noted as a deficiency in the most recent internal *Fannie Mae Audit Report*.[395] OFHEO also considers the absence of documentation to support the process for establishing the tax reserve to be a deficiency, especially since a 1996 memo from Ms. Spencer to Mr. Howard suggested that management may have recorded amounts into this tax reserve for inappropriate earnings management purposes.[396]

Without proper policies, procedures, and documentation in place it is not possible to determine whether the recorded tax reserve was appropriate at the end of any given quarter. In at least one instance in 1996, however, we do know that the weakness in the control process provided the opportunity for Ms. Spencer to record an amount to the tax reserve that was not directly connected to a known tax liability. The absence of a written policy and robust controls around tax reserves was an unsafe and unsound practice.

Conclusion

The examples discussed in this chapter illustrate a number of ways in which certain members of senior management at Fannie Mae deliberately exploited accounting weaknesses to manipulate the public image of the Enterprise and further their own economic interests. They avoided making the investments needed to develop systems and policies adequate to ensure compliance with applicable accounting standards. Senior executives provided selective and misleading information to regulators and other oversight authorities, consciously misapplied accounting standards, and engaged in transactions with no legitimate business purpose. By masking impairment losses, eliminating or deferring current expenses and income, and minimizing earnings volatility, they were able to achieve announced earnings-per-share goals year after year. In so doing, they perpetuated the image of the Enterprise as reliably generating smooth and predictable double-digit earnings at low risk and, at the same time, ensured that the maximum funds would be allocated for their annual performances bonuses. Those actions violated numerous statutory, regulatory, and other standards, constituted unsafe and unsound practices, and created unsafe and unsound conditions at Fannie Mae.

References

[1] 12 U.S.C. § 1723a(k).
[2] 12 U.S.C. § 4514.
[3] See 12 C.F.R. § 1730.

[4] OFHEO Policy Guidance, Minimum Safety and Soundness Requirements, PG-00-001 (December 19, 2000); OFHEO Policy Guidance, Safety and Soundness, 12 C.F.R. § 1720 App. A (August 30, 2002). See also Corporate Governance Regulation, 12 C.F.R. § 1710.15, requiring the Board of Directors to assure the integrity of accounting and financial reporting systems including independent audits and systems of internal control.

[5] OFHEO Policy Guidance, Minimum Safety and Soundness Requirements, PG-00-001 (December 19, 2000). OFHEO Policy Guidance, Safety and Soundness, 12 C.F.R. § 1720 App. A (August 30, 2002). See also Corporate Governance Regulation, 12 C.F.R. § 1710; OFHEO Examination Guidance Examination for Corporate Governance, PG-05-002 (May 20, 2005).

[6] OFHEO Policy Guidance, Minimum Safety and Soundness Requirements, PG-00-001 (December 19, 2000); OFHEO Policy Guidance, Safety and Soundness, 12 C.F.R. § 1720 App. A (August 30, 2002).

[7] OFHEO Policy Guidance, Minimum Safety and Soundness Requirements, PG-00-001 (December 19, 2000); OFHEO Policy Guidance, Safety and Soundness, 12 C.F.R. § 1720 App. A. (August 30, 2002). See also 12 C.F.R. § 1710.15, requiring the Board of the Enterprise to have in place policies and procedures to assure the integrity of accounting and internal controls.

[8] OFHEO Policy Guidance, Minimum Safety and Soundness Requirements, PG-00-001 (December 19, 2000); OFHEO Policy Guidance, Safety and Soundness, 12 C.F.R. § 1720 App. A (August 30, 2002). See also 12 C.F.R. § 1710.15, requiring the Board of the Enterprise to have in place policies and procedures to assure the integrity of accounting and internal controls.

[9] Report and Recommendations from Public Oversight Board's Panel on Audit Effectiveness, p. 77, 3.13 (August 31, 2000).

[10] Michael R. Young, Accounting Irregularities and Financial Fraud: A Corporate Governance Guide (2000 Edition), p. 13 n.1, cited in Report and Recommendations from Public Oversight Board's Panel on Audit Effectiveness, p. 77, 3.13 n.5 (August 31, 2000).

[11] While core business earnings is not a substitute for GAAP net income, we rely on core business earnings in operating our business because we believe core business earnings provides our management and investors with a better measure of our financial results and better reflects our risk management strategies than our GAAP net income. Fannie Mae Form 10-K, 2002, pp. 23.

[12] As directed by the Sarbanes-Oxley Act of 2002, SEC adopted a new disclosure regulation, Regulation G, which requires public companies that disclose or release such non-GAAP financial measures to include, in that disclosure or release, a presentation of the most directly comparable GAAP financial measure, and a reconciliation of the disclosed non-GAAP financial measure to the most directly comparable GAAP financial measure. See 17 CFR PARTS 228, 229, 244 and 249.

[13] Fannie Mae Form 10-K 2002, pp. 47, 49.

[14] Fannie Mae 2002 Annual Report, p. 108. See Chapter V for further details.

[15] SFAS No. 145, Rescission of FASB Statements No. 4, 44, and 64, Amendment of FASB Statement No. 13, and Technical Corrections, April 2002, p. 2.

[16] SEC Rule 10b-5 makes it unlawful for any person, "to make any untrue statement of a material fact or to omit to state a material fact necessary in order to make the statements made, in light of the circumstances under which they were made not misleading." See 17 C.F.R. § 240.10b-5, 15 U.S.C. § 78j.

[17] See the discussion under "Debt Repurchases," infra, for further information on that topic.

[18] If the insurance contracts have the effect of transferring significant risk, then they could potentially be accounted for as an insurance agreement and not as a financing agreement (similar to a loan).

[19] As you know Fannie Mae is not an SEC registrant [and] therefore is not subject to SEC reporting rules, however, we do strive to make every effort to follow SEC guidelines where we believe they are applicable. As such, our Annual Report is structured much like a 10-K.

[20] Presentation to the Audit Committee of the Fannie Mae Board of Directors, "The Year in Review -- The 1998 Annual Report," February 16, 1999.

[21] Memorandum from Ken Russell to Julie Theobald and Eric Smith, "Meeting with Tim Howard – August 11, 1998," August 25, 1998, KPMG-OFHEO-070221-222. Page two of the memorandum is dated September 3, 1998.

[22] Arthur Levitt, "The Numbers Game," speech delivered at New York University September 28, 1998, pp. 1-5.

[23] Lynn Turner speech delivered to AICPA Bank and Savings Institution Annual Conference, November 6, 1998.

[24] OFHEO's September 17, 2004, Report of Findings to Date on the Special Examination of Fannie Mae (Report of Findings to Date) contains the following information about the unrecorded $200 million of amortization expense: [Management of the Enterprise] ...[i]nappropriately] deferred $200 million of estimated expense in 1998, and established and executed a plan to record this expense in subsequent fiscal years. Furthermore, the deferral of such amount enabled management of the Enterprise to receive 100% of their annual bonus compensation. Without such deferral, no bonus would have been paid out. Fourth Quarter of 1998 The genesis for many of Fannie Mae's philosophies, policies and methods began at a time of financial stress for the American economy. The genesis for many of Fannie Mae's philosophies, policies and methods began at a time of financial stress for the American economy. In the third quarter of 1998, the Russian Financial Crisis (among other things) caused dramatically lower interest rates. The resulting interest rate environment increased the propensity of consumers to prepay their existing home mortgages and refinance them at more favorable rates. The manifestation of faster prepayments adversely impacted the Enterprise. The impact of changing rates of prepayments on deferred price adjustments is a function of cumulative life to date amortization itself, and whether prepayment rates are increasing or decreasing, and whether aggregate premiums are greater or lesser than aggregate discounts with respect to the associated loans and securities. Since prepayments were increasing, Fannie Mae's amortization models showed that an estimated expense of approximately $400 [based on current information, the exact number is $439] million had been incurred. This estimated expense was the adjustment necessary to recognize the impact of changing prepayments on deferred price adjustments, consistent with the constant effective yield calculation required under

GAAP. Rather than recognizing the full amount of this estimated adjustment to income, Enterprise management decided to defer recognizing approximately one half (or $200 million) of the estimated expense. Finally, in performing their audit of the Enterprise's 1998 financial statements, Fannie Mae's independent auditor, KPMG, identified the $200 million deferred expense (the unrecorded amount) as an audit difference. As it turns out, the unrecognized estimated $200 million negative catch-up was a pre-tax effect on net income. Adjusted for taxes at the 35% statutory federal corporate income tax rate, the after tax impact on net income – upon which calculations of EPS are –made – was approximately $130 million. The tax-affected amount of deferred expense therefore, only slightly exceeded the $125 million difference between no bonus being awarded and the maximum amount being awarded. Report of Findings to Date, pp. iii, 7, 8, 9, and 12.

[25] External auditors post or cite audit differences for errors or misstatements in a client company's financial statements. Errors may result from mathematical mistakes, classification errors, or deviations from generally accepted accounting principles. When errors or misstatements are identified, the external auditor must decide whether they, individually or in the aggregate, are material to the financial statements. If not material, the external auditor may waive or not take exception to unrecorded differences that are immaterial. In February 1994, nearly four years before 1998 audit differences were posted by the KPMG external auditors, the American Institute of Certified Public Accountants (AICPA) Division for CPA Firms' Professional Issues Task Force, issued Practice Alert No. 94-1, Dealing with Audit Differences, to provide information to external auditors on the handling of audit differences. The Practice Alert reminded auditors to view audit differences in light of factors in addition to earnings and equity. As of December 31, 1998, the accumulated amount of audit differences posted by KPMG, largely attributable to the unrecorded $200 million net premium expense, was $134.3 million on an after-tax basis. On an earnings per share (EPS) basis, the 13 cents ($134.3 million ÷ 1,037 million shares) was material given the effect that recording the accumulated audit differences would have had on Fannie Mae's 1998 EPS targets and bonus compensation. KPMG workpaper BM9 dated January 1999, "Fannie Mae Audit Differences, 12/31/98," KPMG-OFHEO-443378; Fannie Mae 1998 Annual Report, p. 40.

[26] The years 1999 through 2004 represent the period OFHEO considered in its special examination of Fannie Mae. The actions discussed in this chapter are only a sample of the accounting improprieties OFHEO identified during the course of the special examination.

[27] Fannie Mae 12b-25 notification of late filing with the Securities and Exchange Commission, March 13, 2006.

[28] For details on Fannie Mae's implementation of FAS 133, see Report of Findings to Date, p. 82.

[29] Id.

[30] Timothy Howard, "Response to Recent Challenges in Risk Management, Accounting & Regulatory Oversight," speech, October 16, 2003, OFH-FNM00003774.

[31] Memorandum from Jonathan Boyles, March 3, 2003, FMSE 078540-42; "Operating earnings" was a term developed by Fannie Mae that it subsequently changed to "core business earnings." See Report of Findings to Date, p. 84.

[32] Id., p.V.

[33] Id., pp. 82-136.

[34] Form 12b-25 filing for the period ending December 31, 2005, p. 9.

[35] There are specific rules for transferring securities between categories, and removing securities from the Held-to-Maturity category is the most restricted. See Financial Accounting Standards Board, Accounting for Certain Investments in Debt and Equity Securities, Statement of Financial Accounting Standards No. 115, 1993 (FAS 115).

[36] See the Report of Counsel for the Special Review Committee (CSRC Report), pp. 238-249 for a complete discussion of misapplication of GAAP.

[37] Memorandum from James Parks to Timothy Howard and Michael Quinn, April 15, 1993, FM SRC OFHEO 00311349-00311351.

[38] OFHEO Interview, Leanne Spencer, December 9, 2004, pp. 103-103 (VI.22000); OFHEO Interview, Jonathon Boyles, December 7, 2004, pp. 90-94. The Intra-Month Redesignation is the process of reclassifying certain Held-to-Maturity securities to Available-for-Sale at month end.

[39] FAS 115, Accounting for Certain Investments in Debt and Equity Securities, (May1993), paragraphs 68-70.

[40] Consolidation under FIN 46 would require (among other things) valuing and recording in the financial statements the loans that underlie the MBS Trust.

[41] Draft memorandum, Accounting for MBS Wholly-Owned by Fannie Mae, July 30, 2003, OFH-FNM00161128, p. 2.

[42] Id.

[43] Whole Pools Update, June 19, 2003, p.2, OFH-FNM00010222,; Portfolio AFS Whole Pool Movement Analysis, May 27, 2003, p. 2, FMSE081259.

[44] Memorandum from Jennifer Liber to distribution list,, "Accounting for PPs Pools, Whole Megas and Portfolio REMICS," November 2, 2004.

[45] Memorandum from Christine LeBel to Ilene Topper, "Accounting Changes for Resecuritizations (Megas, OOP REMICS & PPS Pools) - REVISED," November 11, 2004, FM SRC OFHEO 01563003-09.

[46] OFHEO and Fannie Mae Weekly Controller Meeting Summary, February 21, 2006; Minutes of the meeting of the Audit Committee of The Board of Directors of Fannie Mae, January 23, 2006, FMSE 697412-417, p. 2.

[47] Jonathan Boyles noted that consolidation of the thousands of individual mortgage-backed security trusts would be an enormous undertaking, and that the creation of mega pools and similar strategies was a means of avoiding that burden. See CSRC Report, February 23, 2006, p. 299

[48] SFAS 140, Accounting for Transfers and Servicing of Financial Assets and Extinguishments of Liabilities – a Replacement of FASB Statement 125, paragraph 48, and SOP 90-3.

[49] See CSRC Report, February 23, 2006, pp 197-214 for a complete discussion of misapplication of GAAP. (VI.40)

[50] First Quarter Review Workpapers, Dollar Rolls/Error in Amortization of Securities and Original Acquisition Date, April 20, 2004, KPMG-OFHEO-119174--177.

[51] The error resulted in a maximum cumulative impact of $38 million and $21 million for years 2003 and 2002, respectively. See memorandum entitled "Error in Amortization of Securities Used In Dollar Rolls," FMSE-SP008397-FMSE-SP-403.

[52] Anthony Lloyd, "Dollar Rolls—STATS Overview on Process Improvements of Business Line," undated presentation.

[53] All errors which are referenced in this section as acknowledged by the Enterprise were acknowledged in their memorandum, "Accounting for Foreclosed Property (Single Family REO)" dated August 26, 2005, FMSE RST 002743 to 773.

[54] SFAS No. 15, Accounting by Debtors and Creditors for Troubled Debt Restructurings (FAS 15), Paragraph 34, which states that if a "creditor receives physical possession of the [collateral], regardless of whether foreclosure proceedings take place," then a foreclosure should be recorded.

[55] OCC's Bank Accounting Advisory Series, Topic 5A: Real Estate, #3, September 2004.

[56] CSRC report, Allowance for Loan Losses, pp. 182-188.

[57] REO assets which are designated as Held For Sale and which are carried at lower of cost or market after being recorded at cost value must be monitored for impairment. If the market value of the asset is less than its cost/carrying value, the entity must recognize the loss in value by reducing the asset to its market value from its cost basis. If market value rises back up again, then the asset can be marked back up to the new market value as long as it does not go above the cost basis, because the asset is carried at the lower of cost basis or market value.

[58] FAS 66, paragraph 3.

[59] 2004 Performance Plans for Appraisal Analysts obtained from the office of James Sartor, Manager for Valuation.

[60] Statement of Auditing Standards 99, "Consideration of Fraud in a Financial Statement Audit, SAS 99, October 2002, p. 20.

[61] OFHEO Interview, Patricia Wells, November 30, 2004, p. 161.

[62] Id., p. 163.

[63] Id., pp. 155-156.

[64] Id., p. 100.

[65] OFHEO Interview, Leanne Spencer, December 9, 2004.

[66] OFHEO Interview, Patricia Wells, November 30, 2004, p. 104.

[67] Id., p. 226.

[68] OFHEO Interview, Patricia Wells, November 30, 2004, p. 226.

[69] OFHEO Interview, Richard Stawarz, December 14, 2004, p. 229-230.

[70] Id., p. 222-230.

[71] OFHEO Interview, Patricia Wells, November 30, 2004, pp. 103-106.

[72] Id., p. 93-101.

[73] OFHEO Interview, Richard Stawarz, December 14, 2004, p. 219.

[74] OFHEO Interview, Leanne Spencer, December 9, 2004, pp. 75-76; OFHEO Interview, Patricia Wells, November 30, 2004, pp. 97-98; OFHEO Interview, Richard Stawarz, December 14, 2004, pp. 66-67.

[75] In SAB 59, SEC staff noted that the phrase "other-than-temporary" should not be interpreted to mean permanent, as has been used elsewhere in accounting practice. Whether or not an impairment is considered other-than-temporary requires investigation on the part of management. Staff Accounting Bulletin No. 59, Accounting for Noncurrent Marketable Equity Securities (SAB 59).

[76] OFHEO Letter (Armando Falcon to Franklin Raines) related to asset impairments, May 6, 2004.

[77] Fannie Mae Form 10-Q, August 9, 2004.
[78] OFHEO Memorandum from Wanda Deleo to Armando Falcon, "Accounting for Fannie Mae's Manufactured Housing Securities Portfolio," May 4, 2004.
[79] Conseco was the servicer of a large proportion of the MH securities in Fannie Mae's portfolio. It provided a certain amount of credit support for the MH securities it issued via a low servicing fee that, unlike other MH security servicers, it subordinated to the rights of the bond holders. See Conseco Manufactured Housing Bonds, FMSE 408306.
[80] Draft Memorandum, from Kenneth Barnes to Paul Saft and Angela Hairston, "Potential Impairment on Aircraft ABS and Zurich Auction Rate Preferred Stock", March 14, 2003, FMSE 047044-53 at 45.
[81] SFAS No. 107, Disclosures about Fair Value of Financial Instruments, paragraph 11.
[82] Mark to Market Comparison Schedules, FMSE 068609-068616 and E-mail: from Thomas M. Gargan to Steve Shen, "Private_Label_with_Marks.xls," September 24, 2002, FMSE 351432-433.
[83] OFHEO Draft Memorandum, "Fannie Mae's Manufactured Housing Security Cash Flow Projections," April 7, 2005.
[84] Id.
[85] CSRC also investigated Fannie Mae's impairment accounting practices. For details related to the facts of the impairment issue, see CSRC report, p. 257.
[86] Evaluation of the FAS 115 Investment Impairment Policy: pre adoption of the 4-step impairment methodology April 1, 2004, October 24, 2005, FMSE-RST-004793–819 at 797.
[87] Id., at 004798.
[88] Letter from Jonathan Boyles to Donald Nicolaisen, "Policies Related to Certain Investments in Debt Securities," April 28, 2004, FMSE 112556–66 at 64 and Memorandum from Ilene Topper to Leanne Spencer, et al., "Implementation of IO/PO Accounting in Q3 2004," October 14, 2004. KPMG OFHEO 207110-13.
[89] Memorandum from Richard DePetris to Sampath Rajappa, Leanne Spencer, et al., "Meeting on Synthetic MBS," November 27 1995, FM SRC OFHEO 00141240-41.
[90] Accounting rules would allow for combining IO securities with PO securities in certain limited circumstances. However, Fannie Mae did not disclose to KPMG the plan to combine IO securities with other securities that would not have met the accounting criteria. See EITF 98-15.
[91] E-mail from Richard DePetris to James Park, "IOs," November 27, 1995, FM SRC OFHEO 00141243.
[92] As discussed in the following section, Fannie Mae tracked potential impairments of its buy-up portfolio (buy-ups are interest-only assets, and economically equivalent to IO securities.) The Enterprise calculated impairments on buy-ups at year end 1998, under proper GAAP accounting, of approximately $500 million. It is reasonable to expect that impairments on the IO portfolio would have been of a similar order of magnitude.
[93] IO/REMIC Package Briefing, March 2, 1998, FM SRC OFHEO 00142114-19 at 15-16.
[94] CSRC Memorandum, "4/15/05 Meeting with Jonathan Boyles," May 10, 2005, p. 9.
[95] Fannie Mae Risk Assessment – Servicing/Management Process Financial Reporting 12/31/98, KPMG-OFHEO-062395.
[96] Letter from Jonathan Boyles to Donald Nicolaisen, "Policies Related to Certain Investments in Debt Securities," April 28, 2004, FMSE 112556–66 at 64.

[97] Memorandum from Ilene Topper to Leanne Spencer, et al., Implementation of IO/PO Accounting in Q3 2004, October 14, 2004. KPMG-OFHEO-207110-113.

[98] FAS 91, Accounting for Nonrefundable Fees and Costs Associated with Originating or Acquiring Loans and Initial Direct Costs of Leases – an amendment of FASB Statements No. 13, 60, and 65 and a rescission of FASB Statement No. 17, issued December 1985, effective date, December 15, 1986

[99] See, e.g., Fannie Mae Catch-up Summary, January 8, 1999, FMSE SP 0000502.

[100] Letter from Jonathan Boyles to Donald T. Nicolaisen, February 24, 2004, "A lender may wish to adjust the guaranty fee up or down … to permit the MBS to have a more tradable coupon rate (that is a pass-through rate based on a whole or half percent)." FSME 068834-47.

[101] Under the level-yield method, unamortized premiums and discounts are taken into income so as to recognize accounting income—coupon interest plus amortized premium or discount—at a constant yield over the life of an investment.

[102] FAS 125, Accounting for Transfers and Servicing of Financial Assets and Extinguishments of Liabilities, issued November 1995, effective December 15, 1995.

[103] Letter from Scott Lesmes to Scott Taub, SEC, November 15, 2005. EITF 99-20, Recognition of Interest Income and Impairment on Purchased and Retained Beneficial Interests in Securitized Financial Assets, effective March 15, 2001.

[104] FAS 125.

[105] Memorandum from Sampath Rajappa to Timothy Howard, "Buyup Accounting,." March 20, 1997. FM SRC OFHEO 00302716-17.

[106] EITF 93-18, Recognition of Impairment for an Investment in a Collateralized Mortgage Obligation Instrument or in a Mortgage Backed Interest-Only Certificate (EITF 93-18).

[107] Id..

[108] Id..

[109] Id.

[110] Email chain from Sampath Rajappa to Leanne Spencer, Jonathan Boyles, and James Parks, "Buyup Accounting," March 22, 1997, FM SRC OFHEO 00302715.

[111] FM SRC OFHEO 025747

[112] Id.

[113] Id.

[114] FM SRC OFHEO 00302714.

[115] FMSE-SP 068084.

[116] Id.

[117] Id.

[118] FMSE-SP 068085; "the market value calculations utilized "OAS values … calculated on 30yr IO trusts with wacs [weighted-average coupons] and wams [weighted-average maturities] similar to (Fannie Mae's) 30 yr FRM buyup book …. The OAS analysis used standard volatility and prepayment parameters." FMSE-SP 068042.

[119] FMSE-SP 068043-4.

[120] FM SRC OFHEO 00302696. In that document and others focusing on those issues, buy-ups are referred to as "IOs," further suggesting Fannie Mae believed that FAS 125, rather than FAS 91, should apply.

[121] Memorandum from Leanne Spencer to Rob Levin, "Enhanced Buyups," April 8, 1998, FM SRC OFHEO 00302679.

[122] FM SRC OFHEO 00302640.

[123] FM SRC OFHEO 00302643.

[124] FM SRC OFHEO 00302645.

[125] Fannie Mae considered a similar strategy as early as November 1995, when Debbie Cohen asked Richard Depetris about the feasibility of bundling IO securities with whole loans for evaluation under FAS 91. See 11/27/1995 e-mail chain among Debbie Cohen, Sampath Rajappa, James Parks, Leanne Spencer, Jonathan Boyles, Richard Depetris and Thanasis Simos, November 27, 1995, FM SRC OFHEO 00141243.

[126] FM SRC OFHEO 00302675.

[127] E-mail chain among Tom Lawler, Rob Weiss, Timothy Howard, Robert Levin, Leanne Spencer, and Adolfo Marzol, "Buyups," May 13-21, 1998, FM SRC 00196019-021.

[128] Id.

[129] Id.

[130] Russia declared a debt moratorium on August 17th; Roger Lowenstein, When Genius Failed, (New York: Random House, 2000), p. 144.

[131] FMSE-SP 068092-95, FMSE-SP 068085.

[132] Documents available to OFHEO do not explain the differences among the three market valuation methodologies. The lower figures appear in a document identified as FMSE-SP 068085.

[133] Roger Lowenstein, op cit., pp. 181, 209, 218.

[134] "Market OAS & Impairment based [on] Fannie Mae [yield] curve, zero vol. [volatility], Treasury discounting [i.e., present value calculations using the risk-free rate]," FMSE-SP 068090-91.

[135] "Applying long run OAS & Impairment based on Rate Forecast in Plan" FMSE 068088-089.

[136] FMSE-SP 068067-70; According to a December 10, 1998, note from Matt [Douthit] to Leanne [Spencer], the increase may have been due to Fannie's early October revision of its prepayment model parameters "to reflect higher observed refi sensitivity and lower observed burnout effect." FMSE-SP 068060.

[137] $310.3 vs. $308.9 million for October and December, respectively, for 30- and 15-year FRMs; FMSE-SP 068067-70, 068061-62.

[138] Note from Jonathan [Boyles] to Leanne [Spencer], December 10, 1998, FMSE-SP 068059.

[139] FMSE-SP 068061.

[140] FMSE-SP 068059.

[141] FM SRC 00269113-17 at 14.

[142] Memorandum from Matt Douthit to Leanne Spencer, "I/O Book (buyups)", January 15, 1999, FMSE-SP 068078–83 at 83.

[143] Memorandum to File from David Berman, "7/1/05 Meeting with Jonathan Boyles," August 22, 2005, FM SRC OFHEO 712448.

[144] Fannie Mae document, "Buyup Accounting History," undated and unsigned, likely dating from early 1999, FMSE-SP 068084-100.

[145] FMSE-SP 068059-60.

[146] Memorandum from Matthew Douthit to Leanne Spencer, January 15, 1999, FMSE-SP 068078-79.

[147] Memorandum from Thomas Harmon to Leanne Spencer, "IO Book (buyups)," April 5, 1999, FM SRC OFHEO 025202.

[148] FM SRC OFHEO 00311251-57 dating of the document is based on a reference to "an unamortized book balance of about $1.9 billion of buyups," the book balance as of September 30, 1998.

[149] Proposed Transaction Related to Pre FAS 122 MSRS, June 1999, FMSE-040307--040309.

[150] E-mail chain among Karen Pallotta, Leanne Spencer, and Jonathan Boyles, July 12, 1999, FMSE-SP 040305–306.

[151] Id.

[152] Id.; Fannie Mae proceeded with the IO purchase, accounted for it under FAS 125, and booked a $5 million impairment on it in June 2003. E-mail chain among Jeff Juliane, Pat Wells, and Karen Lee, January 8, 2004, FMSE-SP 027157–158.

[153] EITF 99-20, Recognition of Interest Income and Impairment on Purchased and Retained Beneficial Interests in Securitized Financial Assets, effective March 15, 2001.

[154] FAS 120, Accounting and Reporting by Mutual Life Insurance Enterprises and by Insurance Enterprises for Certain Long-Duration Participating Contracts – an amendment of FASB Statements 60, 97, and 113 and Interpretation No. 40, effective December 15, 1995.

[155] Under EITF 93-18 other-than-temporary impairment occurred when projected future cash flows, discounted at the risk-free rate, fell below amortized cost. Under 99-20 it occurs when "the present value of the remaining cash flows as estimated at the initial transaction date (or at the last date previously revised)" exceeds "the present value of the cash flows estimated at the current financial reporting date, discounted at a rate equal to the current yield used to accrete the beneficial interest.

[156] Statements of Financial Accounting Standards Nos. 125 and 140, paragraph 14.

[157] "KPMG and Freddie," FMSE 487130.

[158] FIN 45 required that guarantors such as Fannie Mae recognize a liability on its balance sheets for the fair value of the obligations associated with its guarantees. Although FIN 45 did not provide guidance concerning the required book-keeping entry offsetting a guarantee obligation (GO), both Fannie Mae and Freddie Mac chose to recognize an offsetting guarantee asset (GA) equal to the fair value of its guarantee fees. The GA consists of the fair value of guarantee fees remaining to be collected, offset by unamortized buy-up balances. Under FIN 45 buy-ups became a component of the GA—explicitly an asset—further undermining any rationale for Fannie Mae's continued application of FAS 91 accounting, based on its concept that buy-ups were not assets subject to FAS 125 and 140.

[159] See "Results of our Review of Freddie Mac Disclosures," attached to e-mail from Jonathan Boyles, November 26, 2003, OFH-FNM 00801313-319.

[160] E-mail from Jonathan Boyles to Paul Salfi, Leanne Spencer, and Scott Lesmes, March 4, 2004, OFH-FNM 00739129.

[161] Letter from Jonathan Boyles to Jackson Day, undated, follow up of earlier letter, September 5, 2002, FMSE-SP 065240.

[162] http://www.freddiemac.com /investors/ restatement/pdf/ appendix2_112103.pdf, p.15. and http://www.freddiemac.com/investors/ restatement/pdf/appendix4_112103.pdf.

[163] Draft Memorandum distributed to Franklin Raines, Timothy Howard, Daniel Mudd, Thomas Donilon, Ann Kappler, Leanne Spencer, Scott Lesmes, and KPMG. Jonathan Boyles wrote that buyups represented "the largest difference in accounting between Fannie Mae and Freddie Mac as a result of Freddie Mac's recent announcement." January 14, 2004. FMSE 326434.

[164] FMSE-E 2222929.

[165] E-mail from Jonathan Boyles to Franklin Raines, Leanne Spencer, et al., "Heard back from the SEC – follow-ups," February 20, 2004, OFH-FNM 0011602.

[166] E-mail string from Paul Salfi to Leanne Spencer, copied to Harry Argires, KPMG, "SEC," March 3, 2004," FMSE-E 2223237.

[167] E-mail from Jonathan Boyles to Paul Salfi, no subject, March 4, 2004, OFH-FNM 00739129.

[168] E-mail string among Harry Argires, Leanne Spencer, Scott Lesmes, Paul Salfi, Jonathan Boyles, et al., "sec responses," March 4, 2004, OFH-FNM 00749857-58.

[169] Letter from Jonathan Boyles to Greg Faucette, March 15, 2004. FMSE SP 103189-94.

[170] FMSE-E 2228799-805.

[171] FSME-E 2228797.

[172] Letter from Jonathan Boyles to Greg Faucette, March 15, 2004, FMSE SP 103189–94.

[173] Memorandum from Sampath Rajappa to Timothy Howard, "Buyup Accounting.," March 20, 1997, FM SRC OFHEO 00302716.

[174] Letter from Jonathan Boyles to Greg Faucette, March 15, 2004. FMSE SP 103189-94.

[175] Letter from Thomas Carberry, IRS, to Felix Laughlin, Dewey Ballantine LLP (Counsel for Fannie Mae), "Federal National Mortgage Association Tax Years: 1996-1998," February 22, 2005 states that 75% of STIS transaction is not allowed. The increase to taxable income for 1998 is $730,625,285. The taxable increase of $730,625,285 times 1.3333 (which is 1.00/ .75 the amount of the disallowed portion of the STIS deduction) results in a total taxable adjustment without the STIS for Fannie Mae of $974,167,046. The corporate tax rate for 1998 is 35%. The total reduction in taxes for 1998, attributed to the STIS transaction, is $340,958,466. FMSE 528369.

[176] An undated IRS form 886-A shows an proposed adjustment to Fannie Mae's Year 2000 taxable income of $349,726,187. FMSE 524058. Using the same logic and formula described in the preceding footnote, the year 2000 tax liability was reduced in year 2000 by $163,205,553.

[177] E-mail from Mariam Vrnikia to James Harrington, "STIS", April 1, 1998, FMSE 525647.

[178] Memorandum from William Einstein and Sampath Rajappa to Timothy Howard, "Short-Term Interest Securities (STIS): An Executive Summary," March 19, 1998, FSME 519904-906.

[179] Spreadsheet, "STIS Capitalized Expenses," shows an entry for KPMG under GL 1661-53, "Deferred STIS Program Setup," of $1.8 Million, Undated. FMSE 522210. An IRS Form 886-A regarding the STIS 2000 transaction taxable income review shows an entry for a KPMG fee of $250,000, undated. FMSE 521016.

[180] Internal Revenue Code par. 1.1286-1(a) (as quoted in an Ernst & Young letter to Lehman Brothers), June 27, 1996. FMSE 527213-23 at 220.

[181] Letter from Thomas Carberry, IRS, to Felix Laughlin, Dewey Ballantine LLP, "Federal National Mortgage Association Tax Years: 1996-1998," February 22, 2005. FMSE 528369.

[182] See IRS Form 886 Undated, description of FNMA 2000 STIS transaction, FMSE 524058-61.

[183] E-mail chain from Deborah Cohen to Carolyn Swift and Michael Daze, "Re:Help", July 14, 1997, FMSE 527717

[184] Powerpoint presentation to Fannie Mae by Lehman Brothers, "Money Market STRIPS," May 12, 1997, FMSE 520149–158 at 158.

[185] E-mail from William Einstein to Deborah Cohen, "RE(2): Meeting w/Lehman and E&Y," May 14, 1997, FSME 520419; OFHEO Interview, Sampath Rajappa, February 23, 2006, pp. at 113-15.

[186] FMSE 520248–49.

[187] OFHEO Interview, Sampath Rajappa, February 23, 2006, pp. at 115-16.

[188] Id., p. 117.

[189] Id., pp. 113-15

[190] FMSE 520233

[191] FMSE 520235-238 at 235.

[192] OFHEO Interview, Sampath Rajappa, February 23, 2006, p. 126.

[193] The notes are written on fax transmittal memorandum addressed to Mr. William Einstein; they match the handwriting of other notes he appears to have written.

[194] FMSE 520213.

[195] FMSE 519904-06.

[196] FSME 520686.

[197] STIS Capital Expense Analysis, FMSE 522210; Form 886, FMSE 521016; Fannie Mae Short-Term Interest Securities – Opportunity for Pre-Tax Economic Profit, FM SRC OFHEO 00973814.

[198] FMSE 519904-06.

[199] Id.

[200] Side letter signed by Paul Friedman for Bear Stearns, and Debbie Cohen for Fannie Mae, March 31, 1998, FMSE 522307-13.

[201] A REMIC is a vehicle for issuing multi-class mortgage-backed securities which allows the issuer to treat the transaction as a sale of assets for tax and accounting purposes.

[202] Figures for REMIC 2001-81 from "Summary of $20 billion December REMIC Transaction, FMSE 479807 figures for REMIC 2002-21 from "Summary of $30 billion REMIC Transaction Across March, April, and May" ("March deal" column) FSME-SP 010188.

[203] E-mail from Ramon DeCastro to Peter Niculescu, Tom Lawler, Andrew McCormick, Laurie Zeller; copies to Timothy Howard and Sharon Stieber, December 19, 2001, FSME 490136-7.

[204] Figures for REMIC 2001-81 from "Summary of $20 billion December REMIC Transaction FMSE 479807 figures for REMIC 2002-21 from "Summary of $30 billion REMIC Transaction Across March, April, and May" ("March deal" column) FSME-SP 010188.

[205] Statement of Financial Accounting Standards No. 140, paragraphs 56, 58, and 182.

[206] Id., paragraph 58.

[207] Id., paragraph 36.

[208] FAS 140, paragraph 17.

[209] CSRC Memorandum, "Summary of 3/2/05 Interview with Tom Lawler," March 14, 2005, pp. 9-10.

[210] CSRC Memorandum "Interview of Andrew McCormick on March 8 and March 15, 2005," April 6, 2005, p. 6.

[211] FMSE 503623-34.

[212] FMSE 503625.

[213] OFHEO Interview, Thomas Lawler, June 24, 2004, p. 102.

[214] CSRC Memorandum, "Summary of 3/2/05 Interview with Tom Lawler," March 14, 2005, FM SRC OFHEO 00142019-28, at 28.

[215] E-mail string between Jeffrey Juliane and Christine LeBel, April 24, 2003, FSME 022526.

[216] OFHEO Interview, Thomas Lawler, June 24, 2004, p. 103.

[217] CSRC Memorandum, "Summary of 3/2/05 Interview with Tom Lawler," March 14, 2005, p. 9. FM SRC OFHEO 00142019-28, at 28. Since the mid-1990's, Freddie Mac had been issuing far more REMICs than Fannie Mae. Although REMIC issuance was an insignificant factor in terms of earnings, and not nearly as important as relative portfolio size to an Enterprise's competitive position, it was a matter of corporate pride. In 2000, a slow year for REMICs, Freddie Mac issued $48.2 billion vs. Fannie Mae's $39.5 billion. Toward the end of 2001, the most active year for REMICs issuance since 1993, Fannie Mae trailed Freddie Mac badly. The December transaction boosted Fannie Mae's REMIC issuance to $139.4 billion, still far behind Freddie Mac's year-end total of $192.4 billion. OFHEO 2005 Annual Report, pp. 29, 45.

[218] CSRC Memorandum, "Summary of 4/30/05 interview of Ramon DeCastro re: REMIC transactions", May 9, 2004, p. 8. FM SRC OFHEO 00142029.

[219] CSRC Memorandum, "Interview of Andrew McCormick on March 8 and March 15, 2005," April 6, 2005, p. 6. FM SRC OFHEO 00226642.

[220] Id., p. 5.

[221] CSRC Memorandum "Summary of 4/30/05 interview of Ramon DeCastro re: REMIC transactions," May 9, 2004, Op. Cit. p. 4. FM SRC OFHEO 00142019, 00142027-29 at 28-29. The other Portfolio executives were Thomas Lawler and Andrew McCormick.

[222] FMSE 479847.

[223] OFHEO Interview, Thomas Lawler, June 24, 2004, p. 104.

[224] CSRC Memorandum, "Summary of 03/02/05 interview with Tom Lawler", March 14, 2005, p. 11. FM SRC OFHEO 00142029.

[225] OFHEO Interview, Thomas Lawler, June 24, 2004, p. 106.

[226] E-mail exchange between Laurie Zeller and Jonathan Boyles, December 27, 2001, FMSE 490147.

[227] CSRC Memorandum, "Summary of April 14, 2005 interview with Sharon Stieber, "re: REMIC transactions", May 6, 2004, p. 4. FM SRC OFHEO 00227017.

[228] CSRC Memorandum, "Interview of Andrew McCormick on March 8 and March 15, 2005," April 6, 2005, p. 9 FM SRC OFHEO 00226646, and CSRC Memorandum, "Summary of 03/02/05 interview with Tom Lawler", March 14, 2005, p. 11. FM SRC OFHEO 00142029.

[229] CSRC Memorandum, "Summary of April 14, 2005 interview with Sharon Stieber, "re: REMIC transactions," May 6, 2005, p. 4.

[230] E-mail from Ramon DeCastro to Peter Niculescu, Thomas Lawler, Andrew McCormick, Laurie Zeller; copies to Timothy Howard and Sharon Stieber, December 19, 2001, FSME 490136-37.

[231] E-mail string among Timothy Howard, Peter Niculescu, Ramon DeCastro, Jayne Shontell, Janice Daue, and Sharon Stieber, "Re: Rumors on December REMIC" and attachments, December 20, 2001, FMSE 490140-44. `

[232] FMSE 490430-31.

[233] CSRC Memorandum, "Summary of 4/30/05 interview of Ramon DeCastro re: REMIC transactions," May 9 2004, p. 14.

[234] OFHEO Interview, Sharon Stieber, May 5, 2004, p. 2.

[235] Fannie Mae Guaranteed Grantor Trust Pass-Through Certificates, Fannie Mae Grantor Trust 2002-T8, Prospectus, p. 19.

[236] Telephone conversation with OFHEO on August 15, 2005, memorialized in an internal OFHEO e-mail message of September 8, 2005.

[237] Fannie Mae 2002 Annual Report, p. 100.

[238] Testimony Concerning Transparent Financial Reporting for Structured Finance Transactions by Annette L. Nazareth, *www.sec.gov/news/testim ony/121102tsan.htm.*

[239] Fannie Mae 2003 Annual Report, pp. 100-101.

[240] Fannie Mae 2001 Annual Report, p. 55.

[241] E-mail exchange between Laurie Zeller and Jonathan Boyles, December 27, 2001, FMSE 490147 (VI.233A)

[242] "In these instances we measure our retained interests by allocating the carrying amount of the assets we retained based on their fair value at the transfer date relative to the assets we sold." Fannie Mae 2002 Annual Report, p. 100.

[243] At a minimum, Fannie Mae should have considered whether the changing value of the residual interest--negative in the early years of the transaction and positive in the later years - might at some point disqualify the QSPE. In instances when Fannie Mae sold the residual interest, given its increasing value over time, it might reasonably assume, when its retained interests represented pro rata shares of collateral cash flows, that its ownership interest would never exceed 90 percent. However, when the Enterprise retained residual interest as part of its 90 percent retention at inception, the increasing value of the residual eventually might cause Fannie Mae's ownership to exceed 90 percent. Although Fannie Mae sold the residual interest from the $20 billion December 2001 REMIC, it retained the residual from a relatively small, $1 billion income-shifting REMIC it completed the previous month. That $1 billion transaction was something of a dry run for the December deal.

[244] "Summary of $20 billion December REMIC Transaction," FMSE 479807.

[245] CSRC Memorandum "Summary of 4/30/05 interview of Ramon DeCastro re: REMIC transactions," May 9 2004, p. 9. Mr. DeCastro stated "that there was no special approval process in place for OOPS [out of portfolio securitization] transactions, such as the GS [Goldman Sachs] REMIC transactions," and he did not recall anyone raising any issues or concerns about that.

[246] E-mail from Ramon DeCastro to Al Barbieri, et al., "Fwd: December REMIC transaction," December 12, 2001, FMSE 490178-80.

[247] Because the pricing differential on the various maturity REMIC securities was affected through premium and discount pricing, realization of the varying yields of the securities over time depended on the accurate amortization of the varying premiums and discounts.

[248] E-mail from Jeff Juliane to Distribution, "June PDI Numbers," July 15, 2002, FMSE 024211.

[249] June 27, 2003 E-mail from Rene Le Rouzes to Roger Barnes, "Fwd: Re: (no subject)," June 27, 2003, FMSE 024211-12.

[250] E-mail from Roger Barnes to Stephen Spivey, "Items Today," May 7, 2002, "I was informed today, by an analyst in the Finance Division, that Fannie Mae is consciously using the REMICS to reduce short-term income. This is not illegal but calls into question our duty to shareholders and investors. Top management is creating the structured transactions to take losses now. Per Janet, Frank and Tim feel there is enough income locked in for 2002 that we do not need to worry about meeting this year's goals. Further, indicated the amortization of deferred items provides a vehicle to manage to 'Plan.'" FMSE 341795.

[251] Fannie Mae Form 10-K 2003, p. 38.

[252] Calculated by dividing the loss amount by the Weighted Average Diluted Common Shares from Fannie Mae's Annual Reports.

[253] Fannie Mae 1998 Annual Report, p. 43, and 2000 Annual Report

[254] SFAS No. 145, Rescission of FASB Statements No. 4, 44, and 64, Amendment of FASB Statement No. 13, and Technical Corrections, April 2002, p. 2, and SEC Rule 10b-5 makes it unlawful for any person, "to make any untrue statement of a material fact or to omit to state a material fact necessary in order to make the statements made, in light of the circumstances under which they were made not misleading." See: 17 C.F.R. § 240.10b-5, 15 U.S.C. § 78j.

[255] Among other things, risk management involves portfolio rebalancing activity in response to changes in interest rates, so Fannie Mae can better match the durations of its assets and liabilities. When falling interest rates stimulate mortgage refinancings, accelerating mortgage prepayments and shortening the duration of Fannie Mae's mortgage portfolio, the Enterprise may wish to shorten the duration of its liabilities to achieve better matching. To accomplish that, it may redeem its callable long term debt at par, and/or repurchase non-callable long-term debt at its market price, and replace it with new, shorter-term debt. The exercise of cancellation options for fixed-pay swaps is equivalent to the redemption of callable debt. The cancellation of swaps without a cancellation option in exchange for a payment to the counterparty equal to their market value is the financial equivalent of the repurchase of non-callable debt.

[256] Off-the-run securities are securities trading in the secondary market at premiums and discounts, with yields-to-maturity higher than those of newly-issued, current-coupon securities of the same maturity.

[257] CSRC Memorandum, "Summary of 1/4/06 CSRC interview with Peter Niculescu," p. 5, February 23, 2006, FM SRC OFHEO 0153091-115.

[258] OFHEO Interview, Dave Benson, March 6, 2006.

[259] E-mail exchange between Timothy Howard and Leanne Spencer, "Fourth Quarter Earnings (urgent)", December 10, 2001, OFH-FNM 00154731

[260] CSRC Memorandum, "Summary of 1/4/06 CSRC interview with Peter Niculescu," p. 4, February 23, 2006. FM SRC OFHEO 01563094.

[261] OFHEO Interview, David Benson, March 13, 2006. Mr. Benson said that historically Fannie Mae focused its buyback activity toward the end of the quarter when its financial position was clearer.

[262] E-mail exchange between Timothy Howard and Leanne Spencer,, "Re EPS AND BUYBACK LOSSES FOR THIRD QUARTER," September 24, 2003. Franklin Raines, Timothy Howard and Leanne Spencer had primary roles in determining the amount and timing of the debt repurchases to achieve specific earnings targets, OFH-FNM00124614.

[263] E-mail, from Timothy Howard to Leanne Spencer, Peter Niculescu, Thomas Lawler, William Quinn, et al., "EPS and buyback losses for third quarter," September 24, 2003, OFH-FNM 00129205.

[264] Id.,

[265] E-mail from David Benson to Donald Sinclair, "Buybacks," December 10, 2003, OFH-FNM 00560256.

[266] Fannie Mae 1999 Annual Report, p. 20.

[267] Fannie Mae 2000 Annual Report, p. 24.

[268] Fannie Mae 2003 10-K p. 38-39.

[269] Fannie Mae smoothes income say unconcerned analysts, July, 15, 2003 FMSE 083032.

[270] E-mail from Anne Kappler to R. Bruemmer (Wilmer Hale) and Scott Lesmes, "Fwd: Fannie Mae smoothes income say unconcerned analysts," July 15, 2003, FMSE 083032-34 at 33.

[271] FASB Statement No. 113, Accounting and Reporting for Reinsurance of Short-Duration and Long-Duration Contracts (applicable to financial statements for fiscal years beginning after December 15, 1992), specifies the accounting and reporting framework for reinsurance contracts (a pool insurance policy is a form of reinsurance). FAS 113 establishes that contracts that do not result in the reasonable possibility that the reinsurer may realize a significant loss from the insurance risk assumed, in either the amount (underwriting risk) or timing (timing risk), generally do not meet the conditions for reinsurance accounting and are to be accounted for as deposits. Paragraph 9. A deposit from the insurer's standpoint is a loan from the standpoint of the insured.

[272] "Ace to Restate 5 Years of Earnings to Correct Accounting," New York Times, July 22, 2005.

[273] E-mail from James Carey to Robert Schaefer, "Follow-Up, "May 11, 2001, FMSE-IN 001472-74.

[274] FMSE-IN 001479-80.

[275] FMSE-IN 001497-98.

[276] E-mail from Brian Graham to Carlos Perez and Robert Schaefer, "subj: Loss Mgt," June 25, 2001, FMSE-IN 001512.

[277] E-mail from Brian Graham to Robert Schaefer, "Subj: Loss Insurance P&L Pro forma.xls," June 29, 2001, FMSE-IN 001516-7.

[278] E-mail chain among Michael Goldberg, Kieran Gifford, J. Morgan Whitacre, David Kightlinger and Rob Schaefer, "Re: Loss Smoothing," July 3, 2001, FSME-IN 001518-19.

[279] In its March 25, 2004, draft of a paper entitled "Accounting Rule Guidance Statement of Financial Accounting Standards No. 113, Considerations in Risk Transfer Testing (1st DRAFT)", KPMG asserts that "risk transfer tests are only defined in broad, vague terms" and that "auditors need to be able to recognize risk transfer when they see it, and hence the '10-10' rule evolved .... This 10/10 rule has become de facto current practice." KPMG-OFHEO-214742-54 at 54.

[280] E-mail chain among Michael Goldberg, Kieran Gifford, J. Morgan Whitacre, David Kightlinger and Rob Schaefer, "Re: Loss Smoothing," July 3, 2001, FSME-IN 001518.

[281] E-mail from Michael Goldberg to Morgan Whitacre, "Loss Insurance Initiative," FMSE-IN 002041-063.

[282] Memorandum from Leanne Spencer to Jonathan Boyles and Ilan Sussan, "Securites and Exchange Commission's Issuance of Staff Accounting Bulletin No. 102 – Selected Loan Loss Allowance Methodology and Documentation Issues,", July 30, 2001, FMSE 528570-72.

[283] E-mail from Brian Graham to Carlos Perez and Rob Schaefer, "Hmmmmmmm,", October 3, 2001, FMSE-IN 002730.

[284] Id.

[285] E-mail from Brian Graham to Robert Schaefer et al.,"Loss Mgmt Meeting," October 17, 2001, FMSE-IN 002733.

[286] E-mail from Carlos Perez to Robert Schaefer, et. al., "Re: Radian EATPR 1st loss bid," November 30, 2001, .FMSE 529305.

[287] E-mail from Michael Goldberg to Robert Schaefer and Carlos Perez, "RE: Spreadsheet for Loss Insurnace Proposal," November 1, 2001, FMSE-IN 002737.

[288] E-mail from Robert Schaefer to Brian Graham, et al., "Loss Insurance Update," November 28, 2001, FMSE-IN 003247-49.

[289] Id.

[290] Memorandum from Harry Argires to File, "Summary of DDP Consultations Related to 2001 Audit," KPMG-OFHEO-031594.

[291] E-mail from Brian Graham to Robert Schaefer, "Re: Radian EATPR 1st loss bid," November 26, 2001, FMSE-IN 001348 (VI.274)

[292] E-mail from Michael Goldberg to Robert Schaefer, "EATPR", December 11, 2001, FMSE 529357.

[293] E-mail from Michael Goldberg to Robert Schaefer, "Failure Rate," December 13, 2001, FMSE 528633.

[294] E-mail from Michael Goldberg to Robert Schaefer, "Debt vs. Equity," December 14, 2001, FMSE-IN 001382.

[295] E-mail from Robert Schaefer to Carlos Perez, et. al., "Radian Low Stop Loss bids," December 14, 2001, FMSE-IN 001385-87 at 87.

[296] E-mail chain between Timothy Howard, Brian Graham, and Janet Pennewell, "Fwd: credit transaction," December 21, 2001, FMSE-IN 001397.

[297] E-mail chain between Louis Hoyes and Adolfo Marzol, copies to Daniel Mudd, Timothy Howard, Thomas Donilon, Robert Levin, Brian Graham, et al., " Re: Insurance/Stop-loss Policy Purchase," January 9, 2002, FMSE-IN 001398-401 at 398.

[298] "Dedicated Channel, Application of pmiSELECT, Introduction," FMSE-IN 007825.

[299] Memorandum to Daniel Smith, "Deductibility of premiums paid for PMI mortgage insurance," May 2, 2000, FMSE 529358-359.

[300] E-mail from Brian Graham to Robert Schaefer, October 17, 2001, FMSE-IN 002733; see also Undated, unsigned outline, "Loss Insurance Ideas," likely generated in the summer of 2001, "Experience based: variant of PMI select" FMSE 528597-99.

[301] E-mail from Michael Goldberg to Robert Schaefer, et al, "Re: Spreadsheet for Loss Insurance Proposal," November 1, 2001, FMSE-IN 002737-738.

[302] E-mail from Sue Sprague to Robert Schaefer, "draft question," November 15, 2001: Fannie Mae is talking with a variety of insurance companies about a policy ... by which we would be able to purchase a loss risks policy/coverage in which we pay a premium that would be more or less fully expensed in 2002, but any further premium would be calculated on a performance basis ... which ... would result in little to no premium payment in future years, and the upfront premium more or less offset by claims paid .... If the deal has to bear a large premium tax, that probably would skew the economics and kill the deal ... is there an alternative to insurance that would give us the same accounting treatment? FMSE-IN 002751.

[303] PowerPoint presentation, "Enhanced Primary Insurance: Discussion Purposes Only," August 8, 2003, FMSE-IN 008465-75.

[304] E-mail chain among Paul Salfi, Angela Hairston, and Harry Argires, "Insurance Deposit Accounting," September 8, 2003, OFH-FNM 00785991.

[305] E-mail chain between Paul Salfi and Angela Hairston, "Re: Insurance," October 8, 2003, OFH-FNM 00769547.

[306] Memorandum from Dan Smith to Thomas Donilon, "Mortgage Insurance from Ace Capital Mortgage Reinsurance Company ("Ace")," November 10, 2003, FMSE 533847-51 at 47-48.

[307] Memorandum from Roger Wade to the Record, "Review of PMI Select Transaction," March 24, 2004, KPMG-OFHEO 113380-82.

[308] E-mail exchange between Harry Argires and Roger Wade, "Re: Primary Risk Transfer Analysis," March 25, 2004, KPMG-OFHEO-239992- 999 at 992.

[309] E-mail from Robert Schaefer to Allison Herrick, "finite risk policies," March 28, 2005, "I never had gotten a memo from KPMG on any of these policies. We had discussed the pmiSELECT policy with KPMG last year ... I don't know if they or our internal Accounting Standard group memorialized their approval ...."; FMSE-IN 001142.

[310] FMSE-IN 001146-1149.

[311] E-mail from Brian Graham to Leanne Spencer, Janet Pennewell, Adolfo Marzol, and Joseph Sakole, "'Business Management' Strategies," December 18, 2001, FMSE-E-2341110-111.

[312] E-mail from Brian Graham to Timothy Howard, Adolfo Marzol and Leanne Spencer, "COLI," December 21, 2001, FMSE-E_2341108.

[313] Journal Entry, May 2, 2002, FM SRC OFHEO 00769886-88.

[314] See AICPA Audit and Accounting Guide, Chapter 12. Suspense accounts usually contain amounts related to items recorded and held pending classification and transfer to the proper account and may originate from a variety of sources such as loan remittances, branch clearing transactions, automated teller machines (ATM) transactions, and payroll transactions.

[315] Fannie Mae Analysis of Account 1622-00 at September 30, 2003, KPMG-OFHEO-008153.

[316] AICPA Audit and Accounting Guide, loc. cit.

[317] CSRC Memorandum, "Summary of January 6, 2005, Interview with Gary Robinson," August 24, 2005, FM SRC OFHEO 00712118.

[318] CSRC Memorandum, "Summary of February 16, 2005, Interview with Richard Stawarz," August 25, 2005, FM SRC OFHEO 00712128-36 at 31. Mr. Stawarz was unable to recall specifics about the account such as KPMG's proposed audit adjustment for $22.4 million and the accrual reversal for $3.9 million. He also did not recall the $26 million reversal in October 2003 because he was on a leave of absence.

[319] E-mail from Roger Barnes to Stephen Spivey, "Announcement," July 15, 2002, FMSE 341816.

[320] Undated letter from Leanne Spencer to Timothy Howard, FM SRC 00310836-38 at 37. While the document does not specifically refer to the 162200 account by account number, it refers to a "bucket" account and states that the "cushion" is mostly related to net interest income. When shown that document, Ms. Pennewell stated her belief that the "bucket account" referred to the 162200 account. Further, an analysis of the composition of the 162200 account from 1999 indicated that the vast majority of the items in the account related to net interest income. Analysis of Account 162200, November 30, 1999, FMSE-IR 307790.

[321] ARB No. 43, Chapter 3 covers the appropriate accounting and reporting of current assets such as accounts receivables. A current asset is cash or an asset that will be turned into cash or consumed within one year or the normal operating cycle, whichever is longer. The dates of the entries reflect that many of the items were held in this temporary account beyond one year from recordation.

[322] "FNM Audit Differences 12/31/98." KPMG-OFHEO0-063136.

[323] FM SRC OFHEO 00713761 reflects FNM journal entry in the amount of $3,923,476.71 to record miscellaneous income with a debit to Other Accounts Receivable 1622-00 and a corresponding credit to Miscellaneous Income account 7474-39 prepared on January 9, 1999 and effective for December 28, 1998, FMSE-IR 024915-99. The final reported 1998 EPS of $3.2309 was just enough to trigger maximum bonus payouts under AIP. Under Fannie Mae's AIP for 1998, minimum bonuses would have been triggered by an EPS of $3.1300, the target bonus would have been triggered by an EPS of $3.1800, and maximum bonus triggered by an EPS of $3.23. Materials for Jan. 19, 1999 Meeting of the Compensation Committee, FMSE-IR 276226-73, at 33.

[324] It appears that management inappropriately deferred the recognition of income over several periods instead of recognizing the income for the period in which it was earned. SFAC 6 prescribes that matching of costs and revenues should occur simultaneously. Revenues and expenses are generally related to each other and require recognition at the same time; however, when expenses are not related directly to the particular revenues, the expenses can be related to a period on the basis of the transactions or events occurring in that period or by allocation. FM SRC OFHEO 00669802-05 at 02.

[325] CSRC Memorandum, "6/30/05 Interview of Huong Pham", September 26, 2005, p. 5, FM SRC OFHEO 00713747.

[326] There was no written policy prior to early 1999. Policies were proposed in March 1999. FMSE-SP 000110-111 and September 1999 FMSE-SP 000106-109. The official policy was promulgated in December 2000. FMSE 336598.

[327] Id.

A. Yamini, "Purchase Discount Documentation for the Year Ended 12/31/93," FM SRC OFHEO 00714648-52.

[328] "PDAM Analysis and Recommendation, November 7, 1995," FM SRC OFHEO 00141279-81.

[329] E-Mail from Leanne Spencer to Timothy Howard, undated, FM SRC OFHEO 00311203-5

[330] Memorandum from Emily Passeri to File, "Deferred Pool Analysis," November 11, 2004, FM SRC OFHEO 00714505 -11.

[331] The issue of manual adjustments to amortization factor arrays was raised by OFHEO in a letter to Fannie Mae Chairman Stephen Ashley on February 11, 2005.

[332] CSRC Memorandum, "8/23/05 Meeting with Rene LeRouzes," March 16, 2006, FM SRC OFHEO 01563223 – 242 at 227.

[333] Memorandum, from PDA Task Force to Distribution, "Long-Term Objective for New Amortization System," March 12, 1999, FNM SEC-EC 035211.

[334] KPMG's record of Julie Theobald, Ken Russell and Eric Smith meeting on January 8, 1999 with Leanne Spencer, Jim Parks and Jonathan Boyles, FM SRC OFHEO 00140736-741, at 37.

[335] CSRC Memorandum, "1/13/05 Meeting with Leanne Spencer," February 23, 2005, Page 26, FM SRC OFHEO 00140704-706, at 705. Some documents refer to the $199 million as $200 million.

[336] KPMG's record of Julie Theobald, Ken Russell and Eric Smith meeting on January 8, 1999 with Leanne Spencer, Jim Parks and Jonathan Boyles, FM SRC OFHEO 00140736-741, at 38; In his July 1, 2005 meeting with Paul Weiss, Boyles denied attending any meeting with KPMG in 1999 in which the rationale for the nearly $200 million catch-up deferral was discussed and denied that LIHTC was discussed at the 1999 KPMG meeting that he attended. See CSRC Memorandum, "Summary of 7/1/05 meeting with Jonathan Boyles", August 22, 2005, p. 23. FM SRC OFHEO 00712450.

[337] The amount of the KPMG audit difference was a $199 million increase in interest expense and a tax effect of $57.71 million, reflecting a 29 percent tax rate, FM SRC OFHEO 00140738.

[338] KPMG workpaper BM9 dated January 1999, "Fannie Mae Audit Differences, 12/31/98," KPMG-OFHEO-443378. In 2004 Fannie Mae staff decided to revisit the company's failure to record the full amount of the PDA expense in 1998. See Memorandum from Suzanne Barr to Scott Lesmes, "Materiality Considerations for 1998 Amortization of Guaranty Fees," June 22, 2004. FM SRC OFHEO 01398956-958. Suzanne Barr assumed that the $200 million should have been expensed in the fourth quarter of 1998.

[339] Line 13 of OFHEO calculations of the EPS impact.

[340] Pages 3 to 6 of KPMG's October 14, 1998 Professional Practice Letter 98-081, EARNINGS MANAGEMENT AND SEC ENFORCEMENT ISSUES , included a discussion of the September 28, 1998, speech of SEC Chairman Levitt. KPMG-OFHEO-708874-899, at 879. KPMG's May 1998, planning and strategy memorandum for the 1998 audit makes the following statement on the relevance of SEC reporting requirements to Fannie Mae: ...securities issued by Fannie Mae are considered exempt under laws administered by the Securities and Exchange Commission (SEC), thereby eliminating SEC requirements such as periodic filings and registration of securities

(Fannie Mae generally follows the deadlines and reporting requirements that would apply to an SEC registrant and files information with the New York Stock Exchange (NYSE)). KPMG workpaper, "Fannie Mae 1998 Planning/Strategy Memorandum 12/31/98," KPMG-OFHEO-472230-54, at 30.

[341] KPMG Professional Practice Letter 98-110, "DISPOSITION OF AUDIT DIFFERENCES," December 29, 1998, p. 2, KPMG-OFHEO-709101-103, at 102; See remarks of SEC Deputy Chief Accountant, Jane B. Adams in KPMG Professional Practice Letter 98-111, AICPA'S 26TH ANNUAL CONFERENCE ON CURRENT SEC DEVELOPMENTS.KPMG-OFHEO-709041-100, at 95.

[342] 1998 Annual Report to Shareholders, p. 63; January 13, 1999, Independent Auditors' Report; Fannie Mae's January 14, 1999, news release.

[343] CSRC Memorandum, "1/13/05 Meeting with Leanne Spencer," February 23, 2005, p.31, FM SRC OFHEO 00140710. The February 1994 Practice Alert No. 94-1, by the American Institute of Certified Public Accountants (AICPA) Division for CPA Firms' Professional Issues Task Force, Dealing with Audit Differences, included the following caution about not recording or making audit committees and outsiders aware of waived audit differences: Audit committee and outsiders (attorneys, regulators, other auditors, etc.) who become aware of waived audit differences sometimes question why those differences were not recorded, especially if they are marginally below materiality thresholds, are errors and /or are clear deviations from generally accepted accounting principles. Audit committees may become upset that they were not previously informed of these differences.

[344] Minutes of the Audit Committee, February 16, 1999, pp. 7, 14, KPMG-OFHEO-208857 and KPMG-OFHEO-208864.

[345] In the case of Fannie Mae's LIHTC investments, on a cash basis the earnings for the current or latest year were not recorded, i.e., their recognition was deferred to the following year. That body of unrecognized LIHTC earnings for the current year therefore represented an off-balance sheet cookie jar of deferred earnings. Generally accepted accounting principles (GAAP) do not permit that deferral of earnings.

[346] Information about legislation found in the 1/20/94 Issue Summary prepared January 6, 1994 by Deloitte & Touche for the FASB Emerging Issues Task Force regarding EITF Issue 94-1, Accounting for Tax Benefits Resulting from Investments in Affordable Housing Projects.

[347] Description taken from the Abstract for EITF Issue 94-1. If the project owner does not maintain low-income occupancy requirements over the 15 year period or disposes of its interest before the end of the 15 years, the owner must repay a portion of the credits taken. That is termed tax credit "recapture." LIHTC "Year 15" Strategies by The Enterprise Social Investment Corporation.

[348] Fannie Mae made its first LIHTC investment on August 15, 1987, FMSE1 001828. KPMG letter dated November 17, 1993, FMSE 520534.

[349] Information about Fannie Mae investing in 1987 and its accounting for LIHTC from 1987 to 1998 is found in an undated power point presentation that James Parks made on January 8, 1999, to the KPMG auditors about the yearend 1998 change from cash to accrual accounting, FM SRC OFHEO 00141610 and FM SRC OFHEO 00141658.

[350] Cover note, "LMI Tax Credits" May 23, 1996, by "lgs", whom we believe is Leanne G. Spencer, FM SRC OFHEO 00287319-321, at 319.

[351] Draft Memorandum from Leanne Spencer and Janet Pennewell to Timothy Howard and Robert Levin, "1998 Plan – Round 1," January 9, 1998 contains a forecast that LMI (Low to Moderate Income) tax credits would be $85.67 million for 1998 and $223.75 million for 1999. SRC OFHEO 023399-438 at 409, "1998-2001 Four Year Plan, Income Tax Analysis;" Memorandum from Janet Pennewell to Larry Small, et. al, "Your Question on 1999 EPS Growth," November 25, 1998, FM SRC OFHEO 00141649. Memorandum from Leanne Spencer to Timothy Howard, December 2, 1998, FMSE-IR 182499; Memorandum from Shaun Ross to Timothy Howard, with copies to Leanne Spencer and Janet Pennewell, "LIHTC Partnerships," December 22, 1998, FM SRC OFHEO 00141609 and FM SRC OFHEO 00141655.

[352] E-mail from Leanne Spencer and Janet Pennewell to Lawrence Small, November 30, 1998. FM SRC OFHEO 01398917-920, at 919.

[353] While the document shows an intent to keep KPMG in the dark about plans to book the accounting change in 1999, the external auditors had been expecting the accounting change to be made for 1998.

[354] KPMG's record of J. Theobald, K. Russell and E. Smith meeting on January 8, 1999 with Leanne Spencer, Jim Parks and Jonathan Boyles quotes FAS 91 paragraph 19 as follows: ...if the enterprise anticipates prepayments in applying the interest method and a difference arises between the prepayments anticipated and actual prepayment received, the enterprise shall recalculate the effective yield to reflect actual payments to date and anticipated future payments. The net investment in the loans shall be adjusted to the amount that would have existed had the new effective yield been applied since the acquisition of the loans. The investment in the loans shall be adjusted to the new balance with a corresponding charge or credit to interest income. FM SRC OFHEO 00140736-741, at 736-737; November 3, 1998 Third Quarterly Earnings Forecast, from Janet Pennewell to Franklin Raines, Lawrence Small, Jamie Gorelick, Timothy Howard, Robert Levin and Ann Logan, FM SRC OFHEO 00286888-892.

[355] It is customary for companies to make adjustments and close their books after the end of a fiscal year. However, late adjustments that are material can be problematic. Practice Alert No. 94-1, "Dealing with Audit Differences," issued by the American Institute of Certified Public Accountants (AICPA) Division for CPA Firms' Professional Issues Task Force, February 1994, included the following caution: Last-minute entries oftentimes need an even higher degree of audit challenge, particularly if they seem to offset unfavorable proposed audit differences. Journal Entry, "JE21362," January 8, 1999, with the description "Adj. LIHTC Acctg Change" made at 6:23pm and 6:35 pm, FM SRC OFHEO 00713763-764. The JE recorded $123.2 million of tax credits and $22.4 million of associated net operating losses (NOLs). On an after tax basis the NOLs were $14.5 million ($22.4 million @ 65% [100% less the 35% statutory federal corporate tax rate]), producing a net of tax LIHTC gain of $108.7 million ($123.2 million - $14.5 million). In a document summarizing the components of the LIHTC adjustments, Fannie Mae used the 35% statutory rate to calculate the NOL portion of the after-tax gain of $108.7 million on the LIHTC accounting change. There is no tax effect on LIHTC tax credits since each dollar of credit reduces the company's income taxes dollar for dollar. For purposes of references to the amount of the LIHTC gain in this document, the amount is rounded to $109 million. Undated, handwritten draft of "Year-end adj. JE to make LIHTC accounting changes" with supporting

tabulation entitled "Cumulative Catch-up at 12/31/98…" KPMG-OFHEO-709338-339; The use of the term "catch-up" in referring to the LIHTC journal entry was explained in Leanne Spencer's January 28, 2005, meeting with Paul Weiss. Ms. Spencer was asked about the handwritten note regarding LIHTC accounting changes and a chart containing "Cumulative Catch-up at 12/31/98." Spencer identified the handwriting on the document as belonging to [Rick] DePetris, and identified the handwritten note "year-end adjustment" on the top of the first page as belonging to herself. She said that this document pertained only to LIHTC and explained that the use of the term "catch-up" referred to the change from cash to accrual accounting. FM SRC OFHEO 00141624.

[356] The year end $240 million PDA adjustment that was recorded was $156 million after-tax using the 35% statutory federal corporate tax rate.

[357] Senior management presented to the Office of the Chairman, on the morning of January 8, 1999 a proposal to record the $240 million PDA adjustment and the offsetting LIHTC adjustment. Those adjustments – but not the 1998 earnings alternatives proposals were presented later on January 8, 1999 to KPMG as company conclusions on the appropriate year-end adjustments. FM SRC OFHEO 00140701-709, FM SRC OFHEO 00140726-745 and FM SRC OFHEO 00712546-548. KPMG's memo of its January 8, 1999, meeting with Ms. Spencer, Mr. Parks and Mr. Boyles indicates that Ms. Spencer had already met with Franklin Raines, Lawrence Small, Jamie Gorelick, and Timothy Howard. FM SRC OFHEO- 00140736.

[358] In February 2006, Fannie Mae was unable to advise OFHEO how much of the LIHTC accrual accounting adjustment related to 1998 and each of the prior years. Record of February 9, 2006, Telephone Teleconference. OFHEO believes that a majority of the 10.5 cents impact of the LIHTC adjustment related to years other than 1998. Cumulative Catch-up at 12/31/98, FM SRC OFHEO 00141773, and Profile of Tax Credit Business, FM SRC OFEHO 000141660.

[359] In his November 1998 speech, SEC Chairman Arthur Levitt noted that the market was unforgiving of companies that miss Wall Street's consensus estimates. November 16, 1998, Remarks by Chairman Arthur Levitt, Securities and Exchange Commission, "A Financial Partnership." The Financial Executives Institute, New York, NY; Line 22 of OFHEO calculations of the EPS impact. Notes for January 19, 1999, Board of Directors Meeting, FMSE-IR 182240.

[360] Line 26 of OFHEO calculations of the EPS impact. Notes for January 19, 1999 Board of Directors Meeting, FMSE-IR 182240.

[361] In the Notes for the January 14, 1999, Conference Call, Timothy Howard is shown as stating that the $3.23 EPS for 1998: …was not only a penny higher than the analysts' consensus, it also was several cents above the consensus for our EPS at the beginning of the year. FM SRC OFHEO 0134663. The headline in Fannie Mae's January 14, 1999, news release is: Fannie Mae Reports Record 1998 Earnings of $3.418 Billion and $3.23 Per Common Share; 1998 Earnings Per Common Share Up 14.1 Percent Over 1997 While page 2 of the news release mentions a nonrecurring reduction in federal income tax expense from LIHTC and additional amortization of net premiums or discounts and deferred or prepaid guaranty fees that lowered net interest income and guaranty fees, the release did not disclose the dollar amounts recorded in the fourth quarter or the company's $199 million understatement of amortization expense.

[362] KPMG workpaper "Cumulative Catch-up at 12/31/98," showing pretax and after tax components of the adjustment for the LIHTC accounting change, KPMG-OFHEO 512212.

[363] Paragraph 13 of Accounting Principles Board Opinion No. 20, Accounting Changes, (July 1971) provides that: "[a] change from an accounting principle that is not generally accepted to one that is generally accepted is a correction of an error for purposes of applying this Opinion." Paragraph 36 of that opinion provided guidance on how corrections of errors should be recorded in the financial statements: The Board concludes that correction of an error in the financial statements of a prior period discovered subsequent to their issuance (paragraph 13) should be reported as a prior period adjustment. (Paragraph 18 of APB Opinion 9 covers the manner of reporting prior period adjustments.)

[364] Memorandum from Kim Rawls to the file, "Accounting for change in depreciation recognition," with copies to L. Spencer, R. DePetris, J. Boyles, D. Stawarz, B. Harris and KPMG, April 14, 1998, KPMG-OFHEO-698285-286. Rawls' memorandum does not disclose the basis for concluding that the adjustment is immaterial. A January, 28, 1997, E-mail from Rick DePetris states "There is a line on form K-1 which calculates the difference between tax depreciation (27 years) and gaap [sic] (40 years). . . ." The difference in the lives used, e.g., 27 or 27.5 years vs. 40 years, account for a difference between tax and GAAP accounting for LIHTC depreciation. FM SRC OFHEO 00214625.

[365] KPMG workpaper, "Fannie Mae 1998 Planning/Strategy Memorandum 12/31/98," KPMG-OFHEO-472230-253, at 48.

[366] On January 13, 1999, the date that KPMG signed an unqualified or clean opinion on Fannie Mae's 1998 financial statements, KPMG senior manager, Eric Smith, and partner, Julie Theobald, performed procedures and inquiries with Richard Stawarz and Leanne Spencer of Fannie Mae. The workpaper record includes KPMG's acknowledgment that the LIHTC adjustment was significant or unusual: There were no significant or unusual adjustments, except for the recognition of additional amounts of premium amortization ($240 million) and recognition of $120 million of investment tax credits based on improved information systems. "QTR 4-7 Fourth Quarter Down to Date January 13, 1999, Review of Accounts and Related Matters related to the 4th Quarter Press Release," KPMG-OFHEO-063965-967, at 965.

[367] According to EITF 94-1, Accounting for Tax Benefits Resulting from Investments in Affordable Housing Projects, (May 1995), a liability should have been recognized for delayed equity contributions that are unconditional and legally binding. A liability also should be recognized for equity contributions that are contingent upon a future event when that contingent event becomes probable. The need to recognize delayed equity contributions was recognized by Richard DePetris before 1998. His February 2, 1997, E-mail, "Policy issues related to tax credit partnerships," included a statement that said: "[m]y personal opinion is that ...we will need to start grossing up our balance sheet for the full commitment amount." FM SRC OFHEO 00214624. On February 18, 1999, a little more than a month after the LIHTC adjustment was recorded, Leanne Spencer, James Parks and Richard DePetris met to review the accounting policy for LMI (Low to Moderate Income, another term for LIHTC) investments. They decided not to gross up Fannie Mae's balance sheet for future equity contributions because of

the operational problems associated with adopting that accounting method outweighed the benefits and because adding both assets and liabilities of approximately $700 million was immaterial to Fannie Mae's balance sheet. Memorandum from Jonathan Boyles to the file, "LMI," February 18, 1999, FM SRC OFHEO 00292570.

[368] Fannie Mae's March 13, 2006 Form 12b-25 Notification of Late Filing of 2005 Form 10-K to the SEC, page 13.

[369] Fannie Mae 1998 Annual Report, pp. 22, 54.

[370] Id., pp. 20, 21.

[371] Timothy Howard, notes for the January 19, 1999, Meeting of the Fannie Mae Board of Directors, FMSE-IR 182240-264, at 40.

[372] Id., at 41.

[373] While not stating the dollar amounts, Mr. Howard's notes for the January 14, 1999, conference call with analysts indicated that system improvements which gave improved information enabled Fannie Mae "to record in the fourth quarter the tax credits earned for 1998 as well as 1997. The notes indicate that Mr. Howard mentioned the fourth quarter PDA adjustment and "electing to make" the lump-sum changes to net premiums and deferred fees. FM SRC OFHEO 0134663-670, at 64-65.

[374] The net of tax effect amount calculated using the 35 percent statutory federal corporate rate.

[375] In the January 14, 1999, Conference Call with analysts, the transcript has Mr. Howard responding to a question about the fourth quarter LIHTC and PDA adjustments with the answer, "They're comparable in size" on an after-tax basis. FM SRC OFHEO 0134672. As indicated by the CSRC summary of the January 13, 2005, interview with Leanne Spencer, Franklin Raines was aware that the $199 million of 1998 PDA expense was not booked. FM SRC OFHEO 00140705.

[376] The two primary sources of accounting guidance for the allowance for credit losses are FAS No. 5, Accounting for Contingencies (paragraphs 8 and 22) and FAS No. 114, Accounting by Creditors for Impairment of a Loan. Statement 5 provides the basic guidance for recognition of all impairment losses, and Statement 114 provides more specific guidance for a subset of loans— those individually identified as impaired.

[377] Fannie Mae 10-K, 1999, p. 47.

[378] Loss forecast process, first quarter 2000 through third quarter 2002, p. 2, 2nd full paragraph, FMSE-RST-002883.

[379] Note from Leanne Spencer to Sampath Rajappa, Jonathan Boyles, Richard Stawartz and Janet Pennewell, September 24, 1997, FMSRC OFHEO 00311294.

[380] Memorandum from KPMG to Julie Theobald, Sampath Rajappa, Leanne Spencer, and Jonathan Boyles, "Fannie Mae Allowance for Losses Methodology," October 6, 1997," FMSE 189121-189125.

[381] Undated exhibit, "Selected Fannie Mae Loan Loss allowance Statistics," FMSE SRV OFHEO 119085

[382] Note from Morgan Whitacre to Timothy Howard, October 9, 1998, FM SRC OFHEO 00318700-702 The proposed change depicted the allowance representing 3 time trailing charge-offs.

[383] E-mail from Morgan Whitacre to Leanne Spencer, with attachment, "allowance presentation", December 5, 2000, OFH-FNM 01089690-711.

[384] PowerPoint presentation, "Recommendation to Change Loss allowance Methodology," November 2001, FMSE 413305-314.
[385] E-mail exchange between Leanne Spencer, and Adolfo Marzol, "RE: MH Bond P/L Risk," November 17, 2002, FM SRC OFHEO 01377738-39.
[386] The amounts actually provided for losses were obtained from the notes to the financial statements for the years 1997 to 2000, respectively. Foreclosed property expenses represent charge-offs. The planned amounts for the provision for losses as well as the three alternative plans were obtained from a document dated January 7, 1999, FM SRC OFHEO 000001-4.
[387] OFHEO Interview, Morgan Whitacre, January 18, 2006, p. 80.
[388] KPMG workpaper, "GAAP Accounting–Allowance for Loan Losses, period end 12/31/03," KMPG-OFHEO 004068-96.
[389] id..
[390] OFHEO Examination Analysis Memorandum, October 28, 2004.
[391] Fannie Mae Audit Report Office of Auditing Allowance for Loan Losses Audit, December 15, 2003. KPMG OFHEO 004040-48.
[392] FAS No. 5, Accounting for Contingencies, (1975).
[393] Id., paragraph 8.
[394] CSRC Memorandum, "Interview with Carolyn Swift on December 19, 2005," p. 4, FM SRC OFHEO 01602473.
[395] Fannie Mae Audit Report, Office of Auditing, Corporate Tax Audit, June 30, 2005.
[396] Memorandum from Leanne Spencer to Timothy Howard, 1996, "I have now held nothing back such as the previous earnings management items that I've been plugging to the tax line over the last several forecasts, with the reversing of the tax entry." FM SRC, OFHEO 00311203.

VII. THE ROLES OF THE OFFICE OF AUDITING AND THE EXTERNAL AUDITOR

The standards to which auditors are held arise from a variety of sources. OFHEO guidance with respect to audits highlights the obligations of both internal and external auditors:

> An Enterprise should establish and implement internal and external audit programs appropriate to the nature and scope of its business activities that, at minimum, provide for:
>
> i. Adequate monitoring of internal controls through an audit function appropriate to the Enterprise's size, structure and scope of operations;
> ii. Independence of the audit function;
> iii. Qualified professionals and management for the conduct and review of audit functions;
> iv. Adequate testing and review of audited areas together with adequate documentation of findings and of any recommendations and corrective actions; and
> v. Verification and review of measures and actions undertaken to address identified material weaknesses.[1]

Internal and external audits play a fundamental role in the control environment of a corporation. OFHEO guidance with respect to internal controls places the following responsibilities on an Enterprise:

> An Enterprise should maintain and implement internal controls appropriate to the nature, scope and risk of its business activities that, at a minimum, provide for:
>
> i. An organizational structure and assignment of responsibility for management, employees, consultants and contractors, that provide for accountability and controls, including adherence to policies and procedures;
> ii. A control framework commensurate with the Enterprise's risks;
> iii. Policies and procedures adequate to safeguard and to manage assets; and
> iv. Compliance with applicable laws, regulations and policies.[2]

In addition, the Audit Committee of Fannie Mae's Board of Directors, in chartering the Enterprise's Office of Auditing, tied the conduct of internal auditors to professional standards:

> Auditing is performed in compliance with the Institute of Internal Auditors' [International] Standards for the Professional Practice of Internal Auditing and, when appropriate, the American Institute of Certified Public Accountants' Generally Accepted Auditing Standards. Internal control is evaluated against criteria for effective internal control established by the Committee of Sponsoring Organizations [COSO]. Auditors are expected to conduct themselves in compliance with the Code of Conduct of The Institute of Internal Auditors.[3]

The COSO framework of criteria for evaluating internal control systems defines internal control as a "process, effected by an entity's board of directors, management, and other personnel, designed to provide reasonable assurance regarding the achievement of objectives in the following categories: (1) effectiveness and efficiency of operations, (2) reliability of financial reporting, and (3) compliance with applicable laws and regulations."[4]

The Institute of Internal Auditors Performance Standards for internal auditing affirms that:

The internal audit activity should evaluate risk exposures relating to the organization's governance, operations, and information systems regarding the

- Reliability and integrity of financial and operational information;
- Effectiveness and efficiency of operations;
- Safeguarding of assets; and
- Compliance with laws, regulations, and contracts.[5]

One of those standards is to insure that internal audits are performed with "proficiency and due professional care." The Institute of Internal Auditors standards state, in part:

> Internal auditors should possess the knowledge, skills and other competencies needed to perform their individual responsibilities. The Internal auditor should exercise due professional care by considering the extent of work needed to achieve the engagement's objectives, relative complexity, materiality, or significance of matters to which [professional] assurance procedures are applied.[6]

Fannie Mae's audit charter asserts that the Office of Auditing is responsible for reviewing processes to ensure compliance with laws and regulations. Specifically, the Office is charged with:

> [r]eviewing the systems established to ensure compliance with those policies, plans, procedures, laws, and regulations that could have a significant impact on operations and reports and determining whether the organization is in compliance…[7]

The Board of Directors established the Office of Auditing at Fannie Mae to provide management and the Board of Directors with information, analyses, appraisals, recommendations, and counsel, and to promote effective control.[8] KPMG, LLP served as the Enterprise's external auditor from 1998 through 2004, the period covered by this report. The external auditor is responsible for confirming that Fannie Mae's financial statements taken as a whole conform with GAAP in all material respects. Together, internal and external auditors serve to ensure financial and operational integrity. Internal and external audits build on financial information and disclosures provided by management. Internal auditors assess the operational integrity of the processes management uses to prepare and disclose that information. External auditors express an opinion on whether or not the financial statements taken as a whole conform to GAAP in all material respects, based on their analysis and testing of the disclosures of management and the assessments made by internal auditors.

The respective responsibilities of management, internal auditors, and external auditors do not alter the Enterprise's ultimate responsibility for financial statements and related disclosures. Fannie Mae is mandated by its enabling statute, the Charter Act, to submit periodic reports of financial condition and operations, which must include financial statements, prepared in accordance with GAAP, and must contain a declaration that the report is true and correct.[9] Fannie Mae is also required to have periodic audits in accordance with generally accepted auditing standards.[10] Standards of prudent business operation, as set forth in OFHEO guidance and regulations on audits and on internal controls, dictate that the Enterprise be responsible and accountable for internal and external audit programs.[11] In addition, OFHEO Corporate Governance regulations establish minimum standards regarding the conduct and responsibilities of the Board of Directors in furthering the safe and sound operations of each Enterprise. The responsibilities of the Board of Directors include having in place adequate policies and procedures to assure its oversight of, among other things, the "integrity of accounting and financial reporting systems of the Enterprise, including independent audits and systems of internal control" and the "process and adequacy of reporting, disclosures, and communications to shareholders, investors, and potential investors."[12]

The Office of Auditing contravened both OFHEO standards and the responsibilities outlined in its Board-approved charter. This chapter documents the Office of Auditing's failure to ensure proficiency; due professional care; adequate internal controls; meet its stated audit report objectives to assess compliance with generally accepted accounting principles (GAAP) and truthful and complete communications to management, the external auditor, and the Board of Directors. External audits performed by KPMG contravened OFHEO's requirements for external audits in that those audits failed to review adequately Fannie Mae's significant accounting policies for GAAP compliance. KPMG also improperly provided unqualified opinions of financial statements that contained significant departures from

GAAP. The failures and limitations of both internal and external audit procedures further contravened safety and soundness guidance by critically impairing Fannie Mae's ability to detect and correct accounting deficiencies and internal control weaknesses.

The Office of Auditing

Fannie Mae's internal audit unit, the Office of Auditing, failed to meet OFHEO safety and soundness standards with respect to (1) the reliability and integrity of financial and operational information, (2) the effectiveness and efficiency of operations, and (3) meeting its stated audit report objectives. The Office also failed to adhere to standards established by both the Institute of Internal Auditors and the Committee of Sponsoring Organizations, including those pertaining to auditor proficiency and the exercise of due professional care. As a result, the Office also failed to meet the responsibilities assigned to it by Fannie Mae's Board of Directors.

The Office of Auditing's failures manifested themselves in a variety of ways. The Office's audit program failed to properly confirm compliance with GAAP as specified in its audit objectives or to consistently audit critical accounting policies, practices, and estimates in a timely way. When shortcomings were found they were not adequately addressed or communicated. Internal audit reports prepared by the Office consistently understated problems and overstated work accomplished. Rather than undertaking independent work to confirm compliance with policies and procedures, the Office often relied on the managers of units under audit to confirm compliance.

During the period covered by this report, the Office of Auditing had insufficient staff and insufficient expertise. While many auditors were experienced, many others did not have sufficient skills to evaluate satisfactorily many of the deficiencies of the Enterprise. Staff levels did not keep up with the changing or increasing risks, products, and activities of the company, or the increasing responsibilities of the Office. The need for staff in the Office expanded as the retained portfolio grew, new products required different risk measurement methodologies and controls, and major information technology (IT) projects were launched. The staff of the Office was assigned to calculate and report key performance indicators, to manage the self-assessment questionnaire program, and to build and maintain a system to comply with the Sarbanes-Oxley requirement to test internal controls. Those increased responsibilities took resources away from the core mission of the Office.

Those staffing and resource problems contributed to incomplete identification of deficiencies, and ratings for audits related to the Office of the Controller that did not sufficiently reflect the significant issues in processes and controls. At the same time the Office of the Controller was establishing and implementing flawed policies and practices, the Office of Auditing was providing that Office with too many clean audits. For audits between 2002 and 2004 related to the Office of the Controller, about 69 percent resulted in satisfactory ratings and 31 percent identified areas that needed improvement.[13]

The audit program exhibited deficiencies in nearly every process, which affected the scope, frequency, and quality of the audits. Those deficiencies include the following:

- The risk assessment model used auditable entities that were insufficiently granular.

- The ratings often covered a group of too many activities, masking higher risk activities within the group and generating less severe and less accurate risk ratings.
- Model risk auditors often validated the models rather than assessing the effectiveness of the controls surrounding model production, use, and validation.
- Audit procedures often focused on transactions rather than testing controls.
- Accounting audits focused on determining compliance with the Enterprise's accounting policies rather than with GAAP, in accordance with its audit report objectives.
- Sampling methodology often generated insufficient sample sizes.
- Audit reports did not include deficiencies noted during the audit if the business unit corrected them before the audit was done. Thus, audit reports provided an incomplete and inaccurate view of the audited area.
- Auditors often recorded deficiencies as fully corrected if the business unit had a plan to correct the problem, or had begun correction.
- The audit program provided insufficient focus on the monitoring and management of the IT environment. Audits failed to identify all key IT applications and the linkages of those applications to the business purposes they supported.
- The Office of Auditing established a risk-based audit approach, but did not set a maximum period in which all areas within the Enterprise must be audited. The lack of a maximum audit frequency allowed several areas to remain unaudited for extended periods and may have masked the significance of the staffing and resource issues within the Office.

Poor report content and format adversely impacted the communication of audit results. Audit reports provided a list of deficiencies, but often did not explain the root cause of an issue or group issues by root cause. Audit reports provided overall ratings, but did not rate the individual deficiencies noted in the audits.[14] Auditors often did not classify severe deficiencies as "pervasive internal control weaknesses" in work papers because that classification automatically resulted in an overall weak or "red" rating for the audit.

The Office of Auditing designated audits as covering large organizational units to exaggerate the completeness of the audit program's coverage of the Enterprise's activities. The Office counted an entire business group or process as audited no matter how much or how little was reviewed within that unit. Through that method, the Office misleadingly represented that it had audited a significant portion of the balance sheet each year.

The remainder of this section documents failures of the Office of Auditing to properly discharge its responsibilities. The following subsections document the failure of the Office to acknowledge its responsibility to test for GAAP compliance and its failure to ensure proficiency and the exercise of due professional care in auditing critical accounting policies and investigating allegations of accounting improprieties. Those subsections are followed by two that discuss the communications failures of the Office. The first of those subsections focuses on the misrepresentation by the Office of its audit reviews for GAAP compliance. The final subsection focuses on the failures of the office to discharge its obligations to communicate fully with the Audit Committee of the Board of Directors.

Failure to Confirm Properly Compliance with GAAP

As demonstrated below, the audit objectives outlined in the audit reports frequently referenced that audit procedures were performed to assess compliance with GAAP. However, during interviews with OFHEO, Fannie Mae executives maintained that the Office of Auditing was only responsible for conducting audit test work to assess Enterprise accounting processes relative to internally developed accounting policies rather than GAAP. Sampath Rajappa, Senior Vice President for Operations Risk and head of the Office of Auditing from 1999-2004, described responsibilities of the Office of Auditing for reviewing accounting policies for compliance with regulatory standards as follows:

> Q: Are audit procedures directed at determining whether or not the company has been in compliance with GAAP?
> A: Audit procedures are directed at auditing to the standards established by Financial Standards [the group within Fannie Mae responsible for developing accounting policies] and approved by KPMG.[15]

Furthermore, Chief Financial Officer Timothy Howard testified that the Office of Auditing has no role in evaluating the Enterprise's accounting policies to assess compliance with GAAP:

> Q: What is Internal Audit's responsibility for evaluating the company's accounting policies?
> A: Their primary responsibility is to do audits to ensure that the policies are followed by those they govern in a fashion consistent with our [internal] standards.... I don't look to Internal Audit to opine on whether an accounting policy is correctly specified--that's not their background, their job--so if you're asking does Internal Audit say, this is GAAP or non-GAAP, that isn't their job. I mean I look to KPMG to do that, the outside auditor.[16]

Another indication that the Office of Auditing assumed some responsibility for assessing GAAP compliance was an e-mail dated December 10, 2003, from Ann Eilers, Director, Office of Auditing, and Mr. Rajappa to Senior Vice President and Deputy General Counsel Anthony Marra, Senior Vice President and General Counsel Ann Kappler, and Controller Leanne Spencer. That e-mail was issued as a result of the review by the Office of Auditing of the December 2003 OFHEO *Report of the Special Examination of Freddie Mac*.[17] In response to an inquiry from management, Ms. Eilers responded:

> ... we (internal audit) review accounting entries to ensure financial reporting is in compliance with Generally Accepted Accounting Principles (i.e., FAS 133, FAS 115, FAS 91, etc.).[18]

In his interview Mr. Rajappa indicated that Ms. Eilers misspoke.[19] However, even assuming that the misstatement was made in good faith, there is no question that the Office of Auditing and the Audit Committee did not have a common understanding of the scope of the Office of Auditing examinations. Making sure that there is a common understanding is a fundamental part of the roles of the head of Internal Audit and the Audit Committee.

As shown below, the objectives specified by the Office of Auditing in its audit reports (related specifically to audits of controls over accounting and financial reporting) indicate that audits are performed to determine compliance with GAAP financial accounting standards. However, despite the reference to GAAP, Fannie Mae executives maintained that procedures were actually performed to ensure compliance with internal policy. Fannie Mae management and internal auditors disregarded the responsibility of the Office of Auditing to confirm the Enterprise's compliance with GAAP and did not meet the audit objectives. As a result, the Office of Auditing failed to comply with auditing standards and meet the responsibilities outlined in the Audit Charter.

Failure to Perform Internal Audits with Proficiency

OFHEO safety and soundness standards establish that each Enterprise should have audit programs that, at minimum, provide for qualified professionals and management for the conduct and review of audit functions.[20] In addition, the Institute of Internal Auditors standards obligated Fannie Mae to ensure that its internal auditors possessed or obtained the knowledge, skills, and other competencies needed to carry out their audit responsibilities. Mr. Rajappa was neither a CPA nor did he have prior auditing experience.[21] During his tenure as Senior Vice President, the Office of Auditing had insufficient human capital when measured in terms of staff size, auditing and technical skills, and staffing mix. In addition, the Office of Auditing required enhanced skills and competencies as its responsibilities expanded.[22] The additional regulatory requirements that accompanied Fannie Mae's decision to register with the SEC and the implementation of the Sarbanes-Oxley Act (SOX) added to the burden on the already insufficient resources of the Office.

After OFHEO began its special examination of Fannie Mae, the Enterprise engaged Ernst & Young to assess the internal audit function. At the Audit Committee Meeting of January 17, 2005, Ernst & Young reported observations about the Office's strengths and weaknesses.[23] Suggestions for improvements included a need for additional specialty expertise, enhanced training, and the development of work plans for individuals.[24]

While there is some evidence that Mr. Rajappa occasionally discussed with management the staffing challenges in the Office of Auditing, there was no meaningful effort to address those needs until March 2005. At an Audit Committee meeting on March 28th, the Enterprise and Ernst & Young described a three-phase project to strengthen the internal audit function.[25] One of the phases involved a review of staffing.

In June 2005, Ernst & Young made a variety of staffing recommendations to the Audit Committee, including:

- Expansion of the headcount;
- A change in the staffing mix;
- Increased production;
- Expansion of the expertise of both auditing and technical skills;
- Identification of resources to supplement the Office of Auditing staffing needs; and
- Enhancement of training programs.[26]

Those weaknesses existed for the entirety of Mr. Rajappa's tenure. They resulted from Fannie Mae not investing sufficient resources into what should have been viewed as essential functions.

The understaffing of the Office of Auditing became particularly problematic as it became apparent that compliance with Section 404 of SOX (SOX 404) would significantly impair the Office's ability to conduct its core audit activities effectively. Effective March 31, 2003,

Fannie Mae voluntarily registered its stock with the SEC. As a result, the Enterprise was required to comply with SOX, effective in 2004.[27] Although the Office of Auditing lacked the requisite knowledge, skills, and resources, Fannie Mae delegated to the Office the responsibility of building and maintaining the SOX 404 compliance system.

The addition of responsibility for Fannie Mae's SOX 404 compliance to the existing duties of the Office of Auditing was overwhelming.[28] Compliance with SOX 404 required large commitments of time and effort from both management and the Office. Prior to implementation, many companies anticipated that SOX compliance would create resource-related challenges and took the appropriate steps to ensure they possessed the expertise and personnel necessary to perform the required assessment of internal controls.[29] The stress was evident from the dramatic fall-off in deliverables produced by the Office during 2004. From 1999 through 2003, internal audit issued about 100 audit reports and memoranda each year; in 2004, less than 50 were issued.

Following the 2004 OFHEO report, Fannie Mae replaced some members of senior management and engaged PricewaterhouseCoopers to identify deficiencies in the existing internal audit program and develop a new SOX 404 compliance program.[30] PricewaterhouseCoopers identified numerous problems in the existing system, including:

- Incomplete control documentation;
- Lack of linkage to financial statement assertions;
- Identification only of key controls;
- Overly broad control descriptions of internal control areas; and
- Excessive delegation to Internal Audit.[31]

PricewaterhouseCoopers concluded not only that the Sarbanes-Oxley Act-related work performed by the Office of Auditing was inadequate and had to be redone, but also that such work had distracted the Office from its core function of conducting operational, systems, and special project audits for the purpose of ensuring the reliability and integrity of financial and

Failure to Expedite Audit. During 2003, the Office of Auditing conducted its first substantive audit of the Enterprise's FAS 91 policy. Contemporaneously, details of accounting irregularities related to critical accounting policies at Freddie Mac were emerging.[34] In fact, in a press release dated June 25, 2003, Freddie Mac provided additional insight, stating:

> The principal factors thus far identified by Board Counsel are lack of sufficient accounting expertise and internal control and management weaknesses as a consequence of which Freddie Mac personnel made numerous errors in applying Generally Accepted Accounting Principles (GAAP).[35]

On an annual basis, Mr. Rajappa presented the audit plan of the Office of Auditing to the Audit Committee. That plan was approved by the Committee and served as the roadmap for audit activities for the year. Review of key control areas and critical accounting policies were prioritized based on a risk assessment.[36]

After experiencing significant audit differences[37] related to the amortization of discounts and premiums in both 1998 and 1999, and after being told by KPMG that a written policy was an absolute necessity, the Enterprise developed a formal policy for the application of FAS 91 in December 2000. Since FAS 91 was a critical accounting estimate, the Office of Auditing should have made that audit a top priority. Nonetheless, a substantive audit was not done until 2003, more than two years after issuance of the policy, more than four years after the unprecedented 1998 catch-up of $440 million, and more than 10 years after the effective date of the accounting standard. Further, FAS 91 audits were not addressed in either the 2001 or 2002 Audit Plans. The delay in evaluating the application of FAS 91 is a failure to exercise due professional care and an unsafe and unsound practice.

Incomplete Analysis of Realignment Adjustment. As described in the September 2004 OFHEO report, limitations in the timing and quality of data fed from transaction sub-ledgers to Fannie Mae's amortization system created differences between source systems and the amortization system. Reconciliation of those differences was handled in either of two ways. At times they were capitalized and reamortized as assets and, at other times, staff made manual adjustments to the amortization results.[38] Both approaches were referred to as realignment adjustments. Fannie Mae made realignment adjustments related to both portfolio and guarantee fee amortization results.

During the course of its amortization audit, the Office of Auditing discovered that management had adjusted the catch-up results by an estimated expense of $118 million, the estimated impact of correcting MBS misclassifications (premiums classified as conventional discounts), for the first quarter of 2003.[39] As a result of that adjustment, the Enterprise avoided recognizing any catch-up income in the first quarter of 2003. In addition, management inappropriately reduced the amount of catch-up that should have been recorded in the second quarter of 2003 (as a result of including $94 million estimated expense for the Security Master Project) and in the third quarter of 2003 (as a result of including $80 million estimated expense for that project). However, in the Amortization Audit report of July 9, 2003, the Office only noted the lack of a written policy with respect to realignments.[40]

Such discretionary adjustments by management demonstrate a clear failure of internal controls. The Office of Auditing failed to conclude that the realignment differences were inappropriate and disregarded this unsafe and unsound practice. Rather than investigate further, the Office relied on the representations of management that "all material actions and changes are well documented and appropriately reviewed with management."[41] As a result, no immediate corrective action was taken other than a commitment by management to improve documentation. Mr. Rajappa failed to report that unsafe and unsound practice to the full Board or the Audit Committee. Moreover, Fannie Mae failed to implement a policy prior to OFHEO's special examination in 2004.

Since the realignments should have been treated as a correction of an error under APB 20,[42] the Office of Auditing missed yet another opportunity to identify a violation. Furthermore, Mr. Rajappa failed to include the realignment adjustment on the Audit Tracking List[43] and failed, once again, to communicate findings adequately to the Audit Committee.

Incomplete Analysis of Guarantee Fee Adjustment. The Office of Auditing also identified a questionable $20 million guarantee fee adjustment recorded in May 2003. The audit report states:

> For Q3 2003 GF Base Catch Up number, an amount of $20 mm was manually adjusted directly to the AIMS summary data report instead of being disclosed on the Catch Up Sensitivity Analysis report as an adjustment. Some support was available; however, it was not very intuitive since management judgment was used in applying the amount of $20 mm.[44]

Since one of the assigned responsibilities of the Office of Auditing under the Charter was to ensure the reliability and integrity of financial and operating information, the Office had a duty to further investigate that issue further. Having discovered an undocumented, unsupported adjustment that was a policy departure and a potential GAAP violation, the Office elected to forego further investigation and not report the finding to the Audit Committee. Despite the fact that the Office concluded that "management judgment was used in applying the amount of $20 mm," the Office only included the item on the final audit report of July 9, 2003, as part of a broader discussion of the need for enhanced documentation and minimization of key-person dependencies, and relied on management's commitment to implement improved procedures.[45]

The report of the Office of Auditing ignored the effect of the adjustment on Fannie Mae's core business EPS, an effect that was admittedly material, since it enabled the Enterprise to meet analyst expectations for the quarter.[46] The adjustment followed hard upon the $118 million adjustment to the catch-up in the first quarter of 2003, which the internal auditors had observed to lack supporting documentation.[47] As noted further below, the undocumented and unexplained nature of those adjustments was not reported to the Audit Committee.

FAS 91 Audit Improperly Indicates Compliance with GAAP. The "Objectives and Scope" section of the audit report dated July 9, 2003, related to the FAS 91 audit indicated that "[o]ur audit was performed to determine the adequacy of controls … including policies and procedures and *compliance with financial accounting standards* [emphasis added] …"[48] In the Significant Accounting Policies section of the same audit report, a detailed discussion outlined the provisions of FAS 91, including the required accounting, and reporting and the promulgated method for calculating constant effective yield. In performing audit work to comply with the above stated objectives and policies, the Office of Auditing did not obtain sufficient evidence to show compliance with GAAP. For example, there is no documentation that the Office of Auditing staff independently verified the Enterprise's compliance with the standard regarding the acceptability of the three alternative treatments for handling reconciliation differences under GAAP in performing the FAS 91 audit. Rather, Joyce Philip, Manager, Office of Auditing, said that she relied on an oral confirmation from the Financial Standards Group Vice President that the accounting was acceptable. She did not request or obtain documentation from the Financial Standards Group that would support that opinion.[49]

Failures Related to the FAS 133 and Derivatives Control Audits. Management recognized derivatives controls as a critical policy and required the Office of Auditing to audit them annually and provide the Audit Committee with an audit opinion regarding internal controls over non-mortgage derivatives.

Incomplete Analysis of FAS 133 Policy. The 2003 audit concluded that the Enterprise "maintain[ed] effective internal controls over non-mortgage derivatives and is in compliance with the provisions of Board Resolutions that set forth Board strategy for derivatives …"[50] That conclusion was purportedly reached after "testing a sample of transactions for adequate segregation of duties, timely and accurate documentation, data entry, [and] confirmation of terms with dealers …" OFHEO's review of the Office of Auditing's analysis revealed two failures to exercise due professional care.

The first failure relates to inadequate hedge documentation. Work papers revealed that the Office of Auditing tested a sample of 20 derivatives transactions as a component of the derivatives audit for 2003. Out of the sample of 20, the Office identified four transactions with incomplete or insufficient documentation, which represented a 20 percent error rate.[51] Hedge documentation is a key requirement in qualifying for hedge accounting under FAS 133. Lack of appropriate documentation would invalidate the Enterprise's ability to account for those transactions as hedges. Instead of highlighting what should have been deemed a significant finding, the Office of Auditing chose only to reference the problem in a section entitled "Other Discussion Items."[52] Mr. Rajappa failed to report that significant finding to the Audit Committee.

The second failure involves inadequate sampling methodology. A test of 20 derivatives—representing 0.02 percent of the total notional value of derivatives outstanding as of January 17, 2003—was insufficient to enable the Office of Auditing to draw a statistically significant conclusion. Based on audit work papers, the Office used an inappropriate sampling methodology to form its opinion. That opinion misled the Audit Committee by representing that the derivatives sign-off for 2003 was based in part on a statistically significant evaluation of the accuracy of documentation. Following OFHEO's report of September 2004, Fannie Mae engaged Ernst and Young to assess the Enterprise's Office of Auditing. Ernst & Young called into question the testing methods of the Office and made the following statement: "The existing sampling methodology should be amended to be more consistent with generally accepted sampling standards."[53]

Improper Indication of Compliance with GAAP. The Office of Auditing made several representations related to Fannie Mae's compliance with GAAP as it pertained to FAS 133. Mr. Rajappa signed an annual certification for the Audit Committee which represented that the work of the Office included "testing for compliance with FAS 133 requirements to determine whether transactions reported as qualifying for hedge accounting treatment have been properly classified and accurately recognized in the Income Statement and Balance Sheet."[54] The March 31, 2003, Derivatives Control Audit report contained an observation that "… retroactive re-linkages do not conform to FAS 133 requirements."[55] Additionally, work papers for the same audit state that the documentation produced at inception was not consistent with the required accounting treatment.[56] However, when asked whether documentation was inconsistent with the hedge accounting requirements of FAS 133, Joyce Philip, a Director in the Office, responded that she did not have a personal opinion on that topic, and that she would be guided by the internal policy provided by the Financial Standards Group.[57]

Improper Indication of Compliance with GAAP of Loan Loss Allowance. The "Purposes and Scope" section of the Loan Losses Audit report represents that the Office of Auditing "[r]eviewed the overall methodology used by Fannie Mae to ensure compliance with Generally Accepted Accounting Principles including Statement of Financial Accounting Standards No. 5 …"[58] Despite maintaining that the Office did not audit to GAAP, Mr. Rajappa begrudgingly acknowledged that this and other representations imply that it did.[59]

Incomplete Analysis of Barnes' Allegations of Accounting Improprieties

In August 2003, Roger Barnes, a former Manager in Fannie Mae's Controllers' Office, approached the Office of Auditing to raise concerns regarding Fannie Mae's accounting practices related to FAS 91. By that time, the Baker Botts report had been released, detailing accounting manipulations at Freddie Mac. OFHEO had also announced plans to commence a special investigation of Fannie Mae's accounting practices. Against that backdrop, Mr. Barnes questioned the propriety of a manual $6.5 million accounting adjustment and asserted his belief that the adjustment was used to make the amortization amounts recorded in the financial statements "agree" with forecasted amortization expense.[60] Such actions would constitute inappropriate earnings management. The Office of Auditing was responsible for investigating those allegations. In the September 2004 Report, OFHEO found that the Office conducted a hurried investigation into Mr. Barnes' allegations that culminated in Mr. Rajappa certifying GAAP compliance to the Board of Directors. [61]

In response to Mr. Barnes' allegations, the Office of Auditing reviewed the data he provided and concluded that while his concerns highlighted control weaknesses related to documentation, his claims of GAAP noncompliance were not well-founded. The Office indicated that the issues raised by Mr. Barnes were more reflective of a lack of understanding on his behalf rather than a departure from GAAP in Fannie Mae policy. In conducting its investigation, the Office ignored allegations of intentional misstatement of earnings. Ms. Eilers claimed that she was unaware of such allegations.[62] The Office did not perform further follow-up work. Instead, the Office accepted the explanation provided by Jeff Juliane, Director for Financial Reporting, who stated that the adjustment, for which he was personally responsible, was correct.[63]

An independent and objective internal auditor should not accept management explanations without obtaining sufficient evidence to address stated audit objectives. Contrary to professional audit standards, the internal auditors did not insist on obtaining adequate written documentation to form a conclusion on the correctness of the $6.5 million adjustment alleged to be fraudulent by an employee of the Office of the Controller. For that reason, the Office was unable to determine a reasonable basis for the adjustment or whether it was correct or incorrect.

Given the allegations of possible fraud, the Office of Auditing should not have relied on oral representations from Mr. Juliane, since he was the party that Mr. Barnes had indicated had inappropriately authorized the adjustments in the first place.[64] Given the questionable nature of the entry and in the wake of the disclosure of accounting violations and inappropriate earnings management at Freddie Mac, the Office should have expanded the scope of the audit work to review other journal entry adjustments, including reconsidering both the $20 million adjustment that the Office had previously noted as unsupported and the $118 million adjustment to the catch-up. In a decision that calls into question the objectivity and professional judgment of the Office of Auditing, Mr. Rajappa failed to inform the Audit Committee and chose not to initiate a full review.

The internal auditors completely ignored Mr. Barnes' allegations of possible intentional misstatement. Rather than pursue a further investigation, the Office of Auditing concluded that the issue was a documentation problem. Despite the fact that the minutes of the meeting of August 8, 2003, clearly state that Mr. Barnes' concern with the $6.5 million manual change was that "it appeared that the factor change was used to make iPDI 'agree' with forecasted amortization expense,"[65] personnel from the Office claimed that they were unaware of that allegation.66 As a result, the Office treated the entry as an isolated incident and failed to critically evaluate the substance of the entry and expand the review to ensure no other similar entries existed.

Moreover, both the $20 million undocumented adjustment and the $6.5 million manual factor change are examples of unsupported manual entries which affected reported net income. Those entries were the result of key-person dependencies and weak internal controls. The Amortization Audit report even concluded that controls needed strengthening;[67]

however, the annual certification by the Office of Auditing of controls over financial reporting for that year stated that "Fannie Mae maintained effective internal control over financial reporting."[68] Since key-person dependencies and unsupported entries resulted in undocumented factor changes, the Office failed to communicate obvious material weaknesses. Instead, Mr. Rajappa told the Audit

Committee Chairman that he did not believe that the adjustments were an attempt to manage earnings.[69]

In its conduct of that investigation, the Office of Auditing failed in its duty to evaluate the substance of the accounting adjustments and to ensure that the adjustments were in compliance with GAAP. It failed to establish and implement an audit program that was independent, and that adequately tested and reviewed audited areas with documented findings and recommendations for further action, and to provide for qualified professionals and management to conduct and review audit functions, as required by OFHEO safety and soundness standards.[70] The failures of the Office of Auditing represented larger failures of the Enterprise's internal controls and of management responsibilities and functions. OFHEO guidance requires management both to maintain and implement internal controls that among other things provide for compliance with laws, regulations and policies and to establish and maintain an effective risk management framework, to monitor its effectiveness, and to take appropriate action to correct any weaknesses. The Office of Auditing's Board-approved charter charged it with ensuring the reliability and integrity of financial and operating information. The Office had an affirmative duty to investigate the allegations of fraud raised by Mr. Barnes. As noted in the OFHEO September 2004 *Report of Findings to Date*,"[t]he lack of diligence on behalf of the Office of Auditing in the matter of the manual factor change is inconsistent with their responsibility to exercise due professional care." [emphasis in original][71]

Misrepresentation of Accounting Policy Reviews for Conformity with GAAP

Although the internal audit reports of the Office of Auditing indicated that its objectives included assessing compliance with GAAP, the Office did not evaluate GAAP compliance as was noted above. Referencing compliance with regulatory standards when, in fact, referring to Fannie Mae's internal policies misled internal and external users of the financial information.

Ann Eilers, former Vice President of Audit, stated that the discussion of financial standards contained in the audit reports referred to internal Fannie Mae accounting guidelines:

> Q: Okay. On page 1 of the document, in the box that is contained in the middle of the page, under conclusion, labeled conclusion, rather, the first sentence reads:
>
> Fannie Mae's implementation of FAS-149, FIN 45 and FIN 46 is consistent with FASB requirements. [emphasis added]
>
> And would the reference to FASB requirements here— could that reference be inferred as indicating that the implementation of the system was in compliance with GAAP?
>
> A: No. It is the implementation of operational controls at Fannie Mae was in compliance with our policy around 149, 45, and 46.
>
> Q: So the reference to FASB requirements is referring to your internal policy as developed by Financial Standards?
>
> A: Yes….[72]

When audit report objectives indicated that audit procedures were performed to assess compliance with relevant regulatory standards, a reasonable reader would assume that GAAP compliance is included. When this was not the case, the Office of Auditing failed to perform due diligence in meeting stated audit objectives. Moreover, referencing GAAP standards in audit reports and correspondence with the Audit Committee and the Board of Directors intentionally misled them. The misleading references to GAAP overstated the extent of the audit procedures the Office performed. The misrepresentations of the extent of the reviews by the internal auditors violated safety and soundness standards.

Failures to Communicate Appropriately to the Audit Committee

According to the October 1987 Report of the National Commission on Fraudulent Financial Reporting, "[p]roperly organized and effectively operated, internal auditing gives management and the audit committee a way to monitor the reliability and the integrity of financial and operating information."[73] That control is only effective to the extent that a corporation's internal auditors communicate openly and accurately to its audit committee. At Fannie Mae, the Office of Auditing was bound by its Charter to provide the Audit Committee with periodic reports

> describing the scope of planned and actual audit activities, the more significant observations and recommendations, the status of management's corrective actions, and the Office of Auditing's overall opinion on the adequacy and effectiveness of Fannie Mae's system of internal controls.[74]

Despite those expectations, the communications by the Office of Auditing to the Audit Committee were frequently incomplete and inadequate.

Failure to Clarify the Scope of Duties of the Internal Auditors

Perhaps the most serious communication failure concerned the scope of the duties of the Office of Auditing. Audit Committee Chairman Thomas Gerrity stated emphatically to OFHEO that both the external auditor and the Office of Auditing were to serve as "watchdogs for GAAP."[75] Mr. Gerrity stated that it was his understanding that internal audit understood GAAP and would report any instances of noncompliance with GAAP.[76] He also stated that he would be surprised if the Office of Auditing did not audit to GAAP.[77]

In contrast, Mr. Rajappa indicated in his OFHEO interview that the Office of Auditing's role was simply to audit for compliance with internal policies and procedures and that evaluation of GAAP compliance was the joint responsibility of KPMG and the Enterprise's Financial Standards group. Mr. Rajappa stated that, as the head of the Office of Auditing, he did:

> ... not have responsibility for determining if they're [the Enterprise financial reporting or policies] general accounting principles...

I'm not a CPA, so I do not opine on accounting principles or GAAP.[78]

Mr. Rajappa stated further:

> As far as compliance with GAAP, that's for KPMG and Financial Standards. And, again, like I said before, if my auditors, who are certified CPAs, if they had issues with the treatment of GAAP, I have confidence in them that they would either ask the question of Jonathan Boyles, our Financial Standards person, or brought it up with me.[79]

Nevertheless, the Office of Auditing made numerous representations related to Fannie Mae's compliance with GAAP, which likely contributed to Mr. Gerrity's perception of the internal auditor's role. For example, Mr. Rajappa signed an annual certification for the Audit Committee that represented that the Office of Auditing's work included "testing for compliance with FAS 133 requirements to determine whether transactions reported as qualifying for hedge accounting treatment have been properly classified and accurately recognized in the Income Statement and Balance Sheet."[80] Another example is the misleading statements contained in the Derivatives Control Audit report for March 31, 2003, discussed above.

Other Inaccurate, Incomplete, and Misleading Communications

In addition to misrepresenting the scope of its audits in audit reports and other deliverables, the Office of Auditing sent other inaccurate, incomplete, or misleading communications to the Audit Committee. Three examples are discussed below.

Amortization Audit of July 9, 2003. In addition to representing that compliance with FAS 91 standards had been evaluated, the Office of Auditing identified an undocumented, unsupported manual adjustment of $20 million to guarantee fee income, as noted above. The Office failed to include that undocumented adjustment within the Audit Report and failed to inform the Audit

Committee. The Office was required to communicate all significant findings to the Committee. Rather than report the specific $20 million unsupported entry, the Office treated it as part of a larger documentation problem and concluded that "[c]ontrols need strengthening. Requires attention during normal course of business."[81]

Failure to Communicate Insufficient Resources. Fannie Mae's business grew tremendously from 1999 through 2004, which greatly increased the complexity of the workload of the Office of Auditing. Additional demands arose from new and enhanced accounting standards as well as Securities and Exchange Commission (SEC) and Sarbanes-Oxley Act of 2002 (SOX) requirements. Nonetheless, the personnel counts of the Office remained essentially unchanged through 2002, with small increases in 2003 and 2004. Furthermore, the Office suffered from high turnover and reduced training. Nevertheless, the Audit Committee was not informed about resource constraints until August 2004. By that time audits were being postponed or cancelled even as Fannie Mae implemented critical accounting policies.[82] The failure to procure additional resources prevented the Office from adequately and appropriately performing audits of activities that had a material impact on the Enterprise's financial statements.

Failure to Communicate Control Weaknesses. The Office of Auditing had a duty to communicate any significant concerns about Fannie Mae's internal controls directly to the Audit Committee. In August 2003 for the second quarter of 2003, just after completing the investigation into Roger Barnes' allegations and certifying the financial statements, Mr. Rajappa instead sent directly to Mr. Raines a letter that highlighted several concerns regarding the state of affairs at the Enterprise, including the following:

...some frustration with lack of robust operational systems and adequate staff.

[m]ore money needs to be spent on beefing up finance staff & systems.

[g]ive them robust operational tools (not endless workarounds and spreadsheets)...

... data security needs to be strengthened significantly.

... [i]nsufficient access controls to critical applications combined with some of the other frustrations cited above can lead to unfortunate outcomes. 83

Considering that Freddie Mac had just recently detailed its accounting problems, OFHEO had announced a special examination, and the Office of Auditing had just completed an investigation into allegations regarding improper amortization and earnings management, Mr. Rajappa should have communicated his concerns directly to Mr. Gerrity and the other members of the Audit Committee, as required by the Audit Charter as well as best practices. Instead, Mr. Rajappa elected to share the information with Mr. Raines. Neither Mr. Raines nor Mr. Rajappa appears to have communicated those concerns to the Audit Committee.

Omission of Issues from Reports to the Audit Committee. The Audit Charter required that the Office of Auditing provide the Audit Committee with periodic reports detailing significant findings.[84] In order to fulfill that duty, the Office had a responsibility to report any audit items that substantially prevented Fannie Mae from meeting its primary financial, operational, and compliance goals.[85] The primary vehicle for that communication was the monthly Audit Tracking List (ATL). Based on the guidance provided within the Internal Audit Manual, audit issues meeting the following criteria, for example, were to be included within the ATL and communicated to the Audit Committee:

- Items equal to or greater than $1 million;
- Weaknesses in primary control; and
- Systemic weaknesses in controls.[86]

On several occasions, the Office of Auditing failed to include certain items that should have been added to the ATL. For example, despite the recommendation in the Amortization Audit report for strengthening controls, the August 2003 ATL failed to list a need for better documentation or written policies related to the realignments or guarantee fee adjustments described above. Those items exceeded the $1 million threshold established by the manual, and the lack of documentation and key-person dependencies were systematic weaknesses in control. One month later, the Office of Auditing concluded that the reporting change associated with Jeff Juliane's promotion from manager to director potentially further weakened "the segregation of functions"[87] The March 2003 derivatives control audit identified violations of GAAP, a clear violation of a compliance goal.[88] None of those items were included on the ATL. In fact, Ms. Eilers stated that despite the existence of significant control weaknesses, the Office classified the Amortization Audit as "yellow" instead of "red" because management "initiated timely actions to resolve the issues."[89]

The Office of Auditing's failures to highlight the control weaknesses and its failures with respect to communications and reporting generally are not consistent with prudent business operations. These failures directly contravene OFHEO safety and soundness standards with respect to information reporting, documentation, and internal controls.[90] The failures were exacerbated by the complacency of the Audit Committee in its oversight activities, and its failure to discuss diligently or inquire adequately with respect to these incomplete representations as more fully discussed in Chapter IX.

External Audit

OFHEO safety and soundness standards highlight the important role of the external auditor of the Enterprise. While OFHEO has no direct relationship with external auditors, OFHEO guidance requires Enterprise management to establish and implement external audit programs that, among other things, provide for "adequate testing and review of audited areas together with adequate documentation of findings and of any recommendations and corrective actions."[91] OFHEO's interest in external audit involves the Enterprise's compliance with OFHEO standards and guidance. It is the responsibility of Fannie Mae's Board of Directors and management to take reasonable steps to confirm that the external audit complies with OFHEO requirements.

To better understand the safety and soundness failings at Fannie Mae, OFHEO assessed the work of KPMG as Fannie Mae's external auditor. Our assessment of KPMG focused on the review by the external auditor of the Enterprise's accounting policies related to (1) FAS 91,

Accounting for Nonrefundable Fees and Costs Associated with Originating or Acquiring Loans and Initial Direct Costs of Leases and (2) FAS 133 Accounting for Derivative Instruments and Hedging Activities. The purpose of OFHEO's assessment was to gather factual information in order to verify assertions made by Fannie Mae staff regarding assurances provided by the external auditor related to those accounting standards.

Failure to Review Adequately Accounting Policies for Conformity to GAAP

The September 2004 OFHEO report criticized Fannie Mae's accounting policies related to FAS 91 and FAS 133, which govern accounting for key areas of Fannie Mae's primary business activities. FAS 91 applies to loan premium and discount amortization, whereas FAS 133 applies to derivatives and hedge accounting. Both FAS 91 and FAS 133 were identified as "critical accounting policies" in Fannie Mae's filings with the SEC.

In response to that criticism of its accounting policies and practices, Fannie Mae asserted that the non-GAAP provisions identified in the OFHEO report had not only been reviewed by KPMG, but also accepted by KPMG's Department of Professional Practice (DPP). In fact, Leanne Spencer, Fannie Mae's former Controller, stated that the Enterprise "liberally use[d]" KPMG to review accounting policies.[92] In the September 2004 report, OFHEO criticized Fannie Mae for over-reliance on its external auditor to review accounting policy.[93]

KPMG did not have an adequate process for reviewing Fannie Mae's accounting policies for compliance with GAAP. A formal process for reviewing accounting policies would include making a determination of key accounting policies and performing a periodic, systematic, and thorough review of the accounting treatments outlined in those policies for compliance with GAAP. During interviews with OFHEO, KPMG partners indicated that their audits did not include a formal annual process for a comprehensive review of all accounting policies. KPMG explained that policy reviews depended on several factors and were decided on a case-by-case basis.[94] At times, Fannie Mae specifically requested that KPMG review a policy, whereas at other times, KPMG would independently initiate a policy review. As a result, KPMG's review of those critical policy areas was not consistent.

The lack of a formal process for the external auditor's review of accounting policies resulted in inconsistent reviews of those policies. While the Enterprise asserted that the external auditor was conducting a thorough review of accounting policies, KPMG's work papers did not document consistent and detailed policy reviews. The lack of a formal accounting policy review process and the inadequate documentation of the reviews, coupled with the failure of the Enterprise to adequately oversee and administer the auditing process, resulted in unsafe and unsound practices at the Enterprise.

FAS 91

OFHEO concluded in the September 2004 report that Fannie Mae's accounting for purchase premium and discount amortization was inconsistent with GAAP and designed to provide earnings flexibility and minimize earnings volatility.[95] The Enterprise's Purchase Premium and Discount Amortization (PPDA) policy, dated December 2000, details the Enterprise's FAS 91 accounting treatment for deferred fees. FAS 91 was issued by the Financial Accounting Standards Board (FASB) in 1986 and outlines the accounting treatment for nonrefundable fees and other costs associated with purchases of loans. The guidance established that purchase premiums and discounts on loans should be recognized as an adjustment of the yield over the life of the related loans, using the interest method of accounting. According to FAS 91, at each accounting period an entity is required to recalculate the constant effective yield to reflect the cumulative difference between the estimated and actual yield. The guidance requires an entity to recognize immediately in income the cumulative difference in the amortization.[96] Fannie Mae referred to this cumulative adjustment as the "catch-up."

Fannie Mae's purchase premium and discount amortization (PPDA) policy is divided into three sections: (1) The catch-up position, (2) Determining our target, and (3) Managing our Catch-up Position.[97] The first section indicates that the Enterprise's catch-up position will be calculated using the average of five interest rate scenarios. The second section establishes "+/-1%" of related revenue as a materiality threshold for recording amortization adjustments. Finally, the third section provides a three-year time horizon for the Enterprise to record the constant effective yield adjustment.

In the September 2004 report, OFHEO found that the FAS 91 accounting policy did not adhere to GAAP.[98] OFHEO noted, among other things, that the policy (1) improperly applied a materiality threshold to the constant effective yield adjustment, which allowed the Enterprise to avoid recording the required amortization expense under FAS 91; (2) improperly calculated its materiality threshold on an annual basis but applied that annual calculation to quarterly results; (3) inappropriately permitted the Enterprise to record discretionary constant effective yield adjustments within the materiality threshold, allowing the Enterprise to target amortization expense and (4) improperly allotted a three-year time horizon within which to record the constant effective yield adjustment.

Fannie Mae personnel asserted to OFHEO that KPMG had reviewed its FAS 91 policy and was aware of its purchase, premium, and discount amortization practices. The Enterprise insisted that it relied on assurances from the external auditor that its PPDA policy and practices were consistent with GAAP. For example, Controller Spencer made the following statement regarding the KPMG review of the Enterprise's FAS 91 policy:

> A: There is an accounting policy that states that our revenue recognition for deferred fees is FAS 91. This, in essence, was an attempt to document how that's operationalized or how it's applied.
> Q: Is it your understanding that KPMG approved this policy?
> A: Yes.[99]

Additionally, in an interview on August 24, 2004, Jonathan Boyles, Senior Vice President for Financial Standards, commented as follows regarding the review by KPMG of Fannie Mae's FAS 91 policy:

> Q: Do you recollect having discussions with KPMG whereby KPMG agreed that the establishment of a plus or minus one percent target range is appropriate under Generally Accepted Accounting Principles?
> A: Yes, we had. When we met with them and this was presented to them, they were very comfortable with that, and we have met with them every quarter since, and they have audited, you know, the heck out of FAS 91 over the years, and we've had many partners roll through. So presumably they're very comfortable with it. It's a policy they're well aware of.[100]

Finally, in a statement prepared for testimony before the House Subcommittee on Capital Markets, Insurance and Government Sponsored Enterprises given October 6, 2004, CEO Franklin Raines made the following comments regarding KPMG's review of the policy:

> Second, the report alleges that we misapplied GAAP with respect to the two accounting standards, FAS 91 and FAS 133. We believe we applied those standards in accordance with GAAP, and our independent auditor, KPMG, reviewed our application of those standards and concurred.[101]

The Former Chairman and CEO Continued by Stating:

Given these imprecisions [of assumptions underlying the calculation of constant effective yield], Fannie Mae decided to use a range of possible outcomes for our FAS 91 amortization. KPMG reviewed our FAS 91 policy when it was implemented in 2000. Our internal accounting experts believed that using a range was consistent with GAAP. In preparing our financial reports, as recently as last quarter's SEC Form 10-Q, KPMG told us they concurred with our use of a range.[102]

KPMG maintained that despite requests, the Enterprise never provided them a written FAS 91 policy for review. When presented with copies of the PPDA policy, KPMG partners, managers, and staff interviewed by OFHEO testified that they had never seen the policy and were not aware of all of the provisions contained therein.[103] KPMG personnel testified that they gained an understanding of Fannie Mae's accounting treatment for amortization of premiums and discounts through discussions with management and were only informed of certain aspects of the policy.[104]

Despite KPMG's testimony that it was not aware of the policy, OFHEO found copies of the policy included in KPMG's 2003 audit work papers[105] related to the allegations of fraud made by Roger Barnes which are discussed in detail later in this chapter. Furthermore, despite KPMG's assertion that it was never provided a formal FAS 91 amortization policy for review, KPMG reviewed at least two of the non-GAAP provisions criticized in the September 2004 OFHEO report as part of its regular audit procedures: (1) discretionary adjustments and (2) annual adjustment calculation.

Discretionary Adjustments. As noted above, one problematic aspect of Fannie Mae's purchase premium and discount amortization (PPDA) policy is that it establishes a materiality threshold for recording the constant effective yield adjustment. The policy states that "the target catch-up for the NII will be +/-1% of related Portfolio NII on a tax equivalent basis." Additionally, the policy states that "for guaranty fee income, the target catch-up will be +/-2% of related Gfee revenue." As written, the PPDA policy did not require the Enterprise to record an accounting adjustment when the calculated effective yield remained within those thresholds. However, if the calculated effective yield exceeded the materiality threshold Fannie Mae was required to record an adjustment, according to the policy.[106]

During its annual audit procedures, however, KPMG identified some instances in which Fannie Mae made discretionary adjustments for amortization and violated its FAS 91 policy. For instance, a KPMG work paper contained handwritten comments by Michael Tascher, a KPMG Audit Senior Manager, written on a Fannie Mae Audit Committee presentation dated November 17, 2003. The presentation, entitled "Critical Accounting Policy - Deferred Price Adjustments," provided an overview of the requirements of FAS 91. The auditor's handwritten comments read as follows:

> Management records catch-up to return catch-up position to end point of range. Management does not select an arbitrary amount w/n range. Except for Q1 2003, Mgmt did not record NII catch-up of $77.6 million due to an offsetting amount expected to be recorded in Q2 '03....[107]

That comment suggests that KPMG was aware of at least one instance in which the Enterprise did not make an adjustment as required by its PPDA policy. When questioned about that incident, Mr. Tascher stated that the occurrence did not conform to Fannie Mae's PPDA policy.

> Q: I would like to introduce to the record Tascher 3, which is labeled "FAS 91 Amortization Catch-up Adjustment for Net Interest Income," Bates stamped pages KPMG 000892 through KPMG 000894.

> Q: ... Okay. I would like to direct your attention to the bottom of page one labeled KPMG 00892, and it appears to have referred to the incident, the Security Master project that we were discussing from Exhibit two. And I will just read beginning at the bottom of that page:

> ...Through 3/31/03 and as documented in the Q1 work papers, Fannie Mae had completed an analysis of a portion of the data that resulted in a quantified adjustment of $118 million. This amount was not recorded in Q1 as documented in the review work papers, but was considered in light of the overall catch-up adjustment analysis performed by the company. In other words, Fannie Mae would have recorded a large increase in income in the first quarter in order to be within the catch-up parameters discussed in paragraph one to the memo. Given management's awareness of the [$118 million] adjustment to the expense, no catch-up was recorded in Q1. As of 6/30/03, management had substantially completed their analysis as of the remaining portion of the remaining data. As a result, an additional required adjustment of $37 million was deemed necessary to correct the remaining data

cleanup and a total adjustment of $155 million (118 plus 37) was recorded with the amortization catch-up adjustment in Q2.

And I just want to quickly revisit what we were discussing before. So, it appears as though in Q1 there was an adjustment that exceeded the plus-or-minus 1 percent threshold which was not recorded in that period; is that correct?

A: Can I refer back to this?

(KPMG Attorney): Sure.

A: Q1, it looks like the catch-up was 177, and the upper limit was a hundred.

Q: So the answer to my question is, is that a yes?

A: Can you repeat the question.

Q: Sure. It appears as though in Q1 the catch-up amount that was calculated exceeded the plus-or-minus 1 percent threshold. However, an adjustment was not recorded.

A: In Q1, I think that's right.[108]

Mr. Tascher testified that KPMG identified, during the course of audit work, another instance in which Fannie Mae did not record a necessary amortization adjustment as required by the internal policy.

Q: Okay. I'm going to move on to tick mark C, which appears to reference Q3 2002, and it reads:

Net catch-up to record amortization to upper bound of policy band was $8 million. Management decided against recording the entry. KPMG passed as amount is immaterial. See Q3 2002 work papers.
It appears in this instance just from a reading of this tick mark that this hearing of Q3 of 2002, again, the mean catch-up that was calculated exceeded the 1 percent threshold by $8 million. However, management decided, however, Fannie Mae did not record an adjusting entry. Is that consistent with your recollection?

A: Yes, because of the note that I typed here.

Q: ... Does it appear that in this instance Fannie Mae violated the policy as you understood it?

A: Yes, I would say--yes, yes.[109]

In summary, KPMG failed to investigate those instances further based on its determination that the items identified would have an immaterial effect on Fannie Mae's financial statements. The external auditor was aware that Fannie Mae violated its PPDA policy by failing to make required adjustments. Mr. Serock, KPMG Audit Engagement Partner, stated that he recalls having discussion with Fannie Mae management regarding the $8 million adjustment and that ultimately the amount was recorded in 2002; however, OFHEO found no documentation in the audit work papers that the adjustment was recorded.

Additionally, OFHEO found no documentation that KPMG indicated to Fannie Mae that such adjustments violate GAAP until 2004.

Annual Adjustment Calculation. The September 2004 OFHEO report noted that Fannie Mae improperly calculated its materiality threshold based on annual related revenue and applied those calculations to its quarterly results.[110] OFHEO cited that practice as a departure from GAAP. In an SEC filing dated November 15, 2004, Fannie Mae acknowledged that the practice was not consistent with GAAP as follows:

> In addition to the issues presented to OCA [the Office of the Chief Accountant of the Securities and Exchange Commission] regarding FAS 91, Fannie Mae recently determined that its methodology for performing calculations to measure the catch-up adjustment required by FAS 91 for balance sheet dates in the periods 2001 through 2002 was not consistent with GAAP. During those periods, Fannie Mae should have been calculating its catch-up adjustment with reference to its quarter-end position rather than its projected year-end position and recording amounts solely on the basis of those quarterly calculations ....[111]

OFHEO questioned KPMG regarding its awareness of the annual view taken by Fannie Mae in calculating the FAS 91 materiality threshold. Mark Serock, Audit Partner, maintained that KPMG was unaware that the Enterprise was using an annual amortization calculation for purposes of quarterly financial reporting:

> Q: .... As it relates to the plus or minus one percent target range aspect of Fannie Mae's amortization policy, do you have an understanding as to whether or not that plus or minus one percent of net interest income was being calculated as a percentage of annual net interest income or quarterly net interest income?
>
> A: It was my understanding that it was being calculated based upon quarterly net interest income.
>
> Q: Do you recall how you gained that understanding?
>
> A: The understanding was gained through discussions with the previous engagement team and review of, you know, memorandum contained in our work papers.[112]

KPMG year-end 2003 audit work papers, however, contain an analysis to support Fannie Mae's "+/-1%" materiality calculation. As part of that analysis, the Enterprise's quarterly recorded amortization was compared to the quarterly calculated materiality threshold as a test for reasonableness. The threshold amounts calculated in the auditor's analysis, as a benchmark for the amortization recorded in the financial statements, is based on annual net interest income (NII) amounts. The audit work paper contained the review signatures of Messrs. Serock and Tascher. The analysis contained in the FY 2003 audit work papers has been replicated in table VIII-1.[113]

During the interview Mr. Tascher confirmed the significance of the above schedule, as follows:

> Q: I would like to introduce for the record Tascher 2, labeled "Fannie Mae Analysis of FAS 91 Mean Catch-up for Historical Periods," Bates stamp KPMG 000898.
>
> (Tascher Exhibit No. 2 was marked for identification.)

Q: Mike, I will give you a chance to review the document.

Table VII-1. Analysis of FAS 91 Mean Catch-up for Historical Periods (dollars in millions)

Accounting Period	Mean Catch-up(Rounded)	1 percent of NII – Upper Limit
Q1 2001	72	72
Q2 2001	58	76
Q3 2001	58	76
Q4 2001	0	81
Q1 2002	(7)	103
Q2 2002	68	94
Q3 2002	100	92
Q4 2002	65	93
Q1 2003	177	100

Source: KPMG audit work paper titled, Fannie Mae Analysis of FAS 91 Mean Catch-up for Historical Periods, June 30, 2003, KPMG 000898.

(Witness reviews document.)

A: Okay.

Q: Do you recognize this document?

A: I remember the document, yes.

Q: Okay. Did you prepare this document?

A: I did.

Q: And the tick mark that's in the bottom right-hand corner that's an identifying mark, can you identify whose mark that is.

A: I believe that's the mark of one of the engagement partners, Mark Serock.

Q: Okay. And did he have an understanding what the notation represents?
A: Yes. It's the mark he puts on when he's reviewed a work paper.

Q: Okay. I would just like to walk through this document to get an understanding of what's being discussed here. It appears as though there are nine quarters listed consecutively for--beginning Q1 2001 and ending in Q1 2003 in the first column. The second column appears to be--it's labeled mean catch-up rounded. It's our understanding that that column represents the catch-up amount that was calculated for each respective quarter; is that consistent with your understanding?

A: I believe it was.

Q: Okay. The third column is labeled 1 percent of NII-upper limit, and it also has--it's our understanding that this column represents the 1 percent threshold that would have been calculated for each of the respective quarters; is that consistent with your understanding?

A: It is.[114]

Table VII-2 shows a comparison of the +/- 1 percent threshold amounts listed in the audit work paper with Fannie Mae's quarterly and annual financial statements submitted to the Securities and Exchange Commission (SEC). That comparison demonstrates that the threshold amounts calculated by the external auditor more closely reflect the Enterprise's annual NII results than its quarterly results. Thus, KPMG performed its 1 percent materiality threshold analysis based on the Enterprise's annual NII amounts, indicating that KPMG reasonably should have been aware that the Enterprise was improperly applying an annual materiality threshold calculation to quarterly financial results. OFHEO found no documentation that the external auditor raised that issue with Fannie Mae as a violation of GAAP at that time.

Table VII-2. KPMG Upper Limit Calculations (dollars in millions)

Accounting Period	1 percent of NII – Upper Limit calculated by KPMG	1 percent of Annual NII Financial Statement Results	1 percent of Quarterly NII Financial Statement Results
Q1 2001	72	81	17
Q2 2001	76	81	19
Q3 2001	76	81	21
Q4 2001	81	81	24
Q1 2002	103	106	24
Q2 2002	94	106	25
Q3 2002	92	106	26
Q4 2002	93	106	30
Q1 2003	100	136	34

Sources: KPMG audit work paper titled, Fannie Mae Analysis of FAS 91 Mean Catch-up for Historical Periods, June 30, 2003, KPMG 000898. OFHEO calculations based on Fannie Mae SEC filing Form 10-K, for the periods ended December 31, 2003 and December 31, 2002.

In summary, KPMG was or should have been aware of two of the non-GAAP provisions of Fannie Mae's PPDA policy criticized in the September 2004 OFHEO report. However,

OFHEO found no documentation that KPMG raised any concerns with Fannie Mae management or the Board of Directors regarding those non-GAAP provisions contained in that policy. Enterprise personnel asserted that KPMG did not communicate to them that the provisions of the PPDA policy were not in compliance with GAAP. The lack of a formal process for reviewing accounting policies resulted in a critical impairment of Fannie Mae's ability to identify and correct the non-GAAP provisions contained in the policy. This failure created significant legal, operational, and reputational risks to the Enterprise.

FAS 133

Fannie Mae began developing policies and procedures to implement FAS 133 during 1998. In preparation for implementation of that standard, the Enterprise diagramed each of its derivative transactions and compiled internal guidance outlining accounting treatments. Fannie Mae initiated a three-part FAS 133 implementation process. In the first phase, undertaken in 1998, the Enterprise developed the derivative strategies and related accounting treatments. In the second phase, undertaken in 1999, it developed its FAS 133 Accounting

System to process the transactions and related accounting transactions. In the final phase, undertaken in 2000, the Enterprise performed a test run of its FAS 133 Accounting System to ensure preparedness for implementation of the standard on January 1, 2001.

The September 2004 OFHEO report highlighted several instances where the Enterprise's FAS 133 accounting policies and procedures did not conform to GAAP.[115] During testimony Fannie Mae personnel asserted that KPMG was heavily involved in the Enterprise's FAS 133 implementation process. The Enterprise insisted that KPMG engagement partners and members of the Department of Professional Practice (DPP) of the national office of the firm reviewed the Enterprise's derivative strategies and gave assurances regarding their compliance with FAS 133. Additionally, the Enterprise claimed that KPMG reviewed its FAS 133 accounting system and gave assurances regarding the sufficiency of controls surrounding the system and the operating effectiveness regarding conformity to the guidance of FAS 133.

Fannie Mae asserted that KPMG was contracted to perform additional review procedures with respect to the implementation of the FAS 133 policies and accounting system as part of the normal audit procedures. OFHEO questioned KPMG regarding the extent of its review of the Enterprise's FAS 133 accounting policies and procedures. KPMG indicated that the firm did, in fact, perform a detailed review of the Enterprise's derivative transactions. KPMG personnel also noted that the firm performed detailed test procedures over the FAS 133 accounting policies and system. In each case, the firm mentioned that it made a determination that the Enterprise's policies and procedures were in compliance with the requirements of FAS 133.

> Q: To your knowledge, did KPMG review Fannie Mae's hedge transactions and the related accounting treatments for those transactions to make a determination that they complied with FAS 133 during 2000?
>
> A: I'm sorry. Did we look at the hedge transactions?
>
> Q: And the related—
>
> A: To reach a conclusion?
>
> Q: Yes. And the related accounting treatment to make a determination that they complied with FAS 133?
>
> A: I believe we did.
>
> Q: During 2000?
>
> A: I believe our conclusion at the end of the audit in 2000 was that their 133 accounting was appropriate and that their transition adjustment was reasonable at that date.[116]

Fannie Mae officials and KPMG partners agree that during 1998 and 1999, KPMG reviewed all of the proposed derivative and hedging transactions prior to the Enterprise's implementation of FAS 133.[117] KPMG audit work papers show that it had identified many of the non-GAAP practices highlighted in the September 2004 OFHEO report. KPMG regarded the practices as "practical applications" of FAS 133 and determined that the improprieties would result in minimal financial statement impact. However, the SEC determined that the Enterprise's "practical applications" of FAS 133 represented material misrepresentations of GAAP.[118] For example, Fannie Mae had a practice of inappropriately applying the "shortcut method" under FAS 133 to hedge transactions in which the maturity date of the hedged item and the corresponding interest rate swap, in cash-flow hedging relationships, were mismatched by up to seven days. Comments contained in the KPMG 2003 work papers suggest that the external auditor was not only aware of the Enterprise's practice, but also recognized it as a departure from FAS 133, as follows:

> Fannie Mae uses the shortcut method to apply FAS 133 provisions to an interest rate swap in a cash flow hedge when it is assumed that there will be no hedge ineffectiveness.... Fannie Mae assumes no ineffectiveness and applies the shortcut method, if the rollover date of the discount note and reset in the interest rate swap are within +/-7 days of each other or a maximum of 5 business days (Practical Application #1). Although this policy is not in strict compliance with FAS 133 and DIG [Derivatives Implementation Guidance issued by the Financial Accounting Standards Board (FASB)], Fannie Mae goes through the exercise to determine that the departure from strict compliance is clearly inconsequential[119]

The audit work papers indicate that although KPMG identified the practice as a "practical application," and not in strict compliance with GAAP, the external auditor failed to investigate further because the resulting ineffectiveness was deemed to be immaterial. Other instances in which the external auditor failed to disallow identified departures from the requirements of FAS 133 were highlighted in the audit work papers. For example, the 2003 audit work papers contained discussion of Fannie Mae's accounting treatment for anticipatory hedge transactions where the practice was described as a "practical application" of GAAP. The Enterprise inappropriately applied alternative measures to qualify that hedge strategy as highly effective.

> For anticipatory hedge transactions, obtain management's analysis of the calculation of the hedge ineffectiveness that was recorded in the income statement during 2003. Historically, Fannie Mae used the duration and deminimus [sic] measures (which were practical applications of FAS 133) to determine whether the assumption of no ineffectiveness could be assumed. During 2003, Fannie Mae ceased using these practical applications and accounted for anticipatory hedge transactions under the long haul method.[120]

OFHEO questioned the external auditor regarding its acceptance of the Enterprise's "practical applications" of FAS 133. OFHEO examiners found that although KPMG recognized that some of the Enterprise's policies were not in strict compliance with the standard in all respects, the external auditor maintained that "the application of FAS 133 was in accordance with GAAP."[121]

While KPMG performed a detailed review of Fannie Mae's FAS 133 accounting policies to determine compliance with the standard in 1999, the external auditor did not perform another detailed review of those policies until 2003.

> Q: Okay. Could you describe in detail the review of Fannie Mae's FAS 133 policies and operational procedures that was performed upon implementation of FAS 133?
>
> A: It's my understanding that dating back to 1998, Fannie Mae developed what are their transactions and how those transactions would be accounted for under FAS 133; and that

prior to my arrival in late fall of '99, KPMG had concurred with those accounting treatments, and that they were consistent with FAS 133.

Q: So Fannie Mae had developed transactions and the accounting treatment that it would employ for those transactions prior to the time that you arrived in 1999; is that correct?

A: The individual transactions, yes.

Q: ... Okay. Is it your understanding that Fannie Mae contracted with KPMG to perform procedures surrounding the implementation of FAS 133 during 2000?

A: It's my understanding that KPMG as part of the audit process enhanced the scope of procedures that we would perform. I don't recall a separate engagement letter related to that matter.

Q: Okay. As part of the enhanced procedures that were performed in 2000, did you review Fannie Mae's Derivatives Accounting Guidelines [DAG] in its entirety?

A: I reviewed the front section of the Derivative Accounting Guide.

Q: So by that you mean the writing as opposed to the transactions and the schematics of those transactions that are outlined in the back of the Derivatives Accounting Guidelines?

A: That is correct.

Q: Did you review the DAG in its entirety in 2001? A: I don't recall. Q: Did you review the DAG in its entirety in 2002?

A: I don't recall.

Q: ... So to your understanding--so it's your understanding that the only policy review that KPMG performed was as part of its audit procedures for 2003.

A: I believe as part of our audit procedures and as they were enhancing or amending the data, we would have reviewed sections of it.

Q: Okay.

A: In conjunction with that process.

Q: Okay. Now, you mentioned you would have reviewed sections of it. Did you review the DAG in its entirety in 2003?

A: I don't recall.[122]

FAS 138, *Accounting for Certain Derivative Instruments and Certain Hedging Activities*, was issued in June 2000 as an amendment to FAS 133, prior to Fannie Mae's implementation of that standard. Among other things, the statement amended FAS 133 such that Fannie Mae's term-out transactions would no longer qualify for either the "short-cut" or "critical terms matched" approach to hedge accounting because the fair value of the derivative would not be zero at the time of the re-designation. Those changes had significant implications for Fannie Mae's accounting treatment for derivative transactions. As documented in the September 2004 OFHEO report, Fannie Mae personnel indicated that the Enterprise was aware of the major impact that FAS 138 would have on its accounting treatment for term-out transactions; however, the Enterprise did not change its accounting policies to incorporate the amended guidance because an analysis performed indicated that the change would result in minimal ineffectiveness.[123] KPMG failed to conduct a formal review, express concern, or require changes to Fannie Mae's hedge accounting to incorporate the change. Julie Theobald, retired Audit Partner, described the effects of FAS 138 as follows:

> Q: Do you recall FAS 138, which was an amendment to FAS 133 having been issued during 2000?
>
> A: I recall it being issued.
>
> Q: Do you recall--and I'm not trying to put you on the spot--do you recall any discussions with Fannie Mae regarding the effects that FAS 138 would have on their hedge transactions?
>
> A: No. I recall that over this period and specifically in 2000 that there were implementation questions being addressed I guess by the FASB, by this DIG Committee? And I remember that there was an amendment that came out and that we were looking at new interpretations or different interpretations as well as the amendment in making our ultimate conclusion about their adoption of 133.[124]

KPMG failed to identify adequately the impact of FAS 138 on Fannie Mae's existing derivative accounting policies. Given the criticality of derivatives accounting to Fannie Mae's operations, KMPG's failure to do so represented a major weakness that contributed to Fannie Mae's failures to conform to GAAP. In addition, Enterprise management, having knowledge of the effect of FAS 138, did not fulfill its responsibility to disclose and discuss the accounting treatment with its external auditor. The failure by the officers and directors of Fannie Mae to oversee properly the external audits conducted by KPMG contravened the requirements of OFHEO and resulted in unsafe and unsound conditions at the Enterprise.

KPMG Assurances that Accounting Policies Complied with GAAP

KPMG provided an unqualified opinion each year to the Enterprise and its Board of Directors that the financial statements did not contain material deviations from GAAP. Professional auditing standards require the external auditor to make determinations regarding the presentation of financial statements, in all material respects, taken as a whole.

With respect to Fannie Mae's FAS 91 amortization accounting practices, KPMG performed audit procedures around the non-GAAP accounting practices highlighted in the September 2004 OFHEO report and concluded that the purchase premium and discount amortization expense amounts reported in the financial statements were materially correct. KPMG performed a detailed review of the FAS 133 derivatives and hedge accounting practices and noted that the policies contained departures from GAAP. Again, KPMG determined that those departures would not have a material impact on the financial statements. During 2004, the SEC determined that Fannie Mae's accounting practices related to amortization and derivatives and hedge accounting "did not comply in material respects with the accounting requirements in Statement Nos. 91 and 133" for the review period 2001 to mid-2004. [125] Fannie Mae's Board of Directors relied on those improper assurances from KPMG and failed to adequately monitor KPMG. Thus, as more fully discussed in Chapter IX, the Board failed to detect and require correction of accounting deficiencies and internal control weaknesses, and to meet its obligation to ensure compliance with laws, regulations, and standards. Although the complacency of the Board and the efforts of management to obfuscate the seriousness and existence of GAAP failures also contributed to the errors, there is no question that KPMG failed multiple times to surface serious accounting deficiencies that have contributed to the current problems at Fannie Mae.

KPMG's Review of the Barnes Investigation

KPMG also performed review procedures related to the allegations of fraud made by Roger Barnes. Fannie Mae asserted that KPMG had reviewed Mr. Barnes' concerns and concluded that the transactions and accounting practices identified by Barnes were in compliance with GAAP.[126] Despite the Enterprise's assertion that KPMG concluded that the items identified by Mr. Barnes had been recorded in accordance with GAAP, Mark Serock, Audit Partner at KPMG, told OFHEO that they did not perform procedures to review for GAAP compliance.

During an interview with OFHEO, Mr. Serock denied reviewing the issues raised by Mr. Barnes for compliance with GAAP and asserted instead that Fannie Mae made the determination that the transactions highlighted as part of Mr. Barnes' concerns had been recorded in accordance with GAAP:

> A: The involvement of KPMG was not to express a conclusion as to whether Mr. Barnes' matters were being amortized properly. It was we were [sic] in attendance in order to observe the information that had been provided as it related to the investigation, and to hear the discussion of that particular matter at that meeting.
>
> Q: So is it your testimony that KPMG did not make a determination as to whether or not the amortization--the items identified by Roger Barnes were being amortized in compliance with GAAP?
>
> A: Well, our conclusions were directed towards the financial statements as to whether we could issue a review opinion on the financial statements for that particular quarter. They weren't directed towards reaching any individual conclusions relating to any specific matters.
>
> Q: So given that this was a consideration of a possible illegal act, is it your testimony that KPMG did not form a conclusion as to whether or not the issues raised were in compliance with GAAP?
>
> A: Well, the point is, is that we, as I said, observed, heard and saw the company's investigation, and the company concluded that the matters were being recorded in accordance with Generally Accepted Accounting Principles.[127]

The testimony of the external auditor that Fannie Mae reviewed the amortization issues raised by Mr. Barnes for compliance with GAAP highlighted an inconsistency, as Fannie Mae personnel testified that the Office of Auditing did not perform audit procedures to opine on GAAP. During testimony to OFHEO, Mr. Rajappa insisted that the Office did not perform procedures to determine GAAP compliance:

> Q: Are audit procedures directed at determining whether or not the company has been in compliance with GAAP?

A: Audit procedures are directed at auditing to the standards established by Financial Standards and approved by KPMG.[128]

Noting the inconsistency, OFHEO questioned Mr. Serock regarding the reliance of KPMG on the determination of the Office of Auditing that the transactions had been recorded in accordance with GAAP. The external auditor expressed his belief that testing accounting policies for compliance with GAAP was within the scope of the function of the Office of Auditing, contradicting statements by Mr. Rajappa.

Q: I had another question I wanted to follow up on. It's something we talked about before the break. Before the break I understood your testimony to be that KPMG was not charged with making the determination as to whether or not the issues raised by Roger Barnes were in compliance with GAAP, but rather Internal Audit made that determination; is that correct?

A: The determination regarding Mr. Barnes was conducted by the investigation team, which Internal Audit was part of, and their conclusion was that they were in accordance with GAAP I believe in reading the memo.

Q: ... It's our understanding from testimony from Fannie Mae personnel that the Internal Audit Department does not generally perform audit procedures to determine compliance with GAAP as it relates to, you know, their general performance of their internal audit procedures. Is that consistent with your understanding?

A: My understanding would be is [sic] that the procedures which they perform in part determine whether transactions are recorded in accordance with GAAP.[129]

Additional factors limited KPMG's forensic review of Fannie Mae's investigation of Mr. Barnes' allegations. Ron Forster, a Forensic Partner on the review, described how he became involved:

In November 2003, he received a phone call from KPMG's lead engagement partner with FM [Fannie Mae], Harry Argires, requesting that Forster immediately come to FM's headquarters for a meeting.... Forster arrived in Washington the next day and met with Argires, Mark Serock, an audit partner on the FM account, Michael Tascher, an auditor on the FM account, and Pam Verick-Stone, a forensic accountant, all of KPMG.... Argires brought in Forster and Verick-Stone because KPMG forensic teams are used to ensure that KPMG auditors fulfill their [SEC section] 10A obligations. Forster stated that this practice was new at the time of the Barnes review, and it was modified during the pendency of that review in December 2003, but these modifications did not affect his work with FM. Forster noted that this was one of the first investigations of this kind conducted by KPMG Forensic.[130]

KPMG indicated that Mr. Rajappa briefed the review team about Roger Barnes' allegations and discussed the actions taken by Fannie Mae. OFHEO questioned Mr. Serock regarding the manner in which the Office of Auditing characterized Mr. Barnes to assess how seriously the Enterprise was reviewing the allegation of fraud as follows:

Q: ...Did you ever get the perception that Fannie Mae, you know, was not giving full weight to Mr. Barnes' concerns given that he may have been characterized as a disgruntled employee?

A: My feelings about that is that, just upon my discussions with Sam, Mr. Rajappa, is that he very much took the allegation seriously.[131]

However, Ron Forster described Mr. Rajappa's characterization of the issue very differently. Mr. Forster recalled the characterization of Roger Barnes by the Office of Auditing as follows:

First, they [KPMG] met with Sam Rajappa, FM's Senior Vice President of Operations Risk, and Ann Eilers, Vice President of Internal Audit [footnote omitted]. Rajappa described Barnes's allegations, which he characterized as the complaints of a disgruntled, low-level accountant. Rajappa also stated that Barnes did not understand the issues about which he complained and had been seeking to build a discrimination lawsuit against FM for years.[132]

During his interview, Mr. Forster testified that after KPMG completed its review of Mr. Barnes' allegations, additional evidence provided by Fannie Mae revealed that the Office of Auditing had previously mischaracterized Roger Barnes during its initial briefing on the matter. Additionally, Mr. Forster testified that Fannie Mae withheld information that would have been relevant to his review:

> Forster stated that because KPMG's engagement team agreed with Rajappa's assessment of Barnes, Forster came to believe that Barnes lacked the knowledge and skills to fully understand the accounting issues he raised. In November 2004, however, Wilmer, Cutler [Fannie Mae Counsel] provided Forster with certain documents prepared by Barnes that Forster learned FM had possessed but not disclosed to KPMG at the time of the review. Upon reviewing these documents, which consist primarily of Barnes's e-mails to himself and another FM employee, he realized that FM had not been forthright in its dealings with KPMG Forensic and that Barnes had a greater understanding of the accounting issues than Forster had been led to believe. He believes that Verick-Stone asked Tascher and Serock whether they had seen the documents at the time, and they replied in the negative. By the time he saw the documents, however, Paul Weiss had already begun its investigation, so KPMG did not address the matter with FM.[133]

Another limitation of KPMG's review of Mr. Barnes' allegations was that none of the KPMG personnel who reviewed those allegations fully understood FAS 91. In Fannie Mae's Final Report documenting the matter, the Enterprise stated that "Fannie Mae's implementation of FAS 91 was at the heart of Mr. Barnes' concerns."[134] Mr. Forster indicated to Fannie Mae that he relied on the comfort level that KPMG Audit staff had regarding the Enterprise's FAS 91 accounting.

> Forester [sic] stated that he is not familiar with FAS 91, and so he relied on KPMG's auditors, who had examined the amortization issues in question and were comfortable with FM's practices.[135]

By relying on KPMG's earlier assessment of FAS 91, KPMG missed an obvious opportunity to find the errors in that accounting, particularly as the accounting had since been impugned by the allegations of fraud. Safety and soundness standards require that Fannie Mae retain a forensic team that is competent and sufficiently motivated to assess the work of the audit staff. As a result of the failure to do so, the integrity of the forensic review was compromised.

KPMG's determination regarding the Barnes matter was impugned also by its failure to review the Enterprise's FAS 91 policy. OFHEO questioned Mr. Serock regarding his review of the Enterprise's written FAS 91 policy in connection with the Barnes matter. He indicated that KPMG did not request a copy nor was it necessary to do so to make a determination regarding Mr. Barnes' allegation of fraud:

> Q: Did you request a copy of a written--did you request a written copy of Fannie Mae's amortization policy at this time?
>
> A: Did we request a written copy of Fannie Mae's amortization policies at this time. Which time are you referring to?
>
> Q: As a result of the allegations raised by Roger Barnes.
>
> A: No, I did not.
>
> Q: ... Do you believe that it would have been important to have requested a written copy of Fannie Mae's purchase premium and discount amortization policy in order to ascertain all of the factors necessary to explain the complete amortization process?
>
> A: No.
>
> Q: The next sentence [of Exhibit 2] reads: "Fannie Mae's implementation of FAS 91 was at the heart of Mr. Barnes' concerns." Given that Fannie Mae's implementation of FAS 91 was at the heart of this issue, do you still believe that it was not important to have reviewed a copy of, a written copy of the policy in order to ascertain that all the factors necessary to explain the complete amortization process were understood?
>
> (KPMG Attorney): He just answered that question.
>
> Q: Having read this sentence does it change your answer?
>
> A: No.[136]

The final limitation of the external auditor's determination is regarding the lack of independence of, and thus, inherent conflict of interest in, Fannie Mae's investigation. When questioned about the independence and objectivity of the Fannie Mae's internal investigation, Mr. Forster stated that in light of Sarbanes-Oxley requirements and recent developments, having the Enterprise conduct its own investigation may not have been appropriate.

> When asked if KPMG was concerned that IA [Internal Audit] effectively was asked to audit itself in the investigation of Barnes's allegations, Forster replied that the larger concern was whether FM [Fannie Mae] should have used an internal department of any kind to investigate allegations of fraud. He believes that if such allegations were made today, in light of both Sarbanes-Oxley and recent revelations regarding FM, KPMG would look much more carefully at the decision to use IA for the investigation. Forster stated that KPMG was not concerned with generally accepted auditing standards *per se*, but instead sought to ensure that the process followed by the [internal] auditors was thorough and proper.[137]

The internal and external auditors performed a cursory review, at best, of the allegations of fraud raised by Roger Barnes. The review procedures performed by the external auditor were not sufficient to make a determination regarding the reasonableness of the investigation performed by Fannie Mae or to evaluate the Enterprise's conclusions regarding Mr. Barnes' assertions. Furthermore, the evidence suggests that neither Fannie Mae nor KPMG performed a review sufficient to make a determination regarding whether the transactions identified by Mr. Barnes actually complied with GAAP. Thus, another control failed that might have led to discovery of major accounting violations and control deficiencies at Fannie Mae. KPMG's failure to review and investigate adequately the Barnes allegations was a material weakness that contributed to the unsafe and unsound accounting practices of Fannie Mae.

Conclusion

This chapter documents contraventions of OFHEO safety and soundness guidelines and other unsafe and unsound practices associated with the work performed by Fannie Mae's internal and external auditors. The Office of Auditing contravened OFHEO safety and soundness guidance and its own Board-approved charter by failing to assess accounting and operational compliance with GAAP. In addition, the Office represented that its review of critical accounting policies included such assessments when they did not. The intentional misrepresentations of the extent of the internal auditors' reviews violated safety and soundness standards.

The Enterprise also failed to oversee external audits performed by KPMG as required by OFHEO guidance and regulations. Those audits failed to include an adequate review of Fannie Mae's significant accounting policies for GAAP compliance. KPMG also improperly provided unqualified opinions on financial statements even though they contained significant departures from GAAP. Both the failure to review adequately significant accounting policies and procedures for GAAP compliance and representations regarding GAAP compliance indicate that Fannie Mae's external audits contravened requirements for external audits established by OFHEO. The failure of KPMG to detect and disclose the serious weaknesses in policies, procedures, systems, and controls in Fannie Mae's financial accounting and reporting, coupled with the failure of the board of Directors to oversee the external auditors properly, contributed to the unsafe and unsound conditions at the Enterprise.

Both the internal investigation of alleged fraud and KPMG's external review of that investigation contravened safety and soundness standards that require an Enterprise both to maintain and implement internal controls that among other things provide for compliance with laws, regulations and policies and to establish and maintain an effective risk management framework, to monitor its effectiveness, and to take appropriate action to correct any weaknesses. The internal investigation was tainted by conflicts of interest and by an incomplete review of the accounting issues. The procedures used by the external review were not sufficient to make a determination regarding the reasonableness of the investigation performed by Fannie Mae or to evaluate the Enterprise's conclusions regarding Mr. Barnes' assertions. KPMG had insufficient independent understanding of the accounting issues involved, failed to review Fannie Mae's internal accounting policy for compliance with GAAP, and relied on the auditors that had already assessed the questioned accounting practices.

References

[1] 12 C.F.R. § 1720, App. A, B, VI; OFHEO Policy Guidance, Minimum Safety and Soundness Requirements PG-00-001, Subpart B(9), (Dec. 19, 2000).
[2] 12 C.F.R. § 1720, App. A, B, V; OFHEO Policy Guidance, Minimum Safety and Soundness Requirements PG-00-001 Subpart B(8), (Dec. 19, 2000).
[3] Fannie Mae Office of Auditing Internal Audit Manual which includes the Charter approved by the Board on April 21, 1998, p. A-3.7.
[4] The Committee of Sponsoring Organizations of the Treadway Commission – "Internal Control — Integrated Framework Executive Summary," http://www.coso.org/publications/executive_summary_integrated_framework.htm. In 1985 the National Commission on Fraudulent Financial Reporting, also known as the Treadway Commission, was formed to study the financial reporting system in the United States. As part of that effort, the Committee of Sponsoring Organizations (COSO) performed a study of internal control to provide a broad framework of criteria against which companies could evaluate the effectiveness of their internal control systems.
[5] The Institute of Internal Auditors, International Standards for the Professional Practice of Internal Auditing, Performance Standard 2110 – Risk Management, Implementation Standard 2110.A2 – Assurance Engagements.
[6] The Institute of Internal Auditors, International Standards for the Professional Practice of Internal Auditing, 1210 - Proficiency and 1220 - Due Professional Care.
[7] Fannie Mae Office of Auditing Internal Audit Manual which includes the Charter approved by the Audit Committee on April 21, 1998, p. A-3.7.
[8] Id. at p. A-3.6.
[9] 12 U.S.C. § 1723a.(k). See also 12 C.F.R. § 1730.3 (each Enterprise must prepare periodic disclosures relating to its financial condition that include supporting financial information and certifications).
[10] 12 U.S.C. § 1723a.(a)(l).
[11] 12 C.F.R. Part 1720, App. A, B, V and VI; OFHEO Policy Guidance, Minimum Safety and Soundness Requirements PG-00-001, Subparts B(8) and (9), (Dec. 19, 2000).
[12] 12 CFR §§ 1710.15 (b)(4) and (b)(5).
[13] OFHEO analysis of Fannie Mae Audit report records between 2002 and 2004.
[14] Meeting Notes, "Meeting with Jean Hinrichs and John Kerr," April 19, 2006.
[15] OFHEO Interview, Sampath Rajappa, June 17, 2004, p.10.
[16] OFHEO Interview, Timothy Howard, August 5, 2004, pp. 36-37.
[17] E-mail from Ann Eilers to Anthony Marra, Ann Kappler, and Leanne Spencer and copied to Sampath Rajappa, December 10, 2003, OFH-FMS00837285.
[18] Id.
[19] See Paul Weiss Memorandum from Douglas Burns to Fannie Mae Team, "Interview of Sam Rajappa on January 12, 2005," February 15, 2005, FMSRC OFHEO 0135121. See also OFHEO Interview, Sampath Rajappa, February 23, 2006, pp. 62-64.
[20] 12 C.F.R. § 1720 App. A, B, VI; OFHEO Policy Guidance, Minimum Safety and Soundness Requirements PG-00-001, Subpart B(9), (Dec. 19, 2000).
[21] OFHEO Interview, Sampath Rajappa, June 17, 2004, p. 10.

[22] Ernst & Young Report, which includes findings, recommendations, and action plans in connection with human capital improvements, Fannie Mae Office of Auditing: Internal Audit Transformation – Recommendations, June 30, 2005, FMSE 510811–33 at 22.
[23] Audit Committee Minutes, January 17, 2005, FMSE 506214–25.
[24] Id. at 23.
[25] Audit Committee Minutes, March 28, 2005, FMSE 503042–46 at 42.
[26] Ernst & Young Report, Fannie Mae Office of Auditing: Internal Audit Transformation – Recommendations, June 30, 2005, FMSE 510811–33 at 15.
[27] Sarbanes-Oxley Act of 2002, Pub. L. No. 107-204, 116 Stat. 745 imposed various governance and internal controls requirements on SEC registrants. Section 404 of the Act requires each annual report of a public company to include a report by management on the company's internal control over financial reporting.
[28] A study co-sponsored by Jefferson Wells International and The Institute of Internal Auditors in May 2004 found that out of the 53 percent of internal audit functions with direct SOX project management responsibility, nearly a third of internal audit groups devoted between 70 percent and 100 percent of their staff time to SOX work.
[29] Many large firms enlisted the help of external consultants to assist in the development of the SOX compliance structure. See e.g., Sarbox: Year 2 – The second time around promised more headaches, but some best practices are emerging, Bob Violino, CFO IT, September 15, 2005 (www.cfo.com/article.cfm/4390933?f=options,).
[30] Memorandum from Kathryn Rock to Robert Levin, "Management's 2004 Assessment of Internal Control Over Financial Reporting," August 12, 2005, FMSE 519599–616.
[31] Audit Committee Minutes, May 23, 2005, FMSE 510105–23 at 19.
[32] Memorandum from Kathryn Rock to Robert Levin, "Management's 2004 Assessment of Internal Control Over Financial Reporting," August 12, 2005, FMSE 519599–616.
[33] Audit Committee Minutes, May 23, 2005, FMSE 510105–23 at 14.
[34] See e.g., Freddie Mac press releases dated January 22, 2003, March 25, 2003, June 9, 2003 and June 25, 2003.
[35] Freddie Mac Press Release, June 25, 2003.
[36] OFHEO Interview, Sampath Rajappa, June 17, 2004, pp. 14-16.
[37] A significant audit difference is one where the difference between the auditor's expectation and the recorded amount exceeds the auditor's materiality threshold.
[38] OFHEO Report of Findings to Date of the Special Examination of Fannie Mae, September 2004, pp. 68-69.
[39] Amortization Audit Workpaper, 2003, FMSE 118808–09 at 08.
[40] Amortization Audit Report, July 9, 2003, FMSE 023746-52 and Amortization Audit Workpaper, 2003, FMSE 118808–09.
[41] Amortization Audit Workpaper, 2003, FMSE 118808-09 at 09.
[42] Accounting Principles Board Opinion No. 20 (As Amended), Accounting Changes, (July 1971). APB 20 defines various types of accounting changes and establishes guides for determining the manner of reporting each type. It also covers reporting a correction of an error in previously issued financial statements.
[43] The Audit Tracking List included audit issues that meet the following criteria: items equal to or greater than $1 million; weaknesses in primary control; and systemic weaknesses in controls. Fannie Mae, The Office of Auditing Charter, Approved by the Audit Committee April 21, 1998, p. C-3.1-C-3.2.

[44] Amortization Audit Work Papers, 2003, FMSE 118808–09.

[45] Amortization Audit Report, July 9, 2003, FMSE 023746–52 at 49.

[46] Mr. Rajappa admits that a "[c]hange in EPS by 1 cent is material $15-16 mm pre-tax; $10mm after tax," in a discussion of internal audit policies and procedures presented in an insurance risk assessment submitted to Marsh in the fourth quarter of 2002 or the first quarter of 2003, FM SRC OFHEO 01379701–02 at 02.

[47] Amortization Audit Work Papers, 2003, FMSE 118808–09.

[48] Amortization Audit Report, July 9, 2003, FMSE 023746–52 at 46, and Amortization Audit Plan/Program, January 2003, at FMSE 122314.

[49] OFHEO Interview, Joyce Philip, July 21, 2004, p. 95.

[50] Memorandum from Sam Rajappa to Audit Committee of the Board of Directors, "Audit Opinion of Internal Controls over non-Mortgage Derivatives," March 31, 2003, FMSE 016125.

[51] OFHEO Interview, Joyce Philip, July 21, 2004, p. 206.

[52] Derivatives Control Audit Report, March 31, 2003, FMSE 102390.

[53] Ernst and Young Report, Fannie Mae Office of Auditing: Internal Audit Transformation and Recommendations, June 30, 2005, FMSE 510811-510833 at 510819.

[54] Memorandum from Sampath Rajappa to Audit Committee of the Board of Directors, "Audit Opinion of Internal Control over Non-Mortgage Derivatives," April 6, 2001, March 29, 2002, and March 31, 2003, FMSE 014893, FMSE 015316, FMSE 016125, respectively.

[55] Derivatives Control Audit Report, March 31, 2003, FMSE 102388.

[56] Derivatives Controls Audit work paper, 2003; FMSE 186468–72 at 71.

[57] OFHEO Interview, Joyce Philip, July 21, 2004, p. 205.

[58] Allowance for Loan Losses Audit, Audit Report, , December 15, 2003, FMSE 130362.

[59] OFHEO Interview, Sam Rajappa, February 23, 2006, p. 64.

[60] Written Testimony of Roger Barnes, For the U.S. House of Representatives Committee on Financial Services Subcommittee on Capital Markets, Insurance and Government Sponsored Enterprises Hearing on "The OHFEO [sic] Report: Allegations of Accounting and Management Failure at Fannie Mae," October 6, 2004, pp. 7-8, FM SRC OFHEO 01538903-904.

[61] "Summarized Minutes of the Meeting (8/8/03) Unamortized Balances and Factor Analysis," August 8, 2003. FMSE 021264–65.

[62] OFHEO Interview, Ann Eilers, July 23, 2004, p.222.

[63] Office of Corporate Compliance Decision #2203-1 (Part A, Amortization and Documentation Issues), Attachment B, September 29, 2003, FMSE 024417-19.

[64] Written Testimony of Roger Barnes, For the U.S. House of Representatives Committee on Financial Services Subcommittee on Capital Markets, Insurance and Government Sponsored Enterprises Hearing on "The OHFEO [sic] Report: Allegations of Accounting and Management Failure at Fannie Mae," October 6, 2004, pp. 20-21, FM SRC OFHEO 00140417–18.

[65] "Summarized Minutes of the Meeting (8/8/03) Unamortized Balances and Factor Analysis," August 8, 2003 FMSE 021264–65 at 65.

[66] OFHEO Interview, Joyce Philip, July 21, 2004, p. 222.

[67] Amortization Audit Report, July 9, 2003, FMSE 023746–52 at 46.

[68] See e.g., Memoranda from Sampath Rajappa to Franklin Raines and Timothy Howard, "Opinion on Internal Control over Financial Reporting," January 31, 2000, January 31, 2001, January 30, 2004, FMSE 014714, FMSE 095393, FMSE-KD 081843, respectively.
[69] OFHEO Interview, Sampath Rajappa, June 17, 2004, p. 138.
[70] 12 C.F.R. § 1720 App. A, B, VI; OFHEO Policy Guidance, Minimum Safety and Soundness Requirements PG-00-001, Subpart B(9), (Dec. 19, 2000).
[71] OFHEO, Report of Findings to Date Special Examination of Fannie Mae, September 2004, p. 78.
[72] OFHEO Interview, Ann Eilers, July 23, 2004, pp. 50-51.
[73] Report of the National Commission on Fraudulent Financial Reporting, October 1987, p. 37.
[74] Fannie Mae, Office of Auditing Charter, Approved by the Audit Committee April 21, 1998, p. A-3.7.
[75] OFHEO Interview, Thomas Gerrity, February 28, 2006, p. 101.
[76] Id. at p. 101.
[77] Id. at p. 102.
[78] OFHEO Interview, Sampath Rajappa, June 17, 2004, pp. 9-10.
[79] Id. at p. 30.
[80] Memoranda from Sampath Rajappa to Audit Committee of the Board of Directors, "Audit Opinion of Internal Controls over Non-Mortgage Derivatives," April 6, 2001, March 29, 2002, March 31, 2003, FMSE 014893, FMSE 015316, FMSE 016125, respectively.
[81] Amortization Audit Report, July 9, 2003, FMSE 023746–52 at 46.
[82] E-mail from Ann Eilers to Daniel Mudd and Louis Hoyes and copied to Sampath Rajappa, "FW:2004 audits," August 23, 2004, wherein Ann Eilers states she informed Thomas Gerrity that the Office of Auditing was postponing and canceling audits due to the work demands, OFH-FNMNR 00036648.
[83] "Letter to Chairman (from a 30 year veteran)," August 19, 2003, FM SRC OFHEO 0134778–79. It appears that Mr. Raines received this letter from Sampath Rajappa, as the document was sent to and held by Mr. Raines as custodian.
[84] Fannie Mae Office of Auditing Internal Audit Manual which includes the Charter approved by the Audit Committee, April 21, 1998, p. A-3.7.
[85] Fannie Mae Office of Auditing Internal Audit Manual which includes the Charter approved by the Audit Committee April 21, 1998, p. C-3.1-C-3.2.
[86] Id. pp. C-3.1-C-3.2.
[87] "Review of Amortization Results-Audit Analysis of Unamortized Balances and Factors," FMSE 023283.
[88] Derivatives Control Audit Report, March 31, 2003, FMSE 102385–91 at 88.
[89] OFHEO Interview, Ann Eilers, July 23, 2004, p. 242. Since the Board of Directors Audit Committee only read 'red' reports, changing the color to 'yellow' by promising timely resolution was an easy means to avoid Audit Committee scrutiny.
[90] 12 C.F.R. § 1720 App. A, B, V and VI; OFHEO Policy Guidance, Minimum Safety and Soundness Requirements PG-00-001, Subparts B(8) and (9), (Dec. 19, 2000).
[91] 12 C.F.R. § 1720 App. A, B, VI.OFHEO Policy Guidance, Minimum Safety and Soundness Requirements PG-00-001, Subpart B(9), (Dec. 19, 2000).

[92] OFHEO Interview, Leanne Spencer, August 12, 2004, pp. 24-25.

[93] OFHEO Report of Findings to Date of the Special Examination of Fannie Mae, September 2004, p.155.

[94] For example, see OFHEO Interview, David Britt, February 9, 2005, o. 56 and OFHEO Interview, Marissa Wheeler, January 11, 2005 pp. 134-135.

[95] OFHEO Report of Findings to Date of the Special Examination of Fannie Mae, September 2004, p. ii.

[96] Financial Accounting Standards Board, FAS 91, Accounting for Nonrefundable Fees and Costs Associated with Originating or Acquiring Loans and Initial Direct Costs of Leases, December 1986, paragraph 18.

[97] Fannie Mae Purchase Premium and Discount Amortization Policy, December 2000, FMSE 074523–24.

[98] OFHEO Report of Findings to Date of the Special Examination of Fannie Mae, September 2004, p. ii.

[99] OFHEO Interview, Leanne Spencer, June 22, 2004, p. 121.

[100] OFHEO Interview, Jonathan Boyles, August 24, 2004, pp. 36-37.

[101] "Testimony by Franklin D. Raines Before the House Subcommittee on Capital Markets, Insurance and Government Sponsored Enterprises (Written Testimony)," Washington, DC, October 6, 2004.

[102] Id.

[103] OFHEO Interview, Mike Tascher, KPMG Partner, January 13, 2005, pp. 26-27: Q: I would like to introduce for the record Tascher 1, entitled the "Purchase Premium and Discount Amortization Policy," Bates stamped FMSE 074523 through FMSE 074524. Q: I will give you a chance to review the document and then and [sic] ask you some specific questions about it. (Witness reviews document.) Q: Are you familiar with this document? A: I don't believe I have seen this document. Q: Okay. Were you ever provided this policy as part of your audit work for 2001? A: This particular document? Q: Um-hmm. A: I haven't seen--I have not seen this document … A: (KPMG Attorney) Actually, what he's saying is he hasn't seen this written document that articulates this policy. Q: Have you seen it in a different form? A: I have seen components of what's written on this paper on this paper [sic] in a different form.

[104] During testimony, KPMG personnel referenced meeting notes prepared by the Audit Partner following their discussion with Fannie Mae as the basis for their understanding of the policy. KPMG meeting notes entitled Fannie Mae Accounting for FAS-91, December 31, 2000, KPMG 000547–52.

[105] Letter from Donald Remy to Michael Tascher, November 25, 2003, FMSE 024267. The correspondence is excerpted as follows: Dear Mr. Tascher: As discussed, in response to your e-mail of November 21, 2003, enclosed you will find certain information you requested regarding the matters involving Mr. Roger Barnes. You noted that in connection with KPMG's financial statement audit, and for purposes of performing the procedures required by a professional standard (SAS 99 "Consideration of Fraud in a Financial Statement Audit"), you will involve members of KPMG's Forensic practice in the review of this specific matter. To assist with KPMG's review, we provide you with the following: a. A copy of an email and supporting documentation in which Mr. Barnes raised concerns regarding accounting practices. b. A copy of the final Office of

Corporate Compliance Report regarding Mr. Barnes concerns, along with the Purchase Premium and Discount Amortization Policy

[106] Fannie Mae Purchase Premium and Discount Amortization Policy, December 2000, FMSE 074523–24.

[107] Handwritten notes by Michael Tascher on page 9 of Audit Committee Update, Critical Accounting Policy Deferred Price Adjustments, Leanne Spencer, November 17, 2003, KPMG 000533–46 at 42.

[108] OFHEO Interview, Michael Tascher, January 13, 2005, pp. 61-65.

[109] OFHEO Interview, Michael Tascher, January 13, 2005, pp. 58-61.

[110] "The Functional Equivalent of 16%," OFHEO Report of Findings to Date of the Special Examination of Fannie Mae, September 2004, p. 26.

[111] Form NT 10-Q Federal National Mortgage Association Fannie Mae – FNMPRN, filed November 15, 2004 (period: September 30, 2004), p. 4.

[112] OFHEO Interview, Mark Serock, March 9, 2005, pp. 170-171.

[113] KPMG audit work paper, "Fannie Mae Analysis of FAS 91 Mean Catch-up for Historical Periods," June 30, 2003, KPMG 000898.

[114] OFHEO Interview, Michael Tascher, January 13, 2005, pp. 52-54.

[115] OFHEO Report of Findings to Date of the Special Examination of Fannie Mae, September, 2004, pp. 90-92.

[116] OFHEO Interview, Julie Theobald, retired KPMG Partner, February 16, 2005, pp. 193-194.

[117] OFHEO Interview, Julie Theobald, retired KPMG Partner, February 16, 2005, pp.88-89.

[118] Form 8-K, Federal National Mortgage Association Fannie Mae – FNM, filed December 16, 2004 (period: December 15, 2004).

[119] KPMG Memorandum, "Process and Analysis Document-US Derivatives & Hedging," for the period ended December 31, 2003, KPMG-OFHEO-002822.

[120] KPMG Memorandum, "Audit Programme-US Derivatives & Hedging," for the period ended December 31, 2003, KPMG-OFHEO-002872.

[121] OFHEO Interview, Harry Argires, KPMG Partner, February 1, 2005, p. 79.

[122] OFHEO Interview, Harry Argires, KPMG Partner, February 1, 2005, pp. 89-94.

[123] Jonathan Boyles, was unable to produce the analysis related to FAS 138. He stated that the files were inadvertently discarded during his move between offices. OFHEO Interview, Jonathan Boyles, August 3, 2004, pp. 226-227.

[124] OFHEO Interview, Julie Theobald, February 16, 2005, pp. 194-195.

[125] Form 8-K, Federal National Mortgage Association Fannie Mae – FNM, filed December 16, 2004 (period: December 15, 2004).

[126] Memorandum from Donald Remy, Senior Vice President, Deputy General Counsel and Chief Compliance Officer to File, "Final Report on Matters re: Mr. Roger Barnes," February 28, 2004, KPMG-OFHEO-000094–105 at 97. An excerpt from a memorandum prepared by Donald Remy, SVP, Deputy General Counsel and Chief Compliance Officer, February 28, 2004, documents the Enterprise's response and conclusion regarding the Barnes matter as follows: On August 8, 2004 [sic] members from the Office of Corporate Compliance, Internal Audit, the Controller's office, and KPMG met, along with Mr. Barnes, to discuss the amortization analysis. Internal Audit, the Office of Corporate Compliance, and KPMG concluded that Fannie Mae had

properly amortized the items identified by Mr. Barnes and that they were in compliance with GAAP.

[127] OFHEO Interview, Mark Serock, KPMG Partner, March 9, 2005, p. 82-83.

[128] OFHEO Interview, Sampath Rajappa, June 17, 2004, p. 10.

[129] OFHEO Interview, Mark Serock, KPMG Partner, March 9, 2005, pp. 111-112.

[130] Memorandum from Adav Noti, Paul Weiss Attorney, to File, "Summary of January 28, 2005 interview of Ron Forster, Forensic Partner, KPMG," February 22, 2005, FM SRC OFHEO 00141044–60 at 45-46.

[131] OFHEO Interview, Mark Serock, KPMG Partner, March 9, 2005, pp. 95-96.

[132] Memorandum from Adav Noti, Paul Weiss Attorney, to File, "Summary of January 28, 2005 interview of Ron Forster, Forensic Partner, KPMG," February 22, 2005, FM SRC OFHEO 00141044–60 at 47.

[133] Id. at 00141052.

[134] Memorandum from Donald Remy, SVP, Deputy General Counsel and Chief Compliance Officer to File, "Final Report on Matters re: Mr. Roger Barnes," February 28, 2004, KPMG-OFHEO-000094–103 at 96.

[135] Memorandum from Adav Noti, Paul Weiss Attorney, to File, "Summary of January 28, 2005 interview of Ron Forster, Forensic Partner, KPMG," February 22, 2005, FM SRC OFHEO 00141044–60 at 50.

[136] OFHEO Interview, Mark Serock, KPMG Partner, March 9, 2005, pp. 75-78.

[137] Memorandum from Adav Noti, Paul Weiss Attorney, to File, "Summary of January 28, 2005 interview of Ron Forster, Forensic Partner, KPMG," February 22, 2005, FM SRC OFHEO 00141044–60 at 50-51.

VIII. The Role of Senior Management

Previous chapters of this report have reviewed how Fannie Mae senior management contravened minimum standards of safety and soundness, statutory requirements, and OFHEO guidance and regulations. Chapter V described how Chairman and Chief Executive Officer (CEO) Franklin Raines modified the Enterprise's executive compensation program to give senior executives a strong incentive to engage in improper earnings management. Chapter VI provided examples of how senior management executed the earnings management strategy that enabled Fannie Mae to report earnings results that met analyst expectations and maximized annual bonuses and other executive compensation, and illustrated the roles of Mr. Raines, Chief Financial Officer (CFO) Timothy Howard, Controller Leanne Spencer, and other senior executives. Chapter VII described how the Enterprise's Office of Auditing failed to perform its designated responsibilities and how management's inadequate oversight of, and excessive reliance on, KPMG LLP, Fannie Mae's external auditor, contravened requirements for external audits established by OFHEO.

Fannie Mae senior management engaged in other unsafe and unsound practices to facilitate its earnings management strategy and limit internal and external criticism of the Enterprise. This chapter reviews those practices, which included:

- Failing to establish and maintain a sound internal control system;

- Failing to maintain the independence and objectivity of Fannie Mae's Office of Auditing;
- Failing to disclose accurate information to the Enterprise's Board of Directors, its external auditors, OFHEO, the Congress, and the public;
- Failing to investigate properly employee allegations and expressions of concern about Fannie Mae's accounting and financial reporting that, if properly investigated, could have led the Enterprise to restate its financial reports;
- Failing to give members of the Board of Directors unrestricted access to members of Enterprise management; and
- Attempting to interfere with OFHEO's special examination.

Failure to Establish and Maintain a Sound Internal Control System

An effective system of internal control is the foundation of the safe and sound operation of a financial institution. Internal control consists of the policies, procedures, processes, and systems effected by the board of directors, management, and other personnel to safeguard an institution's assets, limit or control risks, and achieve its objectives. OFHEO guidance indicates that each Enterprise should "maintain and implement internal controls appropriate to the nature and scope of its business activities." Those controls must provide for

i. An organizational structure and assignment of responsibility … that provide for accountability and controls, including adherence to policy and procedures;
ii. A control framework commensurate with the Enterprise's risks;
iii. Policies and procedures adequate to safeguard and to manage assets; and
iv. Compliance with applicable laws, regulations, and policies.[1]

OFHEO guidance also indicates that the responsibility for establishing an effective internal control system lies with Enterprise management:

Management of the Enterprise [shall set] policies and controls to ensure the Enterprise's strategies are implemented effectively … and … the Enterprise's organizational structure and assignment of responsibilities provide clear accountability and controls ….[2]

During his tenure as Chairman and CEO of Fannie Mae, Franklin Raines was ultimately responsible for ensuring an adequate internal control system for the Enterprise. That expectation was consistent with best practice in corporate America and OFHEO's supervisory standards. In evaluating the performance of Mr. Raines, the list of factors considered by the Board of Directors included adequate infrastructure and controls, adequate business process controls, adequate internal controls to ensure that goals and objectives are met, and appropriate resource use.[3] Also sharing responsibility for the Enterprise's internal control system were CFO Timothy Howard and Controller Leanne Spencer, who along with Mr. Raines signed the annual certifications of Fannie Mae's financial statements; Daniel Mudd, who became Chief Operating Officer in February 2000; and Chief Technology Officer Julie St. John.

During the period covered by this report, Fannie Mae's internal control system was grossly inadequate and contravened OFHEO's supervisory standards. Chapter VI documented numerous severe internal control weaknesses related to the Enterprise's accounting and financial reporting. Those weaknesses included, but were not limited to:

- An absence of policy guidance and requirements for supporting documentation or independent review of journal entries;
- Weak internal control and accounting policies relating to dollar rolls;
- Weak internal controls and accounting policies relating to real estate owned (REO);
- No formal procedures for the approval of structured transactions;
- An absence of a formal process for assessing the economic benefits and costs of debt repurchases or formal procedures for approving such transactions;
- Serious weaknesses in accounting policies and practices for low-income housing tax credits (LIHTC) and the amortization of purchase discounts and premiums under FAS 91; and
- Inadequate internal control, policies, practices and procedures for determining the adequacy of the allowance for loan losses (ALL), which provided management with the opportunity to use the allowance to manage earnings.

The existence of those and other deficiencies in internal control at Fannie Mae resulted from actions and inactions of Enterprise senior management that contravened OFHEO standards and were in themselves unsafe and unsound practices. That conduct included:

- A failure to ensure appropriate segregation of duties;
- A failure to provide adequate resources to accounting and financial reporting;
- Tolerance of key person dependencies;
- A failure to implement sound policy development and oversight; and
- A failure to avoid conflicts of interest within the Legal Department. This section discusses each of those failures. Failure to Ensure Appropriate Segregation of Duties

Segregation of duties is an important element of a corporation's internal control system that reduces "the opportunity for an individual to be in a position to both perpetrate and conceal errors or irregularities in the normal course of his duties …."[4] The Basel Committee on Banking Supervision has observed:

> In reviewing major banking losses caused by poor internal controls, supervisors typically find that one of the major causes of such losses is the lack of adequate segregation of duties. Assigning conflicting duties to one individual (for example, responsibility for both the front and back offices of a trading function) gives that person access to assets of value and the ability to manipulate financial data for personal gain or to conceal losses. Consequently, certain duties within a bank should be split, to the extent possible, among various individuals in order to reduce the risk of manipulation of financial data or misappropriation of assets.[5]

As documented in OFHEO's September 2004 *Report of Findings to Date*, there was insufficient segregation of the duties of Chief Financial Officer (CFO) and later Vice Chairman Timothy Howard, of the credit risk assessment and financial reporting functions, and of the duties of key staff in the Controller's Office.[6] Chief Executive Officer (CEO) Franklin Raines was directly responsible for the first two of those failures. Responsibility for failing to segregate the duties of executives in the Controller's division rested with Ms. Spencer and Mr. Howard, to whom she reported, and ultimately with Mr. Raines. Those failures were critical weaknesses in the Enterprise's internal control system and contributed to the unsafe and unsound practices related to accounting and financial reporting documented in Chapter VI.

The Duties of Chief Financial Officer Timothy Howard

Timothy Howard, as the CFO of Fannie Mae from 1990 to 2004 and as Vice Chairman in 2003 and 2004, was responsible for an extremely broad range of financial activities at the Enterprise. Mr. Howard made recommendations on Fannie Mae's overall financial objectives—especially the targets for growth in core business earnings per share (EPS) on which executive compensation depended—that were typically adopted by the Office of the Chairman and the Board of Directors. He supervised business units responsible for acquiring mortgages and mortgage-backed securities for the retained portfolio and non-mortgage assets for the liquid investments portfolio. Mr. Howard also supervised personnel responsible for issuing debt and derivatives to fund those assets, was responsible for managing the interest rate risk of portfolio assets and liabilities, and was responsible for recommending how Fannie Mae disclosed that risk. In addition, he supervised the Controller's Office, which is responsible for accounting, budgeting, forecasting, and financial reporting. Further, Mr. Howard supervised departments responsible for credit policy and modeling, investor relations, and capital management. He had responsibility for evaluating and making compensation recommendations for the head of the Office of Auditing, Sampath Rajappa, who reported to him on a dotted-line basis beginning in 2002.

Mr. Howard's responsibilities allowed him to recommend Fannie Mae's core business EPS targets, approve asset acquisition and hedging transactions, approve the strategies used to manage the risks posed by those transactions, approve the risk measures used to report that risk, and approve accounting policies that established how the transactions were reported in the Enterprise's financial statements and whether core business EPS targets were achieved. His relationship to Mr. Rajappa gave Mr. Howard an ability to control Mr. Rajappa's communications with the Audit Committee of the Board of Directors. Thus, Mr. Howard was in a position to determine the overall level of interest rate risk Fannie Mae took, how much the public knew about that risk, and how much the Enterprise's financial statements reflected the volatility of the returns from that risk-taking.

Centralization of all of those responsibilities in one senior executive was unusual and inconsistent with best practices in the financial services industry. As noted in the *Report of Findings to Date*, prudent management and best practices require the segregation of risk taking from financial reporting and risk management.[7] Vesting that degree of authority and power in the CFO of a systemically important financial institution was an unsafe and unsound practice.

Mr. Raines, to whom Mr. Howard reported directly from 2000 onward, expanded Mr. Howard's set of responsibilities and was quite comfortable with the risk posed by assigning such a broad range of duties to one executive. The views of Mr. Raines in that regard were demonstrated in 2004, when Mr. Raines consolidated Mr. Howard's authority and responsibility—making him both the Chief Risk Officer (CRO) and the Chief Financial Officer—despite being advised that research by Fannie Mae had found that no companies had CROs and CFOs who were the same person.[8] Mr. Howard's other responsibilities simply did not provide the independence necessary for an effective CRO. Nonetheless, an e-mail dated August 13, 2004 from Jill Blickstein, Vice President and Assistant to the Chairman, a special assistant to Mr. Raines, to Rebecca Senhauser, Senior Vice President for Human Resources, and Emmanuel Bailey, Director for Human Resources, details a discussion between Blickstein ("me") and Mr. Raines ("FDR") regarding the dual roles of Mr. Howard:

This was FDR's feedback to the benchmarking information:

FDR: Well, we're ok, because just as I thought, lots of companies don't have CCOs [Chief Credit Officers].

ME: But, Frank, the companies who do not have CCOs do have CROs.

FDR: But Tim is our CRO.

ME: But we haven't announced that externally yet.

FDR: Well, we can do that.

ME: And no companies have CFOs and CROs who are the same person.

FDR: But that's because in most companies the CFO is a more junior position. So there's nothing wrong with combining the two.

ME: (Sigh.)[9]

Despite his role in increasing Mr. Howard's responsibilities, in sworn testimony before the Congress Mr. Raines failed to describe adequately the true nature of those duties. At a hearing on October 6, 2004, the following exchange occurred between Rep. Kelly and Mr. Raines:

Q: Mr. Raines, which member of the executive management team is responsible for risk management, accounting, on-balance sheet mortgage portfolio, business planning, tax, investor relations, and internal audit? Do you have one member who…

A: There is no one responsible for all those things unless you are thinking of me. But there is no one person responsible for those things.[10]

That statement by Mr. Raines notwithstanding, the person "responsible for those things" was Mr. Howard.[11]

Duties of Staff in the Office of the Controller

OFHEO's September 2004 report noted important instances of inadequate segregation of duties among staff in the Office of the Controller that undermined internal controls over Fannie Mae's accounting and financial reporting. Specifically, the report found the following:

- Beginning in 1999, Janet Pennewell, VP for Financial Reporting and Planning, was responsible for preparing Fannie Mae's financial forecasts, modeling the amortization of purchase premium and discounts and other deferred price adjustments under FAS 91, and the Enterprise's accounting and financial reporting functions. Thus, Ms. Pennewell could affect Fannie Mae planned financial results and the net income the Enterprise reported. Making one executive responsible for those three functions was a major control weakness that undermined the integrity of the financial reporting process.[12]

- In July 2003 Jeff Juliane, Director of Financial Reporting, was given responsibility for modeling the amortization of purchase premiums and discounts and for recording that amortization in the financial statements. Segregation of those functions had previously served as an important check and control point in the amortization process.[13]

The broad range of responsibilities of Controller Leanne Spencer also did not provide an appropriate segregation of duties. For example, Ms. Spencer played a key role in the development of the Enterprise's FAS 91 policy, effectively substituting for the Financial Standards group that reported to her and was responsible for developing accounting policies.[14] Ms. Spencer also approved financial forecasts and participated in the communication of financial results both internally and externally. The centralization of duties in Ms. Spencer seriously undermined Fannie Mae's internal control system and the integrity of the Enterprise's financial reporting.

Failure to Invest Adequate Resources in Accounting and Financial Reporting

Implementation of complex new accounting standards, rapid growth in business volumes, the passage of the Sarbanes-Oxley Act of 2002, and Fannie Mae's decision to register with the Securities and Exchange Commission required senior management to invest significant resources in enhancing the Enterprise's accounting and financial reporting functions. However, senior management failed to invest the necessary resources. That failure—in and of itself an unsafe and unsound practice as a failure of the Enterprise's responsibility to have policies and procedures in place that, at a minimum, safeguard and manage assets—exacerbated existing internal control weaknesses documented in this report, directly contributing to unsafe and unsound practices.[15]

Keeping Fannie Mae's administrative and other infrastructure-related expenses as low as possible during a time of rapid growth was a recurring topic of senior management communications, especially during the Quarterly Business Review sessions, at which budget issues were discussed. As a follow-up to a QBR session in the summer of 2003, Ms. Spencer and Christine Cahn, Vice President for Budgeting and Expense Management, sent a memo to the Strategic Leadership Team and to senior vice presidents to hold down divisional and system costs for 2004. The memo also references two years of high revenue and core business EPS growth and the need to "tighten our belts."[16] That attitude led Fannie Mae to continue to operate with insufficient resources and inadequate systems.

Ms. Spencer failed to reveal to the Board of Directors resource problems and system implementation challenges relative to the implementation of new accounting standards. For example, in February 2004 she attempted to play down the $1 billion computation error related to FAS 149 to the Audit Committee of the Board, instead indicating that automated processes were under way and that a more permanent system was being developed.[17] Later that month, OFHEO expressed concerns about Fannie Mae's reliance on end-user computing systems and the lack of strong controls that led to the $1 billion computational error and directed the Enterprise to take remedial action.[18]

The failure to invest adequately led to critical resource shortages and a lack of technical accounting expertise within the Financial Standards group, which was responsible for understanding new accounting standards and developing Fannie Mae's accounting policies. Ms. Spencer and various staff of the Controller's Department indicated that questions relating to the accounting for derivatives could only be answered by Mr. Boyles himself.[19] The failure to invest adequate resources also led to a shortage of accounting expertise among the accounting and treasury operations staff in the Controller's Department. For example, individuals with responsibility for key aspects of the FAS 133 accounting process (such as ensuring proper hedge designations, or matching critical terms) were not knowledgeable about how such activities met the requirements of GAAP.[20] That lack of understanding led to those individuals relying heavily on the Financial Standards group, which itself was understaffed and lacked technical expertise.

Fannie Mae is a corporation that provides complex financial products and services to mortgage lenders. Ensuring that the Enterprise had proper accounting policies by providing adequate resources to the Financial Standards group should have been central to the decisions of senior management, not an afterthought.

The failure to provide adequate accounting systems rests not only with personnel in the Controller's Office, but also with officers higher in the organization with budgeting responsibilities. With respect to budgeting, EVP and Chief Technology Officer Julie St. John told OFHEO examiners in April 2004 that the Enterprise had a well-defined annual budget cycle where information technology priorities were reviewed. She added that business unit heads met with the Chief Operating Officer (at the time, Daniel Mudd) to review priorities and funding. She added that she believed that the process worked well.[21]

If that process worked well, it is hard to explain why management did not seek to remedy known issues regarding the limitations of securities accounting systems until recently. In a memorandum dated August 1, 2001, Janet Pennewell acknowledged that the securities accounting area is "frequently required to develop temporary 'workarounds' because our systems (STATs and STAMPs) weren't designed to handle the complexity of many of today's transactions."[22]

During the period covered by this report, Fannie Mae staff often viewed the Enterprise's external auditor, KPMG, as the final arbiter of issues related to compliance with GAAP. As noted in Chapter VII, it is ultimately the responsibility of management to determine whether accounting policies comply with GAAP. The tendency to rely on the external auditor to determine the propriety of accounting policies was symptomatic of inadequate technical expertise in the Office of the Controller, especially in the Financial Standards group.

Tolerance of Key Person Dependencies

The failure to invest adequate resources in the departments responsible for Fannie Mae's accounting and financial reporting resulted in significant key person dependencies in those areas, which were documented in OFHEO's September 2004 report. Both Controller Leanne Spencer and Mary Lewers, Director of Accounting and Audit, had limited knowledge of accounting standards. As noted above, critical shortages of qualified accounting specialists existed in the Controller's Department, especially in the area of FAS 133 accounting. As a result of those shortages, the Enterprise relied heavily on a few individuals, especially Vice President for Financial Standards and Taxes Jonathan Boyles, who had the expertise needed to make key decisions related to accounting policy development, and did not have an independent accounting policy review function, since Mr. Boyles reported directly to Ms. Spencer. The September 2004 report found that CFO Timothy Howard was responsible for those key person dependencies.[23] Mr. Howard's extremely broad range of responsibilities also constituted a significant key person dependency for Fannie Mae.

OFHEO requires the Board of Directors and management of each Enterprise to establish and maintain "an effective risk management framework, including review of such framework to monitor its effectiveness and taking appropriate action to correct any weaknesses."[24] The key person dependencies noted above undermined the effectiveness of Fannie Mae's risk management framework.

Failure to Implement Sound Accounting Policy Development and Oversight

OFHEO's 2004 report documented serious weaknesses in Fannie Mae's process for developing, reviewing, and approving accounting standards.[25] A key weakness during the period covered by this report was an absence of formal written procedures governing the development and approval of accounting policies at Fannie Mae. The absence of such procedures contravened OFHEO supervisory standards, which require Enterprise management to set policies to ensure that the Enterprise's strategies are implemented effectively and that such policies be in writing and approved by the Board of Directors or officers designated by the Board.[26] Written, formally approved policies provide a clear foundation for effective internal control of the auditing and financial reporting functions.

During the period covered by this report, OFHEO found no evidence of formal written procedures that governed the development of accounting policy at Fannie Mae. In fact, when questioned about documentation of the accounting policy development procedures, SVP for Accounting Policy and Tax Jonathan Boyles indicated that he was not aware if any existed:

> Q: Jonathan, is there a formal procedure for that to take place?
>
> A: I'm not sure what you mean by a formal procedure.
>
> Q: A formal procedure for the business unit to contact you.
>
> A: There's a policy that they're supposed to contact me.
>
> Q: Is that in writing anywhere?
>
> A: I don't know that it's in a policy manual out to people. I don't know that it's in writing or not.[27]

Mr. Boyles briefed Mr. Howard and Ms. Spencer on significant accounting policies, but they did not, according to Mr. Boyles, provide formal written approval of those policies.

Rather, Mr. Boyles deemed the policies to be approved unless Mr. Howard or Ms. Spencer voiced concerns about them.[28]

An example of the lack of formal procedures for approving accounting policies was evident in the process for developing the key document relating to FAS 91 accounting. Fannie Mae's *Purchase Premium and Discount Amortization Policy* was developed without input from Financial Standards, which is the group in the Controller's Department normally responsible for development accounting policy. Indeed, Mr. Boyles said that key provisions of that document do not comply with GAAP.[29]

The lack of formal procedures for developing and approving accounting policies at Fannie Mae facilitated the adoption of policies that were aggressive and did not comport with GAAP. In addition, the lack of formal policy development procedures resulted in a breakdown in communication regarding the Enterprise's policies and compliance with regulatory standards and less than full disclosure to the Audit Committee of the Board of Directors as well as the external auditors. The failure of management to keep the Board and external auditors informed about accounting weaknesses is discussed later in this chapter.

Failure to Prevent Conflicts of Interest in the Legal Department

One objective of an internal control system is to minimize conflicts of interest.[30] In general, a conflict of interest exists when the personal or business interests of an insider—a member of the Board of Directors, a manager, or an employee—are inconsistent with the continued safe and sound operation of the firm or with a business opportunity of the company.[31] During the period covered by this report, the structure of Fannie Mae's Legal Department posed conflicts of interest that undermined the department's ability to perform its ethics and compliance functions that were contrary to prudent operations, and that contravened OFHEO safety and soundness standards.[32] General Counsel Ann Kappler was responsible for the creation of those conflicts.

In 2001, the Office of Corporate Justice moved from Fannie Mae's Human Resources Department to the Legal Department in order to centralize the Enterprise's ethics and compliance functions. In 2002, the Office of Corporate Compliance was established to consolidate the various corporate compliance programs into a central office within the Legal Department. Donald Remy, Vice President and Deputy General Counsel, supervised both the Office of Corporate Compliance and the Office of Corporate Justice. Mr. Remy was given the title of Chief Compliance Officer, but his duties in that capacity conflicted directly with his responsibilities for managing the employment law, antitrust, and potential criminal and civil liability groups in the legal department.[33] Ms. Kappler's decision to give responsibility for both investigating employee complaints and defending the company in any related litigation to the same litigation team created a potential for conflict of interest. That potential should have led to more stringent oversight of the operation of both areas.

Failure to Maintain the Independence and Objectivity of the Internal Auditor

To comply with OFHEO safety and soundness standards, each Enterprise, at a minimum, should establish and implement internal and external audit programs that provide for the independence of the audit function and for qualified individuals and management to conduct and review that function.[34] In evaluating Fannie Mae's internal audit program, OFHEO considers industry best practices articulated by such authoritative sources as the Institute of Internal Auditors[35] and the October 1987 Report of the National Commission on Fraudulent Financial Reporting. That report noted that independence enables the internal auditor to be objective, which in turn contributes to the effectiveness of the internal audit function:

The effectiveness of a company's internal audit function depends a great deal on the objectivity of the chief internal auditor and his staff. Public companies should ensure that their internal auditors are free to perform their functions in an objective manner, without interference and able to report findings to the appropriate parties for corrective action.[36]

Fannie Mae's Office of Auditing (OA) is bound by the Audit Charter approved by the Enterprise's Board of Directors. That charter states that the purpose of the Internal Audit function is to act as "an independent appraisal activity." The charter further indicates that "the Vice President of Auditing reports to the Chairman of the Audit Committee of the Board of Directors and is accountable for the adequacy and effectiveness of the audit activities."[37] That reporting relationship is intended to promote the internal auditor's independence.

During the period covered by this report, Fannie Mae senior management undermined the independence and objectivity of the Enterprise's internal audit function in three major ways. First, senior management appointed Fannie Mae's former controller to head the Office of Auditing, despite the fact that he lacked auditing experience, was not an accountant, and would be able to audit his own work for one year. Second, senior management required the internal auditor to report to CFO Timothy Howard, who barred him from unfettered communication with the Audit Committee of the Board of Directors. Third, the compensation of the internal auditor and other OA staff depended substantially on core business EPS—the same metric used to compensate other managers whose departments OA audited. Those actions departed from industry best practices, contravened Fannie Mae's audit charter, violated OFHEO's safety and soundness standards, and were, therefore, unsafe and unsound practices.

As the Office of the Comptroller of the Currency has stated, the function of a financial institution's internal auditor is "to help the board and management monitor and evaluate internal control adequacy and effectiveness."[38] By undermining the independence and objectivity of Fannie Mae's internal auditor, senior executives made it much less likely that the auditor would challenge them to address the Enterprise's severe control weaknesses. As discussed in Chapter IX, the Audit Committee of the Board of Directors, by failing to exercise appropriate oversight over senior management and the audit function, was responsible for the lack of independence and objectivity of the Office of Auditing.

Appointment of Former Controller Rajappa to Head Office of Auditing

Fannie Mae's Audit Charter states that the OA is bound by the standards of the Institute of Internal Auditors to ensure that audits are performed with "proficiency and due professional care." Those standards indicate that auditors should possess the requisite knowledge, skills, and other competencies to perform their individual responsibilities.[39] Sampath Rajappa was appointed to the position of SVP for Operations Risk and Head of OA in 1999 even though he had not previously performed any auditing functions and was not a CPA. Given Mr. Rajappa's lack of those necessary qualifications, his appointment contravened the Institute of Internal Auditors' standards and the Enterprise's audit charter and violated OFHEO's regulatory requirement that the Board have in place adequate policies and procedures to assure its oversight of hiring of qualified senior executive officers.[40]

The Audit Charter also bound OA to the Institute of Internal Auditors' Standards for the Professional Practice of Internal Auditing. Those standards provide the following guidance regarding impairments to internal auditor independence:

> Internal Auditors should refrain from assessing specific operations for which they were previously responsible. Objectivity is presumed to be impaired if an internal auditor provides assurance services for an activity for which the internal auditor had responsibility within the previous year.[41]

In an interview with OFHEO, Mr. Rajappa indicated that prior to being appointed the head of the Office of Auditing in January 1999, he held the position of Controller from 1994 through the end of 1998.[42]

Mr. Rajappa's statements indicate that his service as the head of OA, at least in his first year on the job, contravened the Institute of Internal Auditors' standards. As the head of OA, he was responsible for auditing the Controller's department that he had run for several years. That represented a conflict of interest, undermined the objectivity of Fannie Mae's internal audit function, and was an unsafe and unsound practice.

Subordination of the Internal Auditor to the Chief Financial Officer

In his initial years as the head of OA, Mr. Rajappa reported on a "dotted line" basis to Chief Operating Officer (COO) Daniel Mudd, who participated in writing Mr. Rajappa's annual performance evaluation and made compensation recommendations for him. Mr. Rajappa reported directly to the Chairman of the Audit Committee of the Board of Directors, consistent with the requirement of Fannie Mae's Audit Charter and industry best practice.

However, in 2002 Mr. Raines changed Mr. Rajappa's "dotted line" reporting relationship from COO Daniel Mudd to CFO Timothy Howard, the officer to whom Mr. Rajappa had previously reported as Controller. When questioned about their relationship, Mr. Howard confirmed that he had "indirect or dotted line reporting from the auditor [Mr. Rajappa]." Mr. Howard also noted that

> Sam Rajappa reports directly to the chairman of the Audit Committee, but for the last I think year and a half, maybe two years, he has reported on a dotted line basis to me. Previously he also reported to our chief operating officer.[43]

In practice, however, Mr. Howard could and did exert considerable control over Mr. Rajappa's actions as the head of internal audit, in part because Mr. Howard participated in the annual performance evaluation and made compensation recommendations for Mr. Rajappa, which apparently were always accepted, and in part because of Mr. Howard's key role at Fannie Mae. The degree of Mr. Howard's influence was revealed quite clearly in 2004, when he ordered Mr. Rajappa not to communicate with the Audit Committee about accounting-related issues without first talking to Ms. Spencer or him. In an e-mail to Controller Leanne Spencer, Mr. Howard stated:

> I just got off the phone with Sam. I made it "blisteringly clear" to him that on any future calls he gets from the Chairman of our Audit Committee on accounting-related issues he must run the question or issue by you before he or anyone else gets back to Gerrity [Audit Committee Chairman]. He said he got the message and would do so in the future. (He said that he'd agreed to call Tom [Gerrity] back before realizing that you weren't here on Friday, so he spoke with Janet instead. I responded that going forward that wouldn't be good enough. He had to reach either you or me before responding to Gerrity on any accounting-related question he was asked. He said he understood).[44]

Those two actions—Mr. Raines's shift of Mr. Rajappa's "dotted line" reporting from Mr. Mudd to Mr. Howard and Mr. Howard inserting himself between Mr. Rajappa and the Audit Committee—undermined the independence of Fannie Mae's audit function and the effectiveness of the Enterprise's internal control system. An important role of the Office of Auditing is to test the compliance with Enterprise policies and procedures of departments that report to the CFO and to inform the Audit Committee of control weaknesses revealed by that testing. By preventing the head of OA from unfettered communication with the Audit Committee, Mr. Howard undermined the independence of internal testing and the objectivity and effectiveness of Fannie Mae's internal audit program, violated OFHEO guidance and regulation, and engaged in an unsafe and unsound practice.

Inappropriate Participation in Compensation Programs

The Institute of Internal Auditing's standards indicate that auditors must maintain independence both in fact and appearance.[45] Director-level and above Office of Auditing staff members were compensated through the Annual Incentive Plan (AIP) bonus program. From 1999 through 2003, Mr. Rajappa earned bonuses totaling approximately $1 million as a result of his participation in Fannie Mae's Annual Incentive Plan (AIP). All employees received additional compensation as part of the firm-wide drive to double EPS championed by CEO Franklin Raines. As discussed in detail in Chapter V, AIP payouts ("bonuses") to individual employees depended to varying degrees, and compensation under the core business EPS challenge depended solely on the level of core business EPS reported by Fannie Mae.

Participation in those compensation programs compromised the independence of the Office of Auditing, since Mr. Rajappa and his staff were responsible for auditing the departments that produced the Enterprise's financial reports, including the core business EPS measure. There was a conflict between the interest of Mr. Rajappa in maximizing his compensation and the duty to maintain auditor objectivity. For those reasons, Mr. Rajappa's participation in the Annual Incentive Plan and the core business EPS challenge violated OFHEO's requirement that Fannie Mae maintain the independence of its audit function and was an unsafe and unsound practice.

Failures to Disclose Complete and Accurate Information

During the period covered by this report, Fannie Mae senior management systematically withheld information about the Enterprise's operations and financial condition from the Board of Directors, its committees, its external auditors, OFHEO, the Congress, and the public—or disclosed information that was incomplete, inaccurate, or misleading. That prevented others from becoming aware of Fannie Mae's earnings management strategies, the fact that the Enterprise's accounting policies did not comply with GAAP, the pervasive weaknesses of its internal control system, and related safety and soundness issues. Chapter VII discussed the failure by the Office of Auditing to disclose information to the Audit Committee of the Board of Directors and the Enterprise's external auditors. This section provides several other examples of such misconduct, which contravened OFHEO's regulatory requirements and ordinary standards of prudent business operation.

Failure to Provide Complete and Accurate Information to the Board and Its Committees

The provision of complete and accurate information to a firm's board of directors, in a timely manner, is a cornerstone of effective corporate governance of a company. OFHEO requires each Enterprise's management to provide the board with relevant information of an appropriate level of detail to enable the board and its committees to make informed decisions and exercise its oversight function.[46] Fannie Mae management routinely violated that standard, failing to provide the Board of Directors material information that was needed to understand fully the Enterprise's operations and financial performance.

As Chairman of the Board of Directors and Chief Executive Officer from 1999 through 2004, Franklin Raines had a dual responsibility to ensure that the Board was given all information needed to carry out its fiduciary duty. As Chief Executive Officer, he had a responsibility to ensure that management provided the Board with all necessary information. As Chairman of the Board, he had an oversight duty to inquire of management as to why information was not being provided. Mr. Raines' practice, however, was to restrict the amount and type of information that went to the Board. That behavior set an internal standard that the rest of senior management followed. This section provides examples of how senior management failed to inform the Board.

Failure to Inform That Fannie Mae Accounting Policies Did Not Comply with GAAP

Fannie Mae senior management knew that a number of the Enterprise's accounting policies did not comply with GAAP or were aggressive, i.e., close to the line of what would be considered to comply with GAAP. A notable example was Fannie Mae's FAS 133 policy. In an interview with OFHEO, Jonathan Boyles, SVP for Accounting Policy and Tax, was asked:

> Q. With respect to the overall approach and the concept of assuming no ineffectiveness, do you believe there are situations in which Fannie Mae is applying that when it's not consistent with the guidance in FAS 133?
>
> A. We have several known departures from GAAP in our adoption of FAS 133. We have cleared those with our auditors. We have reported to our auditors on an annual basis the effect of those. And they were comfortable when we adopted them, and they were comfortable over the last several years when we reported the results of that work.[47]

Senior management had a duty to disclose to the Audit Committee of the Board of Directors any accounting policies that did not comply with GAAP. It does not appear, however, that senior management ever did so. In an interview with CFO Timothy Howard, the following exchange occurred:

> Q: Has [SVP for Accounting Policy and Tax] Jonathan Boyles ever informed you that the company's accounting policies or interpretation of accounting policy were aggressive?
>
> A: I'm almost certain he has, but I can't recall a specific instance.
>
> Q: Would you ever then inform the Audit Committee of the board of such an opinion held by your Financial Standards head?
>
> A: No, because again, I don't view the label aggressive accounting as being a bad thing. It is descriptive of relative positioning compared to the GAAP line. That's why I want to find out more about the specific incidents. And if it's uncomfortably close to the line, we will change it. It's not take it to the board. It's don't do it.
>
> Q: Have you ever informed the board or Audit Committee of the board of such an opinion held by your Financial Standards Department head?
>
> A: Not to my recollection.[48]

The combination of Fannie Mae management failing to inform the Board of known departures from GAAP and the Board's failure to oversee the Enterprise's accounting polices properly, detailed in Chapter IX, resulted in accounting failures and unsafe and unsound conditions.

Omission of Information on Amortization of Purchase Premium and Discounts

On January 19, 1999, in a Financial Performance Update to the Board, CFO Timothy Howard presented a summary income statement and described adjustments to income (both expense items and reduction in tax liability) that management had elected to take in 1998.[49] It appears that Mr. Howard did not explain to the Board several key facts, including that the expense related to amortization of purchase premium and discounts was only a portion of the Enterprise's best estimate of such amortization, and that KPMG had recorded an audit difference for the remaining amortization required by FAS 91. Mr. Raines, who was familiar with the 1998 adjustments, was present at that meeting but made no effort to inform other members of the Board.[50]

On February 16, 1999, Controller Leanne Spencer omitted information on the same topic from a presentation to the Board's Audit Committee on "The Year in Review, The 1998 Annual Report." Her notes for that presentation explain that the purpose of the meeting was to present highlighted sections of the draft 1998 Fannie Mae Annual Report that might be of interest to the members of the committee.[51] Her notes also discuss adjustments to the Enterprise's year-end results:

> The first adjustment, the $180 million and the $60 million, represent our recording additional amortization of purchase premium and discount balances associated with our net mortgage portfolio and a similar adjustment to prepaid or deferred guaranty fees. The additional amortization reflects OUR estimates of the effects of the sustained decline in interest rates and the high level of 1998 refinancing activity is having on our book to date and going forward.

As interest rates change, we routinely revaluate the rate at which we are amortizing and when appropriate – adjust the rates by speeding these up or down."[52]

That statement misrepresented management's estimates. The adjustment to which Ms. Spencer refers is only the recorded portion of the estimated 1998 catch up. Another $200 million was to be deferred, but she did not discuss that important fact.

Deletion of Significant Information from Audit Committee Minutes

Ms. Kappler was not a member of the Board of Directors, but she regularly attended the meetings of the Audit Committee. As discussed in more detail in Chapter IX, Role of the Board of Directors, Ms. Kappler controlled the level of detail that went into the Audit Committee minutes. During the period in which Mr. Rajappa was head of Internal Audit (January 1999 to January 2005), he was normally responsible for drafting the Audit Committee minutes and would circulate the draft minutes to other key participants at the meeting—typically Ms. Kappler, KPMG, and Ms. Spencer if she had made a presentation. Often, it is unclear as to whether Ms. Kappler made specific changes to the minutes, or delegated that responsibility to her subordinates. However, Ms. Kappler or her subordinates were involved in several cases where Audit Committee minutes were edited to eliminate comments on problems with Fannie Mae operations. For example, Ms. Kappler would have been responsible for the deletion of questions raised by Audit Committee members to the Controller and comments from Mr. Rajappa regarding the skill gaps that he had identified in his staff. Ms. Kappler also had the final say on decisions not to include details about whistleblower complaints in the minutes.[53]

When asked about changes in the draft minutes, neither Mr. Rajappa nor Mr. Gerrity was aware that their questions or comments had been deleted from the final version of the minutes. Often, the minutes were not finalized until right before the materials for the next Audit Committee were distributed to Audit Committee members. Although minutes were approved at each Audit Committee meeting, the time lag between meetings made it more difficult for the Audit Committee members to remember what was actually said, so that the approval of the minutes became, in effect, a routine, not a purposeful one. Nevertheless, Ms. Kappler's alteration of the minutes to omit material information misled the Board, which received the minutes, and was an unsafe and unsound practice.

Failure to Disclose Significant Financial Information to the External Auditors

OFHEO requires Fannie Mae and Freddie Mac to implement internal and external audit programs that provide for adequate testing and review of audited areas together with adequate documentation of findings and any recommendations and corrective actions.[54] Fannie Mae's external auditors may rely on the representations of management in expressing an opinion on whether or not the Enterprise's financial statements taken as a whole conform to GAAP.

Despite representations to the contrary, Fannie Mae management knew of information that might impact the GAAP representation of the Enterprise's financial statements, but failed to provide this to the external auditors. As part of its annual audit procedures, CEO Franklin Raines, COO Daniel Mudd, CFO Timothy Howard, and Controller Leanne Spencer provided a representation letter to KPMG stating that all relevant and material information had been disclosed to the external auditor. The representation letter indicates that

> [i]tems are considered material, regardless of size, if they involve an omission or misstatement of accounting information that, in the light of surrounding circumstances, makes it probable that the judgment of a reasonable person relying on the information would be changed or influenced by the omission or misstatement.[55]

Despite those statements in the representation letter, Mr. Howard and Ms. Spencer neglected to inform KPMG about accounting treatments that they knew did not conform to GAAP. The withholding of such information critically impaired the external auditor's ability to detect and correct accounting deficiencies and internal control weaknesses and was an unsafe and unsound practice.

For example, in notes regarding a presentation given KPMG, Ms. Spencer described what was communicated (and not communicated) to the external auditor regarding Fannie Mae's catch-up position. The omission of information in that case appears to have been intentional.

> LS [Leanne Spencer] and JB [Jonathan Boyles] met with KPMG on December 7. We walked them through the PDAMS projections as of the September book of business and catch-up. We told them this was being aggressively managed. We informed them that the CFO was fully informed and engaged. We reviewed improvements made over the course of the last six months: staff hired; system purchased and implemented (Bancware). LS informed them that while the catchup was projected to be slightly greater than (150) at December, that I was booking on top amortization and I expected the number to be 'somewhat' lower. I was non-specific as the range or amount. I ended the meeting with ...'what I want you to take away from this meeting is that I am all over this – it's being aggressively managed'. KPMG responded: We hear you, loud and clear.

They have not asked Jonathan or myself one more question about the subject. They have met with Dick's people to inquire about the additional amounts we've booked on-top this year."[56]

When, in 1998, Fannie Mae was faced with serious impairments of its interest-only (IO) securities, it failed to remind KPMG that several years earlier KPMG had approved an accounting practice that now masked those impairments. In 1996, when interest rates were reasonably stable and IO impairments were not a focus of attention, Fannie Mae sought, and KPMG approved a practice that allowed Fannie Mae to bundle IO securities together with other mortgage-backed securities and account for them as synthetic single class MBS. Values of the IOs—premiums, since IOs have no principal—were thus mingled with premiums and discounts of the other securities in a bundle. The net premium or discount was amortized into income over the life of the synthetic instrument under FAS 91. IOs were not valued separately, and no impairment analysis was performed.

In 1998, falling interest rates resulted in accelerating mortgage prepayments that caused the values of IO securities to fall substantially. Proper interest-only accounting under GAAP would have resulted in Fannie Mae's recording substantial impairments on its IO securities. Management recognized that new KPMG staff might not be aware of the firm's earlier approval of bundling. Rather than bring it to their attention, management intentionally avoided raising the issue, continued the bundling practice, and avoided substantial impairment losses. In materials prepared for a briefing of Mr. Howard at that time, Mr. Boyles wrote:

> KPMG has apparently forgotten about these transactions [the IO bundles], and we have not brought these issues to their attention. They [KPMG] have experienced significant turnover since we originally adopted the "package" accounting and, as a result, there is currently only one member of the audit team that remaining from the fall of 1995. The accounting team they currently have on the audit is more technically proficient, and if they stumble across these packages, may not be as easily convinced of the current accounting treatment. We have made every effort to keep our analysis confidential.[57]

Further, Fannie Mae kept KPMG in the dark about the Enterprise's misapplication of GAAP to its buy-up portfolio. Buy-ups are up-front amounts that the Enterprise pays to lenders in exchange for excess guarantee fee payments; as such, buy-ups are unsecuritized interest-only (IO) strips subject to IO accounting. As discussed in Chapter VI, with proper accounting, Fannie Mae would have recognized nearly $500 million of impairments on its buy-up investments in 1998.[58] In part to avoid the volatility associated with IO accounting, and in part because it lacked the necessary systems infrastructure to account for them, Fannie Mae treated buy-ups as mortgage premiums and accounted for them under FAS 91. The extent of the impairments Fannie Mae would have recognized in 1998 had it properly accounted for them reflected not only their sensitivity to interest rate swings, but the fact that the Enterprise had paid above-market prices for buy-ups to increase its share of mortgage securitizations versus its competitor Freddie Mac.

Fannie Mae made a point of not calling KPMG's attention to its buy-up accounting. In July 1999, Mr. Boyles wrote that "KPMG has not questioned our accounting treatment for buy-ups even though we have not necessarily been faithful to IO accounting. One of the reasons they have not questioned our treatment is that the cash flows are part of a guarantee fee payment and don't 'sound' like an IO."[59] Fannie Mae opposed Freddie Mac's retention of KPMG to replace Arthur Andersen, in the wake of the Enron scandal, in part because Freddie Mac properly accounted for its buy-ups and KPMG would notice. Referring to buy-ups here as "IOs," Ms. Spencer wrote, "We believe it is a good thing for the 'industry of two' to have different auditors. It gives us a vehicle to get a second opinion at times. . . .There is at least one thing that we know of where we have a favorable accounting treatment and that is on the IOs we have on our books. Freddie is doing IO accounting and we are not. KPMG hasn't figured that out—but Jonathan reminded me of this." 60

In another instance, Christina Immelman, a Director for Corporate Tax, sent an e-mail to Mr. Boyles and distribution indicating that the Enterprise took advantage of KPMG's uninformed position regarding the Enterprise's business:

> One of my take-aways yesterday was to stop focusing on the inadequacies of our KPMG audit team. I should be happy that they don't really understand our business and don't ask more questions.[61]

Provision of Misleading or Incorrect Information to the Congress and the Public

In Fannie Mae annual reports, sworn Congressional testimony, and other public statements, senior management provided misleading or incorrect information or made false statements about the Enterprise's operations, financial condition, or executive compensation. Such miscommunications were an unsafe and unsound practice.

Inaccurate or Misleading Information about Fannie Mae's Operations or Financial Condition

There were numerous occasions on which senior management provided misleading or incorrect information about the Enterprise's operations or financial condition. For example, as discussed in Chapter VI, Fannie Mae failed to disclose in Annual Reports that it utilized two large REMIC transactions to postpone earnings in years when it expected to exceed analyst expectations and earnings targets. CEO Franklin Raines and CFO Timothy Howard bore ultimate responsibility for the content of those reports. The two transactions, a $20 billion REMIC created in December 2001 and a $10 billion REMIC in March 2002, transformed mortgage assets from Fannie Mae's portfolio, on which Fannie Mae would recognize income at a constant yield, into sequential pay REMIC securities with lower yields on the shorter maturities and higher yields on the longer maturities. Without changing the cash flows of the underlying assets, the transactions allowed Fannie Mae to recognize income at a rising rate, in effect pushing income into future years. The transactions had no significant business purpose other than to achieve desired accounting results. In its annual reports Fannie Mae mentioned neither the transactions nor their expected effects on the timing of earnings. The 2002 Report stated only that "[in] some cases, we create REMICs using assets from our mortgage portfolio and retain an interest in the REMICs."[62] The 2001 Annual Report did not even include that language.

The 2002 Annual Report also included a misleading description of how Fannie Mae responded to significant market volatility during that year. During the summer of 2002, interest rates had fallen 100 basis points in 60 days to a 40-year low, and mortgage prepayments had accelerated dramatically. Those developments caused Fannie Mae's duration gap—the difference between the durations of its assets and liabilities—to widen well outside of Board- approved limits. A review of the year by Mr. Raines described the company's response:

> Even though we took actions to rebalance our portfolio, the actions were routine ... and had no material impact on our business or core business earnings. In fact, our core business earnings per share increased by 21 percent during 2002.[63]

Mr. Raines failed to mention that the volatility of Fannie Mae's duration gap directly contradicted the Enterprise's image of itself as a company that took on little risk. Duration gap volatility results from not fully hedging exposure to mortgage prepayments, a significant source of interest rate risk.

In a July 30, 2003 press briefing, Mr. Raines assured investors that Fannie Mae had not done anything to circumvent accounting rules and, by the incompleteness of his response, left the incorrect impression that Fannie Mae's auditor KPMG had no audit difference with Fannie Mae for 1998:

> Q: Just to elicit the clearest statement that you can possibly make on this subject, has Fannie Mae done anything to circumvent accounting rules? Has Fannie Mae used accounting judgments that either its employees or its auditors consider debatable?
>
> A: The answer to that is clearly, no, we have not. If we had, I would have violated the law in certifying our financial results. If we had, our auditors would be obligated to publicly do something about that.[64]

Mr. Raines made other inaccurate statements during the same briefing. As discussed in Chapter VI, in 1998 Fannie Mae failed to record approximately $200 million of premium and discount amortization expense as required by FAS 91. KPMG categorized that failure as an "Audit Difference." The Enterprise refused to book the additional expense on the basis that the KPMG's audit differences were immaterial. At the briefing, Mr. Raines failed to provide that information in response to the question: "Has Fannie Mae used accounting judgments that either its employees or its auditors consider debatable?" Mr. Raines also assured investors: "I can tell you that at Fannie Mae, we took no steps whatsoever to ameliorate the impact of FAS 133."[65] That statement was simply untrue. As discussed in Chapter VI, the Enterprise's senior management implemented FAS 133 in a manner that placed minimizing earnings volatility and maintaining simplicity of operations over compliance with GAAP and led to a multi-year restatement now estimated at $10.6 billion for hedge accounting errors alone.

Mr. Raines also suggested during the briefing that Fannie Mae's internal control systems were automated and easily adjustable, which was not accurate. In comparing Fannie Mae to Freddie Mac, Mr. Raines said:

> But there is a difference in management. Management does matter, and a management that cares a lot about internal control does matter. I think that's really the important difference. It would not take 500 people for us to go back, even if we had made the same mistakes, because we have these systems automated and we can go back and quickly adjust them.[66]

In October 2004 Mr. Raines and Mr. Howard both made inaccurate statements in sworn testimony before the Subcommittee on Capital Markets, Insurance, and Government Sponsored Enterprises of the Committee on Financial Services of the U.S. House of Representatives. When asked if Fannie Mae had, in fact, deferred expenses from 1998 into 1999, Mr. Raines denied that the deferral had been made:

> Baker: Thank you, sir. Mr. Raines, prior to the decision being executed to defer the $200 million in expenses in the end of 1998 into the quarters of 1999, were you consulted or did you have knowledge of that proposed transaction?
>
> Raines: Chairman, first, let me be clear. There was no decision made to defer any expense from 1998 to 1999. Second—and Howard can go into greater detail into how the process actually occurs—but we did not make any deferral. I was part of a discussion, as I always am as the CEO, in our closing process in which the decisions made in our financial area with regard to the calculation of the catch-up provision was discussed. But the determination of that was made through our normal process of closing our books.[67]

The decision to record only $240 million of the $440 million catch-up expense for 1998 was not in accordance with GAAP and, as discussed in Chapter V, was motivated by management's desire to meet 1998 EPS and AIP targets. At the same hearing, Mr. Raines and Mr. Howard asserted otherwise in response to a question from Rep. Barney Frank (D-MA):

> Rep. Frank: Was the fact that bonuses were somehow dependent on earnings a factor in the treatment of earnings? And did you not mean it consciously, might it have affected you, do you think? Mr. Howard?

Howard: If you are referring to the incident reported in the OFHEO report for 1998, as Raines mentioned, we have been looking into that. And so far we have determined that the amount that was determined to be accurately recorded in 1998 was determined as a result of a process that was run in ....

Rep. Frank: I'm going to your motives. You both deny that trying to hit a certain amount so you could get your bonuses was a factor to any extent in your decisions? I think it is important to just ask you that question.

Howard: Yes, in coming up with that number, yes, we do not ....

Raines: We both deny that.

Rep. Frank: You both deny that.

Howard: Yes.[68]

Incomplete Disclosure of Executive Compensation

Fannie Mae disclosed executive compensation in a manner that effectively obscured public understanding of compensation actually received by senior executives through the use of an unduly opaque method of disclosure. In addition, the Enterprise failed to disclose to OFHEO in a timely manner a post-employment agreement with former CEO James Johnson that provided him with substantial compensation in addition to that already provided upon his termination as a Fannie Mae employee.

Opaque Method of Disclosure of Long-Term Compensation. A recent example of the opaque disclosures is illustrative. Shortly after the release of the September 2004 OFHEO report, an article in the December 23, 2004, *Washington Post* entitled "High Pay at Fannie Mae for the Well-Connected," suggested that 1998 compensation for former Fannie Mae CEO James Johnson "was [reported to be] $6 million to $7 million a year," in 1998.[69] The total compensation in 1998 for Mr. Johnson was, in fact, substantially more.

An initial review of the 1999 Fannie Mae Proxy Statement "Summary Compensation Table" suggests the source of the *Washington Post* figure on 1998 compensation for Mr. Johnson.[70] A close read of that proxy, including footnotes, shows that the Table itself listed only a small portion of the actual 1998 long-term compensation of Mr. Johnson. Mr. Johnson used a program available to only very senior Fannie Mae executives (Executive Vice President and above) to defer a sizable amount of earned Performance Share Plan shares. Fannie Mae disclosed in a footnote to the Summary Compensation table that Mr. Johnson deferred 111,623 shares; the actual value of the shares did not show up in the Summary Compensation Table.[71]

Fannie Mae talking points for that period anticipated possible questions about hiding the compensation of Mr. Johnson. The talking points included several questions and answers: (bolded emphasis in original):

16. **Gimme a break**. He's hiding his compensation. To the contrary, its all quite clearly accounted for in the proxy. What he is doing is deferring compensation.
17. **Why is he doing that?** It is not appropriate for me to discuss Mr. Johnson's financial planning.

18. **He's trying to hide how much he's made, isn't he?** Again, we've disclosed all cash compensation and stock-based awards over the past three years. It couldn't be more transparent.
19. **The way you disclose it isn't the easiest thing to follow**. We account for all options ever granted to Mr. Johnson and to our other senior executives. We account for all options they each continue to hold and those they have exercised. There's really no problem following it at all.[72]

An internal Fannie Mae Gross Wage Analysis for Mr. Johnson for 1998 provided a clearer estimate of the actual 1998 compensation of Mr. Johnson. It showed total wages and other earnings to Mr. Johnson of nearly $21 million, including the Performance Share Plan deferral and the deferred benefits related to the exercise of certain stock options.[73]

That opaque public disclosure of Mr. Johnson's 1998 compensation reflected an allowance for ambiguity regarding Fannie Mae executive compensation. Lorrie Rudin, Director for Executive Compensation and Benefits, referred to that ambiguity as "unusual" reporting of deferred Performance Share Plan shares.[74] To cite another example, the value of the 2001 long-term incentive payout to Mr. Raines in the form of Performance Share Plan shares totaled $6.803 million.[75] The Summary Compensation Table included in the proxy statement for that year, however, listed his 2001 long-term incentive plan payouts at $2.779 million—a difference of $4.024 million. A table footnote indicated that the long-term incentive plan payouts reported were net of shares deferred, and that Mr. Raines deferred 49,699 shares.[76]

On December 11, 2001, Mr. Raines received a memorandum from Terri Atwell, Manager for HR Programs, entitled "Draft of Proxy",[77] which included two "decks" of the Summary Compensation Table: one which listed the long-term incentive plan payout for Mr. Raines at the tentative number of $6,708,080, which was close to the anticipated long-term incentive plan payout—and another which listed that payout at a tentative $2,780,080. According to Ms. Rudin, Mr. Raines himself may have requested the two alternative tables for review.

> Q: Okay. I have one last question. Was this—were these things presented to Frank Raines as options? Did he decide himself to report it one way or another? Why was he given two tables?
>
> A: I don't remember, but I believe he simply asked for it. He just—Frank Raines would ask us to run projections of things 10 ways to Sunday for almost anything.
>
> Q: So, he asked for these tables?
>
> A: I believe that happened.[78]

As described above, Fannie Mae chose the option that listed the smaller amount in the Summary Compensation Table. Fannie Mae was not an SEC registrant in 2001.[79] After it became a registrant, the long-term incentive plan net-of-deferral footnotes disappeared. The Summary Compensation Table in the April 23, 2004 proxy statement correctly listed the 2001 long-term incentive plan compensation for Mr. Raines as $6.803 million. In addition, it correctly listed the long-term incentive plan payment for the year 2000 to Mr. Raines as

$4,588,616,[80] a decidedly higher figure than the $2,588,636 listed in the 2001 Summary Compensation Table.[81]

EPS Challenge Grant Disclosure. The convoluted disclosure of the EPS Challenge Grants by Fannie Mae deserves special note. The 2000 proxy "Summary Compensation Table" included no information on the Challenge Grant options awarded by Board of Directors resolution that year by executive officer,[82] nor did such information appear in the 2001 Table.[83] Instead, those proxy statements included a two-paragraph narrative description of the EPS Challenge Grants that listed the number of options awarded to the "top five" executives, but not the grant date present value of those options. That narrative indicated that the options were in addition to those included in the summary tables. The Summary Compensation Table in Fannie Mae's proxy of April 14, 2003 did include the 2000 Challenge Grants.[84] For Mr. Raines, this meant that the Summary Compensation Table in this proxy showed he received 421,358 options in 2000,[85] even though previous proxy compensation tables listed him as receiving only 207,810 options in that year.[86]

Ongoing Compensation to Former Fannie Mae CEOs James Johnson and David Maxwell. Fannie Mae also failed to disclose fully to OFHEO or to its shareholders in a timely manner certain compensation paid to its former CEOs James Johnson and David Maxwell.

James Johnson. Fannie Mae entered into a post-employment consulting agreement with former CEO James Johnson on February 7, 2000, retroactive to January 1, 2000—the day after Johnson completed his service as a member of the Fannie Mae Board of Directors.[87] Fannie Mae determined that the agreement need not be disclosed to shareholders in the proxy. In addition, Fannie Mae withheld information from OFHEO about the ongoing post-employment agreement with Mr. Johnson until 2005, well after the special examination was underway.

Under the agreement, Mr. Johnson provided Fannie Mae with certain defined advisory services (Mr. Johnson was expected to provide advice on corporate strategy and finance, industry relations, public policy, and international securities)[88] and continued his leadership role in educational, cultural and philanthropic institutions for a CPI-adjusted fee, which in 2002 was $390,500 per year.[89] In addition, under that agreement, Fannie Mae provided Mr. Johnson with at least two employees as support staff and a car and payment of the salary of a driver for up to 50 percent of the driver's time. The cost to Fannie Mae, included the consulting fees to Mr. Johnson and the cost of dedicated staff, minus reimbursements, totaled $547,109 in 2001. In 2002, through August 30, the cost was $411,788.[90] An "evergreen" provision in the contract provided that it would be in force unless terminated by Fannie Mae with three year's advance written notice. Mr. Raines delegated to Thomas Donilon, Executive Vice President for Law and Policy and Corporate Secretary, the responsibility to receive advice from Mr. Johnson under the contract.[91]

Anthony Marra, Senior Vice President and Deputy General Counsel, told OFHEO that discussion about the consultant agreement for Mr. Johnson was initiated in the 4th quarter of 1999, and the actual negotiation of the contract was done by Mr. Raines, by Thomas Nides, Senior Vice President for Human Resources, and by Mr. Donilon. Mr. Marra indicated that the Board of Directors was not promptly notified of the contract but that when it was so notified, the reaction was positive.[92]

There were concerns at Fannie Mae about the terms of the contract. An undated analysis pointed out that Mr. Johnson was already receiving a Fannie Mae pension of $71,000 per month for life and noted:

> When executed in 2000, his fee was set so he could pay for an office and overhead expenses at the Watergate. Since then, he has joined Perseus Group and has no need for separate offices.
>
> The agreement has a three-year term with an evergreen clause. We can only terminate with three year's notice.
>
> Instead of Johnson hiring his own staff and funding it from his fees, we provide him with two secretaries to do the defined Fannie Mae services. He reimburses us for any non-Fannie Mae work they do.
>
> We provide him with a car and driver for up to 50 percent of the driver's time, for which we are supposed to get reimbursement. However, in practice, we are only reimbursed for the time Johnson is in the car. We are not reimbursed for the time spent waiting for Johnson or for driving his wife. As a result, most of the driver's time is spent supporting Johnson and we are reimbursed for only about 15 percent of the driver's time.
>
> The consulting agreement cost to us is about $600,000 per year—one of the largest consulting expenditures.[93]

During 2004, the possible use by Mr. Johnson of phone and fax lines for political activity in that election year appeared to cause concern. Fannie Mae developed ground rules regarding appropriate use of Fannie Mae-provided transportation and support staff when Mr. Johnson was engaged in political activity.[94] COO Daniel Mudd spoke to Mr. Johnson about the concerns of Fannie Mae in that area. In an e-mail to Mr. Marra and others dated March 26, 2004, Mr. Mudd noted:[95]

> I spoke to JAJ this morning. He is fine to move the phone lines, I called Brian Cobb and told him to proceed.[96]

Regarding use of Fannie Mae staff, Mr. Mudd in that e-mail went on to discuss the possibility of having Fannie Mae employees assigned to assist Mr. Johnson scale down their hours "for the duration" while those employees continued to accrue Fannie Mae benefits.

By August 2004, in an apparent reference to a possible political appointment for Mr. Johnson following the November 2004 election, Mr. Marra advised Ann Kappler, Senior Vice President and General Counsel, that Fannie Mae should consider an outside review of the contract "in light of issues that could come up during a Senate confirmation, OGE [Office of Government Ethics] or White House review of the consulting contract."[97]

On March 17, 2005, Mr. Johnson contacted Fannie Mae Board of Directors Chairman Stephen B. Ashley by letter and stated that "I should do my part to assist Fannie Mae's efforts to reduce expenditures at this difficult time." In that letter, Mr. Johnson offered a temporary reduction in his consulting payments to $300,000 a year and termination of all administrative and automobile transportation provided by the company, subject to reimbursement.[98]

David Maxwell. The Fannie Mae proxy statement of May 16, 1991, issued shortly after the retirement of former CEO David Maxwell on January 31, 1991, indicated that Fannie Mae would provide him with an office and secretary "until he reaches the age of 70."[99] Notwithstanding that statement to stockholders, Fannie Mae continued to pay for an office and secretary for Mr. Maxwell *after* he turned age 70. In 2002, the estimated annual cost of that benefit was $190,000.[100] Fannie Mae chose not to correct the false statement in the

1991 proxy because it was deemed not material. In a September 20, 2002, letter from Mr. Marra to Stephen Friedman, member of the Fannie Mae Board of Directors, Mr. Marra wrote:

> Even though he turned 70 almost two years ago, we have continued to provide the benefit. Because he is no longer an executive officer and the amount of the expense is not material, there is no legal obligation to disclose that we are continuing to provide this benefit.[101]

Failure to Conduct Appropriate Internal Investigations and Follow Up

Fannie Mae registered with the SEC in 2003. In January 2003, the Board of Directors approved Fannie Mae's revised Code of Business Conduct, which stated that "Employees must report any possible violations of the code to any officer or to the Office of Corporate Justice.... Any officer who has or receives information about a possible Code violation must report it promptly to the OCJ."[102] The Office of Corporate Justice ("OCJ") was a division of the legal department that was responsible for investigating employee complaints and promptly reporting to the Audit Committee of the Board of Directors on all complaints regarding accounting, internal accounting controls, and auditing matters.

In responding to employee complaints, Fannie Mae management was also subject to the minimum safety and soundness requirements set forth by OFHEO.[103] OFHEO requires each Enterprise's board of directors to ensure that management establishes and maintains an effective risk management framework, including review of such framework to monitor its effectiveness and taking appropriate action to correct any weaknesses.[104] OFHEO expects that an effective risk management framework would include procedures that ensure prompt, thorough, and impartial investigation of employee complaints and allegations of misconduct, and appropriate follow up.

In 2003, three Fannie Mae employees expressed serious concerns about the Enterprise's accounting. Roger Barnes, then a manager in the Controller's Department, made serious allegations about Fannie Mae's accounting for deferred price adjustments under FAS 91 to Sampath Rajappa, Senior Vice President for Operations Risk, who then reported these concerns promptly to Ann Kappler, Senior Vice President and General Counsel. Michelle Skinner, Director for E-Business, expressed serious concerns about accounting in several areas to COO Daniel Mudd. Anthony Lloyd, a Securities Analyst in the Controller's Office, echoed those concerns to Mr. Mudd. By failing to follow up in greater detail with Mr. Rajappa, Mr. Mudd missed an opportunity to recognize that there were similarities between Fannie Mae and Freddie Mac. Ms. Kappler was involved in the investigations of the allegations made by Mr. Barnes and the concerns expressed by Ms. Skinner and Mr. Lloyd. Ms. Kappler made statements about the issues raised and their disposition—in one case, to the Audit Committee of the Board of Directors—that were false and misleading.

Chapter VII reviewed the Office of Auditing's mishandling of its investigation of the allegations of improper accounting made by Mr. Barnes. This section reviews the failures of the Legal Department's investigation of Mr. Barnes' allegations, how Fannie Mae management failed to follow up appropriately after that investigation, and the failures of senior management's investigation of Ms. Skinner's and Mr. Lloyd's concerns. Those investigations had the effect of protecting the image of the Enterprise promoted by senior management.

Failures in the Investigation of Roger Barnes' Allegations

As discussed in Chapter VII, Roger Barnes met with Sampath Rajappa and Ann Eilers of Fannie Mae's Office of Auditing and made serious allegations regarding the Enterprise's accounting that had significant financial reporting implications. Mr. Rajappa immediately reported those allegations to SVP and General Counsel Ann Kappler.[105] Ms. Kappler referred the investigation to the Office of Corporate Compliance (OCC), an office within the Legal Department. Realizing that the Office of Corporate Compliance did not have the requisite expertise to investigate Mr. Barnes' allegations of manipulations in Fannie Mae's amortization accounting, Ms. Kappler asked the Office of Auditing to investigate the allegations. That assignment reflected poor judgment on her part. Just one month earlier in July 2003 the Office of Auditing had issued a report on the adequacy of controls over Fannie Mae's amortization accounting.[106] Ms. Kappler should have encouraged the Audit Committee to conduct an independent review of Mr. Barnes' allegations, as provided for by Section 301 of the Sarbanes-Oxley Act.[107]

Poor supervision by the Office of Corporate Compliance and a lack of understanding on the part of the Office of Auditing of the technical accounting issues raised by Mr. Barnes contributed to the flaws in the investigation of his allegations. The procedures employed in the Office of Auditing's analysis were insufficient to assess the breadth of the issues raised by Mr. Barnes or their quantitative impact.[108] Although he had alleged that Fannie Mae's amortization process was not in compliance with GAAP, the analysis by the Office of Auditing was not designed to evaluate that issue.[109] Further, the Office of Corporate Compliance merely accepted that analysis without challenge because of its own lack of accounting expertise. Insofar as the Office of Auditing apparently had, likewise, not intended to determine if the accounting practices alleged by Mr. Barnes were GAAP-compliant, the investigation was flawed and Ms. Kappler clearly should have referred the accounting aspect of the investigation to an independent auditor with the requisite expertise. The failure to do so resulted in conveying the false impression to the Audit Committee of the Board of Directors that the Office of Auditing had, in fact, tested for GAAP.

Despite the flaws that plagued the Office of Auditing's investigation of Mr. Barnes' accounting-related allegations, the investigation revealed information that should have heightened, not lowered, concerns on the part of Ms. Kappler and the Office of Corporate Compliance. A focus of the investigation was the $6.5 million factor adjustment, which Mr. Barnes said he had been ordered to make without any explanation or appropriate documentation. Office of Auditing staff found that there was insufficient documentation to support the adjustment, so that it could not be determined one way or the other whether the adjustment was appropriate.[110] According to the Office of Auditing, implementation of such factor changes with insufficient documentation or justification "reflects a breakdown of a key control."[111]

As the Office of Auditing had, during its July 2003 Amortization audit, raised similar conclusions regarding an adjustment made in the first half of the year and had raised related documentation issues, clearly the Barnes investigation should have been expanded to determine how widespread was the practice of making undocumented adjustments.[112] Instead, the investigation was abruptly brought to a close, apparently because of the purported immateriality of the amount involved,[113] as well as a subsequent explanation provided by Jeff Juliane, a Director in the Office of the Controller, who had caused the undocumented adjustment to be made in the first place.[114] These actions were contrary to SEC Staff

Accounting Bulletin 99 (SAB 99) that stipulates a registrant and the auditors of its financial statements should not assume that even small intentional misstatements in financial statements, for example those pursuant to actions to "manage" earnings, are immaterial."[115]

The Legal Department's investigation into Mr. Barnes' accounting allegations was completed a mere four days after it began, on August 8, 2003. Fannie Mae rushed to conclude that investigation because the Enterprise was scheduled to finalize its June 30, 2003, financial statements by August 14, 2003; delay was not considered desirable because Fannie Mae would have to disclose the reason for the delay.[116] When asked about the timing of the resolution of the Barnes investigation, Ms. Kappler told OFHEO that she:

> had no intention of signing a certification until there was a resolution of Mr. Barnes' allegations and from my perspective that the important thing to get accomplished was to have a judgment by the time we had to do the certifications.[117]

Upon completion of the four-day investigation, a meeting was held on August 8, 2003, to discuss the amortization issues raised by Mr. Barnes. Participants included members of the Office of the Controller (including Mr. Barnes), the Director of Financial Standards, members of the Office of Auditing, and representatives of the external auditor, KPMG. The meeting, which lasted 90 minutes, was not attended by Ms. Kappler, although the head of the Office of Corporate Compliance, Deborah House, did attend.[118]

Before the investigation even commenced, on July 28, 2003, Ms. Kappler had signed the *Internal Control Representation Letter for "Covered Period": April 1, 2003 – June 2003* to be considered as part of the certification process for the June 30, 2003, quarterly financial statements that she eventually presented to the Audit Committee on August 12, 2003. That letter stated:

> To the best of my knowledge, there were no omissions or misstatements of reported amounts or information in my area that would have had a material impact on the financial statements. For purposes of this statement, matters were generally not considered material if they involve an aggregate absolute value of less than $5 million of net income of $3 billion of balance sheet impact. However, I also considered all the factors in determining whether a matter was material and matters involving less than this amount were material if they would otherwise be of interest to a reasonable investor.[119]

What is particularly noteworthy about the certification is that the "investigation" into the $6.5 million factor change, as discussed above, concluded because of purported immateriality. For Ms. Kappler's certification, matters were considered material if they equaled or exceeded $5 million. It is unknown whether Ms. Kappler failed to recognize that inconsistency, or deliberately ignored it, once she was told about Mr. Barnes' allegations. Either way, she did not withdraw her certification, and, as discussed above, failed to recognize or ignored the requirement that allegations of intentional misstatement should not be subject to materiality thresholds.

Ms. Kappler fully recognized the ramifications that the Barnes matter could have for the timely submission of the Form 10-K to the SEC and characterized the Barnes matter to be a mere interference of that timing, as shown below. Ms. Kappler should have been more concerned over the accuracy of the financial statements and the validity of her certification.

On August 11, 2003, the day before the certification meeting with the Audit Committee, Ms. Kappler provided advice to CFO Timothy Howard as he prepared to hold a meeting with the Controller's staff the next day. Her advice included as follows:

> I know your main theme is support for all their hard work to date and to come. Given the broad audience, and the state of the work being done on the issues raised by Roger, I think you are better off not addressing Roger's concerns in this context.
>
> That said, in the course of your comments you can note that we've just met (or willing [qsic] be meeting with) the Audit Comm'ee [sic] to advise them that you and Frank will be certifying the 10Q. Without connecting that action to any resolution of Roger's issues, it would convey to folks that, at a minimum, anything that was raised will not interfere with the reporting of our financials.[120]

Although Ms. Kappler's missteps in August 2003 were significant, they were exceeded by what followed in October 2003, when Mr. Barnes' counsel sent Fannie Mae a letter threatening to file suit against the Enterprise for claims of discrimination and retaliation.[121] That letter alleges, among other things, inappropriate management of earnings by the Office of the Controller in order to meet targets. Attached to the letter from Mr. Barnes' counsel was a memorandum of September 23, 2002, that Mr. Barnes stated that he sent anonymously to Mr. Raines and Mr. Howard. In it, Mr. Barnes listed several "critical areas in the Finance Division where questionable decisions have been made," and he noted that "[t]he possible impact reaches hundreds of millions of dollars and possibly affects the integrity of the current financial statements and those we will issue after beginning compliance with SEC reporting in 2003."[122]

The seriousness of the allegations in the memorandum of September 23, 2002, and the level at which they were directed, clearly called for prompt, independent investigation by the Board, as well as immediate communication with OFHEO. Neither occurred, and Ms. Kappler bears the responsibility for that failure. Instead, in November 2003 Fannie Mae hurriedly settled the matter by agreeing to a substantial amount of cash and stock for Mr. Barnes.[123]

As part of the settlement, Mr. Barnes terminated his relationship with Fannie Mae and returned to the Enterprise documents that he had maintained during his employment, including documents kept apparently to support many of his allegations. Those documents addressed three areas of concern regarding Fannie Mae's amortization policy: (1) the existence of improper amortization factors;[124] (2) significant realignment differences between accounting systems;[125] and (3) undocumented factor changes implemented at the direction of senior management.[126]

It is unclear how or when the Legal Department evaluated the documents left behind by Roger Barnes. It is evident that the department had sufficient information to launch an investigation by an independent party but did not do so. The department waited until February 12, 2004, to share the documents with OFHEO.[127]

Failure to Follow Up on the Remedial Actions Resulting from the Investigation into Roger Barnes' Allegations

Roger Barnes had alleged that there was a negative environment within the Controller's office that discouraged employees from raising accounting-related concerns or issues to management. SVP and General Counsel Ann Kappler assigned this portion of the investigation to the Office of Corporate Compliance (OCC). The OCC concluded that this negative environment did in fact exist. The OCC observed that a significant number of staff in the Office of the Controller "indicated that, to a greater or lesser degree, the environment there is not conducive to the full, open and frank discussion of issues and concerns relating to accounting issues and practices" and that "staff who voice opinions that are contrary to the actions of management of who question the actions of management are not perceived as team players and to be successful in the Controller's office 'you are either on the team or not."[128]

The Office of Corporate Compliance investigation validated Roger Barnes' complaint that the environment in the Controllers office was "unacceptable" and that, instead, the environment "must be one where staff are [sic] comfortable raising and fully vetting all issues," especially because the controller's office is under scrutiny and its continued integrity is essential to the well being of Fannie Mae.[129] The OCC cited the Controller for violating the Code of Business Conduct and recommended a series of remedial actions for her to complete as a result. Ms. Spencer was required to attend, but did not, a mandated workplace-environment seminar, citing scheduling issues. Further, Ms. Kappler, through her oversight of the OCC, failed to enforce the completion of the remedial actions recommended by the OCC, and thus diminished the effectiveness and minimized the importance of the OCC function. The lack of substantive corrective action required by the OCC given the validity of Mr. Barnes complaint and Ms. Spencer's inability to attend the workplace-environment seminar, demonstrates the lack of regard for appropriate disciplinary action for misconduct.

Provision of Misleading Information to the Audit Committee on Allegations by Roger Barnes

Ms. Kappler and Mr. Rajappa misled the Board of Directors Audit Committee on the nature and resolution of the accounting-related concerns raised by Roger Barnes. On August 12, 2003, four days after the completion of the hurried investigation into Barnes's allegations, Ms. Kappler reported in a meeting of the Audit Committee that the allegations were without merit, that KPMG had fully reviewed the allegations, and that Mr. Barnes had expressed satisfaction that his concerns had been addressed.[130] None of those statements were true, Ms. Kappler knew or should have known they were not true, and they undoubtedly had the effect of misleading the Audit Committee. The following paragraphs discuss those misrepresentations in more detail.

Although Ms. Kappler reported to the Audit Committee that the investigation concluded that Mr. Barnes's allegations were without merit, this was not true. OA concluded that the $6.5 million factor change that Mr. Barnes was directed to make indeed had insufficient documentary support, as Mr. Barnes alleged, such that it could not be determined whether the factor change was correct or incorrect. In addition, Ms. Kappler stated that KPMG had fully reviewed the allegations, but in reality, KPMG's involvement in the investigation was minimal and hardly considered to be a full review.

The minutes to the August 12, 2003 Audit Committee meeting include the following statement, "Ms. Kappler noted that a member of the Office of Corporate Compliance has reviewed management's findings with the employee and the employee has expressed satisfaction that this concerns have been addressed." Mr. Barnes neither expressed to the OCC satisfaction that his concerns had been addressed, nor that he was satisfied with the investigation's findings.[131] Whether Ms. Kappler misunderstood Mr. Barnes' level of satisfaction with the response to the concerns he had raised or whether she understood and ignored it before she made the comment to the Audit Committee is unknown. Regardless, right after the Audit Committee meeting, Deborah House, Ms. Kappler's subordinate, sent her an e-mail in order to make sure that Ms. Kappler understood that Mr. Barnes was not satisfied.[132] There is no indication that Ms. Kappler went back and corrected the record with the Audit Committee after she received the e-mail from Ms. House. In fact, years later, Tom Gerrity, Chair of the Audit Committee, was still left with the impression that Mr. Barnes was satisfied by the investigation.[133] Mr. Barnes, however, was never satisfied. Indeed, on August 25, 2003, Mr. Barnes e-mailed Ms. House and complained that he had still not received a summary of the meeting of August 8, 2003, containing "the explanations provided by Controllers," which was supposed to be provided to each attendee.[134] Mr. Barnes advised Ms. House:

> In the absence of seeing a summary, I am not sure there is not ongoing cause for concern. As I noted in an aside to you, after the meeting, with adequate knowledge of the modeling process, the management meetings and discussions which took place in the business unit, amortization accounting, etc. legitimate questions could still be raised about the series of explanations provided.[135]

Ms. Kappler did not alert the Audit Committee to these "legitimate questions;" instead, she misleadingly suggested that Mr. Barnes was satisfied with the investigation.

At best, it is clear that there was a significant failure of communication on her part, as her statements did not convey the investigation's most serious conclusions. In summary, the Office of Auditing had concluded that there was insufficient documentation to support the $6.5 million factor change which Mr. Barnes was directed to make, and that it could not be determined whether this adjustment was correct or incorrect. The Office of Corporate Compliance concurred with the results of the Office of Auditing's investigation. Inexplicably, however, Ms. Kappler did not inform the Audit Committee of what the Office of Auditing called a "breakdown of a key control."[136]

The night before the Audit Committee meeting of August 12, 2003, Ms. Kappler sent an e-mail to CFO Timothy Howard that described the status of the investigation:

> We've struggled with whether there is anything you can say specifically about Roger's complaint, and—in the end—think you should not say anything. Most importantly, there are open issues, in particular surrounding the atmosphere of the group, but also relating to processes and procedures in place. (I understand that Audit will be suggesting some changes; KPMG has indicated that it wants to go back and look at some of the modeling being done in this area; and Corporate Compliance has yet to complete its interviews and make recommendations.) It would be misleading to suggest to people that we are all done here.[137]

The minutes of the meeting of the Audit Committee the next day indicate that Ms. Kappler made statements that were inconsistent with her statements in that e-mail, which suggests that she misled the Committee regarding the closure of the Barnes matter. According to the minutes:

> Ms. Kappler indicated that the Office of Corporate Compliance and internal audit investigated the concerns. Ms. Kappler stated that the accounting concerns, which Mr. Rajappa described,

> had been properly and fully reviewed by internal audit and KPMG, together with the Controller's Office, and determined to be based on inaccurate and incomplete information and without merit.[138]

There is no indication in the minutes that Mr. Rajappa contested Ms. Kappler's misleading statements to the Audit Committee about the investigation. Through Mr. Rajappa's inaction and by certifying Fannie Mae's financial statements for the second quarter of 2003, he provided tacit support for Ms. Kappler's statements. Mr. Rajappa's certification, which addresses the investigation, represented:

> . . . I have therefore concluded that the 2nd quarter financials were prepared in conformance with the company's accounting policies . . . and that those policies . . . are in compliance with GAAP.[139]

Mr. Rajappa told OFHEO that he did not evaluate whether Fannie Mae's financial statements were in compliance with GAAP.[140] Therefore, he was in no position to make such a representation, regardless of the status of the investigation of Mr. Barnes' allegations. The fact that Mr. Rajappa failed to determine why Mr. Barnes was asked to effect a factor change for $6.5 million further highlights the inappropriateness of his representation.

On October 16, 2003, Mr. Barnes' attorney sent Mr. Raines a lengthy letter threatening to file a lawsuit alleging civil rights violations as well as Sarbanes-Oxley Act (SOX) whistleblower violations, the latter on the grounds that retaliatory action had been taken against him and would continue to be taken against him because of the allegations of accounting manipulation he had previously made. The attorney stated that if there was to be a formal settlement, it needed to be completed by November 3, 2003, the deadline for filing a SOX whistleblower lawsuit.

Fannie Mae reviewed the letter and hurriedly settled the threatened lawsuit with the payment of $1 million plus 8,369 shares of Fannie Mae stock, valued at approximately $500,000 as of November 3, 2003. It is clear that the allegations were settled in order to prevent the filing of the whistleblower SOX lawsuit, which would have made public the accounting manipulations that Mr. Barnes had alleged.

Mishandling of Concerns of Michelle Skinner

On September 9, 2003, another employee, Michelle Skinner, expressed serious concerns about Fannie Mae's accounting directly to Daniel Mudd, the Chief Operating Officer and a member of the Board of Directors, during one of a series of meetings that he held periodically with Enterprise employees called "Unplugged" Meetings.[141] Ms. Skinner's concerns related to a number of areas, including amortization accounting, and were similar to the allegations made by Roger Barnes a little over a month before. Ms. Skinner referred to passages from the Baker Botts LLP report, the report of an internal Freddie Mac investigation on accounting misapplications that led to Freddie Mac's restatement of its financial statements, and compared some practices identified in that report to what she felt were practices at Fannie Mae. Excerpts from Ms. Skinner's e-mail to Mr. Mudd follow:

> ... Janet Pennewell once told me that KPMG had given her a "margin" of plus or minus $90 million to work with in calculating PDS [an amortization database] results (not an exact quote,

> just my memory of what she said). I got the distinct impression that the $90 million cushion could be used to make our EPS hit more closely to analysts' expectations.
>
> ... Another concern is the fact that we have difficulty reconciling the information in STATS [an amortization account sub-ledger] to the information in PDS. "Realignments" between the two have periodically occurred, and I do not know the most recent results. But I believe some of the differences have been significant.
>
> ... My comment this morning regarding some of the similarities between what happens at Fannie Mae and the Baker Botts report center around pages 62-67 of the report,...if I were in your shoes...I would ask some folks with history and knowledge ...to walk me through each sentence of that section. And I would ask them to compare and contrast what each sentence says about Freddie Mac, to what Fannie Mae has done...I can only say that when I read that section, for a number of sentences I said to myself, "wow, that sure sounds familiar".[142]

Mr. Mudd asked his special assistant, Pilar O'Leary, to investigate Ms. Skinner's concerns and report back to him. Ms. O'Leary contacted Sampath Rajappa, the head of the Office of Auditing, for assistance. Mr. Rajappa prepared an analysis of Ms. Skinner's concerns and essentially validated the majority of them. Mr. Rajappa provided his analysis to SVP and General Counsel Ann Kappler for her review.

It is not clear whether Mr. Mudd requested Ms. Kappler to prepare a response, but in any event she prepared two responses for him. One was a response that he was to distribute to Ms. Skinner, and the other was a response that he was to distribute to the rest of the participants in that particular "Unplugged" meeting. In both responses, Ms. Kappler disregarded the comments prepared by Mr. Rajappa regarding the validity of Ms. Skinner's concerns and prepared a watered-down message relaying the results of the investigation (i.e., Fannie Mae accounting was proper.)[143] When given an opportunity to comment on Ms. Kappler's second response, Mr. Rajappa offered only editorial suggestions.

On September 26, 2003, Mr. Mudd distributed a single response via e-mail to Ms. Skinner and the other participants in the "unplugged" meeting. Before that e-mail was distributed, Mr. Mudd deleted some of Ms. Kappler's text and added a sentence: "With 400,000 securities involved, amortization cannot be calculated security by security." That new sentence was eventually challenged by one of the "Unplugged" attendees who received Mr. Mudd's email, Anthony Lloyd (Ms. Skinner was aware of Mr. Lloyd's comments because she was copied on his e-mail to Mr. Mudd).[144] To resolve all of the issues that were being raised by Fannie Mae employees, and in line with the Office of Corporate Compliance decision memo on the allegations raised by Roger Barnes, Ms. Kappler suggested that a training session be held on accounting issues.[145] It is unclear as to whether Mr. Lloyd and Ms. Skinner were satisfied with the resolution of their issues by means of the response from Mr. Mudd and a training session.

Mr. Mudd did not comply with Fannie Mae's Code of Business Conduct by referring the case to the Office of Corporate Justice. Neither did Ms. Kappler, to whom that office reported. Additionally, Ms. Kappler disregarded Mr. Rajappa's analysis of Ms. Skinner's concerns and fully denied any problems with Fannie Mae's accounting. Ms. Kappler further failed to ensure that the matter was brought to the attention of the Audit Committee of the Board of Director's attention, as required by the Code of Business Conduct.

Mr. Mudd, on the other hand, was present at Board of Directors meetings in June 2003 where the problems at Freddie Mac were discussed and where the Board requested to be kept informed of the Freddie Mac situation. Further, Mr. Mudd was aware of attempts by Mr. Raines and Mr. Donilon during these meetings to allay the Board's concern that Freddie Mac's troubles were not shared by Fannie Mae. When Ms. Skinner brought her concerns to Mr. Mudd's attention in September, she specifically referenced similarities between what she knew happened at Fannie Mae and how that was similar to what was reported in the Baker Botts report. Therefore, Mr. Mudd missed an opportunity to recognize that perhaps there were similarities between Freddie Mac and Fannie Mae, especially when Mr. Lloyd responded to Mr. Mudd's e-mail by challenging portions of Mr. Mudd's response. At a minimum, Mr. Mudd should have spoken to Mr. Rajappa to determine what the latter's conclusions were, if he, Mudd, was unaware of those conclusions. Clearly, the matter should have been referred to the Audit Committee.

Failure to Allow the Board of Directors Unrestricted Access to Management

OFHEO has informed Fannie Mae that its Board of Directors should exercise oversight to hold management accountable for meeting the Enterprise's goals and objectives.[146] To perform that duty, members of the Board of Directors must have unrestricted access to members of Enterprise management. Senior executives in the Office of the Chairman at Fannie Mae prevented members of the Board from having such access. As noted above, in March 2004 Vice Chairman and CFO Timothy Howard ordered Controller Sampath Rajappa not to communicate directly with the Audit Committee of the Board, despite the fact that Mr. Rajappa ostensibly reported to the chairman of that committee.

The Office of the Chairman (OOC) had previously placed strict controls on the communications with Board members of certain members of management. On June 30, 2003, Chief Operating Officer Daniel Mudd sent an e-mail to Kathy Gallo, SVP for Human Resources. That e-mail, copies of which went to CEO Raines, CFO Howard, Corporate Secretary Thomas Donilon, and Monica Medina, set forth the "Rules of the Road" for Board interaction with Fannie Mae employees.[147] Those controls were not shared with non-management members of the Board, who erroneously believed they had an open working relationship with management. Mr. Mudd, referring to the contents of the e-mail as "a memo," wrote:

> Kathy, this note is to confirm our conversations on Board interactions.
>
> The Office of the Chair, primarily the Chairman, is the reviewing body for any information passing to or from the Board or the Board Committees. This information includes both oral and written material, and in the event we are communicating to the Board, should be reviewed in advance.
>
> The Office of the Corporate Secretary ([Monica] Medina or Donilon) administers and catalogs these communications. Monica, Tom, or their designee should be present during meetings, discussions or phone conversations with the Board or committees. Exceptions can only be approved by the Chairman.
>
> Consultants, such as those working for the Compensation Committee, have an independent relationship with the Committees-and should be considered 'part of the Committee'. Their direct conversations with the Board or Committee—which do not involve management—are

> managed at the discretion of the Committee Chair. To the extent that consultants receive or send communications to/from management (e.g., you or your staff), the rules above apply: inform the Corporate Secretary and involve the OOC depending on the issue.
>
> It is very important to understand that distinct and separate roles played by management (you), management members of the Board (Frank, Dan and Tim), Corporate Secretaries (Monica and Tom), and the independent directors (including Anne Mulcahy) so that our corporate governance remains best-in-class. Thanks for your attention to this process.[148]

On the same date, Ms. Gallo forwarded Mr. Mudd's e-mail to Christine Wolf, Vice President for Compensation and Benefits, and Lorrie Rudin, Director for Executive Compensation and Benefits. Ms. Gallo added the text: "Helpful clarification."[149]

Fannie Mae Audit Committee Chairman Thomas Gerrity told OFHEO he found the exchange "shocking" and that he would consider one of the "rules of the road" for Board interactions to be to give Board members unfettered access to management.[150] Further, the 2004 Board of Directors Evaluation Form suggested shorter, more "unscripted" presentations; informal contact with Management; and more open discussion time, indicating that at least some board members were aware that the flow of information to the Board was not "unfettered."[151]

Imposing restrictions on the access of Fannie Mae management to members of the Enterprise's Board of Directors violated OFHEO's regulation requiring that management shall provide a board member with adequate and appropriate information.[152] In addition, the restrictions furthered Mr. Raines' attempts to prevent the Board from receiving the full story about accounting problems at the Enterprise. Such action was, therefore, an unsafe and unsound practice.

Attempts to Interfere with OFHEO's Special Examination

Fannie Mae's Government and Industry Relations Department had a special relationship of cooperation and support with select Congressional staff. In the spring and again in the fall of 2004, Enterprise lobbyists, with the knowledge and support of senior management, used their longstanding relationships with Congressional staff to attempt to interfere with OFHEO's special examination. This section describes those actions, which were unsafe and unsound practices.

Fannie Mae lobbyists succeeded in generating a Congressional request for the Inspector General of the Department of Housing and Urban Development (HUD) to investigate OFHEO's conduct of the special examination. Between October 2002 and June 2004, there had been three previous Congressional requests for investigations of OFHEO by the HUD Inspector General. The topics of those investigations were

- The compensation levels of OFHEO's public and Congressional relations staff;[153]
- The results of OFHEO's annual examinations and the basis for its conclusions regarding Fannie Mae and Freddie Mac;[154] and
- Whether OFHEO was in compliance with a provision of the VA-HUD-Independent Agencies Appropriation Act for Fiscal Year 2004 that required the

agency to allocate at least 60 percent of its budget to examinations and safety and soundness.[155]

Fannie Mae lobbyists had been directly involved in the initiation of the third investigation. Specifically, staff in the Enterprise's Government and Industry Relations Department helped formulate the language of the provision of the FY 2004 VA-HUD-Independent Agencies Appropriations that provided the rationale for the third investigation.

There was lengthy communication between staff in Fannie Mae's Government and Industry Relations Department and Congressional staff to establish the percentage governing OFHEO's use of appropriated funds.[156]

Generation of Fourth Request for HUD Inspector General Investigation of the Special Examination

In April 2004, the HUD Inspector General received a Congressional request to conduct a fourth investigation. The subject was OFHEO's conduct of its ongoing special examination of Fannie Mae, especially the allegation that the agency had improperly leaked confidential information about the Enterprise obtained during that examination.[157] OFHEO found a draft of the Congressional request letter on Fannie Mae's computer system that was nearly identical to the request letter that was ultimately sent to the HUD Inspector General. That draft is dated April 15, 2004, almost two weeks before the actual request letter was sent.[158]

Duane Duncan, head of Fannie Mae's Government and Industry Relations Department at the time, admitted under oath in his interview with OFHEO that Fannie Mae had generated the request for the fourth HUD Inspector General investigation.

> Q: [T]hen at some point thereafter, another letter went over to the HUD IG to conduct an investigation ....
>
> A: Yes, sir.
>
> Q: I don't want to put words in your mouth, but somebody looking at that would say, you know, it was instituted on the basis of Fannie Mae's request.
>
> A. Yes, sir.
>
> Q: It was?
>
> A. Yes.[159]

In the same interview, Mr. Duncan commented on the strong interest of Fannie Mae senior management in the report on the HUD Inspector General's fourth investigation becoming public. Mr. Duncan received direction from his superiors during Monday morning External Affairs meetings. Franklin Raines, Thomas Donilon, Timothy Howard, and sometimes Daniel Mudd attended those meetings, with Mr. Raines and Mr. Donilon deciding what positions Fannie Mae would take on any given issue. Mr. Duncan implemented the decisions made at those meetings. Mr. Duncan also met with Mr. Donilon at the end of each workday in order for Mr. Donilon to manage the implementation of the decisions.[160]

Senior management hoped that the report of the HUD Inspector General's fourth investigation would accomplish the objective of discrediting OFHEO's anticipated initial report of findings of its special examination of Fannie Mae.

> Q: Okay. I am sort of curious myself. Why would you be, you Fannie Mae, be so interested in seeing the report and getting it out?
>
> A: I think at the highest levels of the company, I think that the opinion was that the HUD IG report, again not knowing its contents until it came out, would serve to put the special exam, at least the preliminary report, in a perspective with a bias or with a—would kind of show that it was done in a way different than full objectivity, I guess, from the company's perspective … I think the company at the highest levels thought that the HUD Inspector General's report would discredit or show the lack of objectivity in the OFHEO report in September or at least the preliminary report.[161]

In fact, Mr. Duncan and, through him, others at Fannie Mae *did* know the contents of the fourth HUD Inspector General report prior to its publication. Mr. Duncan's handwritten notes on a telephone conversation on September 16, 2004, contain a detailed outline of the contents of the report as well as a notation that it would not be finished for about a month.[162]

To achieve its goals, however, Fannie Mae wanted the report published, even if it was legally restricted, nonpublic information. Accordingly, the Enterprise began a campaign to enlist support for the release of the report. Fannie Mae eventually succeeded in getting the document published on a Congressional website for one hour, during which time the Enterprise obtained the report for further dissemination, including to its Board of Directors, analysts, and Congressional staff. Thus, Fannie Mae succeeded in creating a large volume of negative publicity about the OFHEO examination report, in an effort to distract attention from its multi-billion dollar accounting errors.[163]

In summary, it is clear that Fannie Mae sought to use the fourth investigation of OFHEO by the HUD Inspector General to attempt to undermine the special examination.[164] That initiative, although conceived and executed by the Government and Industry Relations Department, was well known by many members of senior management, including Chairman and Chief Executive Officer Franklin Raines, Executive Vice President for Law and Policy Thomas Donilon (to whom Mr. Duncan reported), and Senior Vice President and General Counsel Ann Kappler. The unquestioning execution of the initiative by Mr. Duncan and other lobbyists in the department indicates that corporate-wide policy was to support it. The Board of Directors was notified of the results of the HUD Inspector General's investigation.[165]

Attempt to Use the Appropriations Process to Force a Change in OFHEO Leadership

OFHEO issued a *Report of Findings to Date of the Special Examination of Fannie Mae* on September 17, 2004. In the period immediately preceding and succeeding the issuance of that report, Fannie Mae lobbyists attempted to use the appropriations process to force a change in the leadership of OFHEO.[166] There were repeated discussions and communications involving the Enterprise's lobbyists regarding their effort to insert language into the VA-HUD-Independent Agencies Appropriation Act for Fiscal Year 2005 that would withhold $10 million from the OFHEO agency appropriation until a new director was appointed.[167] Armando Falcon, who was then Director of the agency, had initiated the special examination of Fannie Mae. That strategy of attempting to reduce OFHEO's resources was improper.

Conclusion

This chapter has described Fannie Mae's failures to establish a sound internal control system; maintain the independence and objectivity of the Enterprise's internal auditor; disclose to external parties accurate information about Fannie Mae's financial condition, operations, and executive compensation; investigate employee allegations and concerns; and allow the Board of Directors unrestricted access to members of management. Senior management was responsible for those failures, which were unsafe and unsound practices.

The chapter has also reviewed Fannie Mae's efforts to interfere with OFHEO's special examination of the Enterprise. The Government and Industry Relations Department of Fannie Mae, through coordination and communication with the Enterprise's Legal Department and senior management, undertook actions that were designed, understood, and expected to interfere with that examination. Those actions also constituted unsafe and unsound practices.

The actions and inactions of Mr. Raines and other senior executives reviewed in the chapter allowed Fannie Mae senior management, for a time, to avoid questions or criticism about the Enterprise's improper accounting policies and transactions or the accuracy and integrity of its financial statements. Avoiding those topics benefited those same senior executives by helping to obscure the inappropriate executive compensation they received, which was triggered by the inaccurate core business EPS reported in Fannie Mae's financial statements.

References

[1] OFHEO Policy Guidance, Minimum Safety and Soundness Requirements, PG-00-001 (December 19, 2000), OFHEO Safety and Soundness Regulation, 12 CFR Part 1720 App. A, B, V.

[2] OFHEO Policy Guidance, Minimum Safety and Soundness Requirements, PG-00-001 (December 19, 2000), OFHEO, Safety and Soundness Regulation, 12 CFR Part 1720, App. A.VIII.

[3] Franklin Raines Job Description prepared 12/07/01 FMSE-EC 004986.

[4] American Institute of Certified Public Accountants, 2002 Codification of Auditing Standards and Procedures, Statement of Auditing Standards No. 55, (New York, NY: AICPA, 2002), p. 350.

[5] Basel Committee on Banking Supervision, Framework for Internal Control Systems in Banking Organizations (Basel, Switzerland: September 1998), p. 17.

[6] Safety and soundness guidelines provide that an Enterprise should separate risk management oversight from oversight of accounting and financial reporting, and should establish a position of chief risk officer independent of the chief financial officer. OFHEO Examination Guidance, Examination for Corporate Governance, PG-05-002 (May 20, 2005). That guidance was issued, in part, in response to the unsafe and unsound practices uncovered in the September 2004 report.

[7] See The Group of Thirty, Enhancing Public Confidence in Financial Reporting (Washington, DC: December 2003), 14: "financial control and risk management must be fully independent of the risk taking business."

[8] OFHEO Interview, Jill Blickstein, January 26, 2006, p. 180.

[9] FM SRC OFHEO 00713573-4.

[10] House Committee on Financial Services: Subcommittee on Capital Markets, Insurance, and Government-Sponsored Enterprises Holds a Hearing on Accounting and Management Issues at Fannie Mae, October 6, 2004, FMSE-E EC0009809.

[11] Timothy Howard Job Description prepared 12/7/01 FMSE-EC 004989.

[12] OFHEO, Report of Findings to Date, Special Examination of Fannie Mae, September 17, 2004, 158-9.

[13] Id., 159-160.

[14] OFHEO Interview, Leanne Spencer, June 22, 2004, pp. 8, 10-11; OFHEO Report of Findings to Date, September 17, 2004; Policy on Purchase Premium/Discount Management, FMSE-SP000110-111.

[15] OFHEO Policy Guidance, Minimum Safety and Soundness Requirements, PG-00-001 (December 19, 2000), OFHEO Safety and Soundness Regulation, 12 CFR Part 1720 App. A, B, V.

[16] Memorandum from Leanne Spencer and Christine Cahn to Strategic Leadership Team SVPs, August 8, 2003, FMSE-E_KD0151519.

[17] Minutes of the Meeting of the Audit Committee of the Board of Directors, February 17, 2004, FMSE 504818-30.

[18] Letter from Director Armando Falcon to Chairman of the Board and Chief Executive Officer Franklin D. Raines, February 24, 2004, pp. 1-2.

[19] OFHEO Interview, Mary Lewers (Vice President for Financial Accounting), July 13, 2004, p. 45, in which she stated, "Accounting Standards is what I would refer to as our expert advice regarding the translation of GAAP into appropriate policy….So I would define myself as someone who was learning this, but that the real sort of expert advance (sic) in terms of how to translate this into compliance with GAAP, it really rested within the Financial Standards team."

[20] OFHEO Interview, Katarina Skladony (Senior Financial Analyst – Treasury Middle Office), August 26, 2004, pp. 144-146, in which she stated, among other things, that the Financial Standards Group did not make her aware of the requirements of FAS 133.

[21] OFHEO Interview, Julie St. John, April 22, 2004.

[22] Memorandum from Janet Pennewell to Leanne Spencer and Valaree Moodee, OGC, "Financial Reporting and Planning Organization," August 1, 2001.

[23] OFHEO, Report of Findings to Date, Special Examination of Fannie Mae, September 17, 2004, 162-168.

[24] OFHEO, Safety and Soundness Regulation, 12 CFR Part 1720, App. A, B.

[25] OFHEO, Report of Findings to Date, Special Examination of Fannie Mae, September 17, 2004, 147-155.

[26] OFHEO, Safety and Soundness Regulation, 12 CFR Part 1720, App. A, B, VIII and IX.

[27] OFHEO Interview, Jonathan Boyles, August 3, 2004, pp. 11-12.

[28] Id., pp. 7-12.

[29] OFHEO Interview, Jonathan Boyles, August 24, 2004, pp. 7-8.

[30] Office of the Comptroller of the Currency, Comptroller's Handbook: Internal Control (Washington, DC: January 2001), p. 1.

[31] Office of the Comptroller of the Currency, Comptroller's Handbook: Insider Activities (Washington, DC: March 2006), p. 7.

[32] OFHEO Policy Guidance, Minimum Safety and Soundness Requirements, PG-00-001 (December 19, 2000), OFHEO Safety and Soundness Regulation, 12 CFR Part 1720 App. A, B, V.
[33] Office of Corporate Compliance, Decision #2004-1, dated February 11, 2004. Footnote 1, "Donald Remy, Senior Vice President, Deputy General Counsel and Chief Compliance Officer...." OFH-FNM00485402. Office of Corporate Compliance Presentation, "Meeting with Audit Committee," dated July 15, 2003. That presentation showed the principal responsibilities of the OCC, including Antitrust, Employment Matters, and Potential Criminal and Civil Liability.
[34] OFHEO Policy Guidance, Minimum Safety and Soundness Requirements, PG-00-001 12 CFR § 1710.18, (December 19, 2000), OFHEO Safety and Soundness Regulation, 12 CFR Part 1720 App. A, B, V; OFHEO Examination Guidance, Examination for Corporate Governance, PG-05-002 (May 20, 2005).
[35] The Institute of Internal Auditors, International Standards for the Professional Practice of Internal Auditing (January 2004), available online at www.theaii.org.
[36] Report of the National Commission on Fraudulent Financial Reporting, October 1987, p. 38.
[37] Fannie Mae's Office of Auditing Internal Audit Manual which includes the Charter approved by the Board on April 21, 1998.
[38] Office of the Comptroller of the Currency, Comptroller's Handbook: Internal Control (Washington, DC: January 2001), p. 1.
[39] The Institute of Internal Auditors, International Standards for the Professional Practice of Internal Auditing, 1210 - Proficiency and 1220 - Due Professional Care.
[40] OFHEO Policy Guidance, Minimum Safety and Soundness Requirements, PG-00-001 (Dec. 19, 2000), OFHEO Safety and Soundness Regulation, 12 CFR 1720 App. A, B, V, VIII, as further amplified in OFHEO, Corporate Governance Regulation, 12 CFR Part 1710.15.
[41] The Institute of Internal Auditors, op. cit., Attribute Standards – 1130.A1.
[42] OFHEO Interview, Sampath Rajappa, June 17, 2004, p. 7.
[43] OFHEO Interview, Timothy Howard, August 5, 2004, p. 8.
[44] E-mail from Timothy Howard to Leanne Spencer, "re: Fannie Scolded for Obsolete Accounting Systems," March 3, 2004. OFH–FNM00126929.
[45] The Institute of Internal Auditors, op cit., Attribute Standards – 1130.
[46] OFHEO, Safety and Soundness Regulation, 12 CFR Part 1720, A, B, VII, I; and Corporate Governance Regulation, 12 CFR Part 1710.11.
[47] OFHEO Interview, Jonathan Boyles, August 3, 2004, page 64.
[48] OFHEO Interview, Timothy Howard, August 5, 2004, pp. 50-51.
[49] Notes for January 19, 1999 Board of Directors Meeting FM SRC OFHEO 00226797.
[50] Financial Performance Update – Board of Directors, January 19, 1999, FMSE 000065. Notes for January 19, 1999 Board of Directors Meeting FM SRC OFHEO 00226797.
[51] Power Point Presentation, The Year in Review, The 1998 Annual Report, February 16, 1999, FM SRC OFHEO 029169.
[52] Power Point Presentation, The Year in Review, The 1998 Annual Report, February 16, 1999, FM SRC OFHEO 029174.
[53] E-mail from Ann Kappler to Iris Aberbach, "Fwd: AC Book," February 6, 2003, FMSE-E KDO153695; OFHEO Interview, Thomas Gerrity, March 14, 2006, pp. 86-87;

OFHEO Interview, Sampath Rajappa, February 23, 2006, pp. 32-38; Draft of Audit Committee Minutes with hand written comments to delete discussion of questions from committee members, February 15, 2000, OFH-FNM 00068835-36; Official Minutes of Audit Committee Meeting, February 15,2000, FMSE 014501 – 3, which show what discussion was deleted from minutes.

[54] OFHEO Policy Guidance, Minimum Safety and Soundness Requirements, PG-00-001 (December 19, 2000), OFHEO, Safety and Soundness Regulation, 12 CFR 1720, App. A, B.VI.

[55] This language was excerpted from the Fannie Mae representation letter dated January 20, 2004, KPMG-OFHEO-000804–14. However, similar language is contained in representation letters for all audit periods.

[56] Note from Leanne Spencer's files, "FACTS", undated (likely December 1998), FM SRC OFHEO 00311273.

[57] IO/REMIC Package Briefing, March 2, 1998, FM SRC OFHEO 00142114-19 at 15-16.

[58] Fannie Mae memorandum from Matthew Douthit to Leanne Spencer regarding IO Book (buyups), January 15, 1999, FMSE-SP 068078-068079.

[59] E-mail string among Karen Pallotta, Jonathan Boyles, and Leanne Spencer, "RE: GMACM/ pre-FAS 122 MSRS," July 12, 1999, FMSE-SP 040305-6.

[60] E-mail from Leanne Spencer to Timothy Howard, cc: Jonathan Boyles, "KPMG and Freddie," FMSE 487130.

[61] E-mail from Christina Immelman to Jonathan Boyles and Distribution, July 29, 2004.

[62] Fannie Mae 2002 Annual Report, p. 101.

[63] Fannie Mae 2002 Annual Report, p. 15.

[64] "Fannie Mae." Host. Jessica Outer, July 30, 2003, FMSE-KD 013319-87 at 33-34.

[65] Id., at 26.

[66] Id., at 86-87.

[67] U.S. Representative Richard H. Baker (R-LA) Holds Hearing on Accounting and Management Issues at Fannie Mae, October 6, 2004. FMSE-E_EC0009785.

[68] U.S. Representative Richard H. Baker (R-LA) Holds Hearing on Accounting and Management Issues at Fannie Mae, October 6, 2004. FMSE-E_ EC0009797.

[69] "High Pay at Fannie Mae for the Well-Connected," Albert Crenshaw, Washington Post, December 23, 2004, at E03.

[70] Notice of Annual Meeting of Shareholders. March 29, 1999 at 13.

[71] Id.

[72] "Questions on the 1999 Proxy." FMSE KD 012637 – 012645.

[73] The 1998 Gross Wage Analysis for Mr. Johnson has the initials "JAJ" in the lower right hand corner and includes data on the exercise of stock options granted in prior years. FMSE 177322.

[74] In discussing a 2002 OFHEO inquiry about disclosure of deferred shares, Ms. Rudin indicated in an internal e-mail that Fannie Mae did not include the cash value of deferred Performance Share Plan shares in the Summary Compensation Table, but rather the number of shares deferred, noting that this reporting treatment "is unusual." E-mail from Lorrie Rudin to Saadia Mahmud et al., "Weekly Report---Executive Compensation," June 28, 2002, FMSE E EC0165620–22 at 21.

[75] Notice of Annual Meeting of Shareholders. April 23, 2004 at 25.

[76] Notice of Annual Meeting of Shareholders. April 2, 2002 at 14.

[77] Memorandum from Terri Atwell, manager for human resources programs, to Franklin Raines, "Draft of Proxy," December 11, 2001. FMSE EC 043801–09 at 04 and 06.
[78] OFHEO Interview, Lorrie Rudin, January 31, 2006 at 186.
[79] On July 12, 2002, Fannie Mae agreed to register its common stock with the SEC beginning in 2003. FMSE 085214.
[80] Notice of Annual Meeting of Shareholders. April 14, 2003 at 24.
[81] A footnote to that table indicated that Mr. Raines had deferred 25,458 shares. Notice of Annual Meeting of Shareholders. May 22, 2001 at 14.
[82] Notice of Annual Meeting of Shareholders. April 2, 2001 at 14 and 17.
[83] Id.
[84] Notice of Annual Meeting of Shareholders. April 14, 2003 at 24.
[85] Id.
[86] See Notice of Annual Meeting of Shareholders. April 2, 2002 at 14 and Notice of Annual Meeting of Shareholders. April 2, 2001 at 14.
[87] "During 1999, Mr. Johnson will also serve as a member of the Board of Directors and as Chairman of the Board's Executive Committee." Letter from Pamela Banks, Vice President for Regulatory Compliance, Fannie Mae, to Nancy Hunt, OFHEO, February 2, 1999. FMSE EC- 058515–16 at 16; "Fannie Mae Professional Services Agreement." FMSE-EC 055238–252. Mr. Johnson signed the contract on February 8, 2000.
[88] Memorandum from Anthony Marra to Ann Kappler, "Consulting Contract with Jim Johnson," August 2, 2004. FMSE EC 064047.
[89] "James A. Johnson Consulting Agreement." FMSE EC 056736.
[90] "Ongoing Benefits Provided to Former CEOs." FM SRC OFHEO 00267088 - 00267089.
[91] Memorandum from Anthony Marra to Ann Kappler, "Consulting Contract with Jim Johnson," August 2, 2004. FMSE EC 064047.
[92] Mr. Marra briefed OFHEO on the Johnson post-employment agreement on September 22, 2005. E-mail from Brian Doherty, Principal Compliance Examiner, OFHEO to Chris Dickerson, Chief Compliance Examiner, OFHEO and Deirdre Kvartunas, Principal Compliance Examiner, OFHEO, "Jim Johnson Contract Meeting with Fannie Mae, September 22, 2004, 1pm."
[93] Untitled memorandum. FMSE EC 055232.
[94] E-mail from Anthony Marra to Thomas Donilon et al., Re: "Jim Johnson," March 25, 2004, FMSE-E_KD 0012453–54.
[95] E-mail from Daniel Mudd to Anthony Marra et al., Re: "Jim Johnson," March 26, 2004, FMSE-E KD0012474–75.
[96] E-mail from Daniel Mudd to Anthony Marra et al., Re: "Jim Johnson," March 26, 2004, FMSE-E KD0012474–75.
[97] Memorandum from Anthony Marra to Ann Kappler, "Consulting Contract with Jim Johnson," August 2, 2004. FMSE EC 064047.
[98] Letter from James Johnson to Stephen Ashley, Chairman of the Fannie Mae Board of Directors, March 17, 2005. FM SRC OFHEO 00298898–99 at 98.
[99] Notice of Annual Meeting of Shareholders. March 25, 1991, FMSE 510292 – 510321, at 29. FMSE 510319.
[100] Letter from Anthony Marra to Stephen Friedman, September 20, 2002. FM SRC OFHEO 00267087–88 at 88.

[101] Id.

[102] Fannie Mae Web Site Home Page, dated January 3, 2003. FMSE-E_KD0034795-807, at page 3.

[103] OFHEO Policy Guidance, Minimum Safety and Soundness Requirements, PG-00-001 (December 19, 2000), OFHEO Safety and Soundness Regulation, 12 CFR Part 1720 App. A, B, V.

[104] OFHEO Policy Guidance, Minimum Safety and Soundness Requirements, PG-00-001 (December 19, 2000), OFHEO Safety and Soundness Regulation, 12 CFR Part 1720 App. A, B, VIII (May 20, 2005).

[105] OFHEO Interview, Sam Rajappa, June 17, 2004, at p. 88.

[106] OFHEO previously concluded that this July 2003 Audit Report was flawed in several respects. Report of Findings to Date, Special Examination of Fannie Mae, September 17, 2004, at 79. Specifically, pertinent findings of the July 2003 Audit Report were unclear, did not provide appropriate emphasis, misrepresented certain significant control weaknesses as documentation issues, inappropriately ignored several meaningful findings noted in the auditors' work papers, and "suggest[ed] a pervasive lack of written procedures and documentation for most of the Enterprise's amortization activities." FMSE 121183-90.

[107] Under Section 301 of the Sarbanes-Oxley Act, Audit Committees are required to have the authority to engage independent counsel and advisors as needed. 15 U.S.C. § 78(f).

[108] September 2004 Report of Findings to Date, Special Examination of Fannie Mae, at 74.

[109] OFHEO Interview, Paul Jackson, August 17, 2004, pp. 78-80. See also id., p. 80 ("If it came down to a question about the appropriateness of GAAP, that is ultimately the decision and ownership of senior management as well as our external auditors. They have the expertise, the knowledge base, and it's their job to do that.")

[110] OCC Decision #2003-1 (Part A, Amortization and Documentation Issues) September 29, 2003 (OA concluded that $6.5 million factor "change request submitted by the modeling group (Mr. Juliane) was not properly documented and was processed by the PDI group (Mr. Barnes) even though reasons for the change were not understood by the PDI group."), FMSE 024413; Summarized Minutes of the Meeting (8/8/03) Unamortized Balances and Factor Analysis ("the factor change request did not include sufficient written documentation to support the transaction and . . . was made without the full understanding by the iPDI group of the reason for the change), FMSE 024418; OFHEO Interview, Sampath Rajappa, June 17, 2004, p. 109 ("I don't believe we had a basis to determine based on the documentation to say whether [the factor change] was right or wrong. . . . We looked at the documentation. The documentation seemed inconclusive."); id. at p. 157 ("The documentation [management] gave me was not sufficient for me to come independently to the conclusion [that the $6.5 million adjustment was correct]"); OFHEO Interview, Paul Jackson, August 17, 2004, p. 139 (documentation provided to support adjustment "wasn't sufficiently explanatory from my standpoint"); OFHEO Interview, Joyce Philip, July 21, 2004, p. 119 (concluding "that insufficient support had been provided to Roger Barnes to explain the reason for this particular factor change"); id. at 121 ("The supporting information provided to Roger was inadequate."); id. at 129 ("we did conclude that insufficient information and documentation had been provided to support that particular factor change").

[111] OFHEO Interview, Joyce Philip, July 21, 2004, at pp. 139-140.

[112] Fannie Mae Audit Report, Office of Auditing, "Amortization Audit", July 9, 2003.

[113] Although Sampath Rajappa, the head of the Office of Auditing (OA), stated that OA determined that the $6.5 million adjustment was not material (OFHEO Interview, Sampath Rajappa, June 17, 2004, p. 112), that assertion was directly refuted by Joyce Philip, one of the two internal auditors whom Mr. Rajappa assigned to perform the investigation. Ms. Philip stated that OA did not reach a conclusion regarding the materiality or immateriality of the $6.5 million adjustment. OFHEO Interview, Joyce Philip, July 21, 2004, pp. 147-48.

[114] Internal auditor Joyce Philip stated that the Office of Auditing followed up with Mr. Juliane to understand the reason for the factor change and that Mr. Juliane created a spreadsheet that provided a "reasonable explanation for the change." OFHEO Interview, Joyce Philip, July 21, 2004, 130-31. See also OFHEO Interview, Sampath Rajappa, June 17, 2004, p. 157, ("management felt it was a correct entry" but the documentation they provided did not support that conclusion); OFHEO Interview, Ann Eilers, July 23, 2004, pp. 226-27, (Management gave OA an explanation for the factor change, "based on a conversation," but "[i]t wasn't documented. So for [OA's] control purposes and for the test work that we do, it basically did not meet our Internal Audit test."); FMSE 024415, Review of Amortization Results, Audit Analysis of Unamortized Balances and Factors ("Controller management were able to verbally explain the reasons for the change.").

[115] SEC Staff Accounting Bulletin: No. 99 – Materiality. Securities and Exchange Commission 12 CFR Part 211.

[116] According to the SEC rules PART II—RULES 12b-25(b) and (c), if a Form 10-Q cannot be filed within the prescribed time period, they must state in reasonable detail the reasons why on Form 12b-25, Notification of Late Filing.

[117] OFHEO Interview, Ann Kappler, April 11, 2006, pp. 209-210.

[118] Summarized Minutes of the Meeting (8/8/03) Unamortized Balances and Factor Analysis, FMSE 024417-19.

[119] Memorandum from Ann Kappler to Sampath Rajappa, "Internal Control Representation Letter for "Covered Period": April 1, 2003 – June 30, 2003," July 28, 2003.

[120] Roger Barnes-Fannie Mae Settlement Agreement, November 3, 2003, FMSE 328797–805.

[121] E-mails sent by Mr. Barnes to a confidante stated that: "Negative factors for discount or premium revises current period net income and destroys all integrity of the $9 billion original discount inventory." FMSE 021184; "I am still troubled by the impact I continue to see of the negative factors I located in the last month (April) factor change. Everyone keeps telling me that there is no problem. Yet the big correction due in June includes the $35 million caused by negative factors I located in the last month (April) factor change. Jeff, Dick, and Janet are not worried. I am being told Frank and Tim are happy with income where it is, as a result of the process used." FMSE 021187; "Discussed with Mary several times, also with Dick. Mary agreed it would seem inconceivable to have negative factors. Mary noted I should talk to Jeff." FMSE 021187. Although it appears that the internal auditors were willing to accept the explanations of the illogical amortization factors provided by the Controller's office in August 2003, documents left behind by Mr. Barnes indicate that he rejected Mr. Juliane's proposed remedy: "Either modeling does or does not produce factors which

comply with accounting rules. Jeff showed, in his analysis, how he now intends to revise the factors to suddenly reduce the cumulative factors below 100% without having to disclose there has been any correction taking place." FMSE 022933.

[122] Mr. Barnes observed in file documents that "[a]ccounting issue-management opts not to post over-amortization or under-amortization in the year in which it affected income and financial statements. Management actually adds the income over/under amortization back to the database as a 'new acquisition' to avoid income volatility and amortizes the over-amortization or under-amortization a second time spread out over a number of years." FMSE 021753. The misapplications identified by Mr. Barnes resulted in improper revenue and expense recognition. According to a January 2003 memorandum from Mr. Barnes to File, a difference identified in the STATS realignment process was historically booked as a "BUCKET" amount and reamortized. Mr. Barnes apparently took issue with that treatment, and senior management agreed in 2003 that realignment differences should be booked to income. However, they decided "NOT TO CORRECT the previous incorrect accounting even though the total is almost $200 million in income with approximately $60 million unstated." FMSE 021199. In the same e-mail, Mr. Barnes alleged a $20 million understatement of income related to the STATS realignment. FMSE 021199. The Deferred Pool Analysis report for the month ended September 30, 2003 reflected a credit balance of $21 million in the BUCKET account. FMSE 021754.

[123] Mr. Barnes claimed that he was asked to leave blank journal entries in January 2001 so that adjusting entries could be posted following Mr. Howard's review of 2000 results: "Jeff reiterated that per discussion with VP, Pennewell, they will be prepared to generate any desired results thru the modeling process. He just needs to know what the expectations are and the rate climate to use as justification." FMSE 021164. Mr. Juliane referred to a process whereby he "adjusted the factors to evenly recognize $75 million of additional income in 2001 which is $50 million less than was originally forecasted in the plan," to which Mr. Barnes responded, "Certainly appears to be income management." FMSE 021170.

[124] OFHEO Production Logs.

[125] Office of Corporate Compliance, Decision #2003-1 (Part B, Reporting Environment), dated October 6, 2003. FMSE580964-68.

[126] Id.

[127] Minutes of the Meeting of the Audit Committee of the Board of Directors of Fannie Mae, August 12, 2003, FMSE 504788-504791.

[128] An e-mail exchange between Ms. Kappler and Mr. Rajappa on August 11, 2003 reveals that Ms. Kappler had already briefed the Audit Committee Chairman, Tom Gerrity, and states that she would say in the Committee meeting the next day that "Roger has indicated that he is satisfied." FMSE 02391, E-mail from S. Rajappa to A. Kappler, August 11, 2003.

[129] E-mail from Deborah House to Ann Kappler, dated August 12, 2003. "Ann, I think we discussed this but I just want to make sure we are on the same pg. Roger has indicated that he is not entirely satisfied as to the answers to his questions but that he will "defer" to those who are."

[130] OFHEO Interview, Thomas Gerrity, dated March 14, 2006.

[131] E-mail from R. Barnes to D. House, August 25, 2003. FMSE 021262.

[132] Id.

[133] OFHEO Interview, Joyce Philips, July 21, 2004, pp. 139-140.

[134] E-mail from Ann Kappler to Timothy Howard, "Thoughts for tomorrow," August 11, 2003, OFH-FNM00187270.

[135] Minutes of the Meeting of the Audit Committee of the Board of Directors of Fannie Mae, August 12, 2003, FMSE 504788-91, p. 4.

[136] Audit Committee Quarterly Certification, 8/12/03, FMSE 023185.

[137] OFHEO Interview, Sampath Rajappa, June 17, 2004, pp. 9-10 and 30.

[138] E-mail from Michelle Skinner to Daniel Mudd, "follow up from your 'unplugged' meeting today," September 9, 2003, FMSE 024452-53. Ms. Skinner was Director for Securities Accounting from January 2000 to November 2002 and has been Director for eBusiness Information Management since then.

[139] Id.

[140] E-mail from Ann Kappler to Sampath Rajappa, "draft messages from Dan," cc to Donald Remy, September 25, 2003, FMSE-E_KD0100611.

[141] E-mail from Anthony Lloyd to Daniel Mudd, cc to Michelle Skinner, September 28, 2003. FMSE-KD023102-104.

[142] E-mail chain from Daniel Mudd to Pilar O'Leary, "Re: Unplugged Question," October 6, 2003, FMSE-E 2326737-39.

[143] OFHEO Policy Guidance, Minimum Safety and Soundness Requirements, PG-00-001 (December 19, 2000), OFHEO Safety and Soundness Regulation, 12 CFR Part 1720 App. A, B, VIII.

[144] In an interview with OFHEO, Mr. Mudd asserted that this e-mail applied only to Ms. Gallo and was based on a request by Board member Anne Mulcahy to limit Ms. Gallo's direct contact with the Board. OFHEO Interview, Daniel Mudd, April 18, 2006, pp. 129-132.

[145] E-mail from Kathy Gallo to Daniel Mudd, June 30, 2003, responding to Mr. Mudd's prior E-mail, FMSE-E_KD0000712. In his interview with OFHEO, Mr. Mudd stated that the e-mail was "specifically to and for Ms. Gallo." Id.

[146] FM SRC OFHEO 00909290.

[147] OFHEO Interview, Thomas Gerrity, February 28, 2006, pp. 136-138.

[148] Board Evaluation Form, KMSE-KD 052693-70.

[149] 12 C.F.R. § 1710.11(b)(4).

[150] The HUD Inspector General notified OFHEO of that investigation on November 13, 2002. The report of the investigation stated: "We concluded the Office's compensation levels are comparable to other regulatory organizations." Audit Report Office of Inspector General, Dept. of HUD, 2003-KC-0002 July 29, 2003. That report also found that OFHEO did not ensure that it used its travel funds "at optimum efficiency" and sometimes paid for lodging costs above the maximum per diem. On December 19, 2003, the HUD Inspector General informed OFHEO that all actions taken by OFHEO satisfactorily addressed recommendations made in the report.

[151] On June 13, 2003, Roger Niesen, Regional Inspector General for Audit of the Office of Inspector General for Audit of HUD, informed Director Falcon that his office was beginning an audit of the oversight responsibilities of OFHEO, particularly regarding the "examination results and the basis for its conclusions regarding Fannie Mae and Freddie Mac ...." Memorandum For Armando Falcon, Jr. Director, Office of Federal

Housing Enterprise Oversight from Roger E. Niesen, Regional Inspector General for Audit, June 13, 2003. Eleven months later, Ronald Hosking, the then Regional Inspector General for Audit, informed Director Falcon that the investigation was being terminated. An E-mail from Mr. Hosking to Director Falcon, May 6, 2004, stated: "We notified you on October 7, 2003 that we were suspending our audit of OFHEO.... We took that action in response to pending legislation to transfer oversight of the GSEs from OFHEO to the Department of Treasury."

[152] The HUD Inspector General commenced that investigation on June 10, 2004. The Inspector General issued two reports. The first concluded that OFHEO met the 60 percent requirement but that additional testing was necessary. Office of Inspector General, Audit Report, 2004-KC-0001, September 30, 2004. The second concluded that OFHEO was comparable to other federal financial regulators in its allocation of resources and staffing. Office of Inspector General, Audit Report 2005-KC-0001. March 16, 2005.

[153] E-mail from Ann Kappler to Catherine Smith, April 27, 2004, FMSE-E_KD 028113 – FMSE-E_KD 28114; E-mail from Randall McFarlane to Patricia Milon, November 20, 2003, FMSE-E GIR 0024725 – FMSE-E GIR 0024726; Handwritten notes of Duane Duncan telephone call, undated, FMSE-GIR 0027468.

[154] Office of Inspector General, Special Investigations Division Report, SID-04-0034-I, October 5, 2004. The report states (p. 4): "It appears that the Director has broad authority to release OFHEO agency information, and that the release of information is discretionary."

[155] Draft letter to Kenneth M. Donohue, March 15, 2004, FMSE-GIR-0043558 through FMSE-GIR-0043559.

[156] OFHEO interview of Duane S. Duncan, April 4, 2006, pp. 160-61.

[157] Id., pp. 33-36.

[158] Id., pp 209-10.

[159] Handwritten notes of Duane Duncan: "Timing on IG Report--writing now + done in a month" FMSE-GIR 0025676; Handwritten notes of Duane Duncan on telephone call, September 16, 2004, at 6:00, FMSE-GIR 0048258; Duncan handwritten notes, FMSE-GIR 0043791 et seq.; Duane Duncan handwritten notes of telephone call with Congressional staff, October 8, 2004 at 9:40, with extensive notes on content of the then-unpublished HUD Inspector General report. FMSE-GIR 0043794.

[160] See e.g., James Tyson, Bloomberg News, "HUD Report Portrays OFHEO as Divided; Director Wanted to Be More Aggressive", Washington Post, November 20, 2004, at E1; John R. Wilke, "Fannie, Freddie Regulator Is Split Over Moves to Toughen Oversight", Wall Street Journal, November 22, 2004, at A2; John R. Wilke, "Sharp Divisions Found Inside Fannie, Freddie", Dow Jones Business News, November 22, 2004; "Congress Urges Ouster of 2 Regulators", New York Times, November 23, 2004, at C2; John Connor, "Capital Views: Bumpy OFHEO Trip From 'Afraid' To 'Tough'", Dow Jones Newswire, November 23, 2004.

[161] The allegations reported in the fourth HUD Inspector General report, that OFHEO overstated Fannie Mae's accounting problems, have been discredited.

[162] E-mails from Monica Medina to Stephen Ashley, et al., November 24, 2004, FMSE-E GIR 0121664; FMSE-E GIR 0078004.

[163] "Senate Panel Conditions $10 M of OFHEO Budget On New Director," September 22, 2004, Dawn Kopecki, Dow Jones Newswires.

[164] Handwritten notes of Duane Duncan on telephone call, dated September 16, 2004, at 6:00, FMSE-GIR 0048258. Subsequently, the congressional conference dropped that language and substituted a non-binding rider calling for the dismissal of the OFHEO Director and Deputy Director.

IX. THE ROLE OF THE BOARD OF DIRECTORS

The duties and responsibilities of the Board of Directors of Fannie Mae, which are embodied in the Charter Act[1] and applicable law, are more particularly set forth in the OFHEO corporate governance regulation.[2] The corporate governance regulation charges the Board of Directors (including its appropriate committees) with furthering the safety and soundness of the Enterprise and sets forth affirmative duties that must be undertaken by the Board to meet its safety and soundness obligations.

Specifically, OFHEO requires the Board to

> direct the conduct and affairs of the Enterprise in furtherance of the safe and sound operation of the Enterprise and ... remain reasonably informed of the condition, activities, and operations of the Enterprise. The responsibilities of the Board include having in place adequate policies and procedures to assure its oversight of, among other matters, the following:

(1) Corporate strategy, major plans of action, risk policy, programs for legal and regulatory compliance and corporate performance ...;
(2) Hiring and retention of qualified senior executive officers and succession planned for such senior executive officers;
(3) Compensation programs of the enterprise;
(4) Integrity of accounting and financial reporting systems of the Enterprise, including independent audits and systems of internal control;
(5) Process and adequacy of reporting disclosures, and communications to shareholders, investors, and potential investors; [and]
(6) Responsiveness of executive officers in providing accurate and timely reports to Federal regulators and in addressing the supervisory concerns of Federal regulators in a timely and appropriate manner."[3]

OFHEO's corporate governance regulation also points Boards of Directors to the body of law elected under 12 CFR 1710.10 and to publications and other pronouncements of OFHEO for additional guidance on conduct and responsibilities for the Board of Directors.[4] Thus, additional duties of the Fannie Mae Board arise from Fannie Mae's election to be governed by Delaware

General Corporation Law, Del. Code Ann. tit. 8, as amended.[5] Delaware statutory and case law, however, is supplemental to OFHEO's corporate governance and safety and soundness standards that OFHEO has imposed since OFHEO's inception.[6]

Well-settled principles of good corporate governance hold that, to be observant of the best interests of the corporation, an independent director must "'exercise a healthy skepticism,'" and an alertness to possible wrongdoing on the part of corporate insiders."[7] In fact, a director's independence should be her "most distinguishing characteristic."[8] That said, in order to be effective, a director must do more than simply monitor management's performance. Applicable standards require that a director must actively undertake vigorous scrutiny of the corporation's affairs, and must be unfailingly vigilant in requiring that management continuously provide an adequate and frequent flow of information concerning the goals, objectives, operations, and financial condition of the corporation. For efficiency, a board will delegate its oversight work to various committees. For example, the audit committee, whose members should be independent and free of management influence,[9] is charged with, among other matters, reviewing the internal and external audit functions. It does not follow, however, that by delegating certain duties a board is absolved of responsibility to ensure that a committee does its work and reports adequately on that work. To the contrary, OFHEO's corporate governance regulation[10] specifically provides that "no committee shall operate to relieve the board of directors or any board member of a responsibility imposed by applicable law, rule, or regulation."[11] In the case of Fannie Mae, the Board of Directors imprudently failed to perform those important duties and responsibilities, in contravention of myriad applicable safety and soundness standards.

This chapter chronicles the oversight lapses of Fannie Mae's Board of Directors and, in particular, its Audit and Compensation Committees. In short, the Board of Directors failed to be sufficiently informed and to act independently of its Chairman, Franklin Raines, and senior management. The Board failed to exert the requisite oversight over the Enterprise's operations and to assure that the Enterprise was fully compliant with applicable law and safety and soundness standards. Among the Board's duties was the responsibility to ensure that Fannie Mae's financial reporting and disclosures were in accordance with generally accepted accounting principles (GAAP).[12] In the absence of policies and procedures adequate to safeguard the integrity of the accounting and financial reporting systems, Fannie Mae issued reports of condition containing materially false annual and quarterly financial statements, requiring the restatement of results in prior financial reporting periods in an amount currently estimated at $10.6 billion. On the basis of those falsified financial statements, over a period of several years, the Chairman, the Chief Financial Officer, and various officers realized sizeable bonuses to which they were not entitled.

Senior management attributed Fannie Mae's unerring ability to hit pre-set earnings per share targets, and Wall Street analysts' projections, to its supposedly unique business model. That questionable construct went unchallenged by the Board for years. As discussed below, had the Board inquired into management's practices with appropriate vigor, many of the problems discussed in this report might have been avoided or addressed earlier.

The Board refrained from demanding accountability from the Chairman and other senior executives in numerous ways. Specifically, the Board abandoned its checks-and-balances oversight responsibilities; acquiesced in allowing management unbridled authority over its agenda, materials, and minutes; did not adopt and impose policies requiring that all critical accounting policies and major transactions be vetted before it or its designated committee; and acquiesced in allowing the Chairman to concentrate power in the Chief Financial Officer and then to seat him on the Board, which enhanced the power and influence of executive

Board members. In fact, the Board allowed management to determine with little opposition the information it received and missed many opportunities for meaningful oversight.

Among those missed opportunities was the failure on the part of the Board, and the Audit Committee in particular, to challenge the Chairman and senior management at several critical points during 2003 when the Board should have required a thorough, independent investigation into Fannie Mae financial accounting and reporting practices. Those critical points included the January 2003 announcement by Freddie Mac, whose business model closely paralleled that of Fannie Mae's, that it was restating its financial statements due to misapplications of GAAP and initiating an internal investigation; the certification of Fannie Mae's financial statements in connection with the registration of its stock effective on March 31, 2003; the management shakeup at Freddie Mac in June 2003; the initiation by OFHEO of the special examination in July 2003; and the August 2003 allegation by an employee turned whistleblower, that certain accounting functions had significantly compromised the validity of the Enterprise's financial reporting just prior to the certification of its financial results in connection with its quarterly financial report (10Q) for the third quarter of 2003. The Board did not question the fast-tracked settlement of the employee's whistleblower claims after management had represented the allegations to be unsubstantiated. During the entire period under review, the Board repeatedly failed to discharge its responsibilities properly, engaged in conduct contrary to standards of prudent operation, and failed to ensure the safe and sound operation of the Enterprise.

The Board delegated important safety and soundness responsibilities to its committees. Of particular importance are the Audit and Compensation Committees. The members of the Fannie Mae Board of Directors were all knowledgeable and qualified individuals, fully capable of understanding the business and corporate governance issues with which they were charged. The chapter proceeds by documenting the responsibilities delegated to the Audit and Compensation Committees and the specific safety and soundness failures of those committees. The failures of those committees reflect failures of the entire Board of Directors. The following section focuses on failures of the full Board to discharge its oversight responsibilities as enumerated in statute, regulation, regulatory guidance, and industry best practice. The members of the Fannie Mae Board of Directors failed to stay appropriately informed of corporate strategy; review major business decisions; ensure appropriate delegations of authority; ensure that Board committees functioned effectively; provide an appropriate check on Chairman and Chief Executive Officer (CEO) Franklin Raines; and adequately oversee the risk policies, programs for legal and regulatory compliance, hiring and retention of qualified senior executive officers, compensation programs, and integrity of accounting and financial reporting systems, including independent audits and system of internal control.

Board Structure and Composition

To some extent the OFHEO corporate governance regulation allows the Board to rely, in directing the Enterprise, on reports from committees.[13] However as detailed later in this chapter, that reliance does not relieve Board members of their responsibility to oversee the functioning of those committees or of numerous other duties of the full Board. The Board approves Committee assignments, including the designation of committee chairs on an annual basis.[14] In 1998, the Board had six standing committees: Executive, Assets and Liabilities Policy, Audit, Compensation, Nominating and Corporate Governance, and Technology. In December 2003, the Technology Committee dissolved and its responsibilities shifted to the Audit Committee. Fannie Mae established three new Board committees in 2004: Housing and Community Development, Compliance, and Special Review. In 2005, the Assets and Liabilities Policy Committee dissolved and the Risk Policy and Capital Committee was established as its replacement.

Membership on the Fannie Mae Board of Directors was prestigious and provided members a high degree of visibility. Mr. Raines was recognized as a top CEO and served as the co-chairman of Business Roundtable, a prestigious business group of top executives of nationally renowned companies. The Board was comprised of highly knowledgeable and qualified individuals with extensive experience on corporate boards of directors, fully capable of understanding the business and corporate governance issues with which they were charged. Key current members of the Board who served during the period covered by this report include current Board Chairman Board Stephen Ashley, who is also Chief Executive Officer of the Ashley Group and a former president of the Mortgage Bankers Association. Audit Committee Chair Thomas Gerrity is a former Dean of the Wharton School at the University of Pennsylvania. Compensation Committee Chair Joe Pickett is the former Chief Executive Officer of Homeside International, Inc., and a former president of the Mortgage Bankers Association. Howard University President H. Patrick Swygert chairs the Compliance Committee. Housing and Community Development Committee Chair Kenneth Duberstein served as White House Chief of Staff in the Reagan administration. Former Secretary of Labor Ann McLaughlin Korologos chaired Fannie Mae's Nominating and Corporate Governance Committee from 2001 to 2004, and currently serves as Chairman of the Board of Trustees of the RAND Corporation.

Other key members of the Board that served during the relevant period included Anne Mulcahy, Chairman and Chief Executive Officer of Xerox Corporation, and Vincent Mai, Chairman and Chief Executive Officer of the private equity firm AEA Investors, LLC, and a former managing partner at Lehman Brothers. Both chaired the Compensation Committee during their tenure at Fannie Mae. Appendix A provides more detail concerning the composition of the Board.

Between 1998 and 2004, management members of the Fannie Mae Board of Directors included James A. Johnson, who served as Chairman and Chief Executive Officer until December 1998, and who served as Chair of the Executive Committee until December 1999; Lawrence Small, who served as President and Chief Operating Officer until January 2000; Franklin Raines, who served as Chairman and Chief Executive Officer-designate from May 1998 to January 1999, and as Chairman and Chief Executive Officer from January 1999 until December 2004; Jamie Gorelick, who served as Vice Chair from May 1997 to May 2003; Daniel Mudd, who served as President and Chief Operating Officer from February 2000 until December 2004, and as President and Chief Executive Officer from December 2004 to the present; and Timothy Howard, who served as Vice Chairman and Chief Financial Officer from May 2003 to December 2004. Due to his material relationship with Fannie Mae as a consultant for the Enterprise, Board member Kenneth Duberstein is considered a non-independent non-management director.

Failures of the Committees of the Board

The Audit and Compensation Committees, two of the standing committees of the Board of Directors, failed to meet regulatory and corporate standards in discharging their responsibilities. Of those two, the one with the most far-reaching significance for safety and soundness, both because of the required independence of its members and the scope of its responsibilities, was the Audit Committee. The failures of the Audit Committee were compounded by failures of the Compensation Committee.

Audit Committee

As the standards governing the roles, responsibilities and conduct of audit committees have evolved over the past two decades,[15] one constant has remained: an audit committee acts under the imprimatur of the board of directors pursuant to the delegations of authority and responsibilities in its enabling charter and applicable law. Importantly, a board of directors, having conferred certain duties upon the audit committee by charter, cannot absolve itself of those responsibilities. It follows that any failure by the Audit Committee of the Board of Directors of Fannie Mae to adhere to the requisite standards constituted a failure of the Board.

Chief among the Board's duties was the responsibility to ensure that Fannie Mae's financial reporting and disclosures were in accordance with GAAP, in accordance with the Charter Act.[16] Of all the Audit Committee's responsibilities—including, for example, the oversight of internal and external auditing and internal controls—its principal obligation was to ensure the fidelity of Fannie Mae's financial reporting and disclosures.[17]

The Audit Committee failed to protect Fannie Mae's safety and soundness by not discharging its duties responsibly and effectively. This section reviews those duties and the Committee's failures.

Applicable Standards

Audit committees are subject to myriad legal and industry standards, which were published throughout the relevant time period, including the 1987 Treadway Commission Report, and two studies released in 1999 that called for strengthening an audit committee's role: the so-called Blue Ribbon Report[18] and the study commissioned by the Committee of Sponsoring Organizations of the Treadway Commission (COSO Report).[19]

Among other matters, the Blue Ribbon Report and the COSO Report called for new audit committee disclosure rules and enhanced auditor independence requirements. In response, the stock exchanges promulgated revised rules.[20] As an exchange-listed company, Fannie Mae is subject to the New York Stock Exchange (NYSE) Listing Standards. Thus, Fannie Mae was required to comply with the NYSE rule changes that required audit committees to consist of at least three independent directors, each of whom should be able to read and understand fundamental financial statements, and one of whom should have accounting or financial expertise.[21] The NYSE also outlined requirements of independence and required the adoption of a formal written charter.[22]

Both the SEC and the NYSE again proposed new standards to further strengthen audit committees[23] in response to the enactment of the Sarbanes-Oxley Act (SOX) in 2002,[24] which effectively federalized the role of the public company audit committee. SOX focused more attention on the need for independent oversight by increasing audit committee responsibilities and authority, and by raising committee membership requirements to include a greater number of independent directors.[25]

As discussed below, Fannie Mae's Board revised the Charter of the Audit Committee as new standards proliferated. For example, in early 2000, in response to the newly elucidated 1999 standards, the Board amended the 1996 Audit Committee Charter. The Board again revised the charter in 2003. That those charter revisions were undertaken is not in question; the issue, rather, is whether the Audit Committee complied with them.

In 1998, the responsibilities of the Audit Committee of the Board were set forth in the Audit Committee Charter adopted in 1996.[26] The 1996 Charter delineates the Audit Committee's oversight responsibilities with respect to regulatory compliance, accounting and financial reporting, the external auditor relationship, and internal auditing activities. Among other things, the 1996 Charter required the Audit Committee to:

- Meet with management, internal auditors, and the corporation's independent auditors, and to develop in-depth and specialized knowledge on matters relating to corporate accounting, financial reporting, internal control, auditing, and regulatory compliance activities;
- Review and make recommendations to the Board on the corporation's accounting and financial reporting practices and its annual financial report to shareholders;
- Assess the adequacy and effectiveness of internal controls, including compliance with established limits on derivatives risk;
- Receive periodic reports from management, internal audit, and the corporation's independent auditors on matters relating to corporate accounting, financial reporting, internal control, auditing, and regulatory compliance, and on the activities of management's Business Conduct Committee, including monitoring compliance with the Code of Business Conduct; and
- Recommend to the Board the appointment of the corporation's independent auditors and oversee the activities of the independent auditors.

The Charter seemingly limited some of the Committee's authority by requiring the Audit Committee Chair to consult with executive management in overseeing and evaluating the activities and performance of the "Vice President for Auditing," and "the budgets and staffing of the internal audit department." Additionally, the Charter authorized the Audit Committee to "cause an investigation to be made" into any matter under its scope of responsibility that "is brought to its attention." The Charter later underwent wholesale revisions.

In 2000, the Audit Committee Charter revised the responsibilities of the Audit Committee members to include monitoring the integrity of the corporation's financial statements and the independence of internal and external audit functions.[27] The 2000 Charter further required the Audit Committee to review the corporation's financial reporting practices, including the significant issues and judgments made in connection with the preparation of the audited financial statements, and to receive periodic reports relating to the corporation's business environment, major risks, and risk management processes. Additionally, the importance of independent communication flow was emphasized. Again, the Charter provided authority for the Committee to "cause an investigation to be made into any matter within the scope of its responsibility that is brought to its attention." Here, the Committee's authority was expanded to permit it to "engage such independent resources to assist in its investigations, as it deems necessary." Thus, the Committee had full authority to initiate an investigation into any matter under its purview.

The Charter was again restructured in 2003[28] in conjunction with Fannie Mae's first proxy statement to shareholders upon SEC registration. At that time, the charter was amended to include the responsibilities of audit committees required by the Sarbanes-Oxley Act of 2002. The 2003 Charter clarified the Committee's responsibility to monitor independence of the internal audit function by requiring that the Committee ensure that no limitations or restrictions were placed on that function.

In addition to maintaining the pre-existing oversight responsibilities, the 2003 Charter also provided for heightened financial statement and disclosure responsibilities, including:

- A discussion and analysis of the outside auditor's judgment as to the quality of the corporation's accounting principles, significant financial reporting issues, and MD&A [Management Discussion and Analysis] disclosures;
- Review and discuss with the outside auditors all critical accounting policies, any alternative treatments under GAAP, and material communications with management; and
- Review and discuss with management and the outside auditor any correspondence with regulators or governmental agencies which raises material issues regarding Fannie Mae's financial statements, financial disclosures or accounting policies.

Failures of the Audit Committee

The Audit Committee of the Board of Directors failed to safeguard Fannie Mae's safety and soundness by not discharging its duties responsibly and effectively. Specifically, the Committee failed to evaluate the internal audit function and the performance of the head of the Office of Auditing, to oversee the production of financial statements, to monitor the development and implementation of critical accounting policies, to develop in-depth or specialized knowledge necessary to its oversight responsibilities, and to oversee adequately the work of the external auditor.

The Audit Committee was complacent in the oversight activities required by its Charter and applicable regulations, guidelines, and standards. Members of the Audit Committee exercised little, if any, meaningful or active oversight. They failed to perform disciplined and consistent evaluations of internal audit activities, to probe management of the Office of Auditing, or to discuss diligently or inquire adequately with respect to incomplete representations of management and the Office of Auditing regarding critical accounting issues. Those issues included whether critical accounting policies conformed with GAAP and the uncorroborated representations of management that the external auditor reviewed and approved those policies. The record fails to demonstrate adequate inquiry or thoughtful requests for additional information or explanation from Audit Committee members in their meetings with the external auditor.

The Audit Committee was required to develop in-depth and specialized knowledge on matters relating to corporate accounting and financial reporting in order to serve its oversight role effectively. That role encompassed oversight of both the internal and external auditor relationships as well as responsibility for monitoring the integrity of the Fannie Mae's financial statements. Further, standards during the relevant time period as developed by the Treadway Commission (1987), The Blue Ribbon Commission (1999) and the SEC (1999, 2000, and 2002) required audit committees to engage in vigilant and effective oversight of the Enterprise's financial reporting process and internal controls.

In February 2001, after the Blue Ribbon Report and resulting changes in SEC and NYSE standards, Sampath Rajappa, Senior Vice President for Operations Risk and head of the Office of Auditing, reported to Vice-Chairman Jamie Gorelick, Chairman and CEO Franklin Raines, CFO Timothy Howard, Controller Leanne Spencer, and others that he would address with KPMG how Fannie Mae would "meet all the foregoing requirements at the Audit Committee meeting."[29] Mr. Rajappa also claimed that "[i]n a nutshell, we are/will be in compliance with all the requirements." The requirements to which he referred included American Institute of Certified Public Accountants Statements of Auditing Standards SAS-89 and SAS-90, the NYSE's guidelines on audit committee governance standards, the SEC Final Rules on audit committee requirements, and the SEC independence rules as they pertained to the external auditor. At the

Audit Committee meeting on February 20, 2001, Mr. Rajappa and Ms. Theobald, of KPMG, reported that the Audit Committee either met or exceeded every requirement.[30,31]

In 2002, Fannie Mae Board policies and practices were reviewed with the goal of ensuring that Fannie Mae corporate governance was "best in class."[32] That review included an assessment of Fannie Mae's corporate governance policies and practices against the standards contained in SOX, NYSE listing requirements, OFHEO and SEC regulations, and best practices.[33] In early 2003, the Fannie Mae Board of Directors adopted a variety of enhancements to achieve "best in class" status.[34] Despite those representations and Fannie Mae's desire to be "best in class," both the Audit Committee and its chairman failed to comply with the Audit Committee Charter and professional standards.

Failure to Oversee the Office of Auditing and the Head of the Office of Auditing. The Audit Committee's responsibilities include oversight of both the internal and external audit functions independent of management. Effective execution of fiduciary duty and responsibility requires robust oversight and involvement, including candid discussions, diligent and knowledgeable committee membership, and the use of external consultants as authorized by the Audit Committee Charter. 35

According to its charter, the Audit Committee has the express duty to oversee the internal audit function, which at Fannie Mae was conducted by the Office of Auditing. In that capacity, the Audit Committee is responsible for discussing Office of Auditing activities, including the appointment and replacement of its head, and its budget and staffing. The Audit Committee is also charged with determining the scope and performance of the internal audit function, reviewing the Audit Plan, and ascertaining whether there are any restrictions or limitations on the Office. In order to fulfill its duty, the Audit Committee also has the responsibility of obtaining periodic reports from the head of the Office regarding the findings of internal audits.

The Audit Committee failed to execute its oversight responsibilities adequately. Those failures primarily involved a lack of appropriate concern for safeguarding the independence of the internal audit function from financial reporting and business functions, and a lack of engagement in the planning and evaluation of internal audits.

The Appointment of Mr. Rajappa. While the Board has the overall responsibility for hiring qualified senior officers,[36] the Audit Committee Charter placed the responsibility for hiring and firing of the head of the Office of Auditing on the Audit Committee. In addition to conducting a thorough evaluation of the qualifications and credentials of a candidate, the Audit Committee was responsible for ensuring that the appointment in no way jeopardized the independence of the internal audit function.

As described in Chapter VIII, since Mr. Rajappa served as Fannie Mae Controller directly before his appointment to head the Office of Auditing, his appointment put him in the inappropriate position of auditing his own work. As Controller, Mr. Rajappa was involved in accounting analysis and decisions related to the entire financial operations of Fannie Mae, including Manufactured Housing, Loan Loss Reserves, REMICS, Purchase Premium and Discount Amortization, interest-only securities, impairment and mark-to-market rules, Synthetic MBS, and low-income housing tax credits. Many of those areas will be subject to restatement or have been identified as not in compliance with GAAP.

No discussion of Mr. Rajappa's new position as head of the Office of Auditing appears in the minutes of either the January 19, 1999, Board of Directors meeting or the minutes of the February 16, 1999 Audit Committee meeting. OFHEO found no other evidence of a critical evaluation of the sufficiency of Mr. Rajappa's education, training, experience (for example, the fact that he was not a certified public accountant), or his ability to oversee the internal audit function objectively, given his former position as Controller. Effective, diligent oversight in compliance with the Audit Committee Charter clearly required such a discussion.

When questioned during the OFHEO examination, Mr. Gerrity, the then newly-appointed Audit Committee Chairman, stated that he could not recall specifically whether Ms. Spencer had assumed the position of Controller by the January 1999 board meeting, nor did Mr. Gerrity know why Mr. Rajappa was selected to be the head of the Office of Auditing.[37] Mr. Gerrity also stated that he did not think it was awkward that Mr. Rajappa was formerly the Controller.[38] The Audit Committee clearly was aware of Mr. Rajappa's prior experience as Controller and had a responsibility to ensure there were no known independence violations or conflicts of interest. Instead, the Audit Committee stood silent as the Office of Auditing, under Mr. Rajappa's supervision, conducted audits of his former department.[39] The Audit Committee did not meet its responsibility to question, if not challenge, the appointment of Mr. Rajappa. At a minimum, the Audit Committee should have required Mr. Rajappa to recuse himself from any review function inconsistent with the Institute of Internal Auditors standards discussed in Chapter VII.

Inappropriate Compensation of Office of Auditing Staff. As discussed in Chapters VII and VIII, compensating senior internal auditors on an EPS-basis creates a problem at least as to the appearance of independence—a problem that was exacerbated by Mr. Rajappa's enthusiasm for EPS compensation. Although the Compensation Committee was directly responsible for setting bonuses, the Audit Committee was responsible for insuring the independence and objectivity of the internal audit function. That responsibility required the Committee to consider the independence and objectivity issues created by tying the compensation of the staff of the Office of Auditing to EPS, given the independent oversight role of that office. The Audit Committee's failure to address the inherent conflict of interest created by that compensation ultimately contributed to the inappropriate admonitions of Mr. Rajappa to his staff members to "live, breathe and dream 6.46" and that they should become "obsessed" with seeing to it that they did their part to help Fannie Mae achieve the EPS goal.[40] As evidenced by that communication and supported by a recommendation in Ernst and Young's report dated June 30, 2005 on Internal Audit Transformation-Recommendations,

[41] the Audit Committee should have considered and recommended that an alternate method to determine incentive compensation be applied to Internal Audit.[42]

Other Issues Concerning the Independence of the Office of Auditing. Internal audit best practices require that "[t]he internal auditors' qualifications, staff, status within the company, reporting lines, [and] relationship with the audit committee of the board of directors must be adequate to ensure the internal audit function's effectiveness and objectivity...."[43] In order to fulfill its duty to oversee the internal audit function, the Audit Committee has a responsibility to ensure that the independence of the internal audit function is not jeopardized, either in appearance or fact. The Office of Auditing was supposed to be a direct report to the Audit Committee, with an administrative or "dotted-line" report to management. In practice those relationships appear to have been reversed.

In 2002, the "dotted line" reporting for the head of the Office of Auditing, Mr. Rajappa, moved from COO Mudd to CFO Howard.[44] According to Mr. Rajappa, CEO Raines made the decision that the reporting line should shift to the CFO. That reporting structure had the potential to jeopardize independence and should have been vetted through the appropriate channels, i.e., the Audit Committee. The minutes do not show that the Audit Committee addressed the issue. However, Mr. Rajappa recalled that Audit Committee Chair Gerrity approved of the change without discussing the issue with him. Thereafter, Mr. Rajappa recalls expressing his reservations regarding the reporting shift to Mr. Gerrity.

Mr. Rajappa questioned whether placing the head of the Office of Auditing under the CFO was appropriate from a best practices perspective. He raised those concerns with Mr. Howard who, according to Mr. Rajappa, claims to have unsuccessfully attempted to coordinate a discussion with Mr. Raines on the topic. As Controller, Mr. Rajappa had served as a direct report to Mr. Howard. Review of the integrity of financial information is among the core functions of the Office of Auditing, and Mr. Howard's direct reports (and, ultimately, Mr. Howard) were responsible for the development of accounting policy. Considering those facts, it is easy to understand why Mr. Rajappa was concerned with having the head of the Office of Auditing report to the CFO.

Mr. Gerrity's insensitivity to any perceived or actual breach of independence is evidenced by his failure to conduct any evaluation of the change in reporting or to discuss it with the Audit Committee as a whole. As a result of the inaction of the Audit Committee and the concomitant lack of clear guidelines, Mr. Howard was in a position to exert inappropriate influence on the Office of Auditing.[45] The Audit Committee's failure was further compounded during the annual review process. The Audit Committee Charter dictates that the Audit Committee is jointly responsible for the budget and staffing of the Office of Auditing. However, Mr. Rajappa's performance evaluations were written and presented by his supervisors—COO Small, COO Mudd, and ultimately, CFO Howard—with input from Mr. Gerrity.[46] Those evaluations were the basis for salary increases and bonuses. Mr. Gerrity's involvement in the process appears to have been a limited review of the evaluation prepared by Mr. Howard.[47]

The Scope of Internal Audits. The Audit Committee was directed by the Audit Committee Charter to establish the scope and evaluate the performance of the internal audit function. On an annual basis, the Office of Auditing developed its Audit Plan, which was vetted with the Audit Committee. That Audit Plan identified key risks and established audit priorities. Effective interaction between the Office and the Audit Committee regarding the Audit Plan was paramount to the development of an effective oversight mechanism. The Audit

Committee expected the Office of Auditing to audit accounting and financial reporting areas for GAAP compliance because those internal audit reports indicated as much. However, as documented in Chapter VII, a communication gap existed between expectations of the Audit Committee and the practices of the Office of Auditing regarding the scope of the reviews. For example, Mr. Rajappa and others in the Office of Auditing have stated that testing for GAAP compliance was not within their mandate. Mr. Gerrity, on the other hand, indicated that the Office of Auditing was to serve as a "watchdog" for GAAP compliance in addition to the external auditor.[48] His understanding was based on his belief that the Office of Auditing understood GAAP and that noncompliance with GAAP would represent a material weakness.[49] That fundamental misunderstanding existed for five years, illustrating the lack of communication between the Audit Committee and the Office of Auditing as well as a lack of the robust oversight that applicable standards require.[50]

Lack of Timely Internal Audits of Critical Accounting Policies. In April of each year, the Audit Committee was responsible for approving the Audit Plan. That plan was developed as a roadmap for audit activities and was based on an assessment of critical policies and key control areas.[51] The process of establishing priorities was a function of both the inherent risk of the activity as well as the results of prior audit activities in the respective areas. As described later in this chapter, audit areas were color coded through that process. "Red" audits areas would be reviewed annually, whereas activities deemed "green" would only be examined every three years.[52] The Audit Committee was involved in the process and specifically requested that the Office of Auditing perform an annual review of the accounting for derivatives.[53] Despite audit differences in 1998 and 1999, and after being told by KPMG, in relation to the 1998 audit that a written policy was an absolute necessity, Fannie Mae waited until 2003 to conduct its first substantive review of the implementation of the FAS 91 policy formalized in December 2000.[54] Given that FAS 91 was a critical accounting estimate (as discussed in Chapter VII) and given the magnitude of the reporting errors that could—and did—result from an improper application of FAS 91, the Office of Auditing should have deemed the review of that policy a high audit priority. In the absence of initiative from the Office of Auditing, it was incumbent upon the Audit Committee to require an audit to be done on a more urgent basis prior to 2003.

Failure to Make Adequate Inquiries. Although the Board has the overall responsibility of assuring the integrity of Fannie Mae's accounting and financial reporting systems,[55] the Audit Committee is charged with the specific responsibility of overseeing "the accounting, reporting, and financial practices of the corporation and its subsidiaries, including the integrity of the corporation's financial statements. . . ." Gaining knowledge and making the appropriate inquiries are critical components of any oversight function. Early versions of the Charter even contained an explicit requirement that the Audit Committee "develop in depth and specialized knowledge on matters relating to the Committee's responsibilities . . ." Despite that directive, Mr. Gerrity was aware of neither how Fannie Mae formulated its accounting policies, nor who was responsible for them.[56] Also, as described in detail below, the Audit Committee failed to exhibit an appropriate level of knowledge about several of Fannie Mae's significant accounting policies, such as those related to FAS 91 and the allowance for losses. Furthermore, Mr. Gerrity stated that he "would count on management and/or Internal Audit and/or KPMG to raise [FAS 91, FAS 133, or other FAS issues with the committee]. That's the only way in which we would know."[57] This passive approach to gaining knowledge of critical accounting policies contravenes all applicable governance standards.

Low-Income Housing Tax Credits (LIHTC) Accounting. As detailed in Chapter VI, Fannie Mae realized a one-time earnings-per-share (EPS) benefit of $0.10 ($108.1 million)[58] as a result of a change in the method of accounting for the Enterprise's investments in low income housing tax credits (LIHTC) from a non-GAAP to a GAAP method. Without the LIHTC, Fannie Mae would not have met analysts' expectations or the EPS targets required for executives to receive the maximum AIP bonuses for 1998.

Considering that LIHTC represented a one-time benefit which resulted from a change made late in the fourth quarter that enabled Fannie Mae to pay out bonuses and meet Wall Street expectations, the Audit Committee members had an oversight-related duty to obtain additional information. Neither the Audit Committee nor the broader Board sought additional information regarding that accounting change, nor did they question the effect on reported EPS and thus AIP and long-term compensation payouts to executives. Considering that KPMG identified that issue as an area of disagreement in the Q4 1998 completion memo,[59] a reasonable inquiry to management and the external auditor would likely have yielded some clarity as to the components of the benefit. At a minimum, the Audit Committee would have received additional information regarding the magnitude of the EPS effect. As the change in LIHTC accounting materially affected reported EPS, the Audit Committee should have communicated the one-time nature of the change to the Compensation Committee to determine whether non-recurring or "poor quality" earnings should have had a negative impact on EPS bonus calculations. Mr. Mai, as a member of both the Audit Committee and Chair of the Compensation Committee, should have been particularly sensitive to the significance of EPS in terms of management compensation. By failing to make the appropriate inquiries regarding the nature of the change, the Audit Committee failed in its oversight role.

Allowance for Loan Loss Accounting. During the period covered by this report, Fannie Mae identified its treatment of the allowance for loan losses as a significant accounting policy.[60] The practice of over-reserving for the purpose of establishing an earnings "cookie jar" had been identified by Arthur Levitt and others as fertile ground for earnings management abuses. Therefore, the Audit Committee had a responsibility to gain sufficient knowledge of Fannie Mae's policy in order to evaluate the appropriateness of its application. Had the Committee members made the appropriate inquiries or conducted a review of the financial statements, they would have noticed that the level of the reserve stood essentially unchanged at approximately $800 million for the period 1997 through 2003.[61] In January 1999, CFO Howard presented the result of operations for 1998 to the Fannie Mae Board of Directors.[62] Mr. Howard told the

Board that the swing from a credit loss position to net recoveries allowed the company to record a negative provision for losses of $50 million (another of the adjustments that allowed Fannie Mae to reach its maximum EPS target in 1998); however, outstanding allowance for future losses stayed the same. Mr. Howard even highlighted the size of the reserve to the investment community in a conference call related to 1998 earnings, stating that even though the amount seemed conservative, Fannie Mae intended to hold the level at $800 million dollars until the Enterprise got a better sense of where long-term trends settled out.[63] The Audit Committee failed to discharge its financial oversight responsibilities by not inquiring further regarding the amount of the reserve and not following up in subsequent years as the amount remained unchanged.

As detailed in Chapter VI, Fannie Mae methodology for recording adjustments to the reserve did not conform with GAAP. Controller Leanne Spencer explained to the Audit Committee at the February 20, 2001 meeting that the current methodology for recording charge-offs and recoveries was not the "preferable" accounting treatment. Additionally, she indicated that she would be investigating whether a change in accounting was appropriate.[64] The minutes of the Audit Committee do not reflect any inquiries regarding the appropriateness of the absolute level of the loss reserve despite a 27 percent decrease in the dollar value of credit losses in 2000 to the lowest level since 1984, when Fannie Mae's portfolio was one-tenth the current size. Neither does the record reflect any questions from members of the Committee regarding the possible accounting change. Ms. Spencer again addressed the issue in February 2002, informing the Audit Committee of an "alternative method" to reclassify recoveries.[65]

Fannie Mae did not elect to change its accounting treatment until 2003. Audit Committee meeting minutes do not reflect that the Committee sought more information regarding the necessity for a change or followed up to establish why the change was not implemented for fiscal year 2001. The Audit Committee appears not to have asked either management or the external auditor about the magnitude of the reserve.

"Yellow" Audit Reports. The Office of Auditing color-coded their audits according to importance, with "red" identifying audits with significant issues that required immediate attention. "Yellow" identified audits where controls needed strengthening and corrective action would be taken during the normal course of business, generally 18 to 24 months, according to Mr. Rajappa.[66] "Green" identified audits that were fairly clean, with issues that could be resolved quickly.[67] "Red" audits were reported to the Office of the Chairman and to the Audit Committee,[68] placed on the Audit Tracking List (ATL), and reviewed. That methodology was utilized in order to prioritize follow-up work and assist in the development of the audit plan.[69]

According to Mr. Rajappa, "yellow" audits would go only to the Chairman of Fannie Mae and the Office of the Chairman but not to the Audit Committee.[70]

Several of the "yellow" issues were significant in and of themselves. In fact, with respect to the Amortization Audit dated July 9, 2003, Ann Eilers, Director for Accounting and Audit, indicated that the audit rating was "yellow" simply because management assured the Office of Auditing that they were working on the problem.[71] As a result, management was able to circumvent Audit Committee review.

In order to provide effective oversight of the control environment, the Audit Committee must have a reasonable understanding of the depth and breadth of internal control deficiencies. Simply reviewing the most egregious control failures did not provide the Audit Committee with that knowledge. For example, key-person dependencies and poor documentation might not raise a red flag in an isolated incident; however, a pattern of undocumented decisions (which existed) highlights a more significant breach of internal controls. The Audit Committee should have had a mechanism in place to understand the scope of internal control problems and management's efforts to address those problems. The significant lack of oversight by the Audit Committee enabled the Office of Auditing to conduct audits and issue findings with less than appropriate scrutiny.

Failure to Oversee the Development and Implementation of Critical Accounting Policies. Previous chapters have established that accounting policies and estimates that Fannie Mae designated as critical failed to comply with GAAP. In particular, those related to the amortization of purchase premiums and discounts (FAS 91) and accounting for derivatives and hedging activities (FAS 133). The Audit Committee failed in its responsibility to understand and ensure that appropriate application of critical accounting policies was occurring, as outlined by the Audit Committee charter as well as in standards previously discussed, despite the requirements that audit committees be informed, vigilant, and effective overseers of the financial reporting process and the company's internal controls.

FAS 91. The Fannie Mae Audit Committee did not actively monitor the critical policy of accounting for the amortization of discounts and premiums. The Audit Committee failed to address the implications of the 1998 FAS 91 audit adjustments, and systems control issues that were brought to the attention of Audit Committee Chair Gerrity in early 1999. Audit adjustments are proposed corrections identified through the external audit process. Prior to the issuance of Statement on Auditing Standards (SAS) 89 effective December 1999, there was no requirement that an external auditor inform the Audit Committee of those adjustments deemed immaterial. Following SAS 89, the external auditor was required to notify the Audit Committee of all audit differences, whether or not material.[72] As detailed in Chapter VI, KPMG identified an audit difference of $200 million related to FAS 91, the amortization of premiums and discounts, in 1998. As part of the year-end audit work, KPMG met with Audit Committee Chairman Gerrity in early 1999 and advised him of that audit difference and how it arose and that the FAS 91 systems needed improvements.[73] For several reasons, Mr. Gerrity should have considered the audit difference material. First and foremost, the size of the difference should have been a red flag. Mr. Gerrity has stated that he now would consider a $200 million audit difference to be material.[74] The reduction in amortization expense also had an important effect on executive compensation. It boosted EPS by over 12¢ per share, and without that boost EPS would not have met the minimum needed for an AIP bonus for 1998.[75] That effect on executive compensation alone should have been sufficient to deem the difference material, irrespective of Fannie Mae's quantitative parameters for determining materiality.

Even after the FAS 91 audit differences were disclosed to the Audit Committee by Ms. Spencer in February 2000, the record fails to show that either Mr. Gerrity or the full Audit Committee followed up to confirm that a policy had been implemented or that Mr. Gerrity or the Committee questioned KPMG again. Given KPMG's position that Fannie Mae's practices were imprecise, reasonable inquiry by the Audit Committee would have exposed the lack of a formal policy. In fact, the record fails to show that the Audit Committee members made an effort to familiarize themselves with that critical accounting policy before Ms. Spencer made a presentation to the Audit Committee in November 2003.

The Audit Committee failed in its oversight role by not demanding that a formal policy for FAS 91 be put in place and that such a policy, when put into place, be endorsed by the Financial Standards group of the Enterprise and the external auditor. In doing so, the Committee failed to insure the integrity of financial results. The Audit Committee also failed to adequately oversee the development of the annual audit plan. Armed with the knowledge of KPMG's audit differences in 1998 and 1999 related to amortization of purchase premiums and discounts, the Audit Committee had a responsibility to ensure that the Office of Auditing conducted an internal audit of that area. Such an audit was not conducted until 2003.

FAS 133. The Audit Committee had opportunities to question management's implementation of FAS 133 but failed in its duty to do so.

In an Audit Committee update on the FAS 133 effort in April 2000, the minutes of the meeting reflect comments of KPMG partner Julie Theobold that KPMG intended to perform a significant amount of testing of financial reporting and planning during the year 2000. She stated that KPMG's test work would emphasize the system and accounting changes required to account for hedges under the new standard.[76] In his February 2001 report to the Board of Directors, CFO Howard criticized the standard and focused on the effect the standard would have on Fannie Mae's financial statements.[77] Minutes of those meetings, however, do not reflect any discussion of the principles used to implement FAS 133 at Fannie Mae, the critical decisions that the Enterprise made regarding systems development or accounting, or the results of any KPMG testing that had preceded implementation. The Audit Committee should have inquired about that information in order to gain sufficient understanding to judge whether appropriate accounting decisions had been made and effective systems were in place.

Furthermore, management represented to the Financial Accounting Standards Board (FASB) and the financial community in 1999 that a delay in implementing FAS 133 was imperative because of the extensive accounting changes the Enterprise was facing when, in fact, one of the three major principles of the Enterprise's implementation of FAS 133 was to leverage off existing accounting systems. In Mr. Howard's letter to FASB Chairman Edmund Jenkins, Mr. Howard emphasized the need for more time to develop new accounting systems to address the complex changes that FAS 133 would require. He stated that those changes were further complicated because of requirements resulting from year 2000 system changes.[78] Mr. Boyles, then Director for Financial Standards, headed a letter-writing campaign with other companies and organizations to convince FASB of the need to delay implementation of FAS 133.[79] In addition, the Enterprise represented in its financial statements that the delay granted by FASB would give the Enterprise "adequate time to build the accounting and management systems needed to implement the new standard."[80] The inconsistency between the aggressive lobbying efforts to delay the standard and the ability of Fannie Mae to qualify virtually all of its derivatives for hedge accounting under the "short cut" method, as described in OFHEO's *Report of Findings to Date*, should have prompted the Audit Committee to explore more closely Fannie Mae's implementation of the standard.

Failure to Investigate Allegations Made by Roger Barnes. Section 301 of the Sarbanes-Oxley Act of 2002 (SOX) requires audit committees of companies that register their stock with the Securities and Exchange Commission (SEC) to establish procedures for the receipt, retention, and treatment of complaints regarding accounting, internal accounting controls, or auditing matters; and the confidential, anonymous submission by employees of concerns regarding questionable accounting or auditing matters. Further, SOX requires that each audit committee shall have the authority to engage independent counsel and other advisers, as it determines necessary to carry out its duties.[81]

As described in Chapter VIII, in October 2003 Roger Barnes, a manager in the Office of the Controller, approached Fannie Mae through his lawyer to pursue a settlement of claims of discrimination resulting from allegations he had previously raised regarding Fannie Mae's amortization policies and earnings management. Fannie Mae entered into a settlement agreement with Mr. Barnes on November 3, 2003. Given its responsibilities for regulatory compliance and investigation of complaints related to accounting, internal controls, and auditing matters, the Audit Committee was required to ensure a timely, thorough, and independent investigation into Mr. Barnes' allegations. The allegations, and the subsequent settlement agreement, should have raised the concern of every member of the Audit Committee, especially when considered against the background of the recently released Baker Botts report on Freddie Mac's internal investigation and the initiation of the OFHEO special examination.

The Audit Committee failed to make further inquiries or convene a special investigation after being informed at the November 17, 2003 Audit Committee meeting that Fannie Mae had reached a settlement with Mr. Barnes.[82] The news of the settlement was received by the Audit Committee just three days after the Committee had been convened in order to discuss certification of the third quarter financial statements. Fannie Mae settled the case without bringing the matter to the Audit Committee and elected to postpone discussion of the matter until after the financial statements had been certified. Given that OFHEO had just announced a special examination of Fannie Mae's accounting practices, the Audit Committee was on notice that such allegations warranted further investigation. At a minimum, the Audit Committee had an obligation to ensure that the matter be disclosed to OFHEO. Instead, the matter was ignored until February 2004, when it was reviewed as part of the special examination.

Failure to Question the Assignment of Both Chief Financial Officer and Risk Policy Functions to Mr. Howard. In 2000, Mr. Howard became a member of the Office of the Chairman. At that time, he also assumed responsibility for all credit and interest rate risk policy functions, becoming the equivalent of a chief risk officer for Fannie Mae. That consolidation gave Mr. Howard direct responsibility "of all people who either set risk policy or did risk analytics"[83] in addition to his core role of overseeing financial and accounting policy as CFO.

As discussed in Chapter VIII, the risk assessment function should be independent from the accounting and reporting functions to assure the fullest exchange of views. Consolidation removes an important control. It creates an environment in which mistakes and inappropriate manipulation may go unchecked as financial reporting results can easily be affected or manipulated by the views of the individual with accounting oversight. The assignment of responsibility for risk policy issues to Mr. Howard should not have been permitted by the Audit Committee or the Board. Fannie Mae's own research found no other peer company having a CFO also serving as CRO.[84]

With the reassignment of Adolfo Marzol, the Chief Credit Officer, in 2004, power was further consolidated as Mr. Howard assumed Mr. Marzol's duties as well. With that move, another source of internal control was removed. Upon the announcement of Mr. Howard increased duties, Board member Ashley voiced his displeasure with management, yet no steps were taken to remedy the situation.[85] The record shows no indication of Audit Committee involvement or inquiry. Oversight of the risk management function should have been performed by the Audit Committee by way of the Office of Auditing, according to Fannie Mae's internal audit charter. The record does not show that the Audit Committee reviewed and approved or had any of the required involvement in the consolidation of powers and responsibilities in Mr. Howard. Consequently, the Audit Committee failed in its oversight responsibilities and allowed an inappropriate consolidation of risk and financial accounting and reporting to occur.

Failure to Adequately Oversee Sarbanes-Oxley Section 404 Compliance Implementation. Chapter VII describes the decision of Fannie Mae management to assign responsibility for

Sarbanes-Oxley (SOX) 404 compliance to the Office of Auditing and the inadequacy of the resources of that office relative to the task. Ultimately, the Office was diverted from performing its core functions and was unable to perform its new functions.[86]

The Audit Committee is responsible for the budget and staffing of the Office of Auditing, the establishment of the annual audit plan, and evaluation of any restrictions or limitations placed on that office.[87] Thus, the members should have been aware of the heavy workload placed upon the Office of Auditing and the inadequacy of its resources. In April 2004, the Audit Committee was presented with an opportunity to address the staffing limitations that resulted from SOX activities. In contrast to previous years, the Audit Plan for 2004 only scheduled 54 internal audits, compared with an average of 120 audits performed in past years[88] That reduction should have been a clear indication to the Committee that resources in the Office were stressed. While the Audit Committee inquired as to what more could be accomplished were the Office of Auditing to receive additional resources, the Committee fell short by approving an abbreviated Audit Plan and authorizing only temporary contract employees to assist in technical writing and flowcharting.[89]

Even assuming that the Audit Committee possessed a positive view of the Office of Auditing, the importance of ensuring Fannie Mae's SOX compliance required that it obtain sufficient information as to how those SOX responsibilities at Fannie Mae would be carried out. There is no indication of any discussion, let alone debate, in any of the Board Minutes or Audit Committee minutes that OFHEO reviewed. Rather, it appears that Fannie's Mae's management assigned those new responsibilities to the Office of Auditing without any meaningful Audit Committee participation.

Oversight of the Independent Auditor. As described in Chapter VII, KPMG improperly provided unqualified opinions on financial statements that contained significant departures from GAAP. The Audit Committee failed to oversee the independent audit function of the Enterprise as required by OFHEO guidance and regulation. In addition, the Audit Committee missed critical opportunities for meaningful inquiry into KPMG's audit activities associated with Fannie Mae's implementation of critical accounting estimates and significant accounting policies that may have revealed deficiencies in the independent audit program. Instead, as confirmed by Mr. Gerrity, the Audit Committee passively waited for KPMG to raise issues to the Audit Committee.[90]

The Audit Committee also failed to inquire about the work KPMG performed, or failed to perform, to determine that Roger Barnes' allegations regarding Fannie Mae's amortization accounting were without merit. Had the Audit Committee questioned KPMG, they would have learned that KPMG had not performed sufficient review or test work to make a determination about the merits of Barnes accounting allegations and that KPMG audit partners had misrepresented their position to Fannie Mae staff, to Mr. Barnes, and to the Audit Committee.

As shown in Table IX-1, the fees that Fannie Mae paid its independent auditor for audit related work accounted for a small fraction of the total fees KPMG received annually from the Enterprise.

Table IX-1. Fees paid to KPMG by Fannie Mae, 2000-2003[91]

Year	Audit Fees	Other Fees	Total Fees	Audit as Percent of Total
1998[92]	$ 760,000	**$8,000,000**	$ 8,760,000	9
1999[93]	$ 810,000	$6,879,000	$ 7,689,000	11
2000	$1,199,000	$6,610,000	$7,809,000	15
2001	$1,402,200	$6,774,036	$8,176,236	17
2002	$1,978,955	$7,511,478	$9,490,433	21
2003	$2,721,300	$8,254,807	$10,976,107	25

The increase in audit fees from 9 percent of total fees in 1998 to 25 percent of total fees in 2003 reflects, at least in part, the sharp increase in the number and complexity of accounting policies and practices that the Enterprise had to adopt during that time-frame and dramatic growth in the Enterprise's portfolio business.[94] Furthermore, lower fees before 2002 reflect the fact that

Fannie Mae was not an SEC registrant. For KPMG, Fannie Mae, as one of the largest financial institutions in the country, was a prestigious client; however, the audit engagement was a minor part of the relationship.

One of the primary functions of the Audit Committee is to oversee the engagement of the outside auditors. Over the period covered by this report, that role required the Audit Committee to become increasingly engaged with the outside auditor so it could make knowledgeable, thoughtful, and probing inquiries. Such inquiries are necessary for the Audit Committee to understand the scope and quality of the independent audit work for which they have contracted and to assure the Board that the Enterprise's financial statements present fairly its financial condition and are prepared in accordance with GAAP. The Committee's failure to adequately perform this role contributed to the unsafe and unsound practices of the Enterprise.

Compensation Committee

The duties and responsibilities of the Compensation Committee of the Board of Directors of Fannie Mae (Compensation Committee) are set forth in the Compensation Committee Charter, and OFHEO regulations and guidance,[95] which incorporate the listing standards of the New York Stock Exchange (NYSE) and applicable safety and soundness standards.[96] The primary role of the Compensation Committee is to "discharge the responsibilities of the Board relating to compensation of Fannie Mae executives,"[97] which is achieved principally by overseeing and advising the Board on the adoption of policies governing Fannie Mae's annual compensation and stock ownership plans. The Committee is also responsible for producing the annual report on executive compensation that is included in the Enterprise's annual proxy statement. In accordance with both the Safety and Soundness Act and the Charter Act, Fannie Mae is only authorized to pay compensation that is reasonable and comparable with compensation for employment in similar businesses involving similar duties.[98] Section 309(d)(2) of the Charter Act also requires that a "significant portion of the compensation of all executive officers. . . shall be based on the performance of the corporation."[99] As the Board members charged with oversight of compensation, the

Compensation Committee members have particular responsibility to review the Enterprise's compliance with those statutory provisions.

OFHEO regulations require that the Compensation Committee shall be in compliance with the charter, independence, composition, expertise, duties, responsibilities, and other requirements under the NYSE rules.[100] The corporate governance NYSE listing standards were revised in 2003 to impose new requirements on the composition and proceedings of compensation committees.[101] The NYSE rule provides specific structural and procedural requirements for board compensation committees of listed companies.[102] There are two basic requirements: (1) a compensation committee must consist of independent directors, and (2) the board must adopt a written compensation committee charter.[103] Under the NYSE rule, the charter must include provisions that address the compensation committee's purpose and responsibilities and that provide for an annual performance evaluation of the committee. The committee's purposes and responsibilities, at a minimum, must include direct responsibility to:

(A) review and approve corporate goals and objectives relevant to CEO compensation, evaluate the CEO's performance in light of those goals and objectives, and, either as a committee or together with the other independent directors (as directed by the board), determine and approve the CEO's compensation level based on this evaluation;

(B) make recommendations to the board with respect to non-CEO compensation, incentive-compensation plans and equity-based plans;[104] and

(C) produce a compensation committee report on executive compensation as required by the SEC to be included in the company's annual proxy statement or annual report on Form 10-K filed with the SEC. [105]

Additionally, as in the case of the other independent board committees, and the board as a whole, the charter for the compensation committee of a NYSE-listed company must provide for an annual performance evaluation. The NYSE listing requirements do not prescribe any particular format or procedure for the performance evaluation.[106]

Finally, the NYSE also suggested that the compensation committee have the sole authority to hire, set the compensation and other terms of engagement of, and fire any compensation consultant who assists in the evaluation of director, CEO, or senior executive compensation. While the direct retention and control of compensation consultants is not a legal requirement or even a mandatory listing standard, it has become the recognized best practice.[107]

The Compensation Committee charters reveal a significant bias in the committee's approach to its oversight role in several important respects. First, as described in the Fannie Mae Compensation Committee Charters of 1998, 2003 and 2005, the general role and purpose of the Compensation Committee was to "support" the Enterprise's "core compensation philosophy" of "pay for performance and comparability."[108] Throughout the 1998 to 2005 period, the justification for that core philosophy was to position the Enterprise to compete for available talent in the financial services industry. But while outwardly plausible, that argument belied its true purpose. As demonstrated in the 2003 charter, the pay for performance rationale in fact conditioned the Committee's authority to review and approve the CEO's compensation and its oversight of the Enterprise's compensation programs.[109]

Second, the charter mandates that "the corporation's use of stock-based compensation shall align the interests of employees and directors to those of Fannie Mae stockholders." As discussed in Chapter V, that mandate ultimately went unfulfilled. Third, the charter contemplates the Committee is to keep the Board informed and use independent sources and consultants, providing the Committee with authority to retain outside counsel, experts or other advisors it determined appropriate to assist it in performing its functions. Again, as discussed in Chapter V, the Committee ultimately lacked the independent counsel it required. Finally, the charter did not provide the Compensation Committee with sole authority to retain, supervise, pay, or fire any compensation expert who was to assist Fannie Mae in the evaluation of executive compensation. Had such authority been conferred and implemented, an independent expert could have provided a counterweight to management's control of the information the Committee received.

In sum, the charter aligned the Compensation Committee with management's interests in the development of compensation policies and plans. In supervising the compensation programs, the Compensation Committee failed in three main ways:

- Having approved an EPS-based executive compensation program that provided strong incentives for earnings management, the Compensation Committee failed to monitor it or ensure that the proper checks and balances were in place to prevent manipulation of earning targets or results;
- Together with the Audit Committee, the Compensation Committee permitted executive management to compensate senior internal auditors under the same EPS-biased plans that created the perverse incentives to manipulate earnings and undermined their independence; and
- The Committee allowed management to script its meetings and rubber-stamped executive compensation proposals made by senior management.

Failure to Monitor the Compensation System

As established in Chapter V, the lion's share of the compensation of Fannie Mae's senior management was based on EPS performance. The focus on a single measure creates an incentive to manipulate earnings, particularly for the highest level of senior management, which stands to benefit the most. Once the singular focus on EPS was established, it was incumbent upon the Board of Directors and the Compensation Committee, in particular, to monitor and scrutinize the EPS results. Such actions would have led the Compensation Committee to question the extraordinary success of senior management in consistently and precisely meeting EPS targets associated with maximum AIP bonus payouts. That realization should have led to an Audit Committee inquiry as to how that extraordinary success was achieved. Compensation Committee minutes make no mention of any concern about the connection between the potential manipulation of EPS and executive compensation until 2004. The Compensation Committee's failure to monitor for abuse of the executive compensation system by Fannie Mae management is another example of failed corporate governance.

By the time Compensation Committee Chair Anne Mulcahy raised questions about the pattern of reported earnings relative to targets, it was too late to be a meaningful check on earnings management. A document entitled "Mulcahy Meeting Notes" dated January 13, 2004 provided from the files of Lorrie Rudin suggests some concern within the Compensation Committee about the well-established trend of "maxing out" on AIP bonus awards every year. Remarks attributed to Ms. Mulcahy were as follows:

Ann- 'doesn't look good that maxing out every year.' Be ready to discuss maxing out issue. Want assurances that goals are stretch and that don't max out next year.[110]

Ms. Mulcahy's concern regarding "maxing out every year" in Annual Incentive Plan (AIP) bonuses was not timely. As documented in Chapter V, for the first time in many years, it was highly unlikely that Fannie Mae would come close to "maxing out" on AIP payouts. Senior management in 2004 was stretching to meet *minimum* payout targets.

Further, as discussed in Chapters V and VI, senior management, with full knowledge of the Board, used both stock buybacks and debt buybacks to achieve pre-set earnings-per-share targets. The Compensation Committee should have questioned closely the rationales for these well-publicized transactions due to their significant impact on annual EPS and the ease with which they could be undertaken by company management.

Insensitivity to Office of Auditing Compensation

As discussed earlier in this chapter, the Compensation Committee should have prevented the inappropriate compensation of Office of Auditing staff. Year after year, the Committee approved an EPS-based compensation structure for internal auditors without questioning its propriety or referring the question to the Audit Committee, which was responsible for supervising the Office of Auditing. Despite the sophistication of the Compensation Committee members and its chair, Mr. Mai, who was a former chairman of the Audit Committee, the Compensation Committee failed in its duty to align compensation with appropriate objectives for internal auditors.

The Committee's Passivity

From as early as 1998, as a memorandum from Fannie Mae General Counsel Stasia Kelly to Compensation Committee Chair Mai indicates, Fannie Mae senior management often scripted meetings of the Compensation Committee,[111] which influenced how meetings were conducted.[112] While the Compensation Committee report included in the annual proxy statement was signed by the independent, non-management Board Members who served on the Committee, in 2003 Mr. Raines, who was by far the largest beneficiary of Compensation Committee actions, edited the draft of that Committee's report to shareholders.[113] Nowhere in the minutes of

Committee meetings is there any suggestion that the Committee seriously vetted management's recommendations.

In 2003 the Compensation Committee sought to hire an executive compensation consultant who was to be accountable to the Committee rather than to management. Nonetheless, Mr. Raines played a key role.[114] In an undated letter from that year to Compensation Committee Chair Mulcahy, Kathy Gallo, Senior Vice President for Human Resources, wrote that the Fannie Mae management consultant on executive compensation, Alan Johnson Associates, recommended two firms that could serve as an independent Compensation Committee advisor: Fred Cook and Company and Brian Foley and Company.

Ms. Gallo and Christine Wolf, Vice President for Compensation and Benefits, interviewed candidates from both firms.[115] A subsequent September 2, 2003 letter to Ms. Mulcahy from Ms. Gallo, however, reflected the key role Mr. Raines played in Board decisions, even when it came to the actions of a Board committee on which he did not sit:

> After our last conversation about an independent consultant to serve as the Committee's expert, I updated Frank on your readiness to explore the Brian Foley (of Fred Cook) option. Frank was very much opposed to that idea because he has some significant concerns about both Fred's executive compensation philosophies and the way he sometimes advances his agenda on the topic. Frank's concerns stem from observing Fred in a (distant) past interaction with the Fannie Mae board and more recently in the Business Roundtable meetings. Given that, Frank would strongly prefer that we not introduce anyone from Cook's organization into a compensation advisory role for Fannie Mae. I regret not spotting this issue before I proposed Brian to you.[116]

Cook Consultants had helped design Fannie Mae's first formal compensation philosophy in 1991.[117] Gallo recommended two additional candidates for consideration, one of whom (Semler Brossy) had been the runner-up to Alan Johnson Associates in the selection of management's compensation consultant.[118] Shortly after receiving the recommendation from

Ms. Gallo, the Compensation Committee chose Semler Brossy as its independent consultant.[119] Management thus appears to have orchestrated the selection process to ensure that a consultant CEO Raines opposed did not receive the contract.

Failures of the Full Board of Directors

In addition to the failures of the Audit and Compensation Committees, Fannie Mae's full Board of Directors failed in numerous ways that put the safety and soundness of the Enterprise at risk. The Board of Directors failed to stay informed about Fannie Mae corporate strategy, major plans of action, and risk policy. Having approved an executive compensation program that created incentives to manipulate earnings, members of the Board of Directors failed to monitor against such manipulations. The Board failed to provide delegations of authority to management that reflected the current size and complexity of the Enterprise. The Board failed to ensure the effective operation of its own Audit and Compensation Committees. The Board of Directors failed to act as a check on the authority of Chairman and CEO Franklin Raines. The Board failed to initiate an independent inquiry into Fannie Mae's accounting following the announcement of Freddie Mac's restatement and subsequent investigation or allegations of Roger Barnes, both of which involved earnings management. The Board failed to assure itself that Fannie Mae's regulators were properly informed of Mr. Barnes' allegations. Finally, the Board of Directors failed to ensure timely and accurate reports to Federal regulators.

Failure to Stay Informed of the Corporate Strategy

To carry out the oversight duties and responsibilities of the Board of Directors, OFHEO requires that members of the Board ensure they receive accurate, timely, and sufficient information about the operations and financial condition of Fannie Mae. The Board is also responsible for working with executive management to establish the Enterprise's strategies and goals in an informed manner.

The Board members should have been alerted to the accounting problems at Fannie Mae by the problems at Freddie Mac. By virtue of their status as government-sponsored enterprises, Fannie Mae and Freddie Mac enjoyed a unique position in the market that gave both Enterprises an advantage over other financial institutions. Their charter advantages did not, however, insulate the Enterprises from the interest rate and credit risks inherent in their businesses. It is incumbent on the Board of Directors to understand those risks, the strategies that were available to manage them, and the choices that management made with respect to the trade-off between risks and returns, and the implications and effects of key accounting rules. Fannie Mae and Freddie Mac chose different approaches to managing interest rate risk. Freddie Mac hedged more of its risk than Fannie Mae, as reflected in the differences in the risk-based capital requirements of the two Enterprises. In every quarter that OFHEO has calculated risk-based capital requirements, Fannie Mae's requirement has consistently exceeded Freddie Mac's on both a dollar and percent-of-assets basis. Nonetheless, Fannie Mae consistently reported earnings that were less volatile than Freddie Mac's. In 2003, Freddie Mac admitted manipulating its accounting to report artificially lower earnings volatility. Yet, the Board failed at the time to initiate an independent inquiry even as OFHEO began its own examination.

Over time, Mr. Howard communicated to the Board and to the investor community the consistent message that Fannie Mae was a low-risk, high-return, "best-in-class" company. The Enterprise consistently met or slightly exceeded analyst estimates for earnings per share. Fannie Mae also constantly reinforced the public image of a low-risk, high-return company that provided stable, predictable earnings growth. In its annual reports, Fannie Mae told investors that the company had "been able to deliver double-digit growth in operating EPS, year after year, through all types of economic and financial market environments. . . ."[120] The Enterprise asserted that this performance resulted from its disciplined approach to risk management.

While compelling, that message was not consistent with the real-world relationship between risk and return, and the realities of accounting. First, the most, and perhaps only, comparable firm to Fannie Mae is Freddie Mac. Fannie Mae was taking more interest rate risk than Freddie Mac, yet reporting less earnings volatility. To achieve higher returns, a company normally must take on more risk and expect to experience greater fluctuations in earnings—that is, higher earnings volatility. Taking on more risk does not imply a less disciplined approach to risk management. Discipline in risk management relates to the willingness of a company to define clearly the level of risk it wishes to accept, and the skill with which it subsequently monitors and measures that risk, and limits it within established bounds. Ignoring that reality, and failing to question Fannie Mae's dubious earnings trend, evidences a clear safety and soundness failure on the part of the Board.

As described in Chapter VI, accounting rules have also introduced new sources of earnings volatility that may or may not be related to actual business risk or financial performance. The most significant of those new rules, FAS 133, requires that a company mark certain of its derivatives to market, but not necessarily the assets whose value is hedged with those derivatives if the company intends to hold them for investment. To the extent Fannie Mae used derivatives to hedge the interest rate risk of its retained mortgage portfolio (much of which is classified as held-for-investment), the asymmetrical accounting produced by FAS 133 affected reported earnings in ways that did not accurately reflect its actual earnings or its financial risk. Members of the Board of Directors should have questioned the continued minimal reported earnings volatility after the implementation of FAS 133. Had they done so, they might have identified management's earnings manipulations. Not doing so constitutes a failure to discharge the Board's responsibility to oversee the safety and soundness of Fannie Mae.

Even after well publicized media coverage about earnings management concerns of the SEC, which the Board had heard as early as 1998, there is little evidence that the Board showed any concern over the consistent good news earnings reports of management, never questioning management as to how Fannie Mae was able to meet EPS targets with precision and with little earnings volatility.[121]

> The Board accepted the representations of senior executives that Fannie Mae was the best at doing what it did and that extraordinary financial success was to be expected. The Board failed to question whether the pattern of reported earnings could be an indication of improper earnings management, failed to probe management, and failed in its responsibility to oversee the safe and sound operation of the Enterprise.

At the Board of Directors annual Strategic Review meetings held each July, Fannie Mae executives consistently reported meeting or exceeding planned earnings targets. For example, in 2000, the Board was told:

> Fannie Mae achieved EPS of $2.08 [year to date] June, our 50th quarter of double digit operating EPS growth. EPS is $.01 above plan at $2.08, expected to meet or exceed the target for the year of $4.27, keeping the company on a path to achieve the goal of doubling EPS between 1998 and 2003.[122]

In July 2002, Mr. Howard made a presentation to the Board entitled, "Corporate Risk Appetite."[123] The presentation included a slide of Fannie Mae's EPS growth and showed the reported earnings per share growth pattern against the trend from December 1990 through projections for December 2002. The chart indicates very little earnings volatility over the twelve-year period. For comparison, Mr. Howard also presented EPS growth charts for three other companies: Alcoa, Fifth Third Bank, and Citigroup. Unlike the Fannie Mae EPS growth, these three charts showed significant volatility in the EPS growth.

There are no indications from the minutes of those meetings that Board members questioned Fannie Mae's ability to meet EPS targets so consistently and often to the penny. Nor do the minutes indicate that Board members questioned Fannie Mae's ability to show smooth and rapid earnings when other financial companies subject to the same interest rate environment as Fannie Mae showed significant earnings volatility. When asked about that lack of inquiry, Audit Committee Chairman Thomas Gerrity stated that he believed "it had become a general presumption that the nature of [Fannie Mae's] business allowed for fairly steady earnings per share growth, at least on a core adjusted internal management perspective,"[124] and that if the comparable companies depicted in the presentation "were in the business that Fannie Mae was in, that they could probably achieve similar results."[125]

The oversight responsibilities vested in the Board of Directors should preclude such presumptions. As noted previously, the most comparable firm to Fannie Mae is Freddie Mac, which is in exactly the same business. Fannie Mae management was claiming smoother earnings than Freddie Mac, despite Freddie Mac's more conservative approach to risk management.[126] Further, by January 2003 the Board knew or should have known that Freddie Mac's steady earnings stream was being questioned in a restatement because of issues related to earnings management. Thus, there was no excuse for any such presumption after that date.

At the July 2003 Strategic Board Retreat, Mr. Howard again presented slides that depicted Fannie Mae's low earnings volatility and remarkable EPS growth. In addition, the presentation included a discussion of Fannie Mae's "earnings variability objective," the strategic objective to minimize earnings volatility. According to Mr. Ashley, at the request of the Board, management discussed the sustainability of its business strategy at the strategic retreat. Based on those discussions, management and the Board concluded that the strategy was sustainable.[127] That conclusion failed to consider, however, the conflict between minimizing earnings variability and Fannie Mae's other financial objective of double-digit earnings growth.[128] In order to meet the latter objective, Fannie Mae hedged only part of its prepayment risk. As a result, some earnings volatility should have been expected. Such volatility could (and did) lead management to accounting manipulations to minimize reported earnings variability. Committee minutes for the Strategic Retreat do not reflect candid consideration of or deliberation about the implications of Fannie Mae's strategic objectives.

Given the information available to various committees of the Board, the full Board should have been increasingly aware of the risks of earnings management practices at Fannie Mae. Throughout the year, the Audit Committee routinely received reports on EPS targets and achievements by Mr. Howard and Ms. Spencer, and the Compensation Committee received reports detailing the links between management bonuses and EPS targets. Every year from 1998 through 2004, there was at least one Board member who was assigned to both committees. In fact, in 2003 three Board members (Anne Mulcahy, Taylor Segue, and Joe Pickett) sat on both Committees.[129] Minutes of the meetings of those committees do not reflect that those Directors questioned the compensation structure at Fannie Mae or determined that such a structure could lead to improper earnings management.

Safety and soundness standards require that Board members ensure that they are provided with timely, accurate information about the operations and financial condition of the Enterprise that is sufficient to enable the Board to perform its oversight duties and responsibilities. The Board of Directors is also responsible for working in an informed manner with executive management to establish the Enterprise's strategies and goals. As established in Chapter V, Fannie Mae had an uncanny history of hitting its maximum bonus EPS targets and analyst expectations with precision. That remarkable achievement should have led a reasonably diligent Board to inquire as to how that record was achieved. Despite indications from management and in the wider financial community of the uniqueness of that record, the Board failed to challenge the strategic direction of Fannie Mae (including the risk management strategy) and failed to draw conclusions that the focus on earnings targets could lead to deliberate manipulations by management to circumvent GAAP and enter into dubious transactions to achieve those targets. Until 2004, the minutes lack any indication that the Board addressed such questions.

Failure to Review Major Business Decisions and Ensure Appropriate Delegation of Authority

Fannie Mae operates under a corporate governance model that includes broad delegation of authority to management that was adopted in 1981 under Chairman and CEO David Maxwell. The bylaws grant broad powers to the Chairman of the Board to make virtually all business decisions, with periodic reporting to the Board on major business decisions:

> Chairman of the Board shall have such powers and perform such duties as the Board may prescribe. Except as otherwise provided by law, the corporate charter, these Bylaws, or the Board, the Chairman shall have plenary authority to perform all duties as may be assigned to him from time to time by the Board.[130]

In practice, management does not generally bring issues relating to business operations or major transaction to the Board for deliberation or approval but reports to the Board on initiatives already underway. Management's own review of Board minutes and resolutions resulted in the following conclusion by Senior Vice President and Deputy General Counsel Anthony Marra in a November 2003 memorandum:

> [M]anagement initiates and implements policies, procedures, and programs and then reports back to the Board on its actions. This has permitted management to have substantial flexibility on how it has carried out the company's business strategy. As long as the Chairman consents, management can undertake a wide range of business activities.[131]

In fact, as late as June 2004, Monica Medina, Vice President and Deputy General Counsel for Corporate Governance, recounted Fannie Mae's lack of formal policy for the Board to approve large transactions and management's discretion on whether or not to inform the Board of such transactions.

> In other areas, such as approval of large transactions, there are no firm guidelines or standards, and the board and management have until now made the decision of whether to notify the Board or seek its approval on a case by case basis.[132]

That such broad discretion was accorded to management contravenes corporate governance standards, and despite recommendations from outside advisors in 2001, the Board did not address the delegation issue until 2004, when it was identified as an area to be reviewed as part of continuing efforts of the Nominating and Corporate Governance Committee to benchmark Fannie Mae's corporate governance policies to industry best practices, efforts initiated in 2002.[133] The Board could delegate authority to management; however, delegation that was overly broad, and the failure to revisit and review delegations of authority as the Enterprise's business changed and grew, contravened applicable safety and soundness standards.

During the period covered by this report, the Board was aware of the broad delegation at Fannie Mae. For example, in an interview during the course of the special examination, Board member Donald Marron challenged Fannie Mae's debt buyback program on the basis that there were no boundaries to the repurchases and that management had complete authority to make decisions with respect to buybacks. During an interview, Mr. Marron noted that

> all of [Tim] Howard's presentations regarding debt buybacks had been historical—meaning Howard would present to the Board what the Company did the quarter before, not on its plans for buying back debt in the future. Marron could not recall there being any boundaries on the Company's practice of buying back debt or management looking to the Board for consent as to the size or parameters of the purchases.

When asked about whether Mr. Marron "challenged" management on that issue:

> Marron agreed, and said that he had asked why the company was buying back debt, what it was doing to replace the capital spent and whether the repurchases were made pursuant to normal policy. Marron noted that the transactions sometimes caused the company to incur losses in the magnitude of "billions" of dollars. However, Marron said that he was told that management had "all bases covered" and that the Company's policy regarding buying back debt had been around a long time.[134]

Mr. Marron's challenge to management was summarily dismissed with further assurances by Mr. Howard.

The Board did not respond appropriately in the face of those assurances. That failure to ensure adequate controls of those transactions, which can affect executive compensation directly, is contrary to OFHEO corporate governance regulation. Under applicable law, the Board should not have accepted dismissive assurances from management. Given the oversight responsibility and authority vested in Boards of Directors, it is incumbent on Board members to carefully delegate authority but retain their ability to stay informed of and provide oversight of Enterprise business activities. The Board's failure to insist upon guidelines requiring that such major transactions receive Board approval was a significant dereliction of duty and a safety and soundness violation.

Failure to Ensure that Committees Functioned Effectively

The delegation of duties to its Committees does not absolve the full Board from ultimate responsibility for the Committee activities or from the full Board's own significant operational shortcomings. The Board's lax oversight of key committees contributed to their failures. As documented earlier in this chapter, the Auditing and Compensation Committees failed the Board and Fannie Mae in the performance of their delegated duties. The Committee failures meant that the delegated areas of responsibility were not receiving an appropriate level of attention and care. Further, because of the Committee failures, the full Board received inaccurate reports based upon inadequate information from poorly functioning Committees.

Failure to Act as a Check on Chairman and Chief Executive Officer Raines

As established in Chapters VII and VIII, during Mr. Raines' tenure accounting and internal control irregularities were not disclosed appropriately to the Board of Directors. Many of those irregularities involved inappropriate financial manipulation conducted to attain EPS targets to enrich senior executives. CFO Howard's tight control of accounting personnel and informal control over the Office of Auditing were fundamental to the control of information presented to the Board. That control of information to the Board meant that (i) the accountants were not performing accounting duties appropriately, (ii) the Office of Auditing was not reviewing the accounting operations appropriately, (iii) the Office of Auditing was not reporting adequately to the Audit Committee, (iv) the Audit Committee failed to adequately oversee the internal audit and risk management functions and was not reporting adequately to the full Board of Directors, and (v) the full Board of Directors did not have complete information at its disposal. In short, the Board did not hear about all important issues, particularly financial ones, and often had a distorted view of those issues. Despite those impediments, this chapter has identified instances when it was incumbent upon the Board to either insist upon the receipt of more information or to act upon the information that it was provided.[135]

Mr. Raines violated applicable standards of corporate governance by concentrating excessive power and conflicting responsibilities in the hands of Mr. Howard, who then used that power to stifle criticism and manipulate earnings to enrich senior executives. The Board's acquiescence to that concentration of power was a failure of Board oversight. Key person dependencies and failures to segregate duties are internal control weaknesses and, thus, unsafe and unsound practices. As described earlier, the Board failed to curtail the concentration of authority in Mr. Howard. As CFO, Mr. Howard was responsible for all accounting and financial reporting, policy and financial standards, budgeting, the mortgage and credit portfolio business, treasury operations, and corporate financial strategies. Organization charts showing Mr. Howard's responsibilities were routinely included in packages of materials distributed to Directors before Board meetings. Members of the Board knew of and had the opportunity to object to the extent of Mr. Howard's authority.

In 2000, Mr. Raines increased Mr. Howard's area of responsibility further by consolidating all of Fannie Mae's financial risk responsibilities under the CFO. Mr. Howard informally referred to himself as the Enterprise's "Chief Risk Officer."[136] As described in the discussion of the Audit Committee's failures, the combination those functions is a serious internal control weakness and is contrary to OFHEO regulations, and contravenes industry best practices.

The 2002 change in the administrative reporting relationship of Senior Vice President for Operations Risk and head of the Office of Auditing Sampath Rajappa to Mr. Howard was a signal to the Board that the independence of the internal audit function was an issue. The Office of Auditing is the internal "watchdog" for the Enterprise and, largely, for operations under the CFO's purview.[137] The Board failed to challenge Mr. Raines' reorganization of that reporting relationship. That failure is particularly noteworthy in light of the inherent conflict of an internal auditor reporting to the CFO and the fact that, in his previous position as controller, Mr. Rajappa had reported directly to Mr. Howard.

Mr. Howard's appointment to the Board of Directors provides another example of the Board's failure to check the actions of Chairman and CEO Raines. Board member Mr. Duberstein stated during the Special Examination that he had objected to the idea of having Mr. Howard elevated to the position of Director. He stated that other Board members agreed with his position but were not as vocal. However, there is no record in the Board meeting minutes of any objections from the Board members over that decision. Mr. Duberstein explained that "with rare passion" Mr. Raines stated he needed Mr. Howard's expertise on the Board.[138] Thus, Mr. Raines' passion overcame the initial judgment of some Board members, and Mr. Howard was appointed a member of the Board of Directors during 2003.

In another example, in August 2004, Mr. Howard announced a significant reorganization of Fannie Mae's Credit Policy function that moved the responsibility for all risk management to Finance, which reported to him. Following a presentation by Mr. Mudd to the Board of Directors on the reorganization, Board Member Stephen Ashley contacted fellow Board member and COO Mudd, to express his concerns that Mudd had not clearly identified where the responsibility for credit risk oversight would reside in the organization.[139] The failure to segregate the responsibilities of the Chief Financial Office and Chief Risk Officer eliminated the inherent checks and balances in having different lines of responsibility for those areas. The failure of the Board to adequately address this issue was an abdication of the Board's duties.

Between 1998 and 2004, the ratio of directors considered independent by the Enterprise to insiders fell from 14:4 to 8:4. The change was due primarily to Presidentially-appointed positions remaining unfilled when incumbents left, but the Board never considered that Mr. Howard's appointment would have a significant impact on the ratio of inside directors.

Another cogent issue is the independence of non-management Board members. Although the Board of Directors adopted the NYSE standards for independence and adhered to them in all material respects, both business relationships and donations from the Fannie Mae Foundation created an appearance of less than total independence. For example, Frederic Malek, an independent Director from 2002 through 2004, and whose job it was to oversee the performance of Mr. Raines, was a business partner with Mr. Raines in the Washington Baseball Club, an organization that attempted to bring major league baseball to Washington D.C., during the time Mr. Malek was a director. While the Nominating and Governance Committee took steps to address that appearance of a conflict of interest by changing Mr. Malek's committee assignments, he retained his position as an independent Board member. Another Board member, Kenneth Duberstein, a Director since 1998, continued to have a lobbying contract with Fannie Mae while he was a Director. Although the Fannie Mae proxy statements fully disclose that relationship, Mr. Duberstein participated in Executive Session discussions with independent directors including discussions involving Mr. Raines' compensation, despite recommendations to the contrary from outside consultants.[140]

Contributions of the Fannie Mae Foundation also eroded at least the appearance of independence of other board members. When members of the Board began their service, they filled out forms listing charities and other organizations with which they were affiliated. The form was resubmitted annually to the company and the Foundation.[141] Fannie Mae Foundation grants to organizations to which Board members were affiliated more than doubled from ($4 million to $14 million) after members accepted their assignments to the Fannie Mae Board of Directors. A number of those organizations only received Fannie Mae Foundation grants after an affiliated member was appointed to the Board.[142]

Examples include Mr. Duberstein who has served on the Boards of various organizations which, according to the Fannie Mae Foundation web site, were awarded grants totaling $5.4 million since he joined the Fannie Mae Board of Directors. Similarly, Ann McLaughlin Korologos, an independent, non-management Director since 1994, held senior posts at the Aspen Institute from 1996 through 2000, during which time the Aspen Institute received $280,000 in grants from the Fannie Mae Foundation. Ms. Korologos was also a Visiting Fellow with the Urban Institute, which received approximately $2.6 million in grants since she has been on the Fannie Mae Board. Ms. Korologos also was assigned to Chair of the Board's Corporate Governance Committee and the Special Review Committee charged with the internal investigation resulting from the OFHEO Special Examination Report in September 2004. Both Ms. Korologos and Thomas Gerrity, chairman of the Audit Committee, were affiliated with Wharton School of Business at the University of Pennsylvania which received $687,500. H.

Patrick Swygert, an independent, non-management Director since 2000, is the President of Howard University. Howard University has received more than $225,000 in grants from the Fannie Mae Foundation since 2000.[143]

The Board was aware that donations to director-affiliated charities could compromise independence, but appeared reluctant to allow scrutiny of such donations. In 2003 the Board enacted guidelines to define an "independent" director, which included number of conflicts that would preclude a director from being considered independent. One of these conflicts was defined to be annual donations of $100,000 or more by Fannie Mae or the Foundation to charities affiliated with the Board members. All the other financial conflict provisions (i.e., employment by Fannie Mae or receipt of large contracts from Fannie Mae) looked back 5 years to determine whether the director was independent. The charitable contribution limit alone was prospective--the only one of the guidelines that did not include a five-year look-back period; thus defining board members as independent no matter how large the prior contributions that Fannie Mae had made to their affiliated charities. If the five-year look back period had been applied, at least three directors considered "independent" by Fannie Mae would not have qualified under the guidelines.

Failure to Order Independent Investigations of Fannie Mae

The Board failed to exercise prudent oversight over Fannie Mae as demonstrated by its ineffective and complacent response to the Freddie Mac accounting missteps and subsequent restatement. The similarities between the two Enterprises in terms of markets, business risks, products, and history of uniquely steady earnings growth should have made Board members skeptical about management assertions that Fannie Mae had none of the accounting issues of its sister Enterprise. The Board should have initiated immediately its own independent investigation into accounting practices at Fannie Mae rather than waiting for OFHEO to investigate.

On January 22, 2003, Freddie Mac announced that an accounting restatement of its 2002, 2001, and 2000 financial results was required due to the misapplication of GAAP. The restatement was required after Freddie Mac's newly appointed external auditor, PricewaterhouseCoopers, recommended changing certain accounting policies that were approved by its previous external auditor.[144] (In March 2002, Freddie Mac had hired PricewaterhouseCoopers to replace Arthur Andersen LLP). Freddie Mac publicly reported that the restatement would result in changes to the timing of the recognition of income that related primarily to a change in accounting policies involving the hedge accounting treatment of certain transactions including those occasioned by the implementation of FAS 133.[145] In late January 2003, in response to the audit findings, the independent, non-management members of the Freddie Mac Board of Directors retained Baker Botts, LLP, to investigate the facts and circumstances relating to certain of the principle accounting errors identified during the Enterprise's previously announced restatement process.[146]

Fannie Mae Board meeting minutes reflect no discussion regarding Freddie Mac's restatement for approximately six months after the announcement. That level of complacency on the part of the Board is particularly disturbing since the two Enterprises share the same business objectives and associated risks. The first documented discussion of the Freddie Mac situation is at the June 9, 2003 Board meeting, three days after Freddie Mac had announced the resignations of its CEO and CFO and the firing of its COO. According to the Board minutes:

> Mr. Raines noted the Freddie Mac and related statements released to the public that morning, copies of which were sent to the Board prior to the conference call. He asked Mr. Donilon to brief the Board. Mr. Donilon reviewed the Freddie Mac management announcements with the Board and media, industry, regulatory, and policymaker reactions. Mr. Raines noted that he did not believe that the company had the financial management or accounting issues outlined in the Freddie Mac announcement and was a full SEC registrant having filed Fannie Mae's initial Form 10K on March 31, 2003 and 10Q in May.

Members of the Board discussed the Freddie Mac situation and Freddie Mac's response. Members asked to be kept informed of developments.[147]

The Board minutes do not reflect any actions directed by the Board for management follow-up. The minutes do not reflect any challenge to the assertion made by Mr. Raines that Fannie Mae did not have similar issues to Freddie Mac. That assertion was made without the benefit of sufficient analysis or documentation. The Board met again the following week. According to the Board minutes:

> Mr. Raines asked Mr. Donilon to brief the Board members on the Freddie Mac situation. Mr. Donilon reviewed the regulatory, legal, and congressional developments of the last week arising out of the Freddie Mac management shakeup and accounting announcements. He reviewed Fannie Mae's statements and information provided to investors, policymakers, and the public, differentiating Fannie Mae from Freddie Mac. Mr. Raines and Mr. Donilon answered questions from Board members. Members of the Board noted the importance of close monitoring of the situation by the Board.[148]

Again, the minutes do not reflect any substance of questions asked, management responses, or any specific actions directed by the Board for follow-up.

The next Board meeting took place on June 27, 2003. According to the minutes of that meeting, "Frank Raines asked Tim Howard, CFO, to report and to comment specifically on Freddie Mac accounting issues that have been raised publicly." The minutes reflect that Mr. Howard discussed seven accounting issues that Freddie Mac disclosed in public statements; however, only five were described in the minutes. The five accounting issues described included security classification, accounting for derivative instruments, asset transfers, asset securitizations, and valuation of financial instruments. Mr. Howard "contrasted Freddie Mac practices with Fannie Mae practices, concluding that Fannie Mae did not have the same practices and approaches disclosed by Freddie Mac to date. Messrs. Raines, Howard, and Donilon responded to questions from various Board members."[149] Again, the minutes of the meeting do not document the nature of the questions and the names of the Board members asking questions, and the answers provided by management. Neither do they indicate any action items for management follow-up.

As reported in *The Washington Post* on July 10, 2003, the events unfolding at Freddie Mac showed a Board whose members struggled, and sometimes hesitated, to take tough action against top executives they had known and respected for years. The *Post* also reported that Baker Botts had told the Freddie Mac Board at its March 2003 meeting that the "accounting issues continued to broaden and . . . included the possibility that senior management had made some transactions solely to manipulate reported profits so the company could meet earnings targets expected by Wall Street."[150]

On July 14-15, 2003, at the Fannie Mae Board of Directors Strategic Retreat, Mr. Howard made his annual presentation on risk management objectives. Mr. Howard stressed that a key corporate financial discipline objective of Fannie Mae was to ensure a "high degree of net income stability." Mr. Howard's message to the Board was clear: for Fannie Mae to capitalize on its unparalleled debt market access and capital requirements, Fannie Mae "must be, and be perceived to be, a low-risk company," and must achieve a stable pattern of earnings. Mr. Howard then compared the standard deviation of Fannie Mae's earnings per share to the trend shown by Standards & Poor's 500 Companies. He showed how Freddie Mac had a slightly less than four percent standard deviation from the median, while Fannie Mae was much closer to the trend with a standard deviation of less than one percent.[151]

On July 18, 2003, *The Washington Post* reported that Freddie Mac's former auditor, Arthur Andersen had warned management and key Board members about a lack of accounting expertise at the Enterprise.[152] On July 22, 2003, one week after the above described Strategic Retreat, Baker Botts, LLP, published its report on the internal investigation of Freddie Mac. That report disclosed critical findings regarding Freddie Mac's efforts to defer income recognition and avoid earnings volatility.[153] Despite the media attention surrounding the Baker Botts report and their knowledge that Fannie Mae shared Freddie Mac's objective of mitigating income volatility, members of the Fannie Mae Board of Directors again failed to exercise adequate oversight. They again failed to request all material information necessary to conclude that Fannie Mae was GAAP compliant and was not improperly managing its earnings.

Mr. Gerrity, Chair of the Audit Committee, told OFHEO that he was not aware, at the time that the Board was discussing the Freddie Mac restatement, that Freddie Mac had been criticized for improper earnings management. Mr. Gerrity also stated that he did not read the Baker Botts report.[154] While Mr. Donilon gave the Board a copy of the executive summary of the report, he told the Board members (including Mr. Gerrity) that the full report was publicly available on the Freddie Mac web site.[155] Board member Stephen Ashley also received the executive summary of the report with the reference to the Internet location of the full report, yet he, too, told OFHEO that he did not read the full Baker Botts report.[156]

The Board convened an additional nine times in 2003 after the release of the Baker Botts report, but the minutes to the Board meetings reflect no additional discussion about the Freddie Mac situation and whether Fannie Mae had any similar problems.

On January 23, 2004, almost one year from the date that Freddie Mac announced its intention to restate its financial statements (and one month after OFHEO issued its own detailed report), the Audit Committee reported to the Board on a study conducted by Controller Spencer. That study compared the accounting treatments of Fannie Mae to those of Freddie Mac for four of the 31 specific issues publicly disclosed by Freddie Mac. The Board minutes reflect the following report by the Audit Committee

> Mr. Gerrity reported that the Committee had received a report on a thorough analysis of the Freddie Mac accounting issues and a comparison of Fannie Mae approaches. Mr. Gerrity reported that KPMG was fully involved in the study. The review highlighted differences between Fannie Mae and Freddie Mac securities structures and business processes that can lead to accounting differences. Mr. Gerrity reported that the study identified 31 specific issues with Freddie Mac's accounting; Ms. Spencer reviewed four issues in detail with the Committee. Mr. Gerrity reported that the company was comfortable with its accounting approaches. [157]

In reality, Fannie Mae had many accounting errors in common with Freddie Mac. Freddie Mac was criticized for accounting related to allowance for loan losses, securities classifications, accounting for derivatives, securitizations, and accounting for purchase premium and discount amortization. Each of those accounting areas are listed as significant accounting policies in the Notes to Financial Statements in Fannie Mae's 2003 10-K.[158] Determining the adequacy of the allowance for loan losses and calculating the amortization for deferred price adjustments (purchase premiums and discounts) are critical accounting estimates for both Enterprises. The Board should have required detailed information related to each of those critical accounting policies and estimates that Fannie Mae shared Freddie Mac. The Board should have challenged Ms. Spencer's assertion that only four of the 31 issues identified by Freddie Mac were significant for Fannie Mae.

The Board placed too much reliance on Mr. Howard and Ms. Spencer to identify weaknesses within their own areas of responsibility. As discussed elsewhere in this chapter, Mr. Howard was responsible for the development of the financial policies and standards used at Fannie Mae as well as for financial reporting. The reliance of the Board of Directors on Mr. Howard and Ms. Spencer was particularly negligent given that control weakness. Considering the similarities between the two Enterprises, the Board should have commissioned an independent inquiry into the accounting practices of Fannie Mae. Not until eighteen months later, after OFHEO had issued its report of September 2004 and the Securities and Exchange Commission had ruled against Fannie Mae on determinations made by OFHEO, did the Board initiate its own investigation.

The allegations of earnings manipulation by senior management at Freddie Mac that surfaced publicly in *The Washington Post* on July 10, 2003, were serious. Knowing that its regulator had begun an unprecedented special examination on the same issues announced on July 17, 2003, the Board of Directors contravened statute, regulation, and industry best practices by continuing to rely on the representations of senior management until the SEC's ruling of December 2004.

The entire Board was also derelict when, in October 2003, counsel for Mr. Barnes threatened suit, alleging earnings manipulations by senior management and asserting that Mr. Barnes had written the senior management directly about that manipulation a year before. SEC regulations required the Board to conduct an independent investigation, and OFHEO regulations required Fannie Mae to inform the SEC or OFHEO about the charges.[159] Neither requirement was fulfilled, nor is there any record that either was considered. In its passivity, the Board missed its last chance to require an independent investigation or review that would have allowed the Enterprise to resolve its own problems. Here, as in many other instances, the Board simply accepted representations of senior management and exercised no discernable oversight responsibility.

Failure to Ensure Timely and Accurate Reports to Federal Regulators

OFHEO regulations require the Board to have in place adequate policies and procedures to ensure that executive officers are responsive in providing accurate and timely reports to Federal regulators and in addressing the supervisory concerns of Federal regulators in a timely and appropriate manner.[160] Board members are also responsible for ensuring that Fannie Mae submits timely and complete reports of financial condition and operations to OFHEO and other federal regulators.

The Board failed to discharge those responsibilities in numerous instances, including with respect to required disclosures of executive compensation and the allegations made by Mr. Barnes. Issues related to the disclosure of executive compensation are discussed in Chapter VIII of this report. The allegations by Mr. Barnes, when initially made, were not reported to OFHEO. The Board should have sought assurance that the OFHEO was aware of the issues. No such assurance was sought. The accounting and internal control failures at Fannie Mae have impeded the Enterprise's ability to file timely and complete reports of financial condition and operations to OFHEO and other federal regulators. The Board's failure to ensure timely and accurate reports to Federal regulators is a violation of OFHEO's safety and soundness regulation.

Conclusion

The bedrock principle of OFHEO's regulation of Fannie Mae is that the entity must operate safely and soundly. The Board, in turn, must take reasonable steps to assure itself that senior management is operating the Enterprise in accordance with that principle. That requirement is a very broad one, as a widely quoted definition makes clear:

Generally speaking, an "unsafe or unsound practice" embraces any action, or lack of action, which is contrary to generally accepted standards of prudent operation, the possible consequences of which, if continued, would be abnormal risk of loss or damage to an institution, its shareholders, or the agencies administering the insurance funds.[161]

Judging the actions and inactions of the Fannie Mae Board against that definition, standards of prudent operation clearly were not met. Rather than an active, concerned Board that effectively supervised senior management, the Board of Directors was a passive and complacent entity, controlled by, rather than controlling senior management. As catalogued in this chapter, the Board and its Committees missed a host of opportunities to uncover and control the malfeasance documented in earlier chapters. Instead, Fannie Mae suffered an enormous loss in credibility and reputation and has incurred hundreds of millions of dollars in remedial expense. A Board operating in accordance with generally accepted standards of prudent operation would have prevented much or all of those losses.

Appendix to Chapter IX: Board Composition

BOARD MEMBER	TENURE	BACKGROUND	COMMITTEE ASSIGNMENTS, 1998-2004[1]
Stephen B. Ashley	1995-Present	Chairman, Fannie Mae (2004-present) Chairman & Chief Executive Officer, the Ashley Group (1975-present) President, Mortgage Bankers Association (1993-1994) Board of Trustees o Cornell University Boards of Directors o Exeter Fund, Inc. o The Genesee Corp.	Executive: 2003-2004 N&CG: 1995-2004 Technology: 1996-2002 HCD: Chair, 2003-2004 SRC: 2004
Thomas P. Gerrity	1991-Present	Professor of Management, Wharton School, University of Pennsylvania (1990-present) Dean, Wharton School, University of Pennsylvania (1990-1999) Boards of Directors o CVS Corp. o Internal Capital Group, Inc. o Knight-Ridder, Inc. o Sunoco, Inc. o Hercules, Inc.	Executive: 1996-2004 Audit: Chair, 1998-2004 N&CG: 1996-2004 Technology: 1996-1999
Ann McLaughlin Korologos	1994-Present	Chairman, RAND Board of Trustees (2004-present) Chairman emeritus, Aspen Institute (2000-present) Senior Advisor, Benedetto, Gartland & Company, Inc. (1995-2005) Chairman, Aspen Institute (1996-2000) U.S. Secretary of Transportation (1987-1989) Boards of Directors o AMR Corporation o Microsoft Corp. o Harman International Industries, Inc. o Host Hotels & Resorts, Inc. o Kellogg Company	Executive: 2001-2004 Compensation: 1998-2004 N&CG: 1998-2004, Chair, 2001-2004 SRC: 2004; Chair, 2004

1. A&L= Assets and Liabilities; N&CG= Nominating and Corporate Governance; HCD= Housing and Community Development; SRC= Special Review Committee

Sources: Fannie Mae Annual Reports and Proxy Statements-1998 through 2003. Fannie Mae Web site. Corporate Governance.

Appendix to Chapter IX: Board Composition

BOARD MEMBER	TENURE	BACKGROUND	COMMITTEE ASSIGNMENTS, 1998-2004[1]
Joe K. Pickett	1996-Present	Chairman and Chief Executive Officer, HomeSide International Inc. (1996-2001) President, Mortgage Bankers Association (1994-1995)	Executive: 1998-2004 A&L: 1998-2001 Audit: 2003-2004 Compensation: 2002-2004 Technology: Chair, 1998-2002
Kenneth M. Duberstein	1998-Present	Chairman & Chief Executive Officer, The Duberstein Group, Inc. (1989-present) White House Chief of Staff (1988-1989) Boards of Directors o Boeing Company o Conoco, Inc.	Executive: 2000-2004 A&L: 1989-2004; Chair, 2000-2004 Technology: 1998-2002 HCD: 2003-2004
Daniel H. Mudd	2000-Present	President & Chief Executive Officer, Fannie Mae (2004-present) President & Chief Operating Officer, Fannie Mae (2000-2004) President & Chief Executive Officer, GE-Capital, Japan (1996-1999) Boards of Directors o Fannie Mae Foundation o Ryder Systems, Inc.	None
H. Patrick Swygert	2000-Present	President, Howard University (1995-present) Board of Directors o United Technologies Corporation o The Hartford Financial Services Group, Inc.	A&L: 2000-2004 Technology: 2000 HCD: 2003-2004 N&GC: 2000
Donald B. Marron	2001-Present	Chairman & Chief Executive Officer, Lightyear Capital (2001-present) Chairman & Chief Executive Officer, UBS PaineWebber Inc. (2000-2001) Chairman & Chief Executive Officer, Paine Webber (1981-2000) Board of Directors o Shinsei Bank Chairman, Collegiate Funding Services, Inc.	A&L: 2001-2004 N&GC: 2001-2004 SRC: 2004

Sources: Fannie Mae Annual Reports and Proxy Statements-1998 through 2003. Fannie Mae Web site, Corporate Governance

Appendix to Chapter IX: Board Composition

BOARD MEMBER	TENURE	BACKGROUND	COMMITTEE ASSIGNMENTS, 1998-2004[1]
Leslie Rahl	2004-Present	President & Founder, Capital Market Risk Advisors, Inc. (1991-present) Vice President and Division Head, Citibank (1972-1991) Boards of Directors ○ International Association of Financial Engineers ○ MIT Investment Management Company ○ New York State Common Investment Advisory Committee	A&L: 2003-2004 HCD: 2003-2004
John K. Wulff	2004-Present	Chairman of the Board, Hercules Inc. (2003-present) Member, Financial Accounting Standards Board (2001-2003) Chief Financial Officer, Union Carbide Corporation (1996-2001) Board of Directors ○ Moody's Corporation ○ Republic Financial	
Bridget A. Macaskill	2005-Present	Principal, BAM Consulting LLC (2005-present) Chairman & Chief Executive Officer, Oppenheimer Funds, Inc. (2000-2001) Chief Executive Officer, Oppenheimer Funds, Inc. (1995-2000) Boards of Directors ○ J. Sainsbury PLC ○ Prudential PLC ○ College Retirement Equities Fund	
Greg C. Smith	2005-Present	Vice Chairman, Ford Motor Company (2005-present) Executive Vice President, Ford Motor Company (2004-2005) Chairman & Chief Executive Officer, Ford Motor Credit Company (2002-2004) Boards of Directors ○ Hertz Corporation ○ Detroit Investment Fund	

Sources: Fannie Mae Annual Reports and Proxy Statements-1998 through 2003. Fannie Mae Web site, Corporate Governance.

Appendix to Chapter IX: Board Composition

BOARD MEMBER	TENURE	BACKGROUND	COMMITTEE ASSIGNMENTS, 1998-2004[1]
Franklin D. Raines	1991-1996 and 1998-2004	Chairman & Chief Executive Officer (1998-2004) Director, U.S. Office of Management and Budget (1996-1998) Vice Chairman, Fannie Mae (1991-1996) Co-Chairman, The Business Roundtable (2003-2004) Chair, Corporate Governance Task Force, The Business Roundtable Boards of Directors o Revolution Health Group o Pfizer, Inc. (1998-2004) o AOL Time Warner, Inc. (2001-2004) o PepsiCo, Inc. (1999-2005); Chair, Audit Committee (2003-2005) o TIAA-CREF (1999-2005)	Executive: Chair, 1998-2004
Timothy Howard	2003-2004	Vice Chairman & Chief Financial Officer, Fannie Mae (2003-2004) Executive Vice President & Chief Financial Officer, Fannie Mae (1990-2003) Board of Directors, CarrAmerica Realty Corporation	None
Anne M. Mulcahy	2000-2004	Chairman and Chief Executive Officer, Xerox Corporation (2002-present) Chief Executive Officer, Xerox Corporation (2001-2002) President and Chief Operating Officer, Xerox Corporation (2000-2001) Boards of Directors o Citigroup, Inc. o Fuji Xerox Co. Ltd. o Target Corporation	Executive: 2002-2004 A&L: 2000 Audit: 2001-2004 Compensation: 2000-2004, Chair, 2002-2004

Sources: Fannie Mae Annual Reports and Proxy Statements-1998 through 2003. Fannie Mae Web site, Corporate Governance

Appendix to Chapter IX: Board Composition

BOARD MEMBER	TENURE	BACKGROUND	COMMITTEE ASSIGNMENTS, 1998-2004[1]
Frederic V. Malek	2002-2004	Chairman, Thayer Capital Partners (1991-present) Co-chairman, CB Commercial (1989-1996) President and Vice Chairman, Northwest Airlines (1989-1991) President, Marriott Hotels (1980-1988) Board of Trustees, Aspen Institute Boards of Directors ○ Automatic Data Processing Corp. ○ FPL Group ○ CB Richard Ellis Group ○ Manor Care, Inc. ○ Northwest Airlines	A&L: 2002-2004 Audit: 2002-2004
Victor H. Ashe*	2001-2004	Ambassador, Republic of Poland (2004-present) Mayor, Knoxville, TN (1988-2003) President, U.S. Conference of Mayors (1995)	A&L: 2001-2002 NCG: 2003-2004 Technology: 2001-2002 HCD: 2003-2004
Molly H. Bordonaro*	2001-2004	U.S. Ambassador to Malta (2004-present) Principal, Gallatin Group (2002-present) Associate, Norris, Beggs & Simpson (1999-2002)	A&L: 2001-2004 Technology: 2001-2002 HCD: 2003-2004
William R. Harvey	2001-2004	President, Hampton University (1978-present) Boards of Directors ○ Trigon Blue Cross Blue Shield ○ Signet Bank ○ Newport News Shipbuilding ○ Wachovia Bank (Mid-Atlantic Region) ○ Newport News Savings Bank	Audit: 2001-2004 Technology: 2001-2002 HCD: 2003-2004
Taylor C. Segue, III*	2001-2004	Partner, Fraser Trebilcock Davis & Dunlap, P.C. (2004-present) Partner, Howard & Howard Attorneys P.C. (2002-2004) Partner, Butzel Long, P.C. (1999-2002)	A&L: 2001-2002 Audit: 2001-2004 Compensation: 2003-2004
Manuel Justiz*	2001-2004	Dean, College of Education at the University of Texas at Austin (1990-present)	A&L: 2002-2004 Technology: 2001-2002 HCD: 2003-2004

Sources: Fannie Mae Annual Reports and Proxy Statements-1998 through 2003. Fannie Mae Web site, Corporate Governance

Appendix to Chapter IX: Board Composition

BOARD MEMBER	TENURE	BACKGROUND	COMMITTEE ASSIGNMENTS, 1998-2004[1]
Jamie Gorelick	1997-2003	Partner, Wilmer Cutler Pickering Hale & Dorr (2003-present) Vice Chair, Fannie Mae (1997-2003) U.S. Deputy Attorney General (1994-1997) Member, National Commission on Terrorist Attacks Upon the United States (2003-2004) Boards of Directors o United Technologies Corporation o Schlumberger, Ltd.	None
Vincent A. Mai	1991-2002	Chairman and Chief Executive Officer, AEA Investors, Inc. (1998-present) Chief Executive Officer, AEA Investors, Inc. (1989-present) Lehman Brothers (1975-1989) Chairman of the Board of Directors, Sesame Workshop Vice Chairman, International Center for Transnational Justice	Executive: 1998-2002 Audit: 1998-2002 Compensation: Chair, 1998-2002
Roger E. Birk	1985-2001	President and Chief Operating Officer, Fannie Mae (1987-1992) Chairman and CEO, Merrill Lynch & Co., (1982-1986)	Executive: 1998-2000 N&CG: Chair, 1998-2000 Technology: 1998-2000
Stephen Friedman	1996-2002	Chairman, President's Foreign Intelligence Advisory Board and Chairman of the Intelligence Oversight Board (2005-present) Senior Advisor, Stone Point Capital (2005-present) Assistant to the President for Economic Policy and Director of the National Economic Council (2002-2005) Senior Principal, Marsh & McLennan Capital Corp. (1998-2002) Chairman, Goldman Sachs (1992-1994)	Compensation: 1998-2001 N&CG 1998-2001

Sources: Fannie Mae Annual Reports and Proxy Statements-1998 through 2003. Fannie Mae Web site, Corporate Governance

Appendix to Chapter IX: Board Composition

BOARD MEMBER	TENURE	BACKGROUND	COMMITTEE ASSIGNMENTS, 1998-2004[1]
Eli J. Segal*	1997-2001	Chief Executive Officer, Welfare to Work Partnership (1996-2006) Assistant to the President (1993-1996)	A&L: 1998-2001 Audit: 1998-2001
Jack Quinn*	1998-2001	Co-Chairman, Quinn Gillespie & Associates LLC (2000-present) Partner, Arnold & Porter White House Counsel (1995-1997)	A&L: 1998-2001 Technology: 1998-2001
Garry Mauro*	1999-2001	Attorney (1999-present) Commissioner, Texas General Land Office (1983-1999)	Audit: 1999-2001 Technology: 1999-2001
Maynard Jackson*	2000-2001	Mayor, City of Atlanta, Georgia (1974-1982; 1990-1994) Chairman, Jackson Securities (1987-2003)	A&L: 2000-2001 Technology: 2000-2001
Esteban E. Torres*	2000-2001	Chair, National Latino Media Council (1998-present) Member, US House of Representatives (1982-1998)	A&L: 2000-2001 Technology: 2000-2001
Lawrence M. Small	1991-2000	Secretary, Smithsonian Institution (2000-2006) President and Chief Operating Officer, Fannie Mae (1991-2000) Former Vice Chairman and Chairman of the Executive Committee, Citicorp/Citibank Board of Directors, ○ Chubb Corporation	None
Karen Hastie Williams	1988-1999	Partner, Crowell & Moring (1982-2005) Boards of Directors ○ Chubb Corporation ○ Continental Airlines, Inc. ○ Gannett Company, Inc. ○ Washington Gas Holdings Company ○ SunTrust Bank	Executive: 1998-1999 A&L: Chair, 1998-1999 Compensation: 1998-1999
Jose H. Villarreal, Esq.*	1993-1999	Partner, Akin, Gump, Strauss, Hauer & Feld, L.L.P. Boards of Directors ○ Wal-Mart Corp. ○ PMI Group	A&L: 1998-1999 Audit: 1998-1999

Sources: Fannie Mae Annual Reports and Proxy Statements-1998 through 2003. Fannie Mae Web site, Corporate Governance

Appendix to Chapter IX: Board Composition

BOARD MEMBER	TENURE	BACKGROUND	COMMITTEE ASSIGNMENTS, 1998-2004[1]
James A. Johnson	1990-1998	Vice-Chairman, Perseus, L.L.C. (2001-present) Chairman of the Board & Chief Executive Officer, Fannie Mae (1991-1998) Boards of Directors o Enterprise Foundation o Goldman Sachs Group o KB Home o Target Corporation o United Health Group	Executive: Chair, 1998 A&L: 1998 Technology: 1998
* Director was appointed by the President of the United States.			

Sources: Fannie Mae Annual Reports and Proxy Statements-1998 through 2003. Fannie Mae Web site, Corporate Governance

[1] A&L = Assets and Liabilities; N&CG = Nominating and Corporate Governance; HCD = Housing and Community Development; SRC = Special Review Committee

References

[1] In fact, its Charter Act requires Fannie Mae to make a formal assessment of its compliance with the applicable safety and soundness laws. See e.g. 12 U.S.C. § 1723a(k)(2).
[2] See 12 C.F.R. Part 1710 (2005). OFHEO requires that the "corporate governance practices and procedures of the [the] Enterprise ... shall comply with [its] chartering act ... and other Federal law, rules and regulations, and shall be consistent with the safe and sound operation of the Enterprise...." 12 C.F.R. § 1710.10(a).
[3] Title 12, C.F.R., Part 1710.15 (2004).
[4] 12 C.F.R Corporate Governance § 1710.15, and § 1710.10.
[5] Fannie Mae complied with the election requirement in 12 C.F.R. § 1710.10(b) by electing to be subject to Delaware law for corporate governance purposes.
[6] 12 C.F.R. § 1710.10 (b) makes clear that federal law supersedes state law where there is any inconsistency. The Federal Housing Enterprises Financial Safety and Soundness Act of 1992, makes clear that OFHEO is primarily in charge of assuring the safety and soundness of Fannie Mae.
[7] See Knepper, W. Liability of Corporate Officers and Directors, 1.11, p. 27 (3rd Ed. 1978) (internal citations omitted).
[8] Id., p. 26.
[9] The New York Stock Exchange instituted the requirement that all listed public companies have an independent audit committee effective June 30, 1978. Id., p. 29.
[10] As discussed in Chapter III, the corporate governance and safety and soundness regulations promulgated by OFHEO capture these essential tenets and provide the analytical framework for assessing the Board's conduct.
[11] 12 C.F.R. § 1710.12(a).
[12] See 12 U.S.C. § 1723a(l), (k)(1) and (2).
[13] 12 C.F.R. § 1710.11.
[14] Fannie Mae Corporate Governance by-laws: Article 4 at http://fanniemae.com/ governance/bylaws/article4.jhtml?p=Corporate+Governance&s=Bylaws&t=Artlice=4:+ The+ Board-.
[15] Historically, the standards governing the roles and responsibilities of audit committees evolved in response to a rash of well-publicized cases of fraudulent financial reporting. For example, in 1987, the National Commission on Fraudulent Financial Reporting (the Treadway Commission) recommended that the boards of directors of all public companies be required by Securities Exchange Commission (SEC) rule to establish audit committees composed solely of independent directors, and outlined key recommendations for audit committees to follow in carrying out their responsibilities. See Louis Braiotta, Jr., The Audit Committee Handbook, Third Edition, 353-354 (1999).
[16] See 12 U.S.C. § 1723a(l), (k)(1) and (2).
[17] "Audit committees also help the Board [of Directors] by overseeing the conduct and performance of management with respect to the preparation of the company's financial statements and financial disclosures." See Fenwick & West LLP, "Audit Committee Duties and Best Practices" (March 21, 2002). p. 2.

[18] In 1999, the role of audit committees was revitalized and strengthened by the "Report and Recommendations of the Blue Ribbon Committee on Improving the Effectiveness of Corporate Audit Committees," February 8, 1999, (Blue Ribbon Report). The Blue Ribbon Report outlined ten specific regulatory changes regarding audit committees and five guiding principles for audit committees to follow when developing their own policies.

[19] See "The COSO Report, Fraudulent Financial Reporting: 1987-1997, An analysis of U.S. Public Companies, Commissioned by the Committee of Sponsoring Organizations of the Treadway Commission," March 1999. The COSO Report identified and analyzed instances of alleged fraudulent financial reporting by companies investigated by the commission in the ten-year period following the 1987 Treadway Commission Report and highlighted the need for independent and effective audit committee oversight.

[20] See NYSE, Nasdaq and AMEX, Audit Committee Rule Requirements, September 20, 1999. Those proposed rule changes were approved by the SEC on December 14, 1999. Securities Exchange Act Release Nos. 34-41, 980-982, October 6 and 13, 1999.

[21] See NYSE Audit Committee Rule 303.01(B)(2), September 20, 1999. The rule was approved by the SEC on Dec. 14, 1999.

[22] See NYSE Audit Committee Rule 303.01(B)(1), September 20, 1999. The rule was approved by the SEC on Dec. 14, 1999.

[23] Securities Exchange Release No. 34-48,745, November 4, 2003.

[24] Sarbanes-Oxley Act of 2002, Pub. L. No. 107-204, § 407, 116 Stat. 745, 790 (2002).

[25] Annemarie K. Keinath and Judith C. Walo, "Audit Committee Responsibilities: Focusing on Oversight, Open Communication, and Best Practices," The CPA Journal, November 2004.

[26] The Audit Committee Charter, November 19, 1996, was included in the Audit Committee Meeting Package, as part of the of the April 21, 1998, committee meeting minutes.

[27] See Audit Committee Charter, July 18, 2000, at FMSE 014495-97.

[28] See 2003 Audit Committee Charter included in the Audit Committee Meeting minutes of January 21, 2003. FMSE 504223-228.

[29] E-mail chain from Sampath Rajappa to Jamie Gorelick with a copy to Franklin Raines, Timothy Howard, Leanne Spencer and others, "Re: Audit Committee Requirements," February 12, 2001, FMSE-KD 016986-88 (in which Mr. Rajappa reported that "KPMG and I will address how we meet all the requirements at the audit committee on Feb. 20.")

[30] See Audit Committee Meeting Minutes of February 20, 2001, FMSE 014870-014876 at 73.

[31] While Mr. Rajappa, Senior Vice President for Operations Risk and head of the Office of Auditing, was reporting that Fannie Mae is or will be in compliance with all the requirements, including independent communication and information flow between audit committee and internal audit and external audit as well as candid discussions with management and external auditors, he also indicates that he " will meet with KPMG on Wednesday to go over their exact talking points. . ." and represents to already know "what they (KPMG) intend to say." See e-mail chain from Sampath Rajappa to Jamie Gorelick with a copy to Franklin Raines, Timothy Howard, Leanne Spencer, and others, "Re: Audit Committee Requirements," February 12, 2001, FMSE-KD 016986.

[32] See Minutes of the Meeting of the Nominating and Corporate Governance Committee of the Board of Directors of Fannie Mae, July 16, 2002, FMSE 505365-66, at FMSE 505365.

[33] See Minutes of the Meeting of the Nominating and Corporate Governance Committee of the Board of Directors of Fannie Mae, July 16, 2002, FMSE 505365-66, at FMSE 505365; Fannie Mae Corporate Governance Benchmarking Project: Issues for Consideration dated Aug. 6, 2002, FMSE 12859-87.

[34] See Minutes of the Meeting of the Board of Directors of Fannie Mae, January 21, 2003, FMSE 504202-40, at FMSE 504220-21. See also Draft Working Scorecard for Benchmarking Project, January 16, 2003, FMSE 13512-16.

[35] E-mail chain from Sampath Rajappa to Jamie Gorelick with copies to Franklin Raines, Timothy Howard, Leanne Spencer, et al, "Re: Audit Committee Requirements," February 12, 2001; Mr. Rajappa submits the five guiding principles for Audit Committee best practices from the SEC's chief accountant, including "robust oversight" of management and diligent and knowledgeable committee membership, FMSE-KD 016986-88, at 016987.

[36] Title 12 C.F.R. 1710.15(b(2)

[37] Paul Weiss memorandum of interview with Thomas Gerrity, February 28, 2006, FM SRC OFHEO 00713198-218, at 00713203.

[38] OFHEO Interview, Thomas Gerrity, February 28, 2006, p. 87.

[39] OFHEO Interview, Sampath Rajappa, February 23, 2006, p. 13.

[40] See Sampath Rajappa's address to Audit Group on "what we can do to help achieve $6.46 EPS," FM SRC OFHEO 00142373-74.

[41] See Ernst and Young report, "Fannie Mae Office of Auditing, Internal Audit Transformation – Recommendations," June 30, 2005, FMSE 510811 - 510833.

[42] Id., Also see "Report to the Board Compensation Committee on Appropriate Corporation Structure and Incentives for Fannie Mae Management," February 23, 2005, which recommended that bonus compensation for the head of Internal Audit should not be tied to earnings, FMSE-EC 008826 - 008992, at 909 and 947.

[43] Report of National Commission on Fraudulent Financial Reporting, (Treadway Commission), p.11.

[44] Paul Weiss memorandum of interview with Sampath Rajappa, January 19, 2005, FM SRC OFHEO 00227300-306 at 302. That page of that memorandum is the source for this and the following paragraph.

[45] E-mail from Timothy Howard to Leanne Spencer, "FW: Fannie Scolded for Obsolete Accounting Systems," March 3, 2004, OFH-FNM00126929. In that e-mail, Mr. Howard informed Ms. Spencer that he had made it "blisteringly clear" to Mr. Rajappa that the latter was to run all Audit Committee issues by him before going to the Audit Committee Chair.

[46] Paul Weiss memorandum of interview with Sampath Rajappa, January 19, 2005, FM SRC OFHEO 00227300-306 at 302.

[47] OFHEO Interview, Thomas Gerrity, February 28, 2006, p. 46.

[48] OFHEO Interview, Thomas Gerrity, February 28, 2006, p. 101.

[49] OFHEO Interview, Thomas Gerrity, February 28, 2006 , p.101

[50] See Audit Committee Certification of FAS 133, FMSE 014893, FMSE 015316, FMSE 016125.

[51] OFHEO Interview, Sampath Rajappa, June 17, 2004, pp. 14-16.
[52] OFHEO Interview, Sampath Rajappa, June 17, 2004, pp. 14-16.
[53] OFHEO Interview, Sampath Rajappa, February 23, 2006, p. 85.
[54] Mr. Gerrity apparently never read Fannie Mae's "Purchase Premium and Discount Amortization Policy" as he had no recollection of seeing the written policy and only learned of the major provisions "in the last year or so." OFHEO Interview, Thomas Gerrity, March 14, 2006, p. 77.
[55] 12 C.F.R. 1710.15(b)(4).
[56] Paul Weiss memorandum of interview with Thomas Gerrity, February 21, 2005, FM SRC OFHEO 00713198-3218.
[57] OFHEO Interview, Thomas Gerrity, March 14, 2006, p. 34.
[58] $108.1 million divided by 1,037 million shares outstanding resulted in an EPS impact of 10.5¢.
[59] See Fannie Mae Fourth Quarter Completion Memo, December 31, 1998, KPMG-OFHEO-063945.
[60] See Fannie Mae Annual Report 1998, p. 44.
[61] Mr. Gerrity stated that he did not even believe that loan loss reserves were considered "critical accounting policies" at Fannie Mae. OFHEO Interview, Thomas Gerrity, February 28, 2006, p. 75.
[62] See Notes for January 19, 1999, Board of Directors Meeting, FM SRC OFHEO 00310536-41 at FM SRC OFHEO 00310536-39.
[63] See Notes for January 14, 1999, Conference Call, p.4, FM SRC OFHEO 034016 - 19.
[64] There is significant similarity between Ms. Spencer's scheduled presentation, including a modified handwritten script, and the Audit Committee Minutes of February 20, 2001, concerning credit losses, charge-offs, and recoveries. See minutes at FMSE 014869-76 and Ms. Spencer's notes within The Year in Review Presentation, FMSE 367220-36, at FMSE 367227-28.
[65] See Audit Committee Minutes, February 19, 2002, p. 3 FMSE 015292.
[66] OFHEO Interview, Sampath Rajappa, June 17, 2004, p. 15.
[67] Id.
[68] OFHEO Interview, Thomas Gerrity, February 28, 2006, pp. 27-28.
[69] See Fannie Mae Office of Auditing Audit Manual at FNM 00100541 at p.C-3.2-3.3.
[70] OFHEO Interview, Sampath Rajappa, February 23, 2006, pp. 81-82; Mr. Gerrity confirmed that the Audit Committee did not review the yellow audits. OFHEO Interview, Thomas Gerrity, February 28, 2006, p. 33.
[71] OFHEO Interview, Ann Eilers, July 23, 2004, p. 242. Since the Audit Committee only received reports on 'red' audits, changing the color to "yellow" by promising timely resolution was an easy means to avoid Audit Committee scrutiny.
[72] Under SAS 89, the external auditor is ". . .required to inform the audit committee about uncorrected misstatements aggregated by the auditor during the current engagement and pertaining to the latest period presented that were determined by management to be immaterial, both individually and in the aggregate, to the financial statements taken as a whole. . ." Also See AICPA Practice Alert 94-1: Dealing With Audit Differences, February 1994.
[73] OFHEO Interview, Julie Theobald, February 16, 2005, pp. 47-48.
[74] Paul Weiss Memorandum of Interview with Thomas Gerrity, March 14, 2006, p. 29.

[75] Mr. Gerrity was unaware that there was a "cliff" built into the AIP targets and, as a result, had no understanding of the significance of the audit difference. OFHEO Interview, Thomas Gerrity, March 14, 2006, p. 63.

[76] Audit Committee Minutes, April 18, 2000, p. 5, FMSE 014459-65.

[77] Board Meeting Minutes, February 20, 2001, pp. 9-10 FMSE 004788-800.

[78] Letter from Timothy Howard to Edmund Jenkins, April 12, 1999, p. 2 FMSE-SP 074288-90.

[79] See 1999 self-assessment by Jonathan Boyles, p. 2, FMSE 698829-33.

[80] Quarterly report Q&A excerpt FMSE 417002.

[81] The Sarbanes-Oxley Act, 107 Pub. L. No. 204, 116 Stat. 745, July 30, 2002.

[82] The November 17, 2003, meeting is also the meeting that contained a presentation by Ms. Spencer regarding the critical accounting policy for FAS 91. See Audit Committee Meeting Minutes at FMSE 504796-805.

[83] OFHEO Interview, Timothy Howard, August 5, 2004, p. 7.

[84] E-mails between Jill Blickstein and Rebecca Senhauser, August 12, 2004, FM SRC OFHEO 00713573-74.

[85] E-mail from Daniel Mudd to Franklin Raines with copies to Timothy Howard, Thomas Donilon and Jill Blickstein, August 10, 2004, FMSE-E KD0048713.

[86] Memorandum from Kathryn Rock to Robert Levin, "Management's 2004 Assessment of Internal Control over Financial Reporting," August 12, 2005, FMSE 519599-616, at 606, where PricewaterhouseCoopers (PWC) identified hundreds of potential control problems that the Office of Auditing had not identified in 2004.

[87] 2003 Fannie Mae Audit Committee Charter. FMSE 504223 – 228.

[88] See Head Count Request for 3 FTE in 2003, FMSE-IR 284780-781, and Office of Auditing and KPMG Joint Audit Plan 2004.

[89] See Audit Committee Meeting Minutes, April 19, 2004, pp. 2-3, FMSE-SP 082060 - 68.

[90] OFHEO Interview, Thomas Gerrity, March 14, 2006, p. 34.

[91] Fannie Mae Notice of Annual Meeting of Shareholders, 1998; Fannie Mae Notice of Annual Meeting of Shareholders, March 29, 1999; Fannie Mae Notice of Annual Meeting of Shareholders, March 27, 2000; Fannie Mae Notice of Annual Meeting of Shareholders, April 2, 2001; Fannie Mae Notice of Annual Meeting of Shareholders, April 2, 2002; Fannie Mae Notice of Annual Meeting of Shareholders, April 14, 2003; Fannie Mae Notice of Annual Meeting of Shareholders, April 14, 2003; Fannie Mae Notice of Annual Meeting of Shareholders, April 23, 2004. Other Fees include fees related to REMIC pricing, closing and validation services, due diligence on multifamily loans, assistance on regulatory matters, and tax services.

[92] KPMG Peat Marwick Trend Analysis Economic Indicators and Audit Fees, KPMG-OFHEO-175801; Fannie Mae presentation, "Discussion of the 1998 Audit," February 16, 1999, p. 7, FMSE 014347-014356 at 353.

[93] Letter from KPMG to the Audit Committee, February 9, 2000, FMSE 014701.

[94] Between 1998 and 2004, the Enterprise implemented, among others, the following accounting statements, guidelines, and pronouncements: FAS 133 Accounting for Derivative Instruments and Hedging Activities; FAS 140 Accounting for Transfers and Services of Financial assets and Extinguishment of Liabilities-a Replacement of FASB Statement 125; FAS 148 Accounting for Stock-Based Compensation Transition and

Disclosure – An Amendment to FASB Statement 123; FAS 149 Amendment of Statement 133; FAS 150 Accounting for Certain Financial Instruments with Characteristics of Both Liabilities and Equity; Emerging Issues Task Force Issue 99-20 Recognition of Interest Income and Impairment on Purchas and Retained Beneficial Interest in Securitized Financial Assets; Statement of Position 01-0 Accounting for certain Entities (including Entities with Trade Receivables) That Lend To or Finance the Activities of Others; FIN 45 Guarantor Accounting and Disclosure Requirements for Guarantees, Including Indirect Guarantees of Indebtedness of Others – An Interpretation of FASB Statements N5, 57, and 107 and Rescission of FASB Interpretation No. 34; and Consolidation of Variable Interest Entities – An Interpretation of ARB No. 51.

[95] 12 CFR §§ 1710.12(c)(2), 1720 and Appendix A to Part 1720 – Policy Guidance-Minimum Safety and Soundness Requirements.

[96] See also Schwartz, B. and Goodman, A. L., "Corporate Governance: Law and Practice, Chapter 10: The Compensation Committee," § 10.01 (2005) (Corporate Governance Law & Practice). The 1992 adoption of federal securities regulations requiring proxy statement disclosures about executive compensation and the enactment in 1993 of section 162(m) of the Internal Revenue Code, which eliminated the corporate income tax deduction for compensation over $1million paid to the CEO and other four most highly compensated executive officers (the so-called "Named Executive Officers"), also have substantively affected the responsibilities of compensation committees.

[97] Compensation Committee Charter, set forth by resolution in the Meeting Minutes of the Nominating and Corporate Governance Committee, dated January 20, 2003. See FMSE 505379, 505390-392.

[98] See 12 U.S.C. § 4518 and 12 U.S.C. § 1723a(d)(2), respectively.

[99] 12 U.S.C. § 1723a(d)(2). As discussed in prior chapters, for its performance metric, Fannie Mae elected to use an internally derived accounting target, EPS, which is highly subject to manipulation by executive management.

[100] 12 CFR § 1710.12(c)(2). As stated previously in this chapter, as a listed company, Fannie Mae is subject to the NYSE listing standards.

[101] See Corporate Governance Law & Practice, at §10.02. At the same time, new best practice guidelines were published by a number of influential organizations.

[102] Id. at §10.02.

[103] Id. at §10.04.

[104] Id. The NYSE rule mandates the compensation committee take direct responsibility ("either as a committee or directly with other independent directors") only for CEO compensation; there is no law, regulation or listing rule requiring a listed company's compensation committee be directly responsible for the compensation of anyone other than the CEO. But because compensation plans are designed around the application of IRC §162(m) to the Named Executive Officers, and because plans designed to comply with that provision's exception for performance-based compensation are normally administered by the compensation committee, it is the practice in many companies to have the compensation committee review and approve the overall compensation (i.e., base salary and performance-based incentive plan awards) for all Named Executive Officers.

[105] Id.

[106] Id. In its commentary to the 2003 corporate governance rules, the NYSE suggested that the compensation committee charter also address committee member qualifications; committee member appointment and removal; committee structure and operations (including authority to delegate to subcommittees); and committee reporting to the board. The Compensation Committee charter does not specifically address these issues, other than to state the committee shall make regular reports to the Board on its activities.

[107] Id.

[108] See, Compensation Committee Charter 1998, 2003 and 2005, FMSE-EC 040020-040021, FMSE-EC 019639 and *http://www.fanniemae.com/ governance/committees/ compensation/charter.jhtml?p=Corporate+Governance&s=Board+Committees&t=Compensation&q=Charter, respectively.*

[109] Id.

[110] Lorrie Rudin, Director for Executive Compensation and Benefits, was the custodian of this document. FMSE-EC 015740 – 015745 at EC 015740.

[111] See memorandum from Stasia Kelly to Vincent Mai, "The 'Script' for the July 17, 1998 Compensation Committee Meeting," July 15, 1998, FMSE EC 055725 – 055732. See also memorandum from Stasia Kelly and Thomas Nides to Vincent Mai, "'Script' for the Compensation Committee Meeting of November 16," November 12, 1998, FMSE EC 055749 – 055759; memorandum from Thomas Donilon and Tom Nides to Vincent Mai, "'Script' for Compensation Committee Meeting of January 18," January 14, 2000, FMSE-E EC0071086-0071095; memorandum from Thomas Nides to Vincent Mai, "The 'Script' for the May 18, 2000 Compensation Committee Meeting," May 16, 2000, FMSE-E EC0071134-0071135.

[112] A request by Joe Pickett to chair the January 2002 Committee Meeting resulted in a same day notice to senior Fannie Mae management. Thomas Donilon wrote in an e-mail to Franklin Raines, Timothy Howard and Daniel Mudd: "Joe Pickett called to day to say he is willing to act as acting chair of the comp committee at the January meeting. He said that he has both the time and the interest. Dan, if this is the way we want to go we'll have to get a briefing scheduled for Joe." E-mail from Thomas Donilon to Franklin Raines, Timothy Howard and Daniel Mudd, "Misc.," December 12, 2002, FMSE E EC0090803.

[113] Mr. Raines was a member of the Board of Directors but not of the Compensation Committee. "With FDR Edits- (March 28, 2003) Compensation Committee Report on Executive Compensation." Attachment to an e-mail from Jill Blickstein to Kathy Gallo, March 28, 2003, included in an e-mail chain from Iris Aberbach to Thomas Donilon, "[Fwd. Re: [Fwd. Compensation Committee Report on Executive," April 4, 2003. FMSE-E EC0013686-0013691.

[114] Johnson Associates was viewed as the management consultant for executive compensation purposes. FMSE-E EC0013760.

[115] Letter from Anne Mulcahy to Kathy Gallo, FMSE EC 010102 – 101003.

[116] Letter from Kathy Gallo to Anne Mulcahy, September 2, 2003. FMSE-EC 010106 – EC010108 at FMSE EC 010106. In her letter, Ms. Gallo incorrectly identifies Brian Foley of Foley and Company as an employee of Fred Cook and Company. In a previous undated letter to Ms. Mulcahy, Ms. Gallo indicated that she and Christine Wolf, Vice President for Compensation Benefits, had interviewed Jeffrey Kanter of Fred Cook and

Company and Brian Foley of Brian Foley and Company and recommended that the Compensation Committee meet with Mr. Kanter, of Fred Cook and Company, but not Mr. Foley. FM SRC OFHEO 01027533-534.

[117] "Briefing for Compensation Committee: The Role of the Compensation Committee in the OFHEO/Fannie Mae Agreement," October 19, 2004, p. 4, FMSE-KD 060250.

[118] "When Tim Howard and I searched for our new comp expert, Roger was a close second to our choice of Alan Johnson." Letter from Kathy Gallo to Anne Mulcahy, September 2, 2003, FMSE-EC 010106 – EC010108 at FMSE EC 010106.

[119] E-mail from Monica Medina to Thomas Donilon, "Re: Comp Call," September 23, 2003, FMSE E EC0013670.

[120] 2001 Fannie Mae Annual Report, p. 7.

[121] As described in Chapter VII, in October 1998 KPMG met with the Audit Committee Chairman, Vincent Mai, to discuss, among other things, a recent public speech made the Chairman of SEC and how the SEC had been focusing on earnings management issues.

[122] Mid-Year Corporate Performance Assessment, dated July 2000 and distributed to Board members by Thomas Donilon on July 13, 2000, in preparation for the July 2000 Board of Directors Strategic Review. FMSE 003813.

[123] Fannie Mae Board of Directors Strategic Review, New York, July 16, 2002. FMSE 017408-017426.

[124] OFHEO Interview, Thomas Gerrity, March 14, 2006, p. 93.

[125] OFHEO Interview, Thomas Gerrity, March 14, 2006, p. 99.

[126] Presentation by Timothy Howard to Fannie Mae Board of Directors Strategic Retreat, "Corporate Risk Management Objectives," July 14 & 15, 2003, FMSE 017263-74 at 71;

[127] OFHEO Interview, Stephen Ashley, April 20, 2006, at p. 96-98.

[128] 2003 Corporate Objectives Progress Report.

[129] Fannie Mae Notice of Annual Meeting of Shareholders, 1998; Fannie Mae Notice of Annual Meeting of Shareholders, March 29, 1999; Fannie Mae Notice of Annual Meeting of Shareholders, March 27, 2000; Fannie Mae Notice of Annual Meeting of Shareholders, April 2, 2001; Fannie Mae Notice of Annual Meeting of Shareholders, April 2, 2002; Fannie Mae Notice of Annual Meeting of Shareholders, April 14, 2003; Fannie Mae Notice of Annual Meeting of Shareholders, April 14, 2003; Fannie Mae Notice of Annual Meeting of Shareholders, April 23, 2004.

[130] Fannie Mae Bylaws Article 4, Section 4.08.

[131] Memorandum from Anthony Marra to Thomas Donilon, Ann Kappler, Monica Medina, and Iris Aberbach, "Corporate Governance," November, 2003, FMSE-KD 035147-155 at 148. Minutes of the Nominating and Corporate Governance Committee, July 14, 2004, FMSE 505442-43.

[132] Email from Monica Medina to Michael Useem of the Wharton School of Business, University of Pennsylvania, "draft project description," June 11, 2004, FMSE-KD 035146.

[133] Id.

[134] Paul Weiss Memorandum of interview with Donald Marron, February 8, 2006, FM SRC OFHEO 01561804, p. 11.

[135] The Business Roundtable notes that "[e]ffective directors maintain an attitude of constructive skepticism; they ask incisive, probing questions and require accurate, honest answers; they act with integrity and diligence; and they demonstrate a commitment to the corporation, its business plans and long-term shareholder value." Business Roundtable, "Principles of Corporate Governance 2005," p. 7.

[136] OFHEO Interview, Timothy Howard, August 5, 2004, p. 7. "I also serve informally as the company's chief risk officer."

[137] OFHEO Interview, Sampath Rajappa, February 23, 2005, at page 56.

[138] Paul Weiss Interview with Kenneth Duberstein, November 17, 2005 FM SRC OFHEO 1377890 – 1377898 at 93.

[139] OFHEO Interview, Stephen Ashley April 20, 2006, p. 54-56.

[140] OFHEO Interview of Monica Medina, December 14, 2005, p. 118. Memorandum from Gibson, Dunn & Crutcher dated May 2004, FMSE-KD 078793.

[141] OFHEO Interview of Thomas Donilon April 24, 2006, p. 191 to 205.

[142] www.fanniemaefoundation.org

[143] The Foundation contribution data was taken from the Fannie Mae Foundation Web site in March 2006.

[144] Freddie Mac Press Release, January 22, 2003, available at http://www.freddiemac.com/news/archives/investors/2003/4Q02.html.

[145] Id.

[146] Baker Botts L.L.P. report entitled, Report to the Board of Directors of the Federal Home Loan Mortgage Corporation, Internal Investigation of Certain Accounting Matters-December 10, 2003 – July 21, 2003, July 22, 2003.

[147] Minutes of the Meeting of the Board of Directors of Fannie Mae, June 9, 2003. FMSE 010214.

[148] Minutes of the Meeting of the Board of Directors of Fannie Mae, June 13, 2003. FMSE 010218.

[149] Minutes of the Meeting of the Board of Directors of Fannie Mae, June 27, 2003. FMSE 010995.

[150] Kathleen Day, "A Reluctant Coming to Grips at Freddie Mac: Auditors and Financial Restatements Forced the Board to Reassess its Longtime Executives," The Washington Post, July 10, 2003.

[151] Presentation by Timothy Howard, "Corporate Risk Management Objectives," July 14 & 15, 2003, FMSE 017263.

[152] David S. Hilzenrath and Kathleen Day, "Freddie Was Told it Lacked Accounting Expertise," The Washington Post, July 18, 2003.

[153] Baker Botts L.L.P. report entitled, "Report to the Board of Directors of the Federal Home Loan Mortgage Corporation, Internal Investigation of Certain Accounting Matters-December 10, 2003 – July 21, 2003," July 22, 2003.

[154] OFHEO Interview, Thomas Gerrity, March 14, 2006, p. 120.

[155] Memorandum from Thomas Donilon to the Board of Directors, "The Freddie Mac Report," July 25, 2003, FM SRC M-OFHEO 00020830-842.

[156] OFHEO Interview, Stephen Ashley, April 20, 2006, p. 111.

[157] Minutes of the Meeting of the Board of Directors of Fannie Mae, January 23, 2004, FMSE 504353-90 at 504375.

[158] Several of Fannie Mae's accounting policies include critical accounting estimates. (In accordance with GAAP, such estimates are considered critical if (1) they require significant management judgments and assumptions about uncertain matters, and (2) the use of a different approach to the estimate or underlying assumption would have a material effect on reported results of operations or financial condition.) Those include Fannie Mae's accounting policies for FAS 91, for derivative instruments and hedging activities, for determining the adequacy of the allowance for loan losses, for estimating the time value of purchased options, and for assessing other-than-temporary impairment. Those accounting policies, along with others, are summarized in the "Notes to Financial Statements" of the Enterprise's Form 10-K filed with the SEC as "Significant Accounting Policies," Fannie Mae 2003 10-K, p. 126 – 135.

[159] SEC 17 CFR Parts 228, 229, 249 and 274, RIN 3235-A175; 12 C.F.R. 1710.15(b)(6).

[160] 12 C.F.R. 1710.15(b)(6).

[161] Gulf Federal Savings and Loan Association v. Federal Home Loan Bank Board, 651 F.2d 259, 264 (1981).

X. Remedial Actions and Recommendations

During the period of the special examination, OFHEO has directed Fannie Mae to take a number of actions, both as a result of the special examination and as part of the agency's continuous supervisory program. Those steps have remedied deficiencies, aimed to reduce the recurrence of improper conduct, and sought to enhance the safe and sound operation of the Enterprise going forward. This chapter reviews OFHEO's remedial actions to date and presents recommendations by OFHEO staff based on the special examination.

Remedial Actions to Date

This section summarizes the significant changes put in motion by a written agreement between OFHEO and Fannie Mae executed on September 27, 2004; a Supplemental Agreement executed on March 7, 2005; and other actions by the agency. OFHEO continues its examination and oversight to assure that those commitments have firm deadlines for completion and are completed.

Capital

In the September 2004 Agreement, OFHEO directed Fannie Mae to maintain an additional 30 percent of capital above the minimum capital requirement to compensate for the additional risk and challenges facing the Enterprise. OFHEO directed that Fannie Mae submit for approval a plan to manage the enhanced capital requirements. OFHEO directed that the capital plan include Fannie Mae's strategy to preserve and maintain capital levels at the minimum capital requirement, plus 30 percent to address costs and risks associated with problems facing the Enterprise, and projections for growth and capital requirements based upon a detailed analysis of Fannie Mae's assets, liabilities, earnings, fixed assets, and off-balance sheet activities. In addition, the agreement requires the Enterprise to include contingency plans that identify alternative methods for appropriately achieving and maintaining the necessary capital levels should the primary methods prove to be insufficient, an analysis of proposed or undertaken corporate actions, and the impact of those actions upon Fannie Mae's ability maintain the appropriate capital levels.

OFHEO also directed Fannie Mae to obtain prior written permission from OFHEO before undertaking certain corporate actions. Those actions include engaging in any payment to:

- Repurchase, redeem, retire or otherwise acquire any of its shares, including share repurchases,
- Call any preferred stock,
- Pay any preferred stock dividends above the stated contractual rates, and
- Pay capital stock dividends in excess of the prior quarter's dividend (that requirement is eased upon Fannie Mae achieving the required capital levels).

OFHEO directed that Fannie Mae inform the agency of any other significant action that is likely to impair the ability of the Enterprise to manage its capital position to the required capital surplus levels.

Further, OFHEO directed that Fannie Mae continue to submit to OFHEO month-end minimum capital reports, no later than 30 days after the end of each month. Those reports will be reconciled to the general ledger and will continue to contain an official declaration of their accuracy. Additionally, Fannie Mae submits to OFHEO weekly management reports and projections detailing growth and other criteria that impact the maintenance of the capital surplus. OFHEO monitors and validates those reports.

On February 17, 2005, OFHEO approved a remedial capital restoration plan authorized by the Board of Directors of Fannie Mae on February 10, 2005. OFHEO oversees and monitors the Fannie Mae capital position on a weekly basis to ensure compliance. The Enterprise will keep the enhanced capital position until the Director of OFHEO releases or modifies the requirement based upon satisfactory resolution of accounting and internal control issues that are the subject of OFHEO examination.

As a result of those directives, Fannie Mae has taken significant actions to increase its capital. Those actions included the issuance of $5 billion in preferred stock,[1] a reduction in the Enterprise's common stock dividend,[2] and a reduction in its on-balance sheet assets.[3]

Corporate Governance

OFHEO directed the Board of Directors to separate the Chairman of the Board and the Chief Executive Officer positions and to provide to OFHEO the new written requirements for the Chief Executive Officer and the Chief Financial Officer. OFHEO also directed the Board to cause to be conducted a review of committee structures, resources, reporting requirements, procedures, and quality of financial disclosures, as well as any potential changes to management and internal systems to meet the Board's oversight responsibilities.

OFHEO has directed Fannie Mae to create a new Office of Compliance and Ethics that reports to the Chief Executive Officer and independently to the Compliance Committee. The office is directed by an officer that has no other duties at Fannie Mae and who operates independently, including with regard to communication with the Board and OFHEO, particularly on matters of wrongdoing. The office will have a separate internal investigative function that is adequately staffed and resourced to perform investigations regarding internal complaints, whistleblower reports, ethics matters, and related topics. That investigative function will report on its findings to OFHEO in a prompt manner. The head of the office cannot be removed without Board approval .

OFHEO directed the Board to establish a Compliance Committee, staffed with a minimum of three independent members of the Board. The Committee monitors and coordinates compliance with the September 2004 agreement and the March 2005 Supplemental Agreement and meets with OFHEO representatives regarding compliance with those agreements. OFHEO directed that the Board or the Compliance Committee establish an appropriate tracking system in consultation with OFHEO to allow for the monthly reporting of material events and the monitoring of the implementation of and progress under the agreements.

OFHEO directed the Board to cause an external review to gather recommended changes to the organizational structures, responsibilities, and personnel required to comply with law and regulation, particularly for regulatory reporting and data processing services. The Board shall consult with, and report to, OFHEO on any proposed changes.

OFHEO directed that the Board establish a program for no less than annual briefings to the Board and senior management on legal and regulatory compliance requirements applicable to Fannie Mae. The briefings are to include reviewing any Enterprise policies and practices that inhibit the effective compliance with those requirements.

OFHEO revised its corporate governance regulation in 2005 to address matters raised in its special examinations of Freddie Mac and Fannie Mae and developments in corporate governance practices. Additional duties and requirements for the Board and senior management were added to that regulation, including a requirement to establish compliance and risk management programs.

OFHEO directed the Board to create a procedure, approved by OFHEO, for the General Counsel of Fannie Mae to report directly to the Board any information relating to actual or possible misconduct by an Executive Officer or member of the Board, or the possibility of significant misconduct by an employee, while keeping counsel's professional and ethical duties to Fannie Mae. The procedure will call for the Board to notify OFHEO of the substance of the allegations, with the Board's comments, in a timely manner. Additionally, if the Board fails to notify OFHEO, the General Counsel will notify OFHEO of the information submitted to the Board.

Organization

OFHEO directed Fannie Mae to create a Chief Risk Officer position and required more direct reporting to the Board and OFHEO by that officer and others charged with audit and audit-like functions. OFHEO also directed a review that led to a stronger policy governing risk tolerance and a revision and enhancement of the Enterprise's internal audit function.

OFHEO directed the Board to separate the function of business planning and forecasting from the Controller's function. Additionally, the Board was directed to separate the modeling and accounting functions.

OFHEO directed the Board to report to OFHEO on any planned revisions in the accounting area that would alter reporting lines, the independence of a function to evaluate models employed in accounting, or the role of the external auditor and internal audit procedures; or add new positions to remedy any determined weaknesses.

OFHEO directed the Board to assure the independence of the internal auditor, including the ability of the internal auditor to report directly to the Audit Committee or the Board. OFHEO directed that the Audit Committee have at least one person with sufficient technical expertise to understand the implications of accounting policies for the Enterprise's financial statements.

OFHEO directed that the Board cause an independent review of organizational, structural, staffing, and control issues, focusing on but not limited to the Chief Financial Officer, controller, accounting, audit, financial reporting, business planning and forecasting, modeling, and financial standards functions. OFHEO directed this review in order to enhance accounting and controls and foster a culture of adherence to proper corporate policies and legal and other requirements. Subsequently, Fannie Mae management began a review that addressed the following topics:

- Lines of reporting,
- Independence of functions,
- Segregation of duties,
- Alignment of functions,
- Roles and responsibilities,
- Staff qualifications,
- Key person dependencies, and
- Adequacy of resources.

OFHEO has met frequently and formally with management of Fannie Mae to assess the status of that review. As a result of the review, management has effected significant changes in the organizational structure of the Enterprise. OFHEO will continue to monitor the effectiveness of those changes.

Internal Controls

OFHEO directed Fannie Mae to restate inappropriate past financial statements, meeting all applicable legal and regulatory requirements, including having the new financial statements reaudited by the Enterprise's new external auditor. OFHEO also directed the Board to cause a review of internal controls relating to accounting, staffing, resources, quality, and routine provision of information to senior management and the Board, and of the effectiveness of the corporate code of conduct, and to report the results back to OFHEO. The review scope also includes any planned revisions to avoid actions that do not support appropriate corporate goals and legal requirements.

OFHEO directed the Board to enlist independent outside counsel to conduct a comprehensive review of Fannie Mae's accounting policies and practices to ensure that the policies and practices are in compliance with applicable laws and regulations. The outside counsel reports directly to the Board and has full access to the Enterprise's staff and resources, including records and e-mail. The outside counsel has full access to the company's books and records related to GAAP compliance including, but not limited to, any adjustments made for system/methodology conversion, any "on-top" adjustments, and any other adjustments. OFHEO directed that the agency have full access to all work conducted by the outside counsel, independent of the Enterprise or the Board.

OFHEO directed that Fannie Mae cease inappropriate hedge accounting. The agency also directed the Enterprise to make necessary adjustments to its accounting for derivatives to bring that accounting into compliance with GAAP.

OFHEO directed Fannie Mae to supply a formal, comprehensive summary of existing methods and practices to manage actively the calculation of amortization. OFHEO also directed Fannie Mae to implement an appropriate policy for SFAS 91 accounting that includes amortization of deferred price adjustments in a manner that requires the Enterprise to correctly book the entire amount of the modeled catch-up provision on a quarterly basis.

OFHEO directed the Board to cause a review of the procedures regarding preparing, revising, validating, authorizing, and recording of journal entries and to report back to OFHEO with the results of that review, including a description of how the deficiencies will be corrected. OFHEO also directed the Board to direct management to develop and implement appropriate written policies and procedures for journal entries. Those policies and procedures must include, but are not limited to:

- Prohibition of employees from falsifying signatures in journal entries as well as signing such entries without proper authorization,
- Requirements that any preparer of a journal entry understand the purpose for which the entry is made,
- Requirements that journal entry reviewers and approvers determine that an entry is valid and appropriate,
- Requirements that journal entries be supported with appropriate documentation, and
- Requirements that journal entries are independently reviewed by an authorized person other than the preparer.

OFHEO directed the Board to direct management to develop and implement a plan to address the deficiencies in the accounting systems for Fannie Mae's portfolio. The plan includes, at a minimum, the ability to:

- Automate marking the mortgage-backed securities portfolio to market, to the degree practicable;
- Properly account for mortgage revenue bonds;
- Properly account for dollar roll transactions; and
- Properly account for interest-only strips pursuant to EITF 99-20. Staff

OFHEO directed a complete review of staffing for skills, past performance, and role in a revised corporate structure and reorganization of accounting. Significant personnel changes have been made. By year end 2005, over 35 percent of officers at or above the senior vice president level have separated or announced separation from Fannie Mae.

OFHEO directed the Board to consult with OFHEO on matters relating to organization and staffing pursuant to the September 2004 Agreement and the March 2005 Supplemental Agreement. The Board directed management to make changes expeditiously, particularly regarding disciplinary or other actions to individuals, and to address concerns raised by OFHEO in the course of its examination of the matters under review and covered by those agreements.

OHFEO directed that Mr. Franklin Raines and Mr. Timothy Howard not be engaged, regardless of compensation arrangements, to provide any service to Fannie Mae subsequent to their separation from the Enterprise. Fannie Mae may apply to OFHEO for the services of any employees separated in connection with the special examination and the agreements.

Recommendations

Based on the special examination of Fannie Mae, OFHEO's staff recommends to the Director that the following actions be taken to enhance the goal of maintaining the safety and soundness of the Enterprise.

1. Fannie Mae should be subject to penalties and fines consistent with the findings of this report.
2. Fannie Mae must meet all of its commitments for remediation and do so with an emphasis on implementation—with dates certain—of plans already presented to OFHEO.
3. Fannie Mae must maintain a capital surplus until the Director determines a change in the surplus amount is warranted.
4. Fannie Mae must continue to use independent consultants acceptable to the Director to validate and assure compliance with requirements. Cyclical targeted exams by independent consultants, at least every two years, are needed to assure systems and practices are being implemented properly.
5. Fannie Mae must develop new structures and operational plans for its Board of Directors related to Board reporting, maintenance of minutes, and other changes that will enhance Board oversight of the Enterprise's management.
6. Fannie Mae must review OFHEO's report to determine additional steps to take to improve its controls, accounting systems, risk management practices and systems, external relations program, data quality, and corporate culture. Once OFHEO has approved the Enterprise's plans, an emphasis must be placed on implementation of those plans.
7. Fannie Mae must undertake a review of individuals currently with the Enterprise that are mentioned in OFHEO's report and provide OFHEO a report as to conclusions regarding terminations, transfers, or other remedial steps (such as disgorgement, restitution, or alteration of benefits) in cases of misconduct.
8. Fannie Mae must assure that departments are fully and appropriately staffed with skilled professionals who have available regular training opportunities in financial services industry standards.
9. Due to Fannie Mae's current operational and internal control deficiencies and other risks, the Enterprise's growth should be limited.
10. OFHEO should continue to develop its program of regulatory infrastructure to add additional rules and regulations that enhance the transparency of its supervision of the Enterprises. With the end of the special examination, OFHEO staff should be directed to address additional items raised during the preparation of this report as part of the regular examination program.

11. OFHEO should continue to support legislation to provide the powers essential to meeting its mission of assuring safe and sound operations at the Enterprises.
12. Matters identified in this report should be referred to OFHEO's Office of the General Counsel for determination of enforcement actions that the Director may wish to consider.
13. Matters identified for remediation by Fannie Mae should be considered by the Director for application to both Enterprises.

Appendix Positions of Fannie Mae Senior Executives Mentioned in the Report, 1998-2004*

Last Name	First Name	Position(s)
Boyles	Jonathan R.	2004 - SVP, Accounting Policy and Tax 2003 - VP, Financial Standards and Taxes 2001 - VP, Financial Accounting 2000 - Director, Accounting and Audit 1998 - Director, Financial Reporting
Donilon	Thomas E.	2001 - EVP, Law and Policy 2000 - SVP, Secretary, General Counsel
Gallo	Kathy G.	2004 - Senior Advisor 2002 - SVP, Human Resources
Gorelick	Jamie S.	1998 - Vice Chairman
Graham	Brian J.	2004 - SVP, Regional Management & Housing Partnerships 2001 - SVP, Credit Portfolio 1999 - VP, Credit Portfolio Management 1998 - VP, Single Family Business
Howard	John T.	2003 - Vice Chairman and Chief Financial Officer 1998 - EVP and Chief Financial Officer
Hoyes	Louis W.	2000 - EVP, Single Family Mortgage Business 1998 - SVP, Multi-Family Lending and Investment
Johnson	James A.	1999 - Chairman of the Executive Committee of Fannie Mae 1998 - Chairman of the Board and Chief Executive Officer
Kappler	Ann M.	2004 - EVP and General Counsel 2000 - SVP and General Counsel 1999 - SVP and Deputy General Counsel
Knight	Linda K.	2003 - SVP and Treasurer 2002 - EVP, Capital Markets 1998 - SVP and Treasurer
Lawler	Thomas A.	2004 - SVP, Risk Policy 2002 - SVP, Corporate Financial Strategy 1998 - SVP Portfolio Management
Levin	Robert J.	2006 - EVP and Chief Business Officer 2005 - EVP and Chief Financial Officer (Interim) 1999 - EVP, Housing and Community Development 1998 - EVP, Marketing
Marra	Anthony F.	1998 - SVP and Deputy General Counsel

Appendix (Continued)

Last Name	First Name	Position(s)
Marzol	Adolfo	2004 - SVP, Corporate Strategy 2002 - EVP, Finance and Credit 1999 - EVP and Chief Credit Officer 1998 - SVP, Capital Markets
McCormick	Andrew	2002 - SVP, Portfolio Transactions 2001 - SVP, Portfolio Management 1999 - VP, Portfolio Transactions 1998 - VP and Assistant Treasurer
Mudd	Daniel H.	2004 - CEO (Interim)
		2000 - Vice Chairman and Chief Operating Officer
Niculescu	Peter S.	2002 - EVP, Mortgage Portfolio Business 1999 - SVP, Portfolio Strategy
Nides	Thomas R.	2001 - SVP, Corporate Resources 2001 - SVP, Administration 1998 - SVP, Human Resources
Pennewell	Janet L.	2004 - SVP, Financial Reporting and Planning 1999 - VP, Financial Reporting and Planning 1998 - Director, Financial Reporting
Quinn	Michael A.	2004 - SVP, Missions and Markets 1999 - SVP, Single Family Mortgage Business 1998 - SVP, Credit Loss Management
Quinn	William F.	2004 - SVP, Portfolio Strategy 2001 - VP, Risk Mgmt Strategy 2000 - VP, Portfolio Strategy
Raines	Franklin D.	1999 - Chairman of the Board and CEO 1998 - Chairman of the Board and CEO Designate
Rajappa	Sampath	1999 - SVP, Operations Risk 1999 - SVP, Risk Management 1998 - SVP and Controller
Remy	Donald M.	2002 - SVP and Deputy General Counsel 2000 - VP and Deputy General Counsel
Senhauser	Rebecca C.	2004 - SVP, Human Resources 2002 - SVP Regional Management and Housing Partnership 2002 - SVP, Community Engagement 2000 - SVP Regional Management and Housing Partnership 1999 - VP and Assistant to the Chairman
Shontell	Jayne J.	2002 - SVP, Investor Relations 2000 - SVP Corporate Development and Investor Relations 1998 - SVP, Investor Relations
Small	Lawrence M.	1998 - President and Chief Operating Officer
Spencer	Leanne G.	1999 - SVP and Controller 1998 - VP, Financial Reporting

Appendix (Continued)

Last Name	First Name	Position(s)
St. John	Julie G.	2002 - EVP and Chief Information Officer 2001 - EVP and Chief Technology Officer 2000 - SVP, Mortgage Business Technology 1998 - SVP, Guaranty and Franchise
Williams	Michael J.	2000 - President, e-Commerce 2000 - SVP, e-Commerce 1999 - SVP, Customer Technology Services 1998 - SVP, Customer Applications and Technology

* Senior executives include the Chairman and Chief Executive Officer, the Chief Operating Officer, the Chief Financial Officer, executive vice presidents (EVPs), and senior vice presidents (SVPs).

Note: VP stands for Vice President.

References

[1] SEC Form 8-K, filed by Fannie Mae on January 4, 2005.

[2] Fannie Mae News Release ("Fannie Mae Announces Reduction in First Quarter Common Stock Dividend as Company Builds Capital"), January 18, 2005.

[3] See, for example, Fannie Mae Monthly Volume Summary for December 2005, which shows mortgage portfolio balances declining from $904.6 billion at the end of 2004 to $727.2 billion at year-end 2005.

In: Fannie Mae and Freddie Mac...
Editor: James R. Cristie, pp. 325-331
ISBN: 1-60021-356-1

Chapter 2

LIMITING FANNIE MAE'S AND FREDDIE MAC'S PORTFOLIO SIZE*

Eric Weiss

SUMMARY

Federal Reserve Chairman Alan Greenspan and Treasury Secretary John W. Snow recently have urged the 109th Congress to pass legislation to limit the size of Fannie Mae's and Freddie Mac's portfolio to reduce the risk to the federal government and the economy. In 2003, these government-sponsored enterprises (GSEs) combined retained portfolio had risen to $1.6 trillion from $136 billion in 1990.

One of the more controversial aspects of GSE reform is this proposal to limit the size of the investment portfolios, which consist of mortgages and mortgage-backed securities (MBSs) that are subject to several types of financial risk. If these risks are not managed properly, or if market movements turn dramatically against the GSEs, the government may face two unsatisfactory alternatives: either let the GSE go into default and hope that the financial repercussions can be controlled, or step in and assume payments on the GSE debt at a significant cost to taxpayers. Proponents of portfolio limits argue that shrinking portfolio size reduces the likelihood and cost if this choice will ever have to be made. The GSEs and their supporters argue, on the other hand, that the profits generated by the investment portfolios enhance the GSEs' ability to support affordable housing programs and reduce mortgage interest rates.

S. 190 and H.R. 1461 propose many changes in the rules governing the activities and regulation of Fannie Mae and Freddie Mac. S. 190 includes portfolio limits. H.R. 1461 does not. CRS Report RL32795, *Government-Sponsored Enterprises (GSEs): Regulatory Reform Legislation*, by Mark Jickling, compares them in a side-by-side report.

This report analyzes the types of risk that the GSEs pose to the economy, and the advantages and disadvantages of proposals to limit portfolio size. It will be updated as warranted by significant developments.

---

* Excerpted from CRS Report RS22307, Updated October 21, 2005

Recently Federal Reserve Chairman Alan Greenspan[1] and Treasury Secretary John Snow[2] have warned that the mortgage portfolios of Fannie Mae and Freddie Mac (the housing government-sponsored enterprises, or GSEs for short) present a risk to the nation's financial system and federal government.

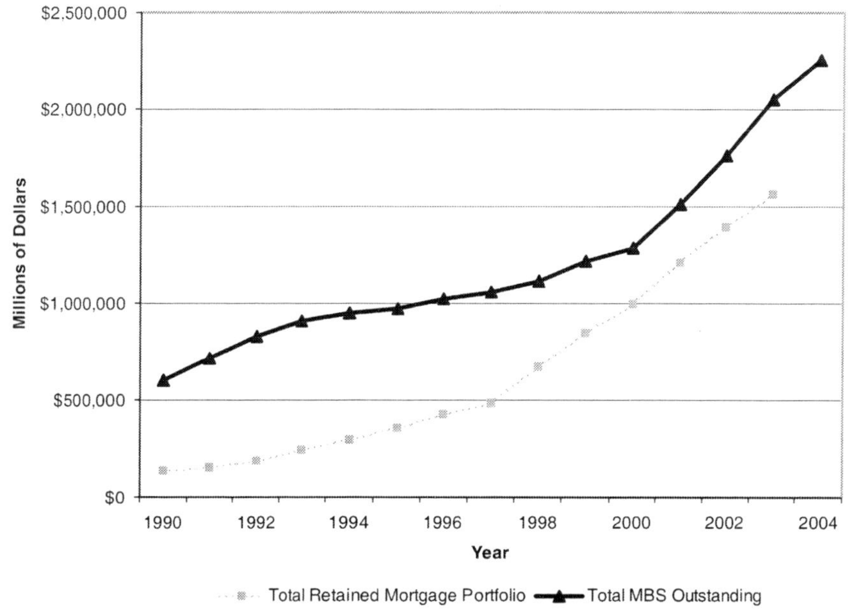

Source: Office of Federal Housing Enterprise Oversight, *2005 Report to Congress*.

Figure 1. Combined MBSs Outstanding and Retained in GSE Portfolios

Fannie Mae and Freddie Mac buy mortgages from the original lenders and package them into mortgage-backed securities (MBSs), which are either sold to investors or held in portfolio by the GSEs themselves.[3] These portfolios are large and have grown rapidly, both in dollar terms and as a percentage of all MBSs outstanding. According to the most current complete information (the end of 2003),[4] Fannie Mae's retained mortgage portfolio was $902 billion[5] and Freddie Mac's was $661 billion.[6] At the end of 2003, their combined portfolios were more than 11 times their size in 1990. Under S. 190, the GSEs could purchase mortgages and MBSs only for the purpose of securitization and sale to others. (Existing portfolios are grandfathered out of this provision.) Figure 1 illustrates the growing size of the combined portfolios and the amount of MBSs outstanding.

Why Are the Portfolios So Large?

The GSEs are designed by their congressional charters to be profit-seeking enterprises. Their portfolios have grown as part of profit maximization. The GSEs have a funding advantage that appears to be unlimited because of the close connection between the GSEs and the federal government. Market forces that limit the size and risk of other financial intermediaries' portfolios do not apply to the GSEs. The GSEs can borrow more money at lower rates. These rates are slightly higher than the comparable Treasuries, but lower than companies (or competitors) with similar financials that lack a federal government connection. Federal Deposit Insurance Corporation staff has estimated that without the implicit guarantee, the GSEs would have credit ratings of AA or A, rather than their current AAA ratings. This reduced cost of borrowing can give the GSEs a profit advantage in any activity they undertake. Relatively little money is required to finance the purchase of mortgages while they are being combined into MBSs. When MBSs are sold, money borrowed can be repaid. Because short-term bonds and loans have lower interest rates than long-term ones, the GSEs use portfolio management techniques to allow them to borrow using short-term bonds to finance long-term mortgages. The key issue is whether the benefits of this portfolio growth to the companies and homeowners exceed their costs to the nation. The main cost is the implied guarantee of GSE debt provided by the federal government without charge. The more GSE debt, the greater the value of the implicit guarantee, the larger the portfolios, and the greater the profit.

There are some benefits to the nation from the GSEs' portfolio. Section 128 of H.R. 1461 would require the GSEs to contribute 5% (3.5% in the first year) of their profits to an affordable housing fund. The higher the profits are, the larger this fund will be. Based on recently available results, CRS has estimated that this contribution will be $380 million in the first year and $540 million in later years.[7]

The GSEs say that large portfolios add liquidity to the secondary mortgage market. Independent analysts do not dispute that a retained portfolio and active trading can help to maintain a liquid market for MBSs and encourage investments in them. (The reason that the portfolios contribute to liquidity is that they allow the GSEs to sell and buy MBS when others are unwilling.) They disagree that the portfolios need to be as large as they are.

The exact distribution of the benefits of the GSEs' status is subject to debate. CBO has concluded that the GSEs retain more than 40% of the subsidy from the implicit guarantee.[8] The larger their portfolios, the more implicitly guaranteed borrowing, and the larger the GSEs' profits. In contrast, the benefit to homeowners is largely independent of portfolio size and is estimated to result in mortgage rates that are lower by 7 to 40 basis points (0.07% to 0.40%).[9] On the maximum single-family loan that Fannie and Freddie may purchase ($359,650) at a currently typical 5.7% rate, this saves the homeowner $0.53 to $3.07 per day, or $195 to $1,120 per year.

GSE Risks

The GSEs share many risks with all business. These risks can affect the companies, stockholders, employees, bondholders, and business partners. The GSEs' risks can also affect the nation's financial system and the economy. There are many ways to analyze these risks. One useful strategy is to look at credit risk, prepayment risk, interest rate risk, and operational risk.

Credit Risk

Credit risk is the risk that the borrowers (mortgagors) will not repay their loan on time — in other words, the risk of delinquency and default. When Fannie and Freddie buy mortgages and combine them into MBSs, they add their guarantee that the loans will be repaid on time. They charge an annual fee of about 20 basis points (0.20%) for this guarantee. Standard & Poor's and most other major observers conclude that because of the different maturity dates, loan-to-value ratios, private mortgage insurance, and geographic diversification, credit risk is not a serious problem.[10]

Prepayment Risk

Prepayment risk is potentially more serious. This is the risk to an investor that a 30-year mortgage will be paid before the full 30 years is concluded. Homeowners prepay for two major reasons: moving, and to obtain more favorable terms. As the cost of refinancing has declined over the last 10 years, the decline in interest rates necessary to justify refinancing (with or without cash out or financing improvements to the home) has been reduced. In recent years, the decline in mortgage rates has caused prepayment rates to increase. This results in uncertainty for lenders and the holders of MBSs.[11] When the GSEs create MBSs and sell them to investors, this is a risk for the investor, not the GSE. When GSEs keep the MBSs, this is a risk to them.

Interest Rate Risk

Interest rate risk comes from financing the MBS portfolios by borrowing money (issuing bonds), and is related to prepayment risk. In 2003, Fannie had $962 billion of debt outstanding; Freddie had $740 billion. Fannie and Freddie use short-term bonds and financial derivatives to finance long-term loans. University of California at Berkeley finance professor Dwight Jaffee has demonstrated how either an increase or decrease in market rates can cause the GSEs' unhedged portfolios to lose value.[12] When interest rates increase, they must roll over their bonds with higher-rate ones. When interest rates decrease, homeowners prepay their mortgages, and the GSEs buy new ones at lower rates. To minimize the losses that occur when interest rates change, the GSEs constantly use sophisticated portfolio management techniques, including derivative securities. One technique they have used involves selling callable bonds that give them the option to pay the bonds off before the stated maturity, much as mortgagors prepay mortgages.

Interest rate risk can be very serious. Many savings and loan associations became insolvent in the early 1980s because of it. During that time, Fannie Mae's portfolio was poorly hedged. According to Secretary Snow, "Fannie Mae became insolvent on a mark-to-market basis. Only a combination of legislative tax relief, regulatory forbearance, and a decline in interest rates allowed Fannie Mae to grow out of its problem."[13] Despite state-of-the-art hedging today, the GSEs' portfolios have significant interest rate risk.

Chairman Greenspan recently wrote: "Moreover, the success of interest-rate-risk management, especially the exceptionally rapid timing necessitated by dynamic risk adjustments, requires that the ultimate counterparties to the GSEs' transactions provide sufficient liquidity to finance an interest-rate-risk transfer that counters the risk. Otherwise, large and destabilizing adjustments will result in sharp changes in the interest rates required to rebalance and hedge a portfolio."[14] In other words, if the GSEs have to make large adjustments to their portfolios, only very large financial institutions will be able to handle the other side of the financial transactions.

Operational Risk

Operational risk is the risk of loss due to inadequate or failed internal procedures and systems. It is addressed by the various reforms in the House and Senate bills that increase regulatory powers, and in S. 190 reducing the size of the GSEs' portfolios. A smaller portfolio would be easier to adjust because the size of transactions would be smaller. It would be possible to find more counterparties for these smaller transactions. In addition, the risk to the financial system from possible future accounting and other operational problems would be less with smaller enterprises. Limitations on portfolio size are consistent with other changes in the proposed legislation.

Fannie Mae's current accounting problems, and those of Freddie Mac in 2003, raise questions about internal controls. Accounting systems provide the basis for portfolio adjustment decisions. If the accounting system is providing inaccurate information, the resulting portfolio adjustment decisions are likely to be incorrect.

Chairman Greenspan has raised the concern that as the GSEs' portfolios have grown, the size and number of transactions needed to rebalance their portfolios have increased. As the size of the adjustments required has increased, the number of financial institutions that can meaningfully participate has decreased.

Reducing Systemic Risk

At a summary level, risk has two dimensions: the probability that the event will occur and the cost if it does. A complete approach to reducing risk works on both aspects. Reducing the size of the portfolios would reduce both dimensions. With smaller portfolios, the GSEs would be able to adjust more nimbly to changing financial markets. The cost of bailing them out would, also, be reduced. Chairman Greenspan summarized the potential for both concerns when he wrote:

> Today, the U.S. financial system is highly dependent on the risk-managers at Fannie and Freddie to do everything right.... The concentrations of mortgage-backed securities at Fannie and Freddie are well beyond what market forces would normally allow because there are no meaningful limits to the expansion of the GSEs' portfolios, which are funded with debt that the market believes to be federally guaranteed.[15]

That is, the implied guarantee allows the GSEs to grow without the usual market forces that would raise their costs as their risks rose. As a result, Fannie and Freddie represent significant systemic risk to the nation's financial system, both because they can make mistakes and because their size and concentration raise the likelihood of high costs for the economy when they do.

Reducing the seriousness of the systemic risk requires reducing the size of the implied guarantee. Some have proposed complete privatization of the GSEs, such as occurred for the college student loan market when Sallie Mae gave up its congressional charter and became entirely private. This would totally eliminate the implied guarantee. The GSEs would be subject to market forces that might drive them to reduce the size of their portfolios. This option is not currently before Congress. Closer regulation along the lines proposed in H.R. 1461 and S. 190 would reduce much of the operational risk, but risks coming directly from the size of the portfolios of mortgages and retained MBSs would remain as long as the portfolios remain larger than necessary to provide a liquid secondary mortgage market.

While it is true that this would distribute the risk more widely, this is less of a concern because the cost of a bailout would be less for any one company. In addition, it is likely that these other companies would use simpler ways to fund their portfolios, which would reduce the risk of hedging errors.

REFERENCES

[1] Letter from Alan Greenspan, Chairman of the Federal Reserve, to the Honorable Robert F. Bennett, U.S. Senate, Sept. 2, 2005, at [http://online.wsj.com/public/resources/documents/Greenspan091505.pdf].

[2] U.S. Department of Treasury, "Testimony of Secretary John W. Snow Before the U.S. Senate Committee on Banking, Housing and Urban Affairs. Proposals for Housing GSE Reform," press release, April 7, 2005, at [http://www.treas.gov/press/releases/js2362.htm].

[3] A relatively small number of mortgages are directly held in the GSEs' portfolios.

[4] Because of accounting problems, Fannie Mae's 2004 financial reports are not available.

[5] U.S. Office of Federal Housing Enterprise Oversight, *2005 Report to Congress*, Table 4, p. 31.

[6] Ibid., Table 14, p. 47.

[7] CRS Report RS21724, *GSE Regulatory Reform: Frequently Asked Questions*, by Loretta Nott and Barbara Miles, p. 6.

[8] U.S. Congressional Budget Office, *Assessing the Public Costs and Benefits of Fannie Mae and Freddie Mac*, May 1996. Available at [http://www.cbo.gov/ftpdocs/0xx/doc13/Fanfred.pdf].

[9] CRS Report RL32795, *Government-Sponsored Enterprises (GSEs): Regulatory Reform Legislation*, by Mark Jickling.

[10] James R. Haggerty, "Mortgage-Securities Drop Will Depend on Economy," *The Wall Street Journal*, Sept. 17, 2005, p. B7.

[11] Since 1986, the GSEs have offered multiclass MBSs, which divide prepayment risk among the different classes. They are customized for investors to match their tolerance and preference for prepayment risk versus anticipated yield.

[12] Dwight Jaffee, "On Limiting the Retained Mortgage Portfolios of Fannie Mae and Freddie Mac," 2005, available at [http://repositories.cdlib.org/iber/fcreue/fcwp/294/].

[13] U.S. Department of Treasury, "Testimony of Secretary John W. Snow Before the U.S. Senate Committee on Banking, Housing and Urban Affairs. Proposals for Housing GSE Reform," press release, April 7, 2005, p. 4, at [http://www.treas.gov/press/releases/js2362.htm]. See also, the Miscellaneous Revenue Act of 1982 (P.L. 97-372, 96 Stat.1726 et seq.), especially Section 102, titled "Adjustment to Net Operating Loss Carryback and Carryforward Rules for Federal National Mortgage Association."

[14] Letter from Alan Greenspan, Chairman of the Federal Reserve, to the Honorable Robert F. Bennett, U.S. Senate, Sept. 2, 2005, p. 1, at [http://online.wsj.com/public/resources/documents/Greenspan091505.pdf].
[15] Letter from Alan Greenspan, Chairman of the Federal Reserve, to the Honorable Robert F. Bennett, U.S. Senate, Sept. 2, 2005, pp 1-2, at [http://online.wsj.com/public/resources/documents/Greenspan091505.pdf].

In: Fannie Mae and Freddie Mac...
Editor: James R. Cristie, pp. 333-338
ISBN: 1-60021-356-1

Chapter 3

ACCOUNTING PROBLEMS AT FANNIE MAE*

Mark Jickling

SUMMARY

On September 22, 2004, the Office of Federal Housing Enterprise Supervision (OFHEO) made public a report that was highly critical of accounting methods at Fannie Mae, the government-sponsored enterprise that plays a leading role in the secondary mortgage market. OFHEO charged Fannie Mae with not following generally accepted accounting practices in two critical areas: (1) amortization of discounts, premiums, and fees involved in the purchase of home mortgages and (2) accounting for financial derivatives contracts. According to OFHEO, these deviations from standard accounting rules allowed Fannie Mae to reduce volatility in reported earnings, present investors with an artificial picture of steadily growing profits, and, in at least one case, to meet financial performance targets that triggered the payment of bonuses to company executives. On November 15, 2004, Fannie Mae reported that it was unable to file a third-quarter earnings statement because its auditor, KPMG, refused to sign off on the accounting results. On December 15, 2004, the Securities and Exchange Commission (SEC), after finding inadequacies in Fannie's accounting policies and methodologies, directed Fannie Mae to restate its accounting results since 2001. Shortly thereafter, the company's CEO and CFO resigned. It is estimated that earnings since 2001 will be revised downwards by as much as $12 billion, but the formal restatement of earnings is not expected before late 2006. This report will be updated as events warrant.

BACKGROUND

Fannie Mae and Freddie Mac, the two government-sponsored enterprises (GSEs) that dominate the secondary mortgage market, are huge and complex financial institutions that play a key role in the financial system. Most home mortgage loans made each year are purchased by one or the other of the GSEs and either held in portfolio or repackaged and sold

* Excerpted from CRS Report RS21949, Updated November 15, 2005

as mortgage-backed securities (MBS). The two GSEs have about $1.6 trillion in debt outstanding, and large quantities of GSE bonds are held by insured banks, pension funds, and investors of all types. While GSE debt is not guaranteed by the government, the "government sponsored" status of Fannie and Freddie leads market participants to put faith in an "implicit" guarantee, a belief that the Treasury will never allow either GSE to default on its obligations.

The savings and loan crisis of the 1980s was a painful demonstration of the risks inherent in mortgage markets. Over a thousand S&Ls failed because their long-term revenues (from mortgage loans) fell below their cost of funds (the interest they paid to savers). When interest rates are volatile, holders of mortgages and MBS face a variety of financial risks, and these risks are now concentrated in the two GSEs. Although both institutions manage risk with sophisticated financial techniques far beyond the capacity of any S&L, the accounting problems at Freddie Mac in 2003,[1] and now at Fannie Mae, raise serious questions. Are accounting irregularities simply a reflection of management's wish to persuade investors and regulators that, despite the volatile nature of the mortgage market, the firm's earnings are predictable and insulated from sudden changes? Or, do they suggest that the firms themselves lack a clear picture of their complex financial positions, risk management strategies, and risk exposures? In either case, improvements in accounting transparency and rigor appear to be needed.

The Accounting Issues

The OFHEO report[2] identifies three major accounting problems at Fannie Mae. Two have to do with failure to comply with accounting rules, and the third focuses on weaknesses in the firm's accounting processes. These issues are summarized below.

Amortization of Purchase Discounts, Premiums, and Fees (SFAS 91)

When Fannie Mae buys mortgages or MBS, it does not pay the exact amount of unpaid premium balance outstanding on the loans. If the interest rate (or coupon rate) paid by the borrower is above current market interest rates, the loan will sell at a premium, above the unpaid balance. If the coupon rate is below current market rates, the loan is less valuable, and will sell at a discount. To calculate the effective yield on the loan, Fannie Mae must take these premiums and discounts into account. (A loan bought at a premium is less valuable than the coupon rate would imply, and vice versa for loans purchased at a discount.) Under SFAS 91, a Financial Accounting Standards Board (FASB) rule, the amount of these premiums and discounts must be amortized, or recognized over the estimated life of the purchased loans (or MBS). The amounts recognized appear on the income statement as an adjustment to current interest income.

When Fannie Mae purchases mortgages that are riskier than usual (i.e., where the borrowers are less creditworthy), it may accept up-front fees from the loan sellers in lieu of credit guarantees. Conversely, Fannie may pay fees to lenders in exchange for greater protection against credit risk. These fees also have an impact on the effective yield that Fannie receives over the life of the loans and must be amortized according to SFAS 91.

As fees, premiums, and discounts are amortized and recognized for accounting purposes, Fannie Mae's quarterly income is increased or lowered. The size of the adjustment to reported income depends upon the estimated life of the loan: other things being equal, the longer the loan, the smaller the adjustment required to each quarter's earnings. A complication is that Fannie Mae does not know at the outset how long a mortgage will last, because borrowers generally have the right to prepay and refinance their mortgages. Critical to the amortization process, therefore, are the assumptions that Fannie Mae makes about the prepayment rate in a group of mortgages. SFAS 91 requires that those assumptions be updated as market conditions change, and that the amounts amortized into interest income be revised accordingly. This is the point, according to OFHEO, at which Fannie Mae has failed to follow accepted accounting practices.

In the fall of 1998, as central banks struggled to contain global financial panic, interest rates fell dramatically. The drop in rates adversely affected Fannie and Freddie by accelerating the rate of mortgage prepayments. The effect of the speed-up in prepayments on Fannie Mae's earnings was a $400 million expense, which according to SFAS 91 should have been recognized and charged against 1998 earnings. However, Fannie chose to recognize only $200 million and deferred recognition of the other half.

The deferred $200 million became known within Fannie Mae as the "catch-up." OFHEO claims that Fannie used "inordinate flexibility" in its handling of the catch-up amount, and used it as an accounting reserve, or "cookie jar," that gave it wide discretion to report or defer amortization income in order to obtain the accounting results it wanted. Fannie adopted polices "specifically intended to manage the catch-up position as a buffer to sudden changes in interest rates and the resultant volatility of amortization accounts."[3]

OFHEO concludes that Fannie Mae's practice was not to produce a single best estimate of prepayment rates, but to generate a range of estimates and choose the one that was most convenient.[4] "[M]odeling of the catch-up was performed for both the current quarter as well as for prospective reporting periods for the purpose of generating results under varying assumptions in order to achieve a specific desired outcome."[5]

OFHEO puts forward two explanations for Fannie Mae's failure to follow SFAS 91. A key company goal was to minimize the volatility of quarterly earnings to create the impression that the company's operations were stable, predictable, and low-risk. For a company like Fannie Mae that issues billions of dollars in debt each year, even a slight increase in the perception of riskiness can be very expensive, as bond investors demand higher yields. Second, the report analyzes Fannie Mae's earnings in 1998 and concludes that if the full $400 million had been charged against earnings, top executives would not have received bonuses linked to earnings per share target levels.[6] The explanations are not mutually exclusive.

Derivatives Accounting (SFAS 133)

Derivatives — including futures contracts, options, forwards, swaps, and caps — are financial instruments whose value is linked to changes in some economic variable, most often interest rates. Fannie Mae uses derivatives extensively to manage risk. For example, if Fannie had a portfolio of bonds that would decline in value if interest rates rose and wished to protect itself against that potential loss, it might purchase a derivative that would gain value by an equal amount as rates went up. The OFHEO report finds major problems in Fannie's accounting for the value of these financial instruments.

Derivatives accounting is governed by SFAS 133.[7] Under SFAS 133, the fair value of all financial derivatives must be calculated ("marked-to-market") at the end of each accounting period. Changes in fair value from the previous accounting period must be reported as current income, unless the derivatives are used for hedging. If a derivative is used to hedge an asset (as in the example above), the value of that asset — the hedged item — will move in the opposite direction to the derivative's value. Thus, a fall in the price of the hedged asset will be offset by a gain in the derivative (or vice versa). Under SFAS 133, the firm can recognize as earnings both the change in the derivative's value *and* the offsetting change in the hedged item's. If the gains and losses are closely correlated, the net effect on reported earnings will be very small or zero.

Hedge accounting has the effect of reducing the impact of changes in derivatives' fair value on current earnings and the bottom line. To qualify for this accounting treatment, however, SFAS 133 requires that there be a close relationship between changes in the value of the derivative and the hedged item. Derivatives that do not meet FASB's hedge test are considered speculative trading instruments, and changes in fair value from period to period must be recognized and reported as current earnings.

The OFHEO report identifies several problems with Fannie Mae's compliance with SFAS 133. The most general problem was also a major issue in Freddie Mac's 2003 accounting restatement: "many of [Fannie Mae's] hedging relationships should not qualify for hedge accounting treatment."[8] Because Fannie Mae does not properly measure the "effectiveness" of its hedges — the correlation between changes in the value of the derivative and the hedged item — they do not meet FASB's hedge test. In many cases, OFHEO finds that Fannie simply assumes perfect effectiveness (that changes in the derivative's fair value and the hedged item's value will exactly offset each other) and fails to perform the calculations and maintain the documentation that SFAS 133 requires.

OFHEO's report analyzes a number of derivatives transactions in detail and finds numerous specific practices that do not conform with SFAS 133. A common theme is the inappropriate use of "short-cuts" that produce the desired result of perfectly effective hedges that will have no impact on the bottom line. OFHEO finds that Fannie Mae's failures to follow SFAS 133 are consistent with the objectives of minimizing earnings volatility and simplifying operations.[9]

Structural Problems in Accounting Operations and Review

The OFHEO report finds significant problems with the way Fannie Mae's accounting results are generated and reviewed. Individuals involved in the process are encumbered by a "heavy workload, weak technical skills, and a weak review environment."[10] Under these conditions, OFHEO finds that accounting operations rely on a few individuals who exercise wide discretion. In this environment, the process for developing new accounting policies is said to be ineffective, and internal controls are called weak or non-existent. The unfortunate result, in OFHEO's analysis, is an accounting culture where methods are chosen to produce the desired results, rather than to produce an objective and transparent view of the firm's financial condition, which is the basic aim of GAAP.

The Supplemental Agreement

On March 8, 2005, Fannie Mae entered into a supplemental agreement to correct further accounting problems identified by OFHEO.[11] Among the accounting issues (and the relevant FASB standards) are

- valuation of mortgage loans held in portfolio (SFAS 65);
- improper classification of securities as either "hold to maturity" or "available for sale" (SFAS 115);
- policies regarding sale and repurchase of securities, called "dollar roles" (SFAS 140);
- failure to account for certain purchase and sale commitments relating to mortgage assets as derivatives (SFAS 149); and
- an accounting policy related to pools of mortgage-backed securities (FASB Interpretation No. 46).

OFHEO also found that several journal entries relating to amortization adjustments between 1999 and 2002 bore falsified signatures, and that the employee whose signature appeared on the journal entries had not in fact prepared them. OFHEO has directed Fannie Mae to determine the full extent and circumstances of such falsifications.

The Financial Impact

How different would Fannie Mae's financial results appear if the deficiencies identified by OFHEO were corrected? Fannie Mae has indicated that correcting its derivatives accounting may result in a reduction in reported income of about $10.8 billion for the years 2001-2004, and recent reports suggest that about $1.5 billion in tax credits may have been improperly recorded.[12] The restatement of earnings called for by the SEC is not expected to be completed until the second half of 2006. Fannie Mae CEO Daniel Mudd has indicated that other accounting problems may surface: "As we work our way to the bottom of the pile, we expect other issues to come to light."[13]

The Regulatory Response

On September 27, 2004, Fannie Mae's board of directors reached an agreement with OFHEO to take a number of actions to address problems identified in the report. Fannie Mae will (1) correct its accounting practices related to SFAS 91 and 133, (2) supplement its capital surplus by an amount equal to 30% of the required minimum capital, (3) review staff structure, responsibilities, independence, compensation, and incentives, (4) appoint an independent chief risk officer and separate key business functions now performed jointly by certain individuals or departments, and (5) put in place new controls and policies to assure adherence to accounting rules.

On November 15, 2004, Fannie informed the Securities and Exchange Commission (SEC) that it could not file a third-quarter earnings report because its outside auditor, KPMG, had declined to sign off on the financial statements. On December 15, 2004, the chief accountant of the SEC issued a statement that Fannie Mae's accounting was not in compliance with SFAS 91 and 133.[14] The SEC directed Fannie Mae to restate its financial statements for the period from 2001 through mid-2004.

On March 8, 2005, OFHEO entered into a supplemental agreement with Fannie Mae, relating to further discoveries of accounting irregularity, as described briefly above.

Congressional Action

House and Senate Committees have held numerous hearings on Fannie Mae's accounting scandal, and on government-sponsored enterprises generally. Two bills — S. 190 (reported by the Senate Banking Committee on July 28, 2005) and H.R. 1461 (passed the House on October 26, 2005) — propose to restructure GSE regulation.[15] The bills would replace OFHEO with an independent agency with authority over Fannie, Freddie, and the Federal Home Loan Banks. The bills would enhance the safety and soundness tools available to the GSE regulator, giving it more flexibility to establish and enforce risk management, operational, and capital standards, and allowing it to put a GSE into receivership, if necessary.

References

[1] See CRS Report RS21567, Accounting and Management Problems at Freddie Mac, by Mark Jickling.
[2] Office of Federal Housing Enterprise Oversight, Office of Compliance, Report of Findings to Date: Special Examination of Fannie Mae, Sept. 17, 2004, 198 p. (Hereafter cited as OFHEO, Report of Findings.)
[3] OFHEO, Report of Findings, p. 13.
[4] Ibid., p. ii.
[5] Ibid., p. 40.
[6] Ibid., pp. 10-12.
[7] See archived CRS Report 98-52, Derivatives: A New Accounting Standard, by Mark Jickling (available from author).
[8] OFHEO, Report of Findings, p. 113.
[9] Ibid., p. 122.
[10] Ibid., p. 168.
[11] For a description of the agreement, see testimony of OFHEO Director Armando Falcon, before the Subcommittee on Capital Markets, Insurance, and GSEs, House Committee on Financial Services, Apr. 6, 2005.
[12] Dawn Kopecki, "New Fannie Mae Violations Surface: Accounting Flaws Include Possible Overvalued Assets, Insurance to Hide Losses," Wall Street Journal, Sept. 29, 2005, p. A3.
[13] James R. Hagerty, "Fannie Mae Taps MCI Finance Chief To Clean Up Books," Wall Street Journal, Nov 11, 2005, p. A3
[14] "Office of the Chief Accountant Issues Statement on Fannie Mae's Accounting," Press Release 2004-172, Dec. 15, 2004.
[15] For a summary of the provisions of these bills, see CRS Report RL32795, Government-Sponsored Enterprises: Regulatory reform Proposals, by Mark Jickling.

INDEX

C

D

E

F

G

Q

R

S

T

U

V

W

Y